LITERARY
CRITICISM

A SHORT HISTORY

WILLIAM K. WIMSATT, JR.
& CLEANTH BROOKS

LITERARY
CRITICISM

A SHORT HISTORY

2: Romantic and Modern Criticism

The University of Chicago Press
Chicago and London

TO RENÉ WELLEK

The University of Chicago Press, Chicago 60637
The University of Chicago Press, Ltd., London

© 1957 by William K. Wimsatt, Jr., and Cleanth Brooks
All rights reserved. Published 1957
Phoenix Edition 1978
Printed in the United States of America

82 81 80 79 78   987654321

ISBN: 0-226-90174-2
LCN: 78-55046

CONTENTS

v

Contents

PART III

PART IV

PART V

PART THREE

CHAPTER 16

POETIC DICTION: WORDSWORTH AND COLERIDGE

§ *"poetic diction" as a critical problem—II. sketch of English poetic diction: the Spenserian strain, the neo-classic: Latinism, adjectives, periphrase, high and low style (Addison, Pope, Johnson), rise of the concept "poetic diction," Dryden to Gray—III. the classical pro-test (Horace, Jonson, Dryden, Pope, Goldsmith, Swift), the romantic protest (more radical), the anonymous po-etic style circa 1797, the diction of the* Lyrical Ballads, *Wordsworth's argument in the* Advertisement *and* Pre-face: *"very language of men," "low and rustic persons," "men in a state of vivid sensation"—IV. Coleridge's cri-tique: distinction between words and manner of combin-ing words, between hackneyed image and nonsense, rela-tion of learning to poetry, Wordsworth's ventriloquism—V. history of poetic diction since Wordsworth: Taylor in 1834, Pre-Raphaelite diction, 20th-century imagistic, realistic, and metaphysical reactions, significance of the debate between Wordsworth and Coleridge—VI. ante-cedents of Wordsworth's primitivism: continental ideas, Homeric theories, the noble savage, Ossian and other forgeries, Duck and other worker poets, Byron's ridicule, the reaction to aristocratic neo-classicism (Swift, Johnson, Goethe, the "bourgeois standard"), varieties of primitiv-ism since Wordsworth: Tolstoy's peasant norm, Saxonism theoretical and practical, concept of false primitives, Celti-cism, folk speech and argots—VII. who invents good new words?—VIII. poetic diction and the language of poetry, intrusion of the chronological norm, social and commer-cial requirement of originality (T. S. Eliot, Gertrude*

Stein), the "Cliché Expert," Gourmont, ingenious and original clichés, Gene Fowler's Barrymore, H. W. Fowler on misapplied quotations—IX. "old saws with new teeth," New Yorker sophistication vs. schoolboy style, tradition and usage, Milton to Pope, Dante to Gray, Wordsworth and 18th-century nature poetry, Blake and Elizabethanism §

AT A LATER POINT IN THIS NARRATIVE (CHAPTER 29) WE SHALL HAVE occasion to consider the question how far a close verbal analysis of poetry may fall short of doing justice to the more massive structural features of such works as novels, epics, dramas. Literary criticism of the mid-20th century in America has been raising that question with an insistence which might even be taken at this point as a discouragement to our dignifying the episode of 18th-century "poetic diction" and the Wordsworthian condemnation of it with very much notice. Both "poetic diction" and the reaction against it, however, stand out conspicuously in critical history, and we choose to dwell upon them with some deliberation. The concept of "poetic diction" is at least a handy one both for the theorist and for the literary historian. It has at least the advantage that it reduces to a nearly definable and testable form a good many other problems of literary criticism. "Poetic diction" is a good small-scale model of the larger problems.

II

THE issue of poetic diction had been growing upon the English literary consciousness steadily since about the time of Chaucer, that is, since the beginning of Renaissance English literature, and with special intensity since the time of Spenser. A new linguistic consciousness, the new linguistic expansiveness of the Renaissance nation, promoted the learned enrichment of vernacular expression and produced a plethora of words.[1] A somewhat different, but closely related, spirit of self-conscious artistry promoted a specifically poetic diction. Such a diction grew rapidly with the tradition of an important poetry in an important language and the development and refinement of this poetry through several generations of poets and critics.

Precisely what kinds of poetic diction were invented and handed on by the succession of English poets and translators—by Spenser, Fair-

[1] Cf. F. W. Bateson, *English Poetry and the English Language* (Oxford, 1934).

fax, Sylvester, Sandys, Milton, Dryden, Pope, Thomson, Collins, Gray? This is a complicated question. One may distinguish minor and major strains. Some kinds of poetic diction (like the Petrarchan flowers that flourished in the lesser Elizabethan sonneteers and were twined with graceful levity by Spenser and Sidney, or the rustic dialect words of Spenser's *Shepheardes Calender*) did not continue into the neo-classic era. Others grew stronger and were consolidated in the English tradition continuously up to Wordsworth's time. Without making a long excursion into what is a matter rather of directly poetic than of critical history, the historian of poetic theory may well note some of the main kinds of poetic diction which became fixed in the 18th-century complex. Slightly to one side perhaps belongs the archaic, melancholy, and variously romantic strain invented by Spenser for the *Faerie Queene*[2] and lavishly repeated in the 18th-century Spenserian imitations. A more distinctly classical diction can be described under three main grammatical headings: (1) With regard to etymology, the most pronounced trend was the continuation of Renaissance Latinism, especially as this was helped by the rise of scientific or "philosophic" ideas and vocabulary and by Ovidian and Virgilian meanings in the translations of Dryden and his predecessors. (2) With regard to parts of speech, the most pronounced trend was the increase of adjectives, both Latin derivatives and a large crowd of scientific and poetic coinages bearing the English termination y.[3] The growth of empirical observation during all this period had an understandably inflationary effect upon descriptive language. (3) With regard to syntax and logical relation, the most pronounced trend was the coupling of the adjective with the noun in a kind of glossy stock phrase, or periphrase, which was sometimes epithetical and redundant, in the Homeric style, sometimes more abstractly definitional (by genera and properties) in a way that is nowadays said to have reflected a philosophy and science of orderly classes in a stable cosmos.[4]

[2] Cf. Ernest De Selincourt, ed. *The Poetical Works of Edmund Spenser* (Oxford, 1932), Introduction, pp. lxi–lxii; F. M. Padelford, "Aspects of Spenser's Vocabulary," *PQ*, XX (July, 1941), 279–83; E. E. Stoll, *Poets and Playwrights* (Minneapolis, 1930), p. 193.

[3] George Gordon, *Shakespeare's English*, S. P. E. Tract No. 39 (Oxford, 1928), p. 274; John Arthos, *The Language of Natural Description in Eighteenth-Century Poetry* (Ann Arbor, 1949), Appendix C.

[4] Cf. Geoffrey Tillotson, *Essays in Criticism and Research* (Cambridge, 1942), p. 84, on "Physico-theological nomenclature"; John Arthos, *The Language of Natural Description*, Chapters IV and V. Other correlatives of 18th-century poetic diction may perhaps be named. The closure and symmetry of couplet verse, for instance, may often have demanded the trochaic or dactyllic adjective. Cf. Thomas Quayle, *Poetic Diction* (London, 1924), Chapter II, p. 29, quoting Shenstone's *Essays*. Personification, as found in the poetry of Johnson, Collins, or Gray, is a kind of abstraction which may be viewed as a special type of poetic diction. Cf. Bertrand H. Bronson, "Personification Reconsidered," *ELH*, XIV (September, 1947), 163–177; Earl R. Wasserman, "The Inherent Values of Eighteenth-Century Personification," *PMLA*, LXV (June, 1950), 435–63.

The definitional type of periphrase stood in a fairly close relation to the standard of universality and abstraction which we have discussed in our last chapter. And the taste for the universal entailed, as we have suggested, a certain mistrust of particularity, the imputation to this of lowness, meanness, or vulgarity. The classical high, middle, and low styles which we have seen transferred by late classical theory from oratory to poetry (becoming the epic, georgic, and eclogue styles) [5] appear by the mid-18th century to have been simplified into the polar concepts of the lofty and the low. Thus Addison could be guilty of saying:

> Since it often happens that the most obvious Phrases, and those which are used in ordinary Conversation, become too familiar to the Ear, and contract a kind of Meanness by passing through the Mouths of the Vulgar, a Poet should take particular Care to guard himself against Idiomatick Ways of Speaking.
>
> —*Spectator* No. 285

And Pope:

> It must also be allowed that there is a majesty and harmony in the Greek language, which greatly contribute to elevate and support the narration. But I must also observe, that this is an advantage grown upon the language since Homer's time: for things are removed from vulgarity by being out of use; and if the words we could find in any present language were equally sonorous or musical in themselves, they would still appear less poetical and uncommon than those of a dead one, from this only circumstance, of being in every man's mouth.[6]

And Samuel Johnson, in a *Rambler* passage on Shakespeare, erected one of the most notorious monuments to the lofty taste.

> Words become low by the occasions to which they are applied, or the general character of them who use them. . . .
> > Come, thick night!
> > And pall thee in the dunnest smoke of hell,
> > That my keen knife see not the wound it makes;
> > Nor heaven peep through the blanket of the dark,
> > To cry, Hold, hold!
>
> . . . the efficacy of this invocation is destroyed by the insertion of an epithet now seldom heard but in the stable, and *dun* night may come or go without any other notice than contempt. . . .

---

[5] See *ante* Chapter 6, p. 103; Chapter 8, p. 146.

[6] Postscript to Pope's translation of the *Odyssey*. Cf. James Sutherland, *A Preface to Eighteenth Century Poetry* (Oxford, 1948), p. 85.

[the] sentiment is weakened by the name of an instrument used by butchers and cooks in the meanest employments. . . . Who, without some relaxation of his gravity, can hear of the avengers of guilt *peeping through a blanket?—Rambler* No. 168

The following positive defense of a special poetic diction is provided by Gray.

The language of the age is never the language of poetry; except among the French, whose verse, where the thought and image does not support it, differs in nothing from prose. Our poetry, on the contrary, has a language peculiar to itself, to which almost everyone that has written has added something by enriching it with foreign idioms and derivations: nay, sometimes words of their own composition or invention. Shakespeare and Milton have been great creators this way; and no one more licentious than Pope or Dryden, who perpetually borrow expressions from the former.[7]

The precise terms "diction" and "poetic diction" seem to have arisen somewhat earlier, in the high Augustan era. Dryden uses "diction" with an apology for Latinism, in the preface to *Sylvae,* 1685. The first person to use the term "poetic diction" is apparently Dennis, in his *Advancement and Reformation of Modern Poetry* (ch. V), 1701. In his Preface to the *Iliad,* 1715, Pope wrote: "We acknowledge him [Homer] the father of poetical diction."[8] As with so many other classic themes, Samuel Johnson wrote a retrospective last word.

There was . . . before the time of Dryden no poetical diction. . . . Those happy combinations of words which distinguished poetry from prose had been rarely attempted; we had few elegancies or flowers of speech.[9]

III

Two kinds of protest against poetic diction have occurred: that of the classicist, hostile to pedantry and affectation, appealing to polite idiom, the educated spoken word; and that of the romantic, hostile to the same things, but appealing to the primitive, the naive, the directly passionate, the natural spoken word. The first of these protests occurs intermittently

[7] To Richard West, April 4, 1742, *Letters,* ed. Leonard Whibley, I, 98. Cf. Lord Chesterfield's recommendation of "poetic diction" to his son seven years old (*Letters,* October 26, 1739).
[8] Thomas Quayle, *Poetic Diction,* p. 7; F. W. Bateson, *English Poetry and the English Language,* p. 71.
[9] *Life of Dryden, Lives* (ed. G. B. Hill), I, 420.

throughout the classical and Renaissance eras. It is the voice of Horace (*usus quem penes arbitrium est et jus et norma loquendi*), of Ben Jonson ("Pure and neat Language I love, yet plaine and customary"),[1] of Dryden in his preface to *Annus Mirabilis* ("'Tis not the jerk or sting of an epigram . . . nor the jingle of a more poor paronomasia"), of Pope in his *Essay:*

> False eloquence, like the prismatic glass,
> Its gaudy colours spreads on ev'ry place;
> The face of Nature we no more survey,
> All glares alike, without distinction gay.
>
> II, 311–314

It is the latter-day voice of Goldsmith, in his *Life of Parnell,*[2] complaining about the "pristine barbarity" of contemporary Spenserians and Miltonists.

The classical protest is more or less unremitting, but it is at the same time moderate, good-tempered, hardly revolutionary. The same Goldsmith who accuses the archaizers of "vainly imagining that the more their writings are unlike prose the more they resemble poetry" will write an essay entitled "Poetry Distinguished from Other Writing." "Certain words" are "particularly adapted to the poetical expression." Jonathan Swift was a consistent classical champion of good prose sense and the idiomatic norm, but the following passage from his satiric *Apollo's Edict*, 1721, illustrates the ambiguity of the classic stand:

> Your tragick Heroes shall not rant,
> Nor Shepherds use *poetick* Cant:
> Simplicity alone can grace,
> The Manners of the rural Race.

Perhaps Swift avails himself of an ironic intimation in that closing periphrase. The "shepherds" become the "rural race" in the course of sixteen syllables saying that they have no right to such a title. Or does Swift accept a certain amount of poetic diction without noticing it? The question evaporates out of the poem itself into the obscure region of Swift's conscious or unconscious intentions.

The final and successful revolt against classical "poetic diction" was more violent—a protest of the second type, primitive, naive, "vegetally"

---

[1] *Timber* No. 118.

[2] *The Miscellaneous Works of Oliver Goldsmith* (London: Globe Edition, 1919), p. 483. "These misguided innovators have not been content with restoring antiquated words and phrases, but have indulged themselves in the most licentious transpositions and the harshest constructions, vainly imagining that the more their writings are unlike prose, the more they resemble poetry."

And see Samuel Butler, *Hudibras*, Part II, Canto I, ll. 591–632.

radical,[3] the first of its kind, at least in English literature, and a thing distinctive of a new social and philosophic era. It is worth while remembering that in the statements which we are about to quote, Wordsworth was reacting immediately not so much against Spenser, Milton, and Pope,[4] the poets who had created English poetic diction, as against his own now anonymous contemporaries who wrote the mélange of dictions which was then poetic staple. The following from the *Monthly Magazine*, for February, 1797, specializes in periphrastic elegance.

> For thee the fields their flowery carpet spread,
> And smiling Ocean smooths his wavy bed;
> A purer glow the kindling poles display,
> Robed in bright effluence of ethereal day,
> When through her portals bursts the gaudy spring,
> And genial Zephyr waves his balmy wing.
> First the gay songsters of the feather'd train
> Feel thy keen arrows thrill in every vein.

From the same issue of the *Monthly* comes this example of the ameliorated pensiveness which had descended in the tradition of Milton's minor poems:

> Oh, far removed from my retreat
> Be Av'rice and Ambition's feet!
> Give me, unconscious of their power,
> To taste the peaceful, social hour.
> Give me, beneath the branching vine,
> The woodbine sweet, or eglantine,
> When evening sheds its balmy dews,
> To court the chaste, inspiring muse.[5]

Beside these let us set down some short examples of the verse which Wordsworth ventured to print in the *Lyrical Ballads* of 1798 and which he defended in his *Advertisement* and in his *Preface* to later editions.[6]

[3] Kenneth Burke, "The Vegetal Radicalism of Theodore Roethke," *Sewanee Review*, LVIII (Winter, 1950), 76, argues that all movements toward a new style are movements toward the "infantile," a way of re-expressing the basic things.

[4] "To this day I believe I could repeat, with a little previous rummaging of my memory, several thousand lines of Pope" (*Letters of the Wordsworth Family*, ed. W. Knight, Boston, 1907, III, 122). The statement is part of a comment made by Wordsworth, in 1836 or later, on Hazlitt's *Spirit of the Age* and recorded in the manuscript *Memoirs* of Barron Field.

[5] Both examples are quoted in Marjorie L. Barstow, *Wordsworth's Theory of Poetic Diction* (New Haven, 1917), pp. 62–3.

[6] The texts of 1800, 1802, 1805 may be conveniently consulted in *Wordsworth, Representative Poems*, ed. Arthur Beatty (New York, 1937), pp. 676–704.

"How many are you then," said I,
"If they two are in Heaven?"
The little Maiden did reply,
"O Master! we are seven."

Few months of life has he in store
As he to you will tell,
For still, the more he works, the more
His poor old ancles swell.
My gentle reader, I perceive
How patiently you've waited,
And I'm afraid that you expect
Some tale will be related.

I heard a thousand blended notes,
While in a grove I sate reclined,
In that sweet mood when pleasant thoughts
Bring sad thoughts to the mind.

And Susan's growing worse and worse,
And Betty's in a sad *quandary*
And then there's nobody to say
If she must go, or she must stay:
—She's in a sad *quandary*

In his *Advertisement* of 1798 Wordsworth called these poems experimental, and he said they were "written chiefly with a view to ascertain how far the language of conversation in the middle and lower classes of society is adapted to the purposes of poetic pleasure." He feared his readers would think he had been "too low" and "too familiar," but he contrasted with his own style "the gaudiness and inane phraseology of many modern writers." [7] In his *Preface* some of the statements are even more downright. He is proud of having uttered "little of what is usually called poetic diction." His purpose has been "to imitate, and, as far as possible, to adopt the very language of men." [8] He asserts "that there neither is, nor can be, any essential difference between the language of prose and metrical composition." [9] His objection to poetic diction is that it is not true to nature—either to external nature or to human nature in

[7] Coleridge, *Biographia*, Chapter I, speaks of the "glare and glitter of a perpetual yet broken and heterogeneous imagery . . . an amphibious something."

[8] Cf. his later note to *Simon Lee the Old Huntsman:* "The expression when the hounds were out, 'I dearly love their voice,' was word for word from his own lips."

[9] The phrasing is that of 1802, a slight alteration from that of 1800.

its responses to the external. "I have at all times endeavored to look steadily at my subject; consequently, I hope that there is in these poems little falsehood of description, and that my ideas are expressed in language fitted to their respective importance." He seems to believe too that even honest expressions can become bad poetry just by being repeated. "I have . . . abstained from the use of many expressions, in themselves proper and beautiful, but which have been foolishly repeated by bad poets, 'till such feelings of disgust are connected with them, as it is scarcely possible by any art of association to overpower." On the genetic side the *Preface* contains a strong statement of the reasons why the language of "low [1] and rustic" persons is likely to be poetic:

> . . . because such men hourly communicate with the best objects from which the best part of language is originally derived; and because, from their rank in society and the sameness and narrow circle of their intercourse, being less under the influence of social vanity, they convey their feelings and notions in simple unelaborated expressions. Accordingly, such language, arising out of repeated experience and regular feelings, is a more permanent, and a far more philosophical language, than that which is frequently substituted for it by poets.

Yet this *Preface* contains a few statements which look like attempts to qualify Wordsworth's main view concerning the "very language of men," the language of "low and rustic" persons. For he speaks also about "a selection of the real language of men in a state of *vivid sensation*," about "a certain *colouring of imagination*, whereby ordinary things should be presented to the mind in an *unusual way*." [2] He wishes to make ordinary situations "interesting" by tracing in them the laws of human nature "as far as regards the manner in which we associate ideas in a *state of excitement*." "All good poetry," as every reader of the *Preface* will remember, "is the spontaneous overflow of *powerful feelings*." [3]

---

[1] "Low" becomes "humble" in 1832.

[2] 1802.

[3] The italics in these quotations are ours. In the same year, 1800, Wordsworth's letter to the critic John Wilson develops his theory as follows: "Please whom? or what? I answer, human nature as it has been and ever will be. But, where are we to find the best measure of this? I answer, from within; by stripping our own hearts naked, and by looking out of ourselves towards men who lead the simplest lives, and most according to nature; men who have never known false refinements." But he says also: "It is not enough for me as a Poet, to delineate merely such feelings as all men *do* sympathize with; but it is also highly desirable to add to these others, such as all men *may* sympathize with, and such as there is reason to believe they would be better and more moral beings if they did sympathize with." Wordsworth's argument is aimed against the distaste felt by Wilson and his friends for *The Idiot Boy*.

IV

THE simplism and primitivism of Wordsworth's poems, and even more of his theoretical views, provoked a considerable volume of immediate protest from his reading public. But the critic who spoke with the shrewdest authority was Coleridge, after a lapse of seventeen years, in his reminiscential *Biographia Literaria.* Coleridge's argument about poetic diction may be summarized under three main heads.

(1) He said that if Wordsworth, in arguing that the language of "metrical composition" is essentially the same as that of prose, meant only that poetry and prose have the same vocabulary, or dictionary, on which to draw, he was uttering a truism. Coleridge concluded that Wordsworth really meant that the poetic manner of combining words was no different from that of prose. And this, he retorted, was patently false.[4] (It is perhaps worth observing that Wordsworth may not in fact have made it quite clear whether he excluded either of the meanings defined by Coleridge—and that it is not necessary, either for justice to Wordsworth, or for the purposes of literary history, to suppose that he had brought himself to the point of facing a sharp distinction.)

(2) Coleridge argued that if a given image or figure (for instance, the "image" of Phoebus as the sun) is used badly by a given poet (for instance, Gray in a sonnet criticized by Wordsworth), the reason for the badness is not that the figure is a repetition of what other poets have done, but that it is in some way a violation of "grammar, logic, psychology," "good sense," or "taste"—the *"rules* of the IMAGINA-TION."[5]

> . . . it is a bad line, not because the language is distinct from that of prose; but because it conveys incongruous images, because it confounds the cause and effect, the real *thing* with the personified *representative* of the thing; in short, because it differs with the language of GOOD SENSE! That the "Phoebus" is hackneyed and a school-boy image, is an *accidental* fault, dependent on the age in which the author wrote.—II, 58

Another poet might be found, for instance Spenser, who had used the Phoebus image well.[6]

[4] Cf. Thomas M. Raysor, "Coleridge's Criticism of Wordsworth," *PMLA,* LIV (June, 1939), 496–510.

[5] Chapter XVIII, (*Biographia,* ed. J. Shawcross, II, 64–5).

[6] Coleridge's master at Christ's Hospital, the Reverend James Bowyer, had been in the habit of saying that "in the truly great poets . . . there was a reason assignable, not only for every word, but for the position of every word" (Chapter I; I, 4).

(3) Coleridge argued that education, and not the lack of it, tends to make a poet. Uneducated men are disorderly in their writing; they lack "surview." If the peasantry of Wordsworth's Westmoreland and Cumberland spoke a pure and vigorous language, this came not from uninstructed communion with nature, but from a spirit of independence and from a solid religious education and acquaintance with the Bible and hymnbook.

One kind of speech (socially defined) could not be more *real* than another.[7] But in a given instance it might be either more or less poetic. In his appreciation of Wordsworth's own poetic performance, Coleridge noted that Wordsworth suffered the difficulties of a ventriloquist in his undue liking for the dramatic form. Either a rustic speaker was invested with a Wordsworthian authority of utterance, or an opposite fault appeared, matter-of-factness, circumstantiality, and a downright prosaism.[8] "I've measured it from side to side; 'Tis three feet long, and two feet wide." It is not possible for a poet, urged Coleridge, especially not for a lyric poet, "to imitate truly a dull and garrulous discourser, without repeating the effects of dullness and garrulity."[9]

V

THE episode of the *Lyrical Ballads* was of course far from settling the business of poetic diction in English. Before many years had passed, a reviewer of Wordsworth's poems would raise his voice to accuse even Wordsworth of having fostered his own kind of poetic diction, more dangerous than the old, because more "covert and surreptitious," more "insidious." A new set of "stock words" seemed to this reviewer to be sprinkled through the "fugitive" poetry of the day "with a sort of feeling senselessness"—words, for instance, like *wild, bright, dark, lonely, light, dream*. The principle of their use was sentimental association lending color to a "pretext of conveying sense"—"in a manner which Mr. Wordsworth's prefaces will be found to explain."[1]

A recent historian of English poetic language has noted the progressive "deliquescence" of diction in English poetry (the development of a

[7] Chapter XVII (II, 39).

[8] Chapter XXII (II, 101, 109).

[9] Chapter XVII (II, 36). Cf. Letter to Southey, July 29, 1802 (*Letters*, ed. E. H. Coleridge, I, 386): "Here and there a daring humbleness of language and versification, and a strict adherence to matter of fact, even to prolixity. . . ."

[1] [Sir Henry Taylor], "Wordsworth's *Poetical Works*," *Quarterly Review*, LII (1834) 318–19. Cf. Theodore Spencer, "Antaeus, or Poetic Language and the Actual World," *ELH*, X (September, 1943), 182–3. Taylor means that Wordsworth's defense of his own diction offers the rationale of a new poetic diction. A close parallel appears between Taylor's argument and Wordsworth's own indictment of earlier poetic diction. See especially the Appendix to the *Lyrical Ballads*. 1802.

certain moonlight norm) during the Tennysonian and Pre-Raphaelite era.[2] In our own century we have experienced several waves of reaction to that era, the imagism of Pound, the realism of Masefield, the metaphysical inclusiveness of Eliot. Nothing is likely to seem more axiomatic to the student of poetry today than statements to the effect that "The poetry of a people takes its life from the people's speech and in turn gives life to it,"[3] that "the language which is good enough for labor and love and marriage, for birth and death, and the friendly breaking of bread, is good enough . . . for the making of poetry."[4]

Nevertheless, the debate between Wordsworth and Coleridge was a significant event in English literary history. It is part of the first romantic revolt against poetic diction in English and it is a more or less adequate monument to two questions: one genetic—Among what kinds of people does poetic language originate? The other critical—How is "poetic diction" in the sense of something undesirably artificial to be distinguished from the valid language—the idiom—of poetry?

VI

THE primitivism of Wordsworth was something which had numerous relations with his immediate background, though some of these are only vaguely implicit. Vico was a fountainhead of which he was certainly unaware. It is not necessary to inquire how directly he was in touch with Herder and other continental writers on the theme of *Volkspoesie*, or with theories of the bardic composition of Homer's epics in English writers like Blackwell, Kames, and Blair.[5] More concrete phenomena are the archaic forgeries of the 18th century (the Ossianic epics of Macpherson, the Rowleyan balladry of Chatterton), the cult of the "noble savage," the "child of nature," and the pathetically exploited worker poets—Stephen Duck the thresher, Henry Jones the Irish bricklayer patronized by Lord Chesterfield, James Woodhouse the shoemaker, Anne Yearsley the milkmaid (Lactilla) who developed airs and fell out with Hannah More.[6] The vogue was recorded in the ridicule of Byron.

[2] F. W. Bateson, *English Poetry and the English Language* (Oxford, 1934) pp. 108–15.

[3] T. S. Eliot, *The Use of Poetry and the Use of Criticism* (Cambridge, Mass.: 1933), p. 5.

[4] Harriet Monroe, quoted in Marguerite Wilkinson, *New Voices* (New York, 1931), p. 113.

[5] Cf. Wellek, *Rise*, p. 87; and Wellek's review of Vico's *Autobiography*, PQ, XXIV (1945), 166–8. Wordsworth's acquaintance with the Abbé Delille and other French georgic poets of the 18th century, shown in his early poems *An Evening's Walk* and *Descriptive Sketches*, is discussed by Arthur Beatty in his *Wordsworth, Representative Poems* (New York, 1937), pp. 31–3, 673.

[6] C. B. Tinker, *Nature's Simple Plan* (Princeton, 1922), pp. 92–103. One difference between Wordsworth and his forerunners of the 18th century was that with

When some brisk youth, the tenant of a stall,
Employs his pen less pointed than his awl,
Leaves his snug shop, forsakes his store of shoes,
St. Crispin quits, and cobbles for the muse,
Heavens! how the vulgar stare! how crowds applaud!
How ladies read, and literati laud!

. . . .

Let poesy go forth, pervade the whole,
Alike the rustic, and mechanic soul!
Ye tuneful cobblers! still your notes prolong,
Compose at once a slipper and a song.[7]

Wordsworth's primitivism was part of a general reaction, setting in well before his own day, against the aristocratic side of neo-classicism. We have seen that Dryden believed the right language of poetry—the very model of correct poetry—to be the language of the king and court. Pope believed the same, at least of the Elizabethan age.[8] About George II he had much difficulty.[9] Swift [1] and Johnson were severe upon the imbecilities of society talk. Johnson spoke of "female phrases," "fashionable barbarisms." [2] It was possible, perhaps usual, during all this time, for the anti-aristocratic tendency to rest short of sheer primitivism in what Marxist criticism would later call the bourgeois standard. Thus Goethe, giving explicit utterance to an idea that was no doubt often implicitly entertained: "A middle rank is much more favorable to talent [than a noble rank], so we find all great artists and poets in the middle classes." [3]

The period from Wordsworth to the present day has been notable for the variety and complexity of its archaizing and primitivistic trends. Some of these, like the peasant standard arrived at by Tolstoy, have had no direct relation to the language. Others, like the theoretical Saxonizing of English essayists and scholars (Macaulay, for instance, and Furnivall), or the practical Saxonizing of the Homeric translator Francis Newman,[4] are quite obviously in the area of "poetic diction." We encounter now, in

---

the latter the preference for nature did not reach the crisis of diction. That was what Wordsworth had against them. The supposedly primitive or natural poets of the 18th century were not distinguished for a Wordsworthian simplicity of language. They used all the ornaments. The point was precisely that they were able to do this. That apparently was thought to reveal something about origins, about natural inspiration.

[7] *English Bards and Scotch Reviewers*, ll. 765 ff.
[8] See his *Preface* to Shakespeare.
[9] See his *Epistle to Augustus*.
[1] See his *Tatler* No. 230.
[2] *Idler* No. 77.
[3] *Conversations*, February 24, 1825. Cf. Wordsworth's phrase "language of conversation in the middle or lower classes of society."
[4] Cf. *post* Chapter 20, p. 443.

contrast to the 18th-century beginnings, a primitivism rather formidably equipped with archeological and philological apparatus. A later special development has been a certain esoteric removal of the primitive locus. This means admitting the existence of fake primitives or bourgeois poseurs (like Robert Burns or Longfellow) but at the same time asserting the existence of a genuine peasant wisdom, an oral tradition from the foundations of the world. This was once in rapport with aristocratic and learned wisdom (the hut with the castle and the cloister) but has now been split off by the wedge of bourgeois culture and is withering away. Theorizing of this kind has had a Celtic and visionary orientation.[5]

So far as any view of poetic origins prevails very explicitly today, it is still likely to be the primitivistic. Our large literature in the departments of dialect, folk speech, argot and slang, is one testimony to a settled primitivistic interest among scholars. And this interest sometimes raises curious problems concerning not only compilation but evaluation. To select one instance from the many: a writer in the magazine *American Speech* argues that during World War II there were two kinds of soldier slang—a small number of terms really invented by soldiers and truly expressive (*shack up, sweat out, latrine rumour, chew ass*), and a much larger number of fake terms invented by newspaper writers, USO workers, and entertainers (*armoured cow,* for canned milk, *scandal sheet,* for payroll, *misery pipe,* for bugle, *homing device,* for furlough, *handgrenades,* for hamburgers, *tire patches,* for pancakes). In the same way there are two kinds of jazz slang—the genuine expressions of jazz musicians and fans (*Tailgate, solid, jam, riff, gutbucket, barrelhouse*), and the spurious inventions of publicity agents, masters of ceremonies, and popular music magazines (*God box,* for organ, *skin-beater,* for drummer, *syringe,* for trombone, *sliver sucker,* for clarinetist, *doghouse,* for bass fiddle, *gitter* or *git box,* for guitar).

> In each case the terms especially invented by persons not familiar through experience with the daily life of soldiers or musicians bear the mark of their artificial origins. They seldom

[5] See W. B. Yeats, "What is Popular Poetry?" in *Ideas of Good and Evil* (London, 1903), pp. 1–15. The classic philological discussion is that concerning the origin of the medieval vernacular lyric, Troubadour and Minnesang poetry. Did its origins lie in courtly scholarship or in folk minstrelsy? See Leo Spitzer, "The Mozarabic Lyric and Theodor Frings' Theories," *Comparative Literature,* IV (Winter, 1952), 1–4, 17–22. "Where within primitive lyricism should we then place the narrative-lyrical love songs of women inferred from the *jarchas* (= *refrains*)? Obviously in that pre-Christian framework of collective, improvised dancing songs of women in springtime which G. Paris, followed therein by Frings, recognized to be at the base of all lyrics in the Romance and Germanic vernaculars." "We are brought ultimately to visualize a primitive world of women dancing and chanting stanzas of love provided for them by the poets (a *Glückslaut* or *Klage* "im Munde des Mädchens, aber von einem Mann, dem Dichter, hineingelegt"), who thus achieve a vicarious pleasure. . . . Such a collaboration of the two sexes is no *creatio ex nihilo.* . . ."

serve a denotive purpose, are laborious, and lack the expressive quality of the terms that have been born of the life experience of the participants themselves.

At the same time, however, this writer notes that jazz musicians and fans tend to discard their own vocabulary when it is taken over by commercial users.[6] In this kind of inquiry, which is inferred from which? The quality of the term from its origin, or the origin from the quality?

VII

THE question about the origins of poetic language seems to allude to a language upon which some sort of special poetic virtue has been conferred before it reaches the poet himself. We are forced to conceive poetic language as a kind of pre-poetically potent vocabulary or vigorous mode of expression. At the same time the history of poetic diction strongly suggests that the main inventors of poetic diction have been professional poets themselves—Spenser, Milton, Dryden, Pope. Who does make up the good new words and phrases—those that add something to our expressive stock and are fitted to survive? Do these occur first in works of creative literature, or in miscellaneous non-literary places? [7] Did the primitive bard write the best poetic language? And if he did, was he an unusually primitive, or an unusually advanced, member of his tribe? Is a modern poet an unusually advanced, or an unusually primitive, member of modern society?

If a dramatic clause be invoked—that is, if we observe that the language of any social class is proper when a writer is representing that class—the inquiry may appear to be translated into something quite different. And indeed it is true that the supposed speaker of any poem is always dramatic, and is always to be conceived as some kind of person, and often as a person not learned or poetically skillful. Nevertheless—as we have heard Coleridge remark about the experiments of Wordsworth—a direct imitation of the uncouth speaker does run a special risk of lapsing into realistic disorder and insignificance. This may be much like what a modern critic has called the "fallacy of imitative form," or like what Dryden called "mechanic humour" in the correctly low-life

[6] Morroe Berger, "Some Excesses of Slang Compilers," *American Speech*, XXI (October, 1946), 196–8.

[7] Cf. Max J. Herzberg, "Who Makes Up the New Words?" *Word Study*, XXIV (October, 1948), 1–9. The modern professionals quoted by Mr. Herzberg make very modest claims as linguistic innovators. As any new expression which becomes a part of the language has to appear in print in order to be recorded, it seems at least likely that a professional phase occurs early in the life of each neologism. But do professional journalists make up their own new words or overhear them in oral discourse?

imitations of Ben Jonson. It is possible also to have correctly tedious imitations of high life. Johnson and Swift were right about this. Anybody who has ever tried to collect brilliant or pungent expressions either at cocktail parties or at diners along truck routes must have been struck by the prevalence of the brassier kind of clichés and the reiterated simplisms of blasphemy.

VIII

IN THE end the only question of critical significance is the second of the two which we have framed above: How is poetic diction in the sense of something false and undesirable to be distinguished from the valid language of poetry? Yet it may not be easy to isolate this critical question. In addition to the concept of origins as we have just attempted to describe it, there is yet another, an intermediate kind of concept, that of chronological staleness, the hackneyed, which is usually associated with that of poetic diction and tends greatly to obscure the critical discussion of the latter. The theoretical issue of poetic diction seemed to Wordsworth an issue between artifice and nature.[8] To Coleridge it seemed more like an issue between propriety and impropriety, congruity and incongruity. In effect he applied the classic norm of decorum. Both Wordsworth and Coleridge assigned a relatively slight role to the chronological concept of the "hackneyed." Yet the notion of the hackneyed, the stereotype, the cliché, today enjoys a strongly established place in habits of critical thinking. It is likely to be among the first appeals of a theorist called upon to explain why poetic diction is undesirable.

The most obvious sense in which the poet is bound to bear the burden of originality is that which relates originality to the social and commercial conditions of success in literature. There is no practical point in repeating the classics, or in repeating their style. Even if some classic had failed to get written on schedule (in its own era) and even if it could be written instead today, the expectancies and demands of publishers and readers preclude the success of the performance. The undergraduate joker who types out a selection of the less well-known sonnets of Shakespeare and submits them over his own name to a New York press does so in full expectation of being rejected.[9] This massive and immovable fact about markets and readers is one of the grounds which supports a kind of statement that often proceeds with great authority from the successful literary person. Thus T. S. Eliot:

> It is exactly as wasteful for a poet to do what has been done already, as for a biologist to rediscover Mendel's discoveries. The French poets in question have made "discoveries" in verse

[8] Cf. Meyer Abrams, *The Mirror and the Lamp* (New York, 1953), p. 120.
[9] Cf. David Daiches, *A Study of Literature* (Ithaca, 1948), pp. 127-8.

of which we cannot afford to be ignorant, discoveries which are not merely a concern for French syntax. To remain with Wordsworth is equivalent to ignoring the whole of science subsequent to Erasmus Darwin.[1]

And Gertrude Stein:

> The whole business of writing is the question of living in that contemporariness. Each generation has to live in that. . . . what I am trying to make you understand is that every contemporary writer has to find out what is the inner time-sense of his contemporaries. The writer, or painter, or what-not, feels this thing more vibrantly, and he has a passionate need of putting it down; and that is what creativeness does.[2]

But the critical problem of poetic diction and the cliché requires a somewhat more precise handling than that. One of the minor comic figures of our time is the "Cliché Expert," who in an early appearance was made to "take the stand" and testified along these lines.

> Q—Mr. Arbuthnot, you are an expert in the use of the cliché, are you not?
>
> A—Yes sir, I am a certified public cliché expert.
>
> Q—Would you answer a few questions on the use of the cliché in ordinary speech and writing?
>
> A—I should be only too glad to.
>
> Q—Thank you. Now just for the record—you live in New York?
>
> A—I like to visit New York but I wouldn't live there if you gave me the place.
>
> Q—Then where do you live?
>
> A—Any old place where I hang my hat is home sweet home to me.
>
> Q—What is your age?
>
> A—I am fat, fair, and forty.
>
> Q—And your occupation?
>
> A—Well, after burning the midnight oil at an institution of higher learning, I was for a time a tiller of the soil. Then I went down to the sea in ships. I have been a guardian of the law, a poet at heart, a prominent clubman and a man about town, an eminent—[3]

[1] 1918. Quoted by N. H. Pearson and W. R. Benét, *The Oxford Anthology of American Literature* (New York: Oxford University Press, Inc., 1939), p. 1636.

[2] Gertrude Stein, "How Writing is Written," a talk before the students at Choate School in 1935 (cf. *The Choate Literary Magazine*, XXI, ii, 5–14), in N. H. Pearson and W. R. Benét, *The Oxford Anthology of American Literature*, pp. 1446–51.

[3] Frank Sullivan, "The Cliché Expert Takes the Stand," *The New Yorker*, August 31, 1935, pp. 15–16.

Here is an ironic frame of reference which makes a series of sorry expressions amusing. But what makes each of the expressions in itself so sorry? Not merely the fact that it is a cold potato, a stereotype (any word in the dictionary enjoys the same status), but the further fact that the expression has a certain special character, even if tame and drab. It attempts to stand up and make a little joke, and the joke is out of place. When the cliché expert took the stand, the context was all against him. There could hardly be any chance for his embroideries, even for the plainest of them. "Fat, fair, and forty" is not an answer for the witness stand.

"In the true notion of the *cliché*," says a French critic, "incoherence has its place by the side of triteness." [4] The logic of the situation would suggest that even ingenuity and originality are no sure proofs against the cliché. The highly ingenious periphrases often employed at certain levels of journalism have a cold ring, like echoes, even though we cannot say of what. A popular biography of a famous actor, for instance, yields a reviewer the following grounds of patronizing complaint.

> For Mr. Fowler, Broadway is inevitably "this street of fickle luster," a distiller a "maker of spirituous delicacies," and Shakespeare "Stratford's first gentleman;" cigarette-smoking is "bronchial debauchery," hair on the chest "torsorial upholstery," and the men's washroom "ammoniac grottos" equipped with "cracked and homely porcelains." When he wants to convey the idea that some white mice were multiplying rapidly, he says that the "snowy rodents were fruitful;" and when Barrymore sets out to play Hamlet, or take on "the Danish assignment," Mr. Fowler says that he "announced . . . his decision to draw on the black tights of the classic Scandinavian." [5]

Some of the expressions quoted here are no doubt clichés in the ordinary chronological sense. Others, however, seem unusual. The real character of their offensiveness (or presumable offensiveness) does not lie in their newness or oldness, but in the difficulty one has in conceiving an excuse for them. There is enough information in the expressions themselves and in their translations by the reviewer to suggest a certain inevitable silliness. They may be saved only on the principle of dramatization—and perhaps even then only at some expense to their author. "The fuzzy

[4] Remy de Gourmont, "Of Style or Writing" (from his *Decadence*, trans. W. A. Bradley, New York, 1921), in *Essays in Modern Literary Criticism*, ed. Ray B. West, Jr. (New York, 1952), p. 62. Cf. Gourmont, *Esthétique de la langue française* (Paris, 1905), pp. 301–38, "Le Cliché."

[5] Edmund Wilson, review of Gene Fowler, *Good Night, Sweet Prince*, in *The New Yorker*, XIX (January 22, 1944), 58; also in Edmund Wilson, *Classics and Commercials* (New York: Farrar, Straus and Company, 1950).

raffish style of this book," says the reviewer, "has its special appropriateness to the subject: it is a literary equivalent for the atmosphere in which the events take place. What we get here is the folklore of the Barrymores."

Bad poetic diction includes a wide range of non-meanings—from the fuzziness or lack of focus that may characterize the whole work of a minor and derivative poet to such grossly misapplied cliché quotations as those noticed by H. W. Fowler in his *Modern English Usage*.[6] A person who actually remembers what goes on in the first act of *Hamlet* will not be guilty of a jocular statement that the Ten Commandments are rules which by and large have been "more honored in the breach than in the observance."

IX

ONE might experiment with the conception that all language is an arsenal of clichés, some expressions, like *man* and *tree*, being only more ordinary and more solidly established than some others,[7] like *umbrageous, prelusive, fleecy kind*, and *finny tribe*. The usual rule of thumb is that a poet should avoid clichés. But a higher rule is that he should be a master of clichés—at all levels. The mastery of the cliché may be illustrated sharply, if simply, in a kind of twisted echo phrase which has been called the "cliché extended."

> At the drop of a brass hat.
> To gild the lily with radiator paint.[8]

A penny saved is a penny to squander.
A man is known by the company that he organizes.[9]

Or the autological expression, which itself sums up the principle:

> Old saws fitted with new teeth.[9]

Such echoes themselves, of course, are not proof against the cliché use. The final worth always depends on a larger context. "Put a beetle in alcohol, and you have a scarab; put a Mississippian in alcohol, and you have a gentleman." This piece of local-color wit has a kind of shoddy

[6] *S.v.* "quotation." Cf. Eric Partridge, *A Dictionary of Clichés* (New York, 1940), Introduction.
[7] There is such a thing as failure to achieve the established clichés of a language. One may have a sense of something like this in reading one of the classics turned into "Basic."
[8] George Arms, "Clichés, Extended and Otherwise," *SRL*, XXIX (November 30, 1946), 9.
[9] Ambrose Bierce, *The Devil's Dictionary, s.v.* "saw," in *Collected Works* (New York, 1911), VII, 310–11.

value which is greatly enhanced in Faulkner's *Sanctuary* through the fact that it echoes the utterance of Gowan Stevens, the collegiate slicker and lady-killer.[1]

Nowadays one may identify a genre of lightly sophisticated magazine poems whose main logic is the slight tilt which they give to a pattern of cliché vocabulary, or the dainty jangle of cross-purposes which they create between intersecting patterns.

> Every soldier is his own architect, a specialist
> In the small home constructed reasonably
> Along pretty traditional lines, complete with
> Smiling wife at ease on screened verandah.[2]

And on the other hand:

> For nineteen years I lived a carefree life
> And pain and toil and grief I never knew.
> Although the world rushed madly on to strife,
> My thoughts of national welfare were but few.[3]

It is not necessary to quote more of either poem to establish the contrast: the simple, unaltered reproduction of clichés by the schoolboy veteran about to tell his experiences on being inducted into the army; and the adroitly proffered series of not-quite clichés from the areas of business and advertising in a competent report from the front on the soldier's day dreams. The first poem is an exercise in a limited kind of whimsy—but within its limits, and in contrast to the second, it shows the difference between dead and live language.

Language gains depth and resonance only by being used, and hence some of the most complete and poetically significant uses of words are just those that occur within a poetic tradition. Beside Milton's

> No light, but rather darkness visible
> Served only to discover sights of woe

we put Pope's

> Of darkness visible so much be lent,
> As half to show, half veil, the deep intent.

Gray was glad to call attention to the origin of

> The curfew tolls the knell of parting day

in Dante's

> . . . *squilla di lontano,*
> *Che paia 'l giorno pianger, che si muore.*

---

[1] *Sanctuary* (New York, 1931), p. 29.
[2] W. W. Gibson, "The Architects," *The New Yorker*, XX (October 1, 1944), 28. Permission the author; © 1944 The New Yorker Magazine, Inc.
[3] Freshman poem.

A recent examination of mid-18th-century English poetry has defined the "major vocabulary" of that poetry as a complex of quite simple words relating to the age's dominant interest in landscape symbols of optimistic divinity. This vocabulary yields the following synthetically typical line:

> Rise, fair day, before the eyes and soul of man.[4]

The poetry of Wordsworth, coming as an artistic climax and renewal, rather than rejection, of this tradition, is in a sense a poetry that turns very simply to nature and the human soul—yet, inescapably, it does this through words, and not entirely through the simple range of words represented in the line just quoted. Wordsworth's poetry is a sound realization and a deepening of certain nature symbols already available to his age in more or less cliché simplifications. It is a dramatization of those symbols by bringing them into contact with select terms from both higher and lower ranges,[5] from the metaphysical and Johnsonian Latinate range and from the range of low, country words.

> Once again I see
> These hedge-rows, hardly hedge-rows, little lines
> Of sportive wood run wild: these pastoral farms,
> Green to the very door; and wreaths of smoke
> Sent up, in silence, from among the trees.
>
> And I have felt
> A presence that disturbs me with the joy
> Of elevated thoughts; a sense sublime
> Of something far more deeply interfused,
> Whose dwelling is the light of setting suns.

A more directly literary—a more artificial—form of such dramatization was no less a part of the romantic movement in English literature. Thus William Blake, in his juvenile *Poetical Sketches*.

> My silks and fine array,
>   My smiles and languish'd air,
> By love are driv'n away. . . .

.   .   .

[4] Josephine Miles, *The Primary Language of Poetry in the 1740's and 1840's* (Berkeley, 1950), pp. 174, 222.

[5] In his *Prelude; or Growth of a Poet's Mind* (VI, 109-12) Wordsworth, speaking, not with complete fairness, of his own early compositions, alludes to a weakness of trading in "classic niceties,"

> The dangerous craft of culling term and phrase
> From languages that want the living voice
> To carry meaning to the natural heart.

I'll pore upon the stream,
Where sighing lovers dream,
And fish for fancies as they pass
Within the watery glass.

Whether on chrystal rocks ye rove,
Beneath the bosom of the sea
Wandring in many a coral grove,
Fair Nine, forsaking poetry!

In these wryly graceful adaptations of an earlier idiom that had come down through the 18th century in Percy's *Reliques* and other collections, Blake gives an advanced demonstration of what it means to be a cliché expert.

SUPPLEMENT

The poet who takes his art seriously will come to his task in a spirit of honest self-criticism. He will not flinch at throwing out whatever words are lacklustre or lack-weight or in any way undeserving—though such words have a way of hanging on hard. A good poet will dig up long forgotten treasures of vocabulary and put them into circulation again, brilliantly old-fashioned terms which lie hidden in the junkpiles of neglect. He will be on the alert to take advantage of the newest creations of shifting usage. His utterance will be urgent and clear, like the spring torrent; he will pour out a wealth of words, he will enrich his mother tongue. At the same time he will cut through stylistic brambles and make smooth and wholesome the paths of meaning; he will be forceful. And all the while, he will make what he is doing look as easy as play, though it keeps his wit on the rack—as he dances through his roles, now Satyr, now boorish Cyclops.—Horace, *Epistle* II, ii, ll. 109–25

A poet ought to avoid the least taint of what we may call low-breeding (*vilitas*) in his vocabulary; he has to assume a style that marks him off from ordinary speakers—let him carry it off with an Horatian "distaste for the crowd and aloofness" (*odi profanum et arceo*). At the same time he has to be careful not to let his wit stick out like an extraneous ornament; it ought to be closely woven into the texture of his argument. Witness Homer! and the Lyrists! and Roman Virgil! And the verbal magic (*curiosa felicitas*) of Horace. . . . The mighty business of a civil war will be a crushing job for any but an exceedingly well educated poet. Civil and military exploits as a matter of fact are hardly to be managed in verse; prose history takes care of them much better. The business of poetry . . . is a free effusion of the spirit . . . through devices of mystery, through divinely contrived interventions, through the torment of wit into forms of fable. Poetry should sound, not like a solemn deposition of fact under oath, but like the utterance of a prophetic mind . . . wildly thrown out, as on first inspiration, without tidying touches.

—Petronius Arbiter, *Satiricon*, Chapter 118

When I travelled, I took a particular Delight in hearing the Songs and Fables that are come from Father to Son, and are most in Vogue among the common People of the Countries through which I passed; for it is impossible that any thing should be universally tasted and approved by a Multitude, tho' they are only the Rabble of a Nation, which hath not in it some peculiar Aptness to please and gratify the Mind of Man. Human Nature is the same in all reasonable Creatures; and whatever falls in with it, will meet with Admirers amongst Readers of all Qualities and Conditions. *Molière*, as we are told by Monsieur *Boileau*, used to read all his Comedies to an old Woman who was his Housekeeper, as she sat with him at her Work by the Chimney-Corner; and could foretel the Success of his Play in the Theatre, from the Reception it met at his Fire-side: For he tells us the Audience always followed the old Woman, and never failed to laugh in the same Place.

I know nothing which more shews the essential and inherent Perfection of Simplicity of Thought above that which I call the Gothick Manner in Writing, than this, that the first pleases all Kinds of Palates, and the latter only such as have formed to themselves a wrong artificial Taste upon little fanciful Authors and Writers of Epigram. *Homer, Virgil,* or *Milton,* so far as the Language of their Poems is understood, will please a Reader of plain common Sense, who would neither relish nor comprehend an Epigram of *Martial,* or a Poem of *Cowley:* So, on the contrary, an ordinary Song or Ballad that is the Delight of the common People, cannot fail to please all such Readers as are not unqualified for the Entertainment by their Affectation or Ignorance; and the Reason is plain, because the same Paintings of Nature which recommend it to the most ordinary Reader, will appear Beautiful to the most refined.

—Joseph Addison, *Spectator* No. 70, May 21, 1711

One touch of Nature may make the whole world kin, but two touches of nature will destroy any work of Art. If, on the other hand, we regard Nature as the collection of phenomena external to man, people only discover in her what they bring to her. She has no suggestions of her own. Wordsworth went to the lakes, but he was never a lake poet. He found in stones the sermons he had already hidden there. He went moralising about the district, but his good work was produced when he returned, not to Nature but to poetry. Poetry gave him "Laodamia," and the fine sonnets, and the great Ode, such as it is. Nature gave him "Martha Ray" and "Peter Bell," and the address to Mr. Wilkinson's spade.

—Oscar Wilde, *The Decay of Lying,* in *Intentions* (London, 1913), p. 19

In writing *The Playboy of the Western World,* as in my other plays, I have used one or two words only that I have not heard among the country people of Ireland, or spoken in my own nursery before I could read the newspapers.

A certain number of the phrases I employ I have heard also from herds and fishermen along the coast from Kerry to Mayo, or from beggar-women and ballad-singers nearer Dublin; and I am glad to acknowledge how much I owe to the folk-imagination of these fine people. Anyone who has lived in real intimacy with the Irish peasantry will know that the wildest sayings and ideas in this play are tame indeed, compared with the fancies one may hear in any little hillside cabin in Geesala, or Carraroe, or Dingle Bay. All art is a collaboration; and there is little doubt that in the happy ages of literature, striking and beautiful phrases were as ready to the story-teller's or the playwright's hand, as the rich cloaks and dresses of his time. It is probable that when the Elizabethan dramatist took his inkhorn and sat down to his work he used many phrases that he had just heard, as he sat at dinner, from his mother or his children. In Ireland, those of us who know the people have the same privilege. When I was writing "The Shadow of the Glen," some years ago, I got more aid than any learning could have given me from a chink in the floor of the old Wicklow house where I was staying, that let me hear what was being said by the servant girls in the kitchen. This matter, I think, is of importance, for in countries where the imagination of the people, and the language they use, is rich and living, it is possible for a writer to be rich and copious in his words, and at the same time to give the reality, which is the root of all poetry, in a comprehensive and natural form. In the modern literature of towns, however, richness is found only in sonnets, or prose poems, or in one or two elaborate books that are far away from the profound and common interests of life. One has, on one side, Mallarmé and Huysmans producing this literature; and on the other, Ibsen and Zola dealing with the reality of life in joyless and pallid words. On the stage one must have reality, and one must have joy; and that is why the intellectual modern drama has failed, and people have grown sick of the false joy of the musical comedy, that has been given them in place of the rich joy found only in what is superb and wild in reality. In a good play every speech should be as fully flavoured as a nut or apple, and such speeches cannot be written by anyone who works among people who have shut their lips on poetry. In Ireland, for a few years more, we have a popular imagination that is fiery and magnificent, and tender; so that those of us who wish to write start with a chance that is not given to writers in places where the springtime of the local life has been forgotten, and the harvest is a memory only, and the straw has been turned into bricks. January 21st, 1907.

—J. M. Synge, Preface to *The Playboy of the Western World*, Boston: J. W. Luce Co., 1911, quoted by permission of Random House, Inc., New York.

The historian of the English language may attach to the word inkhorn *in its Elizabethan context meanings which are no part of Synge's meaning when he uses the word in the Preface here quoted. Synge's mistrust of city language as a literary model can be paralleled, with a different evaluative accent, in a passage quoted earlier in this book (Chapter 11) from Congreve. The aristocratic norm of poetic utterance is in the end true to itself only in aiming to improve on the salon, whereas the peasant norm in being truest to itself drives toward some kind of fidelity to the actual.*

CHAPTER 17

GERMAN IDEAS

§ *early German theory, French classicism, Gottsched, the efforts of Breitinger and Bodmer, Lessing's* Hamburg Dramaturgy, *Herder's radical new interests—II. the historical point of view, Italians, Boileau, Dryden, Shakespeare and Spenser criticism, Vico's* New Science, *comparative studies, the folk—III. rise of term "romantic," A. W. Schlegel, Madame de Staël, nature vs. self, Schiller's* Über naive und sentimentalische Dichtung, *Schelling on pagan and Christian, F. Schlegel, classic beauty, romantic energy, Goethe's reminiscence, Hegel's three stages, Schiller's* Spieltrieb, *Jean Paul—IV. transcendental reconstruction, Novalis on science, the importance of Kant,* Critique of Judgment, *the beautiful and the sublime, the former distinguished from pleasure, interest, and concept, "purposiveness without purpose," symbolism, severe formalism of Kant's view—V. shift from epic and dramatic norms to lyric, Herder, sense media, energy, "music of the soul," synaesthesis, A. W. Schlegel, architecture as music, Schopenhauer, music and will, poet as creator, metaphor and the birth of speech, Herder* Über den Ursprung der Sprache, *later distinction between symbol and allegory—VI. poetry as spiritual regeneration, "myth," F. Schlegel's* Discourse, *Schelling, poetry as philosophy, as absolute reality, Novalis, Fichte, elevation of criticism, poetry as creative dreaming, poetry as fullness, mechanism vs. organism—VII. rationale of the comic, A. W. Schlegel's defence of puns and irony, Jean Paul's* Vorschule, *"infinite incongruity," "humor" and the sublime, F. Schlegel on irony, self-transcendence, the Byronic and dark, metaphysical versions, Heine, K. F. W. Solger, irony the principle of art, Hegel: irony is "Satanic impertinence"—VIII. Goethe on the debt of German literature to English, Kant and English empirical ideas, the German transformation, good for English theory* §

THOUGH THE ISSUE OF POETIC DICTION HAD, AS WE HAVE SUGGESTED, its continental affinities, Wordsworth and Coleridge fought out their quarrel here pretty much on native grounds. It is hardly necessary to go to the contemporary continent to understand English poetic diction of the 18th century and the reaction against it. Certain much larger critical issues centering around what may be called a new idea of poetic "imagination" were, however, more inevitably tied in with continental romanticism. Wordsworth and Coleridge and Shelley did not arrive at their highly important statements in this area without having learned something from abroad, and especially from the Germans.

German literary theory, caught at its outset, during the latter 17th and early 18th centuries, in the rigors of French classicism (see the systematic genre prescriptions of Gottsched's [1] *Versuch einer kritischen Dichtkunst*, 1730) or engaged in the merely emancipatory (Miltonic, Addisonian, neo-Longinian, and pictorialist) counter-efforts of the Swiss professors Breitinger and Bodmer,[2] began with Lessing and some of his friends to rouse itself and threaten more radical announcements. The next two generations of German litterateurs, in league with transcendental philosophers and aestheticians, were to take over the critical leadership which had passed in its classical phases through Italy and France and during the middle part of the 18th century was held by the British empiricists.

Lessing himself in his series of dramatic reviews in the *Hamburg Dramaturgy*, written shortly after the *Laokoon*, turned a destructive scorn on the Voltairean heroic inflation of French classical drama [3] and did much to modulate Cornelian admiration and Voltairean astonishment into the softer norm of 18th-century pity.[4] Yet Lessing was a classical critic, a "new Preceptist," as Saintsbury has called him, a kind of Prot-

[1] He has been called the "German Johnson," but, as Saintsbury (II, 552) points out, the resemblance between the two ends with the fact that each was a neo-classic stalwart. We have observed Johnson's small respect for the genres.

[2] In their imitation of the *Spectator* entitled *Diskurse der Maler* (started in 1721), in four great manifestos: Bodmer's *Von dem Wunderbaren in der Poesie* (1740) and *Über die poetischen Gemählde der Dichter* (1741) and Breitinger's *Von der Natur* (1740) and *Kritische Dichtkunst* (1740), and in Bodmer's translations of Homer, *Paradise Lost*, and English ballads. See Wellek, *History* I, 147.

[3] See, for instance, the comparison in his paper No. 11 between the ghost in *Hamlet* and that in *Semiramis*. "Voltaire's ghost steps out of his grave in broad daylight, in the midst of an assembly of the royal parliament, preceded by a thunderclap. . . . Shakespeare let only Hamlet see the ghost. . . . The spectre operates on us, but through him rather than by itself. . . . At his [Voltaire's] ghost many are frightened, but not much." *Selected Prose Works of G. E. Lessing*, trans. E. C. Beasley and Helen Zimmern (London: Bohn's Standard Library, 1890).

[4] See *Hamburg Dramaturgy* No. 14, on bourgeois tragedy, and Nos. 48, 79, on pity. J. E. Gillet, "A Note on the Tragic 'Admiratio,'" *MLR*, XIII (1918), 233–8, traces the shift from earlier Renaissance "wonder" and "fear" to sympathetic "admiration" and "pity" and the development of these latter in the period from Corneille to Lessing.

estant Aristotelian, one who claimed to be looking back past Voltaire, Corneille, Scaliger, the neo-classic distorters, to the pure classic idea. He did not "hesitate to admit" that he considered the *Poetics* of Aristotle to be as "infallible as the *Elements* of Euclid." "I would dispose of his authority easily enough if I could dispose of his reasons." [5] We have seen how his attempt upon the neo-classic *ut pictura poesis* left that doctrine fundamentally untouched. The degree of romanticism that shows in Lessing consists in the humanitarian and compassionate shading of his ethical views on tragedy.

Between Lessing and the next major figure in the rise of German critical theory, J. G. Herder, a rather distinct line will be drawn by a reader inclined to recognize some antithesis between the "classic" and "romantic." In the voluminous criticism of Herder—for instance, in such representative works as his *Fragmente zur deutschen Litteratur* (1767) and his *Kritische Wälder* (1769),—we find a group of radically new concerns centering in the relations of poetry to race, geography, and history, and in the creative and symbolic powers of verbal expression.[6] These were germinal and explosive ideas.

The criticism of the Italian Renaissance—the annotated editions of the classics, the formal treatises, the "defences" of poetry—had been a relatively deliberate and stolid performance, circumspectly, even legalistically, argued by the savants of that day. The new renaissance of German romanticism was an eruption of notes, fragments, letters, conversations, pamphlets, prize essays, lectures, and systems, enthusiastically thrown out by poets, novelists, translators, oracular professors, and transcendental philosophers. Where the 16th-century Italians had translated Aristotle, the Germans now translated Shakespeare and made him one of the main inspirations. At the same time, Goethe played the role of a contemporary demi-urge and seemed to his fellows the very incarnation of the theories they were developing.[7] Among literary expressions of first importance appear the various essays of Goethe and his retrospectively dramatic *Conversations*.[8]

II

ITALIAN criticism of the 16th century had looked back with reverence to at least one medieval text, the *Commedia* of Dante, and had been

[5] *Hamburg Dramaturgy*, No. 74. Cf. Nos. 101–4.

[6] See Wellek, *History* I, Chapter 9. The notes to the present chapter do not attempt to make explicit acknowledgement of all that is owing to the first two volumes of René Wellek's *History of Modern Criticism: 1750–1950*. The debt is especially large in the passages referring to Herder. The chapter owes much also to Gilbert and Kuhn's *History of Esthetics* and to the help of Richard J. Browne in verifying citations from the German sources.

[7] See especially *Über die bildende Nachahmung des Schönen*, 1788, by Goethe's admirer and fellow traveler in Italy, Karl Philipp Möritz.

[8] Published by J. P. Eckermann in 1836.

much concerned to vindicate the new Ariostan form of epic which had developed out of medieval romance and burlesque. Then this kind of Gothicism had suffered a relative eclipse during the era of French neo-classicism. Boileau's scorn for the Italian tradition was representative.

Évitons ces excès; laissons a l'Italie
De tous ces faux brillans l'éclatante folie.[9]

But at least as early as Dryden's appreciation of Chaucer in the Preface to his *Fables* (1700) a similar vein of archaic taste had begun to appear in English criticism. It ran through the 18th century in Shakespeare and Spenser criticism and in some other notable places like Bishop Hurd's *Letters on Chivalry and Romance,* 1763. There were strong developments in a kind of antiquarianism which was to have special import for methods of literary scholarship.[1] At the same time, a general broadening and deepening of historical interest worked into more exalted notions about the nature of literature. One early continental source, though during the romantic period it was not influential,[2] was the *New Science* of Vico (1725) expounding the patriarchal and monarchic origins of society and along with these the metaphoric and symbolic origins of human thought and institutions.[3] Similar trains of ideas appear in 18th-century books on Homer,[4] such as those in English by Thomas Blackwell (1735) and Robert Wood (1769), leading up to Friedrich Wolf's thesis that the Homeric epics are put together from a number of smaller poems handed down by oral recitation.[5] From the time of Herder on, the appreciation of various folk and Gothic literatures and the comparative study of ancient, eastern, and modern foreign literatures (the criticism of literature by age and race)[6] were strongly established, and these interests profoundly affected theories about the nature of literature as the expression of, or the power that shaped, human cultures or human nature in general. Friedrich Schlegel only accented an already pervasive view when he called poetry the most specifically human energy, the central document of any culture. Developments were partly nationalistic, even chauvinistic (as with the poet Klopstock). Ideas of German

---

[9] *Art Poétique,* I, 43-4.

[1] See *post* Chapter 24.

[2] Vico was scarcely known outside of Italy before Michelet's translation published in 1829.

[3] A devious connection between Vico and Herder has been shown in the notes of the Italian scholar Cesarotti attached to the pseudo-primitive Scottish *Ossian* in the German version by Denis which Herder read. Robert T. Clark, Jr., "Herder, Cesarotti and Vico," *SP,* XLIV (October, 1947), 645-71.

[4] Cf. *ante* Chapter 16, p. 350.

[5] *Prolegomena in Homerum,* 1795.

[6] Herder's main effort on this theme is his Prize Essay of 1773 on the *Causes of the Decline of Taste in Different Nations.* But there is much elsewhere in Herder about climate, landscape, racial customs, politics, and the like.

folk, German literature, and German destiny were rampant. The critics reached out for Shakespeare [7] as a translatable and adoptable expression of the national spirit—even as the 16th-century Italians had exclaimed: "Plunder the ancients and bring home the spoils."

III

ONE historical question with which the German critics were much occupied was that concerning the difference between "classic" and "romantic." The term "romantic" had come a long way from its early neo-classic uses—largely either neutral or pejorative—relating to medieval adventure stories written in the romance languages. During the 18th century the term had gained so much ground that it now became available to the German critics as an honorific, if problematic, name of a central and dynamic literary conception.[8] The Jena professor and Shakespeare translator A. W. Schlegel [9] devoted the first of his Vienna *Lectures on Dramatic Art and Literature* (1808) to rebuking neo-classic exclusiveness and pleading for a "universality of true criticism."

> The groundwork of human nature is no doubt everywhere the same; but in all our investigations, we may observe that, throughout the whole range of nature, there is no elementary power so simple, but that it is capable of dividing and diverging into opposite directions. The whole play of vital motion hinges on harmony and contrast. Why, then, should not this phenomenon recur on a grander scale in the history of man? In this idea we have perhaps discovered the true key to the ancient and modern history of poetry and the fine arts.[1]

Those who have adopted this idea have given "to the peculiar spirit of *modern* art, as contrasted with the *antique* or *classical*, the name of *romantic*." Schlegel's popularization of the "romantic" idea was further broadcast over Europe by Madame de Staël in her *De L'Allemagne.* Coleridge began to use the term and the distinction in his lectures of 1811. "Romanticism" was a highly self-conscious literary movement.

[7] Both Lessing and Herder were main agents for "inoculating" the Germans with Shakespeare (Saintsbury III, 359).

[8] Cf. René Wellek, "The Concept of 'Romanticism' in Literary History," *Comparative Literature*, I (Winter, 1949), 1–23.

[9] The most widely successful propagandist of German romanticism. He was known in England as "our national critic," the "one clear voice out of Germany." He delivered in all four great series of public lectures on literary theory. The *Über schöne Literatur und Kunst*, 1801–03, was superior to, if not more widely known than, the *Über dramatische Kunst und Literatur.*

[1] *A Course of Lectures on Dramatic Art and Literature*, trans. John Black and A. J. W. Morrison (London, 1846), p. 21.

The German critics conceived classical art to be a direct, objective, and happily unsophisticated communion with nature, and romantic (or modern) art to be a view of nature complicated, somewhat unhappily, by various phases of reflexiveness and subjectivity. As long as nature had been sound on the inside of man, he could look at it outside him simply and without tampering. When nature in modern times had gone wrong inside him, he looked on nature outside with nostalgic projections; he invested it with a shimmer of his own yearning personality. Modern art, said Goethe's younger friend, the poet-philosopher of Jena, Friedrich Schiller, in his definitive essay *Über naive und sentimentalische Dichtung* (1795), is a striving toward an ideal synthesis (of intellect and feeling) which is in its very nature unrealizable, but which is nevertheless a higher thing than the once perfect, now irrecoverable, naive.[2] Schelling, in his *Philosophie der Kunst*,[3] dwelt on the harmony between man and nature which had found adequate symbols in pagan mythology, and on the breach between man and God which it was the dialectical role of Christianity to create, and the resulting unsatisfied, infinite yearning of which modern literature was fated to be the inadequate allegory. Friedrich Schlegel, closely echoing the ideas of Schiller, talked about a *progressive Universalpoesie*.[4] Classic art was conceived by the German critics as "beauty;" romantic art as "energy." Classic was universal and ideal; romantic was individual and "characteristic." Classic was plastic (like sculpture), finite, closed, pure in genre. Romantic was picturesque (like painting), infinite, open, mixed.[5]

In a late polemical statement aimed against the French romantics Goethe said:

> I call the classic *healthy*, the romantic *sickly*. In this sense, the *Nibelungenlied* is as classic as the *Iliad*, for both are vigorous and healthy. Most modern productions are romantic, not because they are new, but because they are weak, morbid, and sickly; and the antique is classic, not because it is old, but because it is strong, fresh, joyous, and healthy.[6]

[2] Schiller divided modern "sentimental" poetry into three kinds, according to modes of feeling: satire, which looks down on reality from the height of the ideal; elegy, which mourns the loss of the ideal; idyll, which imagines a past or future ideal as real.

[3] Composed in 1802–03 and circulated in manuscript, though not published until 1859. His *System des Transcendentalen Idealismus* appeared in 1800.

[4] *Athenaeum* No. 116, in Jakob Minor, ed. *Friedrich Schlegel; seine prosaischen Jugendschriften* (Vienna, 1906), II, 220. Cf. Victor Lange, "Friedrich Schlegel's Literary Criticism," *Comparative Literature*, VII (Fall, 1955), 297.

[5] See, for instance, A. W. Schlegel, *Lectures on Dramatic Art and Literature* (London, 1846), pp. 22–7, 340–3, Lectures I and XXII; and René Wellek's account of these passages and of parallel passages in the Berlin Lectures of 1801–04 (*History* II, 48, 58–9).

[6] *Conversations*, April 2, 1829, trans. John Oxenford. See the selections in Bate, *Criticism: the Major Texts*, pp. 400–05.

He was in a somewhat creatively reminiscent mood when he made the following statement—but it will serve here as a summary dramatization of the antithesis we have been describing.

> The idea of the distinction between classical and romantic poetry, which is now spread over the whole world, and occasions so many quarrels and divisions, came originally from Schiller and myself. I laid down the maxim of objective treatment in poetry, and would allow no other; but Schiller, who worked quite in the subjective way, deemed his own fashion the right one, and to defend himself against me, wrote the treatise upon *Naïve and Sentimental Poetry*. He proved to me that I myself, against my will, was romantic, and that my *Iphigenia*, through the predominance of sentiment, was by no means so classical and so much in the antique spirit as some people supposed.
>
> The Schlegels took up this idea, and carried it further, so that it has now been diffused over the whole world; and everyone talks about classicism and romanticism—of which nobody thought fifty years ago.[7]

From a neutrally retrospective standpoint, one might observe that German romantic poetry and criticism were hardly at all primitive or "natural" in the sense that English nature poetry was. German romanticism was historical, Hellenic, actually classic, in an appeal not to Aristotle, but to Homer and the tragic dramatists. It was a spirited and vastly aspiring revision of Winckelmannian classicism. The main paradox of the romantic mind was that it yearned for a primitive or direct nature, yet was compelled to do this through the medium of its own historical awareness and introspective virtuosity.

A further phase in the dialectic of classic versus romantic is marked by Hegel's massively systematic revision of romantic theory, his *Lectures on Aesthetics* (1835) or, as the work is now known in English, *Philosophy of Fine Art*. Hegel divides all art into three stages: first symbolic—where, as in the Egyptian pyramids and temples, the activity of spirit or idea only half struggles forth from the mass of matter; second classic—where, as in Greek sculpture, idea (form) and matter are perfectly fused; and third romantic—where, as in modern music, painting, and (above all) poetry, spirit overflows and envelops matter in self-conscious fulness.[8] There was more moral energy here, less beauty, than in the classic. As Schiller had put it, all art arises out of two impulses and balances these variously—the finite material impulse (*Stoff-*

---

[7] *Conversations*, March 21, 1830.

[8] G. W. F. Hegel, *The Philosophy of Fine Art*, trans. F. P. B. Osmaston (London, 1920), I, 1–5, "Introduction to Second Part."

trieb) and the infinite impulse of the idea (*Formtrieb*). The reconciliation of these is the free "play" of the whole human person (*Spieltrieb*).[9] The novelist Jean Paul Richter in his *Vorschule der Ästhetik* (1804) spoke of two extremes, the materialist and the empty idealist (or nihilist), both of which missed the mean of true form and art.[1] It would not be a great exaggeration to say that all German romantic criticism was devoted to the problem of how literature reconciles sensory experience and ideas (the "particular" and the "universal" of Warton's and Johnson's thinking). Their criticism was hence, at higher levels of speculation, devoted to the problem of how literature reconciles the worldly with the transcendental, the external and dubious material object with the spiritually reliable and self-aware subject, the outer world of "nature" and scientific observation with the inner world of schemes and of will and morals,[2] the contingent world of *history* with the necessary world of *system*.

IV

ALL these antitheses and their attempted resolutions may be described as arising in the due course of historic process out of the empirical and analytic trends of the 17th and 18th centuries. They were the romantic reconstruction, in transcendental terms, of the world successively and resolutely abstracted apart by the Cartesian and the British empirical analyses. German romanticism was a retort to scientism, a program for poetic re-establishment of the analytically dissolved harmony between man and nature and between the parts of man's own consciousness. The most lyric and most visionary of the Jena circle of theorizers, Friedrich von Hardenberg (Novalis), in his essay *Christendom or Europe*, wrote a memorable version of the charge that science was ruining all. Science was making "the infinite creative music of the universe into the dull clappering of a gigantic mill driven by the stream of chance and floating upon it, a mill, without architect and without miller, grinding itself to pieces, in fact a *perpetuum mobile*." [3]

The whole aesthetic trend owed a great deal to Immanuel Kant, whose "Copernican revolution" had recalled thinking from the atomically and externally oriented analyses of Hume and centered it reflexively on an active and unifying creativity of the knowing subject.

[9] Friedrich Schiller, *Letters upon the Aesthetical Education of Man*, Letters XII-XV, in *Essays Aesthetical and Philosophical* (London: Bohn's Standard Library, 1916, *Schiller's Works*, vol. VI), esp. pp. 60-2, 67, 69-72.

[1] *Vorschule*, No. 69, at end, in *Jean Pauls Sämtliche Werke* (Historisch-Kritische Ausgabe, Weimar, 1935), I, ii, 234.

[2] Cf. Schiller, *op. cit.*, pp. 60-3.

[3] Quoted by Carlyle in his essay on "Voltaire," 1829. See his *Critical & Miscellaneous Essays* (Boston, 1860), II, 75-6.

Kant's *Critique of Judgment,* 1790, was a happily aesthetic afterthought, making an intermediate ground and connection between his earlier philosophy of science or *Critique of Pure Reason* and his philosophy of the moral imperative or *Critique of Practical Reason.* His account of *Judgment* was a decisive statement in the history of modern general aesthetics and at once exerted a strong influence upon literary aesthetics. It has a direct reflection in the essays of Schiller, and it is the ghostly paradigm, in *a priori* lines, of many more highly colored utterances by the poets and literary professors. On the one side, Kant had mapped the world of necessary physical events: conditioned by time and space, the spectacles of our sensory intuition (*Anschauung*), unified by imagination (*Einbildungskraft*), ordered according to the categories of scientific understanding (*Verstand*), and in the end only somewhat tentatively and hopefully affirmed under the sanction of the absolute (or thing-in-itself), the soul, the world whole, and God, ideas which were provided by our highest *a priori* faculty, the reason (*Vernunft*). On the other side, the free moral world of our choices, according to the categorical imperative. And then, after a while, the mediational concept of the aesthetic values, the beautiful (*das Schöne*) and the sublime (*das Erhabene*), both subjective. The latter, the more subjective of the two, was an a-prioristically elevated version of the feelings of awe (in the presence of great magnitude) and of self-congratulatory expansion (in safe recoil from the fear of wild natural energy) which had been described empirically by 18th-century British writers and especially by Burke. These feelings yielded Kant the "Mathematical Sublime" and the "Dynamic Sublime." [4] The beautiful, however, was something higher than accidental and private sense pleasure (*das Angenehme*), had a universal claim on human recognition, and was a norm though not a strictly definable norm (it was "without concept"). The appreciation of it was not "interested" in any possessive or practical way.[5] It was a form of order with which nature was "favored" by our own act of knowing, though we looked on it, unlike the subjectively experienced sublime, as something out there, in nature. It was a "purposiveness without purpose" (*Zweckmässigkeit ohne Zweck*). That is, it was not a teleology toward a nameable further end (like nourishment or shelter), but a highly satisfactory fitting of experience precisely to our own faculty of experiencing, to the progress of our knowledge. Our satisfaction in the presence of the beautiful was a feeling of unification, a harmonious interplay of sense and mind, a perfect freedom from scientific and utili-

---

[4] Among the fruits of the Kantian sublime may be listed A. W. Schlegel's view (*Lectures on Dramatic Art and Literature,* III) of tragic endurance as a form of self-assertion, for its own sake, in the face of fate, and the similar view of Schiller.

[5] That is, Kant asserted the "autonomy" of the *aesthetic,* distinguishing it from *pleasure,* from *emotion* and *interest,* and from didactic *knowledge.*

tarian necessity. At the same time the beautiful was "the symbol of the morally good."

> In the faculty of taste the judgment does not find itself, as in judging by experience, constrained by empirical laws; it legislates for itself on the objects of so pure a satisfaction, just as reason legislates autonomously on the faculty of desire in morality. And owing to this capacity in ourselves and to the capacity in external nature to harmonize therewith, the judgment finds in itself a reference to something in us and also outside us, which is neither physical necessity nor moral freedom but is allied to the supersensible conditions of freedom. In this supersensuous reality, the theoretical faculty and the practical faculty are mutually and mysteriously interwoven.[6]

Kant's idea of beauty was severe; it related (so far as human making was concerned) almost exclusively to the formal, decorative, and abstract: to Greek designs, foliation on wallpaper, arabesques (things which "mean nothing in themselves"), music without words. The "charms" of direct sensuous pleasure might fuse with beauty,[7] and beauty *might* be combined with perfect natural forms and purposive human artifacts (the good, the ideal), but in neither of these cases was beauty pure. Beauty allied to the good was not "free beauty" (*pulchritudo vaga*) but dependent beauty (*pulchritudo adhaerens*). The two might help *us* by being together, but strictly speaking neither helped the other. It is worth noting that here was a system which conceived Homer and Shakespeare as less aesthetically pure than wallpaper.

V

CERTAIN technical literary notions which were often repeated by the German critics form a very coherent pattern. This was the time, for instance, when modern literary criticism completed one of its major shifts in preference among the literary genres. The 17th-century norm had been, as we have seen, heroic and epic. That of Lessing, in the third quarter of the 18th century, had been dramatic and Aristotelian. Lessing's high regard for the action, the Aristotelian "fable," was a form of classical objectivity that had a fairly close connection with his preference for the colorlessly ideal forms of sculpture over the mere

---

[6] E. F. Carritt, *Philosophies of Beauty* (Oxford, 1931), p. 123. Cf. *Kant's Critique of Judgement*, trans. J. H. Bernard, 2d ed. revised (London, 1931), p. 251. Our account above uses the terminology of Carritt's translated selections.

[7] Carritt, p. 116; Bernard, pp. 81–2.

phenomenalism of colored painting.[8] Lessing, as we have seen,[9] believed drama to be the most poetic form of literature, and for the reason (related to a distinction made earlier in France by DuBos) that the ordinarily "artificial" signs of language become "natural" signs in drama. They are the direct imitation of persons speaking. But even in the early writings of Herder—and consistently with a general turn of interest from the external world to the knowing and expressing self—we find the notion that not the drama but the lyric is the most poetic kind of poetry, the most direct, free, and unlimited making of the poetic mind. "Lyrical poetry is the perfect expression of an emotion or representation in the highest euphony of language."[1] We have already sampled, apropos of Hegel's division of art into symbolic, classic, and romantic, the more or less normal later romantic view that poetry in general is the expression of mind using itself directly as medium; it is the very energy of mind.

Herder was dissatisfied[2] with the distinction made in *Laokoon* between painting as an art of space and verbal narrative as an art of time (still pictures and moving pictures, as we have suggested earlier). The real difference, said Herder, is that the physical arts work each by its peculiar sense, the ear, the eye, the touch (sculpture is the art of touch),[8] but poetry works by no sense. It is the direct *energy* of the shaping spirit, "immediate of the soul," the "music of the soul."[4] The old *Laokoon* had been written against an external, pictorial analogy between media. The *New Laokoon* of 1910 would look back over a century and a half in which the strong sway of the fascinating spirit had driven toward a general synaesthesis of media or an assimilation of all media to spirit itself and toward their reobjectification in the most intangible

[8] "Mere color and transitory expression have no ideal because Nature has proposed to herself nothing definite in them" (Hugo Blümner, ed. *Laokoon*, Berlin, 1880, 399—cf. 469—notations by Lessing, cited by F. O. Nolte, *Lessing's Laocoon*, Lancaster, Pa., 1940, p. 37).

[9] *Ante* Chapter 13, p. 270.

[1] *Terpsichore*, Part II, in *Werke*, ed. Suphan, XXVII (Berlin, 1881), 171. The earliest fragments of Herder include two sketches for a history of ode and lyric. "The firstborn child of emotion, the origin of poetry, the germ of life, is the ode" (*Werke*, XXXII, 1899, 62).

[2] *Erstes Kritisches Wäldchen*, 1769.

[3] See his *Plastik*, 1778. Cf. *ante* Chapter 13, p. 276.

[4] *Kritische Wälder* I and IV, in *Werke* III, 144, 157; IV, 166. The idea of energy (*energeia*) as a force to be distinguished from its product, a work (*ergon*), may be found in Aristotle, *Metaphysics* IV, 3–8. James Harris, *Three Treatises*, 3d. ed. (London, 1752), pp. 33 ff., uses the terms *energy* and *production*. Cf. Robert T. Clark, Jr., "Herder's Conception of 'Kraft,'" *PMLA*, LVII (1942), 737–52.

The idea of poetry as verbal music is developed by Ludwig Tieck and W. H. Wackenroder, *Phantasien über die Kunst*, ed. Jakob Minor in *Deutsche National-literatur* (Berlin and Stuttgart, n.d.), CXLV, 55–98, esp. 88. Novalis, echoing Diderot, thought of poetry as either inner music or inner painting, "freely modified by the nature of feeling." *Fragmente und Studien*, VI, 21; IX, 3; X, 60, in *Novalis Schriften*, ed. Paul Kluckhohn (Leipzig, n.d.), II, 323; III, 63; III, 290.

or immaterial of media, music. Even so massively solid a thing as architecture might be looked upon as "frozen music." The following statement by A. W. Schlegel summarizes the trend.

> We should once more try to bring the arts closer together and seek for transitions from one to the other. Statues perhaps may quicken into pictures, pictures become poems, poems music, and (who knows?) in like manner stately church music may once more rise heavenward as a cathedral.[5]

In the voluntaristic idealism of Schopenhauer—where the blind *nisus* of will is the noumenal ground of experience—music was to become the fullest and most subtly modulated revelation of that will itself. "The other arts speak only of Shadows." Music "is a copy of the will itself." [6] It has been a commonplace of modern aesthetics—though now somewhat discredited—that music is the center and ideal of all the arts.

If poetic words are the direct energy of spirit, they do not merely present meaning, they create it. Poetry is an "imitation," not of nature, but of the creating, naming Godhead.[7] The poet is a "second creator, *poietes*, maker." This is nowhere more obviously true than in metaphors. The metaphor is conceived as presiding, along with music, at the very birth of speech, of ideas, and of human institutions. Thus Herder in his prize essay of 1770 *Über den Ursprung der Sprache:* The earliest language was a "dictionary of the soul, it was at the same time mythology and a marvelous epic of the actions and speeches of all beings—a constant fable with passion and interest." [8]

> A certain savage sees a lofty tree, with its majestic crown, and is awestruck: the crown rustles! That is stirring godhead! The savage falls prostrate and worships! Behold the history of sensuous Man . . . and the easiest transition to abstract thought! [9]

[5] *"Die Gemählde," Athenaeum* II (Berlin, 1799), 49–50, quoted in Irving Babbitt, *The New Laokoon* (Boston, 1910), pp. 124–5. See p. 125 for relations between A. W. Schlegel and Diderot in the "confusion" of the arts, and p. 61 on the claims of F. Schlegel, Schelling, and Görres to authorship of the phrase "Architecture is frozen music."

[6] *World as Will and Idea,* trans. R. B. Haldane and J. Kemp, 7th ed. (London, 1927), I, 333.

[7] Herder, *Über Bild, Dichtung, und Fabel,* 1787, in *Zerstreute Blätter, Dritte Sammlung (Werke,* XV, 526).

[8] Herder, *Abhandlung über den Ursprung der Sprache,* 1772 (*Werke,* V, 51–3). The theory implies rejection of at least three earlier theories of the origin of language: the theory of divine inspiration, the rationalistic theory of deliberate human compact, and Condillac's sensualistic theory which derived language from brutal cries. Herder's idea of the poet as maker is rather closely anticipated in Shaftesbury's *Moralists,* Part III, end of section 2.

[9] *Werke,* V, 53. *"Jener Wilde sahe den hohen Baum mit seinem prächtigen Gipfel und bewunderte: der Gipfel rauschte! das ist webende Gottheit! der Wilde fällt nieder und betet an! Sehet da die Geschichte des sinnlichen Menschen, das*

Primitive man thinks in symbols, allegories, and metaphors. Combinations of these make fable and myth. And so far as modern man is a poet, he is primitive. Later theory (formulated first by Goethe [1] in 1797 and repeated by Schelling in his *Philosophie der Kunst* and by A. W. Schlegel in his *Dramatic Lecture* on Aeschylus) modified this vocabulary, if not the ideas behind it, by making a very insistent distinction between what was considered the merely conceptualized and finite meaning of "allegory" and the metaphorically full-bodied and infinite meaning of "symbol."

VI

THERE are passages in Herder which suggest that human history shows a uniform degeneracy from the glories of the age of poetry to the civilized weakness of the age of reason,[2] and that, having entered on the age of reason, the human race was committed to further technical progress and hence to the extinction of imagination.[3] But a more optimistic view was more prevalent—namely, that poetry was a new means of spiritual regeneration. With the Schlegels, poetry, and especially metaphor, is a perennial mother speech, a promise and vehicle of future human perfection. An even more formidable concept, that of "myth," comes into its own with several pronouncements by Friedrich Schlegel and the philosopher Schelling. The "main difference between the ancient poets and the modern," says Schlegel in his *Dialogue on Poetry*, is that the moderns "have no mythology. But let me add that we are not far from having one, or rather, that it is time we should make a serious effort to produce one." [4] In the *Discourse on Mythology* which forms part of the *Dialogue*, he issues a ringing invitation to a new world view, a new "synthetic" mythology, a "great mythological poem," which is to rise from some source in modern idealist philosophy or natural science.[5] And Schelling carried this theme even further in an elaborate

---

dunkle Band, wie aus den Verbis Nomina werden—und den leichtesten Schritt zur Abstraktion!" Cf. Ernst Cassirer, *Language and Myth*, trans. Susanne Langer (New York, 1946), p. 85.

[1] In his *Über die Gegenstände der bildenden Kunst;* and later in his *Maximen.*

[2] See, for instance, *Fragmente einer Abhandlung über die Ode*, c. 1765? (*Werke*, XXXII, 69).

[3] For similar views see Vico (with regret) and Fontenelle (with sentiments of welcome to the new age) in his *Traité de la Poésie en Général*. And see the debate between Shelley and Peacock, *post* Chapter 19.

[4] *Gespräch über die Poesie*, 1800, in Jakob Minor, ed. *Friedrich Schlegel: seine prosaischen Jugendschriften* (Vienna, 1906), II, 358, quoted in translation by Victor Lange, "Friedrich Schlegel's Literary Criticism," *Comparative Literature*, VII (Fall, 1955), 301.

[5] *Rede über die Mythologie*, 1800, in Minor, II, 357–63; see Lange, *loc. cit.*, p. 302. "What distinguishes Schlegel's thinking from Herder's," says Lange, "is that . . . at this time, he rejects any temptation to resort to a mere re-creation of past mythological substance."

deification of natural "potencies." Ideas were images of divinity when taken as ideas. When taken as real, they were no less than gods. Thus: the "point of absolute difference" between self and the outer world was Jupiter; the ideal world was Apollo; the formative principle embodied in iron was Vulcan; water, the formless principle, was Neptune.[6] In the aspirations of romantic poetical philosophy, the classic pantheon was always eminent. Schlegel [7] and Schelling were prophetic of a kind of mythology which materialized much more vividly during the later 19th century in the work of Comte, Wagner and Nietzsche.

Poetry conceived along these lines would be a kind of philosophy, the most creative and highest philosophy. It would take the place of ordinary philosophy. Poetry—art—was the supreme fact. "Poetry," wrote Novalis in one of his *Fragments*, "is a genuine absolute reality. This is the gist of my philosophy. The more poetical, the more true." [8] Such speculations soared the more wildly when the subjective idealism of Kant (where the sway of the human intellect was limited to appearances) was stepped up by his followers to the phase of absolute idealism —where all reality is the production of selfhood—of inner, conscious, self and outer, unconscious, self, in conflict with each other (as with Fichte) or reconciled in a higher aesthetic and philosophic self (as with Schelling). There were tensions here between the claims of art and those of philosophy, perhaps most sensitively felt by Schelling, who at first made art the sufficient "organon" of philosophy, an eternal revelation, an infinite satisfaction, but in the absolute phase of his idealism [9] later conceived that, although art mythologized and reflected the absolute, philosophy alone could conceptualize and understand it. A distinctive feature of Friedrich Schlegel's diffusely oracular system was his elevation of criticism itself to a metaphoric and creative status equal to that of the poetry which was its object.[1] The critic must illuminate the original exercise of the poet by transcending it. "Poetry," he said, "can only be criticized by poetry," [2] and the dictum was honored throughout Europe for more than a century in a flourishing tradition of impressionistic criticism.[3]

Nothing could have been less realistic or less naturalistic than the full romantic theory. Poetry as creative dreaming was one of the most

---

[6] *Philosophie der Kunst*, I, B.1, in *Sämtliche Werke* (Stuttgart and Augsburg, 1859), I, 5, 402ff.

[7] Schlegel's essay *Über die Sprache und Weisheit der Inder*, 1808, was to have a considerable influence on the later study of comparative mythology (Lange, *loc. cit.*, p. 303).

[8] *Fragmente und Studien* VI, 468 (*Schriften*, ed. Kluckhohn, II, 411).

[9] In his *Philosophie der Kunst*, written in 1802–03.

[1] Schlegel called his own elaborate review of *Wilhelm Meister* (1798) an *Übermeister* (Lange, *loc. cit.*, p. 296).

[2] Minor, II, 200, quoted by Lange, p. 296.

[3] Cf. *post* Chapter 22, p. 496.

satisfactory conceptions of the era—like the creative dreaming of the Plotinian world soul. In his unfinished novels *Heinrich von Ofterdingen* (about the youth of a medieval Minnesinger) and *Die Lehrlinge zu Sais* (containing the Märchen of *Hyazinth und Rosenblut* or insight through spiritual love) Novalis offers both statement and illustration of his yearning for a single pregnant and reconciling fantasy.[4] Dreaming, said Jean Paul, is involuntary poetry.[5] The photographic naturalism of the later 19th century ("romanticism on all fours") and the direct emotional display which came to represent spontaneity had far less in common with Schiller and the Schlegels and Novalis than with anti-classical phenomena of the earlier 18th century—the emotivism which we have already described in England (in Germany *Sturm und Drang*) and the realism which went with it—the view of "truth" that may be found in Lessing, in Samuel Johnson, in Diderot.

A poetry which is to be truly philosophical will have to be a rounded image of the human spirit. It will have an imaginative fairness and fullness. True simplicity (*Einfachheit*), said Jean Paul, dwells in the organic whole, not in parts. During the era of rationalistic enlightenment, the imagery most often implicit in theories of poetry had been mechanical—imagery of a verbal force working to produce clear impressions on our mental tablets or to pile up handsome aggregations of atomic parts into literary "compositions." The new German imagery of aesthetic theory was botanical and zoological—an imagery of the spontaneously unfolding and articulated self-conscious spirit, in a word, of organism. The poem sprang like a flower from the poetic genius. Organism, said Schelling in his *Philosophie der Kunst*, is the highest "potency" of nature. (Art, the analogue of organism, is the highest potency of the absolute.) In his system of antitheses between classic and romantic, A. W. Schlegel assigned "mechanical" form to the classic,[6] "organic" to the romantic, and though this was not meant as an altogether derogatory judgment upon the "mechanical," the distinction

---

[4] Cf. Eugene E. Reed, "Novalis' *Heinrich von Ofterdingen* as *Gesamtkunstwerk*," PQ, XXXIII (April, 1954), 200–11.

[5] *Sämtliche Werke* (Berlin, 1841), XIII, 262, "*Briefe und bevorstehender Lebenslauf*," postscript to the fifth letter.

[6] At least he managed to suggest that "mechanical" form is what is found in the neo-classic (*Lectures on Dramatic Art*, London, 1846, p. 340, Lecture XXII). "Form is mechanical when, through external force, it is imparted to any material merely as an accidental addition without reference to its quality; as, for example, when we give a particular shape to a soft mass that it may retain the same after its induration. Organical form, again, is innate; it unfolds itself from within, and acquires its determination contemporaneously with the perfect development of the germ. We everywhere discover such forms in nature throughout the whole range of living powers, from the crystallization of salts and minerals to plants and flowers, and from these again to the human body. In the fine arts, as well as in the domain of nature—the supreme artist, all genuine forms are organical, that is, determined by the quality of the work." Cf. Wellek, *History* II, 48, 59.

was one way of honoring the expansive aspiration of a romantic mode which under such aspects as the mixture of its genres might suffer momentary disadvantages in comparison with the purity of the classic.

VII

A HIGHLY distinctive feature of German romantic theory was its concern to develop, under the sanction of such major premises as we have been describing, a rationale of the comic. Rational statements, thought Jean Paul, are one-sided.[7] Sober statements, or painful statements, or tearful statements might well seem to have the same defect. The relation of tragedy to comedy became an important issue, and there was a general tendency to set the comic up and dignify it, either as a separate, yet highly significant, laughable genre of verbal art, or as an integral side of the serious. A moderate version of the argument appears in A. W. Schlegel's defence of puns ("sportive word-play") as a smallscale model of the whole poetic structure, a kind of fullness and directness in verbal representation,[8] and in his guarded view that "irony," though it has no place at all in the "proper tragic," yet permeates the whole fabric of Shakespeare's plays and almost the whole range of literature upward from the "avowed raillery of comedy."[9] More radically, other German critics developed various concepts of the laughable into specific technical literary implementations of the paramount concept of transcendence. Jean Paul (known to English students best as the model of Carlyle's gigantic agility in the laughing style and as a source for

[7] Cf. *Vorschule der Ästhetik*, No. 69 (*Jean Pauls Sämtliche Werke*, 1935, I, ii, 234).

[8] "An imagination which has been powerfully excited is fond of laying hold of any congruity in sound which may accidentally offer itself, that by such means it may, for the nonce, restore the lost resemblance between the word and the thing. . . . We do not mean to say that all playing upon words is on all occasions to be justified. This must depend on the disposition of mind, whether it will admit of such a play of fancy, and whether the sallies, comparisons and allusions, which lie at the bottom of them, possess internal solidity" (*Lectures on Dramatic Art*, XXIII, on Shakespeare).

[9] "Shakespeare makes each of his principal characters the glass in which the others are reflected. Nobody ever painted so truthfully as he has done the facility of self-deception, the half self-conscious hypocrisy towards ourselves, with which even noble minds attempt to disguise the almost inevitable influence of selfish motives in human nature. The secret irony of the characterization commands admiration as the profound abyss of acuteness and sagacity; but it is the grave of enthusiasm. We arrive at it only after we have had the misfortune to see human nature through and through. . . . Shakespeare . . . makes, as it were, a sort of secret understanding with the select circle of the more intelligent of his readers or spectators; he shows them that he had previously seen and admitted the validity of their tacit objections; that he himself is not tied down to the represented subject, but soars freely above it; and that if he chose, he could unrelentingly annihilate the beautiful and irresistibly attractive scenes which his magic pen has produced" (*Lectures on Dramatic Art*, XXIII).

some of Meredith's ideas in his lecture on the *Comic Spirit*) devoted Chapter VI of his *Vorschule* to a theory of comic *contrast* in the vogue prevalent after the statement of Kant.[1] The contrast between the stupidity of the comic action and the ordinary human good sense which the spectator projects upon or "lends" to the comic figure constitutes, in Jean Paul's view, an "infinite incongruity" (*unendliche Ungereimtheit*).[2] We have a lively freedom of choice among three series of thoughts, our own insight, that of the stupid comic figure, and that part or aspect of our insight which we lend. Our intellect toys with these possibilities; it plays and dances back and forth in a delightful freedom.[3] Only man has follies; and only man can recognize them. But on a still higher plane, Jean Paul conceives a phase of the laughable upon which he confers a name dedicated in English theory to an earthier usage—that is, "humor." "Humor" becomes an inverted and sympathetically laughable form of the sublime (treading "in the low buskin of comedy" but carrying the tragic mask in her hand), a measure of the finite against the infinite.

> If man, like ancient theology, glances down from the world beyond on the terrestrial world, the latter looks small and vain; if he measures the infinite world with the small one, as humor does, connecting them with each other, then laughter arises, wherein is, sorrow and greatness.[4]

Humor annihilates not the single object but finiteness as such merely by setting it in opposition to the idea.

One kind of climax to such laughing sympathies appears in the essays of Friedrich Schlegel on the theme of "irony."[5] It was possible to play and dance not only in comparing the stupidity of the comic character and our own projected shrewdness, but in comparing phases of our own stupidity and shrewdness, superior evolutions of the self, moments in that "transcendence of self" developed by Fichte in the higher reaches of the subject-object dialectic. Irony was a succession of contrasts between the ideal and the real, a technique by which the "transcendental ego" was capable of mocking its own convictions and its own productions. It was ultimate self-parody. It remained aloof from fixation or satisfaction at any level of insight. It was an avenue to the

---

[1] To be sampled in English, for instance, in Hazlitt's lecture on "Wit and Humor," introducing his series on the *English Comic Writers*, 1819.

[2] *Vorschule*, No. 28 (*Werke* I, ii, 97).

[3] Cf. Edward V. Brewer, "The Influence of Jean Paul Richter on George Meredith's Conception of the Comic," *JEGP*, XXIX (April, 1930), 243–56.

[4] *Vorschule*, No. 33 (*Werke* I, ii, 116). Kierkegaard's later two-phase transcendence was to move from the aesthetic to the moral (via "irony") and from the moral to the religious (via "humor"). See his *Concluding Unscientific Postscript*, trans. David F. Swenson (Princeton, 1944), p. 448.

[5] *Athenaeum* Nos. 37 and 116 (J. Minor, *op. cit.*, II, 209, 220–1).

infinite, the expression of man's appetite for the boundless; it was expansiveness, it was megalomania. Life at its most incandescent phase destroyed itself as it created.

At the hands of romantic poets, this irony might be very dark, sardonic, misanthropic; the hero stood with cloak pulled round his shoulder thrust out to the cold blast—a Byronic and Poesque figure. "Hot baths of sentiment," says Irving Babbitt, "were followed by cold douches of irony." [6] In its more obvious and emotive phases romantic irony was an engine of self-protection and self-enhancement—the device which the amateur employs when he speaks of his masterpiece as a trifle.

But other phases were hyper-metaphysical. In the essays of the pre-symbolist poet Heine, for example, and in the system of the aesthetician K. W. F. Solger, irony was subtilized until it became coextensive with all art; it was the very principle by which art triumphs over nature, spirit over matter. Looking at even the cruder kind of irony from a metaphysical point of view, Solger accuses it of "conferring a semblance of existence upon nothingness in order to annihilate the latter more easily." Solger conceives the finer irony as an almost mystical energy of artistic insight. It is the creative act by which idea or essence steps into the place of and annihilates phenomenal reality. It is the translation of the world of experience into the artist's ideal dream. The idea, expression of the infinite, surpasses the poverty of its medium. Irony is a transcendental means of contemplative "enthusiasm," a union of impulse and rational lucidity, a poise between the extremes of ecstasy and disenchantment. "Without irony there is no true art." [7] By such stages one emerges again onto the high, transcendentally illuminated plateau of Schiller's impulse of free play (*Spieltrieb*), the reconciliation of *Stoff* and *Form*, the aesthetic equipoise. Hegel, who, like Jean Paul, employed the term "humor" and meant by it something much like what Friedrich Schlegel and Solger meant by "irony," delivered an appraisal which has often been quoted. This activity, he observed, implies the "perversion and overthrow of all that is objectively solid in reality."

> It works through the wit and play of wholly personal points of view, and if carried to an extreme amounts to the triumph of the creative power of the artist's soul over every content and every form. [8]

It is "Satanic impertinence."

[6] *Rousseau and Romanticism* (Boston, 1919), Ch. VII.

[7] Maurice Boucher, *K. W. F. Solger, Esthéthique et philosphie de la présence* (Paris, 1934), pp. 107–10; Kurt Weinberg, *Henri Heine, "romantique défroqué," héraut du symbolisme français* (Paris and New Haven, 1954), pp. 122–5.

[8] *Philosophy of Fine Art*, trans. F. P. B. Osmaston (London, 1920), II, 386; Subsection III, ch. 3, 3, b.

VIII

ONE of Goethe's best-known pronouncements concerns the debt of the Germans to the English.

> Our own literature is chiefly the offspring of theirs! Whence have we our novels, our tragedies, but from Goldsmith, Fielding, and Shakespeare? And in our own day, where will you find in Germany three literary heroes who can be placed on a level with Lord Byron, Moore, and Walter Scott? [9]

Not only German poets and novelists but German literary theorists of the romantic period owed a considerable debt to English writers, though in the latter area the English writers were for the most part less distinguished. We have alluded to the correspondence between Kant's sublime and the empirical ideas of Burke's *Inquiry*.[1] Historians of aesthetic thoery point out how Kant's doctrines about "beauty" are only a reduction to systematic form (though "what a systematic form was that!") [2] of ideas widely current in 18th-century England. In Shaftesbury and Hutcheson, for instance, one finds the disinterestedness of aesthetic pleasure; in Kames, the same disinterestedness and the notion that judgments of taste are immediate; in Addison, the pleasures of the imagination conceived as something intermediate between those of sense and those of understanding.[3]

In the important area of comic theory the Germans had less sufficient antecedents in England than in France, where the leading critical mind of the 18th century, Diderot, after a record of notably *larmoyant* thinking had turned at the end, in his *Paradoxe sur le comédien*, to a view of acting and poetry that laid strong stress on the moment of self-awareness, the ironic reserve of passion. But in general England provided better anticipation of the more solemn themes. The primitivistic ideas of Herder and his successors concerning *Volkspoesie*, lyricism, rhythmic expression, emotion, and the birth of language, were fostered, for one thing, by the very impostures of primitivism, chiefly the Ossianic, that came out of England. The same ideas were available too and were known

---

[9] *Conversations*, December 5, 1824.

[1] A similar correspondence appears in Addison's *Spectator* No. 420, where he speaks of the pleasure to be derived from expanding our imagination by degrees. Kames's use of St. Peter's at Rome and of the pyramids as examples of the sublime is a curious anticipation of Kant's use of the same examples in contradiction to his own principle that works of human art cannot participate in the sublime. See E. F. Carritt, "The Sources and Effects in England of Kant's Philosophy of Beauty," *The Monist*, XXXV (April, 1925), 315 ff.

[2] Gilbert and Kuhn, p. 323.

[3] E. F. Carritt, *loc. cit.* Muratori, the Italian neo-classic critic, had conceived the aesthetic imagination as the harmonious union of the understanding and the imagination in general. (Gilbert and Kuhn, p. 322; cf. E. F. Carritt, *Philosophies of Beauty*, p. 63.)

to Herder in English Homeric theorists and in general aesthetic theorists like Shaftesbury, John Brown, "Hermes" Harris, Hugh Blair, Percy, the Wartons, and Edward Young. And in England the lyric norm had been in serious preparation throughout the 18th century not only in the writings of the theorists but in the practice of numerous "Great Ode" and elegy writers.[4]

The work of the British aestheticians, literary theorists, and writers on genius lay ready for the German transformation. The transformation, the stepping up, was nevertheless a matter of great moment. What was empirical, descendental, down-looking, matter-of-fact in the British pioneering, became with the Germans metaphysical, transcendental, ideal, and absolute. Theories of how human feelings and trains of consciousness *happen* to work became theories of what art *is*, what poetry *is*, and the *is* implied an *ought to be*. This was in a sense a return to classical and neo-Platonic lines of thought, but with a change that made these lines acceptable to a generation that had undergone the disillusioning experience of the "enlightenment." German classico-romantic literary theory bears the same kind of relation to British mid-18th-century aesthetics and criticism as Kant bears to Hume. The *disjecta membra* of experience, subject and object, and parcels of each, were re-assembled by force of spirit—in a philosophy of life that placed human creation, or art, either at or near the pinnacle. The new synthesis and the new faith had a new subjective richness resulting from the long analytic and skeptical decomposition which had preceded. The new idealism was more epistemological than any preceding idealism. It may be true that such thinking, when it occurred in the department of literary criticism, was not always so close as it should have been to its literary object. Saintsbury has taken pleasure in pointing out some mistakes of the Germans in the interpretation of Shakespeare and other Elizabethan texts, even a certain aloofness from the texts, as in the case of Goethe's *Hamlet* criticism in *Wilhelm Meister*. This, says Saintsbury, might have been written about a translation of Shakespeare. It is a commonplace of literary history to observe the heavy schematism of the German critical effort and to believe that the German critics were less

---

[4] See Norman Maclean, "From Action to Image: Theories of the Lyric in the Eighteenth Century," in *Critics and Criticism*, ed. R. S. Crane, pp. 408–60. Eighteenth-century English instances of a desire to push even drama toward a lyric norm may be noted. Kames complained that the Greek drama had more action than feeling. It had "no sentiments except of the plainest kind . . . no intricate or delicate situation to occasion any singular passion; no gradual swelling and subsiding of passion: no conflict between different passions" (letter to Mrs. Montague, June 17, 1771, quoted in Helen W. Randall, *The Critical Theory of Lord Kames*, Northampton, 1944, p. 111). (Cf. *post*, Chapter 20, Hugo, Newman, and Arnold on dramatic norms.) The orientalist Sir William Jones by a simple dichotomy rejected "imitation" in favor of lyric feeling. "The finest parts of poetry, music and painting, are expressive of the passions, and operate on our minds by sympathy. The inferior parts of them are descriptive of natural objects, and affect us chiefly by substitution" (*Poems*, London, 1777, p. 207).

lovingly and immediately in touch with the letter of the literary work than the English literary men of the same generation. Yet the latter took what they could of German philosophy, gratefully, and were improved by it. What came out of British empiricism came back raised to a power where it actually met the critical needs of the literary mind or some of those needs.

CHAPTER 18

IMAGINATION: WORDSWORTH AND COLERIDGE

§ *semantics of "imagination" and "fancy" from 17th century to romantic era, Wordsworth's Preface to* Poems, *1815: elevation of both "imagination" and "fancy," Coleridge's objections, his concern with psychology rather than poems, essential agreement between Wordsworth and Coleridge—II. Coleridge's progress from association to idealism, tabloid treatment of imagination and fancy (*Biographia XIII*), German sources and parallels: Schelling's Oration, Kant, Coleridge's system: Understanding, Reason, Primary and Secondary Imagination, coalescence of inner and outer, creation—III. superior idealism of the artist, symbols, nature and the spiritual life, within us and abroad, various other statements by Coleridge:* Treatise on Method, Semina Rerum, Philosophical Lectures, Anima Poetae, Dejection, *emphasis on coadunation, Schelling, In-Eins-Bildung, reconciliation of opposites (*Biographia XIV*), genesis of* Lyrical Ballads, *"a constitutional malady" —IV. meter and passion, Shakespeare's characters,* Venus and Adonis, *imitation as "mesothesis," Schelling again, transcendental principle and landscape applications, Coleridge on topography, on sonnets, intimate combinations (symbols) vs. formal similes (allegory), "pathetic fallacy," omission of overt statement, reduction of disparity—V. "fancy," Wordsworth's examples, Coleridge on* Venus and Adonis, *on "wit," on metaphysical poets (*Biographia I, XVIII*), canonical content, pantheism, philosophy and poetry, modern objections, Coleridge on "pleasure and truth," difficulties, poems about romantic imagination, Shelley, Coleridge—VI. continuation of 18th-century genius, sublimity, emotion, vagueness, Coleridge at the* *waterfall, Wordsworth's Preface of 1815, Longinianism, numbers consolidated, Johnsonian generality again, infinity and obscurity, emotive congruity, Wordsworth's statements (1800 and 1815), Coleridge: letter to Southey, Biographia on Shakespeare, "predominant passion," "unity of interest" §*

D URING THE 17TH CENTURY THE TERMS "IMAGINATION" AND "FANCY" had often enough been used in a vaguely synonymous way to refer to the realm of fairy tale or make-believe. Yet here and there (as in the opening of Hobbes's *Leviathan*) the term "imagination" had tended to distinguish itself from "fancy" and settle toward a meaning centered in the sober literalism of sense impressions and the survival of these in memory. This was in accord with medieval and Renaissance tradition, where *imaginatio* and *phantasia* had all along been fairly close together, but where, so far as a distinction of this kind had been made, it was *phantasia* which meant the lighter and less responsible kind of imaging.[1] In the light of 17th-century reasonableness, "fancy" suffered the decline in reputation which we have discussed in an earlier chapter. But "imagination" (when it did not mean "fancy") held its own and even slid into a new place of respect in sensationalist aesthetics. It followed that during the 18th century, whenever the distinction between "imagination" and "fancy" was being made—and it often was—honors were likely to fall to the term "imagination." A certain softness and warmth and depth of good feeling grew around the term "imagination" in its Addisonian sense; it stayed close to the heart of 18th-century poetry. A corresponding coldness and brittleness and a suggestion of unreliable frolic invested the related but opposed term "fancy." As 18th-century "imagination" moved through the stages of association theory to which we have alluded in an earlier chapter, the honors accorded the two terms were now and then reversed—"fancy" assuming the higher role of reference to a more creative mental power, imagination, the humbler reference to the mind's more reportorial kinds of drudgework.[2] But such an assign-

---

[1] Cf. Murray W. Bundy, *The Theory of Imagination in Classical and Mediaeval Thought* (*University of Illinois Studies in Language and Literature*, XII, May–August, 1927, Nos. 2–3), p. 266: "Mediaeval usage was, on the whole, unfavorable to any recognition of the creative capacity of *imaginatio*. *Phantasia* implied the loftier functions, the greater freedom—but at the same time the greater liability to error."

[2] See John Bullitt and Walter Jackson Bate, "Distinctions Between Fancy and Imagination in Eighteenth-Century English Criticism," *MLN*, LX (1945), 8–15. Earl R. Wasserman, "Another Eighteenth-Century Distinction Between Fancy and Imagination," *MLN* (January, 1949), 23–5, calls attention to the reversal of the usual roles of the terms in Arthur Browne's *Miscellaneous Sketches: or, Hints for Essays*, 1789. A. W. Schlegel's later assignment of *Einbildungskraft* to the lower and *Fantasie* to the higher role corresponds with the minority English usage.

ment of honors was a little noticed exception. The relative dignity of the two *terms* "imagination" and "fancy" was so well established in English usage by the end of the 18th century that no matter what revised *meanings* Wordsworth and Coleridge and others might assign to them, it was almost inevitable that the superior *term* should be "imagination."

An early and somewhat haphazard attempt on the part of Wordsworth to discriminate between imagination ("Impressive effects out of simple elements") and fancy ("Pleasure and surprise . . . excited by sudden varieties of situation and accumulated imagery") appears in a note to "The Thorn" in the 1800 edition of *Lyrical Ballads*. But the first word in the major critical discussion by Wordsworth and Coleridge occurs in the *Preface* to the *Poems* of 1815, when Wordsworth breaks out in an excited correction of William Taylor's *British Synonyms Discriminated*, 1813. Taylor had unfortunately written:

> A man has imagination in proportion as he can distinctly copy in idea the impressions of sense: it is the faculty which *images* within the mind the phenomena of sensation. A man has fancy in proportion as he can call up, connect, or associate, at pleasure, those internal images (*phantazein* is to cause to appear) so as to complete ideal representations of absent objects. Imagination is the power of depicting, and fancy of evoking and combining. The imagination is formed by patient observation; the fancy by a voluntary activity in shifting the scenery of the mind. The more accurate the imagination, the more safely may a painter, or a poet, undertake a delineation, or a description, without the presence of the objects to be characterized. The more versatile the fancy, the more original and striking will be the decoration produced.

That summed up a century more or less of settled usage and compromise opinion. Wordsworth's objection was in part simply that the terms, as an antithetic pair, were turned upside down. "Imagination," not "fancy," should be used to refer to the creative or poetic principle. Furthermore, and this was really the critical issue (though how far Wordsworth distinguished the merely semantic from the critical may be questioned), the very distinction between the two terms was made at too low a level. The higher power (what Taylor called "fancy") had to be something better than the mere power of wilfully (capriciously) "evoking or combining" images—"shifting the scenery of the mind"—making "decorations." There was a "higher" creative power than that. And this was the "imagination."

> Fancy does not require that the materials which she makes use of should be susceptible of change in their constitution, from her

touch; and, where they admit of modification, it is enough for her purpose if it be slight, limited, and evanescent.

The law under which the processes of Fancy are carried on is as capricious as the accidents of things, and the effects are surprising, playful, ludicrous, amusing, tender, or pathetic, as the objects happen to be appositely produced or fortuitously combined. Fancy depends upon the rapidity and profusion with which she scatters her thoughts and images; trusting that their number, and the felicity with which they are linked together, will make amends for the want of individual value: or she prides herself upon the curious subtilty and the successful elaboration with which she can detect their lurking affinities.[3]

(Even fancy was far from being the uncreative or unoriginal thing, the mere juggler, which William Taylor would have made it.) But imagination! Imagination was a "conferring," an "abstracting," a "modifying," an "endowing" power. The imagination "unites" and "coalesces." It "shapes and creates." [4] In the language of his friend Charles Lamb, the imagination

draws all things to one. . . . it makes things animate or inanimate, beings with their attributes, subjects with their accessories, take one colour and serve to one effect.[5]

Imagination

. . . recoils from everything but the plastic, the pliant, and the indefinite. . . . When the Imagination frames a comparison . . . a sense of the truth of the likeness, from the moment that it is perceived, grows—and continues to grow—upon the mind; the resemblance depending less upon outline of form and feature, than upon expression and effect; less upon casual and outstanding, than upon inherent and internal, properties: moreover, the images invariably modify each other. . . . the Imagination is conscious of an indestructible dominion;—the Soul may fall

[3] Wordsworth's *Preface* of 1815 is quoted from *Wordsworth's Literary Criticism*, ed. Nowell C. Smith (London, 1925), pp. 155–65.

[4] Imagination is "that intellectual lens through the medium of which the poetical observer sees the objects of his observations, modified both in form and colour; or it is that inventive dresser of dramatic *tableaux*, by which the persons of the play are invested with new drapery, or placed in new attitudes, or it is that chemical faculty by which elements of the most different nature and distant origin are blended together into one harmonious and homogeneous whole" ("Conversations and Reminiscences Recorded by the (Now) Bishop of Lincoln," Wordsworth's *Prose Works*, ed. Grosart, III, 465; cf. R. D. Havens, *The Mind of a Poet*, Baltimore, 1941, p. 208).

[5] Wordsworth quotes Lamb's essay "Upon the Genius of Hogarth." See Lamb's *Works* (1811), I, 96.

away from it, not being able to sustain its grandeur; but, if once felt and acknowledged, by no act of any other faculty of the mind can it be relaxed, impaired, or diminished.

In short, where the 18th century had been content with a distinction between a faithfully reportorial imaging faculty, and an unfaithful, or playfully inventive fancy, Wordsworth raised the level of the whole distinction. Simple reproduction interested him not at all. He distinguished two modes of imaging, both inventive.[6] The difference was that one was frolicsome, and inferior, the other was totally serious, and superior.

It was this concession to fancy, though it was only incidental to Wordsworth's aim of elevating the imagination, that became a point of grievance with Coleridge. In Chapter XII of his *Biographia*, he comes down on Wordsworth's venture with a heavy hand.

> If, by the power of evoking and combining, Mr. Wordsworth means the same as, and no more than, I meant by the aggregative and associative, I continue to deny, that it belongs at all to the imagination; and I am disposed to conjecture, that he has mistaken the co-presence of fancy with imagination for the operation of the latter singly.[7]

In Chapter IV of the *Biographia*, after giving Wordsworth the grand credit of having originally inspired his own whole theory of the imagination,[8] Coleridge had already drawn a patronizing distinction between Wordsworth's purpose of considering only the "influences" or "effects" of fancy and imagination "as they are manifested in poetry," and his own more psychologic purpose of investigating "the seminal principle"—that is, the process of imaginative creation, rather than poems themselves.[9] It is our own view that Coleridge did not differ vitally from Wordsworth about "imagination," and that the two may well be considered together,[1]

[6] "To aggregate and to associate, to evoke and to combine, belong as well to the Imagination as to the Fancy." Wordsworth here ventures to object to an opinion expressed by Coleridge in an article contributed to Southey's *Omniana* (London, 1812), II, 13.

[7] *Biographia Literaria*, ed. John Shawcross (Oxford, 1907), I, 194.

[8] "I was in my twenty-fourth year, when I had the happiness of knowing Mr. Wordsworth personally, and while memory lasts, I shall hardly forget the sudden effect produced in my mind, by his recitation of a manuscript poem. . . . It was the union of deep feeling with profound thought, the fine balance of truth in observing, with the imaginative faculty in modifying the objects observed; and above all the original gift of spreading the tone, the *atmosphere*, and with it the depth and height of the ideal world around forms, incidents and situations, of which, for the common view, custom had bedimmed all the lustre, had dried up the sparkle and the dew drops" (*Biographia*, Chapter IV: I, 58–59).

[9] I, 58–64.

[1] For a development of the difference between them, see Clarence D. Thorpe, "The Imagination: Coleridge *versus* Wordsworth," *PQ*, XVIII (January, 1939), 1–18.

although Coleridge no doubt may be conveniently accepted as the more articulate and more theoretical spokesman of the two.

II

IN CHAPTERS V–IX of the *Biographia*, Coleridge traces the growth of his mind from Hartleyan associationism to neo-Platonic and then to German transcendental idealism. Chapter XII lays down in ten Theses the Fichtean and Schellingian phase of ideal realism in which at the moment he finds himself. All this is undertaken in preparation for the grand purpose of expounding "the nature and genesis of the imagination," the literary topic which was laid aside—for want of proper groundwork—at the end of his skirmish with Wordsworth in Chapter IV. Chapter XIII is the well-known Shandean spoof. The tortured exposition abruptly and whimsically gives way to so "completely" convincing a letter of complaint from "a friend" that our author is content to drop the argument and state his "main result" in the following tabloid.

> The IMAGINATION then, I consider either as primary, or secondary. The primary IMAGINATION I hold to be the living power and prime Agent of all human Perception, and as a repetition in the finite mind of the eternal act of creation in the infinite I AM. The secondary Imagination I consider as an echo of the former, co-existing with the conscious will, yet still as identical with the primary in the *kind* of its agency, and differing only in *degree*, and in the *mode* of its operation. It dissolves, diffuses, dissipates, in order to recreate; or where this process is rendered impossible, yet still at all events it struggles to idealize and to unify. It is essentially *vital*, even as all objects (as objects) are essentially fixed and dead.
>
> FANCY, on the contrary, has no other counters to play with, but fixities and definites. The Fancy is indeed no other than a mode of Memory emancipated from the order of time and space; while it is blended with, and modified by that empirical phenomenon of the will, which we express by the word CHOICE. But equally with the ordinary memory the Fancy must receive all its materials ready made from the law of association.[2]

[2] I, 202. For similar but briefer Coleridgean definitions of "imagination" and "fancy," see *Coleridge's Miscellaneous Criticism*, ed. T. M. Raysor, p. 387. For Coleridge's comparison of imagination to delirium (an all-inclusive coloring of the mind) and fancy to mania (a specially channelled response), see *Biographia*, Chapter IV (I, 62) and Shawcross's note (I, 225–6) quoting *Table Talk*, June 23, 1834, and *Aids to Reflection*, Bohn edition, p. 173. Coleridge recognized combinations of imagination and fancy, or shadings between the two. In *Miscellaneous Criticism*, p. 38, Spenser has "fancy under conditions of imagination. He has an imaginative fancy, but he has not imagination."

Does Coleridge mean the same thing that Wordsworth means in the more informal and literary statement of the 1815 Preface? Or does Coleridge mean something far more profound? The question is complicated by the presence of German ideas in Coleridge's mind.

It is not the issue of plagiarism [3] (though that is present for the biographer of Coleridge) which we would here pursue, but the relation of his theory to certain presiding metaphysical notions of his time, and especially to the notions of Kant and Schelling. It is true that a number of clear and even detailed borrowings by Coleridge from the Germans are to be noted, but let us say in advance that the importance of his debt is not always in proportion to its flagrance or its definability.

The lecture *On Poetry or Art* of 1818, for instance, is a fairly close paraphrase of Schelling's Academy Oration *On the Relation of the Formative Arts to Nature* (1807), and this has an importance to which we shall return in a few pages.[4] One of the most amusing betrayals of Coleridge's way with sources is his coinage of the term *esemplastic* (unifying or coadunative) in Chapters X and XIII of the *Biographia* on the model of Schelling's *In-Eins-Bildung* and apparently with the mistaken notion also that the term is authorized by the German word *Einbildungskraft.*[5] One of Coleridge's clearest debts to Kant appears in his *Principles of Genial Criticism* (1814), where both doctrine and examples, concerning pleasure, taste, beauty, and disinterest, are taken directly from Kant's *Critique of Judgment.* Yet this aesthetic borrowing has no very important relation to Coleridge's own literary aesthetic. The main relation of Coleridge's literary theory to Kant is a vaguer one, and lies in the direction not of the *Critique of Judgment* but in that of Kant's general epistemology and ontology in the *Critique of Pure Reason.* "The writings of the illustrious sage of Königsberg, the founder of the Critical Philosophy," says Coleridge in Chapter IX of the *Biographia,* "more than any other work, at once invigorated and disciplined my under-

[3] In Chapter IX of the *Biographia* Coleridge makes a more or less convincing disavowal of "ungenerous concealment or intentional plagiarism," though he admits that his doctrines are likely to show a remarkable coincidence with those of Schelling. "I regard truth as a divine ventriloquist. I care not from whose mouth the sounds are supposed to proceed, if only the words are audible and intelligible" (*Biographia* I, 105). And in *Anima Poetae* under the year 1804 (Boston, 1895, p. 89): "In the preface of my metaphysical works, I should say, 'Once for all, read Kant, Fichte, etc., and then you will trace, or, if you are on the hunt, track me.' Why, then, not acknowledge your obligations step by step? Because I could not do so in a multitude of glaring resemblances without a lie, for they had been mine, formed and full-formed, before I ever heard of these writers." An early instance of the charge of plagiarism against Coleridge appears in De Quincey's article "The Plagiarisms of S. T. Coleridge" in *Blackwood's Magazine* for March, 1840.

[4] See *Biographia*, I, 95, 243, for another free translation from Schelling.

[5] *Biographia Literaria*, I, 107, 195, 249; *Anima Poetae* (Boston, 1895), p. 199; *Letters* (1895), I, 405–406; marginalia to J. G. E. Maass, quoted in Sarah Coleridge, ed. *Biographia Literaria* (1847), I, 173. Cf. Patrick L. Carver, "Evolution of the Term Esemplastic," *MLR*, XXIV (1929), 329.

standing." It may be worth adding that the ideas concerned had been rather widely foreshadowed throughout the neo-Platonic tradition, a tradition in which Coleridge was deeply versed, and one in which Kant himself stood as the theistic and transcendental champion of the age against Spinozan immanentism and pantheism.[6]

We may see the relation of Coleridge's "imagination" and "fancy" to German ideas better if we set beside the definitions already quoted from Chapter XIII of the *Biographia* the following passage, defining two Kantian terms, "Understanding" (*Verstand*) and "Reason" (*Vernunft*), from an early essay by Coleridge in *The Friend:*

> By understanding, I mean the faculty of thinking and forming judgments on the notices furnished by the sense, according to certain rules existing in itself, which rules constitute its distinct nature. By the pure reason, I mean the power by which we become possessed of principles—the eternal verities of Plato and Descartes, and of ideas, not images.[7]

And along with this let us set down the development of these ideas, perhaps not quite consistently, in Coleridge's later religious and philosophic work entitled *Aids to Reflection.*

> 1. Understanding is discursive. 2. The Understanding in all its judgments refers to some other Faculty as its ultimate Authority. 3. Understanding is the Faculty of *Reflection.*

> 1. Reason is fixed. 2. The Reason in all its decisions appeals to itself, as the ground and *substance* of their truth. (Hebrews vi, 13.) 3. Reason of Contemplation. Reason indeed is much nearer to SENSE than to Understanding: for Reason (says our great HOOKER) is a direct aspect of Truth, an inward Beholding, having a similar relation to the Intelligible or Spiritual, as SENSE has to the Material or Phenomenal.[8]

[6] René Wellek, *Immanuel Kant in England,* pp. 115 ff., points out that Coleridge's manuscript *Logic* is largely an elaborate exposition of the *Critique of Pure Reason,* with architectonics, tables of categories, and antinomies taken over literally. The direct relation of this fact to literary matters is no doubt slight. Wellek says (p. 114), "Of the major writings of Coleridge least of Kant's immediate influence is to be found in the *Biographia Literaria.*" Various borrowings by Coleridge from Schiller's *Naive and Sentimental Poetry,* Jean Paul's *Vorschule,* A. W. Schlegel's *Dramatic* lectures, are pointed out by T. M. Raysor in his editions of Coleridge's *Miscellaneous Criticism* and *Shakespeare Criticism.* Shawcross (I, 231) notes that Coleridge's history of association psychology in Chapters V and VI of the *Biographia* is drawn in part from J. G. E. Maass, *Versuch über die Einbildungskraft,* 1797. See also Wellek, *History* II, 151–3.

[7] *Complete Works,* ed. W. G. T. Shedd (New York, 1853), II, 164.

[8] *Aids to Reflection* (London, 1913), p. 148, "On the Difference in Kind of Reason and the Understanding." Joseph W. Beach, *The Concept of Nature in Nineteenth Century Poetry* (New York, 1936), p. 321, believes that Coleridge's dis-

Let four terms, then, "Primary Imagination"↔"Understanding," "Secondary Imagination"↔"Reason," stand as a kind of ascending series, with affinities between the first (or lower) and the second (or upper) pair indicated by the sign ↔. And let "Fancy" ride as a kind of side effort or false parallel to "Secondary Imagination." The Platonic sensory knowledge (*eikasia*), more or less the equivalent of the Kantian immediate sensory intuition (*Anschauung*), does not appear in the Coleridgean system, but so far as it might be distinguished in itself it would be conceived as a shadowy beginning which is substantiated or shaped up into the world of our everyday external experience (horses and houses) by the faculty of Primary Imagination (*Einbildungskraft*) working in accord with the schemes or laws of the scientific Understanding. This "Imagination" is a primary creative act, a willed activity of spirit, a self-consciousness, a "self-realizing intuition," joining and coalescing the otherwise separated parts of our self, the outer unconscious, and the inner conscious, the object and the subject. To support this part of the interpretation, we turn back to the Theses of *Biographia*, Chapter XI and to certain Kantian passages in Chapter VII.

> There are evidently two powers at work, which relatively to each other are active and passive; and this is not possible without an intermediate faculty, which is at once both active and passive. (In philosophical language, we must denominate this intermediate faculty in all its degrees and determinations, the IMAGINATION.[9]

The two powers between which the Imagination mediates are the "subject" and "object" of Chapter XII and the two opposing and counteracting forces described in the involved Schellingian terms of Chapter XIII before it is interrupted by the letter from the friend.[1] Primary Imagination is a human creative act which we may take as a type of and participation in the Divine act, though we are told that Coleridge later deleted that clause in a copy of the *Biographia*—"a repetition in the finite mind of the eternal act of creation in the infinite I AM."

---

tinction is derived, with some misunderstanding, merely from Kant's Preface to his *Critique of Pure Reason*.

Neo-Platonic and Christian writers were accustomed to make a similar distinction between the terms *scientia* and *sapientia*. See, for instance, Augustine, *De Trinitate*, XII, 25. Cf. Aristotle's distinction, in *De Anima*, between the passive and the active intellect.

[9] I, 86.

[1] Cf. Clarence D. Thorpe, "The Imagination: Coleridge *versus* Wordsworth," *PQ*, XVIII (January, 1939), 8.

III

EVERY human being, then, is, so far as he perceives anything at all, a creator and an idealizing agent. What then about the special role of the artist (the poet or maker)? What more can *he* do? What kind of "imagination" does *he* enjoy?

> . . . in common language, and especially on the subject of poetry, we appropriate the name to a superior degree of the faculty, joined to a superior voluntary control over it.[2]

We conceive the "Secondary Imagination," a higher plastic power. This reworks the perceptual products of primary imagination into concrete expressions (symbols) of those "ideas"—the self, the absolute, the world, and God—which are otherwise, conceptually, given by that superior part of the transcendental mind the Reason. Nature, especially as seen by the poet, symbolizes the spiritual life of man and hence too that higher life in which the spiritual life of man participates, "the one life within us and abroad." The ideas of such a life were, as Kant conceived them, framed by the Reason only as regulative hypotheses. But for Coleridge (as for the German post-Kantians, Schelling, Fichte, and Hegel), these ideas were realities (*noumena*) and the Reason was the faculty of philosophic insight into them—as Secondary Imagination gave them symbolic embodiments.[3] Kant had distinguished this imagination, under the name of the "aesthetic," from the "productive" (Coleridge's "primary Imagination") and from the "reproductive" (Coleridge's "fancy").

Various other writings of Coleridge give more poetically colored and less difficult accounts of that higher meaning of nature which he conceived it to be the role of poetic imagination to create and in creating know.

> Certainly the Fine Arts belong to the outward world, for they all operate by the images of sight and sound, and other sensible impressions; and without a delicate tact for these, no man ever was, or could be, either a Musician or a Poet; nor could he attain to excellence in any one of these Arts; but as certainly he must always be a poor and unsuccessful cultivator of the Arts

---

[2] Chapter VI (I, 86).

[3] Coleridge's *Preliminary Treatise on Method*, 1818, assigns to aesthetics a "middle position" between physics, which deals with sensory facts by hypothetical constructions, and metaphysics, which is concerned with "laws" apprehended through the *Ideas* of the reason (J. H. Muirhead, *Coleridge as Philosopher*, New York, 1930, Chapter VII, pp. 197–8). Cf. Shawcross, ed. *Biographia Literaria*, I, lvii–lviii.

if he is not impelled first by a mighty, inward power, a feeling, *quod nequeo monstrare, et sentio tantum;* nor can he make great advances in his Art, if, in the course of his progress, the obscure impulse does not gradually become a bright, and clear, and living Idea! [4]

If the artist copies the mere nature, the *natura naturata,* what idle rivalry! . . . Believe me, you must master the essence, the *natura naturans,* which presupposes a bond between nature in the higher sense and the soul of man. . . . In the objects of nature are presented, as in a mirror, all the possible elements, steps, and processes of intellect antecedent to consciousness, and therefore to the full development of the intelligential act; and man's mind is the very focus of all the rays of intellect which are scattered throughout the images of nature.[5]

To have a genius is to live in the universal, to know no self but that which is reflected not only from the faces of all around us, our fellow-creatures, but reflected from the flowers, the trees, the beasts, yea from the very surface of the waters and the sands of the desert. A man of genius finds a reflex of himself, were it only in the mystery of being.[6]

In looking at objects of Nature while I am thinking, as at yonder moon dim-glimmering through the dewy window-pane, I seem rather to be seeking, as it were *asking* for, a symbolical language for something within me that already and forever exists, than observing anything new. Even when that latter is the case, yet still I have always an obscure feeling as if that new phenomenon were the dim awaking of a forgotten or hidden truth of my inner nature.[7]

Or the emphasis might fall sadly on the waning or loss of that inner power of investiture.

> O Lady! we receive but what we give,
> And in our life alone does Nature live:
> Ours is her wedding-garment, ours her shroud!
>   And would we aught behold, of higher worth,
> Than that inanimate cold world allowed
> To the poor loveless ever-anxious crowd,
>   Ah! from the soul itself must issue forth

[4] *Preliminary Treatise on Method,* 1818, III, 21 (ed. Alice D. Snyder, London, 1934, pp. 62–3).

[5] *On Poesy or Art,* in *Biographia,* ed. Shawcross, II, 257–8.

[6] *The Philosophical Lectures* (*1818–19*), ed. Kathleen Coburn (New York, 1949), p. 179.

[7] *Anima Poetae* (Boston, 1895), p. 115.

A light, a glory, a fair luminous cloud
   Enveloping the Earth—
And from the soul itself must there be sent
  A sweet and potent voice, of its own birth,
Of all sweet sounds the life and element! [8]

All these statements about the meaning of art and the meaning of nature refer to a kind of union between the two. They could all be developed under the aspect of union, the Schellingian emphasis on coalescence, on reconciliation. And it is precisely this emphasis that is the most distinctive feature of Coleridge's theory. This, though it was a tenet of absolute idealism, was capable of working out, and in Coleridge's thinking to some extent did work out, into a dualistic and variously applicable theory of poems. Reconciliation of what? Primarily and generically of the two sides of self, conscious and unconscious, subject and object—and of certain related abstract entities. *In-Eins-Bildung*, said Schelling, *des Einem mit dem Vielen. In-Eins-Bildung des Realen und Idealen.*[9] Or, to give the antithesis a warmer color, *In-Eins-Bildung* (coadunation) of *man* and *nature*. Coleridge's lecture *On Poesy or Art* (1818) is in parts a close paraphrase of Schelling's oration *On the Relation of the Formative Arts to Nature.*

> Art itself might be defined as of a middle quality between a thought and a thing, or, as I have said before, the union and reconciliation of that which is nature with that which is exclusively human. It is the figured language of thought, and is distinguished from nature by the unity of all parts in one thought or idea.[1]

In a passage of the *Biographia* much celebrated recently, Coleridge writes his most enthusiastic and expansive account of the aesthetic "reconciliation."

> Imagination. . . . reveals itself in the balance or reconciliation of opposite or discordant qualities: of sameness, with difference; of the general, with the concrete; the idea, with the image; the individual, with the representative; the sense of novelty and of freshness, with old and familiar objects; a more than usual state of emotion, with more than usual order; judgement ever awake and steady self-possession, with enthusiasm and feeling profound or vehement; and while it blends and harmonizes the natural and the artificial, still subordinates art to nature; the

---

[8] Cf. Wordsworth's *Ode: Intimations.* . . . "There was a time when meadow, grove, and stream. . . ."
[9] Shawcross, I, 249.
[1] *Biographia Literaria*, II, 254–5.

manner to the matter; and our admiration of the poet to our sympathy with the poetry.[2]

The weaving back and forth of Coleridge's syntax and the variation of his phrasing may tend to obscure the generic alignment of the eleven (partially overlapping) pairs of opposites which we now repeat in tabular form.

Imagination reconciles (balances, or harmonizes):

A		B
1. sameness	with	difference
2. general	"	concrete
3. idea	"	image
4. representative	"	individual
5. familiarity	"	novelty
6. order	"	emotion
7. judgment	"	enthusiasm
8. artificial	"	natural

Imagination subordinates:

A		B
1. art	to	nature
2. manner	"	matter
3. admiration of the poet	"	sympathy with the poetry

Column A will come under the head of the "subject," the "human;" Column B under that of the "object," "nature." In the first part of the same chapter Coleridge had given a nice example of reconciliation between familiarity and novelty, treated in such a way as to suggest the intimate relation of these reconcilable opposites with another and more difficult pair, the inner human spirit and the outer transcendental or supernatural. The example is so engaging an incident of English literary history as almost to preclude the possibility of cavil.

> During the first year that Mr. Wordsworth and I were neighbors, our conversations turned frequently on the two cardinal points of poetry, the power of exerting the sympathy of the reader by a faithful adherence to the truth of nature, and the power of giving the interest of novelty by the modifying colors of imagination. The sudden charm, which accidents of light

[2] Chapter XIV (II, 12). Alice D. Snyder, *The Critical Principle of the Reconciliation of Opposites as Employed by Coleridge* (Ann Arbor, 1918), p. 28, was apparently the first modern writer to quote this passage. She was followed by T. S. Eliot in his essay on Marvell (1921), by I. A. Richards in his *Principles of Literary Criticism* (1924). Cf. René Wellek, in *The English Romantic Poets*, ed. T. M. Raysor (New York, 1950), p. 109.

and shade, which moonlight or sun-set diffused over a known and familiar landscape, appeared to represent the practicability of combining both. . . . In this idea originated the plan of the "Lyrical Ballads;" in which it was agreed, that my endeavours should be directed to persons and characters supernatural, or at least romantic; yet so as to transfer from our inward nature a human interest and a semblance of truth sufficient to procure for these shadows of imagination that willing suspension of disbelief for the moment, which constitutes poetic faith. Mr. Wordsworth, on the other hand, was to propose to himself as his object, to give the charm of novelty to things of every day, and to excite a feeling analogous to the supernatural, by awakening the mind's attention from the lethargy of custom, and directing it to the loveliness and the wonders of the world before us.[3]

Coleridge's interest in opposites and their reconciliation was, says Miss Snyder, "a constitutional malady." And she is able to present a very miscellaneous set of topics—foam islands shaping and reshaping below a waterfall, a tooth-ache and the forgetting of it, a cone of loose sand rising and sinking at the bottom of a spring, the movement of ghostlike crowds through the sepulchral fixities of London streets—all of which provoke in Coleridge reflections on this theme.[4]

I V

ONE might expect that the doctrine of reconciliation would be a wide and varied sanction for poetic moods and genres and that it would have a varied and subtle application in Coleridge's practical criticism. Certain more precise technical modulations do appear, for instance the treatment in *Biographia*, Chapter XVIII, of meter as a balance between passion and organization, or in the notes on *The Tempest* an observation about the individuality of Shakespearian women despite their essential sameness, in the notes on *Hamlet* a comment on the tragi-comedy of a semi-feigned madness.[5] In his lecture "Shakespeare, a Poet Generally" (corresponding in part to Chapter XV of the *Biographia*) Coleridge executes a rhapsodic analysis of a couplet from *Venus and Adonis*.

> Look! how a bright star shooteth from the sky;
> So glides he in the night from Venus' eye.

[3] Chapter XIV (II, 5–6). Wellek, *History* II, 177, notes the anticipation of Coleridge's celebrated "willing suspension of disbelief" by Moses Mendelssohn, *Rhapsodie über die Empfindungen*, 1761, and *Morgenstunden*, 1785.

[4] Snyder, pp. 20 ff., quoting *Anima Poetae* (Boston, 1895), pp. 7, 14, 44; *Works*, IV, 434.

[5] Cf. Snyder, pp. 29–30, 37, 48–9.

How many images and feelings are here brought together without effort and without discord, in the beauty of Adonis, the rapidity of his flight, the yearning, yet hopelessness, of the enamoured gazer, while a shadowy ideal character is thrown over the whole!

In other places, he makes a highly reflexive application of the doctrine of reconciliation to the work of art itself conceived as a non-illusory object.

Imitation, as opposed to copying, consists either in the interfusion of the SAME throughout the radically DIFFERENT, or of the different throughout a base radically the same.[6]

Imitation is the mesothesis of Likeness and Difference. The difference is as essential to it as the likeness; for without the difference, it would be Copy or fac-simile.[7]

We have been bringing ourselves, however, to the point of asking an important question about the limits of this doctrine of imaginative reconciliation and hence about the whole theory of poetic imagination entertained by Coleridge and, in fairly close concert, by Wordsworth. Was their theory in fact a general theory of poetry? Or was it not rather a theory slanted very heavily toward a particular kind of poetry, one in which they themselves, and especially Wordsworth, excelled? (The latter status would not have precluded a fairly wide extension of the theory, even by Coleridge and Wordsworth if they had been sufficiently interested.) Let us return for a moment to that lecture of Coleridge's on *Poesy or Art*, so intimately related to Schelling's oration *On the Relation of the Formative Arts to Nature*.

Now so to place these images, totalized, and fitted to the limits of the human mind, as to elicit from, and to superinduce upon, the forms themselves the moral reflexions to which they approximate, to make the external internal, the internal external, to make nature thought, and thought nature,—this is the mystery of genius in the Fine Arts.[8]

Or, we might quote here again that passage which we have quoted just above from Chapter XIV of the *Biographia*, about light and shade, moonlight or sunset "over a known and familiar landscape." In such passages we are confronted in a special way with the important difference between Primary Imagination and Secondary Imagination. We are asked to focus a special attention upon the distinction between the first (a

[6] *Biographia*, Chapter XVIII (II, 56).
[7] *Table Talk, Works*, VI, 468. Cf. Snyder, p. 52.
[8] *Biographia Literaria*, II, 258.

basic and universal power of knowing) and the second (a special power of artistic knowing—yet *not in principle different* from the first). This difficult paradox has haunted all idealistic theory of art from Plotinus to Croce and Susanne Langer. In this crucial instance (crucial because Coleridge and Wordsworth as poet-philosophers did have an eye closely on poems and wished to remain close to them) it may be doubted if the theory succeeds in making the transition from general epistemology to poetics without a leap that largely abandons the epistemology as a formal principle. The theory, at least in some phases, seems to have in mind especially a kind of poetry which will somehow, either by some kind of dramatic figuration, or perhaps by a merely contentual reference, be the appointed representative of the basic philosophy. Yet this poetry, for all that, may not be a sufficient demonstration or illustration of the theory. It is one thing to say that all our knowledge is a "self-realizing intuition" which reconciles subject or conscious self with object or nature. (It is impossible to write a poem which will specially illustrate this transcendental principle. How could any one expression better illustrate or embody it than any other?) It is a vastly different thing to say that the forms of nature are, or are capable of being, suited to moral reflections—or that the latter can be, in any peculiar way, elicited from or superinduced upon the former. This is a very special showing of how "nature" is "thought," and "thought" is "nature." (It may be quite possible to illustrate this in a special kind of poem.)

And so we have such more special statements of preference by Coleridge as that in Chapter XV of the *Biographia.* Images become poetic "when a human and intellectual life is transferred to them from the poet's own spirit, 'Which shoots its being through earth, sea, and air.' "

> Behold yon row of pines, that shorn and bow'd
> Bend from the sea-blast, seen at twilight eve.

In these lines, he says, "There is nothing objectionable, but also nothing to raise them much above the level of a "book of topography" or a "descriptive tour." But the "same image" can be raised to a "semblance of poetry" by being altered thus:

> Yon row of bleak and visionary pines,
> By twilight glimpse discerned, mark! how they flee
> From the fierce sea-blast, all their tresses wild
> Streaming before them.[9]

Or we have the following in the Introduction to the volume of sonnets which Coleridge edited in 1796.

---

[9] *Biographia,* II, 16–17. Cf. Coleridge's lecture *Shakespeare, a Poet Generally.*

Those sonnets appear to me to be the most exquisite in which moral sentiments are deduced from and associated with the scenery of Nature. They create a sweet and indissoluble union between the intellectual and the material world.[1]

Or this in a letter to Southey of 1802.

A poet's heart and intellect should be *combined*, intimately combined and unified with the great appearances of nature. . . .[2]

In this letter, Coleridge is intent on making a distinction between such "intimate" combinations and certain other combinations, or loose mixtures, such as have to be made explicit by "dim" moralizing analogies and "formal similes." [3]

We have similar statements by Wordsworth (with a more genetic accent): that "images and sentiments" should be "wedded" naturally in the mind; images should rise to the mind unsought for, like "exhalations." [4] "The subject and simile should be as much as possible lost in each other," especially in lyric poetry.[5]

In short, we have a theory of "animating" imagery, of romantic anthropomorphism, what Ruskin not many years later termed the "pathetic fallacy" (and one may echo the term without the least hint of derogation), the fallacy, the fiction, of portraying the face of nature so as to invest it with reflections of our own mind and feelings and hence with

[1] *Biographia*, I, 207.

[2] *Letters* (Boston, 1895), I, 403.

[3] Coleridge here verges on the distinction between "symbol" and "allegory" which he was later to make after the example of Goethe and other Germans (cf. *ante* p. 375). "An allegory is but a translation of abstract notions into a picture-language, which is itself nothing but an abstraction from objects of the senses; the principal being more worthless than its phantom proxy, both alike unsubstantial, and the former shapeless to boot. On the other hand a symbol . . . is characterized by a translucence of the special [the species] in the individual, or of the general [the genus] in the special, or of the universal in the general; above all by the translucence of the eternal through and in the temporal" (*The Statesman's Manual*, in *Works*, ed. W. G. T. Shedd, New York, 1884, I, 437). Coleridge and the Germans lay a negative stress on "allegory" which in its broadest application the word will perhaps not bear. If we set aside this semantic difficulty, however, we may recognize in the distinction itself a valid effort to discriminate between various abstractly asserted kinds of imagery and that kind (conveniently called "symbol") which a recent critic of *The Ancient Mariner* has aptly described as "massive," "focal," and "not arbitrary" (R. P. Warren, *The Ancient Mariner*, New York, 1946, p. 76). But Coleridge apparently had no very intent gaze upon the "symbol." In other places he speaks of the symbol as being a part of the whole which it represents, and he seems to be thinking of synecdoche. (See *Miscellaneous Criticism*, p. 99, and *Aids to Reflection*, London, 1913, p. 173 n.) He is sometimes willing to shade his opinion of allegory or to stretch a point to save a poet from the odium of allegorical imputation. *Don Quixote* is "substantial living allegory" (*Miscellaneous Criticism*, p. 102), and Dante is only quasi-allegorical (*Miscellaneous Criticism*, p. 150).

[4] "Letter to Mathetes," *Prose Works*, ed. Grosart, I, 318. Cf. *Prelude*, IV, 113–14.

[5] *Letters of William and Dorothy Wordsworth: The Later Years*, ed. Ernest De Selincourt (Oxford, 1939), I, 158–9.

expressions of the divinity which is the "one life within us and abroad." And this was in fact the way Goethe and Schiller defined modern or "sentimental" poetry. A brilliant host of symbolic nature poems by Blake, by Coleridge, by Keats, by Shelley, and above all by Wordsworth, illustrate the theory and justify it. No poetry before had shaded overt statement of spiritual or psychological meaning (the "still, sad music of humanity," the presence "whose dwelling is the light of setting suns") so curiously, so dramatically, and with such sleights and duplicities of meaning, into the metaphoric intimations of the literally described landscape ("the soft inland murmur," the "one green hue," the "wreaths of smoke . . . as . . . of vagrant dwellers in the houseless woods.") "A puddle," says Hazlitt, speaking of Wordsworth's *Excursion*, "is filled with preternatural faces."

The theory of imagination elaborated by Coleridge, and less precisely but in substantially the same way, by Wordsworth, was an excellent description of their own best poetry in its formal, structural, and metaphoric aspect. One might redescribe this structure approximately in these terms: It is a structure which makes only a restrained use of the central overt statement of similitude which had been so important in all poetry up to that time.[6] Both tenor and vehicle are wrought in a parallel process out of the same material. The landscape is both the occasion of subjective reflection or transcendental insight and the source of figures by which the reflection or insight is defined. In such a structure, finally, the element of tension in disparity may not be prominent. The interest derives not from our being aware of disparity in stated likeness, but in the opposite activity of our discerning the design and the unity latent in a multiform sensuous picture. This is no doubt a form of "reconciliation." At the same time there are certain clearly anti-"metaphysical" tendencies here—the absence of overt definition, the reduction of disparity, the play of phenomena on the one hand and of "spirit" on the other, rather than of entities conceived substantially.

V

THIS is the place to recall that inferior faculty which at the outset was set apart from "imagination"—the "fancy," with its fixities and definites, its capricious, light, playful, and coldly asserted way of connecting these. Wordsworth's examples of "fancy" are Shakespeare's description of Queen Mab, a rather silly couplet by Chesterfield,

[6] Wordsworth's examples of "imagination" in his 1815 Preface are drawn chiefly from his own poems and from Milton. The longest example of his own poetry, from *Resolution and Independence*, is actually framed as an overt similitude—yet, as he himself observes, it is a very subtly complicated "modification" of a natural phenomenon into a human meaning.

> The dews of the evening most carefully shun,
> They are the tears of the sky for the loss of the sun,

and a far from silly, if lighthearted, minor "metaphysical" poem by Charles Cotton, an *Ode Upon Winter*.

> a magazine
> Of sovereign juice is cellared in;
> Liquor that will the siege maintain
> Should Phoebus ne'er return again.

Wordsworth speaks of this poem with considerable affection and even admiration (for the "extreme activity of intellect" displayed and the "correspondent hurry of delightful feeling"). "Though myself a water drinker, I cannot resist the pleasure of transcribing what follows." But the patronage is apparent, and the second-rate status of "fancy" is never for a moment questioned. Coleridge's example of fancy, which does not appear in the *Biographia*, but in the lecture on *Shakespeare, a Poet Generally*, is a quatrain from *Venus and Adonis*.

> Full gently now she takes him by the hand,
> A lily prisoned in a jail of snow,
> Or ivory in an alabaster band:
> So white a friend ingirts so white a foe.[7]

Coleridge's more severe animadversions upon this kind of thing were likely to occur in the immediate context of the word "wit" rather than in that of "fancy." But a close relation is plain enough. In Chapter I of the *Biographia* he observes that "Our faulty elder poets [from Donne to Cowley] sacrificed the passion and passionate flow of poetry, to the subtleties of intellect, and to the starts of wit . . . the heart to the head." They indulged in "the most fantastic out-of-the-way thoughts," though "in the most pure and genuine mother English."[8] In Chapter XVIII a rather bad passage from Cowley's *Pindaric Odes* is rebuked in the following terms:

> . . . such language and such combinations are the native prod-
> uce neither of the fancy nor of the imagination; . . . their opera-

---

[7] Coleridge here defines "fancy" ("the faculty of bringing together images dissimilar in the main by some one point or more of likeness") in a way that goes far to invite the quantitative interpretation which I. A. Richards makes of the difference between "imagination" and "fancy." The difference seems to lie in the *number* of "links of relevance between the units." A great number adds up to mutual modification (*Coleridge on Imagination*, pp. 78–9). Richards admits (p. 19) that he writes "as a Materialist trying to interpret . . . the utterances of an extreme Idealist." Cf. Wellek, in *Romantic Poets*, ed. T. M. Raysor (New York, 1950), p. 110. Both Coleridge and Wordsworth clearly insist in their main arguments that the difference between "imagination" and "fancy" is one "of kind."

[8] I, 15.

tion consists in the excitement of surprise by the juxta-position and *apparent* reconciliation of widely different or incompatible things. As when, for instance, the hills are made to reflect the image of a *voice*. . . . this compulsory juxta-position is not produced by . . . any sympathy with the modifying powers with which the inner genius of the poet had united and inspirited all the objects of his thought . . . it is therefore a species of *wit*, a pure work of the *will*, and implies a leisure and self-possession both of thought and of feeling, incompatible with the steady fervor of a mind possessed and filled with the grandeur of its object.[9]

The truth is that romantic nature poems are all poems of a certain symbolic furniture and of a certain philosophy—the philosophy of immanence or pantheism which appears in Coleridge's *Aeolian Harp* and in Wordsworth's *Tintern Abbey*, and the related idealism of Coleridge's *Dejection*. For Coleridge, as for the Germans, there was a powerful temptation to equate philosophy and poetry. It is notorious that he proposed to write an essay on poetry which would "supersede all the books of metaphysics, and all the books of morals too." It would be in reality a "disguised system of morals and politics."[1] In his chapter of the *Biographia* on Shakespeare, he says, "No man was ever yet a great poet, without being at the same time a profound philosopher."[2] This was Coleridge's dabbling in that grandiose absorption of metaphysics into *Dichtung* and *Kunst*, or into a philosophy of these, such as we have noted among the Germans. The modern intuitional critic will object to this as an over-conceptualization of poetry.[3] The modern "Aristotelian" will say, in his own language, that such a theory of poetry is not a theory of the poetic object as something specifically different from anything else, that the theory deals only with the poetic process and furthermore assimilates this to metaphysics and to other non-poetic mental processes.[4] To which it may be added that Coleridge himself, in Chapter XIV of the *Biographia*, offers his own definition of the poem as a "composition" having "for its *immediate* object pleasure not truth,"[5] but that

---

[9] II, 68.

[1] *Letters* (1895), I, 338, 347 (to Sir Humphry Davy, October 9, 1800, and February 3, 1801).

[2] Chapter XV (II, 19). Cf. Letter to Sotheby, September 10, 1802 (*Letters*, 1895, I, 4–3): Bowles "has no native passion because he is not a thinker."

[3] Cf. A. E. Powell, *The Romantic Theory of Poetry, An Examination in the Light of Croce's Aesthetic* (London, 1926), pp. 111, 117–21. A. C. Bradley, *Oxford Lectures on Poetry* (London, 1950), p. 172, makes the same case concerning Shelley.

[4] R. S. Crane, *et al.*, *Critics and Criticism* (Chicago, 1951), *passim*.

[5] Alba Warren, p. 133, cites the Victorian critic E. S. Dallas's appropriate observation that Coleridge's "pleasure" and "truth" are "objects" of two different orders, subjective and objective. It is scarcely possible to choose either one as an alternative to the other.

by this definition he would have had trouble discriminating between a poem by Wordsworth and one by Bowles. It was only when the general norms of content—passion and thought—were invoked that he could tell a good poem from a bad one.

A difficulty that has always been rather prominent for romantic scholarship lies in the fact that romantic poems do so pronouncedly *contain* and *assert* the philosophy of nature and of art which is supposedly also their formal principle. What the writers in the classical *Ars Poetica* tradition might try to do here and there, as in Pope's little series of handsprings on the theme of sound and sense, the romantic writers may approximate in a whole poem, and more subtly—and this, presumably, one would say they were led to do and were able to do because of the intimate union which they conceived to obtain between art and nature. The theory was endlessly reflexive and self-conscious. The assertion of the romantic poetics seems always to lurk not far from the embodiment in the poems and to be needed for the deciphering of the latter. Romantic poems tend to be about romantic imagination. Shelley's *West Wind* and Wordsworth's *Prelude* are triumphant instances of how the assertion may be dramatized and assimilated into structure. Coleridge's *Ancient Mariner*, which may be read as a poem about imagination, gets along with so little assertion that its theme has perhaps not even been suspected until very recently. The assertion (the content) of a poem is, however, never the same as the embodiment (the poem itself, the achievement), and the first never assures us of the second.

VI

A CONFUSION between poetic theory as operative in poems and poetic theory as their stated content is most often a feat of the historian and critic, rather than of the original theorist or the poet. Yet in his very bias toward illustrating a certain theory the poet-theorist may have done more mischief. The very division between fancy and imagination promoted by Wordsworth and Coleridge, though it was intended as a division between bad and good form in poetry, was responsible for a certain exclusiveness in their view of the thoughts and emotions (the range of psychological materials) which were available for poetry. Nothing too definite, nothing too precisely thoughtful (as tending toward mere scientific understanding), nothing too cool, too playful, too witty. Nothing too "metaphysical." Despite the sharp break with the 18th century which Wordsworth and Coleridge believed themselves to be making and which tradition has credited them with making, their theory of poetic imagination was on its genetic side a continuation of 18th-century "genius," and, with regard to the content of poetry, it prescribed certain items inherited from the 18th-century reaction against metaphysical and neo-classic "wit." These items were the "sublime" and its components the emotive and the vague.

The repeated story of Coleridge at the waterfall[6] and his superior amusement at touristic confusions of the sublime, the beautiful, the pretty, and the picturesque, suggests a great concern to discriminate the "sublime" (in stricter 18th-century and Kantian fashion) from other departments of landscape and hence presumably from other departments of poetry. Yet, when discussing "imagination," both Wordsworth and Coleridge actually place either the "sublime," or its components the emotive and the vaguely grand, very near the center of the complex of qualities by which the imagination and hence poetry are defined.

> The grand storehouses of enthusiastic and meditative Imagination[7] . . . are the prophetic and lyrical parts of the Holy Scriptures, and the works of Milton; . . . . I select these writers in preference to those of ancient Greece and Rome, because the anthropomorphitism of the Pagan religion subjected the minds of the greatest poets in those countries too much to the bondage of definite form; from which the Hebrews were preserved by their abhorrence of idolatry. This abhorrence was almost as strong in our great epic Poet. . . . However imbued the surface might be with classical literature, he was a Hebrew in soul; and all things tended in him toward the sublime.[8]

The Longinianism of the following passage, though not explicit, will hardly be questioned.

> The Imagination also shapes and *Creates*; and how? By innumerable processes; and in none does it more delight than in that of consolidating numbers into unity, and dissolving and separating unity into numbers,—alternations proceeding from, and governed by, a sublime consciousness of the soul in her own mighty and almost divine powers.[9]

[6] The story appears four times in the works of Coleridge himself: *Coleridge's Shakespeare Criticism*, ed. T. M. Raysor (Cambridge, 1930), I, 182; II, 62–63, 352; and *Biographia*, ed. Shawcross, II, 225 (*Genial Criticism*); and once in the *Journals of Dorothy Wordsworth*, ed. W. Knight (London, 1910), I, 195. In *Genial Criticism* Coleridge says the cataract is "in the strictest sense of the word, a sublime object." In Dorothy Wordsworth's *Journal* and in other versions he seems to consider the term "majestic" equally accurate. Cf. C. D. Thorpe, "Coleridge on the Sublime," in *Wordsworth and Coleridge, Studies in Honor of George M. Harper*, ed. Earl L. Griggs (Princeton, 1939), pp. 192–219.

[7] We omit the phrase ". . . of poetical, as contra-distinguished from human and dramatic Imagination," for we are not concerned to tax Wordsworth with this antithesis. "Of human and dramatic Imagination," he says, "the works of Shakespeare are an inexhaustible source."

[8] Preface to 1815, in *Wordsworth's Literary Criticism*, ed. N. C. Smith, p. 162.

[9] N. C. Smith, pp. 160–1. Cf. *Peri Hupsous*, Chapter XXIV: "The conversion of plurals into singulars sometimes conduces in a marked degree to elevation." Words-

In nothing did Wordsworth and Coleridge agree more wholeheartedly than in their association of the "imagination" with the vast, the infinite, the "shadowy ideal character." "Imagination recoils from everything but the plastic, the pliant, and the indefinite." [1] "Imagination [is given] to incite and support the eternal." "The Secondary Imagination . . . dissolves, diffuses, dissipates, in order to recreate." One receives the impression that the spiritual, the divine meaning at which they would get is something nearly identical with the generality, the abstraction. There is something much more Johnsonian here than one might have expected. This is one meaning of the statement sometimes encountered that Coleridge strove to unite with the "organic vitalism" of his day the "traditional rationalistic values of classicism." [2] Wordsworth's later conversations on the theme of imagination seem to have dwelt pretty heavily on "universal ideas or abstractions" embodied in "individual forms" or given a "local habitation." Crabb Robinson, one reporter of such conversations, adds:

> Wordsworth represented, much as unknown to him the German
> philosophers have done, that by the imagination the mere fact
> is exhibited in connection with infinity.[3]

That is, by universal ideas and abstractions, Wordsworth seemed to mean infinity. And for both Coleridge and Wordsworth infinity was not far from obscurity. Coleridge wished to habituate "the intellect to clear, distinct, and adequate conceptions concerning all things that are the possible objects of clear conception." But only in order to put these aside and hence be able

> to reserve the deep feelings which belong, as by a natural right
> to those obscure ideas that are necessary to the moral perfection

---

worth knew both Longinus and his English counterpart John Dennis (*Correspondence of Crabb Robinson with the Wordsworth Circle*, ed. E. Morley, I, 78; undated letter to Southey in N. C. Smith, p. 224). DeQuincey reports that both Wordsworth and Coleridge "had an absurd 'craze' about" Dennis (*Critical Works of Dennis*, ed. E. N. Hooker, II, lxxiii). For the literalness with which Wordsworth pursued this notion of numbers consolidated into unity, see not only the examples from Milton following the passage of the 1815 Preface just quoted but his *Letter to Lady Beaumont*, 1817, defending his sonnet "With ships the sea was sprinkled far and nigh" ("The mind can have no rest among a multitude of objects" . . .), and his "forty feeding like one" ("Written in March," 1802); cf. DeQuincey's comment, concerning "sublime unity," in his essay "On Wordsworth's Poetry," *Tait's Magazine*, September, 1845 (Alden, pp. 336–7).

[1] "You will know that you are dealing with imagination when the edges of things begin to waver and fade out" (F. A. Pottle, "The Eye and the Object in the Poetry of Wordsworth," in *Wordsworth, Centenary Studies*, ed. Gilbert T. Dunklin, Princeton, 1951, p. 38).

[2] W. J. Bate, in *Perspectives of Criticism*, ed. Harry Levin (Cambridge, Mass., 1950), p. 154.

[3] Extracts from Crabb Robinson's *Diary*, 1815 and 1816, quoted by Shawcross, *Biographia Literaria*, I, 227–8.

of the human being, notwithstanding, yea, even in consequence, of their obscurity—to reserve these feelings, I repeat, for objects, which their very sublimity renders indefinite, no less than their indefiniteness renders them sublime: namely, to the ideas of being, form, life, the reason, the law of conscience, freedom, immortality, God! [4]

The 18th-century notion of sublimity as a subjective experience of genius had gotten along well enough with the emerging principle of association by emotive congruity. The latter principle was so well installed in critical thinking by the time of Wordsworth and Coleridge that they could hardly have avoided taking advantage of it. It is true that they did this with delicacy. Wordsworth in his 1800 Preface, after twice invoking the "spontaneous overflow of powerful feelings," adds the tempering phrase "emotion recollected in tranquility," [5] and he touches the same note in his verse.

> And *then* my heart with pleasure fills
> And dances with the daffodils.

> The music in my heart I bore
> Long after it was heard no more.

In one of his later letters he professes: "I have never given way to my own feelings in personifying natural objects without bringing all that I have said to a rigorous after-test of good sense." [6] Like the Germans, both Wordsworth and Coleridge must be largely exculpated as transmitters of 18th-century sentimentalism. Nevertheless the critical theory of each contains some striking statements of the emotive principle. Thus in the 1800 preface:

> Another circumstance must be mentioned which distinguishes these Poems from the popular Poetry of the day; it is this, that the feeling therein developed gives importance to the action and situation, and not the action and situation to the feeling.[7]

"The appropriate business of poetry, . . ." he says later, "and her *duty*, is to treat of things not as they *are*, but as they *appear;* not as they exist in themselves, but as they *seem* to exist to the senses, and to the *passions.*" [8] "You feel strongly," he writes to a minor poet; "trust to

---

[4] *The Friend,* I. Essays: Introductory, Essay XIV (London: Bohn's Standard Library, 1906, p. 66).

[5] N. C. Smith, pp. 15, 34.

[6] Letter to W. R. Hamilton, December 23, 1829, *Letters . . . Later Years,* I, 436–7.

[7] N. C. Smith, p. 16.

[8] *Essay Supplementary to the Preface,* 1815 (N. C. Smith, p. 169).

those feelings, and your poem will take its shape and proportions as a tree does from the vital principle that actuates it." [9]

And Coleridge:

> Association depends in a much greater degree on the recurrence of resembling states of feeling than trains of ideas. . . . A metaphysical solution [like Hartley's] that does not instantly tell you something in the heart is grievously to be suspected. . . . I almost think that ideas never recall ideas, any more than leaves in a forest create each other's motion. The breeze it is runs thro' them—it is the soul or state of feeling. If I had said no one idea ever recalls another, I am confident that I could support the assertion. [1]

What first struck Coleridge about Wordsworth's poetry was

> the union of deep feeling with profound thought . . . and above all the original gift of spreading the tone, the atmosphere and with it the depth and height of the ideal world. . . . [2]

And apropos of Shakespeare:

> Images become proofs of original genius only so far as they are modified by a predominant passion. [3]

He speaks of "modifying a series of thoughts by some one predominant thought or feeling." In the preceding chapter, his phrase is "a tone and spirit of unity." [4] In his dramatic criticism, Coleridge likes to speak about the ruling passion of a character (Capulet or Lear), and, like A. W. Schlegel, he replaces the old unities of time, space, and action by a "unity of interest." [5]

If the Wordsworthian formula "emotion recollected in tranquillity" be taken in an approximately hylo-morphic way, one may suppose that "emotion" refers to a kind of poetic content, and tranquil "recollection" to the control or shaping of this content—the formal poetic principle. In the Coleridgean formulas which we have just quoted, however, the emphasis is reversed. Emotion appears, or attempts to appear, as the organizing principle. The difference is crucial. As organization is a form of intelligibility, it is a basic question of poetic theory whether in fact

[9] *Letters . . . Later Years,* I, 537.

[1] Letter to Southey, August 7, 1803 (*Letters,* 1895, I, 428).

[2] *Biographia Literaria,* Chapter IV (I, 59).

[3] *Biographia,* Chapter XV (II, 16).

[4] *Biographia,* II, 12.

[5] *Shakespearean Criticism,* ed. T. M. Raysor, I, 50, 212–13, 216; II, 73–4, 131. Cf. *post* Chapter 20, E. A. Poe. Both in the *Biographia* and throughout his Shakespearian criticism Coleridge connects poetical figures and meter closely with strong passion. See *Shakespearean Criticism,* I, 96, 206, 209, 218; II, 78, 103.

emotion as such can become the formal or organizing principle of a poem without the disappearance of the principle.

SUPPLEMENT

                              Nor should this, perchance,
Pass unrecorded, that I still had loved
The exercise and produce of a toil,
Than analytic industry to me
More pleasing, and whose character I deem
Is more poetic as resembling more
Creative agency. The song would speak
Of that interminable building reared
By observation of affinities
In objects where no brotherhood exists
To passive minds. My seventeenth year was come
And, whether from this habit rooted now
So deeply in my mind, or from excess
In the great social principle of life
Coercing all things into sympathy,
To unorganic natures were transferred
My own enjoyments; or the power of truth
Coming in revelation, did converse
With things that really are; I, at this time,
Saw blessings spread around me like a sea.
Thus while the days flew by, and years passed on,
From Nature and her overflowing soul,
I had received so much, that all my thoughts
Were steeped in feeling; I was only then
Contented, when with bliss ineffable
I felt the sentiment of Being spread
O'er all that moves and all that seemeth still;
O'er all that, lost beyond the reach of thought
And human knowledge, to the human eye
Invisible, yet liveth to the heart;
O'er all that leaps and runs, and shouts and sings,
Or beats the gladsome air; o'er all that glides
Beneath the wave, yea, in the wave itself,
And mighty depth of waters. Wonder not
If high the transport, great the joy I felt,
Communing in this sort through earth and heaven
With every form of creature, as it looked
Towards the Uncreated with a countenance
Of adoration, with an eye of love.
One song they sang, and it was audible,

Most audible, then, when the fleshly ear,
O'ercome by humblest prelude of that strain,
Forgot her functions, and slept undisturbed.

—William Wordsworth, *The Prelude* (1850),
II, 376–418.

Next, in the serpent we approach the source of a group of myths, world-wide, founded on great and common human instincts, respecting which I must note one or two points which bear intimately on all our subject. For it seems to me that the scholars who are at present occupied in interpretation of human myths have most of them forgotten that there are any such things as natural myths; and that the dark sayings of men may be both difficult to read, and not always worth reading; but the dark sayings of nature will probably become clearer for the looking into, and will very certainly be worth reading. And, indeed, all guidance to the right sense of the human and variable myths will probably depend on our first getting at the sense of the natural and invariable ones. The dead hieroglyph may have meant this or that—the living hieroglyph means always the same; but remember, it is just as much a hieroglyph as the other; nay, more—a "sacred or reserved sculpture," a thing with an inner language. The serpent crest of the king's crown, or of the god's, on the pillars of Egypt, is a mystery; but the serpent itself, gliding past the pillar's foot, is it less a mystery? Is there, indeed, no tongue, except the mute forked flash from its lips in that running brook of horror on the ground.

—John Ruskin, *The Queen of the Air*, Lecture II

The fancy sees the outside, and is able to give a portrait of the outside, clear, brilliant, and full of detail.

The imagination sees the heart and inner nature, and makes them felt, but is often obscure, mysterious, and interrupted, in its giving of outer detail. . . . hear Hamlet:

Here hung those lips that I have kissed, I know not how oft. Where be your gibes now, your gambols, your songs, your flashes of merriment that were wont to set the table on a roar.

There is the essence of lip, and the full power of the imagination. . . . In Milton it happens, I think, generally . . . that the imagination is mixed and broken with fancy, and so the strength of the imagery is part of iron and part of clay:

Bring the rathe primrose, that forsaken dies,	*Imagination.*
The tufted crow-toe and pale jessamine,	*Nugatory.*
The white pink, and the pansy freaked with jet,	*Fancy.*
The glowing violet,	*Imagination.*
The musk rose, and the well-attired woodbine,	*Fancy,* vulgar.
With cowslips wan that hang the pensive head,	*Imagination.*
And every flower that sad embroidery wears.	*Mixed.*

—John Ruskin, *Modern Painters*, Volume II (1846), Section II, Chapter iii

Pope starts with an abstraction or a generalization concerning human nature and then looks for a correlative in the world of nature apart from man. His habit of observation of external nature is not detailed and precise; indeed, he thinks it unimportant whether the "facts" of nature which he alleges in his illustrations are really facts or superstitions. The natural history of Pliny and the old bestiaries are as much grist to his mill as the latest papers of the Royal Society. He appears also to me to have at times no clear, detailed, and consistent mental picture of his own figures. To illustrate: in the couplet near the beginning of the *Essay on Man*,

> The latent tracts, the giddy heights explore
> Of all who blindly creep or sightless soar,

he means, I suppose, moles and birds of some sort. . . . he appears to be making use of the ancient and medieval notion that all birds except the eagle blind themselves by looking at the sun. Surely, by Pope's time it was generally known that the high-flying birds are not "sightless"; that on the contrary they have telescopic vision. . . . Or consider a famous passage from the Second Dialogue of the *Epilogue to the Satires* . . . :

> Ye tinsel Insects! whom a Court maintains,
> That count your Beauties only by your Stains,
> Spin all your Cobwebs o'er the Eye of Day!
> The Muse's wing shall brush you all away. 220–23

"Tinsel" to me means "shining or glittering like cheap metal foil," and my natural image of a "tinsel insect" would be some kind of beetle ("this Bug with gilded wings"). But the word can mean no more than "pretentiously showy" and so may not have been intended to identify the kind of insect Pope has in mind. "Stains," however, can hardly mean anything else than moths or butterflies ("Innumerable of stains and splendid dyes, As are the tiger-moth's deep-damask'd wings"). But the trouble with that is that Pope's insects spin cobwebs, which no butterfly or moth can do. I think we shall do Pope no injustice if we conclude that his insects have the combined characteristics of beetles, moths, and spiders, and hence do not belong to any order known to naturalists. . . .

May I remind the reader again that this essay is descriptive, not judicial? Wordsworth is right in maintaining that many of Pope's images are "false" from the naturalistic point of view, but I should be willing to argue that they are appropriate for the kind of poetry Pope was writing. In the metaphor just discussed, a general idea of insect-ness is what Pope wants, and he can produce it better by eclecticism than by sharp individuation.

—Frederick A. Pottle, "The Eye and the Object in the Poetry of Words-
worth," in *Wordsworth, Centenary Studies Presented at Cornell and
Princeton Universities*, ed. Gilbert T. Dunklin (Princeton: Princeton
University Press, 1951), pp. 34–6. The essay is copyrighted 1950 by Yale
University Press.

CHAPTER 19

PEACOCK VS. SHELLEY: RHAPSODIC DIDACTICISM

§ *romantic theory vs. rationalism, Coleridge and Wordsworth, hopes for reunion, "false secondary power," English empirical and utilitarian philosophy, decline in prestige of poetry (Sprat, Diderot), poetry as "magic," as painting, as insanity (Macaulay), poetry useless (Bentham)—II. Peacock's Four Ages: superficially cyclic, assault on Lake School, modern primitivism, bumptious rhetoric, Shelley's retort, "Reason" and "Imagination," echoes of Plato, Shelley's early naturalism, later idealism, ontologic and epistemologic, plastic power of poetry, an enthusiastic celebration (anthology of passages from* Defense*), parallels in* Ode to the West Wind, *romantic Ars Poetica, emphasis on moral power, similarity to Sidney, profound difference, Aristotle vs. Kant, imagination the absolute—III. Blake, apocalyptic humanism, a literalist of the imagination, Wordsworth's error, outward creation as dirt—IV. international events, social and economic pressures, popular reversion to classical notions, religious and patriotic reviewing, contrast to didacticism of revolution, summary: poetic autonomy during the 18th century, hedonistic direction, romantic theory more ambiguous, 19th-century dual continuation in England: art for art's sake, new didacticisms, rhapsodic and classical, atmospheric influence of Kant—V. De Quincey, journalistic flourishes on Germanic themes, "The Poetry of Pope" (1848), "literature of knowledge," "literature of power," Carlyle, early essays, on poetry and science, enfeeblement of poetry, true poet as visionary,* On Heroes. . . (1840), *from divinity to poet, poet as universal Great Man, generals as poets, Plato's* Ion *again* §

THE GERMAN AND ENGLISH ROMANTICISM WHICH WE HAVE SEEN IN our last two chapters was a late reaction, or a slowly reached culmination of reactionary trends, against the claims of scientific rationalism which had begun to show strength during the latter 17th century. The attitude of protest against scientific encroachment which we illustrated by a passage from Novalis might have been noted too in Wordsworth and Coleridge. The passage in Coleridge's *Aids to Reflection* on the subject of "understanding" associates this lower faculty quite clearly with geometrical, mechanical, and other abstractively scientific modes of thought. In other places Coleridge shared with German Nature philosophers the pious hope that science might some day graduate from its mechanistic bent and become reconcilable with an aesthetic view of the world. Wordsworth's best known thought upon the subject appears in the passage of his 1802 Preface where he laments the contemporary separation of science from everyday life and its consequent repugnance to poetry, but allows himself the hope that at some future day a reunion all round may occur.[1] Wordsworth's allusion, in the *Prelude*, to the abstractive reason as a "false secondary power by which we multiply distinctions" and his lyric phrase "meddling intellect" are also well known.[2] But less well known is the completeness with which he could apply these notions to science—as in his later allusion to the "dull eye, dull and inanimate" of science,[3] and his reported remark that science "waged war with and wished to extinguish imagination," and that he would much rather be a "superstitious old woman" than a scientist ignorant of theology.[4]

It was not as if Wordsworth and Coleridge were engaged with windmills. True, the scientists and inventors of the age were more intent on making discoveries about electricity and steam than on disparaging poetry. The German metaphysicians and aestheticians radiated an authoritative encouragement in the direction of the poetic endeavor. Deep in the mind of the age, however, and solidly settled lay the heritage of the enlightenment—a good hardpan of complacency about the advances of science and its extensive promises. The ideas of German philosophers which invaded England found the ideas of native utilitarian philosophers like Bentham and James Mill very firmly and respectably in possession.

Exhortations by earlier empirical philosophers about what *ought* to be the effect of science on poetry had passed during the latter 17th and

---

[1] Cf. D. G. James, *Scepticism and Poetry* (London, 1937), p. 167. "Such a transfiguration," says James, "is as undesirable as it is impossible, an absurd fiction created for an eloquent argument."

[2] *Prelude*, II, 214–17; *The Tables Turned*, in *Lyrical Ballads*.

[3] *Excursion* IV, 124–5.

[4] R. P. Graves, *Life of William Hamilton* (Dublin, 1882–89), I, 313. The remark is dated August, 1829.

18th centuries, especially among the French, into announcements, more often with a tone of congratulation than with one of regret, that the effect was in the process of being accomplished.[5] Sprat, for instance, in his *History of the Royal Society,* 1672, had described poetry as a technique of primitive pedagogy, now outmoded. "When the Fabulous Age was past, philosophy took a little more Courage; and ventured to rely upon its own strength, without the assistance of Poetry." [6] Fontenelle, in his *Traité de la Poésie en Général* (written apparently in the last quarter of the 17th century though not published until 1751), was well content to witness the end of the age of fable and the retirement of nature and emotion (the essentials of poetry) before the march of civilization. And Diderot in his *Salon de 1767:*

> Poetry always contains a pinch of untruth. The philosophic spirit gives us the habit of noting this untruth, and goodbye poetic illusion, goodbye poetic effect.[7]

In England the idea that poetry is magic might seem during the 18th century a comfortable one, a sufficient compliment to poetry.

> True Poesy is *magic,* not nature; an effect from causes hidden or unknown.[8]

The extent to which this idea is susceptible of a patronizing interpretation—and at the same time the deliquescence of another 18th-century idea, *poesis* as *pictura*—may be observed in the following remarkable passage occurring near the outset of Macaulay's essay on Milton, 1825.

> Perhaps no person can be a poet, or can even enjoy poetry, without a certain unsoundness of mind, if anything which gives so much pleasure ought to be called unsoundness. . . . By poetry we mean the art of employing words in such a manner as to produce an illusion in the imagination, the art of doing by means of words what the painter does by means of colours. . . . Truth, indeed, is essential to poetry; but it is the truth of madness. The reasonings are just; but the premises are false. After the first

[5] The theme appears of course even in classical times. Cf. Atkins, II, 323, on Plutarch's *Why the Pythia does not now give Oracles in Verse,* 406 E. "So, as language also underwent a change and put off its finery, history descended from its vehicle of versification, and went on foot in prose, whereby the truth was mostly sifted from the fabulous. Philosophy welcomed clearness and teachability in preference to creating amazement, and pursued its investigations through the medium of everyday language" (Plutarch's *Moralia,* trans. F. C. Babbitt, vol. V, London, 1936).

[6] *History of the Royal Society of London* (London, 1722), p. 6.

[7] "*Il y a dans la poésie toujours un peu de mensonge. L'esprit philosophique nous habitue à le discerner; et adieu l'illusion et l'effet*" (*Oeuvres,* ed. Tourneur-Assézat, XI, 136).

[8] Maurice Morgann, *Essay of the Dramatic Character of Sir John Falstaff,* ed. W. A. Gill (London, 1912), p. 70.

suppositions have been made, everything ought to be consistent; but those first suppositions require a degree of credulity which almost amounts to a partial and temporary derangement of the intellect. Hence of all people children are the most imaginative. They abandon themselves without reserve to every illusion. . . . Such is the despotism of the imagination over uncultivated minds.

In a rude state of society men are children with a greater variety of ideas. It is . . . in such a state of society that one may expect to find the poetical temperament in its highest perfection. In an enlightened age there will be much intelligence, much science, much philosophy, abundance of just classification and subtle analysis, abundance of wit and eloquence, abundance of verses, and even of good ones; but little poetry. Men will judge and compare; but they will not create. They will talk about the old poets, and comment on them, and to a certain degree enjoy them. But they will scarcely be able to conceive the effect which poetry produced on their ruder ancestors, the agony, the ecstasy, the plenitude of belief. The Greek Rhapsodists, according to Plato, could scarce recite Homer without falling into convulsions. The Mohawk hardly feels the scalping knife while he shouts his death-song. The power which the ancient bards of Wales and Germany exercised over their auditors seems to modern readers almost miraculous. Such feelings are very rare in a civilized community, and most rare among those who participate most in its improvements. They linger longest amongst the peasantry.

Poetry produces an illusion on the eye of the mind, as a magic lantern produces an illusion on the eye of the body. And, as the magic lantern acts best in a dark room, poetry affects its purpose most completely in a dark age.[9]

Poetry in brief is a combination of painting and insanity. In the same spirit and with even more authority Bentham was plastering the arts with the epithets *anergastic* (no-work-producing) and *aplopathoscopic* (mere-sensation-regarding). "The game of push-pin," he said, "is of equal value with the arts and sciences of music and poetry."[1]

---

[9] Macaulay's review of Milton's *De Doctrina Christiana*, August, 1825, paragraphs 14–17 (*Essays*, Everyman's Library, 1907, I, 154–5). Cf. Hazlitt's opinion that the "Necessary advances of civilization are unfavorable to the spirit of poetry" (*Works*, ed. P. P. Howe, V, 9) and that the "greatest poets, the best painters, appeared soon after the birth" of the technological arts "and lived in a state of society, which was, in other respects, comparatively barbarous" (*Works*, IV, 161). Cf. "The Age of Brass," *TLS*, August 11, 1950, p. 50.

[1] Alba Warren, *English Poetic Theory 1825–1865* (Princeton, 1950), pp. 66–7.

II

MACAULAY's too, too solid comment is a serious counterpart to a more notorious, if only whimsical, essay which had appeared five years earlier. This was *The Four Ages of Poetry*, by Shelley's friend the neo-pagan satirical novelist Thomas Love Peacock. Aside from the fact that it is the most sustained account in English of the conflict between poetry and science as it stood in the era of the romantic poets, Peacock's essay is notable for two things: a superficially cyclic account of the history of culture and poetry, and springing out of that a triumphantly unfair assault on contemporary English poetry, especially that of the Lake School. The four ages of poetry in the antique world were, says Peacock, the iron age (when poetry was rude panegyric of rude but real heroes), the golden age from Homer to Sophocles (when poetry was ancestral retrospect—the infancy of history), the silver age of civilization (when poetry was either heroic imitation, the epic of Virgil, or social criticism, the comedy of Aristophanes, the satire of Horace), and the brass age, the second childhood of poetry (a degenerate attempt to regain the primitive). The cause of the steady deterioration of poetry in the ancient world had been the rise of historical and philosophic thinking. First the empire of fact, then the empire of thought had been withdrawn. In the modern world, a second four-phase cycle had occurred: the age of medieval romance, the age of Ariosto and Shakespeare, the age of Dryden and Pope, and now the latest and most ridiculous phase in the history of poetry, that of modern primitivism, the second age of brass, the "patriarchs" of which appear in that "egregious confraternity of rhymesters . . . the lake Poets."

> While the historian and the philosopher are advancing in, and accelerating, the progress of knowledge, the poet is wallowing in the rubbish of departed ignorance, and raking up the ashes of dead savages to find gewgaws and rattles for the grown babies of the age. Mr. Scott digs up the poachers and cattle-stealers of the ancient border. Lord Byron cruises for thieves and pirates on the shores of the Morea and among the Greek islands. Mr. Southey wades through ponderous volumes of travels and old chronicles, from which he carefully selects all that is fake, useless, and absurd, as being essentially poetical; and when he has a commonplace book full of monstrosities, strings them into an epic. Mr. Wordsworth picks up village legends from old women and sextons; and Mr. Coleridge, to the valuable information acquired from similar sources, superadds the dreams of crazy theologians and the mysticism of German metaphysics, and favors

the world with visions in verse, in which the quadruple elements of sexton, old woman, Jeremy Taylor, and Immanuel Kant are harmonized into a delicious poetical compound.

A poet in our times is a semi-barbarian in a civilized community. He lives in the days that are past. His ideas, thoughts, feelings, associations, are all with barbarous manners, obsolete customs, and exploded superstitions. The march of his intellect is like that of a crab, backward.

. . . as if there were no such things in existence as mathematicians, astronomers, chemists, moralists, metaphysicians, historians, politicians, and political economists, who have built into the upper air of intelligence a pyramid, from the summit of which they see the modern Parnassus far beneath them, and, knowing how small a place it occupies in the comprehensiveness of their prospect, smile at the little ambition and the circumscribed perceptions with which the drivelers and mountebanks upon it are contending for the poetical palm and the critical chair.[2]

Peacock's waggishly provocative and bumptious rhetoric gives a vivid enough image of a closing phase in the long process by which the four ages, golden, silver, iron, brazen, of classical myth,[3] were settling into the three (theological, metaphysical, scientific) of 19th-century Comtean positivism. Except for the transvaluation, the accent of rejoicing rather than lament as science is supposed to deprive poetry of its dominion, this evolutionary account of poetic and cultural origins is the same as that which appears in Vico, in the Germans from Herder on, in Rousseau, and in 18th-century British primitivists like Monboddo and John Brown. And substantially the same account appears in the excited retort which Peacock elicited from Shelley.[4]

Shelley's *Defense of Poetry* [5] is not remarkable for metaphysical pre-

[2] Text in P. B. Shelley, *A Defense of Poetry*, ed. A. S. Cook (Boston, 1891), pp. 47–61; available also in *Peacock's Four Ages of Poetry, Shelley's Defense of Poetry, Browning's Essay on Shelley*, ed. H. F. B. Brett-Smith (Oxford, 1945).

[3] Cf. Ovid, *Metamorphoses*, I, 89–127. *Aurea prima sata est aetas. . . . subiit argentea proles, auro deterior. . . . Tertia post illas successit aënea proles. . . . . . duro est ultima ferro.*

[4] Professor Wellek points out that Shelley's immediate source appears to be French. Shelley speaks of the "Celtic" conquerors of the Roman Empire and the predominance of the "Celtic" nations after the fall of Rome. Such a confusion between Celtic and Teutonic occurs in Paul-Henri Mallet, the Swiss propagandist of things Nordic, and among the Celtomanes of the late 18th century, but in English it had been refuted by Bishop Percy, the translator of Mallet (René Wellek, "DeQuincey's Status in the History of Ideas," *PQ*, XXIII, July, 1944, 267).

[5] It was finished and sent to Charles Ollier (the publisher of Peacock's *Four Ages*) by March 20, 1821. With the failure of Ollier's *Miscellany* and then of Hunt's *Liberal*, to which the manuscript had been transferred, it was not published until 1840, in Mrs. Shelley's volume of *Essays, Letters from Abroad, Translations, and*

cision. The opening paragraph expounds a distinction between "Reason" (Coleridgean "Understanding") and "Imagination" (Coleridgean "Secondary Imagination" plus Coleridgean "Reason") along lines so simple as to be almost reminiscent of 17th-century arguments about "judgment" and "wit." [6] The essay contains two or three fairly close echoes of Plato's *Ion* and *Symposium*, both of which Shelley had been recently translating. The most significant of these passages (though Shelley's echo brings over nothing of the jocular spirit by which the words of Socrates in the *Ion* are protected) is perhaps the following:

> The sacred links of that chain have never been entirely disjoined, which descending through the minds of many men is attached to those great minds, whence as from a magnet the invisible effluence is sent forth, which at once connects, animates, and sustains the life of all.[7]

The general course of Shelley's philosophic career had been from French naturalism and necessitarianism (*Queen Mab*,[8] 1813), through a phase of Platonic or ontologic idealism [9] (perhaps more Wordsworthian than actually philosophic—*Mont Blanc* and the *Hymn to Intellectual Beauty*, 1816) to the psychologic or epistemologic idealism (more characteristic of his era) in the *Poems* of 1822.

Thought
Alone, and its quick elements, Will, Passion,
Reason, Imagination, cannot die;
They are, what that which they regard appears,
The stuff whence mutability can weave
All that it hath dominion o'er, worlds, worms,
Empires, and superstitions.[1]

Fragments. In being edited for the *Liberal*, the essay was pruned of its direct references to Peacock.

[6] Cf. *Defense*, ed. Cook, p. 35. Reason is the "calculating faculty."

[7] "This is the language of Plato" (Shelley, at bottom of folio MS. d1. See A. H. Koszul, *Shelley's Prose in the Bodleian Manuscripts*, London, 1910, p. 88, n. 3). Shelley's translation of the corresponding passage in the *Ion* runs as follows: ". . . it is a divine influence which moves you, like that which resides in the stone called magnet by Euripides, and Heraclea by the people. . . . Do you not perceive that your auditor is the last link of that chain which I have described as held together through the power of the magnet. . . ." (*Essays, Letters* . . . 1840, I, 281). In his Preface to the *Symposium* Shelley says that he translated this dialogue from the 9th to the 17th of July, 1818. The only evidence for the date of his translating the *Ion* is a letter to Peacock, February 15, 1821, in which he alludes to reading it.

[8] Of course not *simply* a naturalistic poem. See *Queen Mab*, VI, 32 ff., where "soul" is the only element.

[9] On the sources of Shelley's Platonism, see James A. Notopoulos, "Shelley and Thomas Taylor," *PMLA*, LI (July, 1936), 502–17; *The Platonism of Shelley* (Durham, 1949), pp. 29–77, Ch. III, "The Direct Platonism of Shelley."

[1] *Hellas*, ll. 795–801. Cf. especially *Epipsychidion* and *Adonais*. In her Preface to the 1840 volumes of Shelley's prose Mrs. Shelley became authority for the notion that "Shelley was a disciple of the Immaterial Philosophy of Berkeley." And it is

It would be difficult to show that any one of these philosophies operates decisively in the poetics of the *Defense,* or that any is altogether absent. Even French naturalism may be said to be represented in the conception of poetic origins to which we have alluded just above. Strains of 18th-century primitivism mingle throughout with a Germanically colored romantic excitement about the immediately spiritual and morally plastic power of the poet.

> The savage (for the savage is to ages what the child is to years) expresses the emotions produced in him by surrounding objects in a similar manner; and language and gesture, together with plastic or pictorial imitation, become the image of the combined effect of those objects and his apprehension of them. Man in society, with all his passions and his pleasures, next becomes the object of the passions and pleasures of man; an additional class of emotions produces an augmented treasure of expression; and language, gesture, and the imitative arts, become at once the representation and the medium, the pencil and the picture, the chisel and the statue, the chord and the harmony.—p. 3

> Their language is vitally metaphorical; that is, it marks the before unapprehended relations of things and perpetuates their apprehension.—p. 4

> But poets, or those who imagine and express this indestructible order, are not only the authors of language and of music, of the dance, and architecture, and statuary, and painting; they are the institutors of laws, and the founders of civil society, and the inventors of the arts of life, and the teachers who draw into a certain propinquity with the beautiful and the true that partial apprehension of the agencies of the invisible world which is called religion.—p. 5

· · ·

---

true that Shelley seems to have picked up a good deal of whatever philosophy he had from Sir William Drummond's Berkeleyan handbook of modern philosophy, *Academical Questions* (London, 1805). Yet in one of the few scraps of direct evidence which Shelley left, his fragmentary essay or jottings *On Life,* he follows a Berkeleyan phrase "Nothing exists but as it is perceived" in the same paragraph with the Fichtean monistic pronouncement "The words *I, YOU, THEY, . . .* are merely marks employed to denote the different modifications of the one mind" (*Shelley's Literary and Philosophical Criticism,* ed. John Shawcross, London, 1909, p. 56). See Joseph Barrell, *Shelley and the Thought of his Time* (New Haven, 1947), p. 122, n. 50; cf. pp. 28, 160, 197. And see G. S. Brett, "Shelley's Relation to Berkeley and Drummond," *Studies in English by Members of University College* (Toronto, Canada, 1931); Hans Liedtke, *Shelley durch Berkeley und Drummond beeinflusst* (Greifswald, 1933). Shelley apparently never read Kant. Barrell believes that Drummond taught both Shelley and Peacock (in *Nightmare Abbey*) to scorn the Critical Philosophy. Cf. René Wellek, *Immanuel Kant in England 1793–1838* (Princeton, 1931), pp. 181–2.

> Poetry in a more restricted sense expresses those arrangements of language, and especially metrical language, which are created by that imperial faculty whose throne is curtained within the invisible nature of man. And this springs from the nature itself of language, which is a more direct representation of the actions and passions of our internal being, and is susceptible of more various and delicate combinations, than color, form, or motion, and is more plastic and obedient to the control of that faculty of which it is the creation.—pp. 6–7

What is unique about the essay, and wherein it triumphs, is the overall rhythm of its enthusiasm and the glowing cascade of images which celebrate the magnificent theme.

> Man is an instrument over which a series of external and internal impressions are driven, like the alternations of an ever-changing wind over an Aeolian lyre, which move it by their motion to ever-changing melody.—p. 2

> . . . the mind in creation is as a fading coal, which some invisible influence, like an inconstant wind, awakens to transitory brightness; this power arises from within, like the color of a flower which fades and changes as it is developed, and the conscious portions of our natures are unprophetic either of its approach or its departure. Could this influence be durable in its original purity and force, it is impossible to predict the greatness of the results; but when composition begins, inspiration is already on the decline, and the most glorious poetry that has ever been communicated to the world is probably a feeble shadow of the original conceptions of the poet.—p. 39

> Poetry is the record of the best and happiest moments of the happiest and best minds. We are aware of evanescent visitations of thought and feeling. . . . It is as it were the interpenetration of a diviner nature through our own.—p. 40

> Poetry redeems from decay the visitations of the divinity in man.—p. 41

> It strips the veil of familiarity from the world, and lays bare the naked and sleeping beauty which is the spirit of its forms.
> —p. 42

> The most unfailing herald, companion, and follower of the awakening of a great people to work a beneficial change in opinion or institution, is poetry.—pp. 45–6

Poets are the hierophants of an unapprehended inspiration; the mirrors of the gigantic shadows which futurity casts upon the present; the words which express what they understand not; the trumpets which sing to battle and feel not what they inspire; the influence which is moved not, but moves. Poets are the unacknowledged legislators of the world.—p. 46 [2]

Shelley's *Defense* is written in the vein of his *Ode to the West Wind*, a poem which is a plenary instance of the romantic *Ars Poetica*, where overt enunciation of the cosmic and daemonic poetics is not only supported by imagery but is merged in tumultuous swirls of it and carried in headlong versification.

> Make me thy lyre, even as the forest is:
> What if my leaves are falling like its own!
> The tumult of thy mighty harmonies
>
> Will take from both a deep, autumnal tone,
> Sweet though in sadness.[3] Be thou, Spirit fierce,
> My spirit! Be thou me, impetuous one!
>
> Drive my dead thoughts over the universe
> Like withered leaves to quicken a new birth!
> And, by the incantation of this verse,
>
> Scatter, as from an unextinguished hearth
> Ashes and sparks,[4] my words among mankind!
> Be through my lips to unwakened earth
> The trumpet of a prophecy! [5]

[2] "Earlier laudators of poetry had said the same thing, but it did not mean the same thing; Shelley (to borrow a successful phrase from Mr. Bernard Shaw) was the first, in this tradition of Nature's M.P.'s" (Eliot, *Use of Poetry*, p. 16).

[3] Cf. *Defense*, ed. Cook, p. 35: "Sorrow, terror, anguish, despair itself, are often the chosen expressions of an approximation to the highest good. . . . tragedy delights by affording a shadow of that pleasure which exists in pain. This is the source also of the melancholy which is inseparable from the sweetest melody."

[4] Cf. *Defense*, ed. Cook, p. 11, "a spark of inextinguishable thought"; p. 33, "a spark, a burning atom of inextinguishable thought."

[5] Strains of Shelley's poetic theory, especially in its political and moral aspects, occur throughout his poetry—in *Queen Mab* and *Prometheus*, for instance, in *Mont Blanc*, the *Hymn to Intellectual Beauty*, the *Ode to Naples*, the *Ode to Liberty*. Cf. Melvin Solve, *Shelley, His Theory of Poetry* (Chicago, 1927), pp. 32 ff.

The "undisciplined overflowing of the soul," the "attempt to imitate the untamable wildness" (Preface to Shelley's *History of a Six Weeks Tour*, 1817) which we encounter in this poetry of Shelley's presents a nice problem concerning the formal (i.e., ordered) embodiment of tumult in poetry. As for the genetic question, Shelley speaks against deliberate art in the *Defense* ("I appeal to the greatest poets of the present day whether it is not an error to assert that the finest passages of poetry are produced by labor and study," p. 39). But his record here is not consistent. In the Preface to *Prometheus*, for instance, he confesses that the finest passages of the poem have been the product of laborious revision. Cf. *ante* Chapter 10, p. 181, the relation between genesis and product, ordered or disordered, in the context of Jonson's classical views.

The most definable theoretic tenet in all this looks much like a renewal of one of those practical functions defined in Ciceronian rhetoric, to "persuade" (*persuadere, flectere*). Shelley's emphasis is quite clear.

> A man, to be greatly good, must imagine intensely and comprehensively; he must put himself in the place of another and of many others; the pains and pleasures of his species must become his own. The great instrument of moral good is the imagination; and poetry administers to the effect by acting upon the cause. Poetry enlarges the circumference of the imagination by replenishing it with thoughts of ever new delight. . . . Poetry strengthens the faculty which is the organ of the moral nature of man.—p. 14

> The imagination is enlarged by a sympathy with pains and passions so mighty, that they distend in their conception the capacity of that by which they are conceived; the good affections are strengthened by pity, indignation, terror and sorrow, and an exalted calm is prolonged from the satiety of this high exercise of them into the tumult of familiar life.—p. 18

As Sir Philip Sidney had said, poetry is a feigning "notable images of virtues, vices, or what else, with . . . delightful teaching." Poetry combines the truths of philosophy with the persuasive vividness of history. How, one might be tempted to ask, does Shelley's *Defense* differ from Sidney's? A number of close parallels may be noted. The term "poet," say both Sidney and Shelley, is derived from the verb "to make" (*poiein*); poets are the earliest authors; they are teachers of religion and prophets (or are "called" prophets, as Sidney puts it). Poetry is rhythmic, but rhyming and versification do not make a poet. Aristotle has defined the difference between poetry and history. But great historians and philosophers (the philosopher Plato, for instance) have been poets. A few of Sidney's phrases—"Plannet-like Musick," "low-creeping" objections to poetry—are reborn in Shelley's "planetary music" of poetry and "low-thoughted envy" of contemporaries.[6] The difference between the two *Defenses*, nevertheless, could scarcely be more profound. It lies as deep as the difference between Aristotle and Kant. It amounts to this: that Sidney in all his talking about the teaching and persuading power of poetry would never dream that poetry was teaching or persuading any doctrine which it did not discover in some legislatively competent authority outside itself, either scriptural revelation or ethical philosophy. With Shelley just the opposite is true. When he talks about poetry getting at the motives for good action, touching the heart by enkindling the im-

[6] See *Defense*, ed. Cook, p. xix; ed. H. F. B. Brett-Smith, p. xx.

agination, he may sound for a moment almost pre-Cartesian, forensic, homiletic. The words are, nevertheless, part of an appeal for a vastly creative and autonomous power. There is no appeal to any other authority. The limits of the power come not from outside it but from within. Or, there are no limits. There is no specifically doctrinal commitment. Thus:

> A poet therefore would do ill to embody his own conceptions of right and wrong, which are usually those of his place and time, in his poetical creations, which participate in neither. By this assumption of the inferior office of interpreting the effect, in which perhaps after all he might acquit himself but imperfectly, he would resign a glory in the participation of the cause.
>
> —p. 14

> Milton has so far violated the popular creed (if this shall be judged to be a violation) as to have alleged no superiority of moral virtue to his God over his Devil. And this bold neglect of a direct moral purpose is the most decisive proof of the supremacy of Milton's genius.—p. 31

It is in this spirit that Shelley writes his Preface to *Prometheus* (1820): "Didactic poetry is my abhorrence; nothing can be equally well expressed in prose that is not tedious and supererogatory in verse." [7] The autonomously moral and religious power of poetry stands out much more prominently in Shelley's view than in that of Wordsworth or Coleridge. The Kantian "Reason" which Coleridge, following Fichte and Schelling, improved from a hypothetically constructive to a gnostic faculty does not appear in Shelley's system. The honor conferred upon poetic imagination, though nebulous, is the highest possible. In general import, if not in metaphysical precision, and doubtless not by any direct indebtedness, Shelley's poetic is close to that of Schelling in the "absolute" phase of his idealism and to the mythopoeia of Friedrich Schlegel.

III

ONLY one English poet of this era furnishes a companion theory to Shelley's, and that is Blake, whose apocalyptic humanism, proclaimed in such notations as those collected by modern editors under the title *A Vision of the Last Judgment* and in the gigantic sprawling myths of his

---

[7] A few contrary admissions are to be found in less formal utterances. In a letter of 1811 to Miss Hitchener he said that a large part of *Queen Mab* was overtly didactic. "My opinion is that all poetical beauty ought to be subordinate to the inculcated moral." In a letter of January 1819 he confessed to Peacock: "I consider poetry very subordinate to moral and political science."

canonical prophetic books, can hardly be pressed into literary or even general aesthetic service. Blake connects less with the literary tradition than with cabbalistic and visionary theories of knowledge. He is a "literal realist of imagination"[8] who takes down what is dictated to him by the "Authors in Eternity."[9] Imagination is "the real and eternal World of which even this Vegetable Universe is but a faint shadow."[1] To such an idealism not only the scientific view of nature but nature itself in any simple and external sense is repugnant. Blake, even more than Wordsworth, Coleridge, or Shelley, was an antagonist of scientism—explicitly, repeatedly and contemptuously. Nevertheless, there were moments when he could not quite stomach a nature poet like Wordsworth—or at least not Wordsworth's theory of his own achievement. Blake annotated Wordsworth's 1815 *Poems* thus: "I do not know who wrote these Prefaces: they are very mischievous & direct contrary to Wordsworth's own Practice." "Natural Objects always did & now do weaken, deaden & obliterate Imagination in Me. Wordsworth must know that what he writes valuable is Not to be found in Nature."[2]

> Error is created. Truth is Eternal. Error, or Creation will be Burned up, & then, and not till Then, Truth or Eternity will appear. It is Burnt up the Moment Men cease to behold it. I assert for My Self that I do not behold the outward Creation & that to me it is hindrance & not Action; it is as the dirt upon my feet, No part of Me.[3]

IV

INTERNATIONAL threats (first the republicanism of the French Revolution, then the imperialism of Napoleon) which prevailed during the era of English romantic poetry, and the economic and social troubles internal to England, produced at the level of popular criticism and reviewing, a wholesale resumption of something like the classical didactic mode of criticism, an impassioned appeal to patriotic, religious, and moral norms in the judgment of contemporary poems. "To devote poetry to religious purposes," a reviewer might say, "is to restore it to its original purpose."[4] "It is time," another might say (reviewing Coleridge's *Fears*

[8] W. B. Yeats, "William Blake and His Illustrations to *The Divine Comedy*," in *Essays* (New York, 1924), p. 14.
[9] Blake, *Poetry and Prose*, ed. Geoffrey Keynes (London, 1948), p. 869. ". . . a Grand Poem. I may praise it since I dare not pretend to be any other than the secretary; the Authors are in Eternity" (letter to Thomas Butts, July 6, 1803).
[1] *Jerusalem IV, To the Christians*, in *Poetry and Prose*, 1948, p. 535.
[2] *Poetry and Prose*, 1948, pp. 821–2.
[3] *A Vision of the Last Judgment*, in *Poetry and Prose*, 1948, pp. 651–2.
[4] William S. Ward, "Some Aspects of the Conservative Attitude Toward Poetry in English Criticism 1798–1800," *PMLA*, LX (June, 1945), 386–98. The quotation is from *The Christian's Pocket Magazine*, December, 1819.

in Solitude, during the Alarm of Invasion), "to enthrone reason on the summit of Parnassus; and make poetry the strengthener as well as the enlivener of the intellect;—the energetic instructor as well as the enchanting amuser of mankind." [5] Others might re-activate neo-classic scruples about the relation between instruction and pleasure.

> Poetry has been commonly supposed, indeed, to aim more at the gratification than the instruction of its votaries, and to have for its end rather delight than improvement; but it has not, we think, been sufficiently considered, that its power of delighting is founded chiefly on its moral energies.[6]

The vocabulary of these avowals might sometimes sound like an echo from the ranges of liberal criticism, whose peaks we have examined in Shelley and Blake. There was, however, little consonance between the two. Popular criticism always had in mind a didacticism and exhortation in the service of the tradition—the Church, the state, and the mores. The didacticism of Shelley and Blake, as was necessary for a theory of poetic creativity which had outrun all traditional theological associations, was a didacticism of revolution.

The defence of poetry against the claims of scientism had been during the 18th century an exploratory action, feeling its way toward the formulation of some kind of poetic autonomy. If scientific philosophy maintained that poetic statements did not satisfy scientific criteria, the answer was to be that poetry proceeded according to other criteria. In some way poetry proceeded according to its own criteria. And these were for the most part aligned with principles of sensory ("imaginative") and emotive pleasure. The autonomy was—at least implicitly—hedonistic. The later romantic development in the theory of creative "imagination" afforded, however, a more complex and ambiguous base from which the English defence of poetry during the 19th century could proceed. For one thing, the defence might and did continue along the line of an autonomy oriented toward pleasure—art for art's sake—a theme which we shall notice in a later chapter. But it might also, as we have just been seeing, wax into the assertion of a new, and autonomous, didacticism (more or less revolutionary). And this didacticism had at least two main phases, the rhapsodic (Shelleyan) and a later more calmly classical and cognitive (the Arnoldian—to be seen in our next chapter). The dual defence of poetry during the 19th century—the hedonistically autonomic, and the didactically autonomic—was a thoroughly plausible outcome and illustration of the ambivalent poise achieved in the continental defence of poetry by the end of the 18th century and taken over

[5] Ward, *loc. cit.*, p. 392, quoting *Monthly Review, or Literary Journal*, May, 1799.

[6] Ward, *loc. cit.*, p. 395, quoting *Edinburgh Review*, November, 1820.

by Coleridge and Wordsworth. Kant's beautiful symbols of moral value, his purposiveness without purpose, his judgment by feeling, are a sufficient promise of the whole development. We are speaking of Kant as typical of the thought of an era. Only the vaguest and most atmospheric acquaintance with German ideas (in the case of Shelley a direct dash of Fichte, a general modern philosophical education in Drummond's *Academical Questions*), an awareness of the ideas of Coleridge, or a feeling of sympathy with the neo-Platonic tradition, would be the genetic requirement for a given English literary man's participation in the movement. "Bliss was it in that dawn to be alive."

V

WE MOVE toward a conclusion of this chapter and advance chronologically in the 19th century with quotations from two other authors, both more distinguished for general literary power than for clean lines in literary theory. Coleridge's friend De Quincey was given to ostentatious hints about his understanding of the metaphysics of Kant and performed various journalistic flourishes on the theme of German romantic literature and Germanic neo-Hellenism.[7] His essay of 1848 in the *North British Review* on Alexander Pope contains one of his chief claims to be remembered as a literary theorist—his distinction between a "literature of knowledge" and a "literature of power."

> The function of the first is to *teach;* the function of the second is to *move;* the first is a rudder, the second an oar or a sail. The first speaks to the mere discursive understanding; the second speaks ultimately, it may happen, to the higher understanding or reason, but always through affections of pleasure and sympathy. Remotely, it may travel towards an object seated in what Lord Bacon calls "dry light";—but proximately it does and must operate—else it ceases to be a literature of power—on and through that *humid* light which clothes itself in the mists and glittering iris of human passions, desires, and genial emotions. . . . there is a rarer thing than truth,—namely *power*, or deep sympathy with truth.

> What do you learn from a cookery-book? Something new, something that you did not know before, in every paragraph. But would you therefore put the wretched cookery-book on a

---

[7] René Wellek, "De Quincey's Status in the History of Ideas," *PQ*, XXIII (January, 1944), 250–5, 256 ff. For more about De Quincey's literary aesthetics, see Sigmund K. Proctor, *Thomas De Quincey's Theory of Literature* (Ann Arbor, 1943); John E. Jordan, *Thomas De Quincey Literary Critic* (Berkeley, California, 1952).

higher level of estimation than the divine poem? What you owe
to Milton is not any knowledge, of which a million separate
items are still but a million of advancing steps on the same
earthly level; what you owe is *power*,—that is, exercise and expansion to your own latent capacity of sympathy with the infinite, where every pulse and each separate influx is a step up-
wards, a step ascending upon a Jacob's ladder from earth to
mysterious altitudes above the earth.

It is certain that, were it not for the literature of power, . . .
ideals would often remain amongst us as mere arid notional
forms; whereas, by the creative forces of man put forth in
literature, they gain a vernal life of restoration, and germinate
into vital activities. The commonest novel, by moving in alliance with human fears and hopes, with human instincts of
wrong and right, sustains and quickens those affections. Calling
them into action, it rescues them from torpor. And hence the
preëminency over all authors that merely *teach*, of the meanest
that moves, or that teaches, if at all, indirectly by moving.[8]

The throbbing utterance, the allusion to "discursive understanding" and
the "higher understanding or reason," put this on the grand level of
romantic theory. It sounds sufficiently like the emotive didacticism of
Shelley. At the same time if we read it in the context of Coleridge's
religious influence upon De Quincey and De Quincey's theocratic social
views united with Tory politics in the belief that the British Empire was
the torch-bearer of Christian progress,[9] the passage may sound not un-
reconcilable with the moralistic popular reviewing which we have quoted
from the era of thirty to fifty years before.

In his early miscellaneous essays, Thomas Carlyle was one of the
most powerful and most accurate transmitters of German aesthetic philosophy to England. His program included energetic announcements of
the antagonism between poetry and science and of the paramount claim
which poetry laid to all the truth that mattered. The "polish and lan-
guor," the "external glitter and internal vacuity," of 18th-century literature he blamed squarely on the analytic science of the era. He noted
a continuing prevalence of the enfeeblement even in his own day.

We enjoy, we see nothing by direct vision; but only by reflection, and in anatomical dismemberment. Like Sir Hudibras,
for every Why we must have a Wherefore. We have our little
theory on all human and divine things. Poetry, the workings of
genius itself, which in all times, with one or another meaning,

---

[8] Alden, pp. 340–3. Twenty-five years earlier De Quincey had made the same
distinction in his *Letters to a Young Man*.

[9] Wellek, *loc. cit.*, pp. 253–4.

has been called Inspiration, and held to be mysterious and in-
scrutable, is no longer without its scientific exposition. The
building of the lofty rhyme is like any other masonry or brick-
laying: we have theories of its rise, height, decline and fall,—
which latter, it would seem, is now near, among all peoples.[1]

The power of the true poet, whenever in history it did appear, was quite
another thing.

> The true Poet is ever, as of old, the Seer; whose eye has been
> gifted to discern the godlike Mystery of God's Universe, and
> decipher some new lines of its celestial writing; we can still call
> him a *Vates* and Seer; for he *sees* into this greatest of secrets,
> "the open secret"; hidden things become clear; how the Future
> (both resting on Eternity) is but another phasis of the Present:
> thereby are his words in very truth prophetic; what he has
> spoken shall be done.[2]

Carlyle's lectures *On Heroes, Hero-Worship, and the Heroic in History* were delivered in May, 1840. The diminishing sequence of roles
assigned to the hero in the six lectures—The Hero as Divinity, as
Prophet, as Poet, as Priest, as Man of Letters, as King—represents both
Carlyle's assurance in man's heroic destiny and at the same time a degree
of acquiescence in the philosophy of decline, in the view that civilized
advance means the decay of genius and greatness.[3] The poet is not the
prophet, not the divinity. The opening of the lecture on the Hero as
Poet surveys several phases in the power of the spirit to triumph against
science.

> The Hero as Divinity, the Hero as Prophet, are productions of
> old ages; not to be repeated in the new. They presuppose a cer-
> tain rudeness of conception, which the progress of mere scien-
> tific knowledge put an end to. There needs to be, as it were, a
> world vacant, or almost vacant of scientific forms, if men in
> their loving wonder are to fancy their fellow-man either a god
> or one speaking with the voice of a god. Divinity and Prophet
> are past. We are now to see our Hero in the less ambitious, but
> also less questionable, character of Poet; a character which does

[1] "Signs of the Times," in *Works* (1896–99), XXVII, 76. See Alba Warren,
pp. 79–84.
[2] "Death of Goethe," *Works*, XXVII, 377. Cf. René Wellek, *Immanuel Kant in
England* (Princeton, 1931), pp. 183–202.
[3] See René Wellek, "Carlyle and the Philosophy of History," *PQ*, XXIII (January, 1944), 55–76, for the uncertain kind of resemblance which obtains between
Carlyle's views and the several forms of historical method available in Germany,
France, or England at that day. Wellek argues that Carlyle's ethical normalism and
divinatory impulsiveness are closer to Germanic forms of "historism" and literary
nationalism than to French naturalistic and sociological trends.

not pass. The Poet is a heroic figure belonging to all ages; whom all ages possess, when once he is produced, whom the newest age as the oldest may produce;—and will produce, always when Nature pleases. Let Nature send a Hero-soul; in no age is it other than possible that he may be shaped into a Poet.

But:

> I confess, I have no notion of a truly great man that could not be *all* sorts of men. The Poet who could merely sit on a chair, and compose stanzas, would never make a stanza worth much. He could not sing the Heroic warrior, unless he himself were at least a Heroic warrior too. I fancy there is in him the Politician, the Thinker, Legislator, Philosopher;—in one or the other degree, he could have been, he is all these. So too I cannot understand how a Mirabeau, with that great glowing heart, with the fire that was in it, with the bursting tears that were in it, could not have written verses, tragedies, poems, and touched all hearts in that way, had his course of life and education led him thitherward. The grand fundamental character is that of Great Man; that the man be great. Napoleon has words in him which are like Austerlitz Battles. Louis Fourteenth's Marshals are a kind of poetical men withal; the things Turenne says are full of sagacity and geniality, like sayings of Samuel Johnson.

Admitting not so much as Macaulay in his essay on Milton (that poetry flourishes best in a dark age), claiming not so much as Shelley in his *Defense* (that poets actually perform as legislators), Carlyle is shrewd enough to see the age-old paradox with which he is saddled, energetic enough to bounce it off as of small consequence. "Louis Fourteenth's Marshals are a kind of poetical men withal." On the high tide of Carlyle's plausible eloquence, an ancient moment in the history of the quarrel between rhapsode and dialectician is re-enacted with the victory reversed. One of the passages of Shelley's *Defense* most strongly reminiscent of Plato's *Ion* is that in which the Christian and chivalric poets of the early Middle Ages are credited with having created "forms of opinion and action . . . which, copied into the imaginations of men, became as generals to the bewildered armies of their thoughts." [4] In Plato's *Ion*, the rhapsode, after being pushed gradually into a corner with admissions that he was unfitted to discourse on such professional topics as medicine, charioteering, fishing, and piloting, gave utterance at the very last, under extreme pressure of the Socratic dialectical skill, to the desperate opinion that he might after all have been a successful general of the armies.

[4] *Defense,* ed. Cook, p. 25.

SUPPLEMENT

For the tides are the life of God in the ocean, and he sends his angel to trouble the great DEEP.
For he hath fixed the earth upon arches & pillars, and the flames of hell flow under it.
For the grosser the particles the nearer to the sink, & the nearer to purity, the quicker the gravitation.
For MATTER is the dust of the Earth, every atom of which is the life.
For MOTION is as the quantity of life direct, & that which hath not motion, is resistance.
For Resistance is not of GOD, but he—hath built his works upon it.
For the Centripetal and Centrifugal forces are GOD SUSTAINING and DIRECTING.
For Elasticity is the temper of matter to recover its place with vehemence.
For Attraction is the earning of parts, which have a similitude in the life.
For the Life of God is in the Loadstone, and there is a magnet, which pointeth due EAST.

For FRICTION is inevitable because the Universe is FULL of God's works.
For the PERPETUAL MOTION is in all the works of Almighty GOD.

For Newton nevertheless is more of error than of the truth, but I am of the WORD of GOD.

> —Christopher Smart, *Jubilate Agno*, p. IX, ll. 7–16, 35–6, 45 (written in 1759), quoted from *Rejoice in the Lamb, A Song from Bedlam*, ed. William Force Stead (London, 1939), pp. 83–6, by permission of the editor and Jonathan Cape Limited

His [Thomas Taylor's] first three books, *The Mystical Initiations* (translations of the Orphic hymns, 1787), *Concerning the Beautiful* (a translation from Plotinus, 1787), and *The Philosophical and Mathematical Commentaries of Proclus* (two volumes, 1788–89), provoked immediate criticism in the *Monthly Review* and were apparently widely discussed. . . . A volume containing *The Cratylus, Phaedo, Parmenides and Timaeus of Plato* (1793), following hard upon the *Phaedrus* (1792), was hailed by a writer in the *Analytical Review* as a good beginning toward "a grand *desideratum* in English literature," the translation of all Plato's works. Taylor's efforts, however, were turned for the moment to other tasks, of which the most important were translations of Pausanias's *Description of Greece* (1794), *Five Books of Plotinus* (1794), and *The Fable of Cupid and Psyche* by Apuleius (1795).

These many books, filled as they all were with neo-Platonic ideas, gained Taylor a wide notoriety, if not esteem. For he was militant in thrusting his mystical, polytheistic neo-Platonism before the eyes of a sober and unsympathetic eighteenth-century audience, who in turn ridiculed him as an insane fanatic. The materialism of the age and the concern of classical scholarship at the time with merely textual criticism aroused in Taylor a scorn which he freely expressed. In an eloquent plea for the study of Platonism, appended to his translation of the Orphic hymns, he called on his countrymen to resist these illiberal influences:

> The waters of Thames, heavy laden with the wealth of merchandize, and sonorous with the din of trade, may devolve abundance in a golden tide; but we must remember that the Daemon of commerce is at the same time advancing with giant strides, to trample on the most liberal pursuits, and is preparing with his extended savage arm, to crush the votaries of truth, and depopulate the divine retreats of philosophy. Rise then ye liberal few, and vindicate the dignity of ancient wisdom. Bring truth from her silent and sacred concealments, and vigorously repel the growing empire of barbaric taste; which bids fair to extinguish the celestial fire of philosophy in the frigid embraces of philology, and to bury the divine light of mind, in the sordid gloom of sense.—*The Mystical Initiations*, London, 1787, p. 226

This blunt indictment of contemporary civilization did not increase Taylor's popularity, though it attracted notice. Nor did the remedy which he proposed impress the eighteenth century with his sanity, though it made him famous. If London were found too far sunk in "barbarous ignorance," Taylor advised, the "liberal few" should fly to

> the regions of intellect, those fortunate islands of truth, where . . . we may find a retreat from the storms and tempests of a corporeal life. Let us build for ourselves the raft of virtue, and departing from this region of sense, like Ulysses from the charms of Calypso, direct our course by the light of ideas, those bright intellectual stars, through the dark ocean of a material nature, until we arrive at our father's land. For there having divested ourselves of the torn garments of mortality, as much as our union with body will permit, we may resume our natural appearance; and may each of us at length, recover the ruined empire of his soul.—*The Mystical Initiations*, pp. 226–7

—Frank B. Evans III, "Thomas Taylor, Platonist of the Romantic Period," *PMLA*, LV (December, 1940), 1067–8, by permission of the Modern Language Association of America

CHAPTER 20

THE ARNOLDIAN PROPHECY

§ feeling and image c. 1795, the lyric norm, a French incident: Hugo's Cromwell and Hernani, Coleridge and Poe on the long poem, Mill on mere stories, Newman's Evangelical critique of Aristotle, Keble's Praelectiones, pre-Freudian intimations, "spasmodic" poetry, Aytoun, Tennyson—II. Arnold's brusque resistance, Preface to 1853, all depends on the subject, the "grand style," bad influence of Shakespeare on Keats—III. an altered classicism, Essays, First Series, continental sources, Joubert (clarity and truth), Heine (Philistinism), British parochialism, The Modern Element in Literature, "Wragg is in custody," The Literary Influence of Academies, English proposals for linguistic. authority, Samuel Johnson, The Oxford Dictionary, Arnold's suave anachronism—IV. English violence and individualism, French intelligence and form, poetry and "natural magic," On the Study of Celtic Literature, "moral profundity," vivid disparagement of Shelley, Byron, Coleridge, Keats, On Translating Homer, against Teutonizing, "the object as in itself it really is," The Study of Poetry, "truth and high seriousness"—V. difficulties with Arnold: 1. shift from substance to norm of style, "touchstones," 2. high seriousness, mistrust of "lighter kinds of poetry," what Chaucer lacks, Gray patronized, Burns merely ironic, 3. misunderstanding of anachronism, Merope, literal view of translating, 4. poetry a "criticism of life," detachment vs. application, "laws of poetic truth and poetic beauty"—VI. poetry to replace religion and philosophy, Culture and Anarchy, "sweetness and light," Literature and Science, a new kind of emotivism—VII. other idealist voices, Emerson, James, "The Genteel Tradition," the new humanism in America, P. E. More, humanism with religion, Irving Babbitt, "insight" and "inner check" §

432

FEELING AND IMAGE CAME THROUGH THE EIGHTEENTH CENTURY, AS WE have seen, in close liaison, and they enjoyed at the dawn of the new era a high estate together. Feeling was somewhat indiscriminately treated as either something that welled up in the poet himself or (it made little difference) something that was discernible in the poem or in its images. Among the poetic genres, lyric had moved into the normative place. Or the broader and simpler concept of "poem" (or "poetry," in the soul of the poet) was the norm—it mattered not what "order of composition" the poet elected. The notion of untutored, and hence genuine, utterance was not likely to be far absent from poetic discussion. Let us re-focus momentarily on the situation about 1795 by quoting a letter from a poetess, "The Swan of Lichfield," Anna Seward.

> Our very peasants show that the seeds of poetry exist in the rude soil of their minds. Awaken their passions or excite their wonder, and you will often hear them speaking in metaphor, which is the poetic essence.[1]

Not that anybody said much directly against the classic fable, the story, the structural base of the long poem, but at the same time not much was urged in favor of that element.[2] Poetic theory had passed in the course of the centuries from a classic or Aristotelian focus on drama, through a heroic focus on epic (and then an implicit or hidden focus on satire and burlesque) to the romantic focus on lyric, the songlike personal expression, the feeling centered in the image. The romantic age as the age of lyric is a well enough recognized phenomenon—especially in England.

We have already observed certain lyrist features of the German high theorizing. In France during the 1820's occurred an incident in the history of dramatic literature which may perhaps be relevantly mentioned in this context. A classically regulated French drama, for reasons generated out of both revolutionary republicanism and Napoleonic and

[1] *Letters of Anna Seward* (Edinburgh, 1811), III, 320, October 1, 1793, quoted by Norman Maclean, "From Action to Image: Theories of the Lyric in the Eighteenth Century," in Crane, *Critics and Criticism*, p. 460.

[2] Cf. Donald M. Foerster, "The Critical Attack upon the Epic in the English Romantic Movement," *PMLA*, LXIX (1954), 432–47. "Thus, a writer in the *Reflector* elevates Ferdusi almost to Homer's level despite the fact that the Persian poet had paid little attention to those 'minuter excellences' of the epic, the fable and the three unities; and in the same breath that he says that *Paradise Regained* is really 'a drama of primal simplicity' and the *Odyssey* is not 'a legitimate epic,' Hallam calls it pure 'pedantry' to speak of the *Orlando Furioso* as a romance rather than an epic simply because it lacks a principal hero and a continuity of action. . . . A particular form was not often required; nor did an 'epic' seem to need a great action or a single action, a principal hero or a mighty hero, a race of gods or any other invisible agency. All that was demanded by many critics was a narrative thread which one could detect here and there in a poem of some length" (pp. 435–6).

Bourbon conservatism, had kept up a show of authority for much longer than might now seem understandable in the general retrospect of merely literary history. The revolt came with Hugo's Preface to *Cromwell*, 1827, and with *Hernani*, his first acted play, 1830. This was, to be sure, not officially a lyric movement. But it introduced not only a new taste for enjambed Alexandrines, for a diction coextensive with greater areas of life, and for a juxtaposition of the grotesque with the sublime, but, in part to accommodate the latter ideal, a taste for a profusion of sub-plot and extra incident and for incidentally and lyrically developed characters. The movement was away from the tighter Aristotelian structure. If an audience expected to enjoy anything richer than the traditional pseudo-Racinian austerity, argued Hugo in his Preface to *Cromwell*, the new romantic poet would have to hold the stage for somewhat longer than two hours. He would need no less than the whole evening (all the time usually given to the farce and comic opera which came after the tragedy to relieve it). But such a poet would give a money's worth of character portrayal (an entire hero, with all his genius, beliefs, conflicting passions, tastes, habits, and the crowd of figures who mill around him) as well as the panorama of a whole struggling epoch (its customs, laws, manners, spirit, insights, superstitions, happenings, and people). A gigantic spectacle! (*On conçoit qu'un pareil tableau sera gigantesque.*) A stage crowded with figures of all sizes and shapes. (*Il y aura foule dans le drame.*) [3] One conceives too that an art formed on the principle of a vast assemblage of diversely interesting parts will tend to promote a certain looseness of relationship among such parts and in the parts themselves a certain extravagance of local coloring.

"A poem of any length," Coleridge had said, "neither can be, or ought to be, all poetry." [4] He was echoed about thirty years later by Poe in words which have become even better known: "I hold that a long poem does not exist. I maintain that the phrase, 'a long poem,' is simply a flat contradiction in terms." [5] A modern editor of Poe has paid him an accurate compliment in saying that this pronouncement was "essentially a demand that the poets of his time be themselves and admit that epic themes . . . did not in fact excite their poetic faculties." "What really interested them were emotions of melancholy, nostalgia, puzzled yearning, and the like that could find their proper expression . . . in lyrics of moderate length." [6] In an earlier chapter we have noted J. S. Mill's inheritance of the associational doctrine of feeling—which in full the-

---

[3] Victor Hugo, *"Préface de Cromwell" and "Hernani,"* ed. John R. Effinger, Jr. (Chicago, 1900), pp. 98–9, near the end of the *Préface.*
[4] *Biographia Literaria,* Chapter XIV (ed. Shawcross, II, 11).
[5] *The Poetic Principle,* first paragraph.
[6] W. H. Auden, *Edgar Allan Poe, Selected Prose and Poetry* (New York, 1950), p. xii.

oretical consciousness he adopted as alternative to the utilitarian and scientific rigors of his early training. And so:

> Lyric poetry, as it was the earliest kind, is also, if the view we are now taking of poetry be correct, more eminently and pe-culiarly poetry than any other: it is the poetry most natural to a really poetic temperament, and least capable of being success-fully imitated by one not so endowed by nature.[7]

Mill distinguished [lyric] poetry from certain other and less intense kinds of emotive writing, novels and dramas, mere stories or *imitations* of life. These made an appeal to immature and shallow minds.[8]

A particularly instructive instance in the history of lyric feeling is that of John Henry Newman when he delivers his opinion in an early essay (1829) on no less a topic than Aristotle's *Poetics*.[9] Newman's Evan-gelical background puts him comfortably in possession of the same at-titudes that Mill had to arrive at by struggle. He observes that Aristotle admires *Oedipus the King* for its plot and structure. That is to say, Aristotle conceives a play as "an exhibition of ingenious workmanship." But true poetry is spontaneous expression, the "free and unfettered effusion of genius." Newman goes to Greek drama in order to "listen to harmonious and majestic language, to the voices of sorrow, joy, com-passion, or religious emotion,—to the animated odes of the chorus."

> A word has a power to convey a world of information to the imagination, and to act as a spell upon the feelings; there is no need of sustained fiction, often no room for it.

Newman's argument is a plenary participation in the Longinian double antithesis. The difference between plot and lyric passages is closely tied up with the difference between cold calculation on the part of the author and spontaneous effusion. Within a few years after his essay on poetry, Newman, moving along lines quite different from those of his literary criticism, had reached the opinion that the Evangelicals had landed Protestantism in a bondage to the "feelings." "His many attacks on the Evangelical system," observes a modern commentator, "are an attempt to rescue Evangelicals from a bondage he was willing to keep poets in."[1]

Newman's friend John Keble, Professor of Poetry at Oxford from

---

[7] "Thought in Poetry and its Varieties," in *Dissertations and Discussions* (Lon-don, 1859), I, 85. First published in 1832. Cf. *ante*, p. 308.

[8] Cf. Alba Warren, p. 71. Mill parallels Wordsworth's protest against "gross and violent stimulants," the melodrama of storm-and-stress novels.

[9] "Poetry with Reference to Aristotle's Poetics" appeared in the *London Review*, January, 1829. Cf. Alba Warren, pp. 35-45.

[1] Geoffrey Tillotson, "Newman's Essay on Poetry," in *Perspectives of Criticism*, ed. Harry Levin (Cambridge, Mass., 1950), pp. 161-195.

1831 to 1841, is a priestly poet and theorist whose *Praelectiones Academicae*, collected and published in 1844, turn on the same mistrust of "art," "execution," external medium, and plot construction, the same regard for the poet's spontaneous outburst of inmost feeling. The epigraph to his printed lectures is the image of the rhapsode and the magnetic ring from the *Ion* of Plato. Keble's emotivism invites a specially curious inspection in that it combines Aristotelian cathartic reminiscences with pre-Freudian intimations. He conceives poetry as an indirect strategy, an expression under "certain veils and disguises," whereby sensitive distraught souls may without blame find release from suffering. "It is the function of Poetry to facilitate, yet without prejudice to modest reserve, the expression of glowing motion." [2] The subtitle of his lectures is *De Poeticae Vi Medica.*

A distinct correlation with such minor but characteristic theorizing of the early Victorian era may be observed in the school of violently emotive and pseudo-Elizabethan dramatizing which erupted in the 1840's and was extinguished in the parody by W. E. Aytoun, *Firmilian: A "Spasmodic" Tragedy*, in 1854. Tennyson's *Maud* (1855), a "monodrama" of cloudy "madness," swirling around an all but undescribed action, participates in the spasmodic phase of English poetry. Matthew Arnold's two earliest volumes of poems, in 1849 and 1852, were touched by the same spirit and suffered some disadvantage in competing with it.[3]

II

ARNOLD emerges suddenly, however, the most imposing figure in English mid-Victorian criticism, not as a part of the lyric-spasmodic movement, but in a brusque classical resistance to it. The Preface to his *Poems* of 1853,[4] pitched in the high and confident tone of which he was to become increasingly master, announces the rationale of a valiant negative gesture, that of omitting from the volume of 1853 the long poem which gave the volume of 1852 its title, *Empedocles on Aetna*. Not because it is a poem on an ancient subject, says Arnold, though many may think this a sufficient reason. But because the dark emotions of the protagonist lead to no outcome. "Suffering finds no vent in action." The situation is

---

[2] *Keble's Lectures on Poetry 1832–1841*, trans. E. K. Francis (Oxford, 1912), I, 19–24, 36. See Alba Warren, pp. 46–9; Meyer Abrams, pp. 145–8.

[3] See Arthur Hugh Clough, in the *North American Review*, LXXVII (July, 1853), 4, anonymously reviewing Arnold's *Strayed Reveler* and *Empedocles* along with other volumes of verse including the Glasgow "mechanic" Alexander Smith's spasmodic *Life Drama*. Cf. Lionel Trilling, *Matthew Arnold* (New York, 1939), pp. 146 ff.

[4] The volume appeared in October.

monotonous and morbid. (Empedocles, it will be remembered, concludes his suffering by jumping into Aetna.) It is an ancient story, but it exhibits a modern and merely emotive development. The historical figure Empedocles himself is not a good hero for a poem, not a great example of Greek thought and feeling.

> Into the feelings of a man so situated there entered much that we are accustomed to consider as exclusively modern; . . . The calm, the cheerfulness, the disinterested objectivity have disappeared: the dialogue of the mind with itself has commenced; modern problems have presented themselves; we hear already the doubts, we witness the discouragement, of Hamlet and of Faust.

There is some wavering, some slithering of logic in Arnold's plea. In reaction against recent notions that "the poet must leave the exhausted past," [5] against "spasmodic" champions of "present import," "interest," and "novelty," and no less against the whole contemporary concept of "an era of progress, an age commissioned to carry out the great ideas of industrial development and social amelioration," Arnold wants to say that the "modernness or antiquity of an action . . . has nothing to do with its fitness for poetical representation." "The date of an action . . . signifies nothing." But it comes out pretty clearly before he is done that the great, "permanently" interesting actions, those that involve "permanent problems" and excite the "permanent passions," are all or nearly all to be found in the grand mythic repertories with which Greek epic and tragic writers were concerned. These endure. The occurrences of modern life are transitory. They have an immediate interest, but it is meretricious.

> The Greeks felt, no doubt, with their exquisite sagacity of taste, that an action of present times was too near them, too much mixed up with what was accidental and passing, to form a sufficiently grand, detached, and self-subsistent object for a tragic poem.

Arnold's Preface is an impressive exercise of hauteur at the expense of the thesis that literature has to be up to date.

But even more radically, the Preface is a countercheck quarrelsome to the prevailing lyric trend, a re-affirmation of the classic norm of the

[5] The complaint had been argued more picturesquely during the 17th-century quarrel of the ancients and the moderns. Cowley refers to "The cold-meats of the Ancients," "the threadbare tales of Thebes and Troy" (Preface to *Poems*, 1656; cf. Atkins, II, 173). In our own century the theme is well known. "The more progressive modern poets . . . discard not only archaic diction but also shop-worn subjects of past history or legend, which have been through the centuries a treasure-trove for the second-rate" (Harriet Monroe, ed. *The New Poetry, An Anthology*, New York 1927, p. vi).

fable. The "theory and practice alike" of the ancients, the "admirable treatise of Aristotle, and the unrivalled works of their poets, exclaim with a thousand tongues":

> 'All depends upon the subject; choose a fitting action, penetrate yourself with the feeling of its situations; this done, everything else will follow.'

"They regarded the whole; we regard the parts. With them, the action predominated over the expression of it." Hence the admirably severe style—the "grand style"—of the Greeks. And hence the dangerous influence on modern English poets of Shakespeare, a writer who had, along with his skill in managing "action," "situation," and "character," a further great gift, which, alas! could and did lead even him "astray." That was his power of "expression." "Here has been the mischief." Our modern poets, Keats and others, have been imitating the "attractive accessories," the "richness of imagery," not the central shaping power, the architecture.[6]

> We have poems which seem to exist merely for the sake of single lines and passages; not for the sake of producing any total impression. We have critics who seem to direct their attention merely to detached expressions, to the language about the action, not to the action itself.[7]

III

THE moderns, one might reflect, had been having it all their own way for nearly a century. It was time somebody spoke up for the ancients,

[6] A year before Arnold's Preface of 1853, a lesser if more systematic theorist, Eneas S. Dallas, had published his *Poetics: An Essay on Poetry*, containing a discussion of drama which reveals far more starkly than Arnold's plausibly written argument some of the commitments of a pantomimic regard for the element of dramatic action. "For looking at dramatic speeches in their true light, as the means of imitating character and life, not as a means of as it were by slanting mirrors throwing opinions among an audience, and far less as a running commentary on the whole play, it will be seen that if they convey anything different in kind from what may be conveyed, however feebly, by dumb show, they swerve from dramatic fitness, or at least are more than dramatic." Eneas S. Dallas, *Poetics: An Essay on Poetry* (1852), Book III, pp. 131–2. Cf. Alba Warren, pp. 137–8, and p. 139. Warren neatly locates the Dallas-Arnold fallacy under the rubric "assimilation of the drama to the visual arts."

[7] Arnold's tone becomes distinctly Augustan. "This over-curiousness of expression is indeed but the excessive employment of a wonderful gift—of the power of saying a thing in a happier way than any other man. Nevertheless, it is carried so far that one understands what M. Guizot meant, when he said that Shakespeare appears in his language to have tried all styles except that of simplicity. He has not the severe and scrupulous self-restraint of the ancients, partly no doubt, because he had a far less cultivated and exacting audience. . . . He is therefore a less safe model." "Others abide our question. Thou art free."

even if in overbearing tones, with a kind of kid-gloved arrogance. Not since Lessing perhaps had so keenly whistling a blade been tried on the wind in the classic quarter. But a classicism which had passed through that century of German idealism and German romantic Hellenism was bound to show a profound difference in its commitments. As the Platonism of Sidney stands in relation to that of Shelley, so the Aristotelianism of Lessing to that of Arnold.

Arnold's essays published in the *Cornhill* and other magazines, during the years immediately after he became Professor of Poetry at Oxford in 1857, and collected in 1865 as the first series of his *Essays in Criticism* show his classicism at perhaps its most level development, in the coolest and clearest light. He has gone to continental sources. One of these is the French Catholic, and conservative and Platonic *penseur* Joseph Joubert—a French Coleridge, as Arnold calls him, of less richness and power than the English Coleridge, but of more delicacy and penetration.

> Clearness is so eminently one of the characteristics of truth, that often it even passes for truth itself.

> Ignorance, which in matters of morals extenuates the crime, is itself, in matters of literature, a crime of the first order.

> In literature the one aim of art is the beautiful.

> To accustom mankind to pleasures which depend neither upon the bodily appetites nor upon money, by giving them a taste for the things of the mind, seems to me, in fact, the one proper fruit which nature has meant our literary productions to have.

Another is the German Jewish poet, self-exiled in France, arch-ironist and anti-romantic, Heinrich Heine, from whom Arnold takes up the weapons of a "life and death battle" against the *Philistine*. Arnold's hard-hitting repetitions succeeded in establishing this piece of German student lingo as the right name for the British middle-brow enemy of the noble and lovely.

> *Philistinism!*—we have not the expression in English. Perhaps we have not the word because we have so much of the thing. At Soli, I imagine, they did not talk of solecisms; and here, at the very headquarters of Goliath, nobody talks of Philistinism.[8]

---

[8] *Heinrich Heine*, in *Essays in Criticism, First Series* (London, 1902), p. 162. Cf. the last paragraph of Arnold's Preface to the *First Series*, the apostrophe to Oxford, "Adorable dreamer, whose heart has been so romantic! who hast given thyself so prodigally . . . only never to the Philistines"; and *Joubert* (*First Series*, p. 304), "the great apostle of the Philistines, Lord Macaulay." As early as 1827 Carlyle was using the term "Philistine" in his essays, and in *Sartor Resartus*, 1831, appears "Philistinism." See these words in *The Oxford English Dictionary on Historical Principles*.

Arnold displays a fine scorn for British homebred humour and paro-
chial complacency. He assumes the same kind of anti-domestic and
classical superiority of taste as we have witnessed already in the comic
theory of George Meredith. It is true that he has a great interest in the
national spirit, and, like fashionable thinkers on the continent (Taine
and others) to whom we shall allude in later chapters, he believes in the
race, the milieu, and the moment, in short, in the cultural determination
of literature.

> For a literary masterpiece, two powers must concur, the power
> of the man, and the power of the moment, and the man is not
> enough without the moment.[9]

But Arnold reverses the revolutionary and sociological emphasis of the
continental thinkers. With him it is not as if the march of the historical
process were bound to be working into something superior or more real.
Just the opposite. The English spirit he is so much interested to define
is a mixed potential in the blood and in the culture,[1] capable of being
very badly developed in a bad modern age. In his inaugural lecture at
Oxford, delivered in 1857 and entitled *The Modern Element in Literature,* Arnold appears as a strenuous champion of cultural classicism. He
enjoys a high degree of confidence that the age of Sir Walter Raleigh in
England was but poorly lighted, infested with footpads, over-dressed,
and, compared with the age of Thucydides in Athens, naively incom-
petent to write history. (Distinct, though transvalued, reminiscences of
the Peacockian frame of mind are to be noted in his remarks on the
deficiencies of Roman literature—the Lucretian depression and ennui,
the Virgilian "sweet, touching sadness," the Horatian want of "seriousness.") The progressive vulgarization of English middle-class culture
since the Elizabethan age is a theme to which Arnold never tires of
returning.

> . . . this paragraph on which I stumbled in a newspaper . . . :
> "A shocking child murder has just been committed at Notting-
> ham. A girl named Wragg left her workhouse there on Saturday
> morning with her young illegitimate child. The child was soon
> afterwards found dead on Mapperly Hills, having been strangled.
> Wragg is in custody."

[9] *The Function of Criticism at the Present Time* (*First Series*, p. 4).

[1] "If we had been all German, we might have had the science of Germany; if
we had been all Celtic, we might have been popular and agreeable; if we had been
all Latinised, we might have governed Ireland as the French govern Alsace, without
getting ourselves detested. But now we have Germanism enough to make us Philistines, and Normanism enough to make us imperious, and Celtism enough to make us
self-conscious and awkward; but German fidelity to Nature, and Latin precision and
clear reason, and Celtic quick-wittedness and spirituality, we fall short of" (*On the
Study of Celtic Literature and on Translating Homer,* New York, 1883, p. 132, *On
the Study of Celtic Literature,* VI).

Nothing but that. . . . how eloquent, how suggestive are those few lines! "Our old Anglo-Saxon breed, the best in the whole world!"—how much that is harsh and ill-favoured there is in this best! *Wragg!* If we are to talk of ideal perfection, of "the best in the whole world," has any one reflected what a touch of grossness in our race, what an original shortcoming in the more delicate spiritual perceptions, is shown by the natural growth amongst us of such hideous names. Higginbottom, Stiggins, Bugg! [2]

Among the essays of the 1862 collection, the continental orientation of Arnold's critique stands out nowhere more remarkably than in *The Literary Influence of Academies.* Arnold here throws backward a last glance in the English tradition of wistful regard for the French and Italian academies. The proposals for reducing, refining, and "ascertaining" the Augustan language, the plans for legislative authority and for dictionaries, which appear from the time of the Royal Society on (in essays by Defoe, Addison, Swift, and numerous smaller busybodies and grammarians), had continued up to and even after the time of the greatest English effort to accomplish such dreams, the *Dictionary* of Samuel Johnson published in 1755.[3] But Johnson himself in his Preface had growled out something about the establishment of an academy . . .

which I, who can never wish to see dependence multiplied, hope the spirit of English liberty will hinder or destroy.

And he had followed this up with equally heavy lunges in his *Life of Swift* (". . . an academy; the decrees of which every man would be willing, and many would have been proud to disobey") and in his *Life of Roscommon* ("In this country an academy could be expected to do but little. . . . We live in an age in which it is a kind of public sport to refuse all respect that cannot be enforced. The edicts of an English Academy would probably be read by many, only that they might be sure to disobey them").[4] The idea of a legislated norm of correct linguistic usage was never at home in England. The great Oxford dictionary actually conceived and begun during Arnold's lifetime was a project of a far different order, part of the empirical and investigative spirit of the age. The authority which it sought to establish was strictly a historical

[2] *The Function of Criticism at the Present Time (First Series,* p. 23).

[3] See Albert Baugh, *A History of the English Language* (New York, 1935), Chapter IX, "The Appeal to Authority 1650–1800"; Sterling A. Leonard, *The Doctrine of Correctness in English Usage, 1700–1800* (Madison, 1929); Allen Walker Read, "Suggestions for an Academy in England in the Latter Half of the Eighteenth Century," *MP,* XXXVI (November, 1938), 145–56.

[4] The passage on academies was added to the 1781 *Life of Roscommon* when Johnson constructed this by expanding a sketch published in the *Gentleman's Magazine* in 1748.

authority. But Arnold enjoyed a tall and successful aloofness from the historizing spirit of his times. He broadcast his criticism with a suave assurance that made him seem anything but a gauntly anachronistic and mistaken prophet. "Dryden and Pope," he was to say in one of his later and most notorious pronouncements, "were classics of our prose." It would have been difficult for an Englishman of Arnold's time to participate more fully in the English Augustan spirit than Arnold does in his *Literary Influence of Academies* and *Function of Criticism in the Present Time.* Yet he did this with a difference. Swift in his Proposal to Lord Oxford ("Swift's petty proposal," Johnson called it) and in other essays on the theme had managed to sound no better than the sharp schoolmaster, a sensible, salutary, birch-rod influence, grammatical, philological, precisian. Arnold elevated the academy for which the Augustans had yearned into a vantage point of Olympian vision, a regulator of culture in the lofty creative sense which the German philosophy had by this time made plausible. In place of the Germanic and Carlylean throb of lyric freedom, it is true that he wanted the serenely normative and tempering light from classic France. He spoke of a "sensitiveness of intelligence" which is ready to defer to "authority." [5] But the nature of that authority! Without being very precise about it, he made it sound like a very wise and ultimate thing, something which in other essays he called "culture" and put even higher than religion.

I V

YET an accent of uncertainty appears here and there in Arnold's account of relations between the reasonable classic norm and the individual, non-conformist claims which are likely to be made by poetry—and especially, it would appear, by modern poetry. He entertains a notion that poetry proceeds from a certain honest energy. The English have plenty of this, and hence they do write poetry; for the same reason they write a violent, Corinthian polemic prose; and they write as individuals. The French on the contrary have intelligence and something called "form," and hence they write fine prose (not poetry—poetry has nothing to do with "form"), and they go beyond individual eccentricities, to produce not only prose but schools of prose.[6]

Poetry also has affinities for "magic." The concept takes the form of "natural magic," or "Celtic magic," in Arnold's retrospective expedition into 18th-century Celtomania, the lectures of 1865–1866 entitled *On the Study of Celtic Literature.* "Magic is the word to insist upon,—

[5] *First Series*, p. 49.
[6] *The Literary Influence of Academies (First Series*, pp. 50-2).

a magically vivid and near interpretation of nature." [7] (In its insistence not only on magic but on melancholy, Arnold's pontification was to play a part in determining the color of the actual Celtic revival in Ireland a few decades later.) [8] In some contexts, "natural magic" is Arnold's rendering of the "object" ("nature," the familiar landscape under the charm of moonlight) which stood on one side of the Coleridgean reconciliation of subject and object. The other half of the formula, the "subject," the human and moral kind of meaning, something much more congenial to Arnold, he called "moral profundity." Keats, Shakespeare's imperfect disciple, had an excess of natural magic, not enough moral profundity. Wordsworth had mainly moral profundity. Shakespeare had both qualities to the full.[9]

Arnold's mixed regard for the major English poets of the preceding generation produced some of the most highly colored images which he has left us—Shelley a "beautiful and ineffectual angel, beating in the void his luminous wings in vain," [1] Byron in the act of carrying across Europe "the pageant of his bleeding heart," [2] Coleridge a "poet and philosopher wrecked in a mist of opium," [3] Keats's letters the "love letters of a surgeon's apprentice." [4] The reason for Arnold's dislike of these poets was partly biographical,[5] and to that extent it was purely moral. He gives his most considered poetic reasons in the case of Byron: Byron had personality, talent, sincerity, strength, energy—but he lacked "matter," that is, a serious moral meaning.[6]

Arnold always has less difficulty in knowing what to admire in the classics. His Oxford lectures *On Translating Homer*, 1861, a disdainful reaction against the Teutonized, or Saxo-Norman,[7] translation by Francis William Newman, urge a conception of Homer as "eminently rapid,"

---

[7] *On the Study of Celtic Literature and On Translating Homer* (New York, 1883), *On the Study of Celtic Literature*, VI, p. 122; cf. pp. 102, 126, 128.

[8] John V. Kelleher, "Matthew Arnold and the Celtic Revival," in *Perspectives of Criticism*, ed. Harry Levin (Cambridge, Mass., 1952), pp. 197–227.

[9] *Keats (Second Series*, p. 119). Cf. *Maurice de Guérin (First Series*, pp. 81–2).

[1] *Second Series*, pp. 203, 252, in both *Shelley* and *Byron*.

[2] *Stanzas at the Grande Chartreuse.*

[3] *Second Series*, p. 203, again apropos of Byron.

[4] *Second Series*, p. 103.

[5] And especially in the case of Shelley. Arnold's distaste is a response to unsavory aspects of Shelley's life which had recently been both revealed and defended in Dowden's biography (*Second Series*, pp. 206 ff.).

[6] *Second Series*, p. 193.

[7] The 19th-century Teutonizing camp included such scholars as the Early English Text Society founders F. J. Furnivall and R. C. Trench, the historian E. A. Freeman and the poets William Barnes and Gerard Manley Hopkins. Macaulay's essay on Boswell's *Johnson* contains a good instance of the trend. Cf. Austin Warren, "Instress of Inscape," in *Gerard Manley Hopkins by the Kenyon Critics* (Norfolk, 1945), pp. 82–6. For some 17th-century instances of Teutonizing and a protest against it, see Joseph Glanvill, *An Essay Concerning Preaching*, 1678, in Spingarn, *Essays*, II, 274.

"eminently plain and direct," "eminently noble." [8] The argument is ruled in large measure by a concept of calm objectivity that is closely consonant with the theme of the classic action defined in 1853. Homer composes "with his eye on the object." [9] He thus participates in a virtue which the same lectures define as the main requirement (lacking in the eccentric English) of a good criticism—a "simple lucidity of mind," a capacity "to see the object as in itself it really is." [1]

The concept of a loftily objective aim carries through Arnold's career into his last important general pronouncement on poetics, the essay entitled *The Study of Poetry* which appears as introduction to T. H. Ward's *English Poets* in 1880 and is reprinted as the first of the *Essays in Criticism, Second Series,* in 1888. The Aristotelian phrase *philosophōteron kai spoudaioteron* is cue for the Arnoldian phrase "truth and high seriousness," expressing twin requirements of substance, failing in either of which a very good poet may fall far short of greatness. These requirements are found in the work of the few greatest poets, Homer, Dante, Milton, Shakespeare. Certain other ideas which appear in the essay of 1880 are taken up in the course of our next few pages.

V

"IF HE is not the greatest of English critics," says H. W. Garrod, "his make-up of being so is in itself a piece of greatness; and not to enjoy it is a piece of stupidity." [2] Fair enough. But if a further statement and summary of Arnold's position as developed by the end of his career be permitted a tone of moderate dissatisfaction, we would urge the following points.

1. His argument about Homer relies not only on an idea of dignified substance but rather heavily on another idea—one merely hinted in 1853—that of a classically objective style. Homer writes in the "grand style." This phrase, used in the Preface of 1853 apropos of the Greeks in general and repeated during Arnold's later years in two essays on Milton, expresses a stylistic (and somewhat chastened) version of the 18th-century Michelangelesque sublime. [3] "I think it will be found," he says in some *Last Words on Translating Homer*, "that the grand style

[8] *On the Study of Celtic Literature and On Translating Homer* (New York, 1883), p. 149.

[9] *Op. cit.,* p. 160. "Pope composes with his eye on the style."

[1] *Op. cit.* pp. 199–200. Arnold reiterates the phrase a few years later with heavy emphasis in the opening pages of his lecture on *The Function of Criticism (First Series,* pp. 1, 6). And Sophocles, it will be remembered, "saw life steadily, and saw it whole."

[2] *Poetry and the Criticism of Life* (Cambridge, Mass., 1931), p. 83.

[3] Trilling, *Matthew Arnold,* p. 173, points out Arnold's familiarity with Reynolds' *Discourses.*

arises in poetry, when a noble nature, poetically gifted, treats with simplicity or with severity a serious subject." [4] A similar concern not only
for "substance" or "matter" but for "style" or "manner" runs through
the important essay of 1880.[5] Both the substance and the style must have
their "accent of high beauty, worth, and power." In this complication of
his theory beyond the simple demand for the "excellent" subject of the
1853 Preface, there is a gain in critical insight—and not necessarily any
contradiction. Yet one of Arnold's most memorable new terms in this
essay is "touchstones." By this he means small pieces of poetry—"short
passages, even single lines," a line of Dante, of Chaucer, of Shakespeare,
two lines of Milton—unmistakable examples of great poetry, such as a
critic ought to carry about with him and apply as norms in the estimate
of other poetry. This open appeal to the chunklet, the sample piece of
precious stuff, is a rather startling shift toward the norm of style and
away from the initial classic thesis of 1853 that the "action is all." True,
he says of his touchstone slightly misquoted from Chaucer ("O martyr
souded in virginitee."): "A single line, however, is too little if we have
not the strain of Chaucer's verse well in our memory." Still he is talking
precisely about the "strain" of the *verse*. To make the touchstone test
it would seem we do not have to know much if anything about the story
of the little "clergeon."

2. On the other hand, the lofty purpose, the grand unified exclusive
norm for poetry, the monolithic seriousness, which Arnold proclaims in
1880, is a consistent enough development from the Preface of 1853,
where the requirement of the grand action is completed by a disparaging reference to comedy and the "lighter kinds of poetry." Comedy is
good enough to take care of everyday materials, contemporary trifles.
The "tragic poem," the poem with a seriously useful meaning (*pragmatic*, Arnold actually calls it in 1853, taking the expression from Polyb-
ius) requires the antique heroic subject matter. In 1880 Arnold has a
more extended opportunity to betray his views on the comic modes of
poetry. And we find that Chaucer is a poet of surpassingly fine style (a
"divine liquidness of diction," a "divine fluidity of movement") and even
of superior substance, in one sense (in his "large, free, simple, clear yet
kindly view of human life"), but not in the full sense. He has truth, in
short, but he lacks "high and excellent seriousness." Dryden and Pope,
those two great "classics of our prose," were not "men whose criticism
of life has a high seriousness," or even any "poetic largeness, freedom,.

---

[4] *On the Study of Celtic Literature and On Translating Homer* (New York,
1883), p. 265.

[5] For an earlier gesture at a stylistic definition of poetry, see *Heinrich Heine*
(*Essays, First Series*, p. 161): "Poetry is simply the most beautiful, impressive, and
widely effective mode of saying things." Cf. later *Wordsworth* (*Second Series*, p.
128): "Poetry is nothing less than the most perfect speech of man, that in which he
comes nearest to being able to utter the truth."

insight, benignity." The same low esteem of the Augustan mode works out in the patronizing estimate of Gray.[6] The basic lack of sympathy with the comic produces the meanly anaphoristic emphasis that the trouble with Burns' poetry lies in "Scotch drink, Scotch religion, Scotch manners." Burns' "genuine criticism of life" is merely "ironic." Arnold's stomach for literature suffers limitations of delicacy. "No one can deny," he says in the passage on Scotland, "that it is of advantage to a poet to deal with a beautiful world." And the retort of the 20th-century poet seems highly relevant: "It is an advantage to mankind in general to live in a beautiful world. . . . But the essential advantage for a poet is . . . to be able to see beneath both beauty and ugliness; to see the boredom, and the horror, and the glory." [7]

3. Despite a partial submission to the historistic trend of his age (his congratulation of Shakespeare, for instance, because he "applied freely in literature the then modern ideas"),[8] Arnold never seems to set a correct value on the formal principle of anachronism in poetry, the principle of rebirth in analogy and parody. The theoretical fault may be illustrated, *ad hominem*, in the Oxford Professor's cold fiasco *Merope: A Tragedy*, his most determined attempt as a poet to avail himself of one of those great classically permanent actions described in the Preface of 1853. The return to Messenia in that "period of transition from the heroic and fabulous to the human and historic age of Greece" is made in a spirit all too literal. The noted actress Helena Faucit tactfully shied away from Arnold's invitation to participate in this sort of thing. There were lessons in the metaphoric handling of the antique that Arnold had neglected to learn from Racine or Corneille, from Shakespeare's *Troilus and Cressida*, or from Chaucer's *Troilus and Criseyde*, the last of which one may be doubtful that he had ever read. The same kind of literal demand comes out in his theory of a Homeric translation (if not so flagrantly in the sample passages which he translates). Let the unhappy translator "not trust to his own judgment of his own work; he may be misled by individual caprices."

> Let him ask how his work affects those who both know Greek and can appreciate poetry; whether to read it gives the Provost of Eton, or Professor Thompson of Cambridge, or Professor Jowett here at Oxford, at all the same feeling which to read the original gives them. I consider that when Bentley said of Pope's translation, "It was a pretty poem, but must not be called

[6] F. R. Leavis, "Revaluations (XI): Arnold as Critic," *Scrutiny*, VII (December, 1938), 319–32.

[7] T. S. Eliot, *Use of Poetry*, p. 98. "The vision of the horror and the glory was denied to Arnold, but he knew something of the boredom."

[8] *Heine* (First Series, p. 176).

Homer," the work, in spite of all its power and attractiveness, was judged.[9]

Here again there were lessons of the neo-classic age which Arnold might have read more tolerantly. What Ascham in *The Scholemaster*, what Dryden in his Prefaces to Ovid and the *Sylvae*, said about "metaphrase," "paraphrase," "imitation," might not have provided Arnold with a ready-made and sufficient view. The older school of translation, like Arnold, was looking for a certain spirit, a certain "feeling." But in the freedom of their practice, verging on "imitation," lay an insight, or perhaps merely a habit derived from live classical studies, which was foreign to the age of Arnold. Arnold's arguments about translation (his stern rejection of Newman's effort in search of an idiom) illustrate the growth of the historical sense in his era but also the limitations of that sense as the age applied it to poetry. He was running parallel to the more or less well informed archeologizing of the Shakespearian stage which had begun in the time of Macready.

4. Another 20th-century critic has spoken of Arnold's essays as "higher pamphleteering,"[1] and yet another has called Arnold "rather a propagandist for criticism than a critic."[2] Very simply, very characteristically, and very repetitiously, Arnold spent his career in hammering the thesis that poetry is a "criticism of life." This led to a spectacular involvement in some of the difficulties that have always appeared for didactic theory. In the essay on *The Function of Criticism at the Present Time*, that function is described as the promotion of a lively circulation of the best ideas yet available to humanity,[3] and hence the production of a climate in which poetry can thrive. One "criticism" provides the set-up and encouragement for another "criticism," and the embarrassment of equating poetry with some kind of quasi-philosophic discipline is greatly accentuated. One recent authority[4] on Arnold's thought has interpreted his whole career as a tension between the impulse of detachment and that of practical application, between the Professor of Poetry and the Inspector of Schools. Arnold is frequently aware of the difficulty and attempts to qualify the phrase "criticism of life" as he applies it to poetry. He introduces into the predicate of his definition of "poetry" a safety device of circularity, a kind of short-circuit fuse. A tabular arrangement of the most definite avowals in several of his essays will show the dilemma.

[9] *On the Study of Celtic Literature and on Translating Homer* (New York, 1883), p. 144.

[1] F. R. Leavis, *Scrutiny*, VII, 321.

[2] T. S. Eliot, *The Sacred Wood* (London, 1920), p. 1.

[3] Literary criticism is "a disinterested endeavour to learn and propagate the best that is known and thought in the world, and thus to establish a current of fresh and true ideas" (*First Series*, p. 37).

[4] E. K. Brown, *Matthew Arnold, A Study in Conflict* (Chicago, 1948).

> The end and aim of all literature is . . . a criticism of life.
> —*Joubert*, 1864 (*First Series*, p. 303)

Poetry is at bottom a criticism of life.
> —*Wordsworth*, 1879 (*Second Series*, p. 143)

Poetry [is] a criticism of life under the conditions fixed for such a criticism by the laws of poetic truth and poetic beauty.
> —*The Study of Poetry*, 1880 (*Second Series*, p. 5; cf. p. 48)

I have seen it said that I allege poetry to have for its characteristic this: that it is a criticism of life; and that I make it to be thereby distinguished from prose, which is something else. So far from it, that when I first used this expression, *a criticism of life*, now many years ago, it was to literature in general that I applied it, and not to poetry in especial. 'The end and aim of all literature,' I said, 'is, if one considers it attentively, nothing but that; *a criticism of life*.' And so it surely is; the main end and aim of all our utterance, whether in prose or in verse, is surely a criticism of life. We are not brought much on our way, I admit, towards an adequate definition of poetry as distinguished from prose by that truth; still a truth it is, and poetry can never prosper if it is forgotten. In poetry, however, the criticism of life has to be made conformably to the laws of poetic truth and poetic beauty.[1]
> —*Byron*, 1881 (*Second Series*, pp. 186–7)

VI

ARNOLD's didacticism reaches its mature and accurate formulation in the sentence so often quoted from the opening of the 1880 Essay:

> More and more mankind will discover that we have to turn to poetry to interpret life for us, to console us, to sustain us. Without poetry, our science will appear incomplete; and most of what now passes with us for religion and philosophy will be replaced by poetry.

("But now I only hear Its melancholy, long, withdrawing roar. . . . And we are here as on a darkling plain . . .") Arnold marks out a didactic function for poetry without any of the optimistic frenzy which buoyed the utterances of a Shelley or a Carlyle. He speaks with a level precision and a resolved firmness that make his prophecy all the more appalling. In the essays of broader cultural and quasi-religious scope which oc-

---

[1] The essay on Wordsworth includes lengthy disavowals of anything like an approval of the *doctrines* expressed in Wordsworth's poetry.

cupied his middle period, 1867–1877, especially in *Culture and Anarchy*, 1869, he had expounded in somewhat more detail the kind of new message—the "sweetness and light," the blend of Hebraic spirituality and obedience with Hellenistic critical spirit—which it should be the aim of "culture" and of poetic education to propagate. Religion had once done a fairly good job, but religion now seemed to Arnold to reside mainly in religious "organizations," and these were only "machinery." The highest promotion of the sweet, clear inner life would now be the job of "culture." The text would be the Greek classics.[2]

If we look at Arnold's most direct combat with science, a Cambridge lecture entitled *Literature and Science*, first printed in 1882, we discover the battle positions to be not so much different from those of the Peacock-Shelley incident. We see the names of the new generation of scientific bravos: Huxley, pronouncing a "funeral oration" on literary education at the opening of a college in Birmingham; Renan, Spencer, Darwin, and the liberal politician John Bright. A congress of elementary school teachers at Sheffield hears a proposal that the schools and the universities should come together on the common ground of natural science. On the ground of the dead languages, they can not. Arnold's rebuttal shares much with Shelley. It differs, however, in a more antiseptically confident tone, a quality of assurance that is even quasi-scientific. Arnold is on the stand to testify that literature is not, as Professor Huxley believes, merely *belles lettres*. Literature reaches out and begins with all knowledge, political, social, scientific—it is literally and inclusively "the best which has been thought and said in the world." Literature will be up with the latest scientific data. It will face even Mr. Darwin's proposition that the human ancestor was "a hairy quadruped furnished with a tail and pointed ears, probably arboreal in his habits." But literature (or the humane part of it, "humane letters") will go beyond all mere "instrument" knowledge and all merely "natural" knowledge; it will grasp knowledge in relation with the human "sense for conduct," the human "sense for beauty." Shelley's *Defense* had said much (in richly emotive terms) about "emotion," which was the efficient cause of moral action, even if it was not the faculty of moral definition. But there was no intimation in Shelley that ultimately there were not good enough grounds for the emotions of which he spoke. Arnold's more scientifically circumspect profession of faith does try to keep the tweezers between his truth-searching faculty and that highly desirable yet untruthful element of emotion.

> The middle age could do without humane letters, as it could do
> without the study of nature, because its supposed knowledge
> was made to engage its emotions so powerfully. Grant that the
> supposed knowledge disappears, its power of being made to en-

[2] Consult *Sweetness and Light*, the concluding Oxford lecture of 1867, which becomes the first chapter of *Culture and Anarchy*, 1869.

gage the emotions will of course disappear along with it—but the emotions will remain. Now if we find by experience that humane letters have an undeniable power of engaging the emotions, the importance of humane letters in man's training becomes not less, but greater, in proportion to the success of science in extirpating what it calls "medieval thinking." [3]

VII

ARNOLD was of course not the only voice of his kind to be heard during the long Victorian era. In America the ethical idealism of the New England litterateurs in the "classical" period, notably Emerson, is at least as traceable an influence as that of Arnold in the development of a "Genteel Tradition" [4] that has carried far into our own century. One of the most aesthetically acceptable—brilliantly cautious—statements of a moral perspective upon literature to appear during the whole period was that in the prefaces and other critical essays of Henry James. All art, he would say, is in basis moral. (He was speaking against Gautier's *l'art pour l'art*, and no less against the naturalism of Balzac.) [5] Both in art and in criticism, "the moral sense and the artistic sense lie very near together." "In each of the parts there is something of each of the other parts." [6]

> There is one point at which the moral sense and the artistic sense lie very near together; that is, in the light of the very obvious truth that the deepest quality of a work of art will always be the quality of the mind of the producer. In proportion as that mind is rich and noble, will the novel, the picture, the statue, partake of the substance of beauty and truth. To be constituted of such elements is, to my vision, to have purpose enough. No good novel will ever proceed from a superficial mind; that seems to me an axiom which, for the artist of fiction, will cover all needful ground. [7]

A medley of such voices was very friendly to the rise in academic America shortly after the turn of the century of a new humanistic and ethical school of criticism which, through the resounding efforts mainly of two champions, kept a hearing for about thirty years. It is true that

[3] *Literature and Science,* in *Four Essays on Life and Letters,* ed. E. K. Brown (New York, 1947), pp. 109–10.

[4] Cf. George Santayana, *The Genteel Tradition at Bay* (New York, 1931).

[5] *French Poets and Novelists* (London, 1919), pp. 14, 31–56, 116, essays on Baudelaire, Gautier, Balzac; *Notes on Novelists* (New York, 1914), pp. 122, 126, on Balzac.

[6] *The Art of Fiction,* in *Partial Portraits* (London, 1911), pp. 404–6, 392. Cf. Morris Roberts, *Henry James's Criticism* (Cambridge, Mass., 1929), p. 63.

[7] Beginning of last paragraph of *The Art of Fiction.*

Paul Elmer More in the Seventh volume (1910) of his long series of *Shelburne Essays* utters a lament for the deficiencies of a kind of "culture" which he tries to define by pairing Arnold with a much earlier English critic, the Deist Shaftesbury. "The fault," he says, "lay not in any intrinsic want of efficiency in the critical spirit, nor in any want of moral earnestness." "These men were lacking in another direction: they missed a philosophy which could bind together their moral and their aesthetic sense, a positive principle besides the negative force of ridicule and irony." Thus they left criticism open to subjectivism, impressionism, and moral anarchy.[8] Here was a tightening of the belt—or a promise of sharper teeth for the ethical tradition. In More himself, humanism enjoyed an overt alliance with religion and so of course was not the pure Arnoldian critique of life. But in More's Harvard colleague Irving Babbitt, the concepts of "insight" into the Higher Will through literary symbol and a consequent "inner check" upon romantic emotive expansiveness and naturalistic descendentalism ("romanticism on all fours") received a treatment which in the purity of its withdrawal from revealed religion[9] surpassed even the cultural dreams of Arnold. Babbitt's campaign in its negative phases, his attack on Rousseau, romanticism, and all that, is crowded with richly reported and bizarre incidents and luridly lit up with the flambeaux of his indignant rhetoric. His positive schemes, however, are more thinly delineated, his main illustrative appeals, to the drama of the Greeks, but sketchily intimated. Babbitt showed a heavy hand when late in his career he tried close dealing with an actual work of romantic English literature. His censure of Coleridge's imaginative control in *The Ancient Mariner* seems the all but fanatical result of a theory of literature that was not in fact literary. The twin detonations in 1930 of two anthologies, one for the new humanists and one against them, announced the end of a didactic critical movement which, adequately defined in Arnold's terms of 1880, had in the humanism of his successors moved no nearer to a distinct concern for literature.

SUPPLEMENT

> The history of the creative arts is long
> But the belief in art as the supreme
> Criterion of experience is as new

[8] "Criticism," in *Shelburne Essays, Seventh Series* (New York, 1910), pp. 223-4. Cf. Zabel, *Literary Opinion in America*, p. 30.

[9] More defined Babbitt's kind of humanism as "the study and practice of the principles of human happiness *uncomplicated* by naturalistic dogmas on the one side and religious dogmas on the other" (*On Being Human*, Princeton, 1936, p. 18). Babbitt's parleying with Buddhism was a largely philosophic performance.

As the electric light. Our poets belong
In dangerous numbers to this strange persuasion.
Small wonder that they live like ghosts and perish
Without biographies; small wonder too
That they adopt an adjective for their name
And soberly defer to those who wear
The title of Intellectual. Poets by hosts
Spring fully armed from pure obscurity
To bay like demons at us and to slay
The man in front; our brawls are commonplaces.

. . . .

                     All rime more or less
Has a religious ancestry, for man,
The evidence says, is a believing being.
Nor does it follow that the civilized,
The secular and the profane in art must fail
For lack of faith—thus too the evidence.
What here pertains is the solicitude
Of modern artists for their missing gods,
Our attitude of nervous self-defence
Against the emotions roused by great belief,
Our purely literary use of Christ
In painting, prose and rime, our use of Christ
In any cynical neo-Christian sense
Or even with that perfunctory good-will
Which characterizes Tolerance.

. . . .

By now the plaints of Arnold are too stale
For repetition, yet it is curious
I think to make comparison of his lush
Nostalgia for the Age of Faith with ours
Which is nostalgia madly furious.
In part that deep Victorian melancholy
Is father to our more frantic abnegation
Of all the supernatural. Rime must refer
Anti-religiously to belief and nature,
Or else create the kind of nomenclature
Which hints at natural science.

—Karl Shapiro, *Essay on Rime* (New York, 1945), pp. 52–4, "The Confusion in Belief," copyright 1945 by Karl Shapiro. Reprinted by permission of Random House, Inc.

Poems by Alexander Smith, a volume recently published in London, and by this time reprinted in Boston, deserve attention. They have obtained in England a good deal more notice than is usually accorded there to first volumes of verse; nor is this by any means to be ascribed to the mere fact that the writer is, as we are told, a mechanic; though undoubtedly that does add to their ex-

ternal interest, and perhaps also enhances their intrinsic merit. It is to this, perhaps, that they owe a force of purpose and character which makes them a
grateful contrast to the ordinary languid collectanea published by young men
of literary habits; and which, on the whole, may be accepted as more than
compensation for many imperfections of style and taste.

. . . .

   We do not at all mean to prepare the reader for finding the great poetic
desideratum in this present Life-Drama. But it has at least the advantage, such
as it is, of not showing much of the *litterateur* or connoisseur, or indeed the student; nor is it, as we have said, mere pastoral sweet piping from the country.
These poems were not written among books and busts, nor yet

> By shallow rivers, to whose falls
> Melodious birds sing madrigals.

They have something substantive and lifelike, immediate and first-hand, about
them. There is a charm, for example, in finding, as we do, continual images
drawn from the busy seats of industry; it seems to satisfy a want that we have
long been conscious of, when we see the black streams that welter out of factories, the dreary lengths of urban and suburban dustiness,

> the squares and streets
> And the faces that one meets,

irradiated with a gleam of divine purity.

   There are moods when one is prone to believe that, in these last days, no
longer by "clear spring or shady grove," no more upon any Pindus or Parnassus, or by the shady side of any Castaly, are the true and lawful haunts of the
poetic powers. But, we could believe it, if anywhere, in the blank and desolate
streets, and upon the solitary bridges of the midnight city, where Guilt is, and
wild Temptation, and the dire Compulsion of what has once been done—there,
with these tragic sisters around him, and with Pity also, and pure Compassion,
and pale Hope, that looks like Despair, and Faith in the garb of Doubt, there
walks the discrowned Apollo, with unstrung lyre; nay, and could he sound it,
those mournful Muses would scarcely be able as of old, to respond and "sing
in turn with their beautiful voices."

Empedocles on Etna and other Poems, with its earlier companion volume, The
Strayed Reveller and other Poems, are, it would seem, the productions (as is, or
was, the English phrase) of a scholar and a gentleman; a man who has received
a refined education, seen refined "society," had been more, we dare say, in the
world, which is called the world, than in all likelihood has a Glasgow mechanic. More refined, therefore, and more highly educated sensibilities,—too
delicate, are they, for common service?—a calmer judgment also, a more poised
and steady intellect, the *siccum lumen* of the soul; a finer and rarer aim perhaps, and certainly a keener sense of difficulty, in life;—these are the characteristics of him whom we are to call "A."

   —[Arthur Hugh Clough], review of "Recent English Poetry," *North
American Review*, LXXVII (July, 1853), 1, 4–5, 12

CHAPTER 21

THE REAL AND THE SOCIAL: ART AS PROPAGANDA

§ *dialectic themes: the historical, the scientific, the real-*
istic, the sociological, positivism and the future of art,
study of origins, compromises with idealism—II. "realism,"
pictorial and literary, Courbet, Flaubert, the "democratic
brush," transition to "naturalism," Zola, novelist as scien-
tist, Le Roman Expérimental, *later versions in America,*
Frank Norris, Responsibilities of the Novelist, *environ-*
ment, brutality, Gothic naturalism, a form of "romanti-
cism"—III. early phases of Russian criticism, ideology of
nationalism, Russian novelists, Belinsky and his disciples,
realism and social relevance, hidden meanings, sequence
of literary genres, disapproval of folk poetry, of pure art
and pleasure themes, "The Destruction of Aesthetics,"
psychology and hygiene, paradox of determinism and
revolutionary sacrifice—IV. Tolstoy, "the conscience of
the world," What Is Art?, *Christian anarchy, "infection,"*
religious emotion of this age, *pride, sex, ennui, "pleasure"*
arts caricatured, five-sense aesthetics, "counterfeit" art
(*Wagner's* Nibelungen Ring), *rejection of his own novels,*
peasant boys, Tolstoy's taste in pictures, great art and the
plain man, impressionist pictures and symbolist poetry,
obscurity and immorality, Baudelaire's Le Galant Tireur,
Tolstoy on Shakespeare—V. Marxist criticism, class propa-
ganda, deterministic origins, isolation of modern artist,
bourgeois culture, mirror images, Christopher Caudwell,
Illusion and Reality, *1937, Marxism and historical literary*
studies, party-line mimesis, society the work of art—VI.
American phases, "muckraking," the 1930's, keeping up
with "the vanguard of the Proletariat," Emerson and

454

THE ARNOLDIAN PROPHECY WAS DIRECTED TOWARD THE FUTURE OF SOME autonomous poetic power—appealing for authority, so far as it made any such appeal, to the Hellenic and the Hebraic past. Poetry was not to take orders from, but to take the place of, modern philosophy and religion. Poetry was to tell science what science was working for. The fact was, however, that the most urgently didactic trend in European literary theory of the 19th century aimed at making poetry something far other than an autonomous power or an antique authority. This trend was already well under way in Arnold's time and was destined to arrive at its zenith in the English-speaking world during the earlier 20th century, at about the same time as the less aggressively launched campaign of neo-humanism. This was to be a didacticism committed to the exposition and advancement of a dogma that would receive its definition from a quite unpoetic authority. In its mature phase, it was to issue in a propagandism that far outdid in abstractive solidarity anything ever attempted by poetry in the ages of Christian humanism. In Arnold's day the movement was gaining most headway in continental places somewhat removed from his observation; and nearer home, in France, it was apparently not one of the things which most engaged his attention.

Four main emphases, closely inter-reliant, appear in the post-Hegelian literary thought of the mid-century continent. These are the historical, the scientific, the realistic, the sociological. In place of the Hegelian "spirit" which worked the dialectical play and counter-play of the historical process, post-Hegelianism produced the dialectic of purely material forces, the *mystique* of time and progress. Nevertheless, the idea of a certain kind of function and future for poetry fared not badly. Science with social programs was more inclusive in its tolerance than the simply rationalistic enlightenment of an earlier era. Science with such alliances could even perhaps make better offers than could metaphysical idealism. Whereas Hegel, the idealistic encyclopedist of the arts, had arrived at a view of metaphysical fulfillment which meant the end of art and prophesied for it no future at all, the French positivism of Saint-Simon, Proudhon,[1] and Comte, in a manner curiously akin to the vision

[1] *Du principe de l'art et de sa destination sociale,* 1865.

of Schelling, Friedrich Schlegel, or Shelley, assigned to art a gloriously continuing imaginative function in the phases of human advancement that were to succeed upon the outmoded eras of religion and metaphysics. At the same time, another sort of French positivism, that represented most notably by the literary philosopher and historian Taine, prescribed a rigorous study of literature in its origins (the determining forces of *race, milieu,* and *moment*). And this prescription in the long run had very noticeable effects upon the actual study of literature not only in France but abroad. To construct literary methodologies on the principle of an expansively propagandist future for poetry never became very practicable. But the richly various conditions under which literature had been produced in the past, the economic, the social, the religious, the total of influences on art which Taine called "moral temperature," these made an increasingly inviting field for the application of the "experimental" method.

So far as the definition of art itself was concerned, much was borrowed from German romantic idealism—even by Taine himself [2]—and by other French aestheticians of the romantic generation (Cousin, Jouffroy, and their successors) as they assumed various postures of moderation, compromise, or merger, in response to the increasingly historical, realistic, and social claims of the age.[3]

II

"Realism"—if we may use the term broadly to mean a reaction against a number of things that were thought in the mid-19th-century to be *un*real, not only Gothic romance, picaresque adventure, and allegorical fantasy but classic composure and conservative morality—realism as an aesthetic norm comes into view not only for literary but for pictorial art at about the same time, in the exhibition by Courbet of 1855 and the publication of Flaubert's *Madame Bovary* in 1856. Flaubert's theory of realism was concerned with the professional procedures of a novelist. He conceived a scientific detachment, a coolness and care, in the observation of materials. He made a trip to Egypt to study the scenery for his novel *Salammbô*. "Flaubert, the son and brother of distinguished physicians," Sainte-Beuve would say, "holds his pen like a scalpel." [4] At the same time it can scarcely be said that the novels of Flaubert actually

---

[2] Cf. Iredell Jenkins, "Hippolyte Taine and the Background of Modern Aesthetics," *Modern Schoolman,* XX (March 1943), 141–56.

[3] Victor Cousin (1792–1867), Théodore Jouffroy (1796–1842), Victor de Laprade (1812–83), Jean-Charles Lévêque (1818–1900).

[4] *Causeries du Lundi* (1857–70), XIII, 363; from a manuscript chapter by René Wellek.

exhibit a very servile rendering of natural objects. "People believe I am taken with the real," he said—"whereas I detest it." [5] In the theoretical manifestoes which accompany the realist movement in painting, however, and notably in the codification of Courbet's friend Castagnary, there are no such sophistications.

> The painter of our own time will live our own life, with our own habits and our own ideas. He will take the feelings he gets from the look of things in our society, and give them back to us in pictures where we recognize ourselves and our own surroundings. It will not do to lose sight of the fact that we ourselves are both the subject and the object of art: art is the expression of ourselves for our own sake. [6]

"To make verses," says Courbet himself, in a way that happily shows us the bearing of the doctrine on literature, "is unfair; to speak in a fashion different from all the world, that is an aristocratic pose." [7] Courbet's critics spoke of his "scrupulous imitation of nature," the "signature of nature itself," his "democratic brush." [8] But the Courbet phase of French realism was regarded even by its promoters as a transitional moment. [9] Inherent in its sociological implications, the here and now democratic "truth" which it pursued, was the notion of the ordinary, and hence the notion of the monotonous, the meager, the drab, the underprivileged, even the seamy. And this realism rather quickly intensified into the phase called "naturalism." Of this phase the greatest exponent was Zola. Literary "realism" and "naturalism" constituted an aesthetic centered in the prose novel, which was the literary genre most directly dedicated to the social problems of the 19th century. The naturalistic novelist conceived himself as a scientific sociologist and psychologist, an experimentalist working with his hypotheses like a scientist in a laboratory. The object of the experiment was the social organism. One had to tell the truth about it, not fairy tales. One might admit only (when talking about the "constant evolution of the human spirit") that the eye of the observer did color the picture. The literary artist gave "a corner of

[5] Gustave Flaubert, *Correspondance*, III (Paris, 1892), 67–8. The statement is made apropos of *Madame Bovary*. "*On me croit épris du réel, tandis que je l'exècre, car c'est en haine du réalisme que j'ai entrepris ce roman.*" Melvin Friedman, "Passages on Aesthetics from Flaubert's Correspondence," *Quarterly Review of Literature*, IV [1949], 390–400, gives us a translation of "the total . . . of Flaubert's comments on aesthetics." Cf. Gilbert and Kuhn, pp. 492.

[6] Jules Antoine Castagnary, *Salons* (*1857–70*), I (Paris, 1892), 187. Cf. Gilbert and Kuhn, pp. 481–3.

[7] Emile Gros-Kost, *Courbet, Souvenirs intimes*, 1880, p. 31.

[8] H. d'Ideville, *Gustave Courbet, Notes et documents sur sa vie et son oeuvre*, (Paris, 1878), pp. 107 ff. Gros-Kost and Ideville are quoted from Gilbert and Kuhn (pp. 481–2), to whom our account of Courbet is substantially indebted.

[9] Cf. Harry Levin, "What is Realism?" and Albert J. Salvan, "*L'Essence du réalisme français*," in *Comparative Literature*, III (Summer, 1951), 193–9, 218–3.

nature seen through a temperament." [1] Zola's theoretical treatise, *Le Roman Expérimental*, 1880, describes the setting up of the initial conditions, the release of the action (the life of a libertine, for instance, such as Hulot in Balzac's *La Cousine Bette*), then the patient observation by the scientist-novelist, leading to a sober knowledge,[2] rich in practical implications for the improvement of society.[3] The novelist aimed at nothing less than a supreme knowledge, how to be "master of good and evil, how to rule life, how to rule society." [4] Zola found an authoritative manual of instruction for his new literary procedure in the *Introduction à l'étude de la médecine experimentale* by Claude Bernard. Bernard was so much to the point that in taking over his ideas Zola needed to do little more than change the word "physician" to "novelist." [5]

> The experimental novel is a result of the scientific development which has occurred in this century; it is a continuation and complement to the science of physiology which in turn depends upon chemistry and physics; it substitutes for the study of man as an abstraction, man as a metaphysical entity, the study of the natural man, man as the subject of physico-chemical laws, a being determined by the influences of his environment.[6]

Or, as Zola expressed it in his "Plans" for a vast saga of determinism:

> Study men like simple elements and note the reactions.

> What matters most to me is to be purely naturalistic, purely physiological. Instead of having principles (royalism, Catholicism) I shall have laws (heredity, atavism). . . . I am satisfied to be a scientist, to tell of that which exists, while seeking the underlying reasons. . . . A simple exposé of the facts of a family by showing the interior mechanisms which direct them.[7]

[1] *Le Naturalisme au Théatre*, in *Le Roman Expérimental*, ed. Maurice le Blond (Paris, n.d.), p. 92.

[2] *Le Roman Expérimental*, ed. Maurice le Blond, p. 16: "*Dès qu'il a eu choisi son sujet, il est parti des faits observés, puis il a institué son expérience en soumettant Hulot a une série d'épreuves, en le faisant passer par certains milieux, pour montrer le fonctionnement du mécanisme de sa passion.*"

[3] P. 28. Gilbert and Kuhn, p. 484, quote by contrast the romantic nature worship and fetichism of Zola's *La Faute de l'Abbé Mouret*: "Oh good Earth, take me, thou that art the common mother, the sole source of life, thou the eternal, immortal, where the soul of the world circles. . . ."

[4] P. 28: "*Etre maître du bien et du mal, régler la vie, régler la société, résoudre à la longue tous les problèmes du socialisme.*"

[5] P. 1: "*Ce ne sera donc qu'une compilation de textes;—le plus souvent, il me suffira de remplacer le mot 'médecin' par le mot 'romancier,' pour rendre ma pensée claire et lui apporter la rigeur d'une vérité scientifique.*"

[6] P. 27.

[7] Matthew Josephson, *Zola and His Time* (New York, *The Book League Monthly*, I, 1, November, 1928), pp. 97–8, quoting Zola's manuscript Plans for *La Fortune des Rougon*, in the Bibliothèque Nationale, Paris.

Perhaps the most instructive later variations on the theme occur in America during the years around the turn of the century—where, in the utterances of Howells, for instance, we may observe scientific realism in moderately developed conflict with genteel idealism, or where Frank Norris shows that the lustiest pursuit of naturalism is capable of fantastic, even Gothic, realizations. Norris' *Responsibilities of the Novelist*, 1903, is the American counterpart of Zola's *Le Roman Expérimental* and the vindication of Norris' own novels, with their Zolaesque accumulation of careful detail, their studious concern for environment as the shaper of character, for disease, for brutality and violence. His canvas was crowded not only with weakness and misery but with primitive strong men and robustly animal women. Wheat workers clash with railroad management in a frontier contest of gigantic—nearly cosmic—proportions and implications. He combined an aim at disinterested, scientific objectivity with an evolutionary optimism about the collective future of mankind which it was difficult for readers of Herbert Spencer in that era to escape. And so his theory was not uncorruptly naturalistic. In an early essay he wrote:

> The naturalist takes no note of common people, common in so far as their interests, their lives, and the things that occur in them are common, are ordinary. Terrible things must happen to the characters of the naturalistic tale. They must be twisted from the ordinary, wrenched from the quiet uneventful round of every-day life and flung into the throes of a vast and terrible drama that works itself out in unleashed passions, in blood, and in sudden death.[8]

"Norris," says a recent historian, "knew that naturalistic fiction was a peculiar kind of adventure story. To write such stories, it helped to be able to think of modern business men as the descendants of the aggressive Anglo-Saxons carrying out their fighting instincts, not in war, but in trade." Naturalism, Norris came to believe, "is a form of romanticism, not an inner circle of realism." [9]

"Naturalism" had all along made a strong claim to be socially oriented. It showed a modern conscience for the plight of the working

[8] Editorial in the San Francisco *Wave*, quoted by Franklin Walker, *Frank Norris: A Biography* (New York, 1932), p. 83. Cf. Charles Child Walcutt, "Frank Norris and the Search for Form," *University of Kansas City Review*, XIV (Winter, 1947), 126-36; and "Frank Norris on Realism and Naturalism," *American Literature*, XIII (March, 1941), 61-3, convincing observations on Norris' failure to shape his novels consistently on a philosophy of scientific determinism. Moral responsibility was always breaking in.

[9] William Van O'Connor, *An Age of Criticism, 1900–1950* (Chicago, 1952), p. 42. Our account of Norris is substantially indebted to O'Connor. Cf. Norris, *The Responsibilities of the Novelist* (New York, 1903), pp. 214-15: "Zola has been dubbed a Realist, but he is, on the contrary, the very head of the Romanticists."

classes. It dealt with ordinary folk here and now, or with the kind of
destiny and problems that most people experienced, not with moated
castles, elfin knights, exotic love stories, border outlaws, or any other
fantasies dreamed out of the now irrelevant feudal past or invoked
from parts of the world still under the spell of that past. That is, naturalism was contemporary and socially didactic. But whether it was in
any very strict sense "natural" or "true," or scientifically real or true,
might all along have been considered another question—with obvious
embarrassments to an affirmative answer. Courbet's paintings no less
than Frank Norris' novels exhibit a much clearer relation to a philosophy and a spirit than to either the 19th-century fact of photography
or to any physically determinable features of French peasant life or of
Chicago industrialism.

III

IN Czarist Russia of the mid-19th-century,[1] a didactic theory of literature was strongly invited not only by political and social conditions but
by the actual pre-eminence of a generation of socially conscious novelists. At the same time, Russian police censorship helped to make
literary book reviewing a covert vehicle for much political, social, and
moral criticism. The notion deeply inherent in German romantic
literary historiography and in the ideology of romantic nationalism, that
literature should be the expression of a national spirit (the symbol of
the inner life of the nation, the national physiognomy), carried over
into Russia in the writing of the first Russian critic to attain more than
local importance, Vissarion Belinsky (1811–1848), and in that of his
disciples who wrote during the decades following his death.[2] Marxist
critics of the 20th century have looked back to Belinsky with reverence.
The reviews and essays of Belinsky and his disciples deal with Pushkin,
Gogol, Lermontov, Turgenev, Dostoevsky, and Tolstoy according to increasingly rigorous standards of realism and social relevance. These
critics were on the lookout for empirical reality, for the moment in
history, for social and national needs, and for corresponding responsibilities in literature. They merged the classical norm of the universal

---

[1] This account of pre-Tolstoyan Russian critics follows manuscript chapters
of the third volume of Professor René Wellek's *A History of Modern Criticism*, now
in progress. See his "Social and Aesthetic Values in Russian Nineteenth-Century
Literary Criticism (Belinskii, Chernyshevskii, Dobroliubov, Pisarev)," in *Continuity
and Change in Russian and Soviet Thought*, ed. Ernest J. Simmons (Cambridge,
Mass., 1955), pp. 381–97. Examples of Belinsky's criticism may be found in *Selected
Philosophical Works*, translated anonymously (Moscow, 1948) and of Dobrolyubov's
in *Selected Philosophical Essays*, ed. J. Fineberg (Moscow, 1948).

[2] Nikolay Chernyshevsky (1828–89), Nikolay Dobrolyubov (1836–61), Dmitri
Pisarev (1840–68).

with romantic theories of mythopoeia in a pressing demand that the literary artist create human types according to new patterns of social significance. They considered that the only real literature was the expression of the historically developing national spirit, the dialectic movement of the political and economic idea. That movement provided a norm for distinguishing between the eternal and the ephemeral in literature. The greatest authors were the ones most closely identified with the community and its evolution, those who divined the needs of their time, expressed its spirit, represented their contemporaries. Belinsky's disciple Dobrolyubov was the originator of the idea that novelists might do this independently of, or even contrary to, their conscious intentions. The function of criticism might be to explain hidden social meanings. At the genetic level, these critics shifted the responsibility for the work of art from the artist to his age. They made it a pure result of the historical process. They conceived it more and more as an expression relentlessly forced up out of the national consciousness under pressure exerted by the stream of history. They saw inevitable sequences of literary genres (as from lyric to epic to drama) both in national history and in the growth of individual poets.

On occasions they appeared as reactionaries against romantic primitivism and specifically against folk poetry as a thing socially implicated in a serf-civilization, a survival from an undesirable and irrecoverable past. They were apt also to speak severely against "pure art" or the pleasure art of erotic and convivial themes, dissolute adventures. Pisarev, the most rigidly naturalistic monist of the group, the author of a notorious paper entitled "The Destruction of Aesthetics" (1865), reduced aesthetics to psychology and hygiene, observing that "every healthy and normal person is beautiful." He would concede some usefulness to the art of drawing, but only for the illustration of scientific books. He said that no man of that generation who had genuine intelligence and talent could spend his life "piercing sensitive hearts with iambs and anapests." The main technical emphasis of this whole family of critics was on a faithful naturalistic reporting, a lifelike rendition of the social organism, the stages of its development. Belinsky spoke of Russian writers since Gogol as the "natural school."

Belinsky himself did not propose any simply didactic aim, like the overthrow of autocracy or the emancipation of the serfs—though he moved in this direction and his disciples moved further. Compared with the French positivists, Saint-Simon, Proudhon, Comte, these Russian critics had less to say about the glorious didactic future of art, more about immediate sociological realism, but their social emphasis had deeply and enduringly didactic implications. In the work of Belinsky's disciples, deterministic materialism, hedonistic utilitarianism, and enlightened egoism unite paradoxically with fervor for social reform and a revolutionary spirit of sacrifice and social optimism. They combine the view that any art which has ever been faithful to its historic moment has been for that reason right (even bad taste if pervasive enough expresses a spirit and a time) with a second view, sometimes not distinguished from the first, that the historic development of the mid-19th century is in itself a superior thing. Time and history take on the ambivalent character of an inevitable (blind and neutral) progression which is, however, in its present moment the only truth and is to be promoted with ardent loyalty.

IV

THE greatest Russian literary figure to participate in the 19th-century complex of socio-realistic theory and the writer whose pronouncements on art have impinged with most authority on the English literary mind, was undoubtedly Tolstoy—"the conscience of Russia" in his time, "the conscience of the world," "the conscience of humanity." [3] One might suppose offhand that Tolstoy could not very readily be assimilated to the materialistic trend of Russian social theory. He was in his middle age a violent convert to a certain kind of Christian thinking. A period of furious tractarian activity followed the production of the great novels. And it is a religious theory of literature that near the end of his life issues in his thunderously deliberate denunciation of all that he himself and all that European artists for 300 years had created. Tolstoy's *What Is Art?*, 1898, was published simultaneously in both Russian and English and was widely honored by English readers for its weight and elaboration and for its many passages of profound insight and passionate conviction. It pursued a religious argument—not, however, in the traditional sense. The religious feelings aroused in Tolstoy as he looks back over his career as liberal aristocrat and novelist run heavily counter to the established Christian institutions and to the whole cultural hierarchy related to them. The religion which appears in his tracts, beginning with *A Confession* in 1878,[4] and in all his essays on art, is a form of Christian anarchy, a wide and simple kind of religious feeling for the brotherhood of man and his common relation of sonship to God. Tolstoy's *What Is Art?* fits comfortably enough in the Russian complex, and Tolstoy too has his niche in the Marxist retrospect.

As a literary theorist, Tolstoy appears in the main tradition of emotive art theory developed during the 19th century along rather simple lines from the 18th-century concept which we have noted as late as the essays of Mill. But other versions of emotivism which appear during

[3] Cf. Ernest J. Simmons, *Leo Tolstoy* (Boston, 1946), p. 488; review by E. C. Ross, *Saturday Review of Literature*, XXX (January 18, 1947), 17.

[4] See Matthew Arnold's account of these in his long review of *Anna Karenina* included under the title *Count Leo Tolstoy* in *Essays in Criticism, Second Series*.

this era, and notably the expressionist theory of Véron,[5] have a more aesthetic orientation. Tolstoy's version is strongly anti-aesthetic. Art is to be known by its power of wholesome emotive "infection." He has a theory about the social function of art which invites comparison with the theories of Shelley and Comte. (Science, the pioneer thinker, is a little boat which takes kedge-anchors upstream to new positions; art is the windlass of moral energy which draws the barge up to the new positions. Chapter XX.) [6] And he more or less unwittingly accepts the paradox of the historically emergent new truth which we have noted among the earlier Russians.

There is a chapter (V) where Tolstoy first expounds his infection theory, and here he seems mainly to say that art transmits *emotion*. Then at the end of the same chapter he says that art transmits *religious* emotion. There are several other chapters (VI, IX, XI, XX) where he seems to say that art always transmits the genuine, the "fresh" religious emotion of any age. He uses such phrases as the "highest life-conception of a time" (XI), "the highest conception accessible to their age" (VI), "the highest level of life-comprehension" (IX). Finally, there is a chapter (XVI) where he says that the art of the *present* age must transmit only the progressive religious emotions of this age, those that relate to the universal brotherhood of man.[7]

Thus a problem arises (even though Tolstoy does not see it) concerning that which was once new but is now old.

> From the religious perception of the ancient Greeks flowed the really new, important, and endlessly varied feelings expressed by Homer and the tragic writers.—IX
>
> . . . good, supreme art; the Iliad, the Odyssey. . . . —X
>
> But the Christian idea changed and reversed everything, so that as the Gospel puts it, "That which was exalted among men has become an abomination in the sight of God." The ideal is no longer the greatness of Pharaoh or of a Roman emperor, not the beauty of a Greek nor the wealth of Phoenicia, but humility, purity, compassion, love.—XVI
>
> The artists of the Middle Ages, vitalized by the same source of feeling—religion—as the mass of the people, and transmitting

[5] Eugène Véron, *Aesthetics*, trans. W. H. Armstrong (London, 1879). Véron has optimistic evolutionary and secular millenarian views which are comparable to those of Tolstoy. "What shall we say, then, about the sentiments which are the true glories of our age,—charity, toleration, respect for womanhood, for childhood, and for human life? Pity for animals, is not that, too, a sign of the times?" (p. 353)

[6] See *What is Art? and Essays on Art*, trans. Aylmer Maude (Oxford: World's Classics, 1930).

[7] A second place is given to certain universally accessible, or folk, emotions—namely, merriment, pity, cheerfulness, and tranquillity (Ch. XVI).

. . . the feelings and states of mind they experienced, were true artists; and their activity, founded on the highest conceptions accessible to their age and common to the entire people—though for our times a mean art—was nevertheless a true one, shared by the whole community.—VI

European society [of the Renaissance] went back in their comprehension of art to the gross conception of the primitive Greeks, which Plato had already condemned.—VI

. . . rude, savage, and for us, often meaningless works of the ancient Greeks: Sophocles, Euripides, Aeschylus. . . .—XII

If by art it has been inculcated on people how they should treat religious objects, their parents, their children, their wives . . . and if this has been obeyed through generations by millions of people . . . then by art also other customs more in accord with the religious perception of our time may be evoked.—XX

Presumably the degenerate European art of Tolstoy's time would have been religious art in another era. And we are left with some question whether the religious perception of the new time is a genuine material for art because it is a better perception or because it is the latest.[8]

But Tolstoy is sufficiently compelling in his indictment of the effete emotions—the pride, sexual desire, and ennui which rule the upper-class patrons of the "pleasure arts" in his day. His walloping caricatures of metropolitan fashionable culture—the art show, the salon, the theater, the opera in rehearsal, art schools and art criticism—manage to suggest not only lavish waste and a measure of social injustice but a deplorable perplexity of aesthetic judgment and widespread vitiation of taste. He notices with scorn the new aesthetics of the lower senses— the five-sense aesthetics of gustatory, olfactory, and tactile pleasure which in that day was fulfilling the promise of 18th-century sensationalism and had some connection with the kinds of aesthetic autonomy then in vogue.[9] In short Tolstoy gives pointed expression to the difficult and permanent aesthetic problem whether a non-didactic or autonomous theory of art is bound to be merely a "hedonistic" or pleasure theory of art. He issues us an urgent invitation to ponder the validity of a café-society aesthetic devotion ranging from theater, orchestra, museum, and gallery, through opera and ballet, to the refinements of dinner with chartreuse, cigars, and music. *Aut prodesse . . . aut delectare*—Horace

[8] These paradoxes of post-Hegelian thinking are the paradigm for such quirks in later intellectual history as the appearance on the mid-20th-century American scene of the "premature" anti-communist, or the exclusive sanctity which the *Partisan* kind of liberalism confers upon the repentant Marxist.

[9] Cf. *post* Chapter 22, "Art for Art's Sake."

had given the poet his alternatives. Is there any other—aside from the merely mixed way of "winning all the votes" which Horace suggests? Must the interpretation of *delectare* incline to the frivolity of a merely sensate indulgence?

Tolstoy gives us another impressive set of negative judgments in a chapter (XI) on "counterfeit" art, under four main heads: "borrowing," "imitation," "striking," and "interesting." Or, in terms that may be nearer to our own minds: stock responses, local-color realism, pornography and horror, detective story plots. (Wagner's *Nibelungen Ring* is a model combination of the four ways!) Tolstoy is very pure, very austere, very acute in his opinion of what is not art, and very firm in his will to condemn it.

Yet his sternly exclusive standard would be even more impressive if he had left it less explicitly illustrated. For the application of the standard is horrifying in its sweep. The whole body of medieval, Renaissance, and modern European art—the work of Dante, Tasso, Shakespeare, Milton, Goethe, Raphael, Michelangelo, Bach, Beethoven, for instance (Chapter XII) [1]—is swept away, and with it the great novels of Tolstoy himself. He shows no compunction. "I belong," he says, "to the class of people whose taste has been perverted by false training" (XVI). He is willing to salvage only two of his simplest short stories: *God Sees the Truth but Waits*, the pathetic fable of a man railroaded to Siberia who, after growing old in the prison camp, discovers his enemy and forgives him; and *A Prisoner of the Caucasus*, a tender idyll, full of village and childhood colors, about a Russian officer captured by Tartars and helped to escape by a girl of the tribe. [2] Nearly forty years earlier Tolstoy had set up a school for peasant children in his ancestral estate at Yasnaya Polyana, and two boys Semka and Fedka had written for his school magazine stories which he called "in their way, equal to anything in Russian literature." It seemed to him "strange and offensive" that he "should hardly be able except at a happy moment of excitement to keep up with" these inspired peasant boys. [3] The simplicity, even sentimentality, of the aesthetic norm adopted by Tolstoy may be inspected in the half-tones which embellish Aylmer Maude's large edition of *What Is Art?*, [4] presenting examples of the pictorial art which Tolstoy at various places in his book selects for special commendation:—the peasant boy of Turgenev's story dreaming of the quail, the war widow

[1] Schiller, Hugo, Dickens, Harriet Beecher Stowe, Dostoevski, George Eliot, Cervantes, Molière, Gogol, Pushkin (Chap. XVI) have produced examples of art that *seem* good to Tolstoy, but he attaches no "importance" to his own taste.

[2] Tolstoy's Preface to another short story, Chekhov's *Darling*, argues, according to a principle we have noticed in the earlier Russian critics, that the author expresses humanitarian meaning in his own despite.

[3] Aylmer Maude, *Life of Tolstoy*, vol. I, Chap. viii (World's Classics, c. 1930, , 269–70).

[4] *Tolstoy on Art*, trans. Aylmer Maude (Boston, 1924).

weeping in the room behind the balcony overlooking the victory parade, the peasant girls giggling at a society huntsman, Russian peasants paying out money at a state liquor monopoly. In religious painting Tolstoy preferred N. N. Gay's drably natural *Last Supper* and *What is Truth?* to Manet's Pre-Raphaelite *Angels at the Tomb of Christ.* Millet's *The Man with the Hoe* is an object of his preference which his editor seems to have thought it needless to illustrate.

Tolstoy's exclusiveness raises the difficult aesthetic problem of "communication." Art for whom? [5] A "country peasant of unperverted taste" will detect the genuine work of art easily and unerringly (XIV). And Tolstoy seems to assume that the numerous peasantry are far more likely than the few genteel folk actually to have an unperverted taste. "Unperverted" *means* in fact uncomplicated, ordinary. "Good, great, universal, religious art may be incomprehensible to a small circle of spoilt people, but certainly not to any large number of plain men" (X). The democratic consumers' argument which we have noted here and there in the past, in Longinus, in Castelvetro, in Samuel Johnson, arrives at its fullest realization in Tolstoy.

He applies the norm of easy comprehensibility with special satisfaction against the immediately contemporary "decadent" art which he is most bent on condemning. The truth about this art—the pictures in the Paris impressionist and symbolist exhibitions of 1894, the poetry of Baudelaire, Mallarmé, Verlaine, Maeterlinck—was that it was not only luxurious and effete but also impertinently obscure. It tried to elevate inaccuracy, indefiniteness, lack of eloquence into marks of esteem. Tolstoy's heavily documented attack on symbolist poetry (Chap. X) takes in, along with a difficult sonnet by Mallarmé and a perhaps tenuously rewarding lyric by Maeterlinck, several much easier pieces, including a prose poem by Baudelaire which one finds it almost impossible to believe offered any resistance at all to Tolstoy's penetration. "*Eh bien! cher ange,* je me figure que c'est vous! *Et il ferma les yeux et il lâcha la détente. La poupée fut nettement décapitée.*" The loosely associated ideas of the obscure and immoral in Tolstoy's treatment of symbolist poetry strongly invite us to understand that the flippancy is morally chaotic and, just in that sense, obscure too.[6] The broad thesis

[5] In one place (XV) he wants to make the infectiousness of art depend on "individuality" of feeling, on clarity, and on sincerity. The artist is infected by his own production; writes for himself. Hence he expresses something individual and something which because of its individuality is clear to his audience. The least little stroke, says Tolstoy, makes the difference (XII). But it is difficult to relate this norm to his broad demands for the religious emotion. Cf. his introduction to Semenov's *Peasant Stories.*

[6] The view could hardly be maintained with complete consistency. Tolstoy's Introduction to the *Works of de Maupassant,* 1894, for instance, seems to take Maupassant's intelligibility for granted, though laboring his immorality (*What is Art?* World's Classics ed., pp. 21, 26, 33, 39).

suggested, though never quite stated, is that the fault of obscurity in art is a fault of immorality—and conversely that immorality is a kind of obscurity. Obscurity means obscurantism, confusion, nihilism, the invocation of chaos.

Tolstoy had been reading Shakespeare all his life, in at least three languages, Russian, German, English. At the age of 75, five years after *What Is Art?*, provoked by an English article on "Shakespeare and the Working Classes," he re-read the whole of Shakespeare and responded with a tirade.[7] G. Wilson Knight in an *English Association Pamphlet, Shakespeare and Tolstoy*,[8] has perhaps done as much as anyone to explain some part of Tolstoy's views by relating them to the "rocklike simplicity" of Tolstoy himself as a master of the realistic novel. The symbolic technique and verse conventions of the Elizabethan drama threw him off so badly that he was unable, for instance, to perceive that Shakespeare's characters speak at all differently from one another.

> [Shakespeare] is lacking in the chief, if not the sole, means of portraying character, which is individuality of language—that each person should speak in a way suitable to his own character. . . . All his characters speak, not a language of their own but always one and the same Shakespearian, affected, unnatural language, which not only could they not speak, but which no real people could ever have spoken anywhere.
>
> Lear raves just as Edgar does when feigning madness. Kent and the fool both speak alike. The words of one person can be put in the mouth of another, and by the character of the speech it is impossible to know who is speaking.
>
> The person [9] uttering these various thoughts becomes a mere phonograph of Shakespeare, deprived of any character of his own.

And the deplorable social values reflected in Shakespeare's writing—the feudal respect for kings and dukes, the disesteem of the working classes!

> The content of Shakespeare's plays . . . is the lowest, most vulgar view of life, which regards the external elevation of the great ones of the earth as a genuine superiority; despises the crowd, that is to say, the working classes; and repudiates not only religious, but even any humanitarian, efforts directed toward the alteration of the existing order of society.

The rejection both of Shakespeare's artful intentions and of his artless accomplishment comes near to being total.

[7] *Shakespeare and the Drama*, published in 1906, essay XVII in *Tolstoy on Art*, ed. Aylmer Maude (Boston, 1924).
[8] No. 88, April 1934.
[9] Hamlet.

The third and chief condition—sincerity—is totally absent in all Shakespeare's works. One sees in all of them an intentional artificiality; it is obvious that he is not in earnest but is playing with words.

Whatever people may say, however they may be enraptured by Shakespeare's works, whatever merits they may attribute to him, it is certain that he was not an artist, and that his works were not artistic productions. . . . Shakespeare may be anything you like—only not an artist.[1]

V

THE destruction of the idea "art for art's sake" and the reconstruction of art as a monitor and propagandist for the social process is the gist of Tolstoy's preachment, and this has been also the monotonous burden of subsequent Marxist criticism in Russia and the instructed echoes of this in English and American writing which sounded in the later 1920's and the 1930's. In Marxist writing the basic theme has received a fanatically detailed articulation according to the philosophy of dialectical materialism. Prominent features have been (1) an emphasis on class propaganda and revolutionary didacticism and on the ideological specifications of the total state; (2) a corresponding emphasis on the deterministic origins of art—the economic and social status (proletarian, bourgeois, pseudo-bourgeois, or aristocratic) of artists and artisans in various past eras. Party-line writers have occasionally paused to disclaim any simple deterministic view of art, and they have done this in the name of Marx himself, who said: "Certain periods of highest development of art stand in no direct connection with the general development of society, nor with the material basis and the skeleton structure of its organization."[2] Yet the general mood of Marxism and of other kinds of social criticism, even the most conservative, does not make much room for such refinements. Shakespeare appeared because "we were just in a financial position to afford" him; he "flourished in the atmosphere of buoyancy, exhilaration and the freedom of economic cares felt by the governing class, which is engendered by profit inflations."[3] Or, on

---

[1] To Tolstoy's credit stands the following contradictory anecdote. "Once, when his friend Chekhov came to see him when he was ill in bed, he pressed the latter's hand at parting and said, 'Good-bye, Anton Pavlovich. You know how fond I am of you and how I detest Shakespeare. Still, he did write better plays than you do'" (Aylmer Maude, *Tolstoy on Art*, Boston 1924, p. 19).

[2] Ralph Fox, *The Novel and the People* (1937), Chap. I, in Mark Schorer *et al.*, *Criticism, The Foundations of Modern Literary Judgment*, pp. 134-7.

[3] John Maynard Keynes, *A Treatise on Money* (New York, 1930), II, 154, quoted by Wellek and Warren, p. 102.

the contrary: "Shakespeare's tragic outlook on the world was consequential upon his being the dramatic expression of the feudal aristocracy, which in Elizabeth's day had lost their former dominant position." [4]

According to the Marxist theory, English poetry of the 19th century has in one way or another shown the growing isolation of the modern artist from the bourgeois machine culture in which he was for a time seductively protected, his increasing anarchic agony, and his effort to renounce the culture in ways which have been only mirror images of it. He has lacked a systematic revolutionary outlook, the real rationale of insurgency which would have made him something positive, an affirmatively proletarian artist. In the 20th century T. S. Eliot is said to make the last decadent gesture of the mentality which has turned away from the historico-social reality and sought refuge in the ivory tower of poetry and beauty pure. Among the Russians, the socialist Georgi Plekhanov in his *Art and Society*, 1912–1913 (English translation, 1936), and Leon Trotsky in *Literature and Revolution*, 1923, have elaborated this basic view of the modern poet's isolation from reality. And Christopher Caudwell in *Illusion and Reality*,[5] 1937, has made the applications to English literature. In a call to the barricades which echoed for twenty years, Lenin cried out: "Down with supermen-litterateurs. . . . Literature must become a component part of the organized, planned, unified Socialist party work." [6]

Seen from the genetic point of view, Marxist criticism has some curious affinities. The professional literary student will scarcely be horrified by the bourgeois origin of a given literature; he is not likely to evaluate writers according to the degree of their integration in a totalitarian process, or to believe that the Bohemian, the *poète maudit*, the untrammeled genius is necessarily an artistic bungler. Yet the Marxist program for literature—if one leaves out of account its hortatory violence—is able to take its place with some comfort as an application of the historical idea which purely literary scholars in the tradition of Thomas Warton and Hippolyte Taine have worked out so successfully, for their own purposes, during the past 200 years.[7] The specifically Marxist genetic approach takes its place quite gracefully as one of that numerous kind in literary studies which has attended to social and economic origins—to the mark upon his work made by the professional status of the dithyrambic tragedian, the *Minnesänger*, the court dramatist, the Grubstreet hack, or the affluent 19th-century periodical

---

[4] Anatoli V. Lunacharsky, in *The Listener*, December 27, 1934, quoted by Wellek and Warren, p. 102.

[5] See Chapter VI, "English Poets: The Decline of Capitalism," reproduced in Mark Schorer *et al.*, pp. 125–33.

[6] Quoted by W. V. O'Connor, *An Age of Criticism*, p. 115.

[7] Cf. *post* Chapter 24.

novelist.[8] It is less than a paradox that the Marxist critic, in all the severity of his logic, should have driven this method of the modern literary student to a conclusion that completely destroys the literary viewpoint.

Seen as a demand on the character of literature itself, Marxist criticism prescribes the broad picture of social reality, the novel of sound views, the social document, the party-line mimesis, the blue-print for social planning. And it equally proscribes the lyric cry, the personal relation, the individually intricate symbol, the detachment of contemplation, and any engagement that either bypasses or transcends the totalitarian social responsibility. It does not believe in the work of art. There is no good social art of the kind it prescribes. Under Marxism society itself "becomes the work of art." [9]

VI

In America the idea of a socially activist literature appears during the first decades of the 20th century with the "muckraking" movement (of which Upton Sinclair's *Mammonart*, 1924, may stand as the sufficient symbol) and after that in the overtly Marxist criticism of the later twenties and the thirties—the work of such writers as Michael Gold, editor of the *New Masses*, Joseph Freeman, editor of the anthology *Proletarian Literature in the United States*, 1935, and V. F. Calverton, editor of the *Modern Quarterly*. Here we meet a barefaced rehearsal of the whole canon of Marxist ideas—much about the pessimism and decay of the middle class, the inferiority of the "bourgeois sexual code," the modern sell-out of human values to the "burgher," much about the "creative role" of the worker and the need of the novelist to keep up with "the vanguard of the Proletariat." We hear that the experiments of Joyce, Eliot, and Cummings are misguided and incommunicative, that on the contrary Emerson had confidence in the common man, that Whitman enjoyed a kinship with workers and farmers and had glimpses of a collective society.[1] A major monument was Vernon Louis Parrington's three-volume *Main Currents in American Thought* (1927–1930), where "thought" is equated with literature, and the sufficient principle of economic determinism receives a value shading that is "liberal" and "Jef-

[8] Cf. Wellek and Warren, pp. 93–5. Brander Matthews, "The Economic Interpretation of Literary History," in his *Gateways to Literature and Other Essays* (New York, 1912), is a good American instance of this kind of inquiry.

[9] Edmund Wilson, quoted by W. V. O'Connor, *An Age of Criticism*, p. 126.

[1] W. V. O'Connor, *An Age of Criticism*, pp. 119–24, quoting, among other works, Calverton's *The Newer Spirit* (1925) and *The Liberation of American Literature* (1932), Granville Hicks's "The Crisis in Criticism" in the *New Masses* (1933) and *The Great Tradition: An Interpretation of American Literature Since the Civil War* (1933), and Bernard Smith's *Forces in American Criticism* (1939).

fersonian." [2] Parrington gives us the following flowers of the economic and realist spirit in criticism.

> The problem of Poe, fascinating as it is, lies quite outside the main current of American thought, and it may be left to the psychologist and the belletrist with whom it belongs.[3]

> Hawthorne was the extreme and finest expression of the refined alienation from reality that in the end palsied the creative mind of New England.[4]

> In his subtle psychological inquires, . . . [Henry James] remained shut up within his own skull-pan.[5]

Marxism and the forms of social criticism more closely related to it have never had any real concern with literature and literary problems. In this country the cause enlisted some keen journalistic and literary minds. But a number of them, like Max Eastman as editor of *The Masses*, avoided sociology in their literary criticism. Eastman shied away from doctrinal and scientific claims for literature and worked up a theory of vivid sensory realization that belongs rather in the tradition of art for art's sake. Edmund Wilson in *Axel's Castle*, 1931, made gestures acknowledging the social responsibility of the artist but only as if in atonement for his having dwelt at such length among the mysteries of symbolism. As early as the anthology acclaiming *Proletarian Literature* in 1935, the editors of the *Partisan Review* were observing a flow of "gush" and "invective," in place of analysis, and the exercise of Marxism as a "sentiment" rather than a "science." James T. Farrell's *A Note on Literary Criticism*, 1936, is a critique by an "amateur Marxist" of the party-line simplifications. By 1939 it was possible for the *Partisan* editor Philip Rahv to write an essay under the title "Proletarian Literature: A Political Autopsy." [6] Marxist naturalism persists in American letters today less as a proclaimed cause than as a deeply rooted sympathy (a Gnostic utopianism) ready with each shift in political or literary dialectics to exert itself in a new stratagem. Perhaps the notion of "myth," despite its Germanic, Jungian, and quasi-religious orientation, is the latest of these.[7]

[2] Parrington's Introduction to the first volume and E. H. Eby's Introduction to the posthumous third volume, quoted in W. V. O'Connor, *An Age of Criticism*, pp. 119–20; see also p. 123, the passages next quoted from Parrington.
[3] *Main Currents in American Thought* (New York: Harcourt, Brace and Company, Inc., 1927–30), II, 58.
[4] II, 450.
[5] III, 241.
[6] *Southern Review*, IV (Winter, 1939), 616–28. Cf. Morton D. Zabel, *Literary Opinion in America* (New York, 1951), p. 36; Charles I. Glicksberg, *American Literary Criticism* (New York, 1952), pp. 46–52.
[7] Cf. *post* Chapter 31.

VII

THE main critical issue raised by the tradition of socio-realism—and this was apparent at least as far back as the indignation of Tolstoy over symbolist poetry—is that of "expression" and "communication." The bringing together of these two terms, one so strongly invoking the mind and inspiration of the artist, and the other so heavily entailing the receptivity and demands of the audience (what audience? communication to whom?), is today an especially important problem for the critic who believes in objective aesthetic values. But even the discussion of the problem (not to mention its solution) involves ideas of dramatic inclusiveness and artistic detachment which lie far beyond the range-finding sensitivity of the propagandist programs.

So far as the problem of poetic communication is peculiarly a social one, the opposing energies have been defined in our time with the most original insight by the philosopher Ortega y Gasset, in two complementary works. On the one hand he describes *The Revolt of the Masses*, a cultural phenomenon far more complicated than anything envisaged by the Marxist mind, and appearing in one of its aspects as a vast increase in the number and confidence of uneducated readers.

> Today we are witnessing the triumphs of a hyperdemocracy. . . . the present-day writer, when he takes his pen in hand to treat a subject which he has studied deeply, has to bear in mind that the average reader, who has never concerned himself with this subject, if he reads does so with the view, not of learning something from the writer, but rather, of pronouncing judgment on him when he is not in agreement with the commonplaces that the said reader carries in his head. If the individuals who make up the mass believed themselves specially qualified, it would be a case merely of personal error, not a sociological subversion. *The characteristic of the hour is that the commonplace mind, knowing itself to be commonplace, has the assurance to proclaim the rights of the commonplace and to impose them wherever it will.* . . . The mass crushes beneath it everything that is different, everything that is excellent, individual, qualified and select. Anybody who is not like everybody, who does not think like everybody, runs the risk of being eliminated.[8]

And on the other hand, there appears the exclusiveness and withdrawal of the modern artist in search of a fresh vision, a process which Ortega calls *The Dehumanization of Art*.

[8] *The Revolt of the Masses*, Chapter I (Mentor Book, 1952), p. 12. By permission of W. W. Norton & Company, Inc. The Spanish version appeared in 1930.

Romanticism was the prototype of a popular style. First-born of democracy, it was coddled by the masses.

Modern art, on the other hand will always have the masses against it. It is essentially unpopular; moreover, it is antipopular.

. . . . the split occurs in a deeper layer than that on which differences of personal taste reside. It is not that the majority does not *like* the art of the young and the minority likes it, but that the majority, the masses, do not *understand* it.

But such a thing cannot be done after a hundred years of adulation of the masses and apotheosis of the people. Accustomed to ruling supreme, the masses feel that the new art, which is the art of a privileged aristocracy of finer senses, endangers their rights as men. Whenever the new Muses present themselves, the masses bristle.[9]

Marxism considers modern vulgar art to be a feat of the bourgeoisie, and the revolt of the romantic artist to be a weak anarchic effort which mirrors in negative the same standards. The literary critic, or the metaphysician, of more classical perspective is likely to look on the Marxist alternative as itself a mirror revolution of socialized materialism against privately competitive materialism. In the crudity both of its determinism and of its inconsistent propagandism, the socio-realistic tradition of literary criticism has on the whole contributed little to an understanding of the relation which universality bears to individuality in artistic expression.

SUPPLEMENT

A laissez faire economy such as was dominant in the recent past is basically hostile to great art. "As in economics, so in art: laissez-faire within a capitalist economy (or within any economy) merely abandons art to the chances of unrestricted competition, and the devil take the hindmost. It means that art becomes one more commodity on the free market, and that to succeed it must practice all the wiles of salesmanship—mass appeal, sex appeal, adulteration, and the sacrifice of quality to cheapness." (Herbert Read, "Culture and Liberty," *Nation*, CLII, April 2, 1941, p. 438). On the other hand, a general-welfare-society, such as has been lately envisioned widely is, I believe, in principle, fertile soil for the realization of the ideal of art. . . .

[9] *The Dehumanization of Art and Notes on the Novel*, trans. Helene Weyl (Princeton: Princeton University Press, 1948), pp. 5–7. Cf. Q. D. Leavis, *Fiction and the Reading Public* (London, 1932).

Something of this sort, a beginning at least in certain directions, seems to have happened in Russia as it has struggled to its feet, following revolution, in recent decades. The arts there have had a position not unlike that in the best "organic" societies. They have been integrated with institutions enshrining a widely supported unity of belief. They have had not only official but immense popular support. The artist has been held in the highest esteem. His training has been anxiously attended to. He himself has enjoyed great respect and prestige. He has dedicated himself to the enrichment of the life of all the people. Commercialism between artist and audience has been eliminated and the disposition toward official interference, although certainly far from nonexistent, has been felt adversely far less than is commonly believed. The arts have been carried to the factories and farms and the remotest villages, and the great figures of art, such as the Pushkins and the Gorkys, are among the greatest national heroes. Nor have the arts been made the tool of merely "nationalistic" interests, although the relation of the arts to the life of the people has been kept immediate and evident. Traveling historical museums and theaters have penetrated into all parts of the country, the arts of all mankind have been displayed and studied, and sometimes a non-Russian artist has become as great a hero as the greatest of Russians, e.g., Shakespeare as great as Pushkin.

—D. W. Gotshalk, *Art and the Social Order* (Chicago: The University of Chicago Press, 1947), pp. 236–8. Copyright (1947) by the University of Chicago. A footnote on p. 238 cites as authorities for the view presented a generous selection of volumes dated in the 1930's.

CHAPTER 22

ART FOR ART'S SAKE

§ *aesthetic autonomy, early modern hints, German idealism, an ambiguous ground, Benjamin Constant, Bourbon restoration, Madame de Staël, Cousin and Jouffroy, "German aesthetics," freedom, art for art's sake, a commonplace—II. an atmospheric idea, E. A.* Poe, *blend of sources,* Philosophy of Composition, Poetic Principle, *diffuse Kantian elements, "Supernal Beauty," beauty an effect, different from passion and truth, the fate of M. Valdemar, importance of Poe—III. affinity for Baudelaire, beauty and evil, morality penetrates art, Poe and human anomaly, flowers of evil, "Epilogue," original sin, the "magic" of art,* Eloge du Maquillage, *art not illusion, Parnassian formalism—IV. aestheticism in England, Arnold's judgment, Swinburne's* Poems and Ballads (*1866*), *revolt from "middle class" moralism, "practical aestheticism,"* Wilde, De Profundis, *dandyism, "art," "beauty," "sensation," "passion,"* Pater, The Renaissance, *"gem-like flame," theory of moral subject matter (*Ruskin*), aesthetic counter theories: (*1*) "slim gilded feet," (*2*) indifference to subject, "negative capability" (*Keats*),* Poe *again, vita contemplativa—V. pure "form,"* Wilde, Intentions, *craftsmanship, verse technique, English "Parnassians," rondeau, ballade, etc., poetry and other arts again, Gautier's* Emaux et Camées, *Pater,* Améthystes *and Intaglios, Whistler's "Arrangement in Black and Gray," Roger Fry and Clive Bell, exclusiveness and abstraction, "significant form," warning for literary theory—VI. Whistler,* Gentle Art of Making Enemies, *nature imitates art,* Florentine Nights, *Wilde,* Decay of Lying (*anthology of passages*), *impressionist criticism,* Lamb, Hazlitt, Sainte-Beuve, *et al., soul among masterpieces, sensibility,* Wilde, The Critic as Artist, *the argument full circle: Arnold and Wilde the sons of* F. Schlegel §

475

T HE REVOLUTIONARY VINDICATION OF POETRY BY GERMAN ROMANTICS and their followers resulted during the 19th century, as we have been seeing, in at least three main types of poetic theory which made claims upon ethics and politics. These were the Shelleyan and Carlylean rhapsodic retort to scientism, the Arnoldian neo-classic idealism, and the socio-realistic propagandism generated in Germany, Russia, and France. But the reassertion of poetic rights could take yet another turn, antithetic to the didacticism inherent in all those other three. Poetry— or art in general—might draw off by itself and be content with an emphatic assertion of autonomy—its own kind of intrinsic worth, to be understood and savored by its own devotees. It could be set up as a legitimate pursuit, apart from, and perhaps even in defiance of, the rival norms of ethics and politics.

This notion of art as a terminal value had appeared even during antiquity in the alternative offered the poet, *aut prodesse aut delectare*. It had gained a gradual and subtle emphasis in all those Renaissance versions of classic theory which reversed the usual formula to say that pleasing was somehow more important than teaching or was somehow the end aimed at through teaching. And such approaches to a theory of aesthetic autonomy gained greatly during the 18th century as literary theory first retreated from classical didacticism and then, after following Leibnizian and Lockean psychological lines, reacted against these too, shifting an emphasis on sensory and emotive pleasure toward various conceptions of "taste," inner sense, the absolute beauty of order and harmony, and pleasure without desire. The ideas of Shaftesbury, Hutcheson and other British aesthetic writers were paralleled in France and Germany by Diderot, Sulzer, Mendelssohn, and many others.[1] The transcendental synthesis of Kant's *Critique of Judgment* summarized all such trends and first lent weighty metaphysical authority to the pure aesthetic claim. The mythopoeic and symbolist doctrines of German idealist critics, by generally strengthening the position of art, provided an area of mobilization not only for the didactic claims which we have seen but for the characteristically 19th-century reaction to didacticism which moved under the aegis of art for art's sake. Either development was a more or less legitimate, if simplistic, move from the German positions. There was a fundamental uncertainty in the claim of art to create meanings, to mark out pathways of knowledge, which led perhaps inevitably toward multiple forms both of didacticism and of autonomism.

The French *littérateur* Benjamin Constant, attaching himself to

---

[1] Diderot's article *"Beau"* in the *Dictionnaire Encyclopédique*, 1751; J. G. Sulzer, *Allgemeine Theorie der Schönen Künste*, 1771–1774; Moses Mendelssohn, *Die Morgenstunden*, 1785. See Wellek, *History* I, 54, 149; and *ante* Chapter 13, pp. 276–7.

German literary circles in the year 1804, gives us in his *Journal intime*
(not published until many years later) a casual glimpse of how the
phrase "art for art's sake" may have begun to develop out of Kantian
doctrine in Weimar-Jena discussions.

> Schiller calls. He is a man of keen mind in his art but almost
> wholly the poet. . . . I have a visit with [Henry Crabb] Robin-
> son, pupil of Schelling's. His work on the *Esthetics* of Kant has
> some very forceful ideas. *L'art pour l'art* without purpose, for
> all purpose perverts art. But art attains the purpose that it does
> not have.[2]

With the return to Paris of intellectualist emigrés (among them Constant and his friend Madame de Staël) and the Bourbon restoration in
1814, began the era of a new and vaguely Kantian aesthetic in France.
In the account of Kantian thought contained in Madame de Staël's *De
l'Allemagne*,[3] first brought to Paris from England in 1813, in the exciting
lectures of Victor Cousin at the Sorbonne during 1816–1818,[4] and in
those of his pupil Jouffroy, the key ideas, or at least the key rubrics,
of the new aesthetics were first popularized. On a tide of vaguely
simplified Kantian thinking such terms as "German aesthetics," "Kant's
aesthetics," "freedom," "disinterestedness," "pure art," "pure beauty,"
"form," and "genius" were floated into currency, and along with them
the term "art for art's sake." It appeared in print perhaps for the first
time in a journalistic skirmish of 1833.[5] In the Preface to his *Premières
poésies*, 1832, Gautier, it is true, was able to pronounce his defiance of
economists, utilitarians, utopians, Saint-Simonians, and all others of
their purposeful kind without once invoking the term. ("What end
does this book serve? It serves the end of being beautiful?") But in his
article entitled *"Du Beau dans l'art,"* appearing in the *Revue des
deux mondes* during 1847, *l'art pour l'art* seems to enjoy the status of a
recently established commonplace—"cette formule devenue *célèbre par
des polémiques.*"[6]

II

It is not, however, in the history of the term "art for art's sake" only,
nor in the French school of aesthetic thinking only, that we may observe

---

[2] D. Melagari, *Journal Intime de Benjamin Constant* (Paris, 1895), p. 7, entry
for February 10, 1804. Quoted by John Wilcox, "The Beginnings of *L'Art pour
l'Art*," *JAAC*, XI (June, 1953), 360.

[3] *De l'Allemagne* (Paris, 1820), II, 290 ff. Wilcox, p. 365.

[4] Cousin's lectures were edited by his pupils from his class notes and printed
twenty years later, 1836–42. See the exposition by Wilcox, pp. 367–8.

[5] Hippolyte Fortoul, in *La Revue Encyclopédique*, LIX, 109. Wilcox, p. 371.

[6] Wilcox, pp. 371, 376. Cf. Gautier's Preface to *Mademoiselle de Maupin*,
1834.

the development of that formula. The new idea spread out pervasively and subtly; it was atmospheric. Shortly before the middle of the century, one of the most theatrical presentations occurs in the essays and reviews of the American Gothic story-teller and poet Edgar Allan Poe. Poe's critical origins were at first confusedly Coleridgean and Wordsworthian, with considerable borrowing from the English translation of A. W. Schlegel's *Dramatic Lectures*.[7] He cherished ideas of lyric brevity, unity of interest, "indefinite" pleasure, music, beauty. Later, on reviewing a volume of the new phrenology, he picked up a physico-psychological support for his sympathies, in the notion of a "Faculty of Ideality—which is the sentiment of Poesy." After 1840 he apparently became acquainted with Shelley's rhapsodic defence of romantic imagination. Only in his last efforts, the genetic tour de force entitled *The Philosophy of Composition* (or how he went about thinking up *The Raven*) and his last lecture, posthumously published in 1850, *The Poetic Principle*, does the full luxuriance of Poe's opinion bloom.[8] We discover pronounced, if diffuse and vaporous, Kantian elements in Poe's system: a division of the world of mind into pure intellect, taste, and moral sense (with taste the intermediary between the other two); a Kantian lack of esteem for mere reproduction of "beautiful" sounds, colors, and odors; a general dreamy volume of enthusiasm for the beautiful and the sublime and for the ethereal or supernal—for "Supernal Beauty." (Tennyson [9] is the noblest poet who ever lived, because the most "ethereal.")

> Inspired by an ecstatic prescience of the glories beyond the grave, we struggle, by multiform combinations among the things and thoughts of Time, to attain a portion of that Loveliness whose very elements, perhaps, appertain to eternity alone.

> *That* pleasure which is at once the most pure, the most elevating, and the most intense, is derived, I maintain, from the contemplation of the Beautiful. In the contemplation of Beauty we alone find it possible to attain that pleasurable elevation, or excitement, *of the soul*, which we recognize as the Poetic

[7] Cf. Albert J. Lubell, "Poe and A. W. Schlegel," *JEGP*, LII (January, 1953), 1–12.

[8] See Poe's *Critical Essays*, ed. F. C. Prescott (New York, 1909), pp. xxx, 9–10; Floyd Stovall, "Poe's Debt to Coleridge," *Studies in English*, No. 10, *The University of Texas Bulletin*, July 8, 1930, pp. 70–127; Marvin Laser, "The Growth and Structure of Poe's Concept of Beauty," *ELH*, XV (March, 1948), 69–84.

[9] Poe's book reviews by and large look down upon the poetry of the 16th and 17th centuries. Poetry began for him with Coleridge, Shelley, and Keats (Prescott, p. xxix). The norm of lovely melancholy, developed so dramatically in *The Philosophy of Composition*, appears earlier in his Drake-Halleck review (*Southern Literary Messenger*, April, 1836) along with the dogma that everything ludicrous is "utterly at war with the Poetic Sentiment" and with the sentiments of the "mystical" and the "august," which raise "fancy" to imagination (Laser, pp. 73–4).

Sentiment. . . . I make Beauty, therefore—using the word as inclusive of the Sublime—I make Beauty the province of the poem.[1]

But where is "beauty" located? Where but in the very experience of itself? "When, indeed, men speak of Beauty they mean, precisely, not a quality. . . . but an effect—they refer, in short, just to that intense and pure elevation of *soul . . .* which is experienced in consequence of contemplating 'the beautiful.'"[2] A certain amalgam or association of subject matters—the beautiful and the melancholy when these are "rhythmically created"[3] in a poem—produces in the reader that pleasurable elevation of soul which itself should justly be known as beauty.[4] Such devotion to "supernal beauty" entails a resolute disapproval of "passion" and, of course, a strict anti-didacticism.

> The manifestation of the [aesthetic] Principle is always found in *an elevating excitement of the Soul*—quite independent of that passion which is the intoxication of the Heart—or of that Truth which is the satisfaction of the Reason.

> For, in regard to Passion, alas! its tendency is to degrade, rather than to elevate the Soul.

> I allude to the heresy of *The Didactic*. . . . We Americans, especially, have patronised this happy idea; and we Bostonians, very especially, have developed it in full.[5]

There is much to Poe's credit in these latter Kantian clauses. Still the general picture is hazy. Ethereal vagueness and melancholy, evaporations of languorous and pallid loveliness wreathe the figure of Poe. His poems—*Ulalume, The Raven, Al Aaraaf, The City in the Sea, The Sleepers, Fairy-Land*—are softened and simplified counterparts of Coleridge's *Kubla Khan, The Ancient Mariner, Christabel,* and *Youth and Age.* Poe's theoretical essays bear the same relation to chapters of Coleridge's *Biographia.* Neo-classic theory, in a way peculiar to itself, had rigidified or petrified, then dilapidated. Romantic theory did not do that. But in some of its inheritors it did liquefy or even vaporize. Poe's ideas are Kantian and Coleridgean aesthetic undergoing the fate of M. Valdemar. These writers deserved and got better epigonists. But Poe has become one of the most conspicuous, and his very existence

---

[1] *The Poetic Principle.*

[2] *The Philosophy of Composition.*

[3] "I would define, in brief, the Poetry of words as *The Rhythmical Creation of Beauty*" (*The Poetic Principle*). The emphasis on musicality and rhythm in Poe's last essays no doubt owes something to Shelley.

[4] See the analysis of this circularity by Charles C. Walcutt, "The Logic of Poe," *College English,* II (February, 1941), 438–44.

[5] *The Poetic Principle.*

says something of the era which they ushered in. It is possible to rate Poe up or down. It is difficult to avoid him. His criticism, said Henry James, is "probably the most complete and exquisite specimen of *provincialism* ever prepared for the edification of men." [6] He was, says T. S. Eliot, "not only an heroically courageous critic . . . but a critic of the first rank." [7]

III

It is a source of wonder to comparatists, but an inescapable fact, that the "exquisite provincialism" of Poe should have been highly relished by a spirit so sophisticated as Charles Baudelaire. The literary connection is underscored by the biographical: the sympathy to the degree of identification which Baudelaire felt for Poe, the reading of his own fate in Poe's supposedly aristocratic and feudal flight from American popular culture and in his supposedly ratiocinative discipline of mind so luridly contrasting to his nervous weakness, his dipsomania and wandering.

The title of Baudelaire's collected poems, *Les Fleurs du Mal*, stands as a ready brief symbol for the aesthetic devotion, the belief in beauty despite evil—in beauty through evil—which makes a large part in the reputation of Baudelaire. Yet Baudelaire was a critical essayist and journalist whose ideas one can hardly constrict within any of the simpler versions of art for art's sake. On the issue, baldly stated, whether art can escape the claims of morality, Baudelaire had a complex view. He alternates between the claim that his own poetry is *"un livre d'art pur"* and the opposite claim that it is a moral statement.[8] In other connections he comes out often enough against the current formulations of pure-art theory.

> The childish utopianism of the school of *art for art's sake,* in ruling out morals . . . was doomed to sterility. Art for art's sake was a flagrant defiance of human nature. On the authority of the higher and universal principles of life itself, we must convict the movement of heresy.[9]

> The feverish passion for art cankers and devours all else. And this . . . means the disappearance of art itself. The wholeness

---

[6] *Hawthorne* (New York, 1879), p. 62. James refers specifically to Poe's criticism of his American contemporaries.

[7] Review of *Israfel* by Hervey Allen, in *The Nation and Athenaeum*, XLI (May 2, 1927), 219.

[8] Marcel Françon, "Poe et Baudelaire," *PMLA*, LX (September, 1945), 841.

[9] *L'Art Romantique*, in *Oeuvres Complètes de Charles Baudelaire*, ed. Jacques Crépet, III (Paris, 1925), 184.

of the human being disintegrates. The specialization of a single faculty contracts toward nothingness.[1]

Morality does not appear with a formal title. Morality simply penetrates and blends itself with art as completely as with life itself. The poet is a moralist in spite of himself, simply through the overflowing abundance of his nature.[2]

Yet it would have been one thing for a Shelley, an Arnold, or a Tolstoy to have uttered statements like these; it was another thing for Baudelaire. Take them in the context of the essays in which they appear and of other essays by Baudelaire, and we see that here is a different enough accent from that of the didactic defenders of poetry. The accent, despite the concern for morals, is in a very special way on art itself. Perhaps the shade of emphasis comes from the cumulative coloring of passages rather than from any definitely abstract key terms.

It is imagination which has taught man the moral values of color, shape, sound, and perfumes. At the beginning of the world, imagination created analogy and metaphor. Imagination dissolves all creation. Remassing and reordering her materials by principles which come out of the depths of the human soul, imagination makes a new world, even a new realm of sensory experience. And as imagination has created this world (one may say this, I think, even in a religious sense), it is appropriate that the same faculty should govern it.[3]

Is there any such thing as a pernicious work of art? There is. It is one which distorts the patterns of living reality. . . . If a novel or a play is well made, it can be an invitation to nobody to deviate from the law of nature. The first requirement for a healthy art is a belief in an ordered whole of experience. I challenge anybody to show me a single work of imagination which satisfies the requirements of beauty and is at the same time pernicious.[4]

A passage from one of the three essays which Baudelaire wrote on Poe shows something of how the doctrine of moral order in art might relate to the artistic use of materials of a strikingly disordered sort. "That peculiar genius" of Poe's, Baudelaire writes, "that unique temperament enabled him—in a style at once impeccable and horribly compelling—to unfold the image of irregularity in the moral order. Let me repeat: no-

[1] *L'Art Romantique, Oeuvres*, III, 296.
[2] *L'Art Romantique, Oeuvres*, III, 382.
[3] *Salon de 1859*, in *Curiosités Esthétiques, Oeuvres Complètes* ed. Jacques Crépet, II (Paris, 1923), 274.
[4] *L'Art Romantique, Oeuvres*, III, 284.

body has had a more magical success in the portrayal of the human anomaly." [5] The magic of the anomaly, the burnished glow of perversion, the flowers out of evil, seem intrinsic to the Baudelairean vision of poetry as moral expression.

Epilogue

With heart at rest I climbed the citadel's
  Steep height, and saw the city as from a tower,
Hospital, brothel, prison, and such hells,

Where evil comes up softly like a flower,
  Thou knowest, O Satan, patron of my pain,
Not for vain tears I went up at that hour;

But, like an old and faithful lecher, fain
  To drink delight of that enormous trull
Whose hellish beauty makes me young again.

Whether thou sleep, with heavy vapors full,
  Sodden with day, or, new appareled, stand
In gold-laced veils of evening beautiful,

I love thee, infamous city! Harlots and
  Hunted have pleasures of their own to give,
The vulgar herd can never understand. [6]

The speaker asserts, without shame, his love for the infamous city, the enormous trull. Without shame? Yes, but not without something else, akin to shame, a luridly stated awareness that here is something shameful. There is more moral interest here than in certain simpler kinds of naturalistic celebration.

The German romantic and the Coleridgean versions of the creative power of poetry had moved toward closing the distance between art and nature, or toward elevating art into a higher and more ideal nature. Art was opposed to the artificial. In some instances the enterprise was to return art to the "nature" of a primitive unspoiled honesty. Such theory was part either of a radical optimism about the progress that could be made by the human imagination, or of an ironic self-assurance in the face of cosmic insufficiency. The romantic imagination did not believe in original sin. Nature was good. Quite the contrary with Baudelaire. The integration of which he speaks in some of the passages quoted above was to be a kind of preternatural transcendence—the "magic" of art—even if diabolical. The morality which Baudelaire conceives is something to

---

[5] *Edgar Poe, Sa Vie et Ses Oeuvres,* in *Histoires Extraordinaires par Edgar Poe, Oeuvres,* ed. Jacques Crépet, VIII (Paris 1932), xxviii–xxix.
[6] The translation of Arthur Symons.

which art may characteristically attain—but not naked nature. The poetry of Baudelaire despises vegetable fertility, clumps of trees and bushes. His ideal city has no plant life.

"Most false ideas about the beautiful," says Baudelaire in his essay *In Praise of Face Paint (Eloge du Maquillage),*[7] "arise from the false idea of morality current during the 18th century. In that age the foundation, source, and archetype of all good and all possible beauty was seen in Nature. In the universal blindness of the age the denial of original sin was a thing that passed without notice."

> Nature! That infallible goddess! It is she who has given us parricide and cannibalism and a thousand other abominations which it would be indelicate even to name. On the other hand we have philosophy (I mean right philosophy) and religion. It is these that tell us to take care of our parents when they are old and poor. (Nature, the voice of our self-interest, tells us to bludgeon them.) Take a critical look at what is natural, the actions and desires of the purely natural man. The view is ghastly. Absolutely everything that is beautiful and noble proceeds from reasonable reflection.

These general principles afford Baudelaire the opportunity to erect an extravagantly gilded little shrine around the civilized figure of the well made-up woman.

> It is the right of woman and her duty to give herself a magical finish, a supernatural lustre. She is expected to astonish and charm us. She is a kind of idol, and she ought to gild herself (*se dorer*) until she is a fit object of our adoration (*pour être adorée*).
>
> Rouge and mascara are the symbols of a heightened, a preternaturally intense mode of existence. The dark framing renders the gaze more profound and individual; it deepens the character of the eye as a window opened into infinity. The hectic color on the cheek increases the brilliance of the eye and creates in a feminine countenance of sufficient loveliness the mysteriously passionate look of the priestess.

Baudelaire is at pains to point out that he is not talking about art as mimesis. "I am not trying to assign art the sterile function of imitating nature." Even less, if possible, can there be any question of art as illusion. "There is no point at all in trying to hide cosmetic or make it pass unnoticed. It ought to proclaim itself—if not boastfully, at least with a de-

---

[7] This appeared in *Le Figaro*, December 3, 1863, as No. 11 in a series entitled *Le Peintre de la Vie Moderne*. The text may be found in *L'Art Romantique, Oeuvres Complètes*, ed. Jacques Crépet, III (Paris, 1925), 95–100.

gree of candor." Art, then, is a magical enhancement. But of what? The end of the argument may entail a certain contradiction of the initially dark view of nature. The anciently enlisted virgins of Crotona play a new role, it is true. But they have not been entirely eliminated from the theory. "Cosmetic artifice cannot improve ugliness. It can only serve what is to begin with beautiful." Baudelaire, in being less than a pure theorist of pure art, is one of the witnesses for the theory most worthy of our respectful attention.

With Baudelaire, the main fight for "art" in 19th-century France was won. After him, the simply aesthetic assertion fritters away into *Parnassien* formalism, the exoticism, the intricate versification of Leconte de Lisle or Théodore de Banville.[8] The main line of French poetry and poetics, with Verlaine and even more with Mallarmé, advances into subtler themes of musical intimation, ironic finesse, and symbol—above all else, symbol.[9] The simpler campaign of art for art's sake during the second half of the 19th century is carried with most flourish into the new territory of England.

IV

AESTHETICISM in England, says a recent writer, "was not a sudden development: the nature of the trend from Keats through Tennyson and Dante Gabriel Rossetti was, even in Arnold's mid-career, not unapparent to the critic who passed the judgment on the great Romantics. The insistence that poetry must be judged as 'criticism of life' is the same critic's reaction to the later Romantic tradition; it puts the stress where it seemed to him that it most needed to be put."[1] Arnold himself has left us such statements as the following in his Preface to Wordsworth (1879):

> Morals are often treated in a narrow and false fashion; . . . they grow tiresome to some of us. We find attraction, at times, even in a poetry of revolt against them; in a poetry which might take for its motto Omar Khayam's words: "Let us make up in the tavern for the time which we have wasted in the mosque." Or we find attraction in a poetry indifferent to them; in a poetry where the contents may be what they will, but where the form is studied and exquisite. We delude ourselves in either case; and the best cure for our delusion is to let our minds rest upon that

[8] The idea of art for art's sake can be seen, of course, in other places. It mixes with realistic theory, for instance, in the letters of Flaubert. See Gilbert and Kuhn, pp. 490–8.

[9] Cf. *post* Chapter 26.

[1] F. R. Leavis, *Scrutiny*, VII (December, 1938), 324–5.

great and inexhaustible word *life*, until we learn to enter into its meaning. A poetry of revolt against moral ideas is a poetry of revolt against life; a poetry of indifference towards moral ideas is a poetry of indifference towards life.[2]

An abrupt separation of the artist from the "middle-class" world, and from "middle-class" moralism [3]—or, as it might be conceived in a somewhat different way, his revolt from subservience to the masses and the norms of industrial civilization—was signalized in England by the publication of Swinburne's *Poems and Ballads*, a volume read aloud with excited devotion by Saintsbury and other undergraduate literati at Oxford in the fall of 1866.[4] The "lithe limbs," the "strange, great sins," the *laus veneris*, the dolors, were the more musically vague and voluptuous counterpart in English of the evils which had recently flowered in France, the paganism of Gautier, the satanism of Baudelaire. During the next three decades the theoretical watchwords of the movement were sounded most loudly by three authors: by Pater, by Whistler (who took legal action against the moralist criticism of Ruskin), and by Wilde. The essays of Wilde collected as *Intentions* in 1891 form perhaps the most imposing theoretical monument.

On the side of "practical aestheticism," the artist's acting out of his theory in his own life, the later phase shows us some repetitions and some prettifications of the earlier. Baudelaire's explorations of vice, his decline, and early death are matched in England by Wilde's perversion, his trial, disaster, and death. "I treated art," he says in his *De Profundis*, "as the supreme reality and life as a mere mode of fiction." [5] De Quincey's essay "On Murder, Considered as One of the Fine Arts" is paralleled from the life in Stevenson's "Villon, Student, Poet and Housebreaker" and in the study "Pen, Pencil, and Poison" which Wilde includes in his *Intentions*. A conspicuous feature of the movement is a kind of aesthetic dandyism, an exquisiteness of dress and carriage no less than of the inner life—men in velvet jackets and knee breeches, with a flower in the hand,[6] women in lovely, flowing Pre-Raphaelite gowns. These pursue the vocation of adoring beauty.

The theory of the art object itself during the English phase dwelt intently on the terms "art" and "beauty." "Beauty" was something very pure, very different from everything else. So was "art." "Beauty," said

---

[2] *Essays in Criticism, Second Series* (London, 1888), p. 144.

[3] In France, the enemies during this period were the positive philosophy of Comte and the "bourgeois" society of the Second Empire.

[4] Cf. Dorothy Richardson, "Saintsbury and Art for Art's Sake in England," *PMLA*, LIX (March, 1944), 245–6.

[5] *De Profundis* (New York, 1950), p. 77.

[6] "With a poppy or a lily in your medieval hand" (W. S. Gilbert, *Patience*, in *Plays and Poems*, New York, 1932, p. 200).

Wilde, "is the symbol of symbols. Beauty reveals everything, because it expresses nothing." [7] And: "All art is useless." [8] Art, said Whistler in his *Ten O'Clock Lecture* of 1888, is:

> selfishly occupied with her own perfection only—having no desire to teach—seeking and finding the beautiful in all conditions and in all times.[9]

Still the "beauty" of art for art's sake was far from being a cold or Platonic idea. It has to be reconciled somehow with two very hot ideas, near the center of the theory; namely, "sensation" and "passion"—or "sensation" intensified by "passion." (So far have we come from Kant and Poe!) The "hard, gem-like flame" of "ecstasy" with which we are asked to "burn" in the well-known Conclusion of Pater's *Renaissance* wears the aura of a flickering sensationalism—a philosophy of the fleeting moment—so scandalous to his contemporaries that this Conclusion was omitted in the second edition.

> Not the fruit of experience, but experience itself, is the end. A certain number of pulses only is given to us of a variegated, dramatic life. How may we see in them all that is to be seen in them by the finest senses? How shall we pass most swiftly from point to point, and be present always at the focus where the greatest number of vital forces unite in their purest energy?

The answer lies in the word "passion." "Great passions may give us this quickened sense of life. . . . Only be sure it is passion. . . . Of such wisdom, the poetic passion, the desire of beauty, the love of art for its own sake, has most." Or, as Wilde would put it:

> Emotion for the sake of emotion is the aim of art, and emotion for the sake of action is the aim of life.[1]

And this, explained Wilde, was the reason why "all art is immoral." The most recurrently anguished cry of the artist was against the claim of society in the voice of the moralist, against the pressure of the Philistine practical environment.[2]

A moral theory of art, we may note in passing, is intrinsically a theory about a subject matter. As the moral critic John Ruskin put it:

> The picture which has the nobler and more numerous ideas, however awkwardly expressed, is a greater and a better picture

[7] *The Critic as Artist*, in *Intentions* (London, 1913), p. 145.
[8] Preface to *Dorian Gray*.
[9] *The Gentle Art of Making Enemies* (New York, 1890), p. 136.
[1] *The Critic as Artist*, in *Intentions* (London, 1913), p. 169.
[2] See, for instance, Whistler, *The Gentle Art of Making Enemies*, p. 143: "Humanity takes the place of Art, and God's creations are excused for their usefulness."

than that which has the less noble and less numerous ideas, however beautifully expressed. No weight, nor mass, nor beauty of
execution can outweigh one grain or fragment of thought.[3]

But the rebuttal by art-for-art's-sake was in some measure only a reflection of the same choice, a capture of a risky gambit pawn, a too easy
triumph over moralistic rigor by the introduction of a rival rigor.

> The only beautiful things . . . are the things that do not con-
> cern us. As long as a thing is useful or necessary to us, or affects
> us in any way, either for pain or for pleasure . . . it is outside
> the proper sphere of art. To art's subject-matter we should be
> more or less indifferent.[4]

The aestheticism of the 19th century had its own ideas about what is
acceptable subject matter for art. This was roughly that complex of
motifs at which we have already glanced in Poe and Baudelaire: the
exotic and bizarre, the morbid and ugly, and the gilded and artificial.[5]
And increasingly the dark area of this triad was acceptable only under
an artifice of gilt. Art for art's sake—the art of the Yellow Book era—
was an art of a "fiery-coloured world," [6] a world out of this world, out
of the 19th-century socio-real and middle-class context. Beauty had "slim
gilded feet." [7] This was one expression of the artist's isolation, the aristocratic exclusiveness of interest, the withdrawal into ivory-tower luxury,
by which he was to earn so much contempt from socio-realist quarters.
    At the same time, it is important to notice that such an exclusiveness
was capable of a somewhat different emphasis. Wilde in the passage
quoted above apparently means that there are some subject-matters which
concern us, and some which do not, and the latter only are artistic. But
a person could use nearly the same words and convey the different
meaning that all subject matters, even those which concern us most
acutely, should somehow be treated by the artist with detachment. "To
art's subject-matter, we should be more or less indifferent." This would
be a continuation and a degeneration of "negative capability," the anti-

---

[3] *Modern Painters*, Part I, Section I, Chapter 2. Ruskin differed from Arnold in
that his interests were more confessedly practical and sociological, and again he differed from the French or Russian socio-realist critics in the direction of his thinking
toward medievalism and the cultivation of a handicraft norm of values. But even
more than Arnold, Ruskin stood in the public mind as a symbol of the moral critic.
"The great arts," he said, ". . . have had, and can have, but three principal directions
of purpose, first, that of enforcing the religion of men; secondly, that of perfecting
their ethical state; thirdly, that of doing them material service" (*Lectures on Art*,
New York, 1880, p. 37). Cf. Charles A. Yount, *The Reaction Against Ruskin in Art
Criticism* (Chicago, 1941).
    [4] Wilde, *The Decay of Lying*, in *Intentions*, pp. 16–17.
    [5] Cf. William Gaunt, *The Aesthetic Adventure* (London, 1945), pp. 1–10.
    [6] *The Critic as Artist*, in *Intentions*, p. 145.
    [7] *The Critic as Artist*, in *Intentions*, p. 186.

partisan conception as entertained by Keats, the tolerance of "uncertainties, mysteries, doubts." "We hate poetry that has a palpable design upon us." [8] Art for art's sake may be seen as a kind of aesthetico-scientific detachment, an intellectual reaction against the romantic letting down of the hair and flood of personal emotion. Poe's *Philosophy of Composition*, making a parade of rational deliberacy and professional efficiency with regard to the most melancholy and lovely emotion a human being can experience, that for the death of a beautiful woman, combined an extremely exclusive view of subject matter with an aesthetic remoteness that would become typical. Art for art's sake has been described with some insight as a kind of return to the *vita contemplativa*, the *Bios Theōrētikos*, of the Christian ages. Schopenhauer's early exposition of such a notion lay for a while in obscurity but became popular toward the end of the century.[9] This approach to asceticism, in the literary men and painters at least, was a close kin of 19th-century medievalism—with the difference between the Middle Ages and the 19th century that the latter, especially under the rubric of art for art's sake, offered less to contemplate.

V

IN THE later era of art for art's sake, the argument sometimes became an appeal to a supposedly pure aesthetic element of "form." "Form," said Wilde, "is everything. It is the secret of life." "Start with the worship of form, and there is no secret in art that will not be revealed to you." [1] The term "form" might now and then be somewhat mysterious, but for one thing it had a close relation with the idea of craftsmanship so far as the latter was conceived as a quality discoverable in the art work itself. This meant in one sense, a literal sense, the craftsmanship of verse technique. Thus Wilde waxed ecstatic over the powers of rhyme.

> Rhyme . . . in the hands of the real artist becomes not merely a material element of metrical beauty, but a spiritual element of thought and passion also. . . . rhyme . . . can turn man's utterance to the speech of gods; rhyme, the one chord we have added to the Greek lyre.[2]

The matter may be plentifully, if more trivially, illustrated in the practice of the English "Parnassian" poets and translators (the "Rondelier" set) Payne, Lang, Dobson, Henley, Gosse—who followed Théodore de

[8] John Keats, *Letters*, ed. M. B. Forman, 2nd ed. (Oxford, 1935), pp. 72, 96: Nos. 32 and 44 (December 21, 1817, and February 3, 1818); cf. his advice to Shelley, p. 507: No. 227 (August 9, 1818).
[9] Gilbert and Kuhn, p. 472.
[1] *The Critic as Artist*, in *Intentions*, pp. 201–2.
[2] *The Critic as Artist*, in *Intentions*, pp. 102–3.

Banville in a devotion to French medieval and Renaissance poets (Villon, Charles d'Orléans, Marot, Ronsard) and the intricately fixed forms which they had perfected, *rondeau, ballade, villanelle, chant royal,* triolet.[3] "I intended an ode, And it turned to a sonnet."

But in another, and perhaps in the long run more significant, sense, the 19th-century pursuit of fine craftsmanship and "form" was working all along to establish a new kind of liaison, both literal and metaphoric, between poetry and the musical and visual arts.[4] The concept of poetry as "music" in the later 19th century arrived at a new subtlety, far refined beyond mimetic views of the 18th century, and in France this was a notable part of symbolist thinking.[5] The relation with visual art in the special mode of art for art's sake, going back perhaps to Hugo's *Les Orientales* (1829) and Gautier's *Emaux et Camées* (1853), was in a peculiar way more metaphoric and perhaps more fallacious. In a remark on his *Emaux et Camées* Gautier had written:

> This title . . . expresses the plan of treating tiny subjects in a severely formal way—like working on a gold or copper surface with brilliant enamels, or using a graver's wheel on precious stones, agate, cornelian, or onyx. Each piece would have to be as finely chased as an image for the cover of a jewel box or seal ring—something reminiscent of ancient medals such as painters and sculptors keep about their studios.[6]

In the same spirit Pater spoke of making language "a serious study, weighing the precise power of every phrase and word, as though it were precious metal." [7] *Améthystes, Rimes Dorées, Intaglios,* "Thoughts in Marble," *Proverbs in Porcelain, Ballades in Blue China* are characteristic of the period. They represent a passion for smooth surface and sharp outline, the poem as nearly as possible conceived as a thing, a hard shape, not a discourse. If this was an ideal difficult for literature to achieve, nevertheless the general aesthetic theory might look intently in that direction. Wilde praised purely decorative, or arabesque, art in virtue of its "deliberate rejection of Nature as the ideal of beauty, as well as of the imitative method of the ordinary painter." [8] During this era, visual art, reacting against the new claims of photography, tried to move closer to music, which was considered as a nearly pure form and hence an artistic ideal. The sufficient instance for the moment, if on the inten-

[3] See James K. Robinson, "A Neglected Phase of the Aesthetic Movement: English Parnassianism," *PMLA,* LXVIII (September, 1953), 733–54.

[4] Cf. *ante* Chapter 13.

[5] Cf. *post* Chapter 26, pp. 590–6.

[6] *Les Progrès de la Poésie Française depuis 1830,* in *Histoire du Romantisme,* 3d ed. (Paris, 1874), p. 322.

[7] *Marius the Epicurean,* Chapter VI (London, 1893), p. 71.

[8] *The Critic as Artist,* in *Intentions,* p. 200.

tionalist side, is Whistler's painting of his mother, bearing the title: "Arrangement in Grey and Black." [9]

The most flourishing descendant of art for art's sake during the early 20th century has been the school of pure "formalist" criticism in the graphic arts. Much more than any kind of literary criticism, this school has continued and accentuated the aesthetic trend not only toward purity of form but toward exclusiveness of appeal. "In proportion as art becomes purer," says Roger Fry, "the number of people to whom it appeals gets less. . . . It appeals only to the aesthetic sensibility, and that in most men is comparatively weak." [1] "The representative element in a work of art," says Clive Bell in his classic treatise entitled *Art*, "may or may not be harmful; always it is irrelevant." [2] And he tells us much of a "peculiar emotion provoked by works of art," "the aesthetic emotion," the correlative of which is something called "significant form."

> What quality is shared by all objects that provoke our aesthetic emotions? What quality is common to Sta. Sophia and the windows at Chartres, Mexican sculpture, a Persian bowl, Chinese carpets, Giotto's frescoes at Padua, and the masterpieces of Poussin, Piero della Francesca, and Cézanne? Only one answer seems possible—significant form. In each, lines and colours combined in a particular way, certain forms and relations of forms, stir our aesthetic emotions. [3]

The theory, despite a more overt tendency to tautology than is apparent in most art theories, might be a good enough theory if it could be compelled to answer the question whether lines and colors ever have their complete "significance" in a state purged entirely of our concrete optical experience—the resemblance of a circle to the sun and the moon and the wheel, the contrast between the geometrically ruled straight line and the whole world of organic nature. The problem, as we have suggested, may not have a very precise counterpart in literature,[4] yet it may offer some instruction, *a fortiori*, to literary theory. What is not quite possible in lines and colors may be even less possible in words. Again, the difference between aesthetic formalism and any ideas which the historian of metaphysics may be willing to impute to Kant will not quite eliminate the fact that this formalism (a theory of non-empirical, geometric art

[9] See Gaunt, *The Aesthetic Adventure*, p. 82, on Whistler's *Nocturnes*. Wilde said that "music is the perfect type of art" because it "can never reveal its ultimate secret" (*Intentions*, p. 148); and Pater: "All art constantly aspires towards the condition of music" (*The School of Giorgione*, in *The Renaissance*, Modern Library edition, p. 111).
[1] *Vision and Design* (London, 1920), p. 10.
[2] *Art* (New York, c. 1914), p. 25.
[3] *Art* (New York, c. 1914), p. 8.
[4] Twentieth-century Italian and French versions of "pure poetry" (syllables without sense) and Russian experiments in "trans-sense" language provide parallels.

values) stands in a fairly direct, if blurred line of descent from the Kantian *a priorism*.[5]

VI

IN THE didactic theories of the 19th century, art, even though it took a creative leadership, had to be somehow true to the way things basically are. In Arnold's formula—art is a "criticism of life"—the criticism would obviously have to be somehow faithful to, or limited by, its object. But art for art's sake, both early and late, wanted very much to say something nearly the opposite. Thus Whistler, in terms sufficiently reminiscent of Baudelaire:

> That Nature is always right is an assertion artistically as untrue as it is one whose truth is universally taken for granted. Nature is very rarely right, to such an extent even, that it might almost be said that Nature is usually wrong: that is to say, the condition of things that shall bring about the perfection of harmony worthy of a picture is rare.[6]

The mythopoeia of Schelling and Friedrich Schlegel and the Arnoldian neo-humanism, as well as some forms of the socio-realistic claim, were instances of a lofty view of the artist's power of reshaping reality. The morally didactic principle, the recognition of the artist's undoubted power over the wills and hearts of men, shaded off subtly into idealistic concepts of creative imagination or creative will. All along, too, the notion of art as creator was susceptible of receiving a more purely aesthetic, a more playful, twist. A French historian of romanticism and its effects on real life points out that the 19th century was filled with sins copied from the poets and novelists. For example, a plague of suicides that swept France during several decades of the mid-century followed a pattern of feeling set in romances like *Werther* and *René* and in the morbid verse and prose of writers like Petrus Borel, Philothée O'Neddy, and Alphonse Rabbe.[7] Heine in his *Florentine Nights*, 1836, shows how far the argument might sometimes facetiously venture when he maintains that the beauty of the Italian women is a clear instance of the influence of the fine arts on human physique. There may have been

[5] Formalist art critics frequently make an appeal to the mathematical elements in Plato's theory. Cf. *ante*, Chapter 1, p. 17.

[6] *The Gentle Art of Making Enemies*, p. 143.

[7] Louis Maigron, *Le Romantisme et les Moeurs* (Paris, 1910), Chapter II, "Le Romantisme et le Suicide," esp. pp. 314–15, 324, 332–3, 337, 347. "*En voici un, par exemple, Marcel V***, qui se vante d'avoir 'tout goûté, tout épuisé' de la vie conformément aux meilleurs principes romantiques. . . . Il relit* Obermann, René, Joseph Delorme; *et avant de se tuer, juge original de chanter un 'hymne à la Mort'* (p. 324). "*Je lègue à notre cher Club la petite bibliothèque de vous bien connue. A vous particulièrement j'ai réservé* Werther, René, Obermann, les Oeuvres de Rabbe, *et* Jacques. . . . *C'étaient mes bréviaires*" (p. 347).

a time when nature supplied models for art, but now it is the other way round. "A feeling for the beautiful has penetrated the whole people." "Spirit works on flesh." [8] More moderately, the theorist might observe that art teaches us what to see in nature, that it is characteristic of the human being, as Goncourt put it, "to see nothing in nature that is not a remembrance and recollection of art." [9]

The twin notions which we have just been sketching—that nature is inferior to art (so that art is forced to be untrue) and that art has power to anticipate and modify nature—are developed with fine paradoxical abandon by Wilde in his dialogue *The Decay of Lying* (1889). As to the matter of art and truth:

> My own experience is that the more we study Art, the less we care for Nature. What Art really reveals to us is Nature's lack of design, her curious crudities, her extraordinary monotony, her absolutely unfinished condition. Nature has good intentions, of course, but, as Aristotle once said, she cannot carry them out.[1]

> If something cannot be done to check, or at least to modify, our monstrous worship of facts, Art will become sterile, and beauty will pass away from the land.

> Even Mr. Robert Louis Stevenson, that delightful master of delicate and fanciful prose, is tainted with this modern vice, for we know positively no other name for it. There is such a thing as robbing a story of its reality by trying to make it too true, and *The Black Arrow* is so inartistic as not to contain a single anachronism to boast of, while the transformation of Dr. Jekyll reads dangerously like an experiment out of the *Lancet*.[2]

> Wordsworth went to the lakes, but he was never a lake poet. He found in stones the sermons he had already hidden there. He went moralising about the district, but his good work was produced when he returned, not to Nature but to poetry. Poetry gave him "Laodamia," and the fine sonnets, and the great Ode, such as it is. Nature gave him "Martha Ray" and "Peter Bell," and the address to Mr. Wilkinson's spade.[3]

· · ·

[8] *Florentinische Nächte* (Vienna, 1945, Amandus-Edition), pp. 19–20, "Erste Nacht." "*Die Natur hat hier den Künstlern das Kapital zurückgenommen, das sie ihnen einst geliehen, und siehe! es hat sich aufs entzückendste verzinst. Die Natur, welche einst den Künstlern ihre Modelle lieferte, sie kopiert heute ihrerseits die Meisterwerke, die dadurch entstanden. Der Sinn für das Schöne hat das ganze Volk durchdrungen, und wie einst das Fleisch auf den Geist, so wirkt jetzt der Geist auf das Fleisch.*"

[9] Albert Cassagne, *La Théorie de l'Art pour l'Art en France* (Paris, 1906), p. 325.

[1] *Intentions* (London, 1913), p. 1.

[2] *Intentions*, pp. 8–9.

[3] *Intentions*, p. 19. A critique of Shakespeare introduced by Wilde (p. 21) makes a startling comparison to that which we have quoted from Tolstoy in our last chap-

As a method Realism is a complete failure, and the two things
that every artist should avoid are modernity of form and modernity of subject-matter. To us, who live in the nineteenth century, any century is a suitable subject for art except our own.
. . . it is only the modern that ever becomes old-fashioned. M.
Zola sits down to give us a picture of the Second Empire. Who
cares for the Second Empire now? [4]

They will call upon Shakespeare—they always do—and will
quote that hackneyed passage forgetting that this unfortunate
aphorism about Art holding the mirror up to Nature, is deliberately said by Hamlet in order to convince the bystanders of
his absolute insanity in all art-matters.[5]

And secondly, the matter of art's priority to nature.

Where, if not from the Impressionists, do we get those wonderful brown fogs that come creeping down on our streets,
blurring the gaslamps and changing the houses into monstrous
shadows? To whom, if not to them and their master, do we
owe the lovely silver mists that brood over our river, and turn
to faint forms of fading grace curved bridge and swaying barge.
The extraordinary change that has taken place in the climate of
London during the last ten years is entirely due to a particular
school of Art. You smile. Consider the matter from a scientific
or a metaphysical point of view, and you will find that I am
right. For what is Nature? Nature is no great mother who has
borne us. She is our creation. It is in our brain that she quickens
to life. Things are because we see them, and what we see, and
how we see it, depends on the Arts that have influenced us. To
look at a thing is very different from seeing a thing. One does
not see anything until one sees its beauty. Then, and then only,
does it come into existence. At present, people see fogs, not because there are fogs, but because poets and painters have taught
them the mysterious loveliness of such effects. There may have
been fogs for centuries in London. I dare say there were. But
no one saw them, and so we do not know anything about them.
They did not exist till Art had invented them.[6]

And if so much was true of art itself, what of art criticism? The
notion of an art criticism for its own sake—of a criticism that was itself
a kind of artistic exercise—was strongly invited. "Impressionistic" crit-

---

ter. From the viewpoint of art for art's sake one of Shakespeare's faults is "the over-
importance assigned to character" in his later plays, his uncouthness and vulgarity,
his "realism."

[4] *Intentions*, pp. 52–3.
[5] *Intentions*, p. 28.
[6] *Intentions*, p. 39.

icism of considerable brilliance had begun to appear in English at least as early as the work of Lamb and Hazlitt—Hazlitt's "gusto" and his *bravura* appreciation of *Elizabethan Literature* or *English Comic Writers,* Lamb's baroque whimsicalities concerning Shakespeare's tragedies or English "Artificial Comedy." We encounter there a use of metaphor, an overt personal reference, and a Longinian evocation of feeling such as cannot be matched in earlier English criticism. In a note on the *Revenger's Tragedy* Lamb confessed: "I never read it but my ears tingle, and I feel a hot blush overspread my cheeks." [7] And Hazlitt: "I say what I think: I think what I feel. I cannot help receiving certain impressions from things; and I have sufficient courage to declare (somewhat abruptly) what they are." [8] Later on Sainte-Beuve would say that for him criticism was only a way of "exhaling a hidden poetry in an indirect way." "Criticism as I intend it and want to practise it, is invention and perpetual creation." [9] The heyday of this kind of profession was not reached, however, until the end of the 19th century and the first three decades of the 20th, with critics like Anatole France and Jules Lemaître in France, Saintsbury and Quiller-Couch in England, and their cosmopolite disciples in America, Huneker, Mencken, Nathan, or Van Vechten—souls adventuring among masterpieces. The candor of Anatole France is perhaps best known. "To be quite frank, the critic ought to say: 'Gentlemen, I am going to speak about myself apropos of Shakespeare, apropos of Racine.' " [1]

At least three distinguishable propositions seem to be present in the philosophy of impressionist criticism and to call for notice if our account is to be accurate.

(1) That the most necessary, or the only necessary, equipment of the critic is his sensibility. The classic statement is that of Pater in the Preface to his Renaissance *Studies.*

> What is important . . . is not that the critic should possess a correct abstract definition of beauty for the intellect, but a certain kind of temperament, the power of being deeply moved by the presence of beautiful objects.[2]

---

[7] *Characters of Dramatic Writers Contemporary with Shakespeare,* 1808, in Charles and Mary Lamb, *Works,* ed. E. V. Lucas, I (London, 1903), 48.

[8] *Works,* ed. P. P. Howe, V (London, 1930), 175.

[9] *Portraits de Femmes* (1870), p. 411; *Portraits Littéraires* (1862-64), III, 546; from a manuscript chapter by René Wellek.

[1] *On Life and Letters, First Series,* trans. A. W. Evans (London, 1911), Preface, p. viii.

[2] See the comparable celebration of the "critic's sensorium," his "intimate personal relation" to the piece of literature, his "prizing" of "the fleeting mood, the passing poignant moment of enjoyment," his refusal "to feel twice alike about the same poem," by the Harvard Professor Lewis E. Gates, in his essay "Impression and Appreciation," in *Studies and Appreciation* (New York, 1900), pp. 208-9; cf. Zabel, p. 21.

"Temperament," said Wilde, "is the primary requisite for the critic—a temperament exquisitely susceptible to beauty." [3]

(2) That, as the artist himself is the person most susceptible to impressions of beauty, the artist himself is the only licensed critic. In his suit against Ruskin, Whistler complained:

> It is not only when criticism is inimical that I object to it, but also when it is incompetent. I hold that none but an artist can be a competent critic.[4]

(This idea comes echoing down even to our own time, in the opinion, for instance, of Mr. Eliot, who has been rebutted by Mr. C. S. Lewis with the observation that the poet by this argument crowns himself "King of Pointland," for he can trust the judgment of those who acknowledge him a poet only in virtue of being a poet in order to judge them. It is true, notes Mr. Lewis, that good reasoning can be recognized only by a good reasoner; yet it is not true that good cooking can be recognized only by a good cook.[5] Poetry would appear to be a type of product—in part like reasoning, in part like cooking—which offers at least a considerable resistance to the theory that only a poet can be a critic.) [6]

(3) That a good critic, in virtue of his very criticism, is a true artist, or the truest artist. This is the extreme impressionistic theory of criticism. It is a theory of autotelic criticism, of criticism for its own sake, and perhaps it is a logical enough outcome of the original paradox of art for art's sake. The thesis was perhaps first distinctly propounded by Friedrich Schlegel.[7] It is developed by Wilde in a companion piece to *The Decay of Lying,* a long dialogue essay entitled *The Critic as Artist.*

> GILBERT: Yes: it has been said by one whose gracious memory we all revere, and the music of whose pipe once lured Proserpina from her Sicilian fields, and made those white feet stir, and not in vain, the Cumnor cowslips, that the proper aim of Criticism is to see the object as in itself it really is. But this is a very serious error, and takes no cognisance of Criticism's most perfect form, which is in its essence purely subjective, and seeks to reveal its own secret and not the secret of another. For the highest Criticism deals with art not as expressive but as impressive purely.

[3] *The Critic as Artist,* in *Intentions,* p. 194.
[4] *The Gentle Art of Making Enemies* (New York, 1890), p. 6.
[5] Cf. *ante* Chapter 5, p. 84. The relevance of such observations is of course perennial.
[6] C. S. Lewis, *A Preface to Paradise Lost* (London, 1942), pp. 9–10.
[7] Cf. *ante* Chapter 17, p. 376.

ERNEST: But is that really so?

GILBERT: Of course it is. Who cares whether Mr. Ruskin's views on Turner are sound or not? What does it matter? That mighty and majestic prose of his, so fervid and so fiery-coloured in its noble eloquence, so rich in its elaborate symphonic music, so sure and certain, at its best, in subtle choice of word and epithet, is at least as great a work of art as any of those wonderful sunsets that bleach or rot on their corrupted canvases in England's gallery.[8]

Hours ago, Ernest, you asked me the use of Criticism. You might just as well have asked me the use of thought. It is Criticism, as Arnold points out, that creates the intellectual atmosphere of the age. It is Criticism, as I hope to point out myself some day, that makes the mind a fine instrument. . . . Considered as an instrument of thought, the English mind is coarse and undeveloped. The only thing that can purify it is the growth of the critical instinct.[9]

This passage closes the cycle of aesthetico-impressionist thought in the appropriate way, showing how in the boundless realm of idealism aesthetic and didactic theory become one, or how impressionistic criticism can be assimilated to didactic art. If nature, reversing our usual conceptions, is to imitate art, then art, continuing the direction of reference, may well imitate criticism. Or one art, that which calls itself Art, will imitate, or at least be greatly influenced by, another art, that which calls itself criticism. This will be easier if criticism in turn calls itself Art. Thus Wilde and Arnold find themselves at one. Wilde and Arnold, the aesthete and the austere moralist, were both descendants of Schelling and Friedrich Schlegel. They were Victorian brothers. Both entertained not only a low opinion of the English mind but a vision of art and art criticism as free activities which were destined to bring about man's salvation from the bondage of philosophy and religion.

SUPPLEMENT

The theological consideration of the working idea clearly shows how foreign to art is the servile imitation of the appearance of nature, for art's most fundamental demand is that the work make apparent not something else already made, but the spirit from which it proceeds. As God makes created participa-

[8] *Intentions*, p. 140–1.
[9] *Intentions*, pp. 209–10.

tions of His being exist outside Himself, so the artist puts himself—not what he sees, but what he is—into what he makes. So anyone contemplating the myriad landscapes bearing God's signature at every revolution of light, or the features of any beast or man whatever, clearly sees that they are literally *inimitable* and that there is more humility in continuing in our own way the creative impulse than in striving to obtain a like effect in a picture.

The truth is, and it is the core of the mystery, that we have nothing but what we have received.

There is considerable truth in Wilde's paradoxes on lying; truth which, needless to say, has nothing to do with the shoddy Hegelianism with which he tricks it out. It is quite true that things are better in the mind than in themselves, that they acquire their full stature only when they have been expressed, and that they themselves pray to be assumed into the heaven of metaphysical or poetical thought, where they proceed to live outside time with a life which is universal. What would have become of the Trojan War without Homer? Unfortunate are the adventures which are never narrated.

But what Wilde, choked by the paper roses of his aestheticism, failed to understand is that our art does not derive from itself alone what it imparts to things; it spreads over them a secret which it first discovered in them, in their invisible substance or in their endless exchanges and correspondences. Take it out of "that blessed reality given once for all, in the centre of which we are situated," and it ceases to be. It transforms, removes, brings closer together, transfigures; it does not create. It is by the way in which he changes the shape of the universe passing through his mind, in order to make a form apprehended in things shine upon a matter, that the artist impresses his signature upon his work. He recomposes for each, *according as the poetry in him changes him*, a world more real than the reality offered to the senses.

So, because it is subjected in the mind of a man, the law of imitation, of resemblance, remains constant for our art, but in a sense purified. It must transpose the secret rules of being in the manner of producing the work, and it must be as faithful and exact, in transforming reality according to the laws governing the work to be done, as science in conforming thereto. What it makes must resemble not the material appearance of things, but some one of the hidden significances whose iris God alone sees glittering on the neck of His creatures—and for that very reason it will also resemble the created mind which in its own way discerned those invisible colours. Resemblance, but a *spiritual* resemblance. Realism, if you like, but transcendental realism.

—Jacques Maritain, "The Frontiers of Poetry," in *Art and Scholasticism,* trans. J. F. Scanlan (New York, 1942), pp. 95–6, quoted by permission of Charles Scribner's Sons

When poetry loses sight of the wonderful, it loses its significance and justification. Poetry cannot thrive in our trivial and commonplace world. The miraculous, the marvelous, and the mysterious are the only subjects that admit of a truly poetic treatment.

This conception of poetry is, however, rather a qualification and limitation than a genuine account of the creative process of art. Curiously enough the great realists of the nineteenth century had in this respect a keener insight into the art process than their romantic adversaries. They maintained a radical and uncompromising naturalism. But it was precisely this naturalism which led them to a more profound conception of artistic form. Denying the "pure forms" of the idealistic schools they concentrated upon the material aspect of things. By virtue of this sheer concentration they were able to overcome the conventional dualism between the poetic and the prosaic spheres. The nature of a work of art, according to the realists, does not depend on the greatness or smallness of its subject matter. No subject whatever is impermeable to the formative energy of art. One of the greatest triumphs of art is to make us see commonplace things in their real shape and in their true light. Balzac plunged into the most trifling features of the "human comedy." Flaubert made profound analyses of the meanest characters. In some of Émile Zola's novels we discover minute descriptions of the structure of a locomotive, of a department store, or of a coal mine. No technical detail, however insignificant, was omitted from these accounts. Nevertheless, running through the works of all these realists great imaginative power is observable, which is by no means inferior to that of the romantic writers. The fact that this power could not be openly acknowledged was a serious drawback to the naturalistic theories of art. In their attempts to refute the romantic conceptions of a transcendental poetry they reverted to the old definition of art as an imitation of nature. In so doing they missed the principal point, since they failed to recognize the symbolic character of art. If such a characterization of art were admitted, there seemed to be no escape from the metaphysical theories of romanticism. Art is, indeed, symbolism, but the symbolism of art must be understood in an immanent, not in a transcendent sense. Beauty is "The Infinite finitely presented" according to Schelling. The real subject of art is not, however, the metaphysical Infinite of Schelling, nor is it the Absolute of Hegel. It is to be sought in certain fundamental structural elements of our sense experience itself—in lines, design, in architectural, musical forms. These elements are, so to speak, omnipresent. Free of all mystery, they are patent and unconcealed; they are visible, audible, tangible. In this sense Goethe did not hesitate to say that art does not pretend to show the metaphysical depth of things, it merely sticks to the surface of natural phenomena. But this surface is not immediately given. We do not know it before we discover it in the works of the great artists. This discovery, however, is not confined to a special field. To the extent that human language can express everything, the lowest and the highest things, art can embrace and pervade the whole sphere of human experience. Nothing in the physical or moral world, no natural thing and no human action, is by its nature and essence excluded from the realm of art, because nothing resists its formative and creative process. "Quicquid essentia dignum est," says Bacon in his *Novum Organum* (Book I, Aphorism CXX), "id etiam scientia dignum est." This dictum holds for art as well as for science.

—Ernst Cassirer, *An Essay on Man* (New Haven, 1944), pp. 156-8, by permission of the Yale University Press

CHAPTER 23

EXPRESSIONISM: BENEDETTO CROCE

§ *nineteenth-century expressionism, context and origin of Croce's idealism, his* Aesthetic, *neo-idealism,* Autobiography—*II. the four activities of spirit, intuition-expression the aesthetic fact, externalization—III. resemblance of Croce to Plotinus, double concept of form and art, ugliness as failure of intuition, simple successful intuition vs. rich or full intuition, the analogy of bronze-casting—IV. duplicity in Croce's basic treatment of the affective, "feeling" in art, "lyrism" in his later theory (the* Britannica *article, the* Essence of Aesthetic)—*V. negative grounds of the system: rejection of the figures, genres, rules, analysis, etc., rejection of specific value terms—VI.* Croce as a practical critic, The Defence of Poetry, *"Poetic Personality" of the author* (Shakespeare, Ariosto, and Corneille), *Croce's anthological reading, neglect of plot and character, resemblance to Longinus—VII. balance sheet for and against the system, Croce's strength and influence* §

A RECENT STUDY ENTITLED *The Mirror and the Lamp* [1] SEES ONE OF the main trends of romantic poetics to have been a turning from Renaissance concepts of art as mechanically effected mimesis toward a new concept of art as organic creation. The mirror gave back the literal image of reality external to itself. The lamp threw out its own discovering and organizing rays into the void of darkness. A somewhat earlier study of the English romantic theory of poetry [2] had attempted to show that the concept of creative imagination entertained by Coleridge, Shelley and other poets was the same as the "aesthetic" concept

[1] M. H. Abrams, *The Mirror and The Lamp: Romantic Theory and the Critical Tradition* (New York, 1953).

[2] A. E. Powell, *The Romantic Theory of Poetry* (London, 1926).

elaborated a century later by Benedetto Croce.[3] The present writers, in undertaking some account of the Crocean aesthetic and in placing it at this juncture in their story, believe that Croce does actually achieve something like an ultimate definition and synthesis of the expressionistic art theory which first came clearly into view with the Germans and Coleridge and which was tested and matured through such 19th-century vicissitudes as in part we have been describing. Croce's aesthetic is a long way from looking like the preciously burnished perversions of a Baudelaire, the Whistlerian study in gray and black, the velvet-coated flippancies of a Wilde. Yet the theory is precisely an "aesthetic," a master theory of art for art's sake, a profound realization of all that might underlie and in part justify the 19th-century cry that art must be pure.

Croce's theory grows out of an initial preoccupation with the historico-social thinking which we have seen to be intrinsic to one sort of 19th-century didactic theory, and it is a partial resolution of the conflict between such theory and the starker versions of art for art's sake. His early studies, centering in the antiquities of Italy and especially of his native Naples, resulted soon in a conviction that the simple accumulation of factual knowledge was futile. He read Vico's *Scienza Nuova*. And there came a time in March, 1893, when "after a whole day of intense thought," he produced an essay entitled "History subsumed under the general concept of art." Shortly afterwards he complemented his historical studies by a period of concentration on economics and a studied rejection of Marxism.[4] In February and May of 1900 he read before the Accademia Pontaniana of Naples a memoir entitled *Fundamental Theses of an Aesthetic as Science of Expression and General Linguistic*, and this, with some amplifications, and the addition of a historical section, became his epoch-making *Aesthetic*, published in 1902. In later years Croce has stressed [5] the importance of his *Essence of Aesthetic* (or *Breviario*), a lecture written for the opening of the Rice Institute in 1912, and his *Encyclopedia Britannica* article "Aesthetic," by which he captured the term "aesthetic" in the English-speaking world for his own concept and system. We shall not overlook these statements. Yet the earlier *Aesthetic* not only opens up the system (and Croce's objections to all other systems) in far more detail but reveals in like detail some of the consequences of the system for literary study. This work joins with Croce's *Logic* and his *Philosophy of the Practical, Economic and Ethic* to compose his *Philosophy of the Spirit*. In his "opinion" this "exhausts the entire field of philosophy." [6]

[3] Croce in his *Conversazioni critiche*, Third Series (Bari, 1932), pp. 7–13, has some doubts about Miss Powell's understanding of his philosophy.

[4] *An Autobiography*, trans. R. G. Collingwood (Oxford, 1927), pp. 56–60.

[5] E. F. Carritt, *Philosophies of Beauty* (Oxford, 1931), p. 223, n. 1.

[6] Croce, *Aesthetic as Science of Expression and General Linguistic*, trans. Douglas Ainslie, 2nd ed. (New York, 1922–29), p. xxix, Croce's Preface of 1907. Croce's

In the Hegelian idealism there was something, a world or nature, on which spirit worked in a dialectical process. Marxism reduced this to a very thoroughly monistic working of material nature in and through itself. Croce, using as his entrance into the metaphysical realm no other than a literary observation, concerning the breakdown of classical rules and genres of art, arrives at an opposite, but equally thoroughgoing, monism of spirit. His criticism of the classical genres, he tells us in his *Autobiography*, enabled him to lay his finger "on the point at which 'nature,' the product of man's own spirit, is introduced into the pure spiritual world of art." Having "thus denied the reality of nature in art," he was led by degrees "to deny it everywhere and to discover everywhere its true character, not as reality but as the product of abstracting thought." [7] "Spirit" in the Crocean philosophy is the "absolute reality." Spirit "generates the contents of experience." [8] Some of these contents of experience, it is true, assume the character (by abstraction) of something external to the knowing spirit and (as we shall see) even become the means by which further acts of spirit are projected and made known to individual spiritual agents external to each other and to the immediate consciousness which we must suppose to be spirit for the philosopher of the system. But it is perhaps easiest just to say that Crocean neo-idealism is not interested in such embarrassments to its sweep. They are looked on as problems arising out of abstraction and hence ulterior to the concretely rich, vital and real intuitive knowledge which is the direct creation of spirit.

II

THERE are only four basic, essentially different activities or "moments" of spirit, four kinds of reality: two theoretical, or knowing activities; two practical, or volitional. They occur in the following order, each one supposing or needing all those that precede it: 1. intuition-expression (the primary imaginative act of individual characterization or forming); 2. conceptualization (the intellective and scientific knowledge of relations between individual intuitions); 3. volition in general (economic activity); and 4. volition of the rationally and universally conceived end—willing the true self of spirit (ethical activity—absolute freedom). These four ultimates, qualitatively and a-prioristically different from one another, take the place of such classical ultimates as the ideas of Plato, the sub-

---

Aesthetic is quoted throughout the present chapter from the translation of Ainslie by permission of the copyright holder, Mrs. G. C. Quinton. Ainslie's widely influential translation first appeared in 1909. It was republished in 1953 by The Vision Press, Peter Owen, London.

[7] *An Autobiography*, trans. R. G. Collingwood (Oxford, 1927) p. 94.

[8] J. A. Smith, *Encyclopaedia Britannica*, 14th edition, VI, 732, "Benedetto Croce."

stantial forms of Aristotle, the categories and ideas of Kant. Only these four have abstract, absolute, conceptual, dialectical validity (Ch. IX, p. 73).[9] All other concepts are distinguished only quantitatively, temporarily, conveniently, and more or less arbitrarily, in the boundless realm of our empirical experience. "What is true in the natural sciences is either philosophy or historic fact" (Ch. III). The four sciences corresponding to the four cardinal activities of spirit are: aesthetic, logic, economics, and ethics.

The aesthetician, then, focuses on the first of the spiritual activities, intuition-expression. This is bounded at two levels, above by the abstracted concept, below by an "obscure region of the soul" (Ch. 1, p. 9), unconscious or subconscious, something which Croce most often calls "impression," "sensation," or "matter." It is less a thing that really exists than a "notion postulated as a mere limit" (Ch. I, p. 6). It is not spiritual activity, but inchoate passivity, a formless nothing, a mere urge of something to be known, to be achieved, to be born.[1] Intuition-expression is individual character, it is form—always different in content, but always form. "The aesthetic fact, therefore, is form, and nothing but form" (Ch. II, p. 16). The system banishes all notion of art as illusion or as mechanical reproduction of, or substitute for, external beauty (Ch. II). It asserts that the notion of external physical beauty (either natural or artistic) is a "verbal paradox" (Ch. XIII). The natural world, be it remembered, exists only at the conceptual and abstract level.

It is of first importance to the system to insist that intuition-expression is *both* intuition *and* "expression," that no intuition can occur without expression. Knowing a thing is simply expressing it to oneself. There are really no mute inglorious Miltons, no geometricians who cannot draw a figure on the blackboard (Ch. I, p. 9). Let us ask ourselves: Do I know anything which I cannot put in words, draw, carve, hum as a tune, or express by some other sign? Try to tell someone what that something is? Try to draw a picture of it. The embarrassments are obvious. If I know anything which I cannot express, at least I cannot communicate it to anyone else or prove its existence to anyone else.

But this admission would scarcely be enough for Croce. He puts the acts of speaking or singing, of drawing or painting, under the aesthetically non-essential head of "externalization"—a merely practical, or willed, activity which may or may not follow on the internal and involuntary activity of intuition-expression. The physical work of art, the statue, painting, or verbal sound, is an external stimulus which for the qualified recipient will produce the same intuition-expression (aesthetic

---

[9] *Aesthetic*, trans. Douglas Ainslie, 1929.
[1] Though at moments Croce is able to speak of it as actually something. "Everyone speaks and should speak according to the echoes which things arouse in his soul, that is, according to his impressions" (Ch. XVIII, p. 150).

experience) as prompted the artist to externalize. "Artistic technique" is no more than a complex of prior knowledge at the service of the artist in his volitional activity of externalizing (Ch. XV). "Expression" itself does not possess means.[2]

But looking inside ourselves again and reversing the direction of inquiry, let us ask: Could I have a poem in my head without writing it on paper or saying it aloud? Unless we are behaviorists enough to insist that the essential thing in silent thinking is some unobserved twitching of the throat muscles as the counterpart of audible speech, we will say we could. But could I have a painting in my head without going through the experimental act of smearing paint on canvas with a brush. Could I really? Answers will differ. Beyond doubt, some painters will say yes. Nevertheless, we would ordinarily think of a poem in the head, though not written down, as a bird in the hand; but of a painting in the head, though not painted, as a bird in the bush. Croce's insistence that there is no difference between the two cases (that *aesthetic* is identical with *linguistic*, Ch. XVIII) lies close to the heart of his secret, his strength, and his weakness.

In favor of Croce's view we may reflect, provisionally, that not only is it impossible to communicate to anyone else what we cannot put in signs of some sort, but that whatever we know of that kind (and most of us would surely claim to know something, even much, of that kind) is, by the very fact that we cannot manage it in signs, likely to be somewhat vague, ill-formed, and unavailable even for our own thinking. Signs do seem to help knowledge a great deal.

III

A FEATURE of Croce's system which has provoked some complaint from his critics is his strong tendency to assert the equivalence of terms that are ordinarily thought of as separate. "The entire aesthetic system of Croce," says one of his Italian critics, "amounts to merely a hunt for pseudonyms of the word 'art,' and may indeed be stated briefly and accurately in this formula: art=intuition=expression=imagination= fancy=beauty. And you must be careful not to take these words with the shadings and distinctions which they have in ordinary or scientific

---

[2] So far as it has aesthetic relevance, what is sometimes loosely called a new technique (a new kind of romance, a new style of light and shade in painting) is really a new work of art. The technique is part of the vision. Yet perhaps Croce slips for a moment when (Ch. XV, p. 112) he admits that certain theatrical methods (the use of women on the stage, the use of machinery for changing scenes rapidly) are in some more proper sense to be called "techniques." Rosalind as Katharine Hepburn is presumably a different aesthetic experience from Rosalind as boy actor.

language. Not a bit of it. Every word is merely a different series of syllables signifying absolutely and completely the same thing." [3] A counterpart of this sweeping principle of identity might be described as a subtly persistent principle of ambivalence. In this respect Croce's aesthetic is not unlike the few other most radical or metaphysical theories of both beauty and art which one encounters in ancient and modern times—and it is notably like the neo-Platonic identification of beauty with form, the principle of being, and the corollary Thomistic analogical transcendence of beauty. In such systems, what one might attempt to take as a special philosophy of art turns out to be a philosophy of all being, or of all knowledge. The circle defined is expanded to take in the whole horizon. The Plotinian form enjoyed by a piece of stone is beautiful in itself, but the example of an image exquisitely carved on the stone is used to give focus to the very idea of form. And the Crocean neo-idealism, despite a certain contempt for the mystical ad-libbing of Plotinus, is very much like the Plotinian idealism massively inverted; the *nous* "yonder" becomes the *nous* within, and all else is accordingly seen upside down. The Crocean concept of intuition-expression as the fundamental act both of all knowing and of the special kind of knowing called art involves a doubling almost identical with that of the two forms of stone in Plotinus. The difference between "history" and "art" in the Crocean system is the difference between fact and possibility. But within the general area of "art" itself a further distinction is demanded—a distinction between what is merely art in the sense of being not history and what is art in the sense of what is "generally called *par excellence* art." This is the difference between the art of a scribble on the blackboard or an everyday love letter, and on the other hand, the Art of the great masterpieces. And this difference is said to be merely quantitative and empirical; it is something to which philosophy is indifferent. Even the prose of a scientific discourse has its own character as an expressive effort, its own form. Ill-written=ill-thought (p. 24. Ch. III) is a Crocean equation of the most inclusive import.

> The artistic intuition differs from the ordinary not in intensity. The difference is not intensive but extensive.—p. 13

> The intuition of the simplest popular love-song, which says the same thing, or very nearly, as any declaration of love that issues at every moment from the lips of thousands of ordinary men, may be intensively perfect in its poor simplicity, although it be

[3] Giovanni Papini, *Four and Twenty Minds*, quoted by I. A. Richards, in *Principles of Literary Criticism* (New York, 1934), p. 255. We omit from Papini's equation two terms, "feeling" and "lyricism," because we have yet to note their place in Croce's thought.

extensively so much more limited than the complex intuition of
a love-song by Leopardi.—Ch. II, p. 13

The whole difference, then, is quantitative, and as such is indifferent to philosophy, *scientia qualitatum.*—p. 13

The limits of the expression-intuitions that are called art, as
opposed to those that are vulgarly called non-art, are empirical
and impossible to define. If an epigram be art, why not a simple
word? If a story, why not the news jottings of the journalist?

—p. 13

Why not indeed on Croce's major premises? What it all comes to is that
the "aesthetic" of Croce is after all not a philosophy of Art, but a philosophy of all intuitive knowing. Still the fact seems to be never clearly
admitted or even faced by Croce; it can be detected only by resolute
comparison of phrases obviously not meant to be compared. The steady
trend and rhetorical aim of Croce's *Aesthetic* is to suggest that the spiritual act of intuition-expression, as first broadly defined, is in fact the
central and necessary conception for a theory of Art.

The notion of fullness, completeness, success in the achievement of
intuition-expression plays an important role in the system. The "probable" in art is the same as the coherent. We strive with our intuitive
power to master the confusion of passive sensation, the welter of brute
impression, to objectify it and form it in the clear knowledge of spiritual
dominion. When we succeed completely, and only then, beauty appears.
Beauty is thus absolute, formal, unified, perfect. And it follows that the
anti-aesthetic fact is simply lack of intuitional form. Ugliness in art is a
hole in coherence.[4] Ugliness is embarrassment of intuitive activity; it is
multiplicity, failure of knowledge and reality.[5]

But a certain amount of sliding in the use of terms would appear to

[4] As art does not imitate any beauty already existing in the external world, neither does it imitate, nor can it be spoiled by dealing with, what would ordinarily
be called ugliness in the external world. The strong tendency of 20th-century art in
all media to include or even to center on what is ordinarily called both evil and
ugly in the external world is one correlative of the widely prevalent expressionist
aesthetic. Rembrandt's *Anatomy Lesson* gives place in the annual exhibition of 1950
to Hyman Bloom's *Female Corpse, Back View* (*Art News*, XLIX, May, 1950, 17).
This continues the classical and Renaissance opinion that even a dunghill if accurately represented is pleasing and the more modern debate of literary philosophers,
like Lessing (*Laocoon*, Chs. XXIII–XXV) or in the 19th century the Hegelian Karl
Rosenkranz (*Ästhetik des Hässlichen*, 1853) on the aesthetic relevance of the ugly.

[5] "If the ugly were *complete*, that is to say, without any element of beauty, it
would for that very reason cease to be ugly, because it would be without the contradiction in which is the reason of its existence. The disvalue would become non-
value." Unsuccessful art works are said to have "merits," but not beauty. These "merits" are beautiful parts, or beautiful small wholes, in large failures, and furthermore
(though this may be more surprising) they can exist only in failures. The successful whole work, "being a complete fusion," has but one value. It has no beautiful
parts, no merits (Ch. X, pp. 79–80).

accompany the argument. The notion of the successful intuition harbors a certain duplicity. For there is in the first place the struggle of any given intuition, more simple or less simple, to clarify itself upon the welter of half-known impression. And there is in the second place the achievement of the complex and rich Art intuition in all its superiority over the simpler kind. And these two conceptions constantly blend. Thus:

> On the hither side of the lower limit is sensation, formless matter, which the spirit can never apprehend in itself as simple matter. This it can only possess with form and in form. . . . How often do we strive to understand clearly what is passing within us! We do catch a glimpse of something, but this does not appear to the mind as objectified and formed.—Ch. I, p. 5

But a few pages later:

> The world which as a rule we intuit is a small thing. It consists of little expressions, which gradually become greater and wider with the increasing spiritual concentration of certain moments. They are the words we say to ourselves, our silent judgments: "Here is a man, here is a horse, this is heavy, this is sharp, this pleases me," etc. It is a medley of light and colour, with no greater pictorial value than would be expressed by a haphazard splash of colours, from among which one could barely make out a few special, distinctive traits. This and nothing else is what we possess in our ordinary life; this is the basis of our ordinary action. It is the index of a book. The labels tied to things (it has been said) take the place of the things themselves. This index and these labels (themselves expressions) suffice for small needs and small actions. From time to time we pass from the index to the book, from the label to the thing, or from the slight to the greater intuitions, and from these to the greatest and most lofty.
> —Ch. I, pp. 9–10

> This passage is sometimes far from easy. It has been observed by those who have best studied the psychology of artists that when, after having given a rapid glance at any one, they attempt to obtain a real intuition of him, in order, for example, to paint his portrait, then this ordinary vision, that seemed so precise, so lively, reveals itself as little better than nothing.—p. 10

It is to be observed that the dialectical and absolute importance attached initially in the system to the sheer act of intuition-expression becomes by degrees transferred to a special sort of intuition-expression, that which is "greater and wider." The ordinary, slight intuitions are actually described in a way that makes them sound like cliché concepts—"indexes of a book," "labels tied to things." The greater and wider intuition, of the portrait painter, for instance, is then described as a "real intuition," and the "ordinary vision" sinks back into a status "little better than nothing"—i.e. into the status of sensation or impression. Yet in other passages of the book, where it suits him to be more consistent with his basic doctrine, Croce will say that any kind of intuition at all has an aesthetic worth equal to that of any other.

> Not only is the art of savages not inferior, as art, to that of civilized peoples, if it be correlative to the impressions of the savage; but every individual, indeed every moment of the spiritual life of the individual, has its artistic world; none of these worlds can be compared with any other in respect of artistic value.—Ch. XVII, p. 137

A double notion of "form" has extensive ramifications throughout the system. To take one example which may stand in general for the technical bearings of the difficulty: When Croce attempts to explain how it is that the intuition-expressions of Art do after all use a kind of conceptual language, an inheritance of ready-made forms and pre-fabricated bric-a-brac (words themselves, for instance, allusions, old saws, catch-words, aphorisms, and the like in poetry), he says that these elements do not enter into the new poem as forms but are first de-morphosed as it were, reduced and fused back into a state of mere "impression," formless stuff. An analogy from bronze-pouring seems ready to his purpose.

> He who conceives a tragedy puts into a crucible a great quantity, so to say, of impressions: expressions themselves, conceived on other occasions, are fused together with the new in a single mass, in the same way as we can cast into a melting furnace formless pieces of bronze and choicest statuettes. Those choicest statuettes must be melted just like the pieces of bronze, before there can be a new statue. The old expressions must descend again to the level of impressions, in order to be synthesized in a new single expression.—Ch. II, p. 20

But this analogy may not in fact read so smoothly. Do the conceptual materials (the old saws, catch words, and the like) which one finds in a poem really melt out of sight? Or don't they have to retain their form and meaning in order to operate poetically at all? To make the point in another way: there is a certain kind of form in the statuette—a kind that is absent in the "form*less*" pieces of bronze. But on the showing of Croce's own system, those pieces of bronze also have a form, the simpler intuition-expression which is the very form of our knowing them. And on an issue of intuition *versus* conception, there is no ground for discriminating between the statuette and the junk. The statuette does lose much more than the junk in being melted down. But that is an issue of Art *versus* general intuition. We are back with the Plotinian piece of stone, which always has form, but sometimes has form *par excellence* by having an image carved on it.

IV

CROCE's theory is in a sense the most resolutely cognitive of all modern art theories. His fundamental division of spiritual activity into the cognitive and the volitional enables him to proceed with great clarity and authority in his dismissal of the affective art theories which he groups under the headings "hedonistic" (Ch. XI) and "sympathetic" (Ch. XII). Nevertheless, the affective element is one which his system has always had to cope with, and one which comes to have a more prominent role in works written after his *Aesthetic*. To account for the fact that in the presence of works of art one experiences not just aesthetic knowledge but aesthetic *pleasure*, Croce proposes in his *Aesthetic* that each of the four radical spiritual activities, as it succeeds or fails, is accompanied by a "special activity, of non-cognitive nature, having its two poles, positive and negative, in *pleasure* and *pain*" (Ch. X, p. 74).[6] Aesthetic pleasure is simply the feeling of pleasure which accompanies our successful acts of intuition-expression. But let us realize clearly (and this may cost some effort) that *each* one of the four main spiritual activities is accompanied by this special volitional act (or overtone) called "feeling." Not only activities of knowing (poetic and scientific) but activities of volition themselves (economic and ethical) have their accompaniment of volitional pleasure and pain. Not only does the scientist experience delight in the knowledge of his discovery—*eureka*—but he must experience another delight in the success of his wishing to make the discovery. A certain clarity in the cognitive area has been obtained at the expense of a very odd double situation in the volitional area. This perhaps betrays some conflict between the cognitive effort of Croce's art theory and what turns out to be his equally resolute affectivism in general value theory —by which judgments of value "follow instead of preceding the affirmation of the will, and are nothing but the expression of the volition already experienced" (Ch. VI, p. 49). Working back from such empty acts of willing and feeling (which have to be valued themselves by their own echo acts of feeling), we rule out feeling from the aesthetic act by saying that although it accompanies the act it has nothing to do with the character of the act. To put the matter another way, Croce's affective duplicity in the *Aesthetic* is one cost of his attempt to keep practical

---

[6] In another paragraph (p. 75) he says that this activity is just the same as "that more elementary and fundamental practical activity which we have distinguished from the ethical," i.e., just the same as economic or volitional activity in general.

activity, economic and ethical feeling, too severely distinct from aesthetic activity. Perhaps the difficulty has never been completely overcome. The "incipient" or "imaginal" responses of a later psychological theory of literature, for instance, or the purely contemplative pleasure of an earlier metaphysics, may share somewhat the same embarrassment. Yet there would appear to be something oddly maladroit and absentminded about this aspect of Croce's thought.

It is in certain other passages of the *Aesthetic*, where he is concerned with the danger of consulting either author or audience in their moral activities, their feelings of guilt and innocence, that he makes his best comments, negative though they may be, on "feeling."

> Many legends in the biographies of artists have sprung from this erroneous identification [between knowing and willing], since it seemed impossible that a man who gives expression to generous feelings should not be a noble and generous man in practical life; or that the dramatist whose plays are full of stabbing, would not himself have done a little stabbing in real life. Artists protest vainly: *"Lasciva est nobis pagina, vita proba."*
> —Ch. VI, p. 53

> What are these apparent or manifested feelings, but feelings objectified, intuited, expressed? And it is natural that they do not trouble and afflict us as passionately as those of real life, because those were matter, these are form and activity; those true and proper feelings, these intuitions and expressions.—Ch. X, p. 81 [7]

Croce has always been severe upon the mere display and indulgence of feeling in poetry and upon the critical method of being interested in authors themselves as feeling and willing beings.[8] Yet what, after all, of

[7] Three meanings of the term "feeling" are defined by Croce in his *Aesthetic* (Ch. II, p. 18; Ch. X, p. 74): 1. the volitional activity of pleasure or pain with which we have been dealing above; 2. feeling as passivity, matter, impression, inchoate knowledge; 3. feeling as "pure intuition"—i.e., intuition in its character as non-conceptual and non-historical, neither scientific nor factual. In the passage of *Aesthetic*, Chapter X quoted above, meanings 1 and 2 may be seen in fusion. In a passage which we are about to quote from Croce's *Britannica* article, the use of the term "feeling" in a shift from meaning 1 to meaning 3 is to be noted.

[8] Thus in an essay written as early as 1887: "It is not enough to feel. Feeling is nothing if hand is not ruled by intellect. In the work of Gaspara, self-revelation often remains a mere act of will, an intention. Gaspara sheds tears, but is not always in command of enough magic to transform them into pearls" (Luigi Russo, *La Critica Letteraria Contemporanea*, Bari, 1946, I, 133).

For very strong statements against attending to the author himself (under any practical aspect) instead of to his poetry, see Croce's opening Chapter on Shakespeare, *Ariosto, Shakespeare and Corneille* (New York, 1920), pp. 117 ff.; *The Poetry of Dante* (New York, 1922), pp. 27, 32; *Breviary of Aesthetics*, Rice Institute Pamphlets (Houston, 1915), pp. 13–14; and *La Poesia* (1936), p. 297: ". . . *non importa quel che il poeta si propone o vuol fare o crede di fare, ma unicamente quel che esso fa.*"

feeling and its role in art? Does it have only the same minor role as do the feelings of pleasure attendant on a successful scientific conceptualization, or (in the awkward doubling which we have noted) those attendant on the success of our economic and ethical volitions? Even the impropriety of reading the dramatist's own feelings into his play about murder and incest does not obviate the fact that the element of feeling is a very prominent part of the poem. This line of inquiry can lead to a view arrived at by Croce only some years after the writing of his *Aesthetic* [9] —that Artistic intuition-expression is precisely the intuition-expression of "feeling." Not the tumult of feeling felt by an author in his practical life, not feeling simply spilled out, confessed à la Rousseau, or exposed to public view. But precisely feeling intuited and expressed, feeling objectified, embodied and made knowable in the artistic act—in the linguistic act of the poem. The new and more precise name now bestowed upon Artistic intuition-expression was "lyrism" (*liricità*). Thus in his *Britannica* article, "the basis of all poetry is the moral consciousness." But:

> The feeling is altogether converted into images, into this complex of images and is thus a feeling that is contemplated and therefore resolved and transcended. Hence poetry must be called neither feeling, nor image, nor yet the sum of the two, but "contemplation of feeling," or "lyrical intuition," or (which is the same thing) "pure intuition"—pure, that is, of all historical and critical reference to the reality or unreality of the images of which it is woven, and apprehending the pure throb of life in its ideality.[1]

> The lyric is not a pouring forth; it is not a cry or a lament; it is an objectification in which the ego sees itself on the stage, narrates itself, and dramatizes itself; and this lyrical spirit forms the poetry both of epic and of drama, which are therefore distinguished from the lyric only by external signs.[2]

[9] The Preface to the 1907 edition of the *Aesthetic* alludes to the "lyrical nature of art" (trans. Ainslie, 1929, p. xxix). The earliest emphatic development of the idea seems to be the paper on "The Lyrical Character of Art" delivered at the Heidelberg Congress of 1908. A translation of this appears in the first English edition of the *Aesthetic*, 1909. The Italian text may be found in *Problemi di estetica*, 1910. Cf. *Autobiography*, trans. Collingwood, 1927, p. 102, "the concept of intuition in aesthetic now elaborated into that of lyrism."

[1] The end of this passage seems to revert to the special sense of "feeling" as "pure intuition" defined in the *Aesthetic* (Ch. II, p. 18). But the main sense of "feeling" in these *Britannica* passages is clearly closer to the ordinary affective-volitional sense.

[2] *Encyclopaedia Britannica*, 14th Edition, "Aesthetic," vol. I (1937), pp. 265, 268. Cf. *The Essence of Aesthetic* (London, 1921), pp. 32-3, "lyric" as synonymous with "art."

Croce has changed his definition of Art and of Art value by making feeling the required Art content or a prominent part of it. If we find a difficulty in squaring the new definition with his fundamental doctrine that to classify intuition-expressions in any way is to conceptualize and neutralize them, losing sight of the one aesthetically significant fact, the fullness and success of intuition-expression as "form," he will answer, no doubt, that the feeling itself is a kind of intensity or "throb" which has no specific coloration except from the cognitive character of the intuition-expression which it accompanies. On the plateau which he thus erects for himself, raising his early concept of the fullness and richness, the formal success, of the Artistic intuition more clearly into the strata of human ethical concerns, Croce is able to elaborate his views so as to accommodate much that appears more characteristically in other modern systems, those of the romantic Germans before him and those of his later expressionist and affectivist contemporaries. Thus in one of his *New Essays on Aesthetic* first collected in 1920 we find the doctrine of "lyrism" leaping exultantly into such affirmations as these.

> The particular throbs with the life of the whole intuition, and the whole exists in the life of the particular. Every pure artistic image is at one and the same time itself and the universe, the universe in this individual form and this individual form equivalent to the universe. In every word of the poet, in every act of his creative imagination, appears the whole of human destiny, all the hopes, illusions, sorrows and joys, the grandeur and misery, of the human state.

> To give to the contentual feeling an artistic form is to give it also the stamp of totality, the cosmic afflatus.

> Art is essentially free from practical interest, . . . because in art there is no suppression of any interest at all; rather art gives all our interests simultaneous free play in the image. It is only in this way that the individual image, transcending the particular and acquiring a value of totality, becomes concretely individual.[3]

Or in his Oxford lecture *The Defence of Poetry*, 1933, the following:

> The thoughts and actions and emotions of life, when sublimated to the subject-matter of poetry, are no longer the thought that judges, the action effectually carried out, the good and evil, or the joy and pain actually done or suffered. They are all now simply passions and feelings immediately assuaged and calmed, and transfigured in imagery. That is the magic of poetry: the union of calm and tumult, of passionate impulse with the con-

[3] *Nuovi saggi di estetica*, 3d ed. (Bari: Gius. Laterza & Figli, 1948), pp. 122–5, "Il Carattere di totalità dell' espressione artistica."

trolling mind which controls by contemplating. It is the triumph
of contemplation, but a triumph still shaken by past battle, with
its foot upon a living though vanquished foe. Poetic genius
chooses a strait path in which passion is calmed and calm is
passionate; a path that has on one side merely natural feeling,
and on the other the reflection and criticism which is twice removed from nature; a path from which minor talents find it but
too easy to slip into an art either convulsed and distorted by passion, or void of passion and guided by principles of the understanding. Then they are called "romantic" or "classical." [4]

V

LITERARY students have perhaps found their easiest sympathy with Croce,
and their most profitable instruction, in the negative starting points of
his polemic, and notably in his attack on such fixtures of the literary
tradition as the classical "figures" of speech and thought, the classical
literary species or genres and the rules of decorum long attached to these.
(The theoretical part of his *Aesthetic* is here vigorously supplemented
by his historical chapters.) All these classical technicalities, let it be remembered, had been taken at least implicitly, throughout centuries of
criticism, as conceptions of value and prescriptions for obtaining value.
To use a figure was to add an ornament to plainness and hence to score
a point (*punctum*) on the tally sheet of the *dulce*. To violate the decorum of a genre, as in experimenting with a new lyric meter or with the
hybrid of a pastoral tragi-comedy, was to court chaos or at least the
sharply raised eyebrow of the critical arbiter. But to the inviolable general rule Croce opposes the inviolable individual—the individual which
must not be touched by conceptual abstraction if it is to retain its aesthetic validity. (The beginning of his whole philosophy, as he himself
has confessed, was his criticism of the genres.)

Croce takes ruthless advantage of the inescapable fact that no literary
arbiter has ever succeeded in setting up a code which subsequent poets
have not with equal success subverted. Though the poet's materials and
even his forms in the grammatical and prosodic senses be conventional,
yet it is his rule of craft that he must do something different with them.
(Even if the little bronze image be not melted out of all identity, it must
at least be somewhat twisted.) The *verba . . . parce detorta*, the *callida
junctura* of Horace had long ago testified to this much. The most eloquent champion of genre theory in Croce's early days, Ferdinand
Brunetière, was scarcely setting up as a legislator; he was only joining

---

[4] *The Defence of Poetry: Variations on the Theme of Shelley*, trans. E. F. Carritt
(Oxford, 1933), p. 25, by permission of the Oxford University Press, Inc.

classical genre with Darwinism to create a frame of reference for the orderly exposition of literary history—*l'évolution des genres littéraires.* Something like that Croce himself would permit.[5] Yet such an exposition he would relegate to the dubious realm of literary history, a discipline which works "to some extent with generalizations and abstractions."

Croce's dogma is set sternly against all classification of expressions, all notions about the limits of a given art or about combinations of the arts (Ch. XV). It is set against anything like an intellectualization of the artistic meaning—against all analysis, all classification, all grammar,[6] all allegorizing, all rhetorical splits between "form" and "content," "ornament" and business, all conceptions of proper and "improper" ways of saying the same thing, all notions of homonym and synonym, and of literary translation. (If a metaphor is improper or an ornament external to the real meaning of an expression, why should it appear in the expression at all? If, on the other hand, it is really a proper part of the expression, why call it improper or ornamental?)

> Language is a perpetual creation. What has been linguistically expressed is not repeated, save by reproduction of what has already been produced. The ever-new impressions give rise to continuous changes of sound and meaning, that is, to ever-new expressions. To seek the model language, then, is to seek the immobility of motion.—Ch. XVIII, p. 150

> Language is not an arsenal of arms already made, and it is not a vocabulary, a collection of abstractions, or a cemetery of corpses more or less well embalmed.—p. 150

> We can elaborate logically what we have already elaborated in aesthetic form only; but we cannot reduce what has already possessed its aesthetic form to another form also aesthetic. Indeed, every translation either diminishes and spoils, or it creates a new expression, by putting the former back into the crucible and mingling it with the personal impressions of the so-called translator.—Ch. IX, p. 68

Croce makes a very damaging case not only against all the classic "paraphernalia" of criticism, but (and here the theory cuts to the quick

[5] "It may be asserted that the history of aesthetic productions shows progressive cycles. . . . When many are at work in a general way upon the same subject, without succeeding in giving to it the suitable form, yet drawing always more near to it, there is said to be progress, and when appears the man who gives it definite form, the cycle is said to be complete, and progress is ended" (Ch. XVII, p. 136).

[6] The "linguistic unit," says Croce, is the sentence: "Peteriswalkinginacountryroad." Any analysis of this into words, syllables, or syntax is an abstractive and more or less arbitrary act which does violence to its aesthetic integrity. One might be tempted to begin a critique of the Crocean system at just this point—with the question how one distinguishes a sentence from adjacent sentences of a linguistic discourse. And if such a distinction is valid, why not a distinction between words?

of even the modern critical consciousness) against every term that has ever taken on the least specific or technical coloring as a predicate in an attempt to define good poetry. Consider, he says, such opposed pairs of terms as *classical* and *romantic, symbolic* and *realistic.* Each of the four has been used as a term of positive valuing by a critic of a certain temper and can be used by us for the same purpose at a certain moment in a certain light—but blink your eyes, look again, and like the honeycomb cells of ambiguous perspective in the trick advertising sign, slanting now up, now down, the pair of critical terms will shift its value emphasis. *Classical* means either artistically perfect or coldly artificial; *romantic* means either warmly and truly expressive or sentimental and uncontrolled. *Realistic* means either mechanically imitative or vividly life-like; *symbolic* means either something that takes inspired liberties with reality or something that is stiffly allegorical. In short, any one of these terms can mean either *artistic* or *inartistic.* And no one of them, and no other critical term, has any privileged hold on the notion of the *artistic.* There is no such thing as specific, technical praise of an art work. All such terms when used for positive valuing—rhythm, meter, assonance, rhyme, metaphor, or what you please—are only synonyms for artistic form.[7] For neutral and scientific purposes you can move from the individual intuition into such abstractions, but you cannot move back again.

VI

THE total suppression of all critical discourse seems threatened. At the same time (and from Croce's own practice as a literary critic we may see this) he is scarcely in favor of such a suppression. He himself has defined the office of criticism as being to "discern and to point out exactly where lies the poetical motive."[8] Croce is always an interesting practical critic. He has given us some rather fine examples of a certain taste and of a certain critical idiom, the latter of which may or may not be exactly defined in the formula we have just quoted. Thus in his Oxford lecture *The Defence of Poetry*, the following exegesis of a single line by Racine.

> It is a delusion to suppose that a verse delights us by any sounds with which it stimulates our ears to ecstasy. What it stimulates to ecstasy is our imagination, and thereby our emotion. There is a verse of Racine which Théophile Gautier used to scan and declaim with gusto, and which other disciples of preciosity are in the habit of reciting as absolutely unmeaning and yet, or rather

[7] Ch. IX, pp. 70–1.
[8] *Ariosto, Shakespeare and Corneille,* trans. Douglas Ainslie (New York, 1920), pp. 147.

for that reason, the only beautiful verse which the poet ever succeeded in writing:

La fille de Minos et de Pasiphaé

That is certainly beautiful, but not in virtue of the physical combination of its sounds. One might make infinite other combinations of such sounds without producing any effect of beauty. It
is beautiful because these sounds, these syllables and accents,
bring before us, in an instantaneous imaginative fusion, all that
was mysterious and sinister, all that was divine and fiendish, all
that was majestic and perverted, both in the person and in the
parentage of Phaedra. And this is expressed by two epic names,
that of the royal Cretan legislator and that of his incestuous
wife, at whose side rises in our imagination, the brutal figure of
the bull.[9]

Croce's criticism demonstrates a firm grasp on the nature of the verbal
art expression (or in fact on the nature of all art expression as distinct
from simply sensory pleasure). He has a fine flair for exploring the implicit meanings and hence the imaginative unity of poetic passages. Join
with these facts his statements, already quoted, concerning the highly
complex "totality" which he recognizes in a work of literary art—and
we may be led to hope that in Croce has been discovered the patron
theorist of the practical literary critic.

Yet a certain contradictory simplism may have been suggested in
that definition of the critic's office which we have quoted—to "discern
the poetical motive." And despite Croce's many eloquent pronouncements to the contrary, there is more than a hint here too of a genetic
and biographical standard. Though he avoids the "Practical Personality"
of Shakespeare, it is not, after all, the plays which he would take instead,
but the "Poetic Personality." The classification of the spirit, the literary
characterization (*caratteristica*), hovers between the single work and the
author's whole output, the latter seeming to form some kind of necessary
whole. Literary "history" is proper if it confines itself to the work of a
single author, a single spirit, improper if it tries to include more.[1] "Criticism," wrote Croce in a letter not many months before his death, "does
not require anything else than to know the true sentiment of the poet in
the representative form in which he has translated it. Any other demand
is extraneous to the question." [2]

"Sentiment" and "spirit" tend strongly, in Croce's thinking, to be

[9] *The Defence of Poetry*, p. 23, by permission of the Oxford University Press,
Inc. See his glowing analysis of a passage from Virgil in the *Britannica* article.
[1] "*La riforma della storia artistica e letteraria*," in *Nuovi saggi di estetica*, 3rd
ed. (Bari, 1948), pp. 157 ff., cited by René Wellek, "Benedetto Croce," *Comparative
Literature*, V (Winter, 1953), 76.
[2] Wellek, *Comparative Literature*, V, 77.

conceived as indivisible. They may flash out in a short lyric burst as well as in a whole work, perhaps more likely in the short burst. We recall the doctrine of the *Aesthetic* according to which unsuccessful works have, with reference to their wholeness, only "merits," not beauties, though each merit is in itself a beauty. One might have suspected Croce of an extreme fastidiousness with regard to nominal wholes, of a great readiness to look through long works for their most striking merits, their passages of "pure lyrism" (as Edgar Allan Poe thought a long poem a contradiction in terms and the best of "long poems" only a series of short poems linked by prose). And as a matter of fact this kind of anthological reading is quite prominent in Croce's criticism. He treats Goethe's *Faust*, for instance, almost as an album or commonplace book in which Goethe entered his feelings at various times.[3] He writes of Corneille:

> We care nothing for the canvas, but only for what of embroidery in the shape of poetry there is upon it.
>
> The poetry of Corneille, or what of poetry there is in him, is all to be found in the lyrical quality of the volitional situations, in those debates, remarks, solemn professions of faith, energetic assertions of the will, in that superb admiration for . . . personal, unshakable firmness. Here it is that we must seek it, not in the development of the dramatic action or in the character of the individual personages.
>
> We must insist that those four tragedies [*Le Cid, Horace, Polyeucte, Cinna*], like those that followed them, are not to be read by the lover of poetry otherwise than in an anthological manner.[4]

What might not at first come home to the unprepared reader is that Croce is not here speaking of what he supposes to be badly structured plays, in contrast to better structured, which it would be worth while reading as wholes. The truth is that he looks on the grosser architecture of any verbal work at all as a matter of very small moment, even of aesthetic irrelevance. He tends to associate structure with the mere intentions of the author, something to be known only abstractly and apart from the sentiment and imagination which is the poetry.[5] The structure of Dante's *Commedia* is what pertains to the "theological-political romance,"

[3] Wellek, *Comparative Literature*, V, 77.

[4] *Ariosto, Shakespeare and Corneille*, trans. Douglas Ainslie, pp. 407, 408, 414. Copyright, 1920, by Henry Holt and Company. Copyright, 1948, by Douglas Ainslie. By permission of the publishers.

[5] Wellek, *Comparative Literature*, V, 77, citing "*Recenti lavori tedeschi di critica del* Faust," in Croce's *Goethe*, 4th ed. (Bari, 1946), II, 101.

around which the actual poetry clings like luxuriant vegetation.[6] His statement concerning Shakespeare is perhaps the most shocking of all.

> Certainly, it would be possible to take one of the plays of Shakespeare, or all of them, one after another, and . . . to illustrate their aesthetic coherence and to point out the delicacy of treatment, bit by bit, scene by scene, accent by accent, word by word. . . . This insistence upon analysis and eulogy will be of special value to those who do not immediately understand of themselves. . . . But it does not form part of our object in writing this treatise, nor does it appear to form part of the duty of Shakespearean criticism, for Shakespeare is one of the clearest and most evident of poets, capable of being perfectly understood by men of slight or elementary culture.[7]

It would seem to follow that when Croce in his *Britannica* article asserts the unity of lyric, dramatic, and epic poetry, he does not mean that lyric, dramatic and epic are three *different* ways of realizing the same poetic quality (each having its own special features, approximate laws, and the like) but that epic and dramatic are literally to be read as collections of lyric passages framed together in a largely irrelevant structure of plot and character. Despite all his disavowals, then, he takes his place as the ultimate romantic critic, exhibiting a strong similarity to that far-off harbinger, sometimes considered the first romantic critic, the author of the *Peri Hupsous*, who also frankly confessed his belief that the poetic ecstasy is a thing that occurs only in short spurts of energy, sudden flashes.[8]

VII

IN TRYING to assess the Crocean system, one may be tempted to write a kind of balance sheet. To the credit of the system, let it be set down clearly that it is devoted to the discouragement of all didactic criticism, all scientific, realistic, informational, and baldly mimetic norms, and also the overtly intentionalistic, inspirational and biographical. It discourages likewise all kinds of criticism according to the literary species and according to rules, or, as this is nowadays called (in the terminology

[6] *La Poesia di Dante,* 6th ed. (Bari, 1948), p. 59 (Wellek, *Comparative Literature,* V, 77).

[7] *Ariosto, Shakespeare and Corneille,* pp. 280–3.

[8] In the bewildering range of Croce's work one finds of course a certain number of statements in favor of conceptual criticism and of art as artifice or making, and against merely impressionistic criticism. Critics, he says once, should be reminded of the prohibition posted in some German concert halls: "*Das Mitsingen ist verboten.*" Wellek, *Comparative Literature,* V, 80–1, citing *Poesia popolare e poesia d'arte* (1933) and *Nuovi saggi di estetica,* 3rd ed. (Bari, 1948), pp. 233 ff.

promoted by Richards), criticism by technical presuppositions or general
critical preconceptions. It discourages ornamentalism and every other
separation of form from content, means from end. At the same time, if
only certain clauses of the system are consulted (those concerning fullness, richness and unity of intuitions, harmony of interests and totality),
then it will seem to encourage a study of literary parts in relation to
wholes and a synthetic understanding of the art work. And lastly, the
Crocean system more or less encourages the right kind of historical
study, the reconstruction of the conditions, the vocabulary of ready
meanings, which enter into the meaning of the work itself.

But on the other hand, and against the system, it must be set down
that it inclines in some of its clauses to promote an exaggerated respect
for the author himself (if not as a practical personality, yet as a poetic
personality) and that in its emphasis on the unexternalized intuition it
has favorably influenced (at least in the English-speaking world) the
early 20th-century trend toward critical standards of sincerity, spontaneity, authenticity. In the same way, it has contributed its influence to
the sway of critical impressionism. By the mere fact that it is a form of
monistic expressionism and idealism, it has tended to undercut the notion
of real values and hence to remove the background against which even
an idealistic theory of art values must make its claims. Lastly, and this
is the most serious complaint that must be made, in the zeal of his
anathema against the classical paraphernalia, Croce moves on to prohibit
in effect all critical analysis and hence all consideration of literary works
as integrated objects or as complexes of meaning, and all distinctions
between symbolic and literal structures of meaning. He forbids us in
short to do anything for the critical enrichment of our intuitions. We
are asked to remain content with the lightning flash. In the chapters of
his *Aesthetic* on the history of art (XVI and XVII) he seems to face
the fact that we can ultimately arrive at a better intuition of a whole
through a conceptual analysis of its elements, but he does not like to
extend this view into actual criticism—unless perhaps to the criticism of
a short passage, a single line, like that of Racine's which he analyzes
with such fervor. It is as if Croce can observe the fact of synthesis and
contextual modification of elements within a small compass, but that the
same thing in a wider perspective of plot, character, act and scene, forces
the notion of abstractive conception upon him and leads him to speak
of mere structural intentions and argumentative purposes. In insisting
that the statuette must be melted to enter into a larger work of art, he
forgets the gargoyle upon the cathedral—and he forgets that the small
image if only it is allowed to retain its form can be *trans*formed by
various juxtapositions with other objects and by the play of various lights
upon its own shape.

The problems which we have been sketching are not the peculiar product of Crocean thinking. They are rather some of the most permanent problems of criticism, which Croce succeeds in bringing to a stage of acute even painful realization for the literary student who is faced with the practical need of talking about literary works. Croce perhaps more powerfully than any other modern aesthetician sums up and completes an era of idealistic and expressionistic thinking about art. He polarizes the philosophy of the art work as a uniquely individual organization and as an expression of spirit and hence a creation (ordered by its own laws) rather than an imitation (ordered by the laws of something external to itself). This philosophy, if one attempts to take it as all in all, is probably not enough to enable the survival either of art criticism or of art. Yet it is a pole of thought and reality which has always and unremittingly (whether critics were aware of the fact or not) exerted its energy toward the modification of too simple or too rigid norms of external reference or mimesis—just as those classical norms in turn, along with the affective norms which reach full discussion only in modern times, inevitably exert their own energy to subvert the monistic form of expressionism. We may venture the minimal and summary statement that today it has become almost impossible for the literary critic or historian to use classical conceptions of mimetic decorum or rhetorical affectivity without some tempering awareness of the Crocean critique.

Croce's influence in the English-speaking world has been most readily traceable in the names of his British translators and commentators, Collingwood, Carritt, Walkley, Carr, and in the work of expressionist aestheticians like the American C. J. Ducasse in his early phase, and more broadly in other aesthetic thinking, like Bosanquet's quasi-hedonist *Three Lectures on Aesthetic* of 1923, or even in thinking of a distinctly rival cast. A few years before they died, Croce and John Dewey confronted each other in the *American Journal of Aesthetics and Art Criticism*, the former making large claims of paternity upon the experiential and pragmatist aesthetic of the latter, and the latter irritably alluding to the pervasiveness of the concepts at stake. Literary critics have been on the whole less likely to advertise their indebtedness to Croce—though the "new criticism" sponsored in America by the historian J. E. Spingarn about 1910 was clamorously Crocean, and doubtless a number of acknowledgements might be cited as paralleling that made by the Scotch professor Lascelles Abercrombie in his *Theory of Poetry*, 1926—to Aristotle, Croce, and "common sense." The influence of Croce has been like that of Kant in the era 1800 to 1840 in France, of a pervasive and atmospheric kind, blending with a generally favorable climate of opinion so as not always to be clearly distinguishable.

SUPPLEMENT

In Richmond this month, the Virginia Museum of Fine Arts, instead of allowing the customary five-man jury to select its biennial of contemporary U.S.
painting, has set a precedent that could be profitably followed by other and
larger institutions the country over. To avoid what the Richmond director,
Leslie Cheek, Jr., says of the previous juried exhibitions—"the selections inevitably represented compromises"—he invited, for the 1950 event, a one man
jury and special director in the person of James Johnson Sweeney. Mr.
Sweeney's philosophy and operating policy (with full power to select, invite
and hang the exhibition) are set forth by him in the following pages.
. . . the *succès de scandale* of the first night was not an abstract painting at
all, but a distinguished romantic realist, Hyman Bloom, with his *Female
Corpse*. . . . Nobody seemed to take *that* as a metaphor, proving once more
that most Americans can accept their symbolism in the form of anything, including trade-marks and jingling commercials, so long as it isn't symbolical
realism. Even so, it would have been impossible to foresee the violence and
the pathetic rage with which the Bloom was greeted. An editorial the next
morning in the *Richmond Times-Despatch* went a long way toward a U.S.
record for malapropism and bad taste: it began by disqualifying itself in rank-
ing Mr. Sweeney's choice with its own evaluation of Joyce's *Ulysses*, "A tongue-
in-cheek pretense of 'erudition' which must be seen to be properly deprecated."
But it concluded with an attack on the Virginia Museum's source of income
in state funds, implying that they could be cut off for showing "corpses"—
which is serious business indeed.

The Bloom (any similarity in name to characters in James Joyce's *Ulysses*
is entirely accidental) is, in the writer's opinion and that of many others, an
important American picture. In its subject matter, of course, it shares some
identity and apparently a momentary fate with that of Géricault's *Raft of
the Medusa* and Courbet's *Burial at Ornans*. With them, it violates the sacred
bourgeois tabu that the cadaver is never brought into the parlor except for
the actual funeral party. And, with them, its fate will be to remain misunderstood until the metaphor is discovered beneath the superficial reality.

—Alfred M. Frankfurter, *Art News*, XLIX (May, 1950), 17, "Vernissage:
One Man's Corpse"

*Queries: Why is this only a bourgeois tabu? Why isn't it a good tabu?
Who are the people who ordinarily bring the cadaver into the parlor? For
what purposes? What is the metaphor he is talking about? Why isn't this just
pretentious hot air? Is it? A look into* Art News *for May, 1950, where Bloom's
"Female Corpse, Back View, 1947" is reproduced on p. 18, might lead to a
fruitful series of revelations and speculations concerning the "ugly" in graphic
art.*

Let us now stop and restate the ideas which we are considering in relation to one another. The first is that the style of a poem and the poem itself are one; the second is that the style of the gods and the gods themselves are one; the third is that in an age of disbelief, when the gods have come to an end, when we think of them as the aesthetic projections of a time that has passed, men turn to a fundamental glory of their own and from that create a style of bearing themselves in reality. They create a new style of a new bearing in a new reality. This third idea, then, may be made to conform to the way in which the other two have been expressed by saying that the style of men and men themselves are one. Now, if the style of a poem and the poem itself are one; if the style of the gods and the gods themselves are one; and if the style of men and men themselves are one; and if there is any true relation between these propositions, it might well be the case that the parts of these propositions are interchangeable. Thus, it might be true that the style of a poem and the gods themselves are one; or that the style of the gods and the style of men are one; or that the style of a poem and the style of men are one. As we hear these things said, without having time to think about them, it sounds as if they might be true, at least as if there might be something to them. Most of us are prepared to listen patiently to talk of the identity of the gods and men. But where does the poem come in? And if my answer to that is that I am concerned primarily with the poem and that my purpose this morning is to elevate the poem to the level of one of the major significances of life and to equate it, for the purpose of discussion, with gods and men, I hope it will be clear that it comes in as the central interest, the fresh and foremost object.

—Wallace Stevens, *Two or Three Ideas*, Chapbook Published by the College English Association as a Supplement to *The CEA Critic*, XIII (October, 1951), pp. 4–5, by permission of the University of Pennsylvania Press

When gods and men turn into each other, curiously it is the poem (initially the medium for effecting such transvaluations) which begins to have a hard time maintaining its identity and calls out for salvaging. Wallace Stevens' subtly twisted essay in poetico-theology may be consulted as a plenary illustration of what occurs when the idealistic and fictional view of the world makes a present and urgent threat to take over.

CHAPTER 24

THE HISTORICAL METHOD: A RETROSPECT

§ *the idea of history, early bibliographies, history as decline, as progress, Ancients and Moderns, the rationalist stance—II. reactions, Dryden, Gildon, the medical analogy, Thomas Warton on* The Faerie Queene, *Hurd,* Letters on Chivalry and Romance, *the Gothic norm, French parallels, Chatterton, Macpherson—III. Temple, Of Ancient and Modern Learning, cyclic primitivism, Vico, Hurd,* Elizabethan Dialogue, *Thomas Warton's* History, *three ages of English literature, Hazlitt's* Lectures on the English Poets, *Peacock and Shelley again, romantic and classical dialectic—IV. Warton again, studying old poetry, Germanic complications, national spirit, Carlyle, French determinism, Taine,* History of English Literature, *race, milieu, and moment—V. scholarly achievements of 19th century, the personal and the genuine, scientific evidence, alliance of antiquarianism and genius, tough techniques and emotive interests, "expression"—VI. personal studies, Schiller and Goethe, Taine's devotion, Sainte-Beuve, Shandean depth, Browning and the Shelley letters, Furnivall's comment, Percy's folio, Mrs. Brown of Falkland, forged imagination, Ossian, Skeat and Chatterton, Andrew Lang and Sir Walter Scott, Bentley and Cicero—VII. aestheticism again, Oxford Hegelianism, Leslie Stephen, John Morley, Courthope's* History, *the* Cambridge History, *decline in historical theory, art of praise, Gosse et al., literary scientism, Professor Sherman counting words, Johns Hopkins, the Modern Language Association of America, conflux of motives, the new era, Professor Price's address, vogue of Taine and Brunetière, science and the socio-real—VIII. recent complexities,* History of Ideas, *A. O. Lovejoy,* ELH, *affinities for literary criticism, Geoffrey Tillotson,*

*the original meaning, F. W. Bateson, the elite audience,
dissatisfaction of the critic, Lionel Trilling, "The Sense of
the Past," "extra-aesthetic authority," contemporaneity,
dating and genuineness, tabloid of ambiguities* §

IN SEVERAL EARLIER CHAPTERS [1] WE HAVE ALLUDED TO THE ROLE WHICH the idea of history, or the consciousness of history, has played during modern times in determining conceptions of literature and of literary study. We have noticed the questions about literary progress which appeared in the quarrel between the Ancients and the Moderns during the latter 17th century, the notion of poetry as the evolving expression of racial or national history which occupied German romantic thought from the time of Herder on, and the Hegelian complication of historic process into dialectic idealism and the results of such philosophy during the 19th and 20th centuries, especially in Russian and French theories about the sociologically didactic function of literature. The present chapter aims at giving a somewhat more special account of how modern professional literary studies have developed in the direction of historical method.

In a very simple way historical method began to find an entrance into literary study through early modern attempts at writing literary chronicle—early nationalistic inclinations to look back over certain centuries and to catalogue authors, manuscripts, or printed books, as in the bibliographies of English literature compiled by Leland, c. 1545, Bale, 1548 and 1557, Tanner, 1748, or Mackenzie, 1708–22.[2] But such interests could not continue very long without becoming involved in complications.

The medieval and early Renaissance ages of criticism looked on literary norms as very safely fixed and enduring and on the history of literature—like that of civilization in general—as a decline from a Golden Age. The history of the world had exhibited a lamentable decline of "coherence."[3] But the early 17th century in England saw the rapid rise, under Baconian scientific auspices, of the idea that modern pigmy men might by standing on the shoulders of ancient giants reach even a little higher than they. The end of the century moved on the full sweep of

[1] Chapters 11, 17, 21, 22.
[2] See Wellek, *Rise*, pp. 4–5, 135. This chapter owes a great deal in various places not only to Professor Wellek's *Rise of English Literary History* and to various published essays of his which will be acknowledged in the notes but to two manuscript essays: "English Literary History during the Romantic Age" (read at the Indianapolis meeting of the Modern Language Association in 1941) and "English Literary Historiography in the Victorian Age" (read at the New York meeting of the Modern Language Association in 1944).
[3] Cf. Victor Harris, *All Coherence Gone* (Chicago, 1949).

the rationalist theory that history had been a steady progress from barbaric shadows toward the clear light of the new age. In literature, this was the Modernist view of a direct clear progress from the medieval quaintness of Chaucer toward the correctness in diction and verse of the Augustans. France had taken somewhat of a lead and had provided a model. Back toward the beginning of the century Malherbe had arrived ("enfin Malherbe vint") to purify French style. And at the end, Boileau, though he battled against Modernist pretensions and claimed his authority only "in right of Horace," could nevertheless be said to "reign." The concept of a modern progress had to be more or less accommodated (as we have seen, for instance, in Pope's *Epistle to Augustus*) inside a wider panorama of the Ancient and Modern world. The cycle from Chaucer to Pope was paralleled by the ancient Roman cycle from Ennius to Horace. Still the Augustan emphasis was heavily on modern perfection and on the limping steps which preceding generations had taken toward this state. This was classicism stiffened by the Cartesian accent. The same reasonable spirit which when operating by itself would relegate poetry to a role of outmoded enchanter's gibberish, would when it was allied with the literary spirit assert the principle of literary progress and of modern supremacy in correctness. This Augustan attitude, so well known nowadays to literary historians, was to survive throughout the 18th century and, less conspicuously, even into the 19th. The Elizabethanism of a Coleridge, a Hazlitt, or a Lamb was contemporary with numerous antithetic expressions. Elizabethan prose, Nathan Drake would say, was "quaint, uncouth and tedious, insufferably prolix." It was afflicted with a "barbarous and pedantic stiffness." [4] All poets before Surrey, said Surrey's editor of 1815, George F. Nott, "must be read in reference to the particular age in which they lived. . . . But of this allowance Surrey never stands in need." There is "hardly anything in all his writings to remind us that he lived nearly three hundred years ago." [5]

II

THAT was approximately the rationalist stance, or the classical stance as fortified by the scientific spirit. But it had already, for over a hundred years, been serving as a point of departure for several kinds of liberal

[4] *Essays, Biographical and Historical, Illustrative of the Tatler, Spectator and Guardian* (1805), II, 3-4.

[5] *The Works of Henry Howard Earl of Surrey and of Sir Thomas Wyatt the Elder* (London, 1815), I, ccliii. "Entire passages might be quoted which have all the appearance of having been written in the purest times of modern literature; nor could they be distinguished from the most finished periods of either Pope or Dryden. This is an improvement which reason and judgment must approve as one of the highest importance to our literature."

reaction. The least aggressive kind might be described as merely a plea for tolerance, for giving the literature of ruder ages a square deal. Don't let a man be tried by the laws of a country of which he is not a citizen. Ignorance, in literature as in morals, is some extenuation of guilt. This, however, could easily turn into some such more liberal demand as— simply: Let us not dispute about the different tastes of different times and places! Or, again, with the cutting edge turned in a new direction: Perhaps it was the classic law-givers who were ignorant; they might have changed their minds if they had seen what we have seen.

> The climate, the age, the disposition of the people, to whom a poet writes, may be so different, that what pleased the Greeks would not satisfy an English audience.

> It is not enough that Aristotle has said so, for Aristotle drew his models of tragedy from Sophocles and Euripides; and if he had seen ours, might have changed his mind.[6]

Various scientific analogies might support the argument. Charles Gildon, answering an attack by William Walsh on the artificiality of modern love verses, first insinuates a relative aesthetic on the analogy of medical science:

> Our Physicians have found the Prescripts of *Hippocrates* very Defective; And as in Physic, so in Poetry, there must be a re- gard had to the Clime, Nature, and Customs of the People; for the Habits of the Mind as well as those of the Body, are in- fluenc'd by them; and *Love* with the other Passions vary in their *Effects* as well as *Causes*, according to each Country and Age; nay, according to the very Constitution of each Person affected.[7]

But later—shading tolerance into preference:

> Regard must be had to the *Humour*, *Custom*, and *Inclination* of the Auditory; but an *English* Audience will never be pleas'd with a dry, Jejune and formal Method that excludes Variety as the Religious observation of the Rules of *Aristotle* does.[8]

[6] Dryden, *Heads of an Answer to Rymer*, c. 1677, in *Critical and Miscellaneous Prose Works*, ed. Edmond Malone (London, 1800), I, ii, 305–6.

[7] *Miscellaneous Letters and Essays*, ed. Gildon (London, 1694), "An Essay and a Vindication of the Love-Verses of Cowley and Waller," p. 210, quoted by R. F. Jones, "Science and Criticism in the Neo-Classical Age of English Literature," *JHI*, I (October, 1940), 393. Jones cites Marchamont Nedham, *Medela Medicinae*, 1665, for the argument that diseases and remedies vary according to countries, times, and nations. Cf. Jones, *Ancients and Moderns* (St. Louis, 1936), p. 216.

[8] *Miscellaneous Letters*, p. 223, "To my Honoured and Ingenuous Friend Mr. Harrington, for the Modern Poets against the Ancients." In Thomas Killigrew's comedy *Chit-Chat*, 1719, a character remarks that he would as soon receive medical treatment by the rules of Hippocrates and Galen as see a play written by the rules of Aristotle and Horace (Jones, *JHI*, I, 395).

The argument for tolerance of various tastes and times might be used in favor of an earlier time (that of Chaucer or Shakespeare) when that time was criticized too rigorously by modern classical critics, or the same argument for tolerance might be used in favor of the modern time when that time was criticized too rigorously by the norms of classical antiquity. In this variation, the argument, though using comparative or relativistic premises, could actually swing into support of the classico-scientific notion of simple linear progress.

But the argument for the *earlier* time, the apology for Shakespeare or Chaucer as innocent violators of rules they never made, is that which had the greater immediate future. It was this which developed strongly during the 18th century as Thomas Warton and other writers took up apologetic themes invented two centuries earlier by Italian defenders of romance epic, but heard only now and then, as in an essay by Chapelain (*En Lisant les Vieux Romans*) [9] during the century of French classicism. Thus Warton in his *Observations on the Faerie Queene of Spenser*, 1754:

> In reading the works of an author who lived in a remote age, it is necessary, that we should look back upon the customs and manners which prevailed in his age; that we should place ourselves in his situation, and circumstances. . . . For want of this caution, too many readers view the knights and damsels, the turnaments and enchantments of Spenser with modern eyes, never considering that the encounters of Chivalry subsisted in our author's age . . . that romances were then most eagerly and universally read; and that thus, Spenser from the fashion of his age, was naturally dispos'd to undertake a recital of chivalrous achievements, and to become, in short, a ROMANTIC POET.[1]

> But it is absurd to think of judging either Ariosto or Spenser by precepts which they did not attend to. We who live in the days of writing by rule, are apt to try every composition by those laws which we have been taught to think the sole criterion of excellence. Critical taste is universally diffused, and we require the same order and design which every modern performance is expected to have, in poems where they never were regarded or intended. Spenser, and the same may be said of Ariosto, did not live in an age of planning. His poetry is the careless exuberance of a warm imagination and a strong sensibility. It was his business to engage the fancy, and to interest the attention by bold

[9] Cf. Victor M. Hamm, "A Seventeenth-Century Source for Hurd's *Letters on Chivalry and Romance*," *PMLA*, LII (1937), 820–8.

[1] *Observations* (1754), Section X, p. 217.

and striking images, in the formation, and the disposition of which, little labour or art was applied. The various and the marvellous were the chief sources of delight. Hence, we find our author ransacking alike the regions of reality and romance, of truth and fiction, to find the proper decorations and furniture for his fairy structure. Born in such an age, Spenser wrote rapidly from his own feelings, which at the same time were naturally noble. Exactness in his poem, would have been like the cornice which a painter introduced in the grotto of Calypso. Spenser's beauties are like the flowers in Paradise.[2]

Warton teeters from the accent of apology toward the accent of triumph. He wavers between saying that in order to read an old author we ought to know the customs, favorite books, and literary laws of the time when he wrote[3] and saying that if through better historical knowledge we do learn to read an old author, we may find that in him after all, rather than in our classically correct contemporaries, is the true spirit of poetry. How far this wavering represents an indecision on Warton's part (a conflict between the Augustan ideas in which he had been educated and the Spenserian poetry by which he felt himself attracted) or how far it was a strategy of getting a foot in the door before shoving, is a matter scarcely relevant to the present inquiry.[4] In the *Letters on Chivalry and Romance* published by Warton's friend and correspondent Bishop Richard Hurd in the same year (1762) as the second edition of Warton's *Observations*, the accent of apology[5] has become almost incidental to a far more excited manifesto in favor of the Gothic norm.

The greatest geniuses of our own and foreign countries, such as Ariosto and Tasso in Italy, and Spenser and Milton in England, were seduced by these barbarities of their forefathers: were even charmed by the Gothic Romances. Was this caprice and absurdity in them, Or, may there not be something in the Gothic Romance peculiarly suited to the views of a genius, and to the

[2] Second edition, 1762, Section I (I, 21). Cf. the encomium of Chaucer, 1754, Section V, p. 142.

[3] For similar, if more generalized, statements of this part of the historical argument, see Samuel Johnson's *Miscellaneous Observations on Macbeth*, 1745, and *Preface* to Shakespeare, 1765.

[4] Cf. D. Nichol Smith, *Warton's History of English Poetry* (London, 1929), pp. 1–5, 27–9. Modern scholarship concerning Warton and his friend Hurd resounds with the question whether they were really "romantics" and rebels. See, for instance, R. D. Havens, "Thomas Warton and the Eighteenth-Century Dilemma," *SP*, XXV (1928), 50; Odell Shepard, "Thomas Warton and the Historical Point of View in Criticism," *JEGP*, XVI (1917), 153–63; Hoyt Trowbridge, "Bishop Hurd: A Reinterpretation," *PMLA*, LVIII (June, 1943), 450–65.

[5] See Letter VIII on examining a Gothic structure by Grecian rules.

ends of poetry, And may not the philosophic moderns have gone too far, in their perpetual ridicule and contempt of it? [6]

We are upon enchanted ground, my friend; and you are to think yourself well used that I detain you no longer in this fearful circle. The glimpse, you have had of it, will help your imagination to conceive the rest. And without more words you will readily apprehend that the fancies of our modern bards are not only more gallant, but, on a change of the scene, more sublime, more terrible, more alarming, than those of the classic fablers. In a word, you will find that the *manners* they paint, and the *superstitions* they adopt, are the more poetical for being Gothic.[7]

We arrive, then, at romantic primitivism—the notion that the poetry of uncivilized times, or poetry written about uncivilized times, is the most natural, the most directly human, the most powerfully emotional—pathetic and sublime—and is hence the best. It was about this time that in France Rousseau exploited the political and educational idea that human suffering proceeds from the artificiality of civilization. Diderot was saying that the more a people is civilized and polished, the less are its customs poetic. Everything civilized weakens and sweetens.[8] Condillac's *Traité sur l'Art d'écrire* (1775) draws a sharp contrast between the ages of vivid imagination and succeeding ages of analysis, taste and criticism. In England appeared the primitivistic forgeries of Chatterton (giving his age a stronger taste of the 15th century) and of Macpherson (giving the age what it wanted, a Homer of the Celtic dawn).[9] The issue of "poetic diction" (peasant or aristocratic?) which we have noted in the debate between Wordsworth and Coleridge was one of the more precise and grammatically defined issues produced by the trend of primitivism.

III

THE doctrine of primitivism was a stark contradiction to the Augustan notion of linear progress from barbarism. A simple view of progress was

[6] Letter I, p. 81. Cf. Letter VI, p. 108: Homer, had he had the opportunity, would have "preferred" the "feudal ages" for their "improved gallantry" and "the superior solemnity of their superstitions."

[7] Letter VI, p. 113. Cf. Letter XII, p. 154, "a world of fine fabling."

[8] *Oeuvres*, ed. Assézat-Tourneur, VII, 370.

[9] Macpherson's *Dissertation Concerning the Poems of Ossian*, published with *Temora* in 1763, observes that "The nobler passions of the mind never shoot forth more free and unrestrained than in the times we call barbarous. That irregular manner of life, and those manly pursuits, from which barbarity takes its name, are highly favorable to a strength of mind unknown in polished times. In advanced society, the characters of men are more uniform and disguised. The human passions lie in some degree concealed behind forms and artificial manners; and the powers of the soul, without an opportunity of exerting them, lose their vigor" (second paragraph).

countered by an equally simple view of effete decline. Some complication of this procedure was, however, possible. The Augustan view itself, as we have noticed, had required the contemplation of two classical or Augustan ages, the ancient and the modern. In his essays *Of Poetry* and *Of Ancient and Modern Learning*, 1690, Sir William Temple had given this frame of reference a twist toward the primitivistic by arguing that the modern situation was not a peak of poetical achievement but somewhere on a downslope toward effeteness. Such a complication was in effect the meeting of the Augustan and the primitive notions and the reduction of each, as purely conceived, to the status of an inferior extreme. Yet it was a complication too that was almost bound to favor the primitive somewhat over the classical. For if poetry had risen, it could have risen only from some state of uneducated rudeness, and if it had ever declined, it could have declined only into some state of *over*civilized effeteness. The scheme was bound to be viewed from its forward end (no society of theorizers could possibly see themselves as sunk in barbarism). The theorizers were bound to look back to a less theoretical, more imaginative, golden age. The earliest elaborate version of such a cyclic primitivism is perhaps to be found in Vico's theory of the imaginative rise of human institutions (his ages of patriarch and myth, of king and emblem, of society and law) expounded in the *Scienza Nuova* of 1725. Vico was not known in England during the 18th century. But his ideas would not have been out of place. In one of Bishop Hurd's Elizabethan *Dialogues*, often printed along with his *Letters on Chivalry and Romance*, occurs the following very adequate general statement.

> There is, I think, in the revolutions of taste and language, a certain point, which is more favourable to the purposes of poetry, than any other. It may be difficult to fix this point with exactness. But we shall hardly mistake in supposing it lies somewhere between the rude essays of uncorrected fancy, on the one hand, and the refinements of reason and science, on the other.
>
> And such appears to have been the condition of our language in the age of Elizabeth. It was pure, strong, and perspicuous, without affectation. At the same time, the high figurative manner, which fits a language so peculiarly for the uses of the poet, had not yet been controlled by the prosaic genius of philosophy and logic.[1]

Both the simpler primitivistic contrast (between imagination and reason, between elemental passion and social criticism) and some kind of cyclic

[1] *Hurd's Letters on Chivalry and Romance with the Third Elizabethan Dialogue*, ed. Edith J. Morley (London, 1911), pp. 71–2. The dialogue is the third of Hurd's eight *Moral and Political Dialogues*, and the first of two dialogues on Elizabethan topics. The *Dialogues* were first published in 1759.

elaboration were 18th-century commonplaces which carried well through the theorizing of the romantic period. Thomas Warton's *History of English Poetry*, 1774–81, by far the most elaborate venture of its kind up to that date and an authority which remained standard for several generations, is permeated with an assumption that the growth of reason dries up the sources of imagination. The narrative is laid out on a conception of English literature as divided into three main ages, the archaic, the golden or Elizabethan, and the modern age of wit, toward which the Elizabethan declined.[2] This is a scheme which prevails in English literary history during the next half century, either in fairly literal repetitions, or in such modifications as that of Hazlitt in his *Lectures on the English Poets*, 1818, where he talks about the imagination of the Elizabethans, the fancy of the metaphysicals, the wit of the Restoration, the commonplaces of the 18th century.[3] In an earlier chapter [4] we have seen elaborate cyclic views joined with both primitivistic enthusiasm and anti-primitivistic satire in Shelley's *Defense* and in the *Four Ages* of his friend Peacock. Add to the Augustan phase of effete intellectualization a resurgence of poetry in the romantic era itself, and value this negatively as a pseudo-primitive relapse into barbarism, and we have the *Four Ages*. Value the romantic phase as a kind of promising spring-tide in cosmic legislation, and we have the historical conceptions underlying the *Defense*. Repetitions of the 18th-century pattern or protests against it appear in nearly all the English romantic essayists, in Coleridge, in De Quincey, in Carlyle.[5] At the same time, the romantic mind, both German and English, tended to reduce the phases of literary evolution to only two, a natural and an artificial, a romantic and a classical, conceived either as alternating without limit—a series of revolts against nature and of restorations—or as moving forward from the Homeric, directly natural or naive, in the irreversible dialectic of self-awareness or reflexive involution which we have noted in another earlier chapter.[6]

I V

BOTH in his *Observations on the Faerie Queene* and in his *History of English Poetry* Thomas Warton argues for the study of old, barbaric poetry mainly on the grounds that it records the "features" of a past

[2] Gray's scheme for a History of English Poetry, in a letter to Warton, 15 April, 1770 (first printed in the *Gentleman's Magazine*, February, 1783, pp. 100–1) gave Restoration and Augustan literature the name "school of France."

[3] See *Complete Works*, ed. P. P. Howe, VI (London, 1930), 83.

[4] Chapter 19.

[5] See René Wellek, "De Quincey's Status in the History of Ideas," *PQ*, XXIII (July, 1944), 264–5; "Carlyle and the Philosophy of History," *PQ*, XXIII (January, 1944), 63–4. Cf. Wellek, *Rise*, p. 193.

[6] Chapter 17.

time, "preserves the most picturesque and expressive representations of manners," "transmits to posterity genuine delineations of life." [7] During the romantic age the relation of literary study to historical antiquarianism becomes more complicated, participating in the Germanic conception that literature is the organic creation of a national mind, the expression of a certain society, age, and national spirit. Carlyle gives us the following vigorous formulation.

> The history of a nation's poetry is the essence of its history, political, scientific, religious. With all these the complete Historian of Poetry will be familiar: the national physiognomy, in its finest traits, and through its successive stages of growth, will be clear to him; he will discern the grand spiritual tendency of every period, which was the highest Aim and Enthusiasm of mankind in each, and how one epoch evolved in itself from the other. He has to record the highest aim of a nation, in its successive directions and developments; for by this the poetry of the nation modulates itself; this *is* the Poetry of the nation. Such were the primary essence of a true history of poetry.[8]

During the mid-19th century, French versions of this argument are the most prominent. They are less idealistic and patriotic than the earlier German versions, more sociological and deterministic. In what became the classic French instance with regard to England, Taine's *History of English Literature*, 1864, the aim of literary study is to uncover the environmental causes of literature—and these are conceived as falling under the now famous three main heads of *race, milieu*, and *moment*. That is, the study of literature is valuable because literature, even more than religion (which is a combination of poesy and credulity) and even more than philosophy (which is a mere dry abstraction from poetry) is the warmest and fullest revelation of the motives by which civilizations are determined. For the purpose of this study, poetry stands on the same level with all the other forms of direct human revelation, not only dramas and novels but letters, sermons, table talk, memoirs, "confessions." "The proper object of literature is to take note of sentiments." In fact literature cannot fail—it is rigorously determined—to take note of sentiments.

And so for every kind of human production—for literature, music, the fine arts, philosophy, science, statecraft, industries,

[7] The phrases are taken from Warton's *History of English Poetry*, Preface, p. II. Cf. *Observations on the Faerie Queene*, 1762, Postscript, II, 323: "These compositions . . . preserve many curious historical facts, and throw considerable light on the nature of the feudal system. They are the pictures of ancient usages and customs; and represent the manners, genius, and character of our ancestors. . . ."

[8] *Essays* (Chapman and Hall edition, 1907), III, 225. Originally in the *Edinburgh Review*, vol. LIII (1831), no. 105, a review of William Taylor of Norwich's *Historic Survey of German Poetry*, 1831.

and the rest. Each of these has for its direct cause a moral disposition, or a combination of moral dispositions: the cause given,
they appear; the cause withdrawn, they vanish; the weakness
or intensity of the cause measures their weakness or intensity.
They are bound up with their causes, as a physical phenomenon
with its condition, as the dew with the fall of the variable temperature, as dilatation with heat.[9]

V

THE drive toward literary history had begun during the 18th century
in observations and speculations that were primarily evaluative—that is,
they had to do with a re-assessment of neo-classic norms and a turning
back to look at primitive literatures with what was considered a greater
fairness. Such fairness having been established, and along with it an attitude of some unfairness toward the classic spirit which had once held
sway, speculation continued, as we have seen, in the direction of historical rather than explicitly evaluative goals. The pursuit of literary
studies along such lines could not, however, fail to have profound implications concerning literary value. Both the goals themselves and the
more and more efficient historical techniques which were developed in
their pursuit tended to establish such implications. The mere presence of
historical research as a method of ever-increasing efficiency tended to
promote exhibitions of its worth. Expensive tools have to be used.

The notion of a rigorously historical study of literature had, it is
true, a long neo-classic and classic ancestry. Yet this kind of study
flourished during the 19th century as never before. It will be sufficient
for present aims merely to allude to the union of Bentleian and Wolffian
classical philology with Scriptural hermeneutics under the leadership of
Wilhelm von Humboldt and Schleiermacher, the further transfer of these
methods to modern literature in the *Encyklopädie und Methodologie
der Philologischen Wissenschaften* of August Böckh, the Indo-Ger-
manic philological and folklore triumphs of the brothers Grimm, and
somewhat later in France the resuscitation of the epic cycles and romances by such French scholars as Léon Gautier and Gaston de Paris.
Here was the exalted situation of primitive epic (plausible enough outcome of such 18th-century efforts as those of Hurd) against which
Matthew Arnold raised a classical voice in 1881. In our chapter on
Arnold we have alluded already to the contrast between the classical and
critical spirit of Arnold and the contemporary rise of the empirical linguistic studies which launched the *Oxford English Dictionary on Historical Principles*. During the same era occurred the final purification of
the Chaucerian canon by Bradley and Skeat, a work begun in the 18th-

[9] H. A. Taine, *History of English Literature*, trans. H. Van Laun (New York,
1886), Introduction, pp. 20, 18. Cf. esp. pp. 6–8, 10, 13–15.

century dawn by Tyrwhitt, and the multiplication of Shakespearian studies in every historical dimension. It is perhaps relevant to offer here the general observation that English literary scholarship tended to go against the grandiose generalizations, the dynamic aspirations, the sociological significance of the history writers in the German spirit. Resolute literary research avoided wider questions, suspended critical judgment, devoted all its energy to the accumulation of facts. The immediate value of these might be now and then difficult to see; still it would be rash to question their ultimate place in some construction of total learning.

The reversal of classical norms during the 18th century had meant not only a turning back to the primitive (as in itself a concept of value) but, as we have seen in Chapters 14 and 16, a new kind of respect for the original and genuine, and hence for the personal. Classical sophistication inevitably involved, or seemed to involve, a measure of "imitation" and artificiality. The really primitive, on the other hand, was necessarily a form of originality. And the really primitive could be discovered, in the last analysis, only by techniques of historical research. A certain wildness and abandon, a strength of color and emotion, might make out a *prima facie* case for the primitive. But the final test was scientific. Only scientific historical inquiry could justify an experience of pleasure in the emotion and the color.

The peculiar tone of 19th-century literary study, at least in England, would appear to result from a working union between two forces which one might offhand think of as quite disparate—the force of hardheaded, sceptical, factfinding, textual, bibliographical and biographical antiquarianism, and both augmenting this force and being augmented by it, the force of devotion to poetic genius, to the personality, originality, mind and emotion, virtues and vices, life, suffering and death of the literary creator. The concept of life and sufferings included all kinds of influences upon the creator, and hence no contradiction had to arise between personal study and more deterministic conceptions of national history, sociology, or politics. "Expression," as J. E. Spingarn has argued (with only a little exaggeration), was a motif common to all the forms of 19th-century theory. With the Germans and with their evangelists such as Mme. de Staël literature was an "expression of society." In the school of art for art's sake, from Victor Cousin on, "expression" in itself was the simple supreme law of art. In the variation given this philosophy by Sainte-Beuve and other men of letters, literature was the expression of personality. In the historical and deterministic critics deriving from Hegel, like Taine, literature was the expression of race, milieu, and moment. The "extreme impressionists," as Spingarn calls them, the later aesthetes like Pater and Wilde, thought of literature as the "exquisite expression of delicate and fluctuating sensations or impressions of life." [1]

[1] J. E. Spingarn, "The New Criticism," in *Criticism in America, Its Function and Status* (New York, 1924), pp. 19–20.

For all critics and theorists, literature was the expression of something. The norm of expression was the great co-ordinator, harmonizing the toughest and most scientific research techniques with the softest, most personal, and most emotive aesthetic interests.

VI

It is worth pointing out that the German romantic litterateurs, in their distinction between "classic" and "romantic" art, even Schiller in his germinal distinction between "naive" (direct and objective) classical art and "sentimental" (reflexive and subjective) romantic art, entertained no special reverence for authors themselves as persons to be consulted in the discrimination of one sort of art from another or even in the interpretation of the personal, sentimental, or romantic art. Thus Goethe in his *Conversations:*

> The Germans cannot cease to be Philistines. They are now squabbling about some verses, which are printed both in Schiller's works and mine, and fancy it is important to ascertain which really belong to Schiller and which to me; as if anything could be gained by such investigation—as if the existence of such things were not enough. . . . What matters the mine and thine? One must be a thorough Philistine, indeed, to attach the slightest importance to the solution of such questions.[2]

Literary critics of immediately succeeding generations, however (and one finds convincing examples both in France and in England), had no such scruples about the biographical application of the derivatively romantic theories to which they subscribed. Even Taine's vast schemes of cultural psychology were heavily grounded in a devotion to the individual, producing genius. The Introduction to his *History of English Literature* gets under way with the following nicely conceived imagistic strategy.

> What is your first remark on turning over the great, stiff leaves of a folio, the yellow sheets of a manuscript,—a poem, a code of laws, a declaration of faith? This, you say, was not created alone. It is but a mould, like a fossil shell, an imprint, like one of those shapes embossed in stone by an animal which lived and perished. Under the shell there was an animal, and behind the document there was a man. Why do you study the shell, except

---

[2] December 16, 1828. Cf. the complaint by Heine about the appeal to biographical information in reading his poetry and his sweeping rejection of the principle (*Correspondance*, I [Paris, 1867], 73 ff., June 10, 1823).

to represent to yourself the animal? So do you study the document only in order to know the man.[3]

And Sainte-Beuve, a critic moving along on the full tide both of the historical method and of the quasi-Kantian French movement of art for art's sake, exhibited in his numerous lectures and *causeries* the widest range of interest, understanding, and technique, but his most pronounced critical insight and most radical method, so far as he was a methodical critic, lay in the depth of his devotion to the personality of the author behind the work. The work existed mainly to provide him clues to the charting of that rich hinterland. No more deeply committed version of the biographical principle has perhaps ever been written than the following passage of his *Nouveaux lundis:*

> Literature, the literary product, is for me indistinguishable from the whole organization of the man. I can enjoy the work itself, but I find it difficult to judge this work without taking into account the man himself. I say without hesitation: *Like tree, like fruit.* Literary study thus brings me naturally to the study of morals.
>
> One has to ask oneself a certain number of questions about an author, and give answers to them (even though not out loud —and even though the questions may seem quite irrelevant to the nature of the works to be studied). Only after such questions can one be sure about the whole problem one faces. What did the author think about religion? In what way was he impressed by the contemplation of nature? How did he handle himself in the matter of women? How in the matter of money? Was he rich? Was he poor? What rules of living did he follow? What was his daily routine? And so on.—To sum it up: what was his master vice, his dominant weakness? Every man has one. Not a single one of the answers we give to these questions can be irrelevant to forming an opinion about the author of a book and about the book itself—that is, if we suppose we are dealing with something other than a treatise in pure geometry.[4]

[3] *History of English Literature,* trans. H. Van Laun (New York, 1886), Introduction, p. 1.

[4] *Nouveaux lundis* (Paris, 1865), III, 15, 28. The phrase *Like tree, like fruit* renders the French *tel arbre, tel fruit,* the inexplicit syntax of which is well suited to conveying the notion that here is something that will support Sainte-Beuve's line of argument. The Scriptural *arbor fructu cognoscitur,* which lies behind the French saying, points of course exactly in the opposite direction.

Sainte-Beuve wished to study an author in both his genealogy and his living family—in his father, his mother, his sisters and brothers, and even in his children (*Nouveaux lundis,* III, 18 ff.). He would study the author's childhood, his early environment, even the landscape in which he grew up. Taine, for instance, bore the impress of the gloomy Ardennes (*Nouveaux lundis,* VIII, 71).

From the mid-century in England we may take as a capital instance Browning's Introductory Essay to the Shelley letters published by Moxon in 1852. There are two kinds of poetry, wrote Browning, echoing faintly the utterances of the great Germans.[5] There is "objective" poetry, like that of Shakespeare, which does not depend on the personality of its author and does not require that we know anything about him. And there is "subjective" poetry, like that of Shelley, which is all compact of its author's personality and which takes on added richness and resonance with every iota of the author's personal record which we can discover. And so what extraordinarily good luck that these revelations of Shelley's mind have been preserved and are now made public!

> Such being the two kinds of artists [objective and subjective], it is naturally, as I have shown, with the biography of the subjective poet that we have the deeper concern. Apart from his recorded life altogether, we might fail to determine with satisfactory precision to what class his productions belong, and what amount of praise is assignable to the producer. . . . we must in every case betake ourselves to the review of a poet's life ere we determine some of the nicer questions concerning his poetry,—more especially if the performance we seek to estimate aright, has been obstructed and cut short of completion by circumstances,—a disastrous youth or a premature death. . . .

> The responsibility of presenting to the public a biography of Shelley, does not . . . lie with me: I have only to make it a little easier by arranging these few supplementary letters, with a recognition of the value of the whole collection. This value I take to consist in a most truthful conformity of the Correspondence, in its limited degree, with the moral and intellectual character of the writer as displayed in the highest manifestations of his genius.

One trouble with the argument, as all the world now knows, was that the supposed revelations of Shelley's mind were forgeries—throwing non-authentic light on Shelley's poems. Yet Browning we may suppose had his genuine access of pleasure and perhaps even an enhancement of insight into Shelley's art.[6] (There may well have been some insight,

---

[5] Cf. Meyer Abrams, *The Mirror and the Lamp* (New York, 1953), pp. 242–3, 375, n. 50, on the distinction between objective and subjective poetry as entertained by Friedrich Schlegel, Coleridge, De Quincey and others.

[6] See the statement of a recent editor: "The plain fact is that Browning wrote his essay as a foreword to a collection of spurious letters; but in this case the plain fact is less important than usual. Of the twenty-five letters in Moxon's publication of 1852, all but two were utter forgeries, pieced out with a few genuine phrases from Shelley's pen. . . . If here had been the only ground for the editor's enthusiasm, we

through whatever objective vision the forger himself enjoyed, and the forgeries to that extent were happy.) At any rate, Browning's venture was surely not to be written off as a failure in the cumulative history of romantic experience. One of the most scientific of Victorian philologists and one who was characteristically able to merge his science with a passion for the personal revelation, the distinguished Saxonist and Shakespearian F. J. Furnivall, makes, in an Introduction to the Browning Society reprint of the Introduction, published in 1881, the following boast of his own failure to be interested in Browning's poems:

> The interest [in Browning's Introductory Essay] lay in the fact, that Browning's "utterances" here are *his,* and not those of any one of the "so many imaginary persons" behind whom he insists on so often hiding himself, and whose necks I, for one, should continually like to wring, whose bodies I would fain kick out of the way, in order to get face to face with the poet himself, and hear his own voice speaking his own thoughts, man to man, soul to soul. Straight speaking, straight hitting, suit me best.[7]

The intense and precise labors of the Victorian philologists in the service of authenticity and other forms of factuality resulted in a great purification and straightening out of literary canons, and in large accesses of knowledge about the general education and reading habits of various authors. At the same time, the philologists were but moderately interested in the relation of their canonical and genetic discoveries to questions of evaluation and criticism. Furnivall and Hales, for instance, in their editing of the folio MS. from which Bishop Percy had taken his *Reliques of Ancient English Poetry* in 1765, pounced with much righteous scorn on the various prunings, normalizations, clarifications, and civilizations which Percy, not only an antiquarian but a critic, and faced with a real problem concerning the relation between antique fact and poetic value, had taken the liberty of imposing upon the old text. Furnivall and Hales performed their service of restoration and rehabilitation with unswerving rigor. It was an advantage to them not to be disturbed by any scruples about literary value such as had dis-

---

might well be startled at its strength. But it is clear that Browning paid very little attention to the letters he was introducing to the world" (H. F. B. Brett-Smith, *Peacock's Four Ages of Poetry, Shelley's Defence of Poetry, Browning's Essay on Shelley,* Oxford, 1945, p. xxiv).

[7] *Browning Society Papers,* No. 1, London, 1881. A note to this passage contains the further curious confession: ". . . if a reader is thick-headed, or can't spare time to study and think a poem out, should not a poet give him a helping hand by a 'mediate word'?" Quoted by Alba Warren, pp. 112–13. Cf. Warren, p. 90, Carlyle's mistrust of the poetic medium, his view of Shakespeare's works as only a poor glimpse of the man himself—"windows" opening dimly upon him.

turbed the Bishop—or rather it was their advantage to enjoy a serene unification of scientific conscience with a belief that literary value was always and essentially identical with primitive authenticity. They were not coping with the question: Which of more than thirty versions of the ballad of *Sir Patrick Spens* is the most artistic? It would not have occurred to them to raise the question raised by a recent American scholar, whether Mrs. Brown of Falkland, Sir Walter Scott's informant about the text of ballads, may not have showed as much artistry in the recreative effort which went into her recording as had earlier recreators (to whom she had listened as a young woman) in their own efforts.[8]

In that heyday of scientific and conscientious recovery of the English literary past, problems could, however, become curiously complicated by the existence of such forged monuments to sincere imagination as the enthusiastic primitivism of the 18th century had produced. Here and there a stalwart taste, like that of Carlyle, J. S. Mill, or Herbert Spencer, might hold out for the Homeric grandeur of Ossian, but by and large the decline during the 19th century in the reputation of that remote bard kept pace with the growing obviousness that the Celtic magic was spurious. In another crucial instance, a special difficulty for arbitrating between fact and value arose because there was ample opportunity for comparing the forged language with that which philology could demonstrate to have actually prevailed in the literary era which was mimicked. Skeat's essay on the 15th-century English style which the ingenious Chatterton had scrambled together from 18th-century glossaries was one of the clearest triumphs a modern philology might win over the uncertainties which Warton, Ritson, and even Tyrwhitt had to some extent shared with the juvenile hoaxer. "The plan of the present edition," says Skeat, "will now be explained, and can be readily understood. Given the problem, how to edit the Rowley Poems to the most advantage? What must be the answer?" He was quite sure of this answer:

> To do away with the needless disguises, and, on the supposition of their [the poems'] not being genuine, to give them as far as possible in modern English.

> The reader now has a chance, *for the first time*, of judging what the poems are really like, without being continually pulled up, sometimes three times in a line, by hard words which no amount of acquaintance with early MSS. will enable him to solve. The process of thus re-writing the greater part of the poems has been rendered easier by frequently substituting Chatterton's

[8] Bertrand H. Bronson, "Mrs. Brown and the Ballad," *California Folklore Quarterly*, IV (April, 1945), 129–40.

words in his *footnotes* for his words in the *text*. Thus, at p. 29, the second line in the original stands thus;

Throwe halfe hys joornie, dyghte in *gites* of goulde;

but Chatterton's footnote explains *gites* by *robes*. It is therefore quite justifiable to substitute *robes;* indeed, we really thus approximate more closely to the true original text, viz. to the text as first conceived in the poet's brain before it was translated into the Rowleian dialect.

It is important to understand that Skeat undertook this normalization of Chatterton's text not simply as a way of attaining philological truth (at any aesthetic cost) but actually as a way of getting at true aesthetic value—so closely were the notions of philological truth and aesthetic value united in his philosophy.

What is the exact amount of merit to which Chatterton's genius attained, the reader can, in this edition, at last judge for himself. I only wish to say here that I have faithfully striven so to discharge my task as to protect the reader, on the one hand, from being misled by false old English, whilst endeavouring, on the other, to set forth Chatterton's thoughts to the best advantage. . . . That the public does not want *me* but *Chatterton*, is the fact I have endeavoured to keep steadily before me.[9]

Let us add one simple Chattertonian example to that which we have already supplied from Skeat's own Essay. The opening of Chatterton's *Bristowe Tragedie* reads:

The feathered songster Chanticleer
Han wound his bugle horn. . . .

Skeat duly corrects the second line to "Has wound his bugle horn" (without any advertisement of the fact) and so obliterates in the interest of grammar a part of whatever minor charm the tiny clarion of the line may have had.[1] Skeat's editing of Chatterton back to normal modern English is a turning of the knife in the wound; it accomplishes a kind of double forgery. The method carries out to the letter the

9 W. W. Skeat, "Essay on the Rowley Poems," in *The Poetical Works of Thomas Chatterton*, ed. W. W. Skeat (London, 1872), II, xxxvii, xxxix, xlii. See the approving comment of Henry A. Beers, *A History of English Romanticism in the Eighteenth Century* (New York, 1899), p. 363. Skeat gets us "a little closer to the Rowley poems."

1 For some 20th-century comments on Chatterton, written with a more Jabberwockian understanding of the relation between his faking and the exact nature of his poetic merit, see E. H. W. Meyerstein, *A Life of Thomas Chatterton* (New York, 1930), p. 176; Bertrand Bronson, "Thomas Chatterton," in *The Age of Johnson, Essays Presented to Chauncey Brewster Tinker* (New Haven, 1949), p. 246.

legitimate implications of the factual norm of authenticity and originality; but it has the disadvantage that it leaves "Chatterton the Marvellous Boy" with very little explanation of where he stands in the history of English poetic achievement.[2]

Near the end of a long career as translator and popularizer of classical epic and as custodian of native balladry, Andrew Lang wrote a book on the vexed question about the authenticity of the *Border Minstrelsy* which Sir Walter Scott had assembled from such authorities as Mrs. Brown of Falkland and James Hogg the Ettrick Shepherd. And what of Sir Walter's own role as a ballad maker? Of one thing Lang was sure.

> If it [*Auld Maitland*] is a bad ballad, such as many people could compose, then it is not by Sir Walter.[3]

In short, authorship guaranteed quality, and by a legitimate manipulation of the hypothetical syllogism implied, quality was at least a necessary condition for the imputation of authorship. So far as this was a focus on the literary work itself, rather than on external types of information about it, the argument might find its classical analogues. "I wouldn't believe Cicero had written this way," said Bentley, "even if Cicero himself should swear he had."[4] Cicero might have dreamed he had written that way, or he might simply not have remembered not having done so. So far as the emphasis is on the means of establishing who wrote something, the preference in a given case for internal over external evidence is neither peculiarly classical nor peculiarly postromantic.[5] But it will be noticed that Bentley's statement is a greater hyperbole; it contemplates the extreme of discountenancing the very testimony of the author himself about his own writing. The basic supposition on which Lang and his generation were working was the opposite. Clear, irrefutable external testimony that Sir Walter was the author of a ballad would have elicited from Lang the admission that it

---

[2] On the genetic side, R. D. Havens, "Assumed Personality, Insanity and Poetry," *RES*, N.S. IV (1953), 26–37, discusses the resemblance of forger's mask to Bedlam retreat in releasing such 18th-century poets as Chatterton, Macpherson, and Smart from the inhibitions of the neo-classical poetic conscience.

[3] Andrew Lang, *Sir Walter Scott and the Border Minstrelsy* (London, 1910), p. vi.

[4] The question at issue was whether the name of Hermagoras in Latin should end in *as* or *a*. Quintilian quotes Cicero as using *a*. But: "*Repone hic paulisper, Hermagora inventor, & Hermagora habuisset; non sentis vocalium concursum vaste hiantem? Ego vero Ciceronem ita scripsisse ne Ciceroni quidem affirmanti crediderim*" (Richard Bentley, *Epistola ad . . . Millium*, 1691, quoted in part in footnote to Alexander Pope's *Dunciad* IV, 222). Cf. Bentley's *Emendationes in Menandri Reliquias* (Cambridge, 1713), p. [70].

[5] Cf. Thomas Warton's insistence on the internal and aesthetic evidence against the authenticity of the Rowley poems (*An Enquiry into the Authenticity of the Poems Attributed to Thomas Rowley*, London, 1782, p. 90).

was a good ballad. Criticism would be merely the finding of praise in support of the poetic value necessarily entailed by authenticity.

VII

DURING the latter part of the 19th century, the aesthetic movement which we have considered in Chapter 22 took a contemplative, static view of individual art works and so was anti-historical. Also anti-historical was the kind of non-dialectical Hegelian idealism which appeared at Oxford in A. C. Bradley's appreciation of Shakespearian tragedy and in the essays of W. P. Ker.[6] We have observed already that the more ambitiously systematic kind of literary history writing never enjoyed a real vogue in England. Still a modest tradition may be traced during the latter half of the century in works of Leslie Stephen, John Morley, and even so aesthetically removed a litterateur as Walter Pater.[7] This reached its climax and conclusion in W. J. Courthope's great *History of English Poetry*, published from 1895 to 1910. Courthope, reciting the history of the national imagination in close relation to political institutions, conceives a long dialectical conflict between individualism and collectivism—(the collective Middle Ages had been bad for literature, the harmoniously adjusted Renaissance very good, and the romantically individual modern time bad again). He was a master of the long vista into intellectual history.

The decades immediately following Courthope's *History* saw much activity in the simpler chronicle forms of English literary history (in this period the encyclopedic *Cambridge History of English Literature* was begun and completed), but at the same time there was a decline in speculative history-writing and in a theoretical concern for literary history.[8] The movement of art for art's sake, especially as it affected the criticism of such litterateurs as Gosse, Saintsbury, Raleigh, Quiller-Couch, or Garrod, led away both from history and from criticism to the creed of enthusiastic appreciation and in historical effort to the supposedly literal fidelity of the "photographer's plate."[9] A sceptical attitude toward scholarship became fashionable in England early in the

---

[6] Notably that on the "Philosophy of Art" in the Hegelian manifesto *Essays in Philosophical Criticism*, 1883, reprinted in Ker's *Collected Essays* (London, 1925), II, 231–68.

[7] See Stephen's *History of Thought in the Eighteenth Century*, 1876; Morley's *Studies in Literature*, 1891; Pater's *Plato and Platonism*, 1893. Literature, said Stephen, is the "noise of the wheels of history" (Frederick W. Maitland, *The Life and Letters of Leslie Stephen*, London, 1906, pp. 283–4).

[8] Just at the moment when general cultural history was spreading out into wider and wider cyclic panoramas—as in the works of Spengler and Toynbee.

[9] G. E. B. Saintsbury, *History of English Criticism* (Edinburgh, 1911), pp. 499, 521.

20th century and discouraged all but the less reflective kinds of anti-quarianism and the whimsical essay in the "art of praise." Within the field of critical writing in English, it has remained indeed for American scholarship during the 20th century to carry some of the anti-critical trends which we are about to describe to their most systematic extremes.

In America during even the first decades of the 20th century, academic literary criticism was less warmly colored by romantic personalism and the art of praising. Although a Bliss Perry, a William Lyon Phelps, and later a Henry Seidel Canby did appear and flourish, American literary study was much more inclined than the British to borrow rigors from the methods of German philology and in general to undertake a respectful emulation of feats being performed in the laboratories of physical science. The literary scientist tried to set up the rules of his experimental procedure with sober and neutral precision. Consider, for instance, Professor L. A. Sherman of the University of Nebraska. In a series of notes appearing in the periodical *Science* during 1889, he read that conclusions about the average number of words per sentence used by a given author should not be based on a sampling of fewer than many thousands of sentences. Inspired by this conception, he counted the number of words per sentence for all five volumes of Macaulay's *History of England* and demonstrated a "consistent numerical . . . average," of 23.43 words per sentence.

> Here, then, in this 23.43 was the resultant of the forces which had made Macaulay's literary character.[1]

In 1876 the Johns Hopkins University had been founded expressly for the purpose of introducing upon the American scene the graduate seminar on the German model. In 1883 was organized the Modern Language Association of America, which in 1927 voted to change the original definition of its purpose, "the study of modern languages and literature," to a phrasing more consonant with what had long before become its actually dominant purpose, the "advancement of research in the modern languages and literatures." (It was only in 1950 that the members of the Association voted to add to their constitutional statement of purpose the word "criticism.") A new era of American literary studies was carried in triumphantly by a massive conflux of motives which might be named separately as (1) respect for German philology, (2) a native American desire for facts and scientific precision, (3) a social and moral readiness to fall in with the critical relativism invited by the study of literature in its causes and origins, (4) a growing democratic require-

---

[1] L. A. Sherman, "On Certain Facts and Principles in the Development of Form in Literature," *The University Studies of the University of Nebraska*, I (July, 1892), 350–3.

ment of mass production in the qualification of scholar-teachers, and (5) on the side of the warmer emotions a romantic nostalgia for the European past and the Middle Ages. The rigors of scientific antiquarianism were, as we have already suggested, far from incompatible with certain kinds of sentimentalism—both the personal devotions and gossip of biographical research and the various nationalistic limitations of view, the provincial specializations, which by the end of the 19th century had grown out of the romantic German stress on origins and the evaluation of literature as national or racial physiognomy.[2]

Great things were to be expected in America of the newly imported method, the dawn of a new intellectual life. The aspect of joy and celebration, of pioneer triumph, which came with the arrival of the new disciplines may be illustrated from the presidential address delivered by Professor Thomas R. Price of Columbia before the Annual Meeting of the Modern Language Association in 1901:

> . . . we must all feel a certain warmth and exhilaration. With that period of forty years . . . there has been a steady current of progress. . . . There has been, indeed, in this wide enthusiasm for the spreading and elevation of modern language instruction, an intellectual movement that may fairly be compared with the enthusiasm in the days of the Renaissance. . . . In country villages I found the same ardor for our special studies as in great universities. No man that has shared in this movement can fail to feel a noble joy.[3]

American literary scholars were on the whole more favorably impressed than were the British by deterministic and social thinking about literature along the lines that had been laid down by German and French historians, notably by Taine. The name of Taine and that of Brunetière (who had complicated and partly countered the deterministic view by adding to it the idea of the Darwinian evolution of literary genres)[4] were commonplaces of American journalistic criticism around the turn of the century.[5] In a more routine way, without reference to Taine or to other foreign authorities, and with only a more or less complete understanding of what went on, American literary research found wide scope in exercises relating literature to various kinds of influence— social, political, economic, climatic, national, regional, traditional, psychological, and genealogical—all that might be fitted under the most

[2] See René Wellek, "Literary Scholarship," in *American Scholarship in the Twentieth Century*, ed. Merle Curti (Harvard University Press, 1953), esp. pp. 111–17.

[3] *PMLA*, XVI (1901), 77–91, quoted by Wellek, *loc. cit.*, p. 112.

[4] See especially his *L'Evolution des genres dans l'histoire de la littérature*, 1890, and *Manuel de l'histoire de la littérature française*, 1897.

[5] See W. V. O'Connor, *An Age of Criticism 1900–1950* (Chicago, 1952), pp. 4–6, 51–3.

inclusive and most durable of Taine's three headings, the term "milieu." [6]

Let us attempt a brief retrospective statement which will locate the present topic in relation to that of the socio-real in literature which we have already discussed in Chapter 21. The ground of relation is the concept of science in literature. Two divisions of the concept may be distinguished, the creative and the historico-critical: 19th-century science as the religion of reason sponsored an advance from the realism of Flaubert to the highly theorized and self-conscious naturalism of Zola and Frank Norris (literature scientifically faithful to life), and at the same time another advance from the historical principles of literary study laid down by Taine to the literary evolutionism of Brunetière and then to the more generalized and readily available doctrine that literary criticism should be neutral and tolerant and should devote itself to discovering the natural forces by which literature is caused. There were easy enough connections between neutral determinism and sociological interests, and hence between historical science and certain new forms of didacticism. American literary scholarship during the 1920's and 1930's moved along lines that led quite smoothly into companionship with the proletarian criticism that flourished during the second of those decades. The case for literature as class propaganda and social criticism seemed very obvious. The academically established techniques stood clearly ready to support it. The association between the names of New England college professors and organs of doctrinaire liberal opinion like *The New Republic* became a normal phenomenon.

VIII

BUT the course of literary scholarship during the past twenty-five years both in America and in England has been remarkable for the variety and mixture of its historical and historico-critical drives. One of the most complicated contributions during this period from the historical side has been an American version of *Geistesgeschichte*,[7] the new school of the History of Ideas, initiated by Professor A. O. Lovejoy and represented in his numerous essays and in the *Journal of the History of Ideas* which he founded in 1940. (An earlier journal founded also [1933] by Hopkins professors, *ELH, A Journal of English Literary History*, has aspired to make a much more specifically literary application of historical principles.) Professor Lovejoy and his colleagues

[6] See Edmund Wilson's essay "The Historical Interpretation of Literature," in *The Intent of the Critic*, ed. Donald Stauffer (Princeton, 1941).

[7] Wellek, *loc. cit.*, p. 119 points out that the form of *Geistesgeschichte* cultivated in Germany during recent decades was a reaction against positivistic philology. Among the few direct echoes of that movement in America was the hostile *Academic Illusions*, 1933, by Martin Schütze.

have quite openly confessed to being interested in literature only as it is a document of intellectual history, a "dilution" of "philosophical ideas." [8] These historians may be looked upon as frankly dismissing the discussion of literary values and hence as not being in aggressive conflict with that discussion. The technique of the History of Ideas when picked up by literary scholars themselves, however, has produced some new versions of the problems that were posed in their essentials during the 18th century by writers like Warton and Hurd. The history of ideas has turned out to have a special kind of affinity for literary criticism—the reason for this lying not in the emphasis of the discipline on history, but in its emphasis on ideas. Despite the atomistic treatment of "unit" ideas, like slogans or catchwords, which is a first principle of the school, ideas as such do tend to have implications and to be related in systems. It would be difficult, for instance, to expound Pope's *Essay on Man* in the light of Professor Lovejoy's essays on nature, deism, and classicism without implying something about the organization of ideas in the poem itself and hence about its unity and coherence. Much more than the classic types of textual, bibliographical, biographical and source study, the new reduction of "ideas" to historical study has tended to approach the contestable border lines where historical study and literary evaluation interact and must be reconciled. For ideas constitute the more universal and durable meaning of words—meaning as differentiated from momentary suggestion and from the mere denotation of local date, place, and other fact. Ideas are hence lexicography, the history of the meanings which inform and vitalize the poet's medium, his vocabulary. History of Ideas, if it has not created any critical problem which is on principle different from that created by Hurd's desire to re-appraise Gothic manners, has at least subtilized and universalized the problem.

But in the history of ideas, *whose* ideas are of most importance? The historical problem has been made somewhat more difficult in recent years not only by a growing interest in the history of poetic interpretation but by the emergence of a newly emphasized doctrine that the duty of the literary critic is to look only to the initial moment in any given history. A verbal expression will change in time, perhaps it will improve—but *illegitimately*. What a reviewer in the *Times Literary Supplement* called "an uncomfortably strict rectitude," a very pure attitude of reverence toward the historic moment at which the poet wrote and his first readers read, was illustrated vivaciously in the British critic Geoffrey Tillotson's *Essays in Criticism and Research*, 1942. "To read later emotions here and there into a poem," argued Professor Tillotson, "is a tedious error in criticism and worthy only of the insipidly fickle florilegist."

[8] *The Great Chain of Being* (Cambridge, Mass., 1936), p. 17.

The original meaning of a word in a great poem is the only one worth attending to. However delightful the meaning arising out of new verbal connotations, such meaning is irrelevant to the author's poem. He must stand by his poem as he meant it. . . . When Lady Anne Winchelsea wrote

> Nor will in fading silks compose
> Faintly the inimitable rose,

she meant that she disliked the common feminine pastime of embroidery since it can produce only a poor 'imitation' of an actual rose. But following on after the romantic poets and all the talk about pure poetry, those lines have accidentally taken on a beauty which did not exist for their author.[9]

Perhaps so. The wider implications of the argument, its actual stress on history in some public sense rather than on the author romantically *per se*, were more fully brought out only a few years ago by the British critic and historian F. W. Bateson of Oxford. Following up the success of an earlier inquiry into the linguistic determinations of literature (*English Poetry and the English Language*, 1934), this critic accomplishes a reversal of the usual bent of historical studies toward origins.[1] He is willing to think that the author himself and his inspirations can be related to the produced poem only somewhat dubiously and irrelevantly. Not so the audience for whom the author produced the poem and on whom it made its first impact. Here is a more objectively solid point of reference. Studies in literary reputation had appeared before this, and more than a little scattered attention had been paid to such first-hand evidence as that provided by the diaries and letters of novel readers and theater goers (Simon Forman in the day of Shakespeare, Samuel Pepys in the Restoration, Boswell, Fanny Burney, Horace Walpole, and all the memorialists and letter-writers of the 18th and 19th centuries). Bateson, however, has undertaken to manipulate such material into a distinct theoretical dimension. He offers us the proposition—fairly novel in its clarity—that the validity of the literary work is to be decided exactly by its measure of conformity to the understanding of some historically specific audience. Within a given age there will be not one audience but a number of audiences—according to class, sex, coterie, profession—and hence a number of possible frames of reference. Only one of these, however, will be right. The essential function of poetry is "the expression in language of the sense of social solidarity." And Bateson believes, "on the evidence of the poetry," that "at any one

[9] *Essays in Criticism and Research* (Cambridge, at the University Press, 1942), pp. xx–xxi. Cf. *TLS*, April 4, 1942, p. 174.
[1] F. W. Bateson, *English Poetry: A Critical Introduction* (London, 1950), pp. 69 ff.

period" there was "only one social group in England that was functioning healthily." If we modern readers want to understand a poem of the
past, "we need to be able to identify ourselves as far as possible with
its original readers, the poet's contemporaries, whose ideal response to
the poem in fact constitutes its meaning." Here is milieu and moment
with a sharply new twist.

Perhaps Bateson's argument offers as convenient a provocation as
any for concluding our narrative of the historical method with some
hint of the dissatisfaction which it may entail for the critic even in its
most recent and subtle versions. A critic is a person who habitually
finds himself puzzled to know on what grounds (the poem itself? or some
testimony outside the poem?) he is expected to divine what are sometimes referred to as a poet's intentions. And in this matter Bateson is
apparently at one with the critic. But may not a critic find himself
equally puzzled to know on what grounds (poem or something outside
the poem) he is expected to identify the readers the poet *intended* to
address? Or how is the critic to decide who were the elite or "most intelligent" among the poet's actual first readers? And were these elite
the poet's actual best readers? What of Dr. Johnson's response to the
poetry of Gray? What of Milton's readers before Dryden's and Addison's criticism? What of the contemporary readers whom Gerard Manley
Hopkins almost entirely lacked and did not seek? What of most readers
of Eliot's *Waste Land* in 1922? Let the present writers be content to say
here that they believe a critic ought to have in mind not just any response
of a contemporary reader, or the average response, or even the response
of any elite group, but in a more generally human sense an "ideal response." And in this of course we refuse the question, taking the onus
off the shoulders of any empirically identifiable audience and placing
it on the "meaning" of the poem itself.[2]

The American Professor Lionel Trilling's essay entitled "The Sense
of the Past," as it is one of the latest, appears to us also one of the most
delicate complications of the historical problem. "To suppose that we
can think like men of another time," says Professor Trilling, "is as much
an illusion as to suppose that we can think in a wholly different way."
(As if points of view could be put in and out of our minds like lantern
slides—and opaque ones at that.) Yet certain difficulties do attend upon
our making the ideas of the past transparent for our own uses. "In cer-

[2] The view suggested here does not of course attempt to discountenance a dramatically conceived audience as reflected in the poem itself or in its tone—Marvell's
coy mistress, Donne's metaphoric antagonist Death, Shelley's West Wind, or the audience of young ladies and their polite gentlemen admirers to whom Pope's *Rape of
the Lock* (as distinguished, say, from his *Dunciad*) is immediately addressed. The
critical reader of poetry, and especially the reader of a later age, constantly reads
over the shoulder of a dramatic reader who is as much a fiction as the story of the
poem or any of its rhetoric.

tain cultures," says Professor Trilling (and these include obviously our own), "the pastness of a work of art gives it an extra-aesthetic authority which is incorporated into its aesthetic power."

> Wordsworth's Immortality Ode is acceptable to us only when it is understood to have been written at a certain past moment; if it had appeared much later than it did, if it were offered to us now as a contemporary work, we would not admire it.[3]

Here it may be well to note the resemblance of the argument to that at which we arrived in concluding an earlier chapter,[4] on the technical problem of "poetic diction." Eliot's statement about the futility of repeating poetic achievements or Gertrude Stein's about the vital force of contemporaneity might as well appear in the present context as in the earlier. And so might the young joker who typed out some of Shakespeare's less well-known sonnets and submitted them to a New York press, with the result which need not be repeated here. Professor Trilling argues that a certain quality of pastness enters into some works of art with the lapse of time and becomes part of what we enjoy in them. But he seems to argue too—and this may be a somewhat different argument—that we excuse or accept certain masterpieces only because we know they were written in the past—as if we made allowances for the author's deficiency of scientific knowledge or social vision. Perhaps the truth is that we should find it so odd if a poet wrote in certain ways today that we could not help suspecting the poem somehow of being false. That is, any old-fashioned masterpieces that failed to get written in their own day will now never get written. And if they had been written, they would to some extent have changed the poetic tradition and hence would have changed the situation from which the modern poet must write. But none of these unquestionable facts about the genesis of poetry will quite justify the conclusion (which Professor Trilling in fact does avoid) that old masterpieces are to be taken only on tolerance, or that the only poems which are actually good reading today are contemporaneous ones. There is a passage in the *Practical Criticism* of I. A. Richards in which he argues that the date when a poem was written "cannot by itself settle its genuineness, in the sense of its sincerity." But it is good "presumptive evidence." A poet may well enough "write an entirely sincere poem in the manner of a different age, but on the whole the probability is strongly against it."[5] To the

---

[3] Lionel Trilling, *The Liberal Imagination, Essays on Literature and Society* (New York, 1953), pp. 182, 183, 184.

[4] Chapter 16.

[5] *Practical Criticism* (New York; 1935), p. 77. "It is impossible," writes Victoria Sackville West, "to imagine, even after allowing for changes of diction, a Gray's 'Elegy,' or an 'Ode on Intimations of Immortality,' still less a 'Prelude,' or a 'Paradise

ambiguous sense of the word "sincerity" in this passage—sincerity as warmness and innocence of purpose? sincerity as poetic power and achievement?—let us add a third shade of meaning (legitimate by historical and deterministic canons), sincerity as the poet's being in rapport with his age, and we have a tabloid of the whole ambiguously conceived ground which history and criticism are accustomed to dispute.

SUPPLEMENT

On examination mornings, he [Péguy] would ask the student next to him to wake him up in thirty minutes, after he had read the theme of the composition to be handed in. Then he would go to sleep as soundly as a child and upon being awakened would immediately set to work; and exactly on the dot, he turned in a flawless paper which almost always got the highest grade. There was never the slightest mistake in what he wrote and never a correction. Péguy did not believe it was right to make corrections. Whatever went through his mind in connection with the subject was immediately couched in that straightforward style which was already so convincing. Why, he thought, should he turn down a word or a group of words that had come to him as he wrote. They had a right to stand with all the other words on the page. They expressed something in him. He wasn't going to betray them by pretending that they never had been in his mind.

Péguy . . . wrote regularly, but he never knew what he was going to write when he sat down to his sheet of white paper. . . . Not a word was ever scratched out. If a word came to him, he argued, it had as much right to be written down as all its fellow-words in the book. It was there as a witness, like a pebble on the long road he travelled. Péguy considered that what he wrote had been dictated to him. When he wanted to praise a book, or a sentence in a book, he never said: 'It is good,' he said: 'It is dictated.'—Julian Green, Introduction to Charles Péguy, *Basic Verities, Prose and Poetry* (New York, 1943), pp. 17, 30, by permission of Pantheon Books, Inc.

The players have often mentioned it as an honour to Shakespeare, that in his writing, (whatsoever he penn'd) hee never blotted out line. My answer hath beene, would he had blotted a thousand. Which they thought a malevolent speech. I had not told posterity this, but for their ignorance who choose that circumstance to commend their friend by, wherein he most faulted.—Ben Jonson, *Timber: or, Discoveries* (1641)

Lost,' as the product of the twentieth century. . . . I do not believe that even a great poet, were one to arise, could or would move upon the place or breathe the air of Milton and Wordsworth. This is simply another way of saying that sublimity has gone out of fashion" (*Tendencies of Modern English Poetry*, quoted by H. W. Garrod, *Poetry and the Criticism of Life*, Cambridge, Mass., 1931, p. 13).

Rare Monkish Manuscripts for Hearne alone,
And Books for MEAD, and Rarities for Sloane.

—Alexander Pope, *Epistle to Burlington* (1731), ll. 9–10

Rarities! how could'st thou be so silly as not to be particular in the Raritys of *Sloane* as in those of the other five Persons? What knowledge, what Meaning, is conveyed in the Word *Raritys!* Are not some Drawings, some Statues, some Coins, all monkish Manuscripts, and some Books, *Raritys?* Could'st thou not find a Trisyllable to express some Parts of Nature for a Collection of which that learned and worthy Physician is eminent? Fy, fy; correct and write . . . *Butterflys for* SLOANE. *Sir Hans Sloane* is known to have the finest Collection of Butterflys in *England,* and perhaps in the World.

—Thomas Cooke, *The Comedian,* no. 2, May, 1732, p. 15 [Thomas Cooke was saluted by Pope in the *Epistle to Arbuthnot,* in *Dunciad* II, and in *Peri Bathous.*]

Rare Monkish Manuscripts for Hearne alone,
And Books for MEAD, and Butterflies for Sloane.

—Alexander Pope, *Epistle to Burlington* (1744), ll. 9–10

"Chamier once asked him," said Johnson, "what he meant by *slow,* the last word in the first line of *The Traveller:*
'Remote, unfriended, melancholy, slow.'
Did he mean tardiness of locomotion? Goldsmith, who would say something without consideration, answered 'Yes.' I was sitting by, and said, 'No, Sir; you do not mean tardiness of locomotion; you mean that sluggishness of mind which comes upon a man in solitude.' Chamier believed then that I had written the line as much as if he had seen me write it."

—James Boswell, *Life of Samuel Johnson,* 9 April, 1778

An editor of Goldsmith's poems, Austin Dobson, adds the remark: "It is quite possible, however, that Goldsmith meant no more than he said."

—*Poetical Works of Goldsmith,* Oxford, 1939, p. 167

Thomas Gray's *Elegy Written in a Country Churchyard* (1751) has been criticized adversely for being too personal a revelation of the poet's feelings about himself, especially in the Epitaph with which the poem concludes. On the other hand, the poem has been defended against this criticism by the following three lines of argument: (1) that the Epitaph represents Gray's feelings not about himself but about his close friend Richard West, who died in 1742; (2) that the Epitaph actually does not refer to Gray at all or to his friend, but, as may be seen if one reads the poem closely, to a rustic stone-cutter and epitaphic poet, addressed as "Thee" in stanza 24; (3) that the "me" of the first stanza, the "Thee" of stanza 24, and the Epitaph are all to be read, not in the traditional way, as representing Gray the man who is known in his letters to Walpole and other biographical documents, but in a more detached way, as representing a generalized *persona*, the anonymous poet who is the speaker of the poem. (For further light on these arguments, see Frank Ellis, "Gray's *Elegy:* the Biographical Problem in Literary Criticism," *PMLA*, LXVI, December, 1951, 971–1008.)

This problem in practical criticism is a trim realization of certain 18th-and 19th-century trends in theory about poems and poets. The second line of argument (2), a recent invention by Mr. Ellis, introduces a new degree of complication to the "diagonal" shift described in Chapter 6 apropos of Longinus.

.   .   .

It is not defence of the personalist drift, but explanation, that is needed. The personalist deviation is here to stay, not only in programme notes but in serious discussions of literature which, apparently unaffected by recent critical trends, continue to pour from the presses. For some it may be a racking experience to own that the personalist approach is still established as the dominant approach in most classrooms. But there it is, all the same.

However objectionable, the personalist approach manifests a persistency that itself clamours for explanation. If the urn really is the issue, why is it always in peril of being overlooked or tossed aside? If you so much as whisper that there is a jinnee in the urn, most onlookers will be only too willing to drop the urn without further ado. Broken, it will let the jinnee out, and they can ask him a few questions. While decrying the tendency to behave this way, we may be excused for asking what accounts for the presence of the tendency in the first place.

Man's deepest orientation is personal.

The assertion that in works of art it is the object itself which counts thus treads such crucial ground that it must be made with great honesty, which means with circumspection and humility. Not only the truth of the situation, but its awkwardness as well, must be faced. This awkwardness derives from the fact that, far fetched as it may seem when applied to less important works of art, the principle apparently holds that, in a valid but not exclusive sense, each work of art is not only an object but a kind of surrogate for a person. Anything that bids for attention in an act of contemplation is a surrogate for a person. In proportion as the work of art is capable of being taken in full seriousness, it moves further and further along an asymptote to the curve of personality.

—Walter J. Ong, "The Jinnee in the Well-Wrought Urn," *Essays in Criticism*, IV (July, 1954), 311, 315, 319, by permission of the editor.

PART FOUR

CHAPTER 25

TRAGEDY AND COMEDY: THE INTERNAL FOCUS

§ *Hegel's "lyrical" conception of tragedy: the ethical problem, conflict between rival "goods"—II. some modern variants of the Hegelian conception: A. C. Bradley and spiritual waste, Prosser Frye and the hero's guilt, J. W. Krutch and faith in the "greatness of man"—Arthur Schopenhauer's influence upon modern conceptions of tragedy: tragedy as affording insight into the blind striving of the Will—III. Nietzsche's "Musical" conception of tragedy: his distinction between an Apollonian and a Dionysian art: the origin of Greek tragedy in the festival of Dionysus, the union of the two gods in tragedy, Apollo speaks Dionysian wisdom—IV. tragedy as a harmonizing of discords: Nietzsche's stress upon the joyful wisdom of tragedy, upon tension in art generally—V. parallels and contrasts between Nietzsche's conception of tragedy and Bergson's conception of comedy: Bergson's notion that laughter springs from the discrepancy between the mechanical and the natural: sources of the comic in repetition, inversion, and reciprocal interference of series—Bergson's views on the social function of comedy, his relation to the "classical" view of comedy, his denial that comedy is a genuine art —VI. other psychological theories of laughter and the comic, Shaftesbury, Penjon, Kline, Kallen—VII. Freud's conception of wit as a device for conserving psychic energy: its aim to recover the lost euphoria of the child— VIII. the witty, the comical, and the humorous as distinguished by Freud: laughter as the sudden discharge of the conserved energy—IX. criticisms of Freud made by Max Eastman, and by Arthur Koestler: Freud's failure to distinguish the self-assertive and the self-transcending, integrative emotions—Koestler's view of the "bisociative" treatment*

*of phenomena: his argument that comedy, tragedy, and
the process of scientific discovery all involve bisociative
treatment of phenomena, and that since comedy and
tragedy have the same "cognitive layout," they differ only
in their specific emotional "charges"* §

EACH AGE TENDS TO FIND IN SOME ONE OF THE LITERARY GENRES THE norm of all literary art. The 17th century, we have seen, found the highest poetry to be embodied in the epic. The later 18th century saw in the lyric the "most poetic kind of poetry," [1] for men's interests had shifted, with the burgeoning Romantic movement, from an externally known world to the knowing and expressive self. Georg Wilhelm Hegel illustrates the new emphasis, not only in his philosophy of history, which is the story of spirit expressing itself through successive partial revelations until it finally achieves complete self-consciousness, but in his history of art as well. The first stage finds spirit almost overborne by matter, as in Egyptian art; then there comes the perfect balance between spirit and matter, as in Greek sculpture; and finally in modern art, spirit overflows and envelops matter.[2]

When men's minds are dominated by a lyric norm, their conceptions of the other genres are affected. Like metamorphosed rocks, the other genres, under the heat and pressure of lyricism, change their structure and appearance. Tragedy, for example, may be said to have become "internalized," even "lyricized." Terms like "struggle," "tension," and "resolution" shifted their meanings with the new conception of the problem. Consider, for example, how Aristotle characteristically handled the tragic protagonist's power of choice and his responsibility for that choice. The act that precipitated the downfall of the hero had to be more than a simple misadventure—an accident that simply "happened" to him; on the other hand, it had to be less than a calculated crime. The tragic protagonist could be neither passive victim nor obvious criminal. The problem of guilt and responsibility was thus a matter of central importance; but it is characteristic of Aristotle that this ethical problem is treated in the *Poetics* as a function of the plot. That is, the complicated play that Aristotle called for, a play that includes a *peripeteia* and an *anagnorisis*, demands an action by the hero of a certain seriousness and a certain responsibility. Aristotle's approach was to the total action that the tragedy presents—not directly to the ethical standards of the hero.

But Hegel's view of tragedy begins—and, one is inclined to say, ends —with the ethical problem. Whereas Aristotle was content to make

[1] Cf. *ante* Chapter 17, pp. 372–3.
[2] Cf. *ante* Chapter 17.

hamartia a partly responsible act of error without attempting to define the degree of culpability precisely, Hegel defines the hero's error very precisely: the good chosen by the hero is only a partial good though the hero treats it as though it were an absolute good. The characteristic struggle in tragedy is between rival ethical claims: good is set up against good; and the choice is not between good and evil, but between one good and another.[3]

Hegel considered *Antigone* to be the ideal example of Greek tragedy, probably because in this play we have the maximum of ethical tension. Both Creon and Antigone are right in the sense that the ethical loyalties that they acknowledge are valid. But each is wrong in assuming that the ethical principle exerts an *absolute* claim upon his loyalty. The reconciliation comes in our realization that the claims are but partial and that catastrophe has occurred through the human failure of mistaking the part for the whole. But it is well to notice that the reconciliation as envisaged by Hegel occurs in the mind of the spectator or auditor—not necessarily in the mind of the protagonist. Antigone, one has to suppose, goes to her death without ever realizing that she has mistaken a limited ideal for an absolute ideal.

The spectator perceives that though the conflict is dreadful for the human antagonists caught up in it, it is after all simply a stage in the dialectic through which spirit eternally expresses itself. Indeed, the tragic conflict as Hegel defines it fits comfortably into his massive philosophical system. Tragic conflict proves to be simply another instance of the contradiction of thesis by antithesis, a contradiction to be resolved only in a higher synthesis, where the counter claims of thesis and antithesis are admitted, yet any ultimate contradiction between them is shown to be illusory.

Hegel's is a philosopher's definition of tragedy—not necessarily the worse for that, to be sure—but it has provoked the reaction that it is too "intellectual," and it is certainly part and parcel of a theory of art which regards literature as a primitive, and therefore for the mature mind a limited and defective, kind of philosophy. Benedetto Croce, certainly not the least sympathetic critic of Hegelianism, has put this criticism decisively:

> In a greater degree than any of his predecessors Hegel emphasized the cognitive character of art. But this very merit brought him into a difficulty more easily avoided by the rest. Art being placed in the sphere of absolute Spirit, in company with Religion and Philosophy, how will she be able to hold her own in such powerful and aggressive company, especially in that of Philosophy, which in the Hegelian system stands at the summit

[3] See *The Philosophy of Fine Art,* trans. F. P. B. Osmaston (London, 1920), Vol. IV.

of all spiritual evolution? If Art and Religion fulfilled functions other than the knowledge of the Absolute, they would be inferior levels of the Spirit, but yet necessary and indispensable. But if they have in view the same end as Philosophy and are allowed to compete with it, what value can they retain? None whatever; or, at the very most, they may have that sort of value which attaches to transitory historical phases in the life of humanity. The principles of Hegel's system are at bottom rationalistic and hostile to religion, and hostile no less to art.[4]

Hegel's concept of tragedy does not fit all the extant Greek tragedies. *Oedipus Rex*, Aristotle's ideal tragedy, would have to be pulled and twisted more than a bit to make it answer to Hegel's definition: where in that play, for instance, is an ethical good set over against a rival good? Hegel himself admits that practically none of Euripides' tragedies conform to his notion, a matter which he explains by regarding Euripidean tragedy as "modern" in its concern for character and in its ethical laxity.

II

YET Hegel's concept of tragedy, in spite of its forbidding austerity, has had great and lasting influence. A. C. Bradley, for example, in his *Shakespearean Tragedy* (1904) and in his *Lectures on Poetry* (1909) gave us a somewhat softened, though distinctly Hegelian, view. In setting this forth for the English-speaking reader, Bradley was at some pains to defend Hegel against charges of inflexibility. He maintained that Hegel

> does not teach, as he is often said to do, that tragedy portrays only the conflict of such ethical powers as the family and the state. He adds to these . . . others, such as love and honour, together with various universal ends; and it may even be maintained that he has provided in his general statement for those numerous cases where . . . no substantial or universal ends collide, but the interest is centred on "personalities." [5]

But Bradley conceded that Hegel's treatment of the aspect of reconciliation was inadequate. Hegel did not sufficiently notice that more is involved than acquiescence. As spectators of tragedy we feel a positive exultation along with, and indeed because of, our awareness of the fact that "the hero has never shown himself so great or noble as in the death which seals his failure." [6] Our solace at the fall of the hero is, then, not

[4] *Aesthetic* (1901), trans. Douglas Ainslie (London, 1922), p. 301.
[5] *Lectures* (London, 1909), p. 85, by permission of Macmillan & Company, Ltd., and St. Martin's Press.
[6] *Lectures*, p. 84.

so much a reaffirmation of the moral structure of the universe as a heightened awareness of the greatness of man. Though not every tragedy shows ethical powers in conflict with each other, every tragedy does show, so Bradley argued, "a self-division and self-waste of spirit." [7] We see Macbeth's courage and imagination wasted in his defeat—yet their true grandeur is revealed only by his defeat. Thus, Bradley would broaden Hegel's definition: the typical and essential conflict to be found in tragedy is not that of good against good, but rather a conflict within the self: "*any* spiritual conflict involving spiritual waste is tragic." [8]

Bradley's definition has the merit of fixing attention upon an element that is found in a great deal of literature: not only in a tragedy like *Macbeth*, but in *Don Quixote*, in "Sir Patrick Spens," and even in "An Ode to a Nightingale." But the definition will scarcely help us distinguish tragedy as a genre. The tragic conflict is within the soul: tragedy manifests itself in our sense of spiritual waste. In this essentially "lyric" definition, the tragic becomes a personal and subjective quality.

In rejecting, as a ground for tragedy, Hegel's austere idealism in favor of a milder humanism, Bradley certainly acted in the spirit of the age. He praised tragedy for bringing home to us the spiritual qualities of the hero—his self-assertion, his noble endurance, his magnificent vitality—and nearly all recent writers on the subject have joined Bradley in this emphasis. Bonamy Dobrée, for example, regards tragedy as our prime means for testing man's ultimate strength. "Tragedy," he writes, "is man's trial of his individual strength, a trial becoming increasingly unpopular, indeed incomprehensible, with the advance of democracy." [9]

Prosser Frye's *Romance and Tragedy* (1922) also presented a Hegelian view of tragedy, but Frye retained, as the very center of tragedy, Hegel's insistence upon a problem of ethical choice. Like Hegel, Frye found in Greek tragedy the very type of tragedy, and he refused to soften the edges of his definition to admit more comfortably the Shakespearian masterpieces. Shakespeare, great poet though Frye admitted him to be, was dangerously committed to a modern and "Euripidean" interest in character—to the consequent blurring of a proper ethical focus.

Tragedy, as Frye defined it, rests upon the assertion of a universal moral order. The fall of the hero momentarily disturbs that order: the auditor or the reader is shocked. So great is the disproportion between what we feel ought to happen and what actually does happen that we experience a kind of giddiness—what Frye calls "the moral qualm." In genuine tragedy, however, that qualm is overcome: the very fall of the hero confirms the moral order which it had at first shock seemed to call in question. The tragic writer must stress this ultimate stability of the

---

[7] *Lectures*, p. 86.
[8] *Lectures*, p. 87.
[9] *Restoration Tragedy* (Oxford, 1929), p. 9.

moral order, for he is interested as a writer, not in a psychological, but in a metaphysical problem. The question that he must put is this: why does evil occur?

Shakespeare's alleged failure to put this question causes Frye to deny that he is a typically tragic poet. The question that Shakespeare characteristically puts seems to be: by what steps, through what process, did this apparently powerful and virtuous creature come to grief? And so we have the "tragedies" of Othello or of Hamlet, with their inordinate interest in character and their blurred focus on the metaphysical problem.

Sophocles, on the other hand, shows us that the fall of the hero is not an "accident" but is inevitable, the consequence of a certain blindness on the part of the hero. *Antigone*—which Frye follows Hegel in regarding as the ideal instance of tragedy—will illustrate. Antigone in her entire devotion to one ethical claim denies the other. But to defy the *polis* was a terrible thing, no matter what the motive, and no matter even that the motive be one which, like Antigone's, elicits a pitying response. The Greek audience, Frye insists, would have felt Antigone to be involved in criminality. This tension between terror and pity in our attitude toward the protagonist is for Frye the one necessary tension in tragedy. When this tension is relaxed—when we can view the protagonist with unqualified sympathy, then we are no longer in the presence of tragedy. The downfall of the hero has indeed become merely an unfortunate accident, a matter of unpropitious environment, or of some failure of adjustment. The tragic protagonist has to be responsible for his act; but if he is responsible, then he is in some sense culpable.

To this important point, Frye bears able and effective testimony, but he out-Hegels Hegel in the sternness of his ethical demands. His tragic writer is frankly a teacher; and he argues that literature, in so far as it is "true to itself and its own character," is concerned not to "image life" but to "commemorate some idea about it—or in other words interpret it." The interpretation that Frye demands is of a specific kind: it is not to be an economic or a sociological or an anthropological interpretation. It is to be a "humane" interpretation, and for Frye this depends upon the "new humanism" of Irving Babbitt and Paul Elmer More.[1] Indeed, Frye's *Romance and Tragedy* must be regarded as one of the ablest documents produced by the New Humanists. But, as in so much of the work of this group, there is a certain note of desperation. Frye is carrying out a stubborn rear-guard action. He gloomily notes that almost from the very birth of tragedy there has been a falling off, with no real recoveries. Even the classical Racine did not accomplish a return to genuine tragedy. The neohumanist scholar did not really hope for better days: he was simply keeping the record straight.

[1] Cf. *ante* Chapter 20.

Most modern writers on tragedy, however, have found such a diet too rich for their blood. They have not been interested in ultimate metaphysical questions. They are thoroughly secular and man-centered. What they see in tragedy is primarily a glorification of man's power to endure. We have already mentioned Dobrée's emphasis upon this theme, and other names might be added. Thus, W. V. O'Connor in his *Climates of Tragedy* (1943) refuses to allow that certain modern plays are tragedies on the ground that they do not sufficiently stress "the strength of man," but instead merely "offer consolation in a dogma." And Joseph Wood Krutch in *The Modern Temper* (1929) makes "faith in the greatness of man" a necessary condition for producing tragedy. A tragic writer, he says, does not have to believe in God, but "he must believe in man." Thus, our modern failure to write tragedies springs, not from our loss of faith in the supernatural, but from our loss of faith in the worth of human nature.

Modern writers—Krutch certainly and even A. C. Bradley probably —did not, however, arrive at the theme of noble, tragic endurance by simply expanding Hegel's formula. They borrowed generously from Hegel's German contemporaries and followers. Thus the theme of man's endurance as stated by Krutch reads like a secularization of A. W. Schlegel's treatment of tragic endurance as a form of human self-assertion, a gesture, as Schlegel would have it, made in the face of fate in order to assert the mind's proud claim to a participation in the divine.[2] Among the 19th-century German aestheticians, however, one may point to a much more direct and obvious source in the work of Arthur Schopenhauer. He was "for a long time unread and unknown," but by the end of the 19th century he had become "the most popular and influential of writers. Even in authors, like Gautier or Flaubert, who probably never set eyes on one of his books, we may fancy we feel a kindred spirit." [3]

In *The World as Will and Idea* (1818), Schopenhauer utterly rejected Hegel's notion that the universe manifests the force of spirit, *Geist*, unfolding itself through a self-ordained dialectic and revealing its reasonable nature more and more fully in history. Instead Schopenhauer conceived the ultimate reality to be a blind energy, which in its aimlessness actually belied the term *Will* by which he would name it. This "Will" objectified itself at various levels, in inorganic matter, in the vegetable and the animal kingdoms, and of course, in Man himself. But Man's reason does not represent a coming into consciousness of the Will, a stage in its *self*-realization, for the Will is irrational.

Man's reason is simply one more instrument at the disposal of the Will's blind striving. Yet it lies in Man's power to refuse to be an instru-

[2] Cf. *ante* Chapter 17.
[3] Gilbert and Kuhn, p. 472.

ment of the Will. He is able to free himself of desire, and at least at moments, stand aside from the struggle and simply contemplate serenely the innermost nature of reality.

Scientific knowledge, Schopenhauer insisted, does not reveal that reality. Scientific knowledge is eminently practical: it describes phenomena so as to put them at our service—which really means, at the service of the Will. But the knowledge that art gives is impractical, and that is its glory. Tragedy gives us an insight into the heart of the mystery, into the nature of evil, which is the nature of reality and hence of the Will. But Schopenhauer reserved a special function to the art of music. Music, unlike the other arts, is not tied to any objective representation of the Will but "speaks of the Will itself." "The composer reveals the inner nature of the world, and expresses the deepest wisdom in a language which his reason does not understand; as a person under the influence of mesmerism tells things of which he has no conception when he wakes." [4]

III

TRAGEDY is profoundly "musical" in just this sense, so argued Friedrich Nietzsche in his brilliant essay on *The Birth of Tragedy* (1872). But in doing so, Nietzsche rejected Schopenhauer's notion that tragedy was to be associated with serene contemplation. Tragedy did not arise among the Greeks out of any withdrawal from life, nor were the spectators of the tragedies of Aeschylus and Sophocles "detached" observers. On the contrary, only a formal and artificial barrier separated them from the dancing chorus, with whom emotionally they were at one.

Nietzsche, accordingly, repudiated the notion that Greek tragedy was developed under the auspices of Apollo, the god of the poised, harmonious, "classical" art that we traditionally associate with the Greeks. Nietzsche conceded a role to Apollo in Greek tragedy, but it was a role finally subordinate to that of Dionysus, the god of wild flute music, of wine and intoxication, of the dancing throng and of the orgy in which men as satyrs were connected with their darker, subterranean selves and with the primordial unity of nature.

The luminous order and tranquillity that are traditionally associated with Greek art were not the expression of a naturally Apollonian spirit. The Greek was naturally Dionysian; and his art thus represents a victory won over his own nature. As Nietzsche put it in a later essay:

Extravagance, wildness, and Asiatic tendencies lie at the root of the Greeks. Their courage consists in their struggle with their

[4] *The World as Will and Idea*, trans. R. B. Haldane and J. Kemp (London, n.d.), I, 336.

Asiatic nature: they were not given beauty any more than they were given Logic and moral naturalness: in them these things are victories, they are willed and fought for. . . .[5]

Tragedy was thus, for Nietzsche, the product of a fruitful tension between diverse energies. Certain other forms of art contrive to remain relatively pure. For instance, the painter, the sculptor, and the epic poet are characteristically Apollonian: they work under the special patronage of the god of light, of vision, and of dream. And the actor, the dancer, the musician, and the lyric poet are characteristically devotees of Dionysus. They follow a wilder prompting, and create dynamic patterns out of ecstasy and incantation.

To the modern reader imbued with Freud, Nietzsche's association of *dream* with the Apollonian serenity may appear puzzling, even perverse. For the modern reader will be tempted to regard Nietzsche's Apollonian art as that of the conscious mind and the Dionysian as that of the Freudian unconscious, in which case, dream, with its bold violations of space-order and of logic and its connections with the primordial depths of the mind will seem to be Dionysian rather than Apollonian. But Nietzsche uses *dream* primarily in the sense of the seer's vision, the waking dream, an ideal view which represents phenomena not as they are, but as they ought to be. For this very reason the Apollonian dreaming art demands a Dionysian counterbalance. The idealized representation if *too consciously imposed* degenerates into a flaccid and sterile academicism. The detachment proper to great art can come only after passionate involvement.

The timid German bourgeois, Nietzsche scornfully noted, was eager for ideal schemes that flattered his complacency, for solutions that he had not "earned," for harmonies that were trivial because they avoided the very appearance of dissonance. Such a person, Nietzsche insisted, was quite incapable of conceiving what tragic art meant to the audiences that viewed the drama of Aeschylus and Sophocles. To participate in the experience of genuine tragedy, man must put aside the brittle rigidities of his rationality. Man must lose his petty civic identity and become elemental man; he must, before the vision of the god can be vouchsafed to him, become the satyr, the goat-man.

Indeed, according to Nietzsche, this was just what actually happened in the course of history. Ancient Greek tragedy grew out of the worship of Dionysus. The satyr chorus—originally the band of ecstatic worshippers—was "the womb of dialogue." In the plays before Euripides, all the tragic protagonists were types of Dionysus, seen as such by the chorus in their ecstatic state. When Euripides failed to retain the chorus in its primi-

[5] *The Will to Power* (1896), *Complete Works*, XV (trans. A. M. Ludovici, New York, 1910), 417. This and following passages from Nietzsche's works reprinted by permission of the publishers, George Allen & Unwin Ltd.

tive function, he destroyed tragedy. Nietzsche elaborates the point: the "optimistic dialectic" of Euripides—which Nietzsche associates with that of Socrates—"drove *music* out of tragedy." [6] In the Socratic-Euripidean dispensation, there was a "necessary, visible connection between virtue and knowledge"; hence the tragic protagonist necessarily became a dialectician, the dramatist became essentially "an echo of his own conscious knowledge," and the dark, vital wisdom of the chorus was rendered nugatory. In short, Euripidean "tragedy" had moved toward the Apollonian pole.

True tragedy, on the other hand, Nietzsche asserted, could be interpreted only as "a manifestation and illustration of Dionysian states, as the visible symbolization of music, as the dream-world of Dionysian ecstasy." [7] Such a "dream-world" is, of course, in Nietzsche's terms, Apollonian—but in tragedy, Apollo is made to express "Dionysian knowledge."

> . . . the Apollonian illusion is [in the effect of tragedy] found to be what it really is,—the assiduous veiling during the performance of tragedy of the intrinsically Dionysian effect: which, however, is so powerful, that it finally forces the Apollonian drama itself into a sphere where it begins to talk with Dionysian wisdom, and even denies itself and its Apollonian conspicuousness. Thus then the intricate relation of the Apollonian and the Dionysian in tragedy must really be symbolized by a fraternal union of the two deities: Dionysus speaks the language of Apollo; Apollo, however, finally speaks the language of Dionysus; and so the highest goal of tragedy and of art in general is attained.[8]

The spectator of tragedy sees the hero "in epic clearness and beauty" —the epic, we remember, is an "Apollonian" art—nevertheless, wrought up to Dionysian ecstasy, the spectator "delights in [the hero's] annihilation. . . . He feels the actions of the hero to be justified, and is nevertheless still more elated when these actions annihilate their originator." [9]

When Apollo begins to talk with "Dionysian wisdom," he gives us myth, for tragic myth, as Nietzsche defines it, is "a symbolizing of Dionysian wisdom by means of the expedients of Apollonian art." [1] Science, with optimistic belief in "the explicability of nature," destroys myth, and with it, the possibility of tragedy. This notion that tragedy— and by later extension, all art—is grounded in myth was, however, to

[6] *The Birth of Tragedy* (1872), *Complete Works*, I (trans. W. A. Haussmann, London, 1910), 111.
[7] *Birth of Tragedy*, p. 111.
[8] *Birth of Tragedy*, pp. 166–7.
[9] *Birth of Tragedy*, p. 168.
[1] *Birth of Tragedy*, p. 168.

make its main fortune in the next century. Its typical 20th-century modes will be discussed later in Chapter 31.

IV

Science is optimistic, but tragic wisdom is joyful. The zest for life expresses itself through conflict and tension. Though elements of this view were derived from Schopenhauer, Nietzsche, as time went on, attacked with increasing bitterness Schopenhauer's idea that tragedy begot a mood of resignation. Art is "the great stimulus," the "great will to life," [2] and tragedy springs from exultant strength. Nietzsche charged Aristotle with folly in having supposed that the function of tragedy was to purge us of the emotions of pity and fear. Tragedy is not cathartic but tonic. Even a Zola's preoccupation with the ugly and sordid came about because artists like Zola rejoice in the ugly. The ugliness and disorder of the world constitute a challenge to the artist. The artist does not passively record a beauty that he finds rooted in nature. Beauty is not found—it is made by the artist, who imposes it by his own will, and thus wins a victory over disorder. For in beauty, "contrasts are overcome, the highest sign of power thus manifesting itself in the conquest of opposites." [3] The artist creates out of joy and strength—not out of weakness—and the most convincing artists are precisely those "who make harmony ring out of every discord." [4] The great artist is able to acknowledge "the terrible and questionable character of existence" [5] and still affirm the goodness of life. As a poet of our own time has expressed it:

> All perform their tragic play,
> There struts Hamlet, there is Lear,
> That's Ophelia, that's Cordelia;
> Yet they, should the last scene be there,
> The great stage curtain about to drop,
> If worthy their prominent part in the play,
> Do not break up their lines to weep.
> They know that Hamlet and Lear are gay;
> Gaiety transfiguring all that dread.[6]

And again, as he looked out upon the world moving toward the Second World War:

---

[2] *Will to Power*, p. 285.
[3] *Will to Power*, p. 245.
[4] *Will to Power*, p. 288.
[5] *Will to Power*, p. 291.
[6] W. B. Yeats, "Lapis Lazuli," *Collected Poems* (New York, 1951), p. 292. This and following passages from Yeats's writings are reprinted by permission of The Macmillan Company.

> Irrational streams of blood are staining earth;
> Empedocles has thrown all things about;
> Hector is dead and there's a light in Troy;
> We that look on but laugh in tragic joy.[7]

If all art is an affirmation of life, and if the greatest art is that in which the affirmation is made in the face of the terrible and questionable, then tragic art reveals itself as the greatest art:

> The highest state of Yea-saying to existence is conceived as one from which the greatest pain may not be excluded: the tragico-Dionysian state.[8]

The artist, as Nietzsche conceives him, is a projection of the Nietzschean philosopher. He is a man who is hard and lives dangerously, scorning cowardly generalizations and shop-worn solutions, despising syntheses that he has not "earned," daring to subdue to his purpose the most recalcitrant materials, always "setting his chisel to the hardest stone." Yet the artist does deal in illusion—at least his work can be exploited for the illusory comfort that it may seem to give. And so Nietzsche sometimes praised the artist as the man who truly lives "beyond good and evil," but at other times was moved to reproach the artist because he solaced men with lies. Only a hairline would seem to separate the poet's gift of "metaphysical comfort" from the bogus comfort of soporifics and anodynes.

It is probably idle to try to labor Nietzsche's position into entire consistency: Nietzsche was the deliberate iconoclast, using a rhetoric of overstatement, bold metaphor, exhortation, laconic imperatives, and the like; and moreover his philosophy suffered alteration during the course of his career. In making the value of art depend, not upon the work itself but upon the stress in the soul of the artist who produced it[9] or upon the process, strenuous or easy, by which the spectator apprehended it, Nietzsche provided the basis for endlessly shifting subsequent evaluations.

We have earlier spoken of the pervasive "lyric" quality of the German 19th century: the norm of poetry is consciously or unconsciously sought for in the personal and subjective utterance. The fundamental poetic problem became that of the poet's personal expression, and more

---

[7] "The Gyres," *Collected Poems*, p. 291.

[8] *Will to Power*, p. 291.

[9] Substantially this position is taken in a recent essay by a critic whom one would never think of associating with Nietzsche. Lionel Trilling, at the end of his *Liberal Imagination* (New York, 1950), p. 297, writes: "The aesthetic effect which I have in mind can be suggested by a word that I have used before—activity. We feel that Hemingway and Faulkner [as contrasted with Dos Passos, O'Neill, and Wolfe] are intensely at work upon the recalcitrant stuff of life; when they are at their best they give us the sense that the amount and intensity of their activity are in a satisfying proportion to the recalcitrance of their material."

specifically, the problem of how he might, in the midst of a hostile world, preserve his own individuality and set the seal of his own personality upon the pattern of words that he makes. Tragedy, because of the authority of classical Greek literature, was still spoken of by the Germans as the highest of the literary arts. But the soul of tragedy was no longer to be sought in the plot: it was to be sought in the dramatist's own soul. Nietzsche, as we have seen, conceived of tragedy as "musical": it was the greatest of the arts because it involved a "harmonization" of the greatest possible tensions.

The assimilation of tragedy to a "lyric" form through conceiving of it as a pattern of tensions that are "resolved" or of discords that are ultimately "harmonized" suggests a counterdevelopment that was to appear in later criticism; that is, the tendency to see in even the tiniest lyric a kind of "drama," a pattern of conflicts set up, developed, and then resolved. The "musical" structure of poetry, of which the French symbolists were to make so much, is "musical" in something like this Nietzschean sense. Here again Nietzsche proved himself a forerunner. He anticipated brilliantly the course that the age was to take.

V

TRAGEDY and comedy have always been bracketed together, if only in simple opposition—the laughing mask set off by the weeping mask. Nietzsche's conception of tragedy as a pattern of tensions obviously provides a means for bringing tragedy and comedy much closer together. In German romantic theory we have already [1] called attention to the strong concern to provide a rationale for the comic and to dignify it as an integral side of the serious. Nietzsche's theorizing provides, from the side of tragedy, a powerful answering tendency. By boldly asserting that tragedy is "Dionysian," Nietzsche roots it in impulses immemorially assigned to the comic—that is, in the natural and instinctive impulses which reach their apogee in intoxication, revelry, and wild exuberance.

The celebrated essay *Le Rire* (1900) by Henri Bergson yields a sufficiency of parallels to *The Birth of Tragedy*. Bergson found the basis for the comic in the contrast between the mechanical and the organic. It is intelligence that treats everything mechanically; it is instinct that has an affinity for the organic. Like Nietzsche, Bergson traced art ultimately to the dark, instinctive side of the mind.

He asserts in his *Évolution Créatrice* that it is instinct, not intelligence, that is molded on the very form

> of life. While intelligence treats everything mechanically, instinct proceeds, so to speak, organically. If the consciousness

[1] Cf. *ante* Chapter 17.

that slumbers in it should awake, if it were wound up into knowledge instead of being wound off into action, if we could ask and it could reply, it would give up to us the most intimate secrets of life.[2]

The intellect deals with what Bergson terms "extensive manifolds"; thus the intellect produces science and all the systematizations of knowledge that are so useful to us for the practical ordering of our lives. But the intellect distorts reality—freezes it into abstract patterns—breaks it up into discrete data—and so falsifies the essentially dynamic and changing thing that is reality; that is, the intellect is incapable of dealing with an "intensive manifold." For this we require the more subtle instrument of art. Like Schopenhauer, Bergson finds in art, not in science, the means to the knowledge of reality.

Life presents itself to us, Bergson says, as "evolution in time and complexity in space. . . . [There is a] continual change of aspect, the irreversibility of the order of phenomena, [and] the perfect individuality of a perfectly contained series. . . ."[3] Since such are the characteristic traits that distinguish what is alive from what is mere mechanism, their antitheses—*repetition, inversion,* and *reciprocal interference of series*— are the characteristic patterns of the mechanical; and it is the mechanical that prompts our laughter. We laugh at the failure of human response: the man acting like an automaton, mindlessly following a pattern when the situation calls for change (repetition); the man allowing himself to be victimized by mere things (inversion); the man clumsily falling over himself instead of acting gracefully and effectively (reciprocal interference of series).

Bergson valiantly strove to relate every instance of the comic to one of these three categories of the mechanical. Disguise, for example, was to be regarded as comic because the disguising clothes (as distinguished from our "normal" clothing, which seems at one with the body) appear to us to be a "rigid envelope round the living suppleness of the body." Disguise, in other words, constitutes another instance of the impingement of the mechanical upon the vital and organic. Having stretched his theory sufficiently to make disguise an instance of mechanization, Bergson then stretched the category of disguise:

> A man in disguise is comic. A man we regard as disguised is also comic. So, by analogy, all disguise is seen to become comic, not only that of a man, but that of society also, and even the disguise of nature.[4]

[2] *Creative Evolution* (1907), trans. Arthur Mitchell (New York, 1937), p. 165.
[3] From: *Comedy*, "Laughter" by Henri Bergson, "An Essay on Comedy" by George Meredith, introduction and appendix by Wylie Sypher. Copyright 1956 by Wylie Sypher, reprinted by permission of Doubleday & Company, Inc.
[4] *Laughter*, p. 42.

Though maintaining that every comic incongruity is an instance of mechanization, Bergson was aware that not every such mechanization produces a comic effect. We do not laugh, for example, at the automatism of a crippled man, even though his hobbling gait is to the last degree mechanical. The comic response demands that we suppress our sympathies: there must be, in Bergson's phrase, an "anesthesia of the heart." Where, as with the crippled man, we cannot suppress our sympathies, there will be no laughter.

The writer of comedy realizes this. He plays down our sympathy for the individual; he appeals to the assumptions of society; he engages our intelligence rather than our emotions. Thus, he achieves the necessary anesthesia. For the function of comedy is corrective; society punishes by laughter the individual's deviation from the social norms.

Bergson's account of the social function of comedy is substantially the orthodox, "classical" account—quite as much as George Meredith's.[5] But Bergson achieved his orthodoxy by a kind of *tour de force*. For comedy's very commitment to society and its association with the play of intelligence forced Bergson to deny that comedy was a genuine art. He denied it in so many words: comedy, he wrote,

> is not disinterested as genuine art is. By *organising* laughter, comedy accepts social life as a *natural* environment, it even obeys an impulse of social life. And in this respect it turns its back upon art, which is *a breaking away from society and a return to pure nature*.[6]

In such a passage, Bergson's romantic bias is fully declared: genuine art is natural and instinctive. Comedy makes the deviations from social life seem mechanical as if they were deviations from nature and therefore comic in their own right. The parallel with Nietzsche's view of tragedy again invites attention. One might say that whereas Nietzsche's tragedy represents the dark and instinctive (the Dionysian) drawing the luminous and rational (the Apollonian) into its orbit, Bergson's comedy represents a countermovement: our ultimate commitment to the instinctive and natural is drawn into the orbit of the self-conscious and artificial.

Bergson makes his case against the aberrancy of comedy from "genuine art" by exhibiting typical comic characters. Though genuine art is always concerned with what is uniquely individual, the characters that appear in comedies are types. A comic character is generality personified—which is why we can so readily speak of "a Tartuffe," Bergson

---

[5] In Chapter 11 *ante*, we have observed that Meredith's essay—one has to remind oneself of its date, 1877—was a kind of anachronism. It is a brilliant summation of an earlier ideal of comedy—French classical comedy of the great period.

[6] *Laughter*, pp. 170–1. The italics are ours.

says, but never of "a Phèdre" or "a Polyeucte." [7] Plausible as this statement sounds, perhaps we may wonder whether it constitutes a decisive test: it is not altogether clear that we cannot with propriety speak of "a Hamlet," tragic character though he be; and the great comic character Falstaff has appeared to many readers to be anything but mere generality personified. Be that as it may, Bergson has called down upon himself reproaches for what have impressed some critics as strained manipulations of the facts, the better to make them answer to his special theory. Even his basic tenet that all laughter springs from the contrast between what is mechanical and what is natural has been criticized as much too narrow and rigid. Yet it must be conceded that Bergson's conception of the comic as closely connected with the natural and instinctive is fully in the current of 19th-century ideas.

VI

MUCH earlier, in 1709, Lord Shaftesbury, in an essay significantly entitled *"Sensus Communis:* an Essay on the Freedom of Wit and Humor" (I, iv), had observed that

> the natural free spirits of ingenious men, if imprisoned or controlled, will find out other ways of motion to relieve themselves in their constraint; and whether it be in burlesque, mimicry, or buffoonery, they will be glad at any rate to vent themselves, and be revenged on their constrainers. . . .

During the 19th century, the psychologist Bain, whom Bergson quotes, developed the theory of laughter as "the rebound of hilarity," a sudden deliverance from emotional and moral constraints. Charles Renouvier added the notion that laughter was also a deliverance from the constraints of rationality itself. And Auguste Penjon published in 1893, several years before the appearance of Bergson's *Le Rire*, an essay entitled *"Le Rire et la Liberté"* in which laughter is interpreted as the sudden surging up of the sense of freedom. Penjon's theory of humor was summed up by an American psychologist, L. W. Kline, in the following terms:

> The humor stimulus gives glimpses of the world of uncertainties, of spontaneities and of life, and in so doing creates the sense of freedom of which the sense of humor is the obverse side.[8]

The function of humor is to rest and relax the mind. Humor is said to cut "the surface tension of consciousness" and to increase "the pliancy

[7] *Laughter,* p. 163.
[8] "The Psychology of Humor," *American Journal of Psychology,* XVIII (July, 1907), 437.

of [the mind's] structure to the end that it may proceed on a new and strengthened basis." It "spells" the mind, as Kline put it; it permits it a breathing space on "an uphill pull."

How humor accomplishes this ministry is stated in terms reminiscent of Schopenhauer: humor detaches us "from our world of good and evil, of loss and gain and enable[s] us to see it in proper perspective." And Kline's account of how humor has promoted the very evolution of the race seems to echo Bergson:

> Influences that tend to check mechanization and to incline the mind to grapple with the new and with the ideal prolong the possibilities of spiritual development. Humor and play are two such processes, with the honors in favor of humor. It stands guard at the dividing line between free and mechanized mind, to check mechanization and to preserve and fan the sparks of genius.[9]

The sense in which laughter betokens a freedom from constraint has been interpreted more literally and brutally by Horace Kallen.[1] All laughter reflects a sense of triumph and self-enhancement which may or may not also involve the degradation of an enemy. Having conquered its enemy, "the organism," riding on a tide of released energies, finding itself "again in possession of itself," and now apprehending the "lapsed situation," laughs "spontaneously, instinctively." Kallen remarks that the facial expression at the laughable as in smiling bears "a startling re semblance to [that of] an animal about to rend and devour its prey." But he is able to trace the first dawn of humor to a period before even the teeth appear. For he can find a semblance of the "apprehension of the comic" in "the replete child, repeating the pleasurable act of sucking." [2]

The notion of laughter as the expression of triumphant well-being is as old as the speculations of Thomas Hobbes—as old indeed as the Platonic dialogues; and some readers will prefer Hobbes's account of it to Kallen's, finding Hobbes's brand of behaviorism handled with more dignity and with somewhat less facial contortion.

> *Sudden Glory* [Hobbes writes in his *Leviathan*, I, vi] is the passion which maketh those *Grimaces* called LAUGHTER; and is caused either by some sudden act of their own, that pleaseth them; or by the apprehension of some deformed thing in another, in comparison whereof they suddenly applaud themselves.[3]

[9] Kline, *American Journal of Psychology*, XVIII, 439.
[1] "The Aesthetic Principle in Comedy," *American Journal of Psychology*, XXII (April, 1911), 137–57.
[2] Kallen, *American Journal of Psychology*, XXII, 156.
[3] *Leviathan* (1651).

But perhaps one should not dismiss the facial contortions too summarily. Because of the marked physiological reactions that occur in laughter, comedy has from an early date attracted to itself far more affective theorizing than has tragedy. The development of laboratory techniques in the 19th century produced hundreds of physiological studies bearing on the phenomenon of laughter. Even psychologists not notably behavioristic in approach have been interested in and influenced by the physiological character of laughter. For example, Sigmund Freud writes in a passage that anticipates the phraseology of Kallen, "the grimaces and contortions of the corners of the mouth that characterize laughter appear first in the satisfied and satiated nursling when he drowsily quits the breast." But his *Wit and Its Relations to the Unconscious* (1905) elaborates a far more complex theory of the comic than this particular quotation might suggest.[4] Indeed, Freud will not allow that the "sudden glory" of triumphant well-being is comic laughter at all, insisting that children do not have a sense of the comic. Nevertheless, it is in the happiness of the replete child that Freud finds the key to the pleasure that adults take in the comic. Indeed, his monumental essay concludes with the statement that the methods of wit, comedy, and humor all attempt to return us to the state of the child. They

> strive to bring back from the psychic activity a pleasure which has really been lost in the development of this activity. For the euphoria which we are thus striving to obtain is nothing but the state of a bygone time, in which we were wont to defray our psychic work with slight expenditure. It is the state of our childhood in which we did not know the comic, were incapable of wit, and did not need humor to make us happy.[5]

But to understand why the state of euphoria experienced by the child is characterized by a "slight expenditure" of psychic energy requires further examination of Freud's views on the subject.

VII

EARLY in his study Freud remarks that brevity is indeed the soul of wit, quoting Shakespeare's statement and that of the psychologist Theodor Lipps.[6] The brevity manifests itself through various devices of condensation such as "mixed word-formation" and "double meaning with allu-

---

[4] The passages quoted here and on pp. 573-6 and 611 are taken from *The Basic Writings of Sigmund Freud*, trans. and ed. by A. A. Brill, copyright, 1938, by Random House, Inc. Reprinted by permission of the Trustees of the Brill Estate.

[5] *Basic Writings*, p. 803.

[6] Freud writes: " 'Brevity alone is the body and soul of wit,' declares Jean Paul (*Vorschule der Ästhetik* [1804], I, 45). . . . Lipps' description of the brevity of

sion." Freud distinguishes eleven such devices, all of which he regards as simply variant forms of the principle of condensation. What is common to wit, in Freud's conception, is a principle of parsimony in the expenditure of psychic energy. The verbal economy observable in witty expressions—the "use of few or possibly the same words"—points toward a more important kind of economy, this saving of psychic energy.

What is actually saved and how the saving is effected is most easily illustrated by taking our examples from what Freud calls "tendency" wit, that is, wit that is aggressive, whether hostile or obscene. (Freud holds that all obscene wit represents an act of sexual aggression.)

How such wit serves to economize psychic energy, Freud illustrates in this fashion: When circumstances forbid any direct attack upon an enemy or even directly abusive language, as in retort to superior authority, "wit . . . serves as a resistance against such authority and as an escape from its pressure." For wit provides a means for getting around whatever hinders directly hostile expression and thus allows us to express ourselves after all. Such hindrances to expression need not be outward; they may be inward. "Repressions," for example, forbid the civilized man's enjoyment of the obscene. But a witty obscenity allows him to elude the repression and to enjoy what, if expressed directly, would not be tolerated.

> The only difference between the cases of outer and inner hindrances consists in the fact that here an already existing inhibition is removed, while there the formation of a new inhibition is avoided. . . . a *"psychic expenditure"* is required for the formation as well as the retention of a psychic inhibition. Now if we find that in both cases the use of tendency-wit produces pleasure, then it may be assumed *that such resultant pleasure corresponds to the economy of psychic expenditure.*[7]

So much for the pleasure of wit that has a hostile or obscene tendency. The pleasure that we take in "harmless wit" also arises from an economy of psychic expenditure. The reason is not far to seek. All thinking requires effort: it is "easier to mix up things than to distinguish them; and it is particularly easier to travel over modes of reasoning unsanctioned by logic." Children delight, for example, in word play and nonsense games. One of the pleasures of alcohol is that under its influence the adult can become again a "child who derives pleasure from the free

wit is also significant. He states that '. . . [wit] expresses itself in words that will not stand the test of strict logic or of the ordinary mode of thought and expression. In fine, it can express itself by leaving the thing unsaid' [*Komik und Humor*, 1898, *Beiträge zur Ästhetik*, VI, p. 90]." *Basic Writings*, p. 636.

[7] *Basic Writings*, p. 712.

disposal of his mental stream without being restricted by the pressure of logic." [8]

> Ale, man, ale's the stuff to drink
> For fellows whom it hurts to think.

But all of us, Freud would argue, plausibly enough, are fellows whom it hurts to think. Alcohol protects our childish pleasure by dulling the censorship of reason. In harmless wit, the wit-work circumvents this obstacle by offering a sop to reason; that is, the wit-work sees to it that the "senseless combination of words or the absurd linking of thoughts" does "make sense after all." Thus, just as tendency wit circumvents the hindrances set up by suppressions and inhibitions, harmless wit circumvents the hindrances set up by reason and critical judgment. As Freud summarizes the matter, wit

> begins as play in order to obtain pleasure from the free use of words and thoughts. As soon as the growing reason forbids this senseless play . . . , it turns to the jest or joke in order to hold to these sources of pleasure and in order to be able to gain new pleasure from the liberation of the absurd. In the rôle of harmless wit it assists the thoughts and fortifies them against the impugnment of the critical judgment. . . . Finally, it enters into the great struggling suppressed tendencies in order to remove inner inhibitions. . . . Reason, critical judgment, and suppression, these are the forces which it combats in turn.[9]

The semi-automatic reaction of laughter is easily fitted into Freud's scheme, for if wit always involves an economy of psychic energy, it is that "saved" or "gained" energy that is discharged as laughter. Freud borrows, and in the process modifies, Herbert Spencer's view of laughter as the discharge of psychic *irritation*.[1]

VIII

FREUD carefully distinguishes the witty from the comical and the humorous. All three, to be sure, involve a "saving" of psychic energy, and all three discharge the gained energy in laughter. But Freud seeks through a rather intricate argument to differentiate the several ways in which the gain in energy is made and to specify in each case the form of psychic energy that is conserved. In wit, as we have seen, Freud argues that our gain in psychic energy comes about through our not having to expend our energy in sustaining an inhibition. In contemplating the comic, how-

[8] *Basic Writings*, p. 719.
[9] *Basic Writings*, p. 726.
[1] Freud also mentions L. M. Dugas's description of laughter as a release from tension and Bain's conception of laughter as a "freedom from restraint."

ever, our gain comes from finding that we have built up expectative tensions that are redundant. For example, we see someone straining to lift a heavy basket and laugh when the basket proves to be unexpectedly light. We compare the expected effort with the actual effort as we imaginatively project ourselves into the lifter's situation. Such a comparison occurs, Freud insists, in all instances of the comic. We always compare, if only unconsciously, the effort that the fumbling clown or the clumsy child makes in order to perform some action with the effort which we should need to exert. Thus Freud's theory of the comic at some points resembles Bergson's, the clumsily wasteful expenditure of energy reminding one of Bergson's stiffly mechanical actions. Like Bergson too, Freud attempts some remarkable extensions of what he regards as the basic comic situation. The comic, he tells us, is always found first in *persons* and is then transferred to objects, situations, and the like.

In dealing with the third member of his triad, humor, Freud is much less intricate and consequently may seem less strained. The psychic energy that we "save" in the humorous situation is the energy that would otherwise go into feelings of sympathy. The most obvious instance is that furnished by "gallows-humor." The prisoner on the way to execution pretends to worry about catching cold, and we laugh. If "he who is most concerned is quite indifferent to the situation," [2] then we can save our sympathy, and it is this sympathy that we expected to expend but did not expend that we discharge pleasurably in laughter.

Freud assigns humor and the comic to the foreconscious, but wit, to the unconscious. Indeed, at one point Freud describes wit as "the contribution to the comic from the sphere of the unconscious." The techniques used in dream work—displacement, representation by opposite, absurdity, indirect expression, and so forth—are the techniques used in wit. Since the aim of the dream is simply to preserve our sleep, the dream does not need to be intelligible. It is an asocial product. Wit, however, has to be intelligible; we feel the need to impart wit. Hence in wit the amount of distortion through displacement and condensation has its limit. Dream serves "preponderantly to guard against pain," but wit serves "to acquire pleasure"; and that pleasure, as Freud has described it in the passage that we quoted earlier, is an approximation to the euphoria of childhood.

IX

ONE of the most vigorous attacks upon Freud's theory of the comic has been made by Max Eastman.[3] Eastman finds it incomprehensible that Freud should deny a sense of the comic to children, who are, of course,

[2] *Basic Writings*, p. 799.
[3] *The Enjoyment of Laughter* (New York, 1936).

the "greatest laughers of all." But, of course, Freud does not deny that children laugh. The child laughs, and his motives for laughter, Freud says, are "clear and assignable." Someone slips and falls, and the child laughs "out of a feeling of superiority or out of joy over the calamity of others. [His laughter] amounts to saying: 'You fell, but I did not.' " [4] In short, the child's laughter is an instance of Hobbes's "sudden glory." (And this is precisely why Freud denies that it has a part in the comic.) Balzac can be quoted: "As children only do we laugh, and as we travel onward laughter sinks down and dies out like the light of the oil-lit lamp." So true is this, Eastman goes on to say, that most adults will rarely laugh at "a mere nothing . . . unless it is reinforced and sanctioned by some meaning. . . . They demand, in short, that jokes should have a point." [5] But in writing this, Eastman has blundered squarely upon Freud's central idea. Indeed, when Freud writes that "Certain pleasure motives of the child seem to be lost for us grown-ups . . . ," he might be echoing Balzac. His *Wit and Its Relation to the Unconscious* could be fairly described as a study of the manoeuvers by which the adult endeavors to recover the lost infantile laughter.

A much more competent and informed criticism of Freud's theory of the comic is made by Arthur Koestler in his *Insight and Outlook* (1949). Koestler is able to accept most of what Freud has to say about wit, but he finds Freud's comments upon the comic needlessly intricate. Freud attempts to "reduce differences in the quality of the behaviour patterns involved in a comic situation to differences in quantity." Koestler finds that this preoccupation with mere quantitative difference on occasion leads to absurdities, as when Freud writes: "Chance exposures of the body . . . affect us as comic, because we compare this easy way of enjoying what is offered to the eye with the great effort which would otherwise be necessary to attain the same aim." [6] As if, comments Koestler, this were the way to account for our laughter when the dignified gentleman rips his trouser seat as he executes a sweeping bow.

Koestler locates the principal defect of Freud's theory in what he calls a failure to distinguish between the self-assertive and the self-transcending emotions. Neither Bergson [7] nor Freud recognizes the existence of a self-transcending emotion, and as a consequence neither of them

[4] *Basic Writings*, p. 794.
[5] *The Enjoyment of Laughter*, p. 37.
[6] *Insight and Outlook* (New York, 1949), p. 426. Reprinted by permission of The Macmillan Company.
[7] Koestler regards Bergson's theory of the comic as too narrow—Bergson's "comic" is only one sub-category, though a frequently occurring sub-category, of the comic. Bergson also neglects "the emotional dynamics of laughter," but his is "the most stimulating work ever written on the subject" (*Insight and Outlook*, p. 421).

is able to see "the direct connection between the comic and the tragic, between laughter and crying, between humour and art." [8]

In *Insight and Outlook*, Koestler boldly undertakes to demonstrate just these relationships. He would connect not only the comic with the tragic, but the mental processes involved in the creation of wit with those involved in making a scientific discovery. The key to these connections lies in what Koestler calls the "bisociative" treatment of a phenomenon. The comic contrast is bisociative: we see the phenomenon in question under two contrasting aspects. It is linked to two different fields of interest. The phenomenon is regarded as an habitual member of one of these fields, but its affinities with the second field "have hitherto been regarded as adventitious, or have passed unnoticed." [9] This bisociative treatment may be illustrated by the simplest joke ("One swallow does not make a summer, nor quench the thirst"); but it is also illustrated by Archimedes' action when, lying in his bath, he suddenly connected the immersion of a body in water with the problem of measuring the volume of the crown. The pun on "swallow" links two quite different fields through a trivial sound connection; the discovery that sent Archimedes rushing from his bath shouting "Eureka" also connected different fields —and again through a trivial and unimportant link, though the consequences were to be most important. Both wit and the "eureka process" have, as Koestler puts it, the same "intellectual geometry." Metaphor also employs this intellectual geometry: metaphor links up two fields not ordinarily connected and allows us to view the "link" in the perspective of two fields—"bisociatively."

Koestler regards laughter as the discharge of nervous tension, but he gives this notion a twist not to be found in Freud. Emotional processes have greater inertia than cognitive processes. When one line of logic or one chain of association is suddenly intersected by another, our understanding

> does jump from the first field to the second, whereas our emotion, incapable of performing the sudden jump, is spilled. This difference in behaviour implies that emotion tends to persist in the direction of a straight line, like a bull, whereas thought can dance about like a matador; in other words, that emotion has a greater mass momentum.[1]

Laughter is the discharge of the emotion "spilled" when the understanding makes one of its sudden hair-pin turns in traversing the course of the witticism. The emotion suddenly becomes excessive—or to use Freud's

[8] *Insight and Outlook*, p. 430.
[9] *Insight and Outlook*, p. 53.
[1] *Insight and Outlook*, p. 60.

term, there is a sudden "gain"—and the now unneeded emotion can gush out as laughter.

Man alone is capable of laughter; his ability to laugh is a mark of his civilization. "All animals are fanatics," since they cannot emancipate themselves "from the fanaticism of the biological urge."

> The sudden realization that one's own emotional state is "Unreasonable" signalizes the emergence of self-criticism. . . . Thus laughter rings the bell of man's departure from the rails of instinct.[2]

The inert emotions discharged in laughter are the self-assertive, aggressive-defensive emotions. They are to be carefully discriminated from the self-transcending, integrative emotions that underlie tragic art. Any tragedy can be turned into a comedy by altering the emotional charge. "Every story of Boccaccio's" can be transformed into a little tragedy without altering its factual content and "Oedipus Rex can be made to appear as a prize fool who kills his father and marries his mother, all by mistake; the tragedy is turned into a French farce without altering its cognitive layout." [3]

Unlike the self-asserting emotions, the self-transcending emotions

> are capable of following the train of thought round any junctional corner. . . . The emotions of participative sympathy attach themselves like a dog to the narrative and do not become detached from it whatever the surprises, jumps, changes of associative climate through which the narrator leads it. . . . When a bisociation occurs, [they] do not become detached from thought, but follow it loyally to the new field.[4]

Since tragedy, like comedy, makes use of a bisociative technique, Koestler requires some such explanation as this to account for the fact that the emotional charge in tragedy is not also "spilled" en route and discharged in laughter. Koestler frankly would not want it spilled, for the self-transcending emotions have their own value, they are integrative; they move man toward a sympathetic participation in the universe about him. They teach loyalty to the larger whole of which man is a part.

Koestler's position here is that of the modern liberal humanist, with all the appropriate political and social implications. Art is a civilizing influence: through comedy it helps us to jettison the assertive emotions: through tragedy it fosters the integrative emotions; it teaches us to live together; and through its cathartic effects it helps the individual to endure what is otherwise without remedy.

[2] *Insight and Outlook*, pp. 69–70.
[3] *Insight and Outlook*, p. 241.
[4] *Insight and Outlook*, p. 277.

The experience of tragedy is of special therapeutic value for modern man, who is confined "to the arid plane of associative routine," the plane of the trivial. His contacts with tragic reality are so infrequent that, "instead of eliciting original adjustments, [they] throw him completely out of gear. . . . Routine has become man's rusty armour which makes the living flesh rot underneath." [5] Modern man, deadened as he is by "associative routine," stands in special need of viewing himself and his situation "bisociatively." He needs to have the trivial plane on which he lives intersected by the tragic plane.

The prominence that Koestler gives to the self-transcending emotions renders his theory of literature strongly reminiscent of that of 18th-century aestheticians like Shaftesbury and Lord Kames who emphasize sympathy.[6] Koestler's tone is, of course, quite different: he levies upon modern biological and neurological research for evidence, pointing to the basic tendency toward integration in even the most primitive organisms. But his stress upon the affective and his assumption that the greatest and most valuable art civilizes man by extending his sympathies connect him unmistakably with figures like Shaftesbury. Like the 18th-century aestheticians, Koestler holds what is ultimately an optimistic view of man and his arts. The self-transcending emotions, even though they are connected with " 'depersonalization' of consciousness," or with "the self becoming dissolved" or with Freud's "oceanic feeling," are *not* connected with Freud's death-instinct.[7] That, Koestler dismisses as having no biological foundation. ". . . biologically Freud's death-and-destruction drive is a myth—the only one," Koestler somewhat startlingly avers, "which his myth-destroying genius embodied into his system." [8] Cultivation of self-transcendence points, then, not toward death but toward the road of evolution and human progress.

A number of tendencies that have developed through the last seventy-five years seem to culminate in Koestler's *Insight and Outlook:* the stress upon conflict, upon tension, and upon the quality of emotional charge; the drawing together of comedy and tragedy, and their subsumption—along with aesthetic illusion and the "eureka" process—under one pattern, a pattern of bifurcation, of resistances acknowledged but transcended.

Koestler's is an ambitious, and in its promise of neat unification, an attractive scheme. That tragedy and comedy do make use of the same *general* intellectual frame-work—the same "intellectual geometry," in

---

[5] *Insight and Outlook*, p. 379.

[6] Cf. *ante* Chapter 14.

[7] Koestler writes (p. 216) that the "pessimistic, antihumanistic bias" in Freud's system may have been determined by "Freud's life-long work on neurotic patients with infantile fixations and regressive tendencies, against the background of the decaying civilization of the Austro-Hungarian Empire."

[8] *Insight and Outlook*, p. 153.

Koestler's phrase—may perhaps without too much difficulty be conceded. But the concession tends to throw great weight upon the character of the "emotional charge" in a literary work: for the quality of that charge would seem to be the sole means left by which one may differentiate comedy and tragedy. Thus there are difficulties. How one can alter an emotional charge without also altering the "cognitive layout" may not be altogether apparent. We have already noted Koestler's claim that *Oedipus Rex* could be transformed into a French farce without tampering with the cognitive layout. But Koestler hardly tells us how we can know that Oedipus is a tragic hero and not a "prize fool" apart from what Oedipus says and does—apart, that is, from the action of the play. Koestler takes it for granted that the author could manipulate the reader's attitude toward a character without at the same time altering the presentation of the character. There is obviously some loose and easy sense in which an author can do this; otherwise it would not be possible to produce parodies and ironic paraphrases. But Koestler seems to commit himself to a more questionable proposition—namely, that the emotional charge can in fact be quite sharply and cleanly separated from the cognitive "layout." He says flatly that "other attitudes can be produced [by] altering the stimulus . . . in such a way that its cognitive aspect or ground plan remains unchanged while its emotion-evoking aspects are altered," [9] and he goes on to say that his distinction between the "cognitive aspect" and the "emotion-evoking aspects" corresponds to the distinction made in *The Meaning of Meaning* [1] by C. K. Ogden and I. A. Richards between "two uses of language," the referential and the emotive.

This distinction between the referential and the emotive does play an important part in the theorizing of some of the critics to be discussed in a later chapter. Ogden and Richards, like Koestler, are conversant with modern psychology, and again, like him, their theories show a strong affective bias. But just because they are less ambitious to subsume so many various workings of the mind under one pattern, they will provide us with a more specifically literary focus for our examination of the problem.

SUPPLEMENT

Thus Satan's character, as Milton presents it, cannot but inspire feelings of sympathy and admiration. The traditional motive of Satan's fall was pride. Milton had then to describe the pride of Satan. But, as we have seen, pride

[9] *Insight and Outlook*, p. 240.
[1] *The Meaning of Meaning: a Study of the Influence of Language upon Thought and of the Science of Symbolism* (London, 1923).

was the ruling passion in his own soul. Consequently, the character of Satan is drawn with a power unique in literature. In reality, Milton pours out his own feelings. Satan's first speeches are pure Miltonic lyricism.

—Denis Saurat, *Milton: Man and Thinker* (New York, 1925), p. 214

. . . any real exposition of the Satanic character and the Satanic predicament is likely to provoke the question "Do you, then, regard *Paradise Lost* as a comic poem?" To this I answer, No; but only those will fully understand it who see that it might have been a comic poem. Milton has chosen to treat the Satanic predicament in the epic form and has therefore subordinated the absurdity of Satan to the misery which he suffers and inflicts. Another author, Meredith, has treated it as comedy with consequent subordination of its tragic elements. But *The Egoist* remains, none the less, a pendant to *Paradise Lost*, and just as Meredith cannot exclude all pathos from Sir Willoughby, so Milton cannot exclude all absurdity from Satan, and does not even wish to do so. That is the explanation of the Divine laughter in *Paradise Lost* which has offended some readers. There is a real offence in it because Milton has imprudently made his Divine Persons so anthropomorphic that their laughter arouses legitimately hostile reactions in us—as though we were dealing with an ordinary conflict of wills in which the winner ought not to ridicule the loser. But it is a mistake to demand that Satan, any more than Sir Willoughby, should be able to rant and posture through the whole universe without, sooner or later, awaking the comic spirit. The whole nature of reality would have to be altered in order to give him such immunity, and it is not alterable. At that precise point where Satan or Sir Willoughby meets something real, laughter *must* arise, just as steam must when water meets fire. And no one was less likely than Milton to be ignorant of this necessity. We know from his prose works that he believed everything detestable to be, in the long run, also ridiculous; and mere Christianity commits every Christian to believing that "the Devil is (in the long run) an ass."

—C. S. Lewis, *A Preface to Paradise Lost* (Oxford, 1942), pp. 92–3, by permission of Oxford University Press, Inc.

A serious analysis of literary art [such as this] with only an occasional, passing mention of Shakespeare may have seemed to many readers a curious innovation. The reason for it, however, is simple enough, and has been suggested above: Shakespeare is essentially a dramatist, and drama is not, in the strict sense, "literature."

Yet it is a poetic art, because it creates the primary illusion of all poetry —virtual history. Its substance is an image of human life—ends, means, gains and losses, fulfillment and decline and death. It is a fabric of illusory experience, and that is the essential product of poesis. But drama is not merely a distinct literary form; it is a special poetic mode, as different from genuine literature as sculpture from pictorial art, or either of these from architecture. That is to say, it makes its own basic abstraction, which gives it a way of its own in making the semblance of history.

Literature projects the image of life in the mode of virtual memory; language is its essential material; the sound and meaning of words, their familiar or unusual use and order, even their presentation on the printed page, create the illusion of life as a realm of events—completed, lived, as words formulate them—events that compose a Past. But Drama presents the poetic illusion in a different light: not finished realities, or "events," but immediate, visible responses of human beings, make its semblance of life. Its basic abstraction is the act, which springs from the past, but is directed toward the future, and is always great with things to come.

—Susanne K. Langer, *Feeling and Form* (New York, 1953), p. 306. Reprinted by permission of Charles Scribner's Sons.

I have gone into this scene [I, v of *Hamlet*] at some length, since it illustrates so perfectly the relationship between psychology and form, and so aptly indicates how the one is to be defined in terms of the other. That is, the psychology here is not the psychology of the *hero*, but the psychology of the *audience*. And by that distinction, form would be the psychology of the audience. Or, seen from another angle, form is the creation of an appetite in the mind of the auditor, and the adequate satisfying of that appetite. This satisfaction—so complicated is the human mechanism—at times involves a temporary set of frustrations, but in the end these frustrations prove to be simply a more involved kind of satisfaction, and furthermore serve to make the satisfaction of fulfilment more intense. If, in a work of art, the poet says something, let us say, about a meeting, writes in such a way that we desire to observe that meeting, and then, if he places that meeting before us—that is form. While obviously, that is also the psychology of the audience, since it involves desires and their appeasements.

—Kenneth Burke, *Counter-Statement* (New York, 1931), p. 40; also Hermes Publications, 1953, pp. 30–1. By permission of the author.

If the difference between tragedy and comedy is a difference between the emotions they express, it is not a difference that can be present to the artist's mind when he is beginning his work; if it were, he would know what emotion he was going to express before he had expressed it. No artist, therefore, so far as he is an artist proper, can set out to write a comedy, a tragedy, an elegy, or the like. So far as he is an artist proper, he is just as likely to write any one of these as any other; which is the truth that Socrates was heard expounding towards the dawn, among the sleeping figures in Agathon's dining room.

—R. G. Collingwood, *The Principles of Art* (Oxford: Clarendon Press, 1938), p. 116, by permission of Oxford University Press, Inc.

CHAPTER 26

SYMBOLISM

§ *Coleridge's wish to destroy the antithesis between words and things: its partial fulfillment in certain modern philosophies of symbolic form—II. Emerson's Transcendentalism: its relation to Coleridge and to German philosophers, its strength and its weakness, Whitman's optimism and Melville's disquieting doubts—III. Edgar Allan Poe's concern for lyric intensity: his efforts to "purify" poetry, the implications of these efforts for subject matter and form, poetry analogized to music—the influence of Poe's ideas upon Baudelaire: Baudelaire's system of "correspondences," tendencies in Baudelaire toward the irrational and the occult—IV. Mallarmé's poetry as a refinement of thing or event to a "Platonic idea" of itself, poetry as evocation and poetry as ritual—V. Two side developments of French symbolism: Verlaine and lyric impressionism, and Rimbaud and the systematic disordering of the senses, Rimbaud's conception of the poet as voyant—VI. Valéry and his detachment of the poem, as pure meaning, from the realm of reality, his years of silence, the tendency of symbolist poetry to extinguish itself—some attempts to define and summarize the nature of French symbolism—VII. William Butler Yeats as a symbolist poet: his debt to Arthur Symons, the relation of "magic" to poetry, Yeats's attempt to create a personal myth—VIII. Yeats's knowledge of philosophy, his conception of poetry as yielding a peculiar kind of knowledge, parallels between his position and that of R. G. Collingwood—Yeats's saving dualism: his refusal to fall into "angelism"* §

THE DOCTRINE THAT WORDS CREATE KNOWLEDGE IS A PART OF THE romantic theory of the imagination. Coleridge, for example, constantly verges upon such a conception in his speculations upon poetry as a way of mediating between the subject and the object. In a letter to William Godwin (22 September 1800) he writes:

> I wish you to write a book on the power of the words. . . . is *Thinking* impossible without arbitrary signs? And how far is the word "arbitrary" a misnomer? Are not words, etc., parts and germinations of the plant? And what is the law of their growth? In something of this sort I would endeavour to destroy the old antithesis of Words and Things; elevating, as it were, Words into Things and living things too.[1]

Many of the more recent developments in literary theory can be read as attempted answers to the questions which Coleridge puts here to Godwin. Present-day philosophers like Croce, R. G. Collingwood, Ernst Cassirer, and Susanne Langer have concerned themselves with the laws that govern the growth of words and may indeed be said to have gone far to destroy the old antithesis between words and things. Even a theorist like I. A. Richards, who began with the thesis that words were arbitrary signs, in the course of time proceeded toward a correction and modification of that thesis, and in doing so came to argue for a much more organic conception of words, finally arriving at the view that reality itself, as man can know it, is a symbolic construction: "the fabric of our meanings, which is the world," is Richards' way of putting it in 1936.[2] Indeed, the tendency to treat words as things has in our time gone so far as to provoke vehement reactions. Thus, Allen Tate has denounced the

> belief that language itself can be reality, or by incantation can create a reality: a superstition that comes down in French from Lautréamont, Rimbaud, and Mallarmé to the Surrealists, and in English to Hart Crane, Wallace Stevens, and Dylan Thomas.[3]

In Tate's list, the preponderance of French and American names is significant. Though Coleridge prophetically raised the right questions and

---

[1] *Unpublished Letters of S. T. Coleridge*, ed. E. L. Griggs (London, 1932), I, 155–6. A few years later Lord Byron voiced much the same aspiration in his *Childe Harold*.

> I do believe,
> Though I have found them not, that there may be
> Words which are things.

>   —Canto III, stanza CXIV

[2] Cf. *post* Chapter 28.
[3] *The Forlorn Demon* (Chicago, 1953), p. 61.

even implied some of the answers later to be proposed by the symbolist theoreticians, the most direct line of development does lead through French and American thinkers. Coleridge's American followers, more nearly than his English, entered into direct engagement of the problem of symbolic form. We refer to the American Transcendentalists, Ralph Waldo Emerson, H. D. Thoreau, and Herman Melville.

II

IN HIS essay entitled "The Poet" (1844) Emerson boldly pronounced "Words and deeds" to be "quite indifferent modes of the divine energy. Words are also actions, and actions are a kind of words." [4] The poet is not to be sharply set apart from the "practical" man; nor is his work to be thought of as artful in some sense that cuts it off from nature and the natural. ". . . the poet names the thing because he sees it, or comes one step nearer to it than any other. This expression or naming is not art, but a second nature, grown out of the first, as a leaf out of a tree." [5] The last phrase echoes the metaphor that Coleridge used in his letter to Godwin, and to something like Coleridge's purpose. Emerson is insisting that verbal expression is not a wilful and arbitrary thing—as Coleridge put it elsewhere, not "a pure work of the will"—but natural and organic as the growth of the leaf is organic.

We are not to take too seriously, of course, such parallels of phrasing between Emerson and Coleridge. They may be accidental, and the reader in any case soon learns not to put too much reliance upon the letter of the somewhat rhapsodic language in which Emerson habitually expressed himself. Yet there can be no doubt that Emerson has to be accounted one of the forerunners of the conception of literature as symbolic form.[6]

Emerson drew upon Coleridge's sources in neo-Platonism and German idealistic philosophy, and, of course, he drew directly upon Coleridge himself. But he was apparently affected even more deeply than was Coleridge by a sense of crisis in the problem of knowledge. He was sensitized to feel that problem by a number of circumstances—his provincialism, his lack of a rich and sustaining tradition, his "innocence," and his relatively slight interest in aesthetic forms as such.

The old rationalism in which Emerson had been brought up had been routed. The Cartesian dualism between the objects of the world and the spirit which thought about them had suddenly collapsed. Kant had

[4] *Works* (Fireside Edition, Boston and New York, 1909), III, 14.
[5] *Works*, III, 26.
[6] See the convincing argument made by Charles Feidelson, Jr., in *Symbolism and American Literature* (Chicago, published by The University of Chicago Press, 1953. And copyright 1953 by the University of Chicago.) See especially pp. 119–35.

asserted that the mind was no *tabula rasa* on which external objects scratched their impressions: the mind was an active force, which, by its own forms, moulded our conceptions of reality. Emerson and the other intellectual leaders of his culture, starved after two hundred years of the Puritanic attenuation of symbolism and already more than vaguely dissatisfied with abstractions, were ripe for the discovery that the mind was a transcendental force.[7]

But Emerson was not a thinker systematic enough to work out the implications of the position, either for philosophy or for literary criticism. The fact of the mind's transcendence remained for him a kind of overpowering insight to which he recurred in endless variations in his rather high-pitched and evangelistic essays. Emerson wins his victories of reconciliation over the contradictions of experience a shade too easily. William Butler Yeats might have said of Emerson, as he did say of Shelley, that he lacked the vision of evil. One remembers Carlyle's complaint to Emerson that he took "so little heed of the frightful quantities of *friction* and perverse *impediment* there everywhere are; the reflections upon which in my own poor life made me now and then very sad, as I read you." [8] Emerson reminds one of the protagonist in *The Waste Land*, whose eyes failed him at the vision in the hyacinth garden, and who was neither living nor dead, "Looking into the heart of light, the silence." Emerson's vision of the poem fails under excess of light: he sees little more in any poem than the scintillant fact that it *is* a poem—no mere shadow of external objects and no mere subjective fancy, but a coalescence of man with nature in a union that guarantees the participation of both man and nature in something transcendental.

For Emerson the poetic vision, we may say, is a kind of universal solvent: it brings the most refractory and stubbornly contradictory things into unity. Or, as he put it himself in "The Poet," the poet renders the whole realm of phenomena transparent:

> As the eyes of Lyncæus were said to see through the earth, so the poet turns the world to glass, and shows us all things in their right series and procession. For through that better perception he stands one step nearer to things, and sees the flowing or metamorphosis; perceives that thought is multiform . . . and following with his eyes the life, uses the forms that express that life, and so his speech flows with the flowing of nature.[9]

The difficulty of turning the world to glass, however, is that a really transparent world would be quite invisible. Wishing to see everything,

---

[7] *Symbolism and American Literature*, p. 129.

[8] Carlyle to Emerson, April 6, 1870. *The Correspondence of Carlyle and Emerson* (Boston, 1894), II, 360-1.

[9] "The Poet," *Works*, III, 25.

we should actually see nothing. It would be unfair to the spirit of his essay to bind Emerson rigidly by the terms of his own metaphor. The fact of *some* transparency—"We are symbols and inhabit symbols,"[1] he says in the same essay—is evidently all that Emerson really meant to claim. Yet the passage quoted does fairly suggest the weakness in Emerson's conception, and it points to a problem that any thoroughgoing system of symbolism has to face: if there are no fixities and definites at all but only symbolic fluidity, then there would appear to be some danger that everything will disappear into froth and bubbles.

Such is the characteristic weakness of the poetic performance of Walt Whitman, the poet upon whom Emerson's transcendental theory registered with most emphatic force. In Whitman's *Song of Myself* the poet and the universe about him merge so effortlessly that the poem threatens to collapse into tautology. The poet discovers with a kind of jaunty wonder that he is a part of nature and indeed is not to be separated from all those things ordinarily thought of as external to man:

> I find I incorporate gneiss, long-threaded moss, fruits,
> grains, esculent roots,
> And am stucco'd with quadrupeds and birds all over. . . .

The typical problem raised by Herman Melville's work, however, is not that of too easy reconciliation. With Melville the question is rather whether there is any reconciliation at all. Even more than Emerson, Melville was shaken by the crisis in epistemology. And Melville possessed the vision of evil. That the universe was not merely an external and mechanical framework, but was plastic, "organic," and alive was for Melville something more than an innocently exhilarating discovery. The discovery also held an element of terror, for the evil in the world was not thereby canceled; indeed, it was rendered more deeply and ineradicably alive. Moreover, to a mind desperate for truth, the very ambiguity of the universe was horrible.

The heroes of Melville's novels are all concerned with the problem of knowledge. Each of them asks whether we can truly *know* anything, or whether we are not actually caught in a quicksand of our own dreams and imaginative projections, a quicksand into which our struggles to reach objective truth can only mire us deeper. In his masterpiece, *Moby Dick* (1851), Melville frankly accepted a "methodological paradox." That is, he accepted the fact that although the "realm of significance" would seem to deny "the dual reality of subject and object," yet in fact the realm of significance rises from and returns to that duality. The realm of significance is allowed to do so in this novel; for example, the whale is "simultaneously the most solid of physical things and the most

[1] *Works*, III, 24.

meaningful of symbols." [2] But in Melville's later novels, the objects are hazy and the heroes become more and more involved in a frustrating struggle with shadows. The failure of Melville's novel *Pierre: or The Ambiguities* (1852) may be imputed to Melville's having become "contemptuous of literary form in general." Melville as author "suspects from the beginning what his hero discovers in the end, that all literature is meretricious." [3]

> He reached not only a personal, but also a technical, impasse. The logic of his career was the logic of his aesthetic premises; his concept of artistic truth was calculated to lead him into a skepticism of art. [4]

Something of the sort seems to have happened to another extreme proponent of symbolist theory, the French poet Arthur Rimbaud. After publishing *Une Saison en Enfer*, Rimbaud apparently came to an impasse, burned his manuscripts, and left Europe to become an ivory-trader and gun-runner in Abyssinia. [5]

III

THERE are good reasons for grouping Edgar Allan Poe with the Transcendentalists, who were, of course, his contemporaries and fellow-countrymen. Poe, to be sure, had some sharp things to say on the topic of Emerson's obscurantism, and he deplored the general bias of New Englanders toward the allegorical and toward the didactic. "We Americans especially," he writes, "have patronised [the heresy of the Didactic]; and we Bostonians, very especially, have developed it in full." [6] But Poe's literary theorizing was in general derived from the same sources as those of the Transcendentalists.

What sets Poe apart from the Transcendentalists is his special aestheticism, aspects of which have already been discussed in our chapter on "Art for Art's Sake." [7] By contrast with Emerson's attitude toward poetry, Poe's is technical and "professional." Poe envisages the poet not as that vague and splendidly democratic creature, "man speaking," but as a craftsman who brings his intelligence fully, and even coldly, to bear upon the problem of organizing words into specific literary struc-

[2] *Symbolism and American Literature*, p. 184.
[3] *Symbolism and American Literature*, p. 201.
[4] *Symbolism and American Literature*, p. 164.
[5] Enid Starkie in her study, *Arthur Rimbaud* (New York, 1947), p. 294, offers among other conjectures, the suggestion that "perhaps [Rimbaud's] new form of poetry led him to a dead end. . . ."
[6] "The Poetic Principle," *Complete Works*, ed. J. A. Harrison (New York, 1902), XIV, 271.
[7] Cf. *ante* Chapter 22.

tures. Poe was prepared to take quite literally Milton's compliment to Lycidas on his knowledge of how "to build the lofty rhyme." A poem had an architecture and it was well built or ill built. Its shape ought not to be a matter of "accident or intuition" but ought to reveal—at least in the ideal case—"the precision and rigid consequence of a mathematical problem." [8] This aspect of Poe's criticism was to prove, as we shall see, most attractive to Baudelaire and the other French symbolist poets. For them it evidently constituted a special way of focusing upon the pure lyric intensity that Poe argued was the essence of poetry.

There could be no such thing as a *long* poem. That phrase, Poe confidently declared, was "simply a flat contradiction in terms." The "degree of excitement" which entitles one to use the term "poem" simply cannot be sustained throughout a long work, for all such excitements are "through a psychal necessity, transient." [9] This stress upon lyric intensity implied a special kind of subject matter and a special kind of form. The subject matter must be an experience of peculiar intensity. The form must be purely functional, with all that is nonfunctional—all that is merely "prose" connective tissue—eliminated. In short a poem should have the intensity that one finds in a waking dream and its elements should contain as little "inert" matter as the notes of a musical composition. It is "in Music, perhaps," Poe writes, "that the soul most nearly attains . . . the creation of supernal Beauty." [1]

Thus dream and music were used by Poe to suggest the special kinds of purity that he demanded of poetry, and this analogizing of poetry to dream and to music was to run all the way through the speculations of the French symbolists. Poe refers in his *Marginalia* to "points of time where the confines of the waking world blend with those of the world of dreams." [2] Nearly a century later, Poe's very phrasing returns to us in a passage of one of W. B. Yeats's last poems, referring to

> . . . forms that are or seem
> When sleepers wake and yet still dream,
> And when it's vanished still declare,
> With only bed and bedstead there,
> That heavens had opened. [3]

This indeed would be to catch a glimpse of the supernal beauty; and if the modern poet's almost aggressive insistence upon the domestic realism of the bedroom furniture seems oddly out of key with the ornate and mannered Gothic decor that Poe usually provides as the setting for

[8] "The Philosophy of Composition," *Works*, XIV, 195.
[9] "The Poetic Principle," *Works*, XIV, 266.
[1] "The Poetic Principle," *Works*, XIV, 274.
[2] *Works*, XVI, 88.
[3] "Under Ben Bulben," *Collected Poems* (New York, 1951), p. 343, by permission of The Macmillan Company.

such experiences, the contrast itself makes a point: it testifies to the vitality of Poe's key ideas and to their ability to suffer translation from one realm of sensibility to another. Yeats's version of the waking dream, of course, reveals the impress of his own personality and also reflects the modifications the notion received in passing through the succession of French symbolists and then back into English again. Like most other British and American poets, Yeats accepted very little from Poe directly. The poetry that enchanted Baudelaire left Yeats cold. He observed to a friend: "Analyse the Raven and you find that its subject is a commonplace and its execution a rhythmical trick. Its rhythm never lives for a moment, never once moves with an emotional life. The whole thing seems to me insincere and vulgar." [4]

But upon Baudelaire Poe's empurpled rhetoric registered with very different effect. In 1846 or 1847 Baudelaire read his first French translations of Poe, and felt immediately a powerful sense of spiritual kinship with the American poet. In an ecstasy of discovery, he took over Poe's whole doctrine of pure poetry. The poet, Poe had said, had nothing to do with the good or the true, but only with the beautiful. His prime task was to "reach the Beauty above," [5] of which the beauty of this world is a reflection. In Chapter 22 *ante* we have already considered the implications of this statement for the doctrine of art for art's sake. It remains to relate it more specifically to the theories of the French symbolists.

To assert that the beauty of this world is but a "reflection" of a "Beauty above" is in itself to imply a symbolist aesthetic of sorts. But Poe makes it quite plain that we can attain to this eternal beauty—even if to no more than "a portion" of it—only by making use of "multiform combinations among the things and thoughts of Time." [6] The general recipe is old enough: but in Poe's formulation it is worth noting that "things and thoughts" are made to lie down beside each other as if any invidious distinction between them had been obliterated.

Poe's "multiform combinations" finds its parallel and development in Baudelaire's more celebrated "system of correspondences." As Baudelaire wrote in 1859 in an article on Théophile Gautier: ". . . it is our instinct for beauty which causes us to consider the earth and its visibilia . . . 'comme une *correspondance* du Ciel.' " [7] In *Les Fleurs du Mal*

[4] The letter, dated 3 September 1899, is addressed to W. T. Horton. See *The Letters of W. B. Yeats*, ed. Allan Wade (New York, 1955), p. 325. This and following passages from Yeats's writings are reprinted by permission of The Macmillan Company. Aldous Huxley has some acute as well as amusing observations on the fact that French men of letters have so much admired Poe whereas English-speaking readers tend to find him vulgar. See his *Vulgarity in Literature* (London, 1930), pp. 26–36.

[5] "The Poetic Principle," *Works*, XIV, 273.

[6] "The Poetic Principle," *Works*, XIV, 274.

[7] Guy Michaud, *Message Poétique du Symbolisme* (Paris, 1947, 3 vols.), I, 70.

(1857), Baudelaire expresses this conception in a sonnet entitled "*Correspondances*," where all nature is viewed as a temple, a natural temple whose living pillars are the trees. As the wind blows through these "forests of symbols," confused words are now and then breathed forth. The poet, because of his special endowment, is able to apprehend these words, for in all things there is a symbolic sense and every object in nature has its special connection with a spiritual reality.[8]

The correspondences are developed upon several planes. The poet asserts that there are equivalences among the data of the various senses—sounds, colors, odors. ("*Les parfums, les couleurs, et les sons se répondent.*") And he speaks of perfumes "fresh as a child's skin, sweet as oboes, green as meadows."

In the second place,

> Since sensuous data can have "the expansion of infinite things," it follows that a desire, a regret, a thought—things of the mind —can awaken a corresponding symbol in the world of images (and vice versa). . . . From the world of the senses the poet takes the material in which to forge a symbolic vision of himself or of his dream; what he asks of the world of the senses is that it give him the means of expressing his soul. [9]

The neo-Platonic flavor of this conception of poetry is sufficiently evident. In Baudelaire's poetry, this general idealistic tendency reinforces, and is reinforced by, special tendencies toward the irrational and the occult. But Baudelaire showed himself the true disciple of Poe[1] in refusing to be guided by instinct alone. He believed in method; he could even refer to inspiration as "the reward of daily effort." He classed himself among those artists who attempt to "discover the obscure laws by virtue of which they have created, and to draw from this study a number of precepts whose divine goal is the infallibility of poetic production." [2]

IV

PREOCCUPATION with method was, however, far more than with Baudelaire the special concern of Stéphane Mallarmé. Mallarmé took very

[8] Baudelaire's theory of correspondences also derives in part from the notions of the Swedish mystic, Emanuel Swedenborg. In his article on Victor Hugo (1861), Baudelaire writes: "Moreover Swedenborg . . . has already taught us . . . that everything, form, motion, number, color, scents, in the *spiritual* as well as in the *natural* realm, is significant, reciprocal, converse, corresponding. . . ." See Guy Michaud, *La Doctrine Symboliste: Documents* (Paris, 1947), p. 22.

[9] Marcel Raymond, *From Baudelaire to Surrealism* (Paris, 1933, revised 1940); translated into English by "G.M." *Documents of Modern Art Vol. 10*, New York: George Wittenborn, Inc., 1949, p. 18.

[1] Cf. *ante* Chapter 22.

[2] In an article on Richard Wagner. See *From Baudelaire to Surrealism*, p. 21.

seriously Poe's notion of a poem so carefully organized that it possessed "the precision and rigid consequence of a mathematical problem." One finds Mallarmé writing such a passage as the following:

> The further I go, the more faithful I shall be to those severe ideas which my great master, Edgar Poe, has bequeathed me. The wonderful poem *The Raven* was conceived thus, and the soul of the reader enjoys exactly what the poet wanted it to enjoy.[3]

During the 1870's and the 1880's, Mallarmé came to be regarded as the saint and sage of the symbolist movement. He was not a popular poet; he published little; but his Tuesday receptions at which he talked with his friends about poetry became an institution. To his house there came not only the French poets and critics of the period, but writers in English such as Oscar Wilde, Arthur Symons, George Moore, and W. B. Yeats. With Mallarmé, the cultivation of poetry went far toward becoming a ritual and a cult. It also went farthest toward becoming an enterprise engaging all the powers of the mind—not a matter of blind inspiration or of sudden and inexplicable visitations by the Muse, but a problem of craftsmanship and of philosophical theorizing. It is to Mallarmé that one turns, incidentally, for what is probably the most celebrated observation about symbolic methods. In 1891 he wrote:

> . . . the Parnassians, for their part, take the thing as a whole and show it; that's where they are deficient in mystery. They deprive the mind of the delicious joy of believing that it is creating. To name an object is to do away with three-quarters of the enjoyment of the poem which is derived from the satisfaction of guessing little by little; to suggest it, that is the illusion. It is the perfect handling of the mystery that constitutes the symbol: to evoke an object little by little in order to show a state of mind or inversely to choose an object and to disengage from it a state of mind, by a series of unriddlings.[4]

Someone has described Mallarmé's characteristic poetic activity as that of trying to refine and purify any object or event to the "Platonic idea" of that object or event. There was in him a compulsion to reduce to essences by removing the accidental and adventitious. Mallarmé was concerned that nothing in the poem be the effect of mere chance, that the articulation of every part with every other part should be complete,

[3] *Message Poétique du Symbolisme*, I, 165.

[4] *Réponse à une Enquête* (1891), quoted in *La Doctrine Symboliste: Documents*, p. 74. Mallarmé's reference to the "delicious joy" that the mind experiences in "believing that it is creating" recalls Coleridge's remark that the reader feels Shakespeare to be a poet "inasmuch as for a time he has made you one—an active creative being." For more recent instances of this view, see *post* Chapter 28.

each part implying every other part, and that the meaning of the poem should be inseparable from its formal structure. In the Mallarmean poem the words acquire something of the bulk and density of things; the poem is treated almost as if it were a plastic object with weight and solidity and with even a certain opacity. For the words are not *signs*, transparently redacting ideas. Instead they have acquired something like bulk and mass. The poems have become little mysterious worlds whose meaning is to be read with only somewhat less difficulty than the meaning of the great world of which the poems are in a sense analogical copies.

Words for Mallarmé were then much more than signs. Used evocatively and ritualistically, they are the means by which we are inducted into an ideal world. "Poetry is," as Mallarmé defined it in 1886, "the expression by means of human language restored to its essential rhythm, of the mysterious sense of the aspects of existence: it endows our sojourn with authenticity and constitutes the sole spiritual task." [5]

V

THE main line of succession of the French symbolist movement, it is generally agreed, runs from Baudelaire to Mallarmé and thence to Paul Valéry.[6] But before taking up Valéry, it will be useful to examine briefly two important side developments. The first of these has to do with the career of Paul Verlaine. We have already had occasion to cite Poe's observation that it is in music that the soul most "nearly attains . . . the creation of supernal Beauty." The symbolist movement may be described as the effort to bring poetry to the condition of music—indeed Valéry did so describe it in 1926. Mallarmé's poetry is clearly musical in this sense, words being organized and orchestrated almost as if they were musical notes. But Verlaine's poetry is "musical" in a more direct and literal sense. In his poetry, the words tend to be emptied of their intellectual content. As Michaud puts it, in Verlaine's poetry "the language is vaporized and is reabsorbed into the melody." [7] Raymond says of Verlaine that he was "born to bring to its perfection the intimate and sentimental lyricism founded by Marceline Desbordes-Valmore and Lamartine." [8] Verlaine represents a temperament, a mood, rather than a technique. It will be more accurate to call his poetry impressionistic than to call it symbolist.

Yet if Verlaine has to be excluded from the circle of genuine symbolist poets, he had, nevertheless, much to do with bringing symbolism

[5] *Message Poétique du Symbolisme*, II, 321.
[6] See, for instance, *From Baudelaire to Surrealism*, p. 5.
[7] *Message Poétique du Symbolisme*, I, 123.
[8] *From Baudelaire to Surrealism*, p. 22.

to public notice. In 1884 Verlaine published his *Les Poètes Maudits*. The "accurst" poets discussed were Mallarmé, Tristan Corbière, and Arthur Rimbaud. It is easy to see why Verlaine applied the adjective to Corbière and Rimbaud, poets clearly repulsed by the society in which they lived; it is less easy to see how it applies to Mallarmé, and a recent writer on Mallarmé doubts whether Verlaine ever understood Mallarmé's poetry "in any profound way." [9]

The case of Verlaine provides an opportunity to render more precise the sense in which symbolist poetry may be said to be "musical"; that of Rimbaud allows one to develop a little further the sense in which the symbolist poet may be said to give over the initiative to the words themselves. Mallarmé, though he may be said to have given words their heads,[1] never, as the Surrealists were to do later, dropped the reins completely, abandoning the poem to the latent energies of language. Whether Rimbaud may be fairly said to have "abandoned" all conscious control is debatable; but Rimbaud is clearly a precursor of Surrealism. He deliberately cultivated the unconventional and the irrational.

In Rimbaud's conception, the poet is essentially a *voyant*, a seer. He applauded, as the "first voyant," Baudelaire, that "King of poets, a real God," even though he lamented the fact that Baudelaire lived in "too artistic a *milieu*" and encumbered himself with old literary forms.[2] For the new discoveries demanded new forms. The *voyant* perceives those images that the unconscious reveals only fitfully and accidentally to the ordinary man. Rimbaud's poetry was to be the systematic exploitation of such images. To this end the poet would make use of drugs, alcohol, debauchery—anything that broke down the control of reason and freed the faculties from their ordinary inhibitions. Rimbaud's famous recipe for the poet's activity reads thus: "The poet makes himself *voyant* by a long, vast, reasoned derangement of all the senses" (*Lettres du Voyant,* 1871).[3]

VI

VERLAINE, as we have seen, called Rimbaud and Mallarmé "poètes maudits" and himself gloried in the term *décadent*. Théophile Gau-

---

[9] Wallace Fowlie, *Mallarmé* (Chicago, 1953. Copyright [1953] by the University of Chicago). Fowlie goes on to say (p. 255): "The essay on Mallarmé was Verlaine's opportunity to cast opprobrium on those critics and readers who had considered him insane and ridiculous. Although Mallarmé's personal life would never place him with Poe, Baudelaire, Rimbaud, and Verlaine himself, his fate as poet was that of revolutionary, one cursed by the existing society."

[1] "A pure work, Mallarmé has written, gives over the initiative to the words themselves. The deliberate rhetoric of the poet disappears in them."—Fowlie, *Mallarmé,* p. 269.

[2] See *Message Poétique du Symbolisme,* I, 138, and Starkie's *Rimbaud,* p. 128.

[3] See Starkie, *Rimbaud,* p. 129.

tier had used *décadent* in his preface to Baudelaire's *Les Fleurs du Mal*, and Paul Bourget would call Baudelaire the "theoretician of decadence." The *décadent* was a seeker after rare sensation, a dandy, perhaps a roué, a cultivated dilettante, and, as one critic has phrased it, decadence came "to signify a kind of moral solitude of an artist, coupled with an exasperated and perverse form of mysticism." [4] The fashion of decadence was a way of protecting oneself from bourgeois triviality and all the dullness of a world increasingly given over to industrialism. So defined, the term has pertinence for Rimbaud and Verlaine, but less for a poet like Mallarmé. (Valéry observes that although "Verlaine and Rimbaud continued Baudelaire in the order of sentiment and sensation, Mallarmé carried his work forward in the province of perfection and poetic purity.") [5] At any rate, in 1885 some of the younger *décadent* writers repudiated that term and chose to call themselves "symbolists." The latter term certainly answered more nearly to the idealism of men like Mallarmé and Valéry, to their stress upon the intellectual construct, and above all to their attitude toward language. The symbolists, having discovered the non-notational aspect of language, proceed to explore the rich possibilities of intimation, suggestion, and all the other modes of linguistic indirection. Thus, one might attempt to summarize the history of the movement.

But "symbolism" was a rather loose and vague term, as Valéry himself was well aware. It was used to cover various and sometimes conflicting conceptions of poetry. What had been baptized Symbolism, Valéry was to write in retrospect in 1920, is summed up simply in an "intention of several groups of poets (not always friendly to one another) to recover from music the heritage due to them." [6] In music, there is no dross, no inert residue. Form and content coalesce. It was to this purified wholeness that symbolist poetry aspired. Valéry remarks in his essay on Baudelaire that Poe

> understood that [poetry] could claim to realize its own object and produce itself, to some degree, in a *pure state*.
>
> Thus, by analysing the requirements of poetic delight and defining *absolute poetry* by *exhaustion*, Poe showed a way and taught a very strict and fascinating doctrine in which he united a sort of mathematics with a sort of mysticism. . . . [7]

In Valéry's own work this aspiration to absolute purity finally led

[4] Fowlie, *Mallarmé*, p. 257.

[5] "The Position of Baudelaire" (first published in 1924), *Variety: Second Series*, trans. W. A. Bradley (New York, 1938), p. 98.

[6] Fowlie, *Mallarmé*, p. 268. Valéry's words are: "*Ce qui fut baptisé le Symbolisme, se résume très simplement dans l'intention commune à plusieurs familles de poètes (d'ailleurs ennemies entre elles) de reprendre à la Musique leur bien.*"

[7] *Variety: Second Series*, p. 92.

on past poetry, considered as a realized structure, to a preoccupation with the poetic activity as such. That is why Valéry could say to his friend André Gide: "They take me for a poet! I don't give a damn about poetry. It interests me only by a fluke. It is by accident that I have written verse. It has no importance for me." [8] Poetry, that is, was interesting only in so far as one could make it an exercise in pure creation. Thus symbolist poetry at its apogee threatens to purify itself out of existence. If the pressure for pure meaning is pressed unremittingly, the poem is finally detached from reality and becomes knowledge of *nothing!* Valéry's poetic masterpiece, "*Le Cimitiere Marin*," derives its power from a candidly tragic apprehension of some final dichotomy between knowledge and life. It is the dichotomy tirelessly echoed, though of course with a different inflection, in the later poetry of William Butler Yeats:

> For wisdom is the property of the dead,
> A something incompatible with life. . . .[9]

That symbolist poetry should, in its yearning for purity, extinguish itself was much more than a merely academic possibility. Valéry did remain silent for some twenty years before he resumed the writing of poetry. We have already referred to Rimbaud's abandonment of poetry in favor of a life of action in Africa.

Any attempt to summarize symbolist doctrine exposes the vagueness of the pronouncements of the various symbolists and critics, not to mention their frequent contradictions. One might be forgiven for coming to doubt whether the term "symbolism" has any specific meaning at all, and to conclude that it is, like the term "romanticism," simply the name for a bundle of tendencies, not all of them very closely related. A definition may be attempted as follows:

> Whether a real school of symbolism ever existed, remains a problem of speculation. . . . Each poet developed and represented a single aspect of an aesthetic doctrine that was perhaps too vast for one historical group to incorporate. . . . But more than on any other article of belief, the symbolists united with Mallarmé in his statements about poetic language. The theory of the suggestiveness of words comes from a belief that a primitive language, half-forgotten, half-living, exists in each man. It is language possessing extraordinary affinities with music and dreams.[1]

This is a just appraisal; yet the phrasing, "primitive language, half-forgotten, half-living," could be misleading to a modern reader. It could

[8] *Message Poétique du Symbolisme*, III, 572.
[9] "Blood and the Moon," *Collected Poems*, p. 234.
[1] *Mallarmé*, p. 264.

suggest certain special developments of our own time which scarcely existed for Baudelaire and Mallarmé and to which, as the context shows, the words do not refer: that is, the tremendous contemporary interest in the pre-logical and primitive mind, whether of children or savages or neurotics, and as treated typically in anthropology and in depth psychology. With this interest, there has arisen a powerful new interest in myth as a "primitive language, half-forgotten, half-living," and there have been bold and sometimes extravagant speculations about the relation of myth to poetry. Such developments of symbolist and expressionist theory will be dealt with in a subsequent chapter. Suffice it to say that the French symbolists were interested in the magic of the Rosicrucians rather than that of the Trobriand Islanders, and in the ritual practices of the heretical sects of the Middle Ages rather than in those of the present-day tribes of the Congo and Amazon. In short, their interests were "philosophical" rather than "psychological," and "traditional" rather than "anthropological."

VII

SUCH also were the interests of the English-speaking poets and critics who were most powerfully influenced by the French symbolists, men like T. E. Hulme, Ezra Pound, and T. S. Eliot, whose ideas we shall consider in a later chapter, and even men like William Butler Yeats, whose attempt to construct a personal myth in *A Vision* (1925) might seem to argue a different concern. The affinities between Yeats and the French symbolists are numerous, and some of them have already been suggested by our recourse to Yeats in several earlier pages in order to illustrate symbolist ideas. Yet the direct influence of the French poets upon Yeats was slight. Though as early as 1894 Yeats took with him on a visit to Paris a letter of introduction to Mallarmé, he seems to have learned about symbolist ideas largely from his friend Arthur Symons, who dedicated to Yeats his *Symbolist Movement in Literature* (1899). A letter that he wrote many years later in 1937 indicates how slight the direct influence of Mallarmé had been. Yeats writes that he has just been looking at

> Roger Fry's translation of Mallarmé. . . . I find it exciting, as it shows me the road I and others of my time went for certain furlongs. It is not the way I go now, but one of the legitimate roads.[2]

What Yeats learned from Symons about symbolism comes out most plainly in Yeats's essay on "The Symbolism of Poetry" (1900). He re-

[2] Written, May 4, to Dorothy Wellesley: see *Letters of W. B. Yeats*, p. 887.

marks that the scientific movement had tended to bring into literature "externalities of all kinds," and that as a consequence, literature had been in danger of losing itself in

> opinion, in declamation, in picturesque writing, in word-painting, or in what Mr. Symons has called an attempt "to build in brick and mortar inside the covers of a book." [3]

Now, however, "writers have begun to dwell upon the element of evocation, of suggestion." Yeats asserts that "the substance of all style" is a "continuous indefinable symbolism," which he chooses to illustrate, not from one of the new writers, but from one of the 18th-century poets, Robert Burns.

> There are no lines [he writes] with more melancholy beauty than these by Burns—
>   "The white moon is setting behind the white wave,
>   And Time is setting with me, O!"
> and these lines are perfectly symbolical. Take from them the whiteness of the moon and of the wave, whose relation to the setting of Time is too subtle for the intellect, and you take from them their beauty. But, when all are together, moon and wave and whiteness and setting Time and the last melancholy cry, they evoke an emotion which cannot be evoked by any other arrangement of colours and sounds and forms.[4]

In the same essay Yeats writes that

> All sounds, all colours, all forms, either because of their pre-ordained energies or because of long association, evoke indefinable and yet precise emotions, or, as I prefer to think, call down among us certain disembodied powers, whose footsteps over our hearts we call emotions.[5]

Yeats's deliberate invocation of some kind of supernaturalism by references to "pre-ordained energies" and "disembodied powers" and the general glitter of his rhetoric should not be allowed to distract us from what is the central issue: though the emotions are "indefinable" yet they are nevertheless "precise." That is, the fact that the emotions cannot be defined in logical and scientific terms does not in the least invalidate their claim to precision.

A year later, in an essay entitled "Magic," Yeats trailed his cloak even more vigorously in the face of the naturalist, flaunting his belief

---

[3] W. B. Yeats, *Ideas of Good and Evil* (London, 1903), p. 240, by permission of The Macmillan Company.
[4] *Ideas of Good and Evil*, pp. 241-2.
[5] *Ideas of Good and Evil*, p. 243.

in the "evocation of spirits" (though he was careful to acknowledge that he did "not know what they are"). He recorded in that essay his belief in three doctrines which have been, he declared, "the foundations of nearly all magical practices." The doctrines were:

(1) That the borders of our minds are ever shifting, and that many minds can flow into one another, as it were, and create or reveal a single mind, a single energy.
(2) That the borders of our memories are as shifting, and that our memories are a part of one great memory, the memory of Nature herself.
(3) That this great mind and great memory can be evoked by symbols.[6]

"To show that past times have believed as I do," Yeats cites Joseph Glanvill's story of the Scholar Gipsy, the story upon which Matthew Arnold founded his poem. Yeats seems to take the Scholar Gipsy's powers quite literally; yet the context makes it plain that what interests him especially is what is summed up in the twice-used phrase, "the power of imagination." Yeats quotes the passage in which the Scholar Gipsy tells his Oxford friends that the gipsies

he went with were not such impostors as they were taken for, but that they had a traditional kind of learning among them and could do wonders by the power of imagination. . . . The scholars . . . earnestly desired him to unriddle the mystery. In which he gave them satisfaction, by telling them that what he did was by the power of imagination, his phantasy leading theirs. . . .[7]

That power, Yeats declares, is alive today, and symbols are still the "greatest of all powers whether they are used consciously by the masters of magic, or half unconsciously by their successors, the poet, the musician and the artist."[8]

The contrast with Arnold could hardly be more complete: the Scholar Gipsy, for the great Victorian critic, is obviously a fabulous creature, part of the folklore of a charmingly naive world toward which the sore-beset modern rationalist can turn back no more than a wistful glance. But for Yeats, the power of imagination possessed by the Gipsy is still valid and is to be claimed to its fullest extent. If to assert one's

---

[6] *Ideas of Good and Evil*, p. 29.
   This conception of the great mind and the great memory sounds like an interesting anticipation of Carl Jung's doctrine of the collective unconscious with its repository of archetypal images which on occasion can well up into individual minds. Jung stated his conception first in 1912.
[7] *Ideas of Good and Evil*, pp. 48–9.
[8] *Ideas of Good and Evil*, p. 64.

belief in this kind of power means to make claims for magic as such, Yeats will do so. But it is worth remarking that Yeats seems to swallow the magic for the sake of possessing the imagination and not the other way around.

Our softening of Yeats's assertions of a literal belief in magic may seem overconfident in view of his membership in organizations boasting such titles as the "Order of the Golden Dawn," his association with Madame Blavatsky, and his lifelong interest in table-rapping, spirit mediums, and clairvoyants. But these more lurid stageprops ought not to distract us from Yeats's other interests—such as the philosophy of history as developed by Vico and Hegel and the epistemology of Plato and Plotinus and Bishop Berkeley. Even *A Vision*, that extravagant attempt to set forth a personal mythology, the substance of which Yeats claimed to have received from the "teaching spirits" through the mediumship of his wife, had an intellectual justification which Yeats could state in sober enough terms. Works like Berkeley's *Principles of Human Knowledge*, Yeats wrote, might prove "to our logical capacity" that there is a "transcendental portion of our being that is timeless and spaceless," and yet "our imagination [may] remain subjected to nature as before." It was otherwise for the ancient philosopher, Yeats maintained, for he "had something to reinforce his thought,—the Gods, the Sacred Dead, Egyptian Theurgy, the Priestess Diotime." [9] *A Vision* was to furnish to the modern philosopher a like imaginative reinforcement.

VIII

ALL symbolist doctrines seem to rest either upon some kind of idealism or else to deny the dualism of ideality and materialism altogether by considering these opposed concepts to be abstractions out of a prior and deeper reality in which they lie undifferentiated. The latter alternative has proved historically a difficult one to sustain. The position of those philosophers of symbolic form who, like Ernst Cassirer and Susanne Langer, seek to avoid moving into any kind of pure idealism, we shall discuss in a later chapter. Most symbolist poets and critics, including those already discussed in this chapter, tend to be rather pure idealists. And so did Yeats.

In 1926 Yeats wrote to his friend Sturge Moore that because the "teaching spirits" had forbidden it, he did not read philosophy until he had completed *A Vision*. But then, he writes, "I read for months every day Plato and Plotinus. Then I started on Berkeley and Croce and Gentile." [1] One of the topics canvassed at length in this correspond-

[9] *A Vision* (London, 1925), pp. 251–2.
[1] *W. B. Yeats and T. Sturge Moore: their Correspondence, 1901–1937*, ed. Ursula Bridge (Oxford University Press, Inc.: New York, 1953), p. 83.

ence (published 1953) has to do with the cat that John Ruskin was alleged to have picked up and thrown out of the window with the explanation that it was really a tempting demon. Yeats wanted to know on what basis, if any, the cat could be regarded as "unreal," and specifically how Ruskin could have distinguished the demon cat from the house cat. His choice of the problem is significant. It provided him with an occasion to talk about the topics that had particularly engaged his interest as he read Plato, Berkeley, Kant, Hegel, and Croce. Some of his arguments turn out to be quite fantastic, but, as Yeats wrote to Moore, the "points most of my fantasies and extravagancies were meant to suggest are . . . that images of the mind and images of sense must have a common root . . . and that whatever their cause or substratum that substratum is not fixed at one spot in space." [2]

In general Yeats was a good—if somewhat unconventional—Kantian. He termed "the vast Kantian argument" the "most powerful in philosophy." From it there descended "two great streams of thought," the "philosophy of will in Schopenhauer, Hartmann, Bergsen [sic], James, and that of knowledge in Hegel, Croce, Gentile, Bradley and the like." [3] Of these "two paths to reality," as Yeats elsewhere refers to them, that "of knowledge" proved the more attractive to him.

Poetry yields a special kind of knowledge. Through poetry, man comes to know himself in relation to reality, and thus attains wisdom. On this theme Yeats's own poetry descants tirelessly. The magi seeking the manger in Bethlehem are conceived of as seekers after knowledge, "hoping to find . . . The uncontrollable mystery on the bestial floor." [4] When Yeats imagines the rape of Leda by the swan, the question that he puts is: "Did she put on his knowledge with his power?" [5] In "The Gift of Harun Al-Rashid," the young bride gives unwittingly to her older philosopher husband that precious gift that is "to age what milk is to a child," "A quality of wisdom" which springs from "her love's Particular quality." [6] Even Yeats's account of the fortunes of the soul after death, as detailed in *A Vision*, is the story of a quest for knowledge. The soul must first relive all the passionate experiences of its life until it understands them, and then it must experience the opposite of all that it actually did and suffered in its life so that it may truly complete its knowledge of itself. Only then is it allowed to drink of the cup of Lethe.

The knowledge that poetry confers is obviously something other than a traffic in "opinions," which the poet associates with competition and intellectual hatred. It is not produced by the "levelling, rancorous, ra-

[2] *Yeats and Moore: Correspondence*, p. 92.
[3] *Yeats and Moore: Correspondence*, pp. 122–4.
[4] *Collected Poems*, p. 124.
[5] *Collected Poems*, p. 212.
[6] *Collected Poems*, p. 444.

tional sort of mind That never looked out of the eye of a saint Or out of a drunkard's eye." [7] It is so completely detached from the life of action that Yeats says more than once that only the dead have true wisdom; or else he regards such true wisdom as the living may enjoy to be something so deep and instinctive that its possessor hardly knows that he possesses it—

> Considering that, all hatred driven hence,
> The soul recovers radical innocence
> And learns at last that it is self-delighting,
> Self-appeasing, self-affrighting,
> And that its own sweet will is Heaven's will. . . .[8]

Perhaps we shall appreciate these scattered "poetic" utterances if we set beside them some comparable passages from a systematic aesthetician. The writings of the late R. G. Collingwood, philosopher and one of the English translators of Croce, will serve our purpose well. Collingwood admired Yeats's poetry, his own position is that of an idealist and symbolist, and like Yeats he was even interested in "magic" and found a place for it in his intellectual scheme. In his *Principles of Art*, he comments upon the artist's concern for knowledge as follows:

> Theoretically, the artist is a person who comes to know himself, to know his own emotion. This is also knowing his world, that is, the sights and sounds and so forth which together make up his total imaginative experience. The two knowledges are to him one knowledge, because these sights and sounds are to him steeped in the emotion with which he contemplates them: they are the language in which that emotion utters itself to his consciousness. His world is his language. What it says to him it says about himself; his imaginative vision of it is his self-knowledge.[9]

Compare with this passage what Yeats wrote in 1900:

> Solitary men in moments of contemplation receive . . . the creative impulse from the lowest of the Nine Hierarchies, and so make and unmake mankind, and even the world itself, for does not "the eye altering alter all"? [1]

And in one of his earliest poems:

[7] *Collected Poems*, p. 236.
[8] *Collected Poems*, p. 187.
[9] *The Principles of Art* (Oxford, 1938), p. 291, by permission of Oxford University Press, Inc.
[1] "The Symbolism of Poetry," *Ideas of Good and Evil*, pp. 246–7.

> . . . words alone are certain good:
> Sing, then, for this is also sooth. . . .
> Dream, dream, for this is also sooth.[2]

Collingwood goes on to say:

> But this knowing of himself [by the artist] is a making of
> himself. . . . The coming to know his emotions is the coming
> to dominate them, to assert himself as their master. . . .
> Moreover, his knowing of this new world is also the making
> of the new world which he is coming to know. The world he
> has come to know is a world consisting of language; a world
> where everything has the property of expressing emotion. In so
> far as this world is thus expressive or significant, it is he that has
> made it so. . . .
> The aesthetic experience . . . is a knowing of oneself and
> of one's world. . . . It is also a making of oneself and of one's
> world, the self which was psyche being remade in the shape of
> consciousness, and the world, which was crude sensa, being re-
> made in the shape of language, or sensa converted into imagery
> and charged with emotional significance.[3]

Beside this passage from the philosopher can be set any number of
passages gleaned from the poet, in which he asserts the creative power
of man's imagination. Out of "poet's imaginings," out of the "memories
of love," out of "Memories of the words of women,"

> Man makes a superhuman
> Mirror-resembling dream. . . .

> From man's blood-sodden heart are sprung
> Those branches of the night and day
> Where the gaudy moon is hung. . . .[5]

More arrogantly still,

> Death and life were not
> Till man made up the whole,
> Made lock, stock and barrel
> Out of his bitter soul,
> Aye, sun and moon and star, all.[6]

And of man's rage for knowledge of what he is, the poet declares:

[2] *Collected Poems*, p. 8.
[3] *The Principles of Art*, pp. 291–2.
[4] *Collected Poems*, p. 197.
[5] *Collected Poems*, p. 247.
[6] *Collected Poems*, p. 196.

> man's life is thought,
> And he, despite his terror, cannot cease
> Ravening through century after century,
> Ravening, raging, and uprooting that he may come
> Into the desolation of reality. . . .[7]

But it is to a letter written by Yeats not long before his death that one turns for what is perhaps the best statement of Yeats's yearning for the "concrete" knowledge that poetry can give, of his sense of the part that man's own expression plays in the determination of that knowledge, and of his recognition of man's limitation with regard to the apprehension of any knowledge:

> . . . I know for certain that my time will not be long. I have put away everything that can be put away that I may speak what I have to speak, and I find "expression" is a part of "study." In two or three weeks—I am now idle that I may rest after writing much verse—I will begin to write my most fundamental thoughts and the arrangement of thought which I am convinced will complete my studies. I am happy, and I think full of an energy, of an energy I had despaired of. It seems to me that I have found what I wanted. When I try to put all into a phrase I say, "Man can embody truth but he cannot know it." I must embody it in the completion of my life. The abstract is not life and everywhere draws out its contradictions. You can refute Hegel but not the Saint or the Song of Sixpence. . . .[8]

An argument is subject to refutation. The noble life, the song, the poem, are none of them subject to refutation. For the poem, like the life of the saint, does not state a proposition but embodies a meaning.

Earlier in this chapter we had occasion to speak of the danger inherent in any thorough-going symbolic system, particularly as held by an idealist: if, as Emerson put it, "the poet turns the world to glass," how shall he be able to show us anything? Will not all shapes and outlines simply disappear into one blur of diffused radiance? Yet this danger, Yeats, in spite of the extravagance of some of his idealistic pronouncements, successfully avoided. Indeed, we have had few poets in history who have stressed more powerfully the density and hard particularity of the objects of the external world. In celebrating the power of words, as all proponents of symbolist-expressionist doctrines must, Yeats did not lose thereby his grip upon things. Or, if we were willing to suppose with the symbolists that we could get at things only through language, then we would still have to say that in Yeats's poetry, language is not de-

[7] *Collected Poems*, p. 287.
[8] Written to Lady Elizabeth Pelham, 4 January 1939: see *Letters of W. B. Yeats*, p. 922.

natured and diluted into a common gray "wordiness." Words retain the
sharp outlines and individual profiles of "things." Yeats's earliest poetry is
indeed vague and dreamy, everything melting imperceptibly into something else; but the poetry of his maturity is angular, precise, and even
shockingly realistic. Because this is true, the poet is able to exploit real
oppositions. The poetry is filled with tensions between stubbornly recalcitrant contraries. Everywhere Yeats finds the drama of the antinomies.

"Donne," Yeats observes in his *Autobiographies* (1916), "could be as
metaphysical as he pleased, and yet never seemed unhuman and hysteri-
cal as Shelley often does, because he could be as physical as he pleased." [9]
Yeats took the lesson to heart. Even in celebrating his hero Bishop Berkeley, in whose clarifying vision "Everything that is not God" was "consumed with intellectual fire," Yeats remembered the lesson. He gives
Berkeley the proud title "God-appointed" because he

> proved all things a dream,
> That this pragmatical, preposterous pig of a world, its farrow
>   that so solid seem,
> Must vanish on the instant if the mind but change its theme.[1]

But the poetry establishes the solidity of the pig. If the intellectual fire
emanating from the Bishop's mind promises to consume pig, bishop, and
all in a blaze that will leave no ash, the poet is too wise to attempt to por-
tray that holocaust in the poem. In the poem, the pig is as real (and for
the poem as necessary) as the bishop.

One can state Yeats's saving physicality in a somewhat different way:
a danger endemic to symbolist doctrine is that of "angelism," the "sin of
a man who rejects human existence and wants to be like God." Raymond,
in his *From Baudelaire to Surrealism*, says that a Catholic would find such
a sin in Mallarmé's poem, "*Les Fenêtres*," where the speaker, unwilling
to accept his limitations as a man, wishing to extend the domain of his
consciousness forever farther, turns his back upon life as a great frustrating force, and facing the casement windows, now "gilded by the chaste
morning of the infinite," exclaims, "I look upon myself and see an angel." [2]
"Angelism" as a sin incurred by Poe is the subject of Allen Tate's essay
entitled "The Angelic Imagination." Tate admits that "strictly speaking,
an *angelic imagination* is not possible. Angels by definition have un-
mediated knowledge of essences." [3] Man, lacking such direct intuition of
essences, is committed to the imagination, for he can take hold of essences
only through analogy—analogy to the natural world. If in his pride, however, he refuses to look at nature, then Tate says, he is "doomed to see

[9] Quoted from *Autobiographies* (New York, 1927), p. 402.
[1] *Collected Poems*, p. 233.
[2] *From Baudelaire to Surrealism*, p. 24.
[3] *The Forlorn Demon*, p. 70.

nothing." Poe "overleaped and cheated the condition of man. The reach of our imaginative enlargement is perhaps no longer than the ladder of analogy. . . . [Poe having kicked the ladder away] sits silent in darkness." [4]

Yeats never scorned the ladder of analogy, and never forgot the relationship of the "masterful images" of his accomplished poetry to the world of "things," even when those images, "because complete," seem to compel the admission that they "Grew in pure mind." In a stanza that is suggestive of Tate's figure of the ladder (and which Tate may unconsciously be recalling), Yeats writes that the "masterful images" began in

> A mound of refuse or the sweepings of a street,
> Old kettles, old bottles, and a broken can,
> Old iron, old bones, old rags, that raving slut
> Who keeps the till. Now that my ladder's gone,
> I must lie down where all the ladders start,
> In the foul rag-and-bone shop of the heart.[5]

These lines may seem too somberly desperate in their acknowledgement of the limitations of the human being. They collide with Yeats's bolder idealistic assertions. They certainly embarrass any attempt to reduce Yeats's critical position to a neat and tidy consistency. But they point to an important fact about Yeats's poetry: there is a real working dualism—real oppositions as distinguished from merely opposed positions in an abstract dialectic. The poetry can aspire to the reduction of all things to "intellectual fire" for the very good reason that the materials to be consumed are not wraiths of uninflammable moonshine. (Like the French symbolists before him, Yeats had learned, in part from Nietzsche, the uses of tension and conflict in art.) The materials that make up the poems have enough substance to resist, and when ignited, to feed, combustion.

SUPPLEMENT

For the poet, language is a structure of the external world. The speaker is *in a situation* in language; he is invested with words. They are prolongations of his meanings, his pincers, his antennae, his eyeglasses. He maneuvers them from within; he feels them as if they were his body; he is surrounded by a verbal body which he is hardly aware of and which extends his action upon the world. The poet is outside of language. He sees words inside out as if he

[4] *The Forlorn Demon*, p. 78.
[5] *Collected Poems*, p. 336.

did not share the human condition, and as if he were first meeting the word as a barrier as he comes toward men. Instead of first knowing things by their name, it seems that first he has a silent contact with them, since, turning toward that other species of thing which for him is the word, touching them, testing them, palping them, he discovers in them a slight luminosity of their own and particular affinities with the earth, the sky, the water, and all created things.

—Jean-Paul Sartre, *What is Literature?*, trans. Bernard Frechtman (New York, 1949), pp. 13–14. Reprinted by permission of the publishers, The Philosophical Library.

It may be well to remind the reader that in the work from which this passage is quoted, Sartre is arguing for an engaged *literature—not at all for art-for-art's-sake.*

Whereas the Neoclassical writers had been taught to observe particular natural objects carefully and accurately and then abstract the general from them, the Romantics reverse the process. Thus Blake says: "All goodness resides in minute particulars" but "Natural objects always did and now do weaken, deaden and obliterate imagination in me" and Coleridge writes in a letter:

> The further I ascend from animated Nature (i.e., in the embracements of rocks and hills), from men and cattle, and the common birds of the woods and fields, the greater becomes in me the intensity of the feeling of life. Life seems to me then a universal spirit that neither has nor can have an opposite.

As long as images derived from observation of nature had a utility value for decorating the thoughts of the mind, nature could be simply enjoyed, for Nature was not very important by comparison with human reason. But if there is a mysterious relation between them, if

> *La Nature est un temple où de vivants piliers*
> *Laissent parfois sortir de confuses paroles;*
> *L'homme y passe à travers des forêts de symbols*
> *Qui l'observent avec des regards familiers.*
>
> *Comme de longs échos qui de loin se confondent*
> *Dans une ténébreuse et profonde unité,*
> *Vaste comme la nuit et comme la clarté,*
> *Les parfums, les couleurs et les sons se répondent.*
>
> —Baudelaire (*Correspondances*)

then the merely visual perception is not the important act, but the intuitive vision of the meaning of the object, and also Nature becomes a much more formidable creature, charged with all the joys, griefs, hopes and terrors of the human soul, and therefore arousing very mixed feelings of love and hatred.

On the one hand, the poets long to immerse in the sea of Nature, to enjoy its endless mystery and novelty, on the other, they long to come to port in some transcendent eternal and unchanging reality from which the unexpected is excluded. Nature and Passion are powerful, but they are also full of grief. True happiness would have the calm and order of bourgeois routine without its utilitarian ignobility and boredom.

Thus the same Baudelaire who writes:

Why is the spectacle of the sea so infinitely and eternally agreeable?

Because the sea presents at once the idea of immensity and of movement . . . Twelve or fourteen leagues of liquid in movement are enough to convey to man the highest expression of beauty which he can encounter in his transient abode.

(Mon Coeur Mis à Nu)

and identifies human nature with the sea:

> *Vous êtes tous les deux ténébreux et discrets*
> *Homme, nul n'a sondé le fond de tes abîmes,*
> *O mer, nul ne connaît tes richesses intimes*
> *Tant vous êtes jaloux de garder vos secrets!*
> *(L'Homme et la Mer)*

also exclaims:

> *Ah! ne jamais sortir des Nombres et des Etres*

and likens Beauty to a dream of stone (cp. the stone of Wordsworth's dream):

> *Je hais le mouvement qui déplace les lignes,*
> *Et jamais je ne pleure et jamais je ne ris.*

—From *The Enchafèd Flood* by W. H. Auden, pp. 84–6, copyright 1950 by The Rector and Visitors of the University of Virginia. Reprinted by permission of Random House, Inc.

We have entered a universe that only answers to its own laws, supports itself, internally coheres, and has a new standard of truth. Information is true if it is accurate. A poem is true if it hangs together. Information points to something else. A poem points to nothing but itself. Information is relative. A poem is absolute.

—E. M. Forster, *Anonymity: An Enquiry* (London, 1925), p. 14

Symbolism in one form or another has been used by nearly every great European poet and Baudelaire's definition could without violence be applied to their practice. The use of symbols is simply one aspect of language; the mistake lies in trying to invest them with some sort of transcendental significance instead of regarding them as a technical device of the same order as simile or metaphor. A symbol is nothing more than a vehicle for imaginative experience. What is essential is that it should correspond to the emotion evoked, and a great deal of Mallarmé's obscurity is due to the fact that he tried to use symbols to convey experiences which had not been transmuted into poetry. Baudelaire himself cannot be altogether exonerated from the charge of adding to the confusion and it is unfortunate that his *Correspondances* have been used by critics as a text instead of being treated as a piece of muddled psychology.

This does not mean that Baudelaire and his followers did not extend and develop the use of symbols. They undoubtedly did. Now the term has a variety of meanings. It includes the expanded image in *l'Albatros*, the use of the "sea" as a symbol of liberation in the work of both Baudelaire and Mallarmé and Mallarmé's way of "working" words in the *Swan*. These are straightforward examples. What is more interesting is Baudelaire's use of the *néant* and the *gouffre* to symbolize the void behind the façade of contemporary civilization.

—Martin Turnell, "The Heirs of Baudelaire," *Scrutiny*, XI (Summer, 1943), 295–6, by permission of the author.

CHAPTER 27

I. A. RICHARDS:
A POETICS OF TENSION

§ *Affective criticism and laboratory techniques—
other forms of psychological criticism: Freud's view of art
as "substitute-gratification"—Max Eastman's concept of
art as "pure realization," and Santayana's hedonism—II.
Richards' evaluation of various psychological views of art:
his rejection of hedonism, of the specifically "aesthetic"
emotion, of empathy, etc., in favor of synaesthesis—III.
synaesthesis defined as the equilibrium of opposed impulses: discriminated from either vacillation on the one
hand or simple resolution on the other—synaesthesis characterized as a readiness to take any action we choose—
this harmonization of impulses related to the principles of
"exclusion" and "inclusion," parallels with Santayana, irony
as a character of this "balanced poise"—IV. Ransom's
criticism of Richards' notion that the poise is in our response and not in the structure of the "stimulating object"
—Ransom's criticism of other art theories that are based
upon some notion of tension and fusion, his criticism of
Eliot—the resemblances and differences between the
theories of Richards and Eliot—V. Richards' series of
cleavages: between two kinds of aesthetic failure, between
evaluative and technical criticism, his later modification of
these views—VI. Richards' separation of two kinds of
"truth," truth of reference and truth of coherence, and his
solution of the problem of the relation of science and
poetry—VII. other dualistic and quasi-dualistic theories of
poetry: Ransom's distinction of structure and texture, his
doctrine of the irrelevance of the texture to the structure,
this notion as criticized by Yvor Winters—Eastman's
parallel doctrine of irrelevance: poetic discourse as "impractical," Ransom's psychologism and his appeal to Freud
—VIII. Freud's general contribution to criticism reassessed
and compared with that of Richards* §*

A FFECTIVE CRITICISM IS, AS WE HAVE SEEN, AS OLD AS CRITICISM ITSELF. It appears, for example, in Plato's view that poetry "feeds and waters the passion" and in Aristotle's doctrine of catharsis. But in the 19th century, the decay of metaphysics and the extraordinary growth of the physical sciences gave a special stress to affective theories. Gustav Fechner, for example, took the problems of aesthetics into the laboratory. Fechner set out to construct an aesthetic theory, not *von oben* but *von unten*. The methods of investigation were to be empirical and inductive. There were to be "controlled" experiments to determine what percentage of human beings find the rectangle a more pleasing shape than the square or what percentage prefer rectangles proportioned to the golden section as compared to rectangles of other proportions. But the future of psychologism in criticism was not to lie with this kind of experimentation, whether carried out by Fechner or by such investigators as Zeising, Wundt, or Helmholtz.[1] The great impact of psychology upon 20th-century criticism was to come through introspective psychologists like Theodor Lipps or through students of abnormal psychology like Sigmund Freud and Carl Jung.

Freud's theory of wit and the comic has been discussed in a preceding chapter. Though Freud did not apply his theory of wit directly to literature, certain parallels clearly suggest themselves. The creation of poetry like the creation of wit draws upon the unconscious; poetry and wit are both in some sense "inspired." Many of the techniques of poetry, like those of wit and dream, are evidently to be subsumed under a principle of condensation. "Rhyme, alliteration, refrain, and other forms of repetition of similar sounding words in poetry" afford us pleasure, Freud writes, for the same reason that "harmless wit" yields us pleasure; and that pleasure, as we have seen in the last chapter, is a pleasure gained through economy of psychic expenditure.[2]

When Freud does address himself directly to the subject, his account of art is disappointingly simple: the pleasure of art is quite baldly reduced to that of a "substitute-gratification." Freud lumps the artist and the neurotic together in their reversion to fantasy. Art represents a vicarious fulfilment of wishes denied to the artist by reality. But the artist differs from the neurotic in several very important ways: [3]

---

[1] Adolf Zeising (*Neue Lehre von den Proportionen des menschlichen Körpers,* 1854) actually preceded Fechner in some of Fechner's characteristic experiments; Fechner's *Vorschule der Ästhetik* was published in 1876. Wilhelm Wundt made researches in sensation and feeling. Herman Helmholtz produced works on *Physiological Optics* (1856–66) and *Tone Sensation* (1862).

[2] "Wit and its Relation to the Unconscious," *The Basic Writings,* pp. 712 ff.

[3] From *A General Introduction to Psychoanalysis* by Sigmund Freud, copyright R 1948 Susie Hoch; copyright 1935 Edward L. Bernays, by permission of Liveright Publishers, New York (Permabook Edition, pp. 384–5).

First of all he understands how to elaborate his day-dreams, so that they lose that personal note which grates upon strange ears and become enjoyable to others; he knows too how to modify them sufficiently so that their origin in prohibited sources is not easily detected. Further, he possesses the mysterious ability to mold his particular material until it expresses the ideas of his phantasy faithfully; and then he knows how to attach to this re-flection of his phantasy-life so strong a stream of pleasure that, for a time at least, the repressions are outbalanced and dispelled by it. When he can do all this, he opens out to others the way back to the comfort and consolation of their own unconscious sources of pleasure, and so reaps their gratitude and admiration; then he has won—through his phantasy—what before he could only win in phantasy: honor, power, and the love of women.[4]

Freud makes pleasure a specific means used by the artist ("attach . . . so strong a stream of pleasure") as well as the general end of his art; moreover the closing sentence of the passage indicates that he was willing to lump together, quite indiscriminately, the various kinds of pleasure to which art may conduce, including the quite solid and ma-terial pleasures which financial success may bring. But Freud, as he him-self more than once pointed out, made no pretense to a total literary theory. He was apparently willing to leave the task of discriminating specific aesthetic pleasure or pleasures to the aesthetician and literary critic.

II

BEFORE examining the special positions argued by typical affective critics, however, it may be well to reiterate that the heavy stress upon affectivity in our time is closely related to our preoccupation with science. Thus, a critic like Max Eastman, who regards poetry as a "pure effort to heighten consciousness," [5] counsels the poet "to yield up to science the task of interpreting experience" and "of finding out what we call truth." [6] Eastman instances a poet like Edna St. Vincent Millay as exhibiting the proper stance with reference to science. She is quite well informed about "complexes" and "ductless glands" and yet does not allow that knowledge to inhibit a burning love poetry. She recaptures the language of the Elizabethans, not to recover their "unscientific" world view, but "only to clothe therein her feelings and her fearless will to have them." [7]

---

[4] Cf. Melvin Rader, *A Modern Book of Esthetics* (1935), pp. 70–2.
[5] *The Literary Mind* (New York, 1932), p. 170, by permission of the publishers, Charles Scribner's Sons.
[6] *The Literary Mind*, p. 239.
[7] *The Literary Mind*, p. 148.

George Santayana had earlier begun with a similar distinction between the emotionally neutral and abstract world as described by science
and the emotions that the objects of that world stir within us. The
beauty that we attribute to objects is merely, Santayana argued, in *The
Sense of Beauty* (1896), the objectification of our own emotions. Though
we insist upon regarding beauty as "the quality of a thing," it is really a
pleasure within us, and indeed in our normal, common-sense view of the
world, it would never occur to us to include in our concept of reality
"emotional or passionate elements." This objectification of our feelings
in the "sense of beauty" is a survival of an "animistic and mythological
habit of thought," once quite universal, as with primitive man, but now
banished from the world of pure science and also from "the intermediate
realm of vulgar day," where "mechanical science" has influenced our
thinking.[8]

> The scientific idea of a thing is a great abstraction from the mass
> of perceptions and reactions which that thing produces; the es-
> thetic idea is less abstract, since it retains the emotional reaction,
> the pleasure of the perception, as an integral part of the con-
> ceived thing.[9]

The need for clarification of our ideas in this realm was pressed with
a special urgency by I. A. Richards, the critic through whose mediation
psychology was to make its greatest impact upon literary criticism. Richards asked his readers to purge their critical thinking of all such animistic
habits as cause us to make unwarranted connections between our inner
feelings and the nature of objective reality. But his specific contribution
lay in his account of the way language bears on the problem. He distinguished "two uses of language."

> A statement may be used for the sake of the *reference*, true or
> false, which it causes. This is the *scientific* use of language. But
> it may also be used for the sake of the effects in emotion and
> attitude. . . . This is the *emotive* use of language.[1]

Science makes statements, but poetry makes what Richards calls
"pseudo-statements": their referential value is nil. Poetry makes an emotive use of language. That is its specific character. But, of course, not
every instance of such emotive use is aesthetically valuable, and Richards
indicts both Eastman and Santayana for not discriminating between emotional intensity and valuable emotional experience. Richards' earliest book,
The Foundations of Aesthetics (1921), written in collaboration with

---

[8] *The Sense of Beauty* (New York, 1896), p. 47.
[9] *The Sense of Beauty*, p. 48.
[1] *The Principles of Literary Criticism* (London, 1924; 4th impression, 1930),
p. 267, by permission of the publishers, Harcourt, Brace and Company, Inc.

C. K. Ogden and James Wood, will provide a convenient scheme for summarizing the more typical affective theories of our century and at the same time setting forth the choices and rejections by which Richards arrived at his own special theory. Richards and his colleagues list sixteen meanings of the term *beauty*, the last seven of which they label "psychological views."

The simplest of these defines the beautiful as anything "which excites Emotions." [2] Such a definition, our authors comment, is much too wide. For "it is not easy to ascribe the highest value to emotions in general, merely as emotions. They may often be experienced without particular significance, and have their place without necessarily being the concern of art." [3]

A somewhat more restricted view specifies pleasurable emotions; that is, "Anything is beautiful—which causes Pleasure." Richards and his colleagues choose to refer this definition of beauty to Santayana, its "most accomplished modern advocate." [4] But the great disadvantage of any pleasure view of art, they point out, "is that it offers us too restricted a vocabulary." [5] Criticism exhausts itself in recording that the art work is indeed pleasing. (Such would indeed seem to be the limitation of a really simple hedonism, but it is a question whether Santayana's hedonism is of this kind. His hedonism, as we shall see, has been subjected to a number of complications and refinements.)

Among the writers who have felt constrained to narrow the field of emotions expressed by art to "some unique emotion," Richards and his colleagues cite Clive Bell and Roger Fry. Bell asserts that the work of art gives us a "peculiar emotion," an "aesthetic emotion" as such. Both Bell and Fry specify that the work of art must possess "significant form." "Significant form," however, can be defined only by the "rather uncommon emotion which it causes." [6]

The difficulty with such a peculiar emotion, Richards points out, is that any attempt to define it is bound to be circular: death-dealing things, for example, do not necessarily have any quality in common except that they all can cause death, and by the same token "beautiful" things need have in common only the fact that they can cause someone to avow that they are beautiful. But if the critic proposes to connect beautiful things by nothing further than the assertion that he feels them all to be beautiful,

---

[2] *Foundations of Aesthetics*, 2nd ed. (New York, 1925), p. 21. The passage refers to what is essentially Eastman's position though Eastman is not mentioned in this book. For Richards's specific comments upon Eastman, see *The Philosophy of Rhetoric* (New York, 1936), pp. 123-4.

[3] *Foundations*, p. 56, by permission of George Allen and Unwin, Ltd., and the authors.

[4] *Foundations*, p. 52.

[5] *Foundations*, p. 53.

[6] *Foundations*, p. 61.

he has not advanced beyond his original assertion: namely, that they provoke in him that "peculiar" emotion.

Richards and his colleagues mention further attempts to characterize the art emotion. The beautiful has been defined as anything that involves the processes of *empathy*. Empathy (*Einfühlung*) was the name that Theodor Lipps gave to a process which he described as "feeling something, namely, oneself, into the esthetic object." [7] In this activity, "the antithesis between myself and the object disappears, or rather does not yet exist." [8]

Vernon Lee (Violet Paget) independently formulated much the same account as that of Lipps. When we say, for example, that the *mountain rises*, we are transferring from ourselves to the looked-at shape of the mountain the idea of rising and the emotions that accompany it.

> . . . it is this complex mental process, by which we (all unsuspectingly) invest that inert mountain, that bodiless shape, with the stored up and averaged and essential modes of our activity— it is this process whereby we make the mountain *raise itself*, which constitutes what . . . I have called *Empathy*. [9]

But since experiences involving empathy are part of the day-by-day experiences of our lives and are by no means confined to aesthetic experiences, Richards points out that we shall have to limit empathic experiences further if we are to distinguish those which are beautiful. Vernon Lee limits the beautiful to those objects which allow empathic projection *and* in which the projection is pleasurable because the process facilitates our vitality. But such a formula is still too vague to represent any real advance over the usual hedonistic account of art. [1]

This review of various affective theories, though not exhaustive, will suggest some of the reasons for Richards' choice of *synaesthesis* as the one affective theory that seemed to him fit to serve as the foundation of an aesthetic. Even projective theories like empathy apply to so much non-artistic experience that they fail to isolate the specific values of art. The element constant to all experiences that have the characteristic of beauty, concludes Richards, is *synaesthesis*—a harmony and equilibrium of our impulses. ·

[7] "*Einfühlung, innere Nachahmung, und Organempfindungen*," *Archiv für die gesamte Psychologie*, Vol. I (1903): quoted from Melvin Rader, *A Modern Book of Esthetics* (1935), p. 302.

[8] Rader, p. 294. Here we are evidently dealing with a psychological version of the metaphysics of Fichte or Schelling—cf. *ante* Chapter 17.

[9] *The Beautiful* (Cambridge, 1913), pp. 65–6.

[1] ". . . the experiences we get from successfully riding a bicycle, which presumably cause pleasure and facilitate our vitality, could clearly be recalled by our projecting similar movements into lines and rhythms, and the resultant state would be neither more nor less aesthetic than the original one, except in virtue of its new origin in recall through projection" (*Foundations*, p. 69).

III

ANY experience must involve the arousal and interplay of various impulses, but in the experience of beauty Richards contends that our impulses are organized in a peculiar way. In this peculiar organization which constitutes synaesthesis, the rivalry of conflicting impulses is avoided, not by our suppressing the impulses, but, paradoxically, by our giving them free rein.

> Not all impulses . . . are naturally harmonious, for conflict is possible and common. A complete systematization must take the form of such an adjustment as will preserve free play to every impulse, with entire avoidance of frustration. In any equilibrium of this kind, however momentary, we are experiencing beauty.[2]

Such a conception, indeed, presents its difficulties, for an equilibrium of conflicting impulses is easily confused with the state of "balance" that one finds in irresolution—that is, an oscillation between two sets of opposed impulses in which the mind, like the fabled donkey poised between the equally attractive bales of hay, can only remain suspended in inaction. Richards and his friends warn us that this is not at all what they mean by synaesthesis. Synaesthesis is no such oscillation but a harmonization: the competing impulses sustain not two states of mind but one. They do not split the ego in two, but complete and enrich it. In the experience of synaesthesis, our "interest is not canalised in one direction,"[3] and there is a sense of detachment and disinterest. Our lack of commitment to any particular course of action means in reality that we are, like the poised athlete, in readiness for any kind of action.

For this special kind of "disinterest," a technical psychological explanation is offered. Our authors say that whereas two perfectly simple impulses must either oscillate or lock, a "more complex initial conflict" may discharge itself "through its branch connections." Such a complex conflict may "solve" itself "in the arousal of the other impulses of the personality."[4] At any rate, whatever the precise nature of the psychological explanation, Richards and his colleagues are confident that the sense of disinterest in the aesthetic experience means, paradoxically, that the maximum number of interests is actually involved, and that the feeling of "impersonality" that synaesthesis induces means that the "whole of the personality" has been brought into play. By the equilibrium of synaesthesis Richards evidently would suggest, then, not the lifeless balance

[2] *Foundations*, p. 75.
[3] *Foundations*, p. 78.
[4] *Foundations*, p. 77, note.

of deadlock but the vibrant poise of the completely co-ordinated personality.

There is a second state of mind which we are also warned not to confuse with synaesthesis. Our authors remark that the feeling of "lucidity, self-possession and freedom" [5] that characterizes the experience of synaesthesis may also attach to the state of mind that arises when one is possessed by an intense emotion such as anger or joy. In one of his later poems, W. B. Yeats admirably describes this state of "simple resolution":

> Know that when all words are said
> And a man is fighting mad,
> Something drops from eyes long blind,
> He completes his partial mind,
> For an instant stands at ease
> Laughs aloud, his heart at peace. . . .[6]

But since this state of mind gains its "harmony" by having no warring impulses to harmonize, its resemblance to synaesthesis is illusory. Richards and his colleagues offer a test by which it can be distinguished from synaesthesis: synaesthesis "refreshes and never exhausts." [7]

In their theorizing about synaesthesis it is evident that Richards and his colleagues have moved beyond any simple pleasure principle. A few years after the publication of *The Foundations of Aesthetics*, Richards asserted that the pleasure that a competent reader feels is "no more the aim of the activity in the course of which it arises, than, for example, the noise made by a motor-cycle—useful though it is as an indication of the way the machine is running—is the reason in the normal case for its having been started." [8] The main value of literature was to be found in its *after*-effects upon the mind.

One more observation on synaesthesis is pertinent here: though Richards deplored Kant's having created a "phantom problem of the aesthetic mode" through his attempt to define the "judgment of taste" as a judgment "concerning pleasure which is disinterested, universal, unintellectual, and not to be confused with the pleasures of sense or of ordinary emotions," [9] Richards' own doctrine of synaesthesis courts, if it does not actually demand, the same series of adjectives. True, the term synaesthesis has a psychological orientation, not a metaphysical, but synaesthesis is certainly disinterested, and this aspect comes out most plainly when Richards tries to distinguish it from the false equilibrium of irresolution or from that of full emotional commitment.

[5] *Foundations*, p. 77, note.
[6] "Under Ben Bulben," *Collected Poems*, p. 342.
[7] *Foundations*, p. 77, note.
[8] *The Principles of Literary Criticism*, p. 97.
[9] *Principles*, p. 11.

Attitudes, as Richards defines them, are incipient or "imaginal" actions. In synaesthesis, these incipient actions are so ordered and so balanced that the maximum number of them is involved and the minimum number is blocked—but they remain incipient; no action occurs. Synaesthesis is defined as our readiness "to take any direction we choose," but in synaesthesis evidently we do *not* choose. Presumably if we did choose and acted upon that choice, that very fact would indicate that the supposed state of synaesthesis was illusory, not real.

> When works of art produce such action, or conditions which
> lead to action, they have either not completely fulfilled their
> function or would in the view of equilibrium here being con-
> sidered be called not "beautiful" but "stimulative." [1]

Synaesthesis, says Richards, is the ground-plan of all aesthetic experience. Many people obviously have had this experience in the past, but they have confused the experience with a revelation of some sort. The arts, he admits, do seem "to lift away the burden of existence" and we do seem "to be looking into the heart of things," but this state of euphoria, he insists, has actually nothing to do with truth. For truth belongs to science, which represents a "different [principle] upon which impulses may be organized," [2] and which has a very different function from that of the arts.

In his *Principles of Literary Criticism*, Richards never makes use of the key term "synaesthesis." Instead the terms "inclusion" and "synthesis" are used to name the character of the greatest and most valuable poetry. *Synthesis* [3] is, of course, fair coin for synaesthesis, and the key passage in which Richards defines synthesis bears a remarkable resemblance to one of the paragraphs in Santayana's *The Sense of Beauty*. It will be useful to set the two passages side by side.

In a section of his book that he significantly entitled "The Liberation of the Self," Santayana had written:

> Now, it is the essential privilege of beauty to so *synthesize*
> and bring to a focus the various *impulses of the self*, so to sus-
> pend them to a single image, that a great peace falls upon that

---

[1] *Foundations*, p. 77. Stephen Dedalus in *A Portrait of the Artist as a Young Man* (New York, 1916), p. 240, makes a comparable point in denying that "kinesthetic" art (i.e., art that provokes us to a particular action) is truly art at all.

[2] *Principles*, p. 265. Compare with this Santayana's assertion that a great work of art leaves us with the sense that "however tangled the net may be in which we feel ourselves caught, there is liberation beyond, and an ultimate peace" (*The Sense of Beauty*, p. 239).

[3] The term may show the influence of Coleridge's description of the imagination as a "synthetic and magical" power. In any case the adaptation of Coleridge's account of the imagination is frankly acknowledged. See the chapter on "The Imagination," in *Principles*, pp. 239–53.

perturbed kingdom. In the experience of these momentary harmonies we have the basis of the enjoyment of beauty, and of all its mystical meanings. But there are always two methods of securing harmony: one is to unify all the given elements, and another is to reject and expunge all the elements that refuse to be unified. Unity by *inclusion* gives us the beautiful; unity by *exclusion*, opposition, and isolation gives us the sublime. Both are pleasures: but the pleasure of the one is warm, passive, and pervasive; that of the other cold, imperious, and keen. The one identifies us with the world, the other raises us above it.[4]

And now for the passage from Richards:

> There are two ways in which *impulses* may be organized; by *exclusion* and by *inclusion*, by *synthesis* and by elimination. Although every coherent state of mind depends upon both, it is permissible to contrast experiences which win stability and order through a narrowing of the response with those which widen it. A very great deal of poetry and art is content with the full, ordered development of comparatively special and limited experiences, with a definite emotion, for example, Sorrow, Joy, Pride, or a definite attitude, Love, Indignation, Admiration, Hope, or with a specific mood, Melancholy, Optimism or Longing. And such art has its own value and its place in human affairs. No one will quarrel with "Break, break, break," or with the *Coronach* or with *Rose Aylmer* or with *Love's Philosophy*, although clearly they are limited and *exclusive*. But they are not the greatest kind of poetry; we do not expect from them what we find in the *Ode to the Nightingale*, in *Proud Maisie*, in *Sir Patrick Spens*, in *The Definition of Love* or in the *Nocturnall upon S. Lucie's Day*.[5]

The two kinds of poetry are not, for Richards as they evidently are for Santayana, on the same level. Richards displays no interest in distinguishing the beautiful from the sublime; his interest is rather to distinguish a richer, deeper, and more tough-minded poetry from a more "limited and exclusive" kind of poetry. Furthermore, Santayana's harmonization of the impulses of the self by rejection and expungement of all "the elements that refuse to be unified" could not, in Richards' terms, qualify as a harmonization at all; instead it rather suggests Richards' state of "simple resolution." [6] But the resemblances between the passages are striking enough.

[4] *The Sense of Beauty*, pp. 235–6. The italics are ours.
[5] *Principles*, pp. 249–50. The italics are ours.
[6] Cf. *ante* p. 617.

Richards proceeds to give a psychological account of the peculiar kind of stability of this second kind of poetry (the poetry of synthesis) and to use the presence of irony as a kind of touchstone for such poetry.

> The difference comes out clearly if we consider how comparatively unstable poems of the first kind are. They will not bear an ironical contemplation. We have only to read *The War Song of Dinas Vawr* in close conjunction with the *Coronach*, or to remember that unfortunate phrase "Those lips, O slippery blisses!" from *Endymion*, while reading *Love's Philosophy*, to notice this. Irony in this sense consists in the bringing in of the opposite, the complementary impulses; that is why poetry which is exposed to it is not of the highest order, and why irony itself is so constantly a characteristic of poetry which is.
>
> These opposed impulses from the resolution of which such experiences spring cannot usually be analysed. When, as is most often the case, they are aroused through formal means, it is evidently impossible to do so.[7]

IV

RICHARDS' confession of the difficulty—not to mention the impossibility—of analyzing the "opposed impulses" throws an interesting light upon the psychological machinery which he has used to account for the effects of this "poetry of inclusion." When we get ready to use the machinery, it evaporates. The poem is before us and is susceptible to analysis, but the psychological goings-on turn out to be below the surface and out of sight. This curious state of affairs is a main object of attack in John Crowe Ransom's criticism of Richards.[8]

Ransom points out that Richards' account of the relevant poetic structure is not only a mere hypothesis, but that this particular hypothesis, if accepted, would destroy criticism. For if the "balanced poise" is, as Richards says it is, in our "response" and not at all "in the structure of the stimulating object," then the labor of criticism in "analysing the poetic object" is vain. Vain also was the labor of the poet in putting the poem into a particular "shape." On Richards' showing, the

> poem is not needed in that shape; and what the proper shape would be we are not likely to know. I for one feel that I cannot know even what it is in the poem which constitutes its stimulus.[9]

---

[7] *Principles*, pp. 250–1.

[8] *The New Criticism* (New York, 1941). Copyright 1941 by New Directions and reprinted by permission of the publisher.

[9] *The New Criticism*, p. 32.

It is indeed questionable whether Richards actually succeeds in cutting his desiderated "balanced poise" cleanly off from all relation to "the structure of the stimulating object." Though Richards is careful to point out that such balanced poise is "not peculiar to Tragedy," significantly it is in tragedy, the form of literature in which conflicts and tensions are obvious structural features, that he finds his clearest illustrations. Nietzsche too had found that in tragedy "contrasts are overcome" and "oppositions" are "conquered," [1] and his insistence that the greatest artists are those "who make harmony ring out of every discord" strengthens the notion that Nietzsche anticipated Richards' conception of a "poetry of inclusion," though Nietzsche gave his "inclusion" a clear structural reference. For the discords are in the composition, and the larger harmony in which these momentary disharmonies are finally resolved is obviously to be referred to the total structure. Not the least important of the "musical" characteristics that Nietzsche attributes to tragedy is this conception of a richer and more intricate harmony, achieved by the resolution of apparent discords, as opposed to the "thinner" harmony of less ambitious works.

Richards himself, when he suggests that one may test the stability of such poetry by exposing it to ironical contemplation, seems to regard the differentia of "inclusive" poetry as structural. For, though the reader supplies the ironical squint, the subsequent collapse in the defective poem is a structural collapse.

Richards' insistence that irony is "so constantly" a characteristic of the highest order of poetry reminds one of Solger's claim that irony is "coextensive with art." [2] It also calls for comparison with T. S. Eliot's notion that the function of wit is to provide an "internal equilibrium" for the poem in which it occurs. If Richards' irony is not made to provide the stability of the experience, it is at least a symptom of the stability. Eliot's notion about wit seems to be the complement of Nietzsche's conception of a "harmony" that is rung "out of every discord." For in saying that witty poetry implies "in the expression of every experience" the recognition of the fact that "other kinds of experience . . . are possible," [3] Eliot is saying that wit calls to our attention the potentially discordant; that is, the unity of the witty poem is not a unity easily won by glossing over the discordant elements of human experience.

Such restatements of Richards' conceptions of "inclusion" and of "tension" would, however, scarcely appease a critic like Ransom. He impartially condemns both Richards and Eliot for talking about the reconciliation of what he insists are in fact irreconcilables:

[1] Cf. *ante* Chapter 25.
[2] Cf. *ante* Chapter 17.
[3] "Andrew Marvell" (1921), *Selected Essays, 1917–32* (New York, 1932), p. 262, by permission of the publishers, Harcourt, Brace and Company, Inc.

My belief is that opposites can never be said to be resolved or reconciled merely because they have been got into the same poem, or got into the same complex of affective experience to create there a kind of "tension"; that if there is a resolution at all it must be a logical resolution; that when there is no resolution we have a poem without a structural unity; and this is precisely the intention of irony, which therefore is something very special, and ought to be occasional.[4]

This statement is of a piece with Ransom's criticism of Eliot's conception of metaphysical poetry: "The aspiration here is for some sort of fusion of two experiences that ordinarily repel one another," and Ransom warns us not to become "the fools of the shining but impractical ideal of 'unity' or of 'fusion.'"[5] Thus, on the special and limited nature of irony, he firmly takes his stand beside Irving Babbitt and the new Humanists.[6] Far from being a "a constant characteristic" of good poetry, irony signifies for Ransom a failure to unify. "In a pointed form of irony," he writes, "the oppositions produce an indecisive effect, just as in tragedy there is an opposition with a negative effect."[7] Richards had been careful to distinguish the poetry of "harmonious equilibrium" (of which irony is "so constantly a characteristic") from mere "irresolution." Ransom's argument is that ironic poetry can represent only irresolution: that is, the oppositions "produce an indecisive effect."

Ransom is no less firm in dismissing Eliot. Though he has called Eliot "The Historical Critic," he says that Eliot's theory of poetry is "equivalent to some version of Richards' psychologistic theory."[8] There is some psychologism in Eliot; and there are certain conceptions that he shares with Richards. One remembers Eliot's statement that for the poet the noise of the typewriter and the smell of cooking, reading Spinoza or falling in love—experiences which for the ordinary man have nothing to do with one another—"are always forming new wholes."[9] And one places beside it this passage from Richards:

> The wheeling of the pigeons in Trafalgar Square may seem to have no relation to the colour of the water in the basins, to the tones of a speaker's voice or to the drift of his remarks. A narrow field of stimulation is all that we can manage, and we overlook the rest. But the artist does not, and when he needs it, he has it at his disposal.[1]

Unless one recognizes the amount of agreement between Richards and Eliot, one will find it difficult to understand the relative ease with

[4] *The New Criticism*, p. 95.
[5] *The New Criticism*, p. 183.
[6] Cf. *ante* Chapter 20.
[7] *The New Criticism*, p. 96.

[8] *The New Criticism*, p. 152.
[9] *Selected Essays*, p. 247.
[1] *Principles*, p. 185.

which Richards' influence upon criticism has merged with that of Eliot, and one will find it difficult to account for some of the later developments in Richards' own criticism—see the next chapter. Nevertheless, the differences between Eliot and Richards are very important, and nowhere more so than in their treatment of thought and feeling. In spite of some waverings and confusions encouraged by an occasional use of affective terminology, Eliot stands by his bold assertion that a poem is a *fusion* of thought and feeling. Richards, on the other hand, from the first has endeavored to maintain a careful distinction between the emotional state produced in the reader (the balance of impulses or state of synaesthesis) and the means used to produce this emotional state.

V

RICHARDS' endeavors to distinguish between the emotional effect produced in the reader and the means by which it is produced give rise in his criticism to a whole series of related separations: between value (content) and communication (as conditioned by form); between the "badness" that results from the communication to the reader of a worthless experience and the "badness" that results from the faulty communication of what was presumably a valuable experience; between technical criticism (which Richards defines as dealing with the make-up of the stimulating object) and evaluative criticism (which deals with the value of the experience communicated). An exploration of some of these topics supplies striking instances of the difficulties with which an affective theory burdens a critic who has genuine literary sensitivity and whose deepest allegiance is evidently to poetry rather than to the psychology of reader response.

In *The Principles of Literary Criticism*, Richards illustrated the two kinds of "badness" by using a tiny Imagist poem by H. D. and a rather glib love sonnet by Ella Wheeler Wilcox. H. D.'s scrap of Imagist verse was said to fail because it did not sufficiently communicate the valuable experience that Richards conceded that the poet might have had. The Wilcox sonnet was said to fail because the experience that it communicated—all too clearly—had no value. The sonnet was dominated by an elaborate analogy between Summer and Love and Friendship and Autumn. And Richards pointed out that those readers "who have adequate impulses as regards *any* of the four main systems [of impulses] involved" in this poem are not "appeased" by the poem. "Only for those who make certain conventional, stereotyped maladjustments instead, does the magic work." [2]

Yet it might have been simpler to deal with adequacy of imagery

[2] *Principles*, p. 202.

rather than with adequacy of "impulses." A critic of the poem could simply have said that any reader who attended to the imagery of the poem would find it absurdly confused. If the reader knew anything about autumn, he would know that an autumn day with a "touch of frost . . . in the air" tends to be crisp and sparkling, not hazy with the mellowness of St. Martin's summer. If he knew anything about love, he would hardly be satisfied with the metamorphosis of Love into "large-eyed Friendship" through a kind of fadeout-dissolve of one obviously trumped up allegorical figure into another.[3]

In spite of a certain superficial plausibility, the distinction between defectiveness of communication and the "worthlessness" of the experience communicated cannot in fact be maintained. We can only speculate about values that are not revealed in the poem itself. That there might have been a valuable experience behind H. D.'s "The Pool" is, and must remain, pure hypothesis. On the other hand, one *could* argue that the alleged clarity of the Wilcox sonnet is actually an illusion since what is inextricably confused cannot have "clarity." The "badness" of this poem consists in a pretension to coherence that is not made good; the analogy between Summer-Autumn and Love-Friendship is asserted but never realized dramatically. The essential act in condemning the poem consists therefore in exposing the basic *incoherence*.[4]

The motive for Richards' various "separations" is, of course, rooted in his desire to discuss poetry in terms of stimulus and response. This fact comes out most clearly in his attempt to distinguish "technical" remarks from "critical" (i.e., evaluative) remarks. He regards the distinction as important because, as he writes, the trick of mistaking "the means for the end, the technique for the value, is in fact the most successful of the snares which waylay the critic." [5] Yet on the same page Richards indi-

---

[3] As a measure of the coherence proper to a genuine poem, one might contrast with the Wilcox sonnet, Keats's "To Autumn," in which the "completeness" of an autumn day is made to subsist *with* a note of melancholy, or with Shakespeare's "How Like a Winter hath mine Absence Been," where there is a responsible alignment of the vicissitudes of love with seasonal change, or with Edna St. Vincent Millay's "The Cameo," which gives a *coherent* rendering of something like the specific theme of the Wilcox poem.

[4] Richards' very proper concern for the pernicious social effects of bad art seems to be as well served by this account as by his own: the reader who asks only that certain of his stock responses be titillated, who is content with certain "conventional, stereotyped maladjustments," is a reader who is oblivious to the kind of incoherence that characterizes the Wilcox sonnet. Such a reader will be baffled by the incoherence of H. D.'s "The Pool," but the incoherence of the Wilcox sonnet, because it mirrors his own distortions and oversimplifications, will probably be seen in quite other terms: as a clear and exalted vision of life. His inability to make sense of a poem—any poem—may well be coterminous with his inability to make sense of his own experiences; but with this latter problem we move from the field of criticism proper into a consideration of education, ethics, and the analysis of popular culture.

[5] *Principles*, p. 24.

cates his belief in an *organic* theory of poetry. There are problems: in what sense can a part of a poem be regarded as the means to an end? There is a sense, to be sure, in which all the parts of an organic whole may be regarded as reciprocally means and ends. The head is a "means" to the functioning of the heart and the heart is a "means" to the functioning of the head. But within the poem, it is not clear how there can be ends and means; the correct relation would seem to be that of parts to a whole.

By 1934 Richards himself had become suspicious of this distinction. In *Coleridge on Imagination* he wrote:

> It is with deceptive ease . . . that the inquiry [into poetic mean-ing] divides into questions about the *what* and the *how*. Or into questions about the *methods* a poet uses and the *feats* he thereby achieves. Or into questions about his *means* and his *ends*. Or about the *way* of his work and the *whither*.[6]

Though he regards the division as for some purposes "necessary" and for other purposes "convenient," he warns that it tends to distort the whole meaning of the work by abstracting "some component to be treated as its *whither* and to be set over against the rest as its *way*." [7]

V I

THE best-known and the most radical of Richards' separations is, of course, that which he made between the emotive and the referential "uses of language." [8] Richards denied to poetry any truth of reference and argued that the "truth" as applied to a work of art could mean only the "internal necessity" or "rightness" of the work of art: that is, whereas scientific truth has to do with correspondence to the nature of reality, artistic "truth" is a matter of inner coherence.

> The "Truth" of *Robinson Crusoe* is the acceptability of the things we are told, their acceptability in the interests of the ef-fects of the narrative, not their correspondence with any actual facts involving Alexander Selkirk or another. Similarly the falsity of happy endings to *Lear* or to *Don Quixote*, is their failure to be acceptable to those who have fully responded to the rest of the work. It is in this sense that "Truth" is equivalent to "internal necessity" or rightness. That is "true" or "internally necessary" which completes or accords with the rest of the experience. . . .[9]

[6] *Coleridge on Imagination* (New York, 1934), p. 198.
[7] *Coleridge on Imagination*, p. 199.
[8] *Principles*, pp. 261 ff.
[9] *Principles*, p. 269.

The "truth" of *Robinson Crusoe* or of *King Lear*, in short, has nothing to do with objective truth. The "effects of the narrative" which determine the "acceptability" of the "things we are told" are psychological effects. The happy ending supplied by Nahum Tate for *Lear* is "false" because it is at odds with the rest of the play; the play as a whole is "true" only in virtue of giving rise to the proper psychological effects, in helping us, that is, to "order our attitudes to one another and to the world." That is why "we need no beliefs" in order to read *King Lear*. Indeed, Richards goes much further and writes that "we must have [no beliefs], if we are to read *King Lear*"; [1] for beliefs, with their claims to objective truth, would disturb the self-contained coherence, the "internal necessity" which is the only "truth" that Richards will allow to the play.

Such was Richards' solution to the conflict of science and poetry: it is as drastic as it is neat. There could be no conflict for the good reason that there was no common ground upon which science and poetry (properly understood) could meet. They were held to utilize radically different aspects of language.

There are, to be sure, certain things that *Robinson Crusoe* cannot do because they would violate our sense of his character as built up in the earlier pages. The happy ending that Nahum Tate clapped onto *King Lear* simply does not accord with the earlier parts of the play. And yet more would seem to be operative in forming our rejections than what is contained in previous chapters or previous scenes of a specific novel or play: we appeal to, and are influenced by, our whole previous acquaintance with human beings. When we decide that Crusoe cannot do this or that, we are relying upon our notions of human psychology—very general notions perhaps—but notions that refer to a world outside the formmal limits of the art work itself. Even the world of Aesop's fables or of the fairy tale or of "science fiction" has not cut all connections with a world of our experience.

There would have been little debate if Richards' severance of poetry from all "reference" had amounted to no more than saying that the reader of Shakespeare did not need to worry about the inaccurate Scottish history in *Macbeth*, or that the reader of Coleridge had no cause to be disturbed by such scientifically impossible descriptions as that which places a star within the nether tip of the moon. On this level, the severance between poetry and history and poetry and science had been made by the ancients. But Richards, going further, seemed to be arguing that poetry was literally nonsense, though, for reasons bound up with his psychologistic theory, a peculiarly valuable kind of nonsense. It was difficult for critics like Allen Tate and John Crowe Ransom to see how one

[1] *Science and Poetry* (London, 1925; 2nd ed. 1926), p. 67.

could deny all truth to poetry, and yet at the same time argue in the fashion of Matthew Arnold that "poetry could save us."

VII

YET the temptation to make such severances and separations as Richards makes is stubbornly persistent in modern criticism. A striking instance occurs in the work of Ransom himself. Earlier in this chapter we have referred to Ransom's denial that there can be any "fusion" of "experiences that ordinarily repel one another" [2]—as that notion is held either by Richards or by Eliot.

Ransom drew a crucial distinction between the *texture* and the *structure* of a poem. The texture of a poem is constituted of its rich local values, the quality of things in their "thinginess." The structure is the "argument" of the poem. It gives the poem such shape as it has; it regulates the assemblage of sensory data, providing order and direction. Science has, properly speaking, no texture; it is content with pure structure and exhibits no rich particularity. A poem, on the other hand, has a texture *and* a structure. Though the texture is strictly irrelevant to the logic of the poem, yet it does after all affect the shape of the poem; it does so by *impeding* the argument. The very irrelevance of the texture is thus important. Because of its presence we get, not a streamlined argument, but an argument that has been complicated through having been hindered, and diverted, and having thus had its very success threatened. In the end we have our logic, but only after a lively reminder of the aspects of reality with which logic cannot cope.

A main source of Ransom's dissatisfaction with Richards' theory was its affectivity, and Ransom stressed the cognitive element in his own theory. But his would have to be described as a kind of "bifocal" cognitive theory: poetry gives us through its structure and texture, respectively, knowledge of universals and knowledge of particulars. Poetry is the complement of science which, restricting itself to universals, can mirror only a world of abstractions. Ransom hands over the realm of the universals to science, and in effect retains for poetry no more than an apprehension of particulars.

There are some problems here: are the two knowledges on the same level? Can they be kept from fusing? Or do they function intermittently, and if they do, is there any reason why they should occur in connection with each other? Ransom has rejected any notion of the union of the levels as an impossible oil-and-water mixture: neither component will dissolve into the other. What he proposes would have to be described as

[2] See *ante* p. 622.

a sort of emulsion—the little droplets of local "knowledge" suspended in, and diffused through, the other "knowledge" of universals.

> [The imagination] presents to the reflective mind the particularity of nature; whereas there is quite another organ, working by a technique of universals, which gives us science.[3]

On a strict interpretation, Ransom would seem to confine the imagination to such matters as the reflection of odors, tactile impressions, tone, colors, and other sensations, leaving out larger patterns such as those woven by the "moral" imagination.

The doctrine of the irrelevance of the texture poses another formidable problem. Yvor Winters has asked why, in view of the irrelevance of all texture, one "irrelevant" detail should be preferred to another.[4] Would not one texture do for any given poem as well as another? Marvell's "To his Coy Mistress" is, in terms of Ransom's thesis, the fine poem that it is because the lover's argument runs such an obstacle race before it can come to its conclusion. But Winters conjectures that in terms of such a theory as this, Crashaw's poem "The Weeper" would prove to be a finer poem still, its argument being even more besettingly impeded by the irrelevance of its texture.[5] Irrelevance, he urges, is irrelevance. To argue that some forms of irrelevant detail are more suitable to the poem than other forms of irrelevant detail would be to admit that *irrelevant* was not, after all, the proper term.

Ransom's theory that "impeding" the argument gives poetry's special knowledge of particularity finds a parallel in Eastman's notion that the hyperconsciousness achieved in poetry comes through "obstruction." As was noted earlier in this chapter, Eastman assumes that the function of art is to heighten consciousness. The artist does this by stimulating a response and yet obstructing it. To invoke an analogy: putting on a coat is a largely automatic action; we need not be conscious, and usually are not fully conscious, of what we are doing. But if the lining of the sleeve is torn and the action of thrusting the arm through it proves unexpectedly difficult, we become intensely aware of what we are doing. And so:

> [Art] must arouse a reaction and yet impede it, creating a tension in our nervous systems sufficient and rightly calculated to make us completely aware that we are living something—and no matter what.[6]

[3] *The World's Body* (New York, 1938), p. 156.
[4] *The Anatomy of Nonsense* (1943), included in and reprinted from *In Defense of Reason* by Yvor Winters by permission of the publisher, Alan Swallow. Copyright 1937 and 1947 by Yvor Winters, pp. 537–9.
[5] *In Defense of Reason*, pp. 538–9.
[6] *The Literary Mind*, p. 205. Richards has made considerable play with the careless abandon of Eastman's "and no matter what." He points out that if one ties a man down and then approaches him brandishing a red-hot poker—stimulating and yet

To pursue this parallelism between Ransom and Eastman: Eastman asserts that the "impractical identifications" made by metaphor and the "luxury of surprising and rich adjectives and figurative expressions . . . do not help to explain like maps or illustrations, but rather obscure the meaning of the sentence in which they occur." [7] Ransom has been careful to make his details of texture "impractical," and to show that, from the point of view of prose discourse, they are a "luxury"; yet he insists that it is just because they are impractical, that they force us to take in the rich particularity of experience. But Eastman's theory of poetry is frankly affective and psychologistic.[8]

On closer examination, the function that Ransom accords to "statement" or "structure" in poetry resembles very closely that accorded to statement in poetry by Richards. Richards makes it plain that referential statements in poetry are not important in themselves, though they frequently occur and indeed usually must occur "*as conditions* for, or *stages in,* the ensuing development of attitudes"—the elements that *are* important.[9] Likewise Ransom stresses the fact that a poem cannot do without structure (i.e., a determining argument): the human mind is so constituted that it has to have an argument to follow. But the arguments of most poems, Ransom concedes to be, in themselves, usually dull affairs;[1] we follow the pathway of the argument really for the sake of the details that border the path. We are tempted to pick a daisy or to investigate an oddly shaped bush (the elements of "texture"). We keep returning to the path and eventually arrive at our elected destination, but we arrive having seen the country—as we would not have had we kept to the strait and narrow path of science. The incidental details give the journey its value.[2] For Ransom as well as for Richards, the statements made in the poem are important only in so far as they are a means to something else.

impeding a response—one will produce a spectacularly heightened consciousness but scarcely anything that can be called art. See *The Philosophy of Rhetoric* (New York, 1936), p. 124.

[7] *The Literary Mind,* p. 183.

[8] Eastman's praise for Richards amounts to commendation for his serious effort to apply psychology to criticism. Eastman has little patience with the actual results. He finds in Richards' "harmonious equilibrium of impulses" no "foundation of aesthetics." If perchance we do find in a work of art a "reconciliation of our conflicting impulses," then that particular art "besides being art . . . is for us a kind of medicine" (*The Literary Mind,* p. 205). But most art is not, and no art need be, medicinal. In general Eastman deplores Richards' attempt to regard the scientific (the referential) apart from the emotive. A scientific interpretation of an event (e.g., that the snake in the path is not a garter snake but a copperhead) can evoke as much emotion and make the percipient jump as quickly as a merely "emotive" interpretation—besides being a better basis for proper action (*The Literary Mind,* p. 302).

[9] *Principles of Literary Criticism,* p. 267.

[1] The paraphrase of a poem, Ransom writes, "is a fair version of the logical structure," and since the paraphrase of even a fine poem usually reveals an undistinguished and commonplace argument, he concludes that the structure is not the valuable element of the poem.

[2] *The New Criticism,* p. 73, and pp. 184–5.

Ransom's justification of poetic structure, no less than Richards', rests upon an appeal to psychology: that is, human beings demand at least an apparent argument; we will not swallow our local detail neat. Ransom remarks that "it is hard to say what poetry intends by its odd structure," and the makeup of poetry, as he has described it, *is* odd— so odd that one must despair of accounting for it in terms of any entelechy of its own. Only the cravings of the human psyche can account for it, and Ransom, in a later phase of his theory,[3] came to seek for the explanation in Freudian psychology. The conscious and reasonable *ego* flourishes upon neat and tidy orderliness, but the unconscious *id* requires the concrete and unpredictable particulars for its sustenance. Poetry thus ministers to the health of the mind, and Ransom's later position tends to approximate in some features the earlier position of Richards. This fact, taken together with the counter-fact that Richards, in *his* own later criticism, has moved toward a cognitive position, is eloquent testimony to the difficulties inherent in any critical theory which begins by slicing apart value and knowledge—whether it be Richards' cutting the emotive use of language free from the referential or Ransom's cutting the valuable illogical "texture" free from logical "structure." The critic may indeed make refinements that push his theory nearer to a cognitive view, but in so far as the value of the poem is something that cannot be figured forth in the poetic meaning before us, psychology will have to be called in, either at the beginning or at the end, to justify the irrational elements in which the value has been made to reside.

Ransom's appeal to Freud is, however, somewhat startling in view of the embarrassing simplicity of Freud's own theory of literature as offering a kind of surrogate gratification, a theory touched upon briefly earlier in this chapter.[4] But it ought to be observed that Freud's concept of the mind and of its workings has exerted a profound influence, even upon critics who are quite willing to dismiss Freud's specific literary theory as inadequate. Lionel Trilling, for example, who admits that Freud has said "many clumsy and misleading things about art," and remarks that Freud "eventually . . . speaks of art" with "what we must indeed call contempt,"[5] nevertheless has urged us not to underestimate the value of Freud's contribution to literary criticism.

VIII

THERE is a certain propriety in ending this chapter as we began it with some observations upon Freud, the more so since those made in the open-

---

[3] See in particular two articles in *The Kenyon Review*, IX (Summer and Autumn, 1947), Nos. 3 and 4.

[4] See *ante* p. 611.

[5] *The Liberal Imagination*, p. 42.

ing pages could scarcely do justice to his influence. We owe to Freud a whole new psychological vocabulary—the *Id*, the *Ego*, the *Super-ego*, *transference*, and *repression* are only a few of its terms—a vocabulary which reflects a new conception of the psyche and its functioning. In elucidating the symbolic content of dreams and the way in which the "dream-work" is performed—through *condensation*, *substitution*, and *displacement*—and in calling attention to typical *motifs* (like the Oedipus Complex) which recur in literature, Freud has enlarged our notions of the richness and complexity to which a literary symbol may attain. In his concept of the *overdetermination* or multiple relevance of accurately used language, Freud has paralleled such more specifically literary concepts of ambiguous verbal riches as those which we shall consider in succeeding chapters. Trilling's summary of Freud's accomplishment on this level is probably not overstated:

> In the eighteenth century Vico spoke of the metaphorical, imagistic language of the early stages of culture; it was left to Freud to discover how, in a scientific age, we still feel and think in figurative formations, and to create, what psychoanalysis is, a science of tropes, of metaphor and its variants, synechdoche and metonymy.[6]

The value of the tools with which Freud has supplied the literary critic ought indeed to be acknowledged, even though the tools are at the mercy of the tool-users, and they in turn are at the mercy of whatever literary theory they may hold. A new "science of tropes" does not necessarily provide a new theory of literature. Suffice it to say that up to this time most Freudian critical studies have devoted themselves to psychoanalyses of the artist[7] while making very questionable assumptions about the nature of his accomplished work, or else they have occupied themselves with the effect of the work upon the reader and have thus tended to move off into studies in reader psychology.

The most fruitful and intensive application to literature of something like a new "science of tropes" has in fact come out of the influence of Richards rather than that of Freud, and this fact itself serves to point a difference between Richards' affectivism and Freud's. (That some of the most brilliant "Freudian" critical studies have been written by critics like William Empson, who are even more deeply indebted to Richards,

---

[6] *The Liberal Imagination*, p. 53.

[7] See, for example, Ernest Jones, *Hamlet and Oedipus* (London, 1911), in which he attempts to probe into "the deeper working of Shakespeare's mind." Trilling's criticism of Jones's assumption is to be found in *The Liberal Imagination*, pp. 48–51. See also Daniel E. Schneider, *The Psycho-Analyst and the Artist*, (New York, 1950); and Ernst Kris, *Psychoanalytic Exploration in Art*, (New York, 1952). Dr. Kris makes the comment (p. 286) that "Literary critics seem of late weary of the intrusion of psychoanalysis. However politely, they assert—and rightly so—their independence."

tends to confirm this point.) As Susanne Langer has put it: to make all art a natural self-expressive function like dream and "make-believe" tends to put good art and bad art on a par. "One does not say of a sleeper that he dreams clumsily, nor of a neurotic that his symptoms are carelessly strung together; but a poem may certainly be charged with ineptitude or carelessness." [8] Richards, on the other hand, has from the beginning focused attention upon the problem of discriminating good art from bad and he has to a remarkable degree, sometimes one feels in spite of his own more extravagant theories, stressed the organic structure of the work itself.

SUPPLEMENT

Selection will be sure to take care of itself, for it has a constant motive behind it. That motive is simply experience. As people feel life, so they will feel the art that is most closely related to it. This closeness of relation is what we should never forget in talking of the effort of the novel. Many people speak of it as a factitious, artificial form, a product of ingenuity, the business of which is to alter and arrange the things that surround us, to translate them into conventional, traditional moulds. This, however, is a view of the matter which carries us but a very short way, condemns the art to an eternal repetition of a few familiar *clichés*, cuts short its development, and leads us straight up to a dead wall. Catching the very note and trick, the strange irregular rhythm of life, that is the attempt whose strenuous force keeps Fiction upon her feet. In proportion as in what she offers us we see life *without* rearrangement do we feel that we are touching the truth; in proportion as we see it *with* rearrangement do we feel that we are being put off with a substitute, a compromise and convention. It is not uncommon to hear an extraordinary assurance of remark in regard to this matter of rearranging, which is often spoken of as if it were the last word of art. Mr. Besant seems to me in danger of falling into the great error with his rather unguarded talk about "selection." Art is essentially selection, but it is a selection whose main care is to be typical, to be inclusive. For many people art means rose-coloured window-panes, and selection means picking a bouquet for Mrs. Grundy.

—Henry James, *The Art of Fiction* (New York, 1948), pp. 16–17

Irony arises when one tries, by the interaction of terms upon one another, to produce a *development* which uses all the terms. Hence, from the standpoint of this total form (this "perspective of perspectives"), none of the participating "sub-perspectives" can be treated as either precisely right or precisely wrong. They are all voices, or personalities, or positions, integrally affecting

[8] *Feeling and Form* (New York, 1953), p. 245.

one another. When the dialectic is properly formed, they are the number of characters needed to produce the total development. Hence, reverting to our suggestion that we might extend the synecdochic pattern to include such reversible pairs as disease-cure, hero-villain, active-passive, we should "ironically" note the function of the disease in "perfecting" the cure, or the function of the cure in "perpetuating" the influences of the disease. Or we should note that only through an internal and external experiencing of folly could we possess (in our intelligence or imagination) sufficient "characters" for some measure of development beyond folly.

People usually confuse the dialectic with the relativistic. Noting that the dialectic (or dramatic) explicitly attempts to establish a distinct set of characters, all of which protest variously at odds or on the bias with one another, they think no further. It is certainly relativistic, for instance, to state that any term (as per metaphor-perspective) can be seen from the point of view of any other term. But insofar as terms are thus encouraged to participate in an orderly parliamentary development, the dialectic of this participation produces (in the observer who considers the whole from the participation of all the terms rather than from the standpoint of any one participant) a "resultant certainty" of a different quality, necessarily ironic, since it requires that all the sub-certainties be considered as neither true nor false, but *contributory* (as were we to think of the resultant certainty or "perspective of perspectives" as a noun, and to think of all the contributory voices as necessary modifiers of that noun).

—Reprinted with permission of publishers from *A Grammar of Motives* by Kenneth Burke. Copyright, 1945, by Prentice Hall, Inc.

It is possible to interpret aesthetic response in a purely subjectivistic manner by denying that aesthetic quality actually characterizes the object of awareness. The subjectivist admits that aesthetic response has psychological characteristics which distinguish it from other types of response. But he denies that some objects of awareness actually possess in greater or less degree an objective aesthetic character of their own. He explains the *apparent* objectivity of aesthetic quality by saying that we unconsciously project our aesthetic feelings into the object of our awareness, and thus ascribe to it a quality which the object itself completely lacks. The subjectivist may admit that some objects occasion this projection more readily than other objects, and that some aesthetic preferences are idiosyncratic, some more general, and some very widespread. But this fact is explained solely in terms of temperamental variations, social habits, and cultural traditions, and not at all in terms of the presence or absence of an aesthetic quality in different objects of awareness. Aesthetic quality is thus asserted to be merely a function of aesthetic evaluation, and evaluation, in turn, is not conceived to be the discovery of an objective quality in things. . . .

Aesthetic quality is, I believe, *as* objective as the secondary qualities of color and sound, and may (following G. E. Moore) be entitled a tertiary quality. It is "objective" in the sense of actually characterizing certain objects of awareness and not others, and therefore as awaiting discovery by the aesthetically sensitive observer. It is correctly described as "objective" because it satisfies the generic criterion of objectivity, namely, coercive order. Aesthetic quality is apprehended by the aesthetically-minded observer as a quality which presents itself to him with compelling power; which characterizes different objects in different degrees and in conformity to certain basic principles; which he can rediscover on different occasions and explore as he explores other objective qualities; and which other aesthetically sensitive observers can also discover and investigate.

I have adopted this position because it seems to me to do full justice to the sensitive layman's and the thoughtful critic's normal interpretation of the aesthetic experience, whereas the subjectivistic interpretation does unnecessary violence to this experience. . . . the burden of proof must rest with the iconoclastic philosopher. And no defense of subjectivism yet formulated seems to me to be compelling or even plausible. I shall therefore presume the objectivity of aesthetic quality in the following analysis.

—Theodore Meyer Greene, *The Arts and the Art of Criticism* (Princeton, 1947), p. 4, by permission of Princeton University Press, Publishers.

CHAPTER 28

THE SEMANTIC PRINCIPLE

§ *Coleridge as a "semasiologist": his verbal analyses of imaginative syntheses—Richards' practical criticism and its cognitive implications—II. Empson's concern for multiplicity of meaning: his concept of ambiguity, his analyses of verbal structures, his psychologism, his ultimate repudiation of Richards' "two uses of language"—III. Richards' contextual theory of meaning—IV. the consequences of the contextual theory for rhythm and for the general interaction of words within a given context—Richards' definition of metaphor as a "transaction between contexts" —W. B. Stanford's account of metaphor as a "stereoscope of ideas"—V. Richards' "poetry of inclusion" related to his contextual theory of meaning: the significance of irony in this connection, as interpreted by Richards, and by R. P. Warren—VI. the problem of the width of context properly relevant to the discussion of a poem, and the related problem of "simplicity"—E. B. Burgum's method of rendering all poetry "complex" by viewing it in "sociological perspectives"—VII. Empsonian-Ricardian complexity and the protests it has evoked—VIII. its bearing upon lyric simplicity: its connection with the problem of simplicity as envisaged by Plotinus* §

RICHARDS' INTEREST IN SEMANTICS [1] HAS BEEN MENTIONED IN THE preceding chapter. In *The Meaning of Meaning*, written in collaboration with C. K. Ogden, the preferred term is "science of Symbolism." Such a science, the authors believed, had now become pos-

[1] In Charles W. Morris' terminology (see *Foundations of the Theory of Signs*, Vol. I, no. 2 of *The Encyclopaedia of Unified Science*, Chicago, 1938) *semantics* proper involves the reference of a sign to its object. It is a subdivision of the general

sible largely through developments in psychology.[2] The function of such a science would be to purify thinking of the errors and distortions forced upon it by the "Power of Words."

> . . . words may come between us and our objects in countless subtle ways, if we do not realize the nature of their power. In logic . . . they lead to the creation of bogus entities, the universals, properties and so forth. . . . By concentrating attention on themselves, words encourage the futile study of forms which has done so much to discredit Grammar; by the excitement which they provoke through their emotive force, discussion is for the most part rendered sterile; by the various types of Verbomania and Graphomania, the satisfaction of naming is realized, and the sense of personal power factitiously enhanced.[3]

But the power of words need not be merely negative; it can be positive and beneficent, and to this positive power Richards turns in his *Principles of Literary Criticism*. That book "endeavours to provide for the emotive function of language the same critical foundation" as *The Meaning of Meaning* attempted to provide "for the symbolic [i.e., referential]." [4]

Even in Richards' earliest work his concern for semantic analysis—the subtle and elaborate examination of verbal complexities—is evident. His discussion of Coleridge will show how closely synaesthesis and semantics are in practice associated in Richards' mind. Richards finds in Coleridge's celebrated description of the imagination as a "synthetic and magical" power an early hint of the doctrine of synaesthesis.[5] Coleridge's discussion of concrete instances of the "synthetic and magical power" reveals him to be a *semasiologist*, that is, a man centrally concerned with "the meanings of words," and as part of this concern, anxious to inquire into "the behaviour of words in poetry." [6] Moreover, Coleridge's account of the behavior of words in certain passages of Shakespeare's *Venus and Adonis* provides admirable instances of poetic analysis. For example, Richards quotes Coleridge's commentary upon the lines:

> Look! how a bright star shooteth from the sky,
> So glides he in the night from Venus' eye.

---

study of linguistics signs, which is *semiotic*. (The other subdivisions of semiotic are the *syntactical*, having to do with the relations of linguistic signs to one another, and the *pragmatic*, having to do with the practical effects of such signs.) Richards occasionally makes use of the term *semiology*, and, as we shall see, he refers to Coleridge as a *semasiologist*.

[2] *The Meaning of Meaning* (New York, 1923), p. 8.

[3] *Meaning of Meaning*, p. 45, by permission of the publisher, Harcourt, Brace and Company, Inc.

[4] See the Preface to the second edition of *The Meaning of Meaning* (1926).

[5] *Principles of Literary Criticism*, pp. 242 ff.

[6] *Coleridge on Imagination*, pp. xi–xii.

Coleridge emphasizes the number of "images and feelings" that

> are here brought together without effort and without discord—
> the beauty of Adonis—the rapidity of his flight—the yearning
> yet helplessness of the enamoured gazer. . . .

And Richards, picking up the theme, enlarges further upon the intercon-
nections among the various images.[7]

A great deal of Richards' practical criticism, much of it incidental
to the stated topic of discussion and scattered through his various books,
is criticism of this kind. For an impressive body of such criticism, however, it is convenient at this point to turn to the work of Richards' pupil,
William Empson. Empson's contributions to this kind of criticism are
more extensive than those of Richards and they are on the whole more
daringly ingenious. They illustrate the substantial achievement of semantic analysis; they also reveal some of the problems that it raises.

II

EMPSON, impressed by the multiplicity of meanings revealed in an analysis by Robert Graves and Laura Riding of Shakespeare's sonnet "The
Expense of Spirit in a Waste of Shame,"[8] set out to explore the applica-
bility of this kind of analysis to English poetry in general. The result
was the publication in 1930 of his brilliant study *Seven Types of Ambiguity*. The choice of the term "ambiguity" was perhaps not altogether
happy, for this term reflects the point of view of expository prose, where
one meaning, and only one meaning, is wanted. The presence of a second or third meaning creates a puzzle. The man habituated to expository
prose asks: which is *the* meaning?[9] Because the term "ambiguity" con-
notes doubt and puzzlement, Philip Wheelwright has argued that we need
a more positive term, and one that will suggest richness of meaning. He
proposes *plurisignation*.[1]

[7] *Coleridge on Imagination*, pp. 82–3. M. H. Abrams in *The Mirror and the
Lamp* (New York, 1953), p. 182, criticizes Richards for translating "the difference
between the products of the faculties [of fancy and imagination as distinguished by
Coleridge] into that of the number of 'links' or 'cross-connections' between their
'units of meaning.'" Cf. *ante* Chapter 18.

[8] Robert Graves and Laura Riding, *A Survey of Modernist Poetry* (New York,
1929).

[9] So also with the literary theorists of the past, including Aristotle. As W. B.
Stanford points out in his *Ambiguity in Greek Literature* (Oxford, 1939), p. 1,
Aristotle was "inclined to consider all ambiguity as a perversion or failing of language instead of its natural and valuable quality. . . . he allowed the danger of dialectical dishonesty in ambiguities to obscure their poetic value—and this even in his
literary criticism." Yet ambiguity is, in Stanford's words, "a natural, subtle and effective instrument for poetry and dramatic purposes," and for that reason it occurs very
frequently in Greek literature.

[1] *The Burning Fountain* (Bloomington, 1954), p. 61.

Whatever the proper term, the phenomenon in question is one of multiple implication, as a typical passage of Empsonian analysis will reveal:

> When a word is selected as a "vivid detail," as particular for general, a reader may suspect alternative reasons why it has been selected; indeed the author might find it hard to say. When there are several such words there may be alternative ways of viewing them in order of importance.

> > Pan is our All, by him we breathe, we live,
> > We move, we are; . . .
> > But when he frowns, the sheep, alas,
> > The shepherds wither, and the grass.
> > > (Ben Jonson, *Pan's Anniversary*)

> *Alas*, the word explaining which of the items in this list we are to take most seriously, belongs to the *sheep* by proximity and the break in the line, to the *grass* by rhyming with it, and to the *shepherds*, humble though they may be, by the processes of human judgment; so that all three are given due attention, and the balance of the verse is maintained. The Biblical suggestions of *grass* as symbolic of the life of man ("in the mornings it is green and groweth up; in the evening it is cut down, dried up, and withered") add to the solemnity; or from another point of view make the passage absurdly blasphemous, because Pan here is James I. The grace, the pathos, the "sheer song" of the couplet is given by an enforced subtlety of intonation, from the difficulty of saying it so as to bring out all the implications.[2]

Empson's classification of ambiguities into *seven* types is not, as he himself makes clear, to be pressed too hard. The types overlap and at points the definitions are highly arbitrary. Some such classification was apparently necessary to allow him to lay out his material and to provide him with a framework for the many acute analyses of particular poems —analyses which brought home to a whole generation of readers the fact of the manysidedness of language. That would be our perhaps biased way of disposing of the scheme itself, and of acknowledging the qualifications of his scheme that Empson himself has made.

Empson has a general psychologistic bias which comes out clearly in such a passage as the following:

> Ambiguities of this sort [he has been discussing Shakespeare's sonnet XVI] may be divided into those which, once understood,

remain an intelligible unit in the mind; those in which the pleasure belongs to the act of working out and understanding, which must at each reading, though with less labour, be repeated; and those in which the ambiguity works best if it is never discovered. Which class any particular poem belongs to depends in part *on your own mental habits and critical opinions.*[3]

This is to classify in terms of the reader rather than the poem. The second kind of ambiguity (in which the "act of working out and understanding . . . must . . . be repeated") would seem to be in fact merely an imperfectly apprehended version of the first kind. That is, if the labor of working out the meaning becomes, on further readings, progressively less, one might plausibly expect that it would eventually disappear. But it is for the third kind of ambiguity that Empson provides a completely baffling definition. Here the reader is required to be *unaware* that he is confronted with an ambiguity, for this third kind is said to work "best if it is never discovered." What Empson has done is to classify three kinds of response—not three kinds of poems, but three grades of reading.

Empson's general psychologistic emphasis has an important negative bearing on the problem of evaluation. His "method" can obviously be applied to a poor poem just as easily as to a good one—a fact of which he himself is well aware. For example, in discussing Eliot's criticism of the first stanzas of Shelley's "Sky Lark," he proceeds to show how the various images which Eliot believed to be unrelated could actually be related; but he goes on to remark of his own analysis:

> At the same time the thought [in Shelley's poem] seems excessively confused; this muddle of ideas clogging an apparently simple lyrical flow may be explained, but it is not therefore justified; and it is evident that a hearty appetite for this . . . type of ambiguity would apologise for, would be able to extract pleasure from, very bad poetry indeed.[4]

In at least one passage in *Seven Types* Empson does attempt to deal explicitly with the problem of value. An ambiguity is valuable, he says, and not merely a bothersome muddle "in so far as [it] . . . sustains intricacy, delicacy, or compression of thought, or is an opportunism devoted to saying quickly what the reader already understands." But ambiguity is a nuisance—Empson's precise phrase is "not to be respected"—in so far as "it is due to weakness or thinness of thought," when it "obscures the matter in hand unnecessarily," or when, because it is so removed from the focus of interest, its presence gives the reader "a general impression of incoherence." A valuable ambiguity is indeed a "plurisignation," add-

[3] *Seven Types* (1947), p. 57. The italics are ours.
[4] *Seven Types* (1947), p. 160.

ing richness and complexity to, but not obscuring, the structure of meaning.

The foregoing justification of ambiguity reflects the strong cognitive tendency that runs throughout Empson's criticism. But he has other passages in which the cognitive element is overshadowed or is suppressed in favor of other interests. Empson's inveterate psychologism constantly makes him put such questions as these: Why would a reader of such and such a kind find this ambiguous? What historical circumstances make the 18th-century reader, say, prone to take this rather than that as the primary meaning? Did the poet put this in by design or by inadvertence? Indeed, Empson's interest sometimes seems to be merely a curiosity as to what could be made of a particular passage if he simply gave his mind to the search for puzzles. His raccoon-like curiosity [5] perhaps goes a long way to account for the hostility toward Empson felt by many scholars and critics who have been able to see in his work only the naughtiness of the little boy who dismembers the clock in order to see what makes it go.

In his latest book,[6] the psychologism continues as a dominant element. In the literary analyses that occupy him here, Empson sometimes works overtly in terms of author psychology, speculating upon the author's unconscious motivations, his private beliefs, his sense of what kind of rhetorical tricks he could play upon his audience; sometimes, in terms of audience response, examining the ideas that the particular audience had inherited, the literary conventions to which it had been conditioned, its sensitivity or its stupidity. In one very important regard, however, *Complex Words* makes a signal advance toward a cognitive position. In his very first chapter, Empson finds it necessary to reject Richards' doctrine that the "Emotions of the words in poetry are independent of the Sense." In fact, Empson argues, whenever you find

> a case where there are alternative ways of interpreting a word's action, of which one can plausibly be called Cognitive and the other Emotive, it is the Cognitive one which is likely to have important effects on sentiment or character, and in general it does not depend on accepting false beliefs. But in general it does involve a belief of some kind . . . so that it is no use trying to chase belief-feelings out of the poetry altogether.[7]

[5] Compare Marianne Moore's lines on Kenneth Burke:

> and Burke is a
> psychologist—of acute, racoon-
> like curiosity.

From "Picking and Choosing," *Selected Poems* (London, 1935). A reviewer of Empson's book complained that: "Quite a number of Mr. Empson's analyses do not seem to have any properly critical conclusion; they are interesting only as a revelation of the poet's, or Mr. Empson's, ingenious mind."—*Criterion*, July, 1931.

[6] *The Structure of Complex Words* (New York, 1951).

[7] *Complex Words*, p. 10. All rights reserved. Reprinted by permission of the publisher, New Directions.

Empson makes the further observation that by the time Richards had come to write *The Philosophy of Rhetoric*, Richards himself "seems to have dropped the idea that a writer of poetry had better not worry about the Sense"; indeed, in this book he finds Richards arguing "that the only tolerable way to read poetry is to give the full Sense a very sharp control over the Emotion."[8]

III

THE comment upon the shift in Richards' emphasis is just. In his *Philosophy of Rhetoric* (1936), Richards seems to have quietly laid aside the distinction between the referential and the emotive aspects of language and to have devoted himself to an account of a new rhetoric founded upon semantic analysis.

> . . . the old Rhetoric treated ambiguity as a fault in language, and hoped to confine or eliminate it[;] the new Rhetoric sees it as an inevitable consequence of the power of language and as an indispensable means of most of our important utterances— especially in Poetry and Religion.[9]

Richards admits that the ambiguity of words is not absolute; a condition of general conformity among users is a condition of communication. "That," he writes, "no one would dream of disputing"; for language is a social fact as well as a part of personal experience.[1] Stable meanings derive from stable contexts. The meaning of a word like *knife* is rather stable, because the situations in which *knife* occurs are much the same. Stability may be imposed artificially. The stability of the meaning of *mass* as a technical term in physics has been established by limiting and specializing the contexts which we will take into account in using the word technically. Scientific terms are thus limited by convention to one "right or good use"—one proper meaning that the term always and invariably bears.

But this tidy arrangement, Richards goes on to say, is impossible outside of the technical language of the sciences, and most of our discourse, including some of our most important discourse, is not technically scientific. In nontechnical discourse, words "must shift their meanings." If they did not, "language, losing its subtlety with its suppleness, would lose also its power to serve us."[2] The last sentence is worth careful inspection. Not only does Richards see ambiguity as normal; he

[8] *Complex Words*, p. 14.
[9] *Philosophy of Rhetoric*, p. 40, by permission of the publishers, Oxford University Press, Inc.
[1] *Philosophy of Rhetoric*, p. 54.
[2] *Philosophy of Rhetoric*, p. 73.

couples "suppleness" of language with "subtlety." Terms that have lost their pliability, their capacity for being stretched or wrenched a little so as to apply to a new context, are no longer subtle terms. As terms become incapable of ambiguous use they become incapable of precise use.

This view runs quite counter to our conventional notions of precision of meaning, which are founded for the most part on the nature of scientific terminology. Richards had written much earlier in the *Principles* that "Words, when used . . . scientifically, not figuratively . . . , are capable of directing thought to a comparatively few features of the more common situations," [3] and he is making the same point here. Scientific language has its own kind of precision; but another kind of precision, or if not precision, then "subtlety," is required for "the topics with which all generally interesting discussion is concerned." [4]

Richards extends this view of meaning to include rhythm. Poetic rhythm, he had already argued in *Practical Criticism* (1929), influences and is influenced by meaning: ". . . the difference between good rhythm and bad is not simply a difference between certain sequences of sounds; it goes deeper, and to understand it we have to take note of the meanings of the words as well." [5]

We commonly think of rhythm as making a direct appeal to the emotions: a vigorous march is stirring, certain minor airs are plaintive. And, it should be pointed out, Richards does not take the extreme position of denying that the rhythm of a poem *as such* may have emotional efficacy. The actual sounds are important. They are the stuff with which the poet works—comparable, one supposes Richards would say, to the "dictionary" meanings of the words that the poet uses. But the "actual sounds . . . do not carry the whole responsibility for the rhythm." And if we want to praise or condemn the rhythm of a particular poem, we shall not be able, except in the loosest sort of way, to deal with rhythm apart from meaning.[6]

Richards exhibits a phonetic dummy in nonsense syllables of Stanza XV of Milton's "On the Morning of Christ's Nativity." He challenges the reader to find in the dummy the aesthetic virtues which are sometimes ascribed to the "mere sound" of Milton's stanza, including its "expressiveness" as mere sound. If the reader of the dummy finds in it as a

[3] *Principles*, p. 131.
[4] *Philosophy of Rhetoric*, pp. 72–3.
[5] *Practical Criticism* (New York, 1929), p. 227.
[6] In *Practical Criticism*, p. 229, Richards says that the rhythm that we admire and feel that we detect in the sounds themselves is something that we "ascribe" to them. Later, in *Coleridge on Imagination*, p. 119, he puts the matter in terms nearer those of Coleridge: "The movement of the verse becomes the movement of the meaning; and prosody, as a study of verse-form apart from meaning, is seen to be a product of unwary abstraction. In saying that 'the sense of musical delight . . . is a gift of the imagination,' Coleridge set aside the conventional conception to restore a wholeness to our view of the act of speech. . . ."

mere series of sounds the phonetic virtue characterizing Milton's stanza, then successful verse must be amenable to a formula, for one can make up such dummies *ad infinitum*. If, on the other hand, the reader protests that the dummy is not a phonetic replica of Milton's sonnet, he is in reality arguing that the difference *in sound* between the dummy and original is what deprives the dummy of all merit. "In which case," Richards points out, the reader "will have to account for the curious fact that just those transformations which redeem it as sound, should also give it the sense and feeling we find in Milton. A staggering coincidence, unless the meaning were highly relevant to the effect of the form." [7]

I V

AT THIS point it may be well to summarize some of the consequences of what Richards calls broadly a "context" theory of meaning.

First, words interanimate one another. They are qualified by the whole context in which they figure, and they bring to that context powers derived from other contexts in which they have figured in the past. Much of modern criticism devoted to the "close reading of texts," including that of Empson, illustrates the subtle and rich complex of meaning which a finely wrought poetic context can yield.

Second, the problem of meaning—especially *the* meaning of a poem or drama or piece of fiction—is seen to be a matter not easily and summarily determined. It is not enough to seize upon one or two "statements" as indicating the thesis and to relegate everything else to the role of ornament or detailed illustration. "Statements" (such as "Beauty is truth" or "Ripeness is all") may indeed bear importantly upon the meaning of the whole work and may in some instance summarize that meaning, but not necessarily: they are subject to all the pulls and attractions of the other elements of the work.

Third, the poet necessarily tailor-makes his language as he explores his meaning. He does not (and cannot) "build up the meaning of his sentences as a mosaic is put together of discrete independent tesserae." The senses of the author's words are not such "fixed factors" as these. Instead, what we call the "meanings" of his words "are resultants which we arrive at only through the interplay of the interpretative possibilities of the whole utterance." [8]

---

[7] *Practical Criticism*, pp. 232–3. T. S. Eliot, following the main line of French symbolist doctrine, affirms the interconnection between rhythm and meaning quite as emphatically. In *The Music of Poetry* (Glasgow, 1942), he writes (p. 13): "the music of poetry is not something which exists apart from the meaning. Otherwise, we could have poetry of great musical beauty which made no sense. and I have never come across such poetry."

[8] *Philosophy of Rhetoric*, p. 55.

Fourth, the reader, like the writer, finds the meaning through a process of exploration. "Inference and guesswork!" Richards exclaims. "What else is interpretation? How, apart from inference and skilled guesswork, can we be supposed ever to understand a writer's or speaker's thought?" [9]

Fifth, in the light of the context theory, metaphor is seen to be a typical instance of the merging of contexts. A metaphor is more than a mere "comparison" that illustrates a point, or recommends a doctrine by lending it an attractive coloring. A metaphor is the linchpin joining two contexts, contexts which may be quite far apart and, in conventional discourse at least, utterly unrelated. The meaning achieved by a metaphor —and certainly by the most vigorous and powerful metaphor—is not simply a prettified version of an already stated meaning, but a new meaning in which imagination pushes itself forward and occupies new ground.

Mere vividness has never been the aspect of imagery that has interested Richards. He has countenanced neither Max Eastman's quest for intense realization, nor even T. E. Hulme's insistence that poetic language should "hand over sensations bodily." Poetry's inveterate concern for concrete particulars has for Richards a very different importance: concrete particularity means heterogeneity; it means difference; and it insures the sort of confrontation of unlike elements that is necessary to prevent discourse from collapsing into literal statement.

In fact, what determines that a given usage is metaphorical rather than literal is this linkage with a second context. As a test case, Richards instances Hamlet's question: "What should such fellows as I do crawling between earth and heaven?" Is *crawling* to be taken literally or metaphorically? Metaphorically, Richards answers. A baby literally crawls, and, on occasion, a man may literally crawl, but here "there is an unmistakable reference to other things that crawl," such things as cockroaches or snakes. If we substitute for *crawling*, *walking*, or more decisively still, the more general word *moving*, we shut out the context of *crawling* creatures and the use becomes literal. Metaphors die into fixed and literal terms when habitual usage confines them to one context: the *eye* of a needle or the *leg* of a table have lost all metaphoric force. They are no longer what Richards calls metaphor, "a transaction between contexts."

This last definition has a bearing on the problem of triteness, a topic we have touched upon in an earlier chapter.[1] It would be oversimple to conclude that every trite expression has become so through simple repetition. The attrition by repetition is only one, and perhaps not an essential, factor. Some expressions may attain triteness, and some have undoubtedly had triteness forced upon them, but some again are born trite. Even at a first hearing some phrases seem "shopworn." On the other hand, many

[9] *Philosophy of Rhetoric*, p. 53.
[1] Cf. *ante* Chapter 16, pp. 354–60.

readings do not impoverish Shakespeare's *King Lear*. Even passages like Hamlet's "Something is rotten in the state of Denmark," which may be said to have had triteness forced upon them, slough off their triteness at once when set back into the context of the whole play.

W. B. Stanford (whose *Ambiguity in Greek Literature* has been mentioned earlier in this chapter) calls metaphor a "stereoscope of ideas." [2] Stanford offers this definition:

> The term metaphor is fully valid only when applied to a very definite and a rather complicated concept, *viz.* the process and result of using a term (X) normally signifying an object or concept (A) in such a context that it must refer to another object or concept (B) which is distinct enough in characteristics from A to ensure that in the composite idea formed by the synthesis of the concepts A and B and now symbolized in the word X, the factors A and B retain their conceptual independence even while they merge in the unity symbolized by X. . . . [3]

Stanford says that the objects or concepts related by the metaphor must be sufficiently "distinct" to retain conceptual independence. Consider such an example as the following: "The dog raged like a wild beast." This sentence has almost no metaphoric force, for the dog, a tamed beast, is not sufficiently distinct from a wild beast. "The man raged like a wild beast" or "The sea raged like a wild beast" are poor enough as metaphor, but with the substitution of *man* or *sea*, a trace of metaphoric power begins to be perceptible.

Stanford's own metaphor of a stereoscope insists upon this necessary maintenance of difference: only by keeping the two pictures distinct can the stereoscope use them to create a third thing, the depth picture, which is a "synthesis" of the two flat pictures, a picture in which the flat pictures may be said to "merge" but which is in fact a third thing, quite different from either.

Metaphor "means" a third thing, different from the meaning of either of its terms taken in isolation. "The traditional theory," notes Richards, made metaphor seem to be only "a shifting and displacement of words," whereas "fundamentally it is a borrowing between and intercourse of *thoughts*, a transaction between contexts." [4] Metaphor is not merely "a grace or ornament or *added* power of language"; it is "its constitutive form." [5] And again, "*Thought* is metaphoric, and proceeds by comparison, and the metaphors of language derive therefrom."

[2] See his *Greek Metaphor* (Oxford, 1936), p. 105, by permission of the publishers, Oxford University Press, Inc.

[3] *Greek Metaphor*, p. 101.

[4] *Philosophy of Rhetoric*, p. 94.

[5] *Philosophy of Rhetoric*, p. 90.

V

WE ARE invited to apply the contextual theory of meaning as elaborated by Richards in his *Philosophy of Rhetoric* to his earlier distinction between a poetry of "exclusion" and a poetry of "inclusion." [6] That which is "excluded" for the sake of unity, one might argue, is a different "context." A sentimental love poem, to take an easy and obvious example, systematically excludes from its context such matters as doctors' bills, squalling babies, and the odors of the kitchen. Its unity depends upon the reader's viewing it from a certain perspective and in a certain light. When the reader, because of the enlargement of the relevant context, is forced to view such a poem from a different perspective, the essential flimsiness of the poem is revealed. The altered perspective reveals that the recalcitrant and contradictory elements of the experience in question have not been taken into account—they have simply been ignored. The poetry of "inclusion," on the other hand, systematically draws upon other and larger contexts. It has already made its peace with the recalcitrant and the contradictory. That is why it is, as Richards says, "invulnerable" to "ironic contemplation."

Thus might a sympathetic critic be expected to relate certain key terms of Richards' earlier critical theory to the "context" theory elaborated in his *Philosophy of Rhetoric*. Such an interpretation of Richards' views has the merit of implying a conception of irony congenial to that held by many critics of the present and of the recent past. For example, Henry James, in his Preface to *The Lesson of the Master*, declared that "operative" irony "implies and projects the possible other case" [7]—an observation possibly echoed by T. S. Eliot in his definition of wit as involving "a recognition, implicit in the expression of every experience, of other kinds of experience which are possible." [8] Such also is the function of irony described in R. P. Warren's "Pure and Impure Poetry" (1943). The unwillingness to face up to the "other possible case" constitutes for Warren the characteristic weakness of the "pure" poetry that avoids on principle any manifestation of irony and witty intellection.

Why, Warren asks, should a love poem, for instance, include in its make-up "self-contradictions, cleverness, irony, realism—all things which call us back to the world of prose and imperfection"? [9] He answers his

[6] Cf. I. A. Richards, *Principles of Literary Criticism* (New York, 1929), p. 240, the discussion of metaphor as "the supreme agent by which disparate and hitherto unconnected things are brought together in poetry."

[7] *The Art of the Novel*, introduction by R. P. Blackmur (New York, 1953), p. 222.

[8] "Andrew Marvell," *Selected Essays*, p. 262.

[9] "Pure and Impure Poetry," *The Kenyon Review*, V (Spring, 1943); reprinted in R. W. Stallman, *Critiques and Essays in Criticism, 1920–1948* (New York, 1949), p. 86, by permission of the author.

question by making a comparison of three love poems: Tennyson's "Now sleeps the crimson petal, now the white," Shelley's "Indian Serenade," and *Romeo and Juliet*. The first two poems aspire to purity of effect: they "exclude" the sordid and the realistic. *Romeo and Juliet* does not: it "includes" the bawdy jests of Mercutio, just outside the wall of Juliet's garden, and it includes the earthy and common-sense nurse who also has her bawdy jests and who will offer her counsel of half-measures and compromises. It is, as Warren puts it, as if the

> poet seems to say: "I know the worst that can be said on this subject, and I am giving fair warning. Read at your own risk."
>
> Let us return to one of the other gardens, in which there is no Mercutio or nurse, and in which the lady is more sympathetic. Let us mar its purity by installing Mercutio in the shrubbery, from which the poet was so careful to banish him. You can hear his comment when the lover says:
>
>> And a spirit in my feet
>> Hath led me—who knows how?
>> To thy chamber window, Sweet!
>
> And we can guess what the wicked tongue would have to say in response to the last stanza.
>
> It may be that the poet should have made his peace early with Mercutio, and have appealed to his better nature. For Mercutio seems to be glad to cooperate with a poet. But he must be invited; otherwise, he is apt to show a streak of merry vindictiveness about the finished product.[1]

Warren, for the sake of making his point, has proposed to "install" Mercutio "in the shrubbery." But in suggesting that poets should always make their peace with Mercutio, he implies that Mercutio is actually lurking in Shelley's poem all the time—and that he lurks in all poems. Mercutio, the implied argument runs, had best be invited for the simple reason that it does not lie in the poet's power to keep him away. The many-sided complexity of reality and the nature of language are facts that have to be reckoned with: only technical language—that is, language that allows a systematically literal reading—would seem to offer a setting quite bare of any cover in which a Mercutio might lurk. Looked at in this fashion, the exclusions made by a poetry that strains after purity reveal themselves as failures to develop and exploit latent meanings, meanings which, since they are in the words, must be brought to bear positively or else must be neglected in the hope that the neglect will not be noticed. In a poetry of "inclusion," the metaphoric potentialities have been taken into account. They have been harnessed to support each other and to sustain

[1] Stallman, p. 88.

the meaning of the whole. In a poetry of exclusion, the unrecognized and unused potentialities are a threat to any superficial unity that the poet has established: a vigorous and imaginative reading brings these elements to life—to the distraction of the poem.[2]

VI

THOUGH Warren's essay seems to invite even a further development along the lines we have just indicated, it is only fair to observe that an exploration in this direction would uncover a series of problems not fully solved in Warren's essay, nor—for they are substantially the same problems—solved in the work of Empson and Richards.

A poetry capable of surviving an ironic contemplation must not, Warren would say, be purged of all "impurities" or, as Richards might put it, draw upon too narrow a context. Thus, these critics would seem to demand a certain complexity as the desideratum of any "good" poem. But, by insisting that poetry is a complex structure capable of richness (ambiguity) and toughness (irony), they have alarmed some readers by seeming to deny any value to simplicity. Their attack—or at least what those readers took to be an attack—upon a virtue so long honored by critics of all schools prompted sharp protests. But before looking directly at such protests, it may be well to notice at this juncture a second, closely related problem. It may be called the problem of relevant context.

This problem may be put as a question: against how wide a context should a given poem be read? A play like *Romeo and Juliet* obviously can appeal to, and make use of, much wider and richer contexts than any lyric can. What, in this connection, is the proper "magnitude" (if we may use Aristotle's term) of an art work? How many competing contexts must be active in a lyric in order for it to be properly and sufficiently complex?

Socially minded critics of our time sometimes dispose of the problem by disposing of simplicity. The Marxist E. B. Burgum, for example, argues[3] that there is no lyric so humble that it need be ashamed of its simplicity. There was nothing wrong with "Empson's method," but only with Empson's "non-social use of it." Burgum's use of the method applies "sociological perspectives" to poetry. Even though the closing choral

---

[2] What happens in such a case is analogous to what happens sometimes in bad prose when dead or benumbed metaphors, unwanted by the author who has failed to take their potentialities into account, waken into life, to the embarrassment of the whole passage. Such prose fares better under a superficial reading: it dare not invite, and may seriously suffer under, a vigorously imaginative reading.

[3] "The Cult of the Complex in Poetry," *Science and Society*, XV (Winter, 1951), 31–48.

lines of Aeschylus' *Prometheus Bound* [4] present no evident ambiguity, a more careful consideration manages to reveal that they imply two Greek philosophical systems, the religious and the materialistic, in conflict. Complexity enters "when it is recognized that the play is ending with this contradiction . . . unresolved." Burgum urges "the fact that the simplest idea becomes complex when related to human experience." [5]

The show-piece of the essay is Wordsworth's lyric "She dwelt among the untrodden ways." Though this poem, according to Burgum, would have to be regarded "in Empsonian terms" as simple and straightforward, it actually involves all sorts of complexity: the speaker is revealed to be conscious of his moral isolation; Lucy herself turns out to be a neurotic personality; [6] the value system as implied in the poem reveals itself as that of an era of rapid social change, and so forth. But in distinguishing the complexity that he finds in this poem from any complexity "in the phrasing (as Empson would put it)," Burgum, of course, has given over any specific literary problem, or rather he has denied that any specific literary problem exists. He treats Wordsworth's poem about Lucy as merely a document of the manners, morals, and value judgments of its age. The "problem of poetic meaning, like all problems of meaning, is fundamentally sociological." [7]

Burgum, in his exploration of complexity, does not stop with the poem conceived as a unit. By relating it to that grand manifold "human experience," he is able to propose that even a single line of poetry—his example is the Arnoldian touchstone "In his will is our peace"—is "complex." He obviously might have gone further still, for it is evident that by this sort of method one will be able to show just as convincingly that a single word possesses "complexity." For if Dante's line about God's will and our peace is "complex," the word "God," or the word "peace," with its varying and manifold implications, is "complex" also.

VII

MOST protests against Empsonian-Ricardian complexity have, however, stopped short of merging all poetic meaning into general psycho-socio-

---

[4] 'Tis Zeus who driveth his furies
To smite me with terror and madness.
O Mother Earth all-honored,
O Air revolving thy light
A common boon to all,
Behold what wrongs I endure.

[5] *Science and Society*, XV, 43.

[6] Burgum's treatment of this poem makes the examples of the application of the historical method that we observed earlier in Chapter 24 seem very conservative indeed.

[7] *Science and Society*, XV, 37.

logical meaning. The protestants, indeed, have tended, when it came to a matter of the relevant context, to be strict constructionists. They have deplored Empson's method, not because it is "non-social" but because they think it implies a license to read "anything one likes" into the text. Such was the nature of the protest made by F. L. Lucas in his *Decline and Fall of the Romantic Ideal* (1937).[8] Another typical protest was that voiced by Donald Stauffer: critics who insisted upon the complexity of poetry were guilty of partial sympathies: they demanded that all poems be "original, spare, and strange" and thus disparaged verses written "with simplicity and sentiment." [9] What, he asked, would such critics do with the simple lyrics of a Wordsworth or a Blake? Or with the simple eloquence of the Psalms?

There is often latent in such protests the misconception that a complex structure must necessarily reflect an equally complex intention on the writer's part. The poem could not be so complex as Empsonian analysis would make it, for that would argue that the writer was intolerably self-conscious. To this criticism, Richards and Empson would no doubt answer that it is naive to equate a theory of structure with a theory of composition.

A second misconception reveals itself when someone offers a great line or a memorable passage of poetry as an example of how truly *simple* great poetry can be, *forgetting* that it depends for its power upon the great literary context from which it has been taken. Thus Herbert Muller, echoing the method of Matthew Arnold,[1] has quoted brief memorable passages from Shakespeare and Dante as proof of the poetic power to be found in the simple statement of a great master.[2] It may be hard for us to realize how powerfully the context of a great literary work may qualify our reading of a passage that we *believe* we are dealing with in isolation. Shakespeare's "Ripeness is all," for example, may seem movingly eloquent because of its very naked simplicity, but if we repeat "Ripeness is all" to someone who *really* knows nothing of its context, especially if we divorce it from all literary contexts by speaking it casually at a fruit-stand, we shall find that its eloquence has been lost upon our auditor. For him it will not be poetry at all.[3]

[8] "In a recent work with the apocalyptic title, *Seven Types of Ambiguity*, it has been revealed to an admiring public that the more ways a poem can be misunderstood, the better it is" (p. 228).

[9] "The *Mesures* Lectures," *Kenyon Review*, IV (Autumn, 1942), pp. 412–13.

[1] Cf. *ante* Chapter 20.

[2] "The New Criticism in Poetry," *The Southern Review*, VI (Spring, 1941), 823.

[3] The whole matter of context is rightly seen by historical critics to be very important. How much can one poem be isolated from the context of the author's work in general? (Blake's "Lamb" taken in isolation is not quite the same poem as when viewed as a part of a whole which is the *Songs of Innocence;* it becomes a third thing when paired with "The Tiger" and viewed as one half of a double poem.)

The problem of "simplicity" has its complications. They begin to emerge as soon as we notice how little a "simple" lyric differs in its general structure from a "complex" poem. Warren urges this consideration in the essay we have previously cited. He argues there very persuasively for a considerable complexity in "Western wind, when wilt thou blow," a tiny four-line lyric usually celebrated as a pure cry of the heart.[4]

VIII

AN AMUSING illustration of the amount of complexity that may lurk beneath a commonly accepted simplicity is provided by Laura Riding and Robert Graves. In their *Pamphlet Against Anthologies*,[5] published one year before their *Survey of Modernist Poetry* which was to send William Empson out upon his career of semantic analysis,[6] they set forth a detailed discussion of the complications of meaning to be found in Wordsworth's "A Slumber Did My Spirit Seal."

Convinced that William Wordsworth was too "simple" and straightforward to have "meant" the logical contradictions that they found in his little poem, they experimented with a rewriting to correct Wordsworth's mistakes.

> The details [of the poem] are even more illogical than the main argument. Apparently what Wordsworth has in his mind is that "I thought once she was non-human in a spiritual sense, but now she is dead I find her non-human in the very opposite sense." But all the words have got misplaced. "Spirit" has got attached to Wordsworth [A slumber did *my* spirit seal] when it should go with Lucy; "no human" [*I* had no human fears] likewise. There is a false comparison made between "A slumber did my spirit seal" and "She neither hears nor sees." "Trees" is an irrelevant climax to "rocks and stones." "Thing" should not qualify the first Lucy [She seemed a thing that could not feel] but should be with the second Lucy among the rocks and stones. . . . [The poem] would run more logically, something like this:

> > A slumber sealed my *human fears*
> >   For her mortality:
> > Methought *her spirit* could withstand
> >   The touch of earthly years.

---

[4] "Pure and Impure Poetry," Stallman, pp. 88–9.
[5] *A Pamphlet Against Anthologies* (London, 1928), by permission of the authors.
[6] See *ante* p. 637.

> Yet now her spirit fails, she is
> Less sentient than a *tree*,
> Rolled round in earth's diurnal course
> With rocks and stones and things.[7]

But the revision reduces the poem to a tidy emptiness: the loss of the rhymes is the very least of the losses incurred. Riding and Graves themselves prefer Wordsworth's own version of the poem, arguing that in spite of its illogical details, it has not a "sublogical" incoherence but a "supra-logical harmony." They justify the form that he has given to his poem by a kind of Longinian argument to the effect that the "inability of the mind to face the actual reality of death" mirrors itself here in the speaker's "inability to get the right words to pair off in a logical prose manner";[8] i.e., the speaker's very incoherence points to the depth of the emotional shock that he has suffered.

But this would seem to be an unnecessarily desperate line of defense. For it can be argued that Wordsworth's "misplacing" of words is the best placing of them. The apparent contradictions and violations of logic turn out to be in fact refinements of meaning and subtleties of statement. The lover, for example, is saying that Lucy's present strange slumber has waked him out of his—out of that strange slumber in which he, unable to conceive that *she* could ever feel the "touch of earthly years," had been indifferent to the possibility of her death. But now Lucy "feels" the touch of earthly years indeed in her very lack of feeling—in the numbing of hearing, sight, and her other senses at the touch of mortality. "No motion has she now," and yet her inert body is hurled in violent motion, along with the stones and the trees, as the planet spins them all in the empty whirl that measures out each earthly day and each of the "earthly years."[9] Be the proper justification of the poem what it may, Riding and Graves by their proposed revisions, clearly showed how far this "simple" poem departs from straightforward statement and how much it partakes of the ambiguous and the paradoxical.

Semantic analysis such as that associated with Richards and Empson does seem to imply a value in complexity itself. The great poems reveal an organic structure of parts intricately related to each other, and the totality of meaning in such a poem is rich and perhaps operative on several levels. In terms of this view of poetic excellence, a principal task of criticism—perhaps *the* task of criticism—is to make explicit to the reader the implicit manifold of meanings. That this view implies a rejection of any *simpliste* notion of art is quite clear; yet it is only

---

[7] *Pamphlet Against Anthologies*, pp. 128-9.

[8] *Pamphlet Against Anthologies*, p. 129.

[9] For the detail of such an interpretation, see Cleanth Brooks, "Irony as a Principle of Structure," *Literary Opinion in America* (New York, 1951), pp. 735-7.

fair to observe that there are senses of the term simplicity which the semantic critic does not need, and presumably does not want, to reject. In any case, the problem is not new. It goes back at least to Plotinus and the third century of our era. In an earlier chapter we noted that the term used for "simple" by Plotinus (*haplous*)

> may describe either *absence* of *internal differentiation* (as with the simplicity or unity of a pebble) or precisely the opposite, a high degree of *internal differentiation*—in other words, organic unity (as with the unity of a living body).[1]

For the semanticist, it is no praise to say that poetry is simple in the first sense. The sheer simplicity of the pebble is to be despised; a high degree of "internal differentiation" is praiseworthy. Our modern semantic criticism has insisted upon its debt (as through Richards) to Coleridge, remembering his emphasis upon organic form. But it might properly also pay its respects to one of Coleridge's masters, Plotinus. It might claim still another ancestor in the person of St. Augustine who wrote:

> Any beautiful object whatsoever is more worthy of praise in its totality as a whole than in any one of its parts. So great is the power of integrity and unity that what pleases as a part pleases much more in a unified whole.—*Contra Manichaeos*, I, xxi [2]

SUPPLEMENT

> We, too, had known golden hours
> When body and soul were in tune. . . .
> And would in the old grand manner
> Have sung from a resonant heart.
> But, pawed-at and gossipped-over
> By the promiscuous crowd,
> Concocted by editors
> Into spells to befuddle the crowd,
> All words like peace and love,
> All sane affirmative speech,
> Had been soiled, profaned, debased
> To a horrid mechanical screech:

[1] Cf. *ante* Chapter 7, p. 118.
[2] Cf. *ante* Chapter 7, p. 123.

> No civil style survived
> That pandaemonium
> But the wry, the sotto-voce,
> Ironic and monochrome:
> And where should we find shelter
> For joy or mere content
> When little was left standing
> But the suburb of dissent.

—"To Reinhold and Ursula Niebuhr," from *Nones* by W. H. Auden, copyright 1951 by W. H. Auden. Reprinted by permission of Random House, Inc.

In the celebrated description of cold weather in the beginning of *The Eve of St. Agnes* [ll. 14–16], the poet intensifies the cold with the added suggestion of silence and immobility. It is not a blustery north-wind that he has described, but the penetrating cold of a still, dead air. In the second stanza of the poem, Keats makes use of three puns, which, *though often unnoticed*, assist in the poetic fusion of ideas.

In the first stanza he begins with the outside world. The sheep are silent; and when the hare moves, it is in a limp, a cataleptic movement from one rigid posture to another. The poet then moves inside to the monk, in the attitude of prayer, or moving down the chapel aisle with the slow shuffle of age, a muffled noise which in the deserted chapel accentuates the stillness and the cold.

Following the first quatrain of the second stanza, however, Keats moves away from all forms of life to the complete immobility of art, "the foster child of silence and slow time." Each of three successive lines contains a pun, but so fused in the imagination are the various suggestions of the three words that *the reader is unaware of the poetic alchemy*. The most obvious perhaps is "freeze" in line 14, which, while establishing the relationship of coldness with the stone figures, at the same time reemphasizes the immobility and imprisonment of the "sculptured dead" by fixing them in a frieze along the chapel walls.

In line 15, in "rails," Keats undoubtedly has in mind a word derived from OE *hrægl*, "garment, dress, cloak," which according to the NED was *last used in this sense in the thirteenth century* in "The Owl and the Nightingale." The more obvious meaning of "rails" as bars strengthens the word "emprison'd" and indeed has a suggestion of coldness; but "purgatorial rails," or the bars which enclose purgatory, a place of punishment and unrest, suggest just the opposite of coldness and immobility, with which Keats is primarily concerned here. The other meaning of "rail" as a garment or a cloak has a subtle influence on the word "purgatory," quieting any suggestion of restlessness and torment, and presenting merely a picture of death and grave clothes.

In line 16, the word "orat'ries" likewise carries a double meaning. In such a poem so particularly concerned with the terminology as well as the atmosphere of the mediaeval church, "orat'ries" suggests other places of devotion, like the cold, deserted chapel Keats has just described, in which the knights and ladies prayed in a dimmer and more distant time. However, with its qualifying adjective "dumb" the word takes on its more obvious meaning in the secular world. The "orat'ries" are the words that might have been spoken in the articulated prayers of the dead figures, but which, frozen in stone, remain "dumb."

In the last two lines of the stanza, Keats returns to the monk to show the effect of the "sculptured dead" on his thin, meagre life. More than before, his weak spirit fails before the idea of death so subtly suggested in the cold silence of the chapel air. The three puns are not only inoffensive *to the point of being unnoticed:* they amplify beyond analysis the fused idea of stillness and cold culminating in death, which Keats wished to establish in the beginning of the poem, as a counterpoint to the happier idea of mobility and warmth leading to life, which in the climax of the poem is expressed in the consummated love of Madeline and Porphyro.

—Elmo Howell, "Keats' The Eve of St. Agnes, 14–16," *The Explicator,* XIV (February, 1956), No. 5, by permission of the editors. The italics are ours—with no real misgivings about the interpretation of them.

Words can be effective only if they have a definite meaning. And what defines the meaning of a word is its undeniable correspondence with certain things, certain feelings, the fact that it necessarily pledges acts. Now this correspondence ceases to be arbitrary only by virtue of a unanimous agreement, which is to say that it can be brought about only in the midst of a living group or community. A common tradition, law, faith and authority alone are capable of defining the meaning of what we call current words. But all these things have disappeared in our century. Then the words that circulate everywhere lead nowhere. Our language is *out of gear.* The more we speak the less we understand one another. Death alone can put everyone into agreement.

The twentieth century will appear in the future as a kind of verbal nightmare, of delirious cacophony: people spoke more often than they had ever spoken (imagine those radio stations which *can* no longer be silent day or night, where words are delivered at so much per minute, whether or not there are listeners, whether or not there are things to say), a time when words wore out faster than in any century of History, a time of prostitution of language, which was to be the measure of the true, and of which the Gospel says that at its source it is "the life and the light of men!"

Alas, what have we done with language! No longer able even to lie in certain mouths, language has fallen lower than the lie, I mean into insignificance. How the Devil rejoices over the pleasant or excited chatter of the radio-speakers! He, the great confusionist, who likes nothing better than flattering equivocation, the drone of official style, the senile incontinence of after-dinner verbiage. He, the romantic, who, when we are stupefied by speeches, suggests to us that the *inexpressible* is perhaps truer than clear, sharp speech! . . . He knows that . . . by . . . debasing the meaning of words he destroys the very basis of our loyalties. He knows that wherever a spade is called a spade, evil recedes and loses something of its prestige; this is why he has invented the language of diplomats and its insane coyness. He knows that nothing in the world can make us be silent, now that we have the radio, and he takes up his post in all the microphones. He finally organizes that verbal inflation, words no longer being "covered" by acts, which he hopes, not without reason, will complete, more effectively than the worst tyrannies, the utter confusion of our moral sense. . . .

I was about to write that the only remedy would be to combat him with *semantics*, which is the science of meanings, of precise and shaded language, guaranteed by a long tradition and by etymologies. A *Ministry of the Meaning of Words*, endowed with discretionary powers—this is what a Democracy needs—since after all it is a regime entirely founded on words.[3] (This ministry was formerly the Church. An analysis of our vocabularies would show that the little common sense which they preserve comes from biblical and liturgical reminiscences.)

—Denis de Rougemont, *The Devil's Share*, trans. Haakon Chevalier (Pantheon Books, 1944), Chapter 64, "The Meaning of Words," pp. 211–13, by permission of the publishers, Pantheon Books, Inc.

[3] The parliamentary regime, social contracts, laws, public opinion, free press, meetings, conferences. The monarchy was founded on ritual, consecrated formulae, plastic ceremony. Dictatorship is the regime of blows where speech has ceased to be anything but planned and directed lying.

CHAPTER 29

ELIOT AND POUND:
AN IMPERSONAL ART

§ *Eliot's classicism: discriminated from that of Matthew Arnold and Irving Babbitt, its relation to the French symbolists and particularly to Remy de Gourmont—II. T. E. Hulme's classicism: his association of the classic view of man with the religious view, his indifference towards kinds of subject matter, his exaltation of craftsmanship, his stress upon metaphor and on the organic character of the poem—III. Pound's insistence that poetry should possess the virtues of good prose, his interest in the Chinese ideograph as a paradigm of the poetic method, and his stress upon poetry as a kind of "inspired mathematics"—IV. Eliot's doctrine of the impersonality of poetry, his association of the method of the 17th century "metaphysical" poets with that of the 19th century French symbolist poets —Eliot's theory of a "dissociation of sensibility" with its implications for a poetics of tension—V. his doctrine of the objective correlative—the attack upon that doctrine by Eliseo Vivas, and by Yvor Winters—VI. Winters' classicism: his indictment of the "fallacy of imitative form," his insistence upon the need for a rational structure, and his attack upon "qualitative progression" as a method for organizing a poem—VII. Winters' reprehension of irony as reflecting either the poet's carelessness or his irresponsibility: this view of irony contrasted with that held by Eliot and by Warren—VIII. Winters' criticism of modern poetry interpreted as a reassertion of the importance of "plot" and of dramatic organization—the implications of this view: the lyric as drama, metaphor as drama—IX. Eliot's doctrine of the impersonality of poetry reconsidered: the view that the poem has a "life" of its own, as interpreted by Eliot, and by Allen Tate* §

W HEN T. S. ELIOT ANNOUNCED IN 1928 THAT HE WAS A ROYALIST
in politics, an Anglo-Catholic in religion, and a classicist in
literature, the reaction was immediate and noisy. The revelation of his political and religious position elicited most of the cat-calls
and solemn protests, but his profession of classicism drew its share too,
mingled with expressions of honest bewilderment. For Eliot's own poetry
was surely "romantic," was it not? And how could a poet who had
obviously derived so much from the French symbolist poets of the
19th century maintain with a straight face that he honored "classicism"?

The line of descent from the classicism of Matthew Arnold to that
of Eliot is certainly neither an evident nor an unbroken one. Of Arnold,
Eliot has remarked that he "might have become a critic," [1] but had in
fact devoted his energies to "attacking the uncritical." Though Irving
Babbitt had been one of his teachers at Harvard, Eliot felt that Babbitt,
like Arnold, had confused literary criticism with something else. Neither Babbitt nor his fellow neo-Humanist, Paul Elmer More, Eliot had
been forced to conclude, was "primarily interested in art." Primarily
they were moralists, and whereas he acknowledged that it was a
"worthy and serious thing to be" a moralist, Eliot had had to write down
Babbitt and More among his "Imperfect Critics." [2]

Yet Eliot made it plain in his essay entitled "The Perfect Critic"
(1920) that he did not consider that the proper alternative to moraliza-
tion was impressionism. A critic like Arthur Symons, for example, undertook to give us his impressions of the work in hand; but Eliot points
out that it is impossible for the critic to rest there; for "the moment
you try to put the impressions into words, you either begin to analyse
and construct, to 'ériger en lois,' or you begin to create something else." [3]
By taking the second alternative, Symons produced, instead of a work of
criticism, a prose poem about his own responses.

Eliot had borrowed the phrase *"ériger en lois"* [4] from the French
critic, Remy de Gourmont. The sentence from which it is taken serves
as an epigraph for Eliot's whole essay, and strikes its keynote: the true
critic will strive to build his impressions up into laws. His impressions
will be subjective and personal—how could they be otherwise?—but
because he will try to refer them to principles. he will move away from
mere impressionism toward objectivity. Aristotle is for Eliot the classic instance of such critical power, and of "all modern critics," he

[1] "Introduction," *The Sacred Wood* (1920), 2nd ed. (London, 1928), p. xiii,
by permission of the author and of the publishers, Methuen and Co., Ltd.

[2] See "Imperfect Critics" (1920), *The Sacred Wood*, pp. 41–4.

[3] *The Sacred Wood*, p. 5.

[4] *"Ériger en lois 'ses impressions personelles, c'est le grand effort d'un homme
s'il est sincère"* occurs in *Lettres à l'Amazone* (1914).

writes, "perhaps Remy de Gourmont [has] had most of the general intelligence of Aristotle." [5]

Eliot's emphasis upon the "generalizing power" and upon the critic's need to objectify gives the clue to his special kind of classicism. Of that we shall have more to say later in this chapter. But his collocation of the symbolist poet and critic, de Gourmont, with Symons, the author of *The Symbolist Movement in Literature*, is in itself significant. It points to the fact that important "classical" elements were to be found in a movement that it has been fashionable to regard as a "second wave" of Romanticism. Ezra Pound, Eliot's friend and fellow literary revolutionist, said flatly: "De Gourmont prepared our era; behind him there stretches a limitless darkness." Despite the fact that he had his beginning "in the symbolistes," de Gourmont becomes for Pound a restorer of "the light of the XVIIIth century." [6]

II

In THIS general connection one ought to mention another conspicuous champion of the classical virtues, T. E. Hulme, who was a companion of Pound's in London during the years before the first World War, in which Hulme was to die in 1917. When Pound launched "Imagism" in 1912, one of his prime exhibits was a group of five short poems, devised by Hulme to illustrate a point in a literary discussion, and published by Pound half-jokingly as "the complete poetical works of T. E. Hulme." Between Hulme's critical theory and de Gourmont's there are numerous parallels, as René Taupin has shown; [7] and de Gourmont himself has commented upon the Imagist poets with special reference to their debt to the French symbolists:

> The English Imagists obviously proceed from the French Symbolists. One sees that first of all in their horror of the cliché, horror of rhetoric and the grandiose, of every oratorical and facile manner with which the imitators of Victor Hugo have always disgusted us; the precision of the language, the nakedness of vision, the concentration of thought which they love to fuse in a dominant image. [8]

[5] *The Sacred Wood*, p. 13.
[6] "Remy de Gourmont: a Distinction followed by Notes" (1919), *Instigations* (New York, 1920), p. 169.
[7] *L'Influence du Symbolisme Français sur la Poésie Américaine, 1910–1920* (Paris, 1929), pp. 84–5.
[8] *La France*, May 5, 1915; quoted by Taupin, p. 87.

Hulme published very little in his short lifetime. His *Speculations* (the source of all the passages that we shall quote below) did not appear until 1924. Much of his influence upon his contemporaries has therefore to be referred to his lectures and conversations. (He and Eliot, by the way, had no personal contact.) It has been argued that Hulme's actual influence upon his immediate generation was much slighter than our present-day reading of *Speculations* would suggest.[9] Yet the parallels between his position and Eliot's are striking.

Hulme, like Eliot's Harvard teacher, Irving Babbitt, referred romanticism to Jean Jacques Rousseau's notion that "man was by nature good, that it was only bad laws and customs that had suppressed him." In the Romantic view man is "an infinite reservoir of possibilities" and not as in the classical view, a creature "intrinsically limited, but disciplined by order and tradition to something fairly decent." Hulme considered the classical view to be "identical with the normal religious attitude." [1]

The traditionalism of Hulme is thus much more thoroughgoing than that of Babbitt or of Arnold. It goes behind Babbitt's "Humanism" and Arnold's participation in the Victorian Compromise, and thus anticipates almost precisely Eliot's criticism of Babbitt and Arnold. Hulme wanted a return to orthodox doctrine. His concern with religion had nothing to do with recapturing "the sentiment of Fra Angelico."

> What is important, is what nobody seems to realize—the dogmas like that of Original Sin, which are the closest expression of the categories of the religious attitude. That man is in no sense perfect, but a wretched creature, who can yet apprehend perfection. It is not, then, that I put up with the dogma for the sake of the sentiment, but that I may possibly swallow the sentiment for the sake of the dogma.[2]

But the relation of such orthodoxy to Hulme's views about actual works of verbal art might not be hit at first guess by an uninitiated person. Unlike Babbitt and unlike Arnold, Hulme is not marshalling

[9] Ezra Pound, for example, writes: "Without malice toward T. E. H. it now [1938] seems advisable to correct a distortion which can be found even in portly works of reference. The critical LIGHT during the years immediately pre-war in London shone not from Hulme but from Ford (Madox, etc.) in so far as it fell on writing at all. . . . It detracts no jot from the honour due Hulme that he had no monopoly of London literary life and did not crowd out other interests. . . . Hulme's broadside may have come later as a godsend when published. I have no doubt that the bleak and smeary 'Twenties' wretchedly needed his guidance, and the pity is that he wasn't there in person to keep down vermin. . . ." (*The Townsman*, January, 1938). Quoted from *The Poetry of Ezra Pound*, by Hugh Kenner (Norfolk, Conn. 1951), pp. 307–9.

[1] *Speculations* (New York, 1924), pp. 116–17, by permission of the publishers, Harcourt, Brace and Company, Inc.

[2] *Speculations*, p. 71.

ethical or religious views as a frame for a didactic theory of literature. On the contrary the classicism of Hulme is a form of objectivism which insists upon clear distinctions between ethical or religious doctrine and poetic composition. Hulme thought that poetry ought to recognize its limitations. In order to compete with religion poetry has to try to lug in the infinite, and the infinite in poetic form may be somewhat less than satisfactory. We encounter here mainly the *emotions* "that are grouped round the word infinite." We enter the area of "spilt religion," a certain romantic "damp." [3] What Hulme is getting round to saying is that if ethics and religion themselves are firm, art too will enjoy its own kind of "dry hardness" [4]—not as a vehicle for, or simple statement of, ethics or religion, but as a human artifact taking shape in the same universe where ethics and religion are sustaining principles. Certain corollaries of this basic view form a cluster of doctrines which we shall see interacting rather tightly in the logic of the neo-classic criticism.

(1) There is no such thing as a "poetic" subject matter. Hulme wants to knock out both Arnold's high seriousness and the romantic distinction between fancy and imagination. "It doesn't matter an atom," he says, "that the emotion produced is not of dignified vagueness, but on the contrary amusing." [5] The Coleridgean "fixities and definites" are apparently just what the poetic fancy *should* be occupied with. For "the great aim is accurate, precise and definite description." [6] Fancy would be the proper faculty for producing the "cheerful, dry and sophisticated" verse that Hulme predicted was to come.

(2) The business of the poet is not personal expression but craft. Hulme's version of this doctrine is, looking toward the reader, an objection to the "sloppiness" which "doesn't consider that a poem is a poem unless it is moaning or whining about something or other." [7] The proper aim of the poet is to "get the exact curve of what he sees, whether it be an object or an idea in the mind." [8]

(3) Poetry is a matter of images, metaphors. That much is entailed in the advice about accuracy just given. "Visual meanings can only be transferred by the new bowl of metaphor; prose is an old pot that lets them leak out. Images in verse are not mere decoration, but the very essence of an intuitive language." [9] And so we are led to dwell on a distinction between prose and poetry, and, borrowing some logical terms from Henri Bergson, to explain the difference as a difference between the "extensive" and the "intensive." Prose—that is, the mode of intellectual exposition—the use of language properly made by writers of cook

[3] *Speculations*, p. 118.
[4] *Speculations*, p. 126.
[5] *Speculations*, p. 137.
[6] *Speculations*, p. 132.

[7] *Speculations*, p. 126.
[8] *Speculations*, p. 132.
[9] *Speculations*, p. 135.

books and legal constitutions and scientific treatises—deals with "extensive manifolds." Prose makes "diagrams, and diagrams are essentially things whose parts are separate one from another. The intellect always analyses—when there is a synthesis it is baffled." But poetry deals with "intensive" manifolds, and "to deal with the intensive you must use intuition," [1] and hence "images," which "are the very essence of an intuitive language." [9]

(4) Finally, the complexity with which poetry deals is not mechanical but organic. Each "part" of a poem is "modified by the other's presence, and each to a certain extent is the whole." [1] Hulme is bound to remind us here of the German romantics and Coleridge rather than of any classical or neo-classical source. His central essay, "Romanticism and Classicism," indeed makes extensive reference to Coleridge. Still Hulme does emphasize the art object more cleanly than Coleridge. And as we have seen he has a positive distaste for that expansive "genius," or mind producing the art object, which was Coleridge's chief distraction. Hulme is guilty of a good many references to the poet's sincerity and to the zest which goes into his poetic activity—yet in the end he seems to refer these experiences to the actual poem and to want to find their validation there if anywhere. He is giving us on the whole the classical and objective version of organicity, which to be sure is what appears in the Schlegels and other German "romantics," if not in Coleridge.

III

HULME'S training as a student of philosophy enabled him to provide a rather systematic account of the new classic reaction. By contrast, Ezra Pound's most vigorous and most influential criticism is *ad hoc* and occasional. It has often taken the form of practical advice to other writers. Pound has not aspired to system-building; he has rather been concerned to "discover" a new author; to help him find his appropriate idiom; to preside over the formation of taste (one of his books bears the characteristic title, *The ABC of Reading*); to assist in the final revision of particular poems. (The most celebrated of these was Eliot's *The Waste Land*, which is dedicated to Pound as *Il Miglior Fabbro*.)

Pound's special critical emphasis reveals itself in a letter that he wrote in 1915 to Harriet Monroe: "Poetry," he says, "must be *as well written as prose*," a sentiment to be echoed by Eliot in his Introduction to Samuel Johnson's *The Vanity of Human Wishes*. In the same letter Pound went on to specify the "prose" virtues that he had in mind:

[9] *Speculations*, p. 135.
[1] *Speculations*, p. 139.

There must be no book words, no periphrases, no inversions. It must be as simple as De Maupassant's best prose, and as hard as Stendhal's. . . . Rhythm MUST have meaning. It can't be merely a careless dash off, with no grip and no real hold to the words and sense. . . .

There must be no clichés, set phrases, stereotyped journalese. The only escape from such is by precision, a result of concentrated attention to what [one] is writing. . . . Objectivity and again objectivity, and expression: no hindside-beforeness, no straddled adjectives (as "addled mosses dank"), no Tennysonianness of speech; nothing—nothing that you couldn't, in some circumstance, in the stress of some emotion, actually say." [2]

For Pound, content and expression are coterminous. In a good poem, where every word performs its function, there is no room for an idle ornament or a vague expression or a mechanical and irrelevant rhythm. Form is expressive of meaning: ideally, form *is* meaning.[3] "Great literature," Pound writes, "is simply language charged with meaning to the utmost possible degree." [4]

Pound's ideal poetry has the "simplicity" (the economy) of good prose; and it has the "hardness" of good prose—as opposed to the vague and imprecise feeling that he like Hulme associated with "romantic" poetry. But poetry has in addition its own characteristic devices for rendering its meanings. Principal among them is something which Pound connects with the method of the Chinese ideogram.[5]

Pound was fascinated with the concrete particularity apparently enjoined by the Chinese written character. In reading Chinese, it seemed to him that one was not attending to a mere "juggling [of] mental counters," but was "watching *things* work out their fate." How did the Chinese write "Man sees horse"?

. . . the Chinese method follows natural suggestion. First stands the man on his two legs. Second, his eye moves through space: a bold figure represented by running legs under an eye, a modified picture of an eye, a modified picture of running legs but unforgettable once you have seen it. Third stands the horse on his four legs.[6]

[2] *Letters of Ezra Pound*, ed. D. D. Paige (New York, 1950), pp. 48–9, by permission of the publishers, Harcourt, Brace and Company, Inc. Compare Coleridge's amusingly similar remarks in his *Biographia Literaria*, Chapters I and XVIII.
[3] Cf. Croce's position, *ante* Chapter 23.
[4] "How to Read" (1929), *Polite Essays* (Norfolk, Conn., 1939), p. 167.
[5] By 1913 Pound had encountered the writings of Ernest Fenollosa and in 1919 edited Fenollosa's "The Chinese Written Character as a Medium for Poetry." This work was reprinted in *Instigations* (New York, 1920).
[6] *Instigations*, p. 363.

Whether in any workable language the discrete elements could retain so much of their original integrity may perhaps be questioned. A comparison with English (which is a manifold of dead metaphors that resist all but the most unremitting attempts to resuscitate them) will be hardly reassuring. But in any case the Chinese ideogram provided Pound with a screen upon which to make a vivid projection of his ideal for a poetic language.

In such a language, the grip upon concrete particulars remains firm. The language resists a tendency (to which Pound believes the modern Western reader is particularly prone) either to slip into woolly abstractions or to take abstractions to be themselves *things*. The ideographic method of juxtaposing picturable elements not only seemed to inhibit shallow and oversimple abstractions: it allowed a skilful artist to define with subtlety and precision what he wanted to say: not this, and not that, but precisely *this*.

Pound's ideographic method is, of course, metaphoric in essence and Pound acknowledges as much: "[The ideographic] process is metaphor, the use of material images to suggest immaterial relations." [7] But it is not hard to see why Pound would welcome a new term, one which would avoid the notions of refinement and decoration that adhere to the term *metaphor*, and which would allow him to stress function and structure. The ideograph is an arrangement of concrete particulars; there is a confrontation of these, yielding not a denatured abstraction, but a precise concrete experience. In constructing his ideograph, the poet is as "impersonal" as the scientist. "Poetry," Pound wrote in 1910, "is a sort of inspired mathematics, which gives us equations, not for abstract figures, triangles, spheres, and the like, but equations for the human emotions." [8]

IV

It was Eliot, however, who brought this matter of impersonality squarely to the attention of his generation. In "Tradition and the Individual Talent" (1919), Eliot stated the position with almost shocking emphasis:

> the poet has, not a "personality" to express, but a particular medium, which is only a medium and not a personality, in which impressions and experiences combine in peculiar and unexpected ways. Impressions and experiences which are important for the man may take no place in the poetry, and those which

[7] *Instigations*, p. 376.
[8] *The Spirit of Romance* (London, 1910), p. 5.

become important in the poetry may play quite a negligible part in the man, the personality.[9]

Such an "impersonal" conception of art is almost belligerently "anti-romantic." It focuses attention, "not upon the poet but upon the poetry." It thus emphasizes the art object as such. It represents a return to something like Aristotelian theory. Hardly since the 17th century had a critic writing in English so resolutely transposed poetic theory from the axis of pleasure versus pain to that of unity versus multiplicity.[1]

The relations among the parts that make up the art work become the important matter for critical investigation. That relationship is conceived to be complex. Eliot even suggests that the work of art is to be regarded as an organism, alive with a life of its own. Thus, in the Introduction to the 1928 edition of *The Sacred Wood*, he writes:

> We can only say that a poem, in some sense, has its own life; that its parts form something quite different from a body of neatly ordered biographical data; that the feeling, or emotion, or vision, resulting from the poem is something different from the feeling or emotion or vision in the mind of the poet.[2]

Such an emphasis was bound to bring down upon Eliot the charge that he had reduced the poet to an automaton who secreted his poem in some unconscious and brainless way, and that he had thus committed himself to the most "romantic" theory possible. We shall notice some of these attacks upon Eliot's theory of art a little later in this chapter. But for the moment we are concerned to round out a little further Eliot's "classicism," particularly in its more general aspects. For Eliot, as for Pound, the essence of poetry is metaphor; but the special insights that he brings to metaphor come, not from Chinese picture writing, but from the French symbolist poets of the 19th century and from the English "metaphysical" poets of the 17th.

Eliot refused to be upset by the notorious "conceits" of a Donne or a Herbert; their admitted failures did not impugn their successes. As for Dr. Johnson's criticism that these poets "yoked by violence together" the "most heterogeneous ideas," Eliot remarked that "a degree of heterogeneity of material compelled into unity by the operation of the poet's mind is omnipresent in poetry."[3] He accepted the

[9] *Selected Essays, 1917–1932* (New York, 1932), p. 8. Cf. also from the same essay (p. 11) "The emotion of art is impersonal. And the poet cannot reach this impersonality without surrendering himself wholly to the work to be done," and (p. 10) "Poetry is not a turning loose of emotion, but an escape from emotion; it is not the expression of personality, but an escape from personality." René Taupin has pointed out (pp. 212–15) the derivation of these notions from Remy de Gourmont's *Problème du Style*.

[1] Cf. *ante* Chapter 7, p. 134.

[2] *The Sacred Wood* (1928), p. x.

[3] "The Metaphysical Poets," *Selected Essays*, p. 243.

incongruity of the elements as inevitable: the perennial problem of the poet was to unite what resists unification; the skilful poet was the poet who could turn to positive account the very resistances set up by his materials.

Eliot found in the bold and often strenuous figurative language of the metaphysical poets the necessary means for achieving "a direct sensuous apprehension of thought, or a recreation of thought into feeling." [4] He saw that the problem of "acceptable" metaphor was continuous with the general problem of poetic unity. Thus he writes:

> A thought to Donne was an experience; it modified his sensibility. When a poet's mind is perfectly equipped for its work, it is constantly amalgamating disparate experience; the ordinary man's experience is chaotic, irregular, fragmentary. The latter falls in love, or reads Spinoza, and these two experiences have nothing to do with each other, or with the noise of the typewriter or the smell of cooking; in the mind of the poet these experiences are always forming new wholes. [5]

This power to "amalgamate disparate experience" was not limited to the metaphysical poets. It was possessed by the great Elizabethan dramatists. Dante possessed it. And coming nearer to our own time, Eliot discerned in some of the French symbolist poets "a method curiously similar to that of the 'metaphysical poets'. . . . Jules Laforgue and Tristan Corbière in many of his poems, are," he declared, "nearer to the 'school of Donne' than any modern English poet." [6]

Any lapse of this power to "amalgamate" results in the separation of thought and feeling, the poetic and the unpoetic, form and content. As applied to figurative language, it has the effect of making metaphor non-structural, a mere echo of the thought (illustration) or emotional excess baggage (ornamentation). A high point of his praise of Andrew Marvell is that Marvell's best verse satisfies "the elucidation of Imagination given by Coleridge: 'This power . . . reveals itself in the balance or reconcilement of opposite or discordant qualities. . . .'" [7] In terms reminiscent of Hulme, Eliot speaks of Marvell's "bright, hard precision," which, as achieved by Marvell, does not render his poetry less but more serious. Marvell's poetry, with its serious wit, challenges Coleridge's distinction between the fancy and the imagination, for many of the devices in Marvell's poetry that Coleridge would have to range under

[4] *Selected Essays*, p. 246.
[5] *Selected Essays*, p. 247.
[6] *Selected Essays*, pp. 248–9.
[7] "Andrew Marvell," *Selected Essays*, p. 258. In the same essay Eliot remarks that "in the verses of Marvell . . . there is the making of the familiar strange, and the strange familiar, which Coleridge attributed to good poetry."

fancy are actually used to achieve effects that show the full power of the imagination.

V

ELIOT's thoughts about an impersonal art arrived at their most celebrated formulation in an essay entitled "Hamlet and his Problems" (1919). Eliot wrote:

> The only way of expressing emotion in the form of art is by finding an "objective correlative"; in other words, a set of objects, a situation, a chain of events which shall be the formula of that *particular* emotion; such that when the external facts, which must terminate in sensory experience, are given, the emotion is immediately evoked.[8]

The phrase "objective correlative" has gained a currency probably far beyond anything that the author could have expected or intended. With the advantage of hindsight, it is easy to see why; the notion of an objective correlative puts the emphasis firmly upon the work itself as a structure. Since the poet cannot transfer his emotions or his idea from his own mind directly to his readers, there must be some kind of mediation —"a set of objects, a situation, a chain of events." It is through these that the transaction between author and reader necessarily takes place. This is where "what the author has to say" is objectified, and it is with the shape and character of this object that the critic is properly concerned. For this object is the primary source of, and warrant for, the reader's response, whatever that may be; and it is also the primary basis for whatever inferences we may draw about what it is that the "author wanted to say."

Yet the doctrine of the objective correlative is a kind of summation of what Eliot, along with Hulme and Pound, derived from the theory and practice of the French symbolists. The symbolists had argued that poetry cannot express emotion directly; emotions can only be evoked. And their studies had canvassed the various means by which this can be done. Baudelaire maintained that every color, sound, odor, conceptualized emotion, and every visual image has its correspondence in each of the other fields. Mallarmé, insisting that poetry was made, not of ideas, but of words,[9] devoted himself to exploring the potentialities of words

---

[8] *Selected Essays*, pp. 124–5. This notion is perhaps anticipated by Pound's phrase "equations for the human emotions": cf. *ante* p. 664.

[9] Degas tried to write sonnets and complained to Mallarmé that he was unsuccessful, despite all the ideas he had. "You don't write poems with ideas, my dear Degas," said Mallarmé, "but with words." P. Valéry, 'Poésie et Pensée Abstraite," in *Variété* V (Paris, 1945), p. 141.

conceived as gesture or as modes of emotive suggestion, and treated the interplay of words as a kind of ballet or a kind of "musical" organization. To name an object was to destroy three-quarters of the delight proper to a poetic evocation of it. Pound, in making acknowledgement of "the great gifts of 'symbolisme,' " mentions specifically "the doctrine that one should 'suggest' not 'present.' " [1]

The doctrine of the "objective correlative" places a thoroughly anti-Romantic stress upon craftsmanship; but Eliot, in the way in which he argues it, manages to involve himself in the language of expressionism. This expressionism and the "language of the emotions" have come in for a vigorous overhauling by the philosopher Eliseo Vivas. [2]

Eliot has implied that Shakespeare knew in advance the particular emotion for which *Hamlet* was to be the "correlative," and has implied further that the reader (or auditor) ought to feel this particular emotion too, if the play is to be considered successful. But Vivas contends that in fact the poet only discovers his emotion through trying to formulate it in words. What the poet "really felt could only be expressed precisely in and through the poem, which is to say that he had to discover it through the act of composition." [3] It is impossible that the reader should ever feel the same emotion as the poet did, and there is no reason why he should. A poem expresses *less* than the emotion with which the poet began, but it also expresses much more. It expresses "all that which the poet presents objectively in it for apprehension." [4] Among the elements making up the poem-object,

> there are some that we find easier to denote. . . . through the terms which we use to denote emotions. But I see no reason to assume that all else in the poem is put there merely to arouse an emotion in us or to bring about its objective denotation. Surface, formal, and ideational elements are all in their own right of intrinsic interest. And while the emotion expressed is also of interest, it is not, and it should not be, of chief or exclusive interest to the reader. [5]

Vivas is confident that such objections have "devastating" consequences for Eliot's "critical approach"; and with special regard to the theory about *Hamlet,* that judgment may well be correct. As regards Eliot's general position, however, Vivas' criticism is a pruning operation that lops off excrescences but can hardly affect the main branches of the theory set forth in "Tradition and the Individual Talent." "Poetry is

[1] *Make It New* (New Haven, 1935), p. 187.

[2] "The Objective Correlative of T. S. Eliot," *The American Bookman,* Winter, 1944; reprinted in *Creation and Discovery* (New York: The Noonday Press, 1955). Reprinted by permission of the author.

[3] *Creation and Discovery,* p. 184.   [5] *Creation and Discovery,* p. 188.

[4] *Creation and Discovery,* p. 188.

not a turning loose of emotion. . . . it is not the expression of personality, but an escape from personality."⁶ "Honest criticism and sensitive appreciation are directed not upon the poet but upon the poetry."⁷ Eliot is at times inconsistent, but he seems never to subscribe seriously to the notion that the poet's main job is to hand over to the reader some determinate content, whether an emotion or an idea, or that the poet's effectiveness is to be measured by the success of this transaction. On the contrary, the weight of Eliot's prestige has been thrown behind a quite antithetical conception: an anti-Romantic, "impersonal" art, in which the claims of the art-object, with all their complexity and indeterminacy have first consideration. A less vulnerable statement of the objective correlative might be found in another of Eliot's essays, that "On the Metaphysical Poets": "[The metaphysical poets] were, at best, engaged in the task of trying to find the verbal equivalent for states of mind and feeling."⁸ The phrase "states of mind and feeling" has the merit of minimizing the notion of some pure emotion, personal to the poet, with which the reader is to be directly infected.

VI

OTHER attacks on Eliot, notably those of Ransom and Yvor Winters, have rested upon more fundamental disagreements. Ransom found Eliot's criticism too psychologistic, too much concerned with affective experience and too little cognitive.⁹ Eliot's classicism, in short, was not classical enough. This was in part Winters' criticism; but Winters' classical reaction, which harks back to that of Irving Babbitt, has in it a strong ethical ingredient. Winters castigates romanticism not merely for its murky indefiniteness but for its moral delinquency. Indeed he regards one as an aspect of the other.¹

In the first place, Eliot's acknowledgement that the poem has in some sense a life of its own seems to Winters a concession that goes far toward making the poet merely an automaton.² And this is very bad for poetry.

> The artistic process is one of moral evaluation of human experience, by means of a technique which renders possible an evaluation more precise than any other. The poet tries to understand his experience in rational terms, to state his understanding, and

⁶ *Selected Essays,* p. 10.
⁷ *Selected Essays,* p. 7.
⁸ *Selected Essays,* p. 248.
⁹ Cf. *ante* Chapter 27.
¹ Compare the position of Tolstoy: see *ante* Chapter 21.
² Ransom makes the same point: "This is very nearly a doctrine of poetic automatism" (*The New Criticism,* p. 152).

simultaneously to state, by means of the feelings which we attach to words, the kind and degree of emotion that should
properly be motivated by this understanding.[3]

Since the poet is making an evaluation, he must remain fully in control
of his poem; there must be no French-symbolist nonsense about letting
the reins lie loose upon the horse's neck, allowing him to find his own
way. Eliot trusts Pegasus too far when he writes: "I do not deny that
art may be affirmed to serve ends beyond itself; but art is not required
to be aware of these ends. . . ."[4] The poet must be aware of where he
is going; it is not enough for him merely to try to "find the verbal
equivalent of states of mind and feeling." Those states of mind and feeling
must be judged and evaluated.

Winters charges that Eliot was too often content merely to reflect
the disorder and incoherence of the age. Instead of mastering his experience and judging it, he simply mirrors it. To do this is to fall into
what Winters has called the "fallacy of expressive, or imitative, form;
the procedure in which the form succumbs to the raw material of the
poem."[5] The modern poet would justify the formlessness of his poem
by saying that he is writing about a chaotic and disordered age. But on
the basis of such reasoning as this one could argue that the proper way
to write a poem about madness is to make the poem itself insanely
irrational, and the proper way to write about dulness is for the poet to
make his *Dunciad* as dull and sleep-provoking as possible.

Winters has urged his indictment relentlessly. Eliot's *Waste Land*
betrays in its "limp" rhythms Mr. Eliot's own "spiritual limpness."[6]
Likewise Pound's "Hugh Selwyn Mauberly," St. John Perse's *Anabase*,
and Joyce's *Ulysses*—all are found guilty in some degree or other of the
fallacy of imitative form. Even a poet like Marianne Moore, whom Winters credits with "unshakeable certainty of intention"[7] as distinguished
from the romantic ironist's "moral insecurity," reveals in her poetry some
of the weaknesses of imitative form.

Fortunately, one does not have to endorse Winters' applications of
his principle in order to endorse the principle itself. Winters is clearly
right in pointing out that confusion cannot be rendered by confusion;
the negative, by the presentation of a slice of negation. This insight has
allowed him to put with special cogency several questions having to do
with the structure of poetry: what is the minimum coherence required
of a poem and by what structural methods is that coherence to be attained?

[3] *In Defense of Reason*, p. 464.
[4] "The Function of Criticism," *Selected Essays*, p. 13.
[5] *Primitivism and Decadence* (1937), included in *In Defense of Reason*, p. 41.
[6] *In Defense of Reason*, p. 22.
[7] *In Defense of Reason*, p. 71.

The poem must have a rational structure, for it is the rational structure that controls the emotion. The rational statement made by the poem is the "motive" for the emotion. Winters, to be sure, does not demand that the poem have an *explicitly* logical organization: it is enough that it be "implicitly rational." The test is whether the poem "can be paraphrased in general terms." [8] The last phrase does a great deal to remove the rigor from Winters' prescriptions. If the terms of the paraphrase be general enough, then any poem that "makes sense" can be paraphrased, including many poems to which Winters would deny a rational structure. Ezra Pound, for instance, has denied Winters' charge that he has abandoned "logic in the Cantos." Much depends upon what person is to apply the test of paraphrasability.

The rational statement that the poem makes—however necessary in Winters' scheme—is not the essence of the poem. Winters himself cites a poem in which the rational content as such says quite the reverse of what the poem taken as a whole "says." [9] The "moral attitude" that Winters insists the poem shall present is defined not by the "logical content alone" but by the feeling as well, and "the feeling is quite specific and unparaphrasable." Yet however indirect the influence of rational structure, it has its final importance, and Winters' censure of Eliot boils down to the charge that he gives "primacy . . . to the emotions." [1]

Certain structural methods yield poems that cannot be paraphrased. Many of our modern poets, laying aside such time-honored methods for organizing a poem as Repetition, Logical Method, and Narrative, have used what Winters calls "Pseudo-reference" and "Qualitative Progression." Pseudo-reference pretends to rational coherence (by retaining the "syntactic forms and much of the vocabulary of rational coherence") [2] but it is not really coherent. Qualitative Progression goes further and abandons even the pretence of rational progression. It is an attempt to build poetry out of the "connotative" (i.e., the suggestive) aspects of language alone, and it actually results in merely a blur of "reverie."

In Qualitative Progression, the transition from image to image is governed by mood: the principle of coherence is that of feeling. Qualitative Progression occurs in traditional poetry, to be sure, but only as an ancillary to the basic method of progression, not as the basic method itself. For example, in Shakespeare

> the qualitative progression . . . is peripheral, the central movement of each play being dependent upon . . . the psychology of the hero, or narrative logic, and so firmly dependent that oc-

[8] *In Defense of Reason,* p. 31.
[9] See his discussion of Allen Tate's "The Subway," *In Defense of Reason,* pp. 19–20.
[1] *In Defense of Reason,* p. 469.
[2] *In Defense of Reason,* p. 40.

casional excursions into the rationally irrelevant can be managed with no loss of force, whereas in [Eliot's] *The Waste Land* the qualitative progression is central: it is as if we should have a dislocated series of scenes from *Hamlet* without the prince himself, or with too slight an account of his history for his presence to be helpful. The difference between Mr. Eliot and Mr. Pound is this: that in *The Waste Land,* the prince is briefly introduced in the footnotes, whereas it is to be doubted that Mr. Pound could manage such an introduction were he so inclined.[3]

Beneath Winters' polemics lurks an important distinction that deserves a clear restatement: emotions may be presented in one of two basic ways. The poet can give the reasons for his hero's emotion, "motivating" the emotion by giving us the events which produced it, or the poet can define the emotion through a symbol or a series of analogies. One method, of course, does not exclude the other. Shakespeare can give us the series of dramatic events that prompt Hamlet's puzzled disgust with himself, but he can also, and does, allow Hamlet to find an analogy for his feelings: "O what a rogue and peasant slave am I!" Winters censures the modern poet for relying too exclusively upon the second method: he moves in an aimless and random reverie from image to image with only a kind of stream-of-consciousness connection between the images. The result is vagueness and obscurity. "The great discovery of the French symbolists," remarks the author of a recent book on Pound, "was the irrelevance, and hence the possibility of abolition, of paraphrasable plot." [4] It is just this abolition that Winters censures.

VII

WINTERS has defined a third structural method that he regards as reprehensible. He calls it progression by Double Mood (i.e., by ironic qualification). He regards Lord Byron as the first poet to use this method on a "pretentious scale," but Jules Laforgue and Tristan Corbière yield striking instances of it in modern poetry. In this kind of progression, the poet alternates moods: he "builds up a somewhat grandiloquent effect only to demolish it by ridicule or by ridiculous anticlimax." [5] Such a method is "the formula for adolescent disillusionment: the unhappily 'cynical' reaction to the loss of a feeling not worth having." [6]

The deflation of the positive mood is accomplished by irony—ro-

[3] *In Defense of Reason,* p. 59.
[4] Hugh Kenner, *The Poetry of Ezra Pound,* p. 91.
[5] *In Defense of Reason,* p. 65.
[6] *In Defense of Reason,* p. 67.

mantic irony,[7] Winters calls it, carefully distinguishing it from the classical irony of a Dryden or a Pope, who was "perfectly secure in his own feelings"[8] and whose irony was used to attack someone else.

The romantic ironist is not morally secure and his irony is thus a reflection of his confusion or of his moral flabbiness or of his lack of concern to focus his poem. It amounts to "an admission of careless feeling, which is to say careless writing." Winters therefore recommends "the waste-basket and a new beginning."[9] For the poet cannot legitimately say: my confused and uncertain poem simply reflects the confusion of the situation which happens to be my subject matter. That would be to embrace the fallacy of imitative form.

Winters' bias toward the logical, the definite, and the unequivocal gives him a certain corrective value. He has refused to be imposed upon by misty and vague meanings, and he has been able to put his finger on tendencies toward incoherence that have escaped the notice of many other modern critics. But one may doubt whether Winters leaves sufficient room for what was once attributed to the superventions and ministering grace bestowed by the Muse. Winters assumes that the poet knows (or ought to know) how to "adjust feeling"[1] to the rational structure of his poem, and that his failure to do so is a kind of moral failure. Thus, he places a great burden upon the poet's conscious intention, more perhaps than it can sustain. For as Vivas, for instance, has pointed out (see p. 668 above) the poet often *discovers* what he has to say in the process of saying it. Furthermore, Winters perhaps needs to be reminded of Mallarmé's dry observation that poetry is written not with ideas, but with words. The poet has to take into account not only the complexities of experience but the recalcitrant qualities of language; he must always depend, to some degree, upon implication and indirection.

Eliot's suggestion that a poem "has its own life" acknowledges its resistance to direct control by the poet. So do Eliot's reiterations that all poetry, even a lyric from the Greek anthology, is *dramatic*.[2] There may be some significance in the fact that Winters defines poetry as a *statement*. (He regards it as a statement of a special kind, to be sure, but a statement, nevertheless.) Winters never quite escapes, nor apparently does he wish to escape, the consequences of this term.

A curious passage in *Primitivism and Decadence* illustrates Winters' suspicion of "dramatic" presentation. He quotes with approval a student's

[7] Winters borrows the term from Irving Babbitt (cf. *ante* Chapter 20), whose use of the term was influenced by his unsympathetic response to the German critics' development of irony: cf. *ante* Chapter 17.

[8] *In Defense of Reason*, p. 70.

[9] *In Defense of Reason*, p. 73.

[1] *In Defense of Reason*, p. 367.

[2] "A Dialogue on Dramatic Poetry" (1928), *Selected Essays*, p. 38.

remark that "Laforgue resembles a person who speaks with undue harshness and then apologizes; whereas he should have made the necessary subtractions before speaking." [3] A considered *statement* does indeed require that one make the "subtractions" first, but the mode of *drama* undertakes to give us the very process by which the final attitude is reached: the "subtractions," the conflicts between rival attitudes, the ironic qualifications, the various stages in the dialectic—all of these are of the essence of dramatic presentation. For Winters, however, the issue comes down to this: "the question of how carefully one is willing to scrutinize his feelings and correct them." [4] So it does, and Winters is right in demanding that the poet refrain from "careless feeling, which is to say careless writing." That is to say, the poet should not correct his poem in public as it goes along. For such botching, Winters' recommendation is surely the proper one: "instead of irony as the remedy for the unsatisfactory feelings," the "wastebasket and a new beginning." But it can be argued that irony has other and more respectable functions.

Once the dramatic character of poetry is admitted, we make room for a very different conception of irony. Irony becomes a recognition of the incongruities with which poetry has to deal. It acknowledges the pressure of the total context upon the individual word or image, the slight warping of signification continually made by the poet as he shades the word to its precise meaning in his context. It registers the tensions set up between the disparate elements of the poem which are being compelled into unity. It concedes the element of compulsion.

If one insists in finding in this structural irony an index of the poet's attitude, that attitude is not necessarily one of carelessness or cynicism or moral slovenliness. The irony might rather point to his humility, to his sense of the limitations of the human mind and of the complexity of experience. Such a poet is willing to qualify his more sweeping generalizations and to undercut his more fervent enthusiasms. [5]

Most of what Eliot has had to say on this specific topic occurs in his essay on Marvell under the rubric "wit." Marvell's wit is "a tough rea-

---

[3] *In Defense of Reason*, p. 72.

[4] *In Defense of Reason*, p. 72.

[5] Much turns here upon whether one accepts the view that some measure of indirection is enjoined upon the poet by the very nature of poetry. To the man habituated to the motorboat of logic, the manoeuvers of a sailing vessel forced to tack against the wind will seem wasteful and silly. He may even accuse the skipper of drunkenness or of moral vacillation.

T. E. Hulme definitely found in his "classical" poetry a manifestation of the poet's humility and of his sense of his own limitations. Hulme wrote that even in "the most imaginative flights" of the classical poet, there is "always a holding back, a reservation. The classical poet never forgets this finiteness, this limit of man. . . . If you say an extravagant thing which does exceed the limits inside which you know man to be fastened, yet there is always conveyed in some way at the end an impression of yourself standing outside it, and not believing it, or consciously putting it forward as a flourish" (*Speculations*, pp. 119–20).

sonableness beneath the slight lyric grace"; it "implies a constant inspection and criticism of experience"; [6] it provides for his poetry an
"internal equilibrium." [7] But R. P. Warren will provide a good instance of
the tendency of critics influenced by Eliot to use the term irony itself as
a structural principle. In an essay from which we have already quoted he
tries to answer the argument that poetry ought to be eloquently simple
without ironic tension:

> Poets *have* tried very hard, for thousands of years, to say what
> they mean. But they have not only tried to say what they mean,
> they have tried to prove what they mean. The saint proves his
> vision by stepping cheerfully into the fires. The poet, somewhat
> less spectacularly, proves his vision by submitting it to the fires of
> irony—to the drama of his structure—in the hope that the fires
> will refine it. In other words, the poet wishes to indicate that his
> vision has been earned, that it can survive reference to the com-
> plexities and contradictions of experience. And irony is one such
> device of reference.[8]

VIII

BUT though Winters seems distrustful of "dramatic" presentation, because of its reliance upon implication and the consequent relinquishment
of the poet's control over his "statement," his choice of the term *motive*
("rational statement . . . is . . . motive to emotion") [9] actually points
toward the mode of drama. For if the emotions are "motivated," the
emotion can only be *inferred* from the context of situation and action.
It cannot be stated directly, and the paraphrasable matter that "motivates"
it is not so much a "statement" as a dramatic situation—a narrative, or
a plot.

Indeed it is possible to interpret Winters' criticism as a powerful reassertion of the importance of plot. One might even compare it to Matthew
Arnold's "classical" protest against romantic "confused multitudinous-
ness" and "exuberance of expression." [1] But Eliot's concern with metaphor
and symbol and even with irony represents a like "classical" reaction.
For these, as Eliot treats them, are all aspects of a dramatic presentation
as distinguished from the *personal* expression of the poet. The distinction
is crucial: once we have dissociated the speaker of the lyric from the
personality of the poet, even the tiniest lyric reveals itself as drama. A

---

[6] *Selected Essays*, p. 262.
[7] *Selected Essays*, p. 263.
[8] "Pure and Impure Poetry," Stallman's *Critiques*, p. 103.
[9] *Anatomy of Nonsense*, p. 13.
[1] Cf. *ante* Chapter 20.

poem is not a "statement about" something, but, as Aristotle said of tragedy, an *action*. Even metaphor is an action is this sense. It is a presentation of discrete entities, and the role of interpreting their relationship is forced upon the hearer or the reader. Since the identification asserted by a metaphor is *literal* nonsense, the interpretation, by implication, directs attention to the situation, the character of the speaker, and the occasion.

If the smallest lyric can be regarded as a drama, conversely the most formidable tragedy can be regarded as symbolic. *Macbeth* is perennially interesting to us, not as a historic incident (even if the history in that play were undistorted history), but because Macbeth is universal; he is in some sense ourselves. If his emotions are "motivated" by the events presented in the play, they are also meaningful symbols of our own emotions. Otherwise we should feel that Macbeth's emotional reactions were indeed "unmotivated": he would seem perverse or incomprehensible.

A realization that Winters' conception of poetry, like Eliot's, is ultimately "dramatic" need not impugn the useful distinction between motive (the reason for an emotion) and objective correlative (the symbol of an emotion). (The perception may indicate, however, why it is difficult to maintain the absolute distinction, especially with reflexive and highly allusive poetry.) It suggests further that Winters' "motive" is itself a kind of objective correlative. If the poet is to "control" emotion by providing "motives" for it, he is indeed compelled to make use of "a set of objects, a situation, or a chain of events." These are objective and can be presented; and since the emotion is generated by these objects and actions and, in so far as it is controlled, is controlled by the selection and rearrangement of these objectified elements, they may fairly be called the "correlative" of the emotion. For whether their "relation" to the emotion is that of cause or of symbolic equivalent, their *cor*relation with the emotion is evident.

IX

THE concern for the poem as an objective thing is the special highlight of the classicism of Eliot. We have mentioned Eliot's observation that the poem possesses a life of its own, and his insistence on the poet's need to extinguish his personality in the poem. Though such remarks as these can be interpreted as an abdication of the poet's proper responsibility, they need not be. Indeed, Eliot's metaphor about the poem's "life" and his suggestion that the poet's primary task is to foster and nurture that life are not incorrigibly irrational. It is possible to argue that the poem, like a growing plant, naturally grows toward the light and unless interfered with tends to grow straight.

This notion that the developing poem furnishes the poet with certain norms for its own nurturing (along with the further implication that poetry gives us a special kind of knowledge) has been spelled out by Allen Tate a little more fully than by Eliot. Tate, rejecting Winters' conception of a poem as a *statement* about something, would define it as an action rendered in its totality. This action is not prescriptive of means (as science is) nor of ends (as religion is). The reader is left to draw his own conclusions: (". . . the vision of the whole," as Tate says, "is not susceptible of logical demonstration.") [2] There can be no *external* verification: the reader grasps it by an act of the imagination or not at all. (The didactic poet, the rhetorician in the service of a cause, the advertising man—all do appeal to some "truth"—some authority, scientific or unscientific—as proof of the case being made.)

But though the poem is not a statement that can be proved, Tate will not allow that it is a whimsical, subjective "projection." He reprehends metaphors and similes that are "imposed upon the material from above," for they should "grow out of the material." [3] The implications of the last clause are significant: the poet, it is implied, does not fashion statements to a prearranged formula. He does not impose his formulas upon experience but reveals the patterns inherent in experience.

As an instance of adequate metaphor Tate adduces "Ripeness is all," as spoken by Edgar in *King Lear*. This figure is not imposed upon the experience "as an explanation" of it. Rather

> the figure rises from the depths of Gloucester's situation. . . .
> Possibly *King Lear* would be as good without Edgar's words;
> but it would be difficult to imagine the play without the passage
> ending in those words. They are implicit in the total structure,
> the concrete quality, of the whole experience that we have
> when we read *King Lear*.[4]

One must be careful in assigning very precise meanings to phrases like "grow out of the material" and "implicit in . . . the whole experience," which are themselves figurative. But surely they seem to discountenance the view that the imagination is merely whimsical. They suggest that the imagination obeys laws implicit in the human psyche. They even seem to demand the assumption that all human experience is finally one.

Tate, it is true, never states these assumptions in so many words, and one supposes that he would have to resist the view that this ultimate

[2] "Three Types of Poetry" (1934), *On the Limits of Poetry* (New York, 1948), p. 113.
[3] *On the Limits of Poetry*, p. 92.   [4] *On the Limits of Poetry*, p. 93.

oneness of the human psyche can be formulated in a set of laws which could then be used to determine the goodness or badness of particular poems. But the assumption that man exists and that his fundamental oneness transcends the innumerable differences that set apart individual men and set apart men of various cultures and periods of history seems implicit here. Perhaps it should be brought to light and stated quite flatly. For it may be the necessary assumption if we are to undertake to talk about poetry at all. Unless we can assume it, we necessarily abandon any concept of an aesthetics of poetry in favor of a tabulation of various kinds of social and personal expressions. '

SUPPLEMENT

. . . Among the things that dramatic action must burn up are the author's opinions; while he is writing he has no business to know anything that is not a portion of that action. Do you suppose for one moment that Shakespeare educated Hamlet and King Lear by telling them what he thought and believed? As I see it, Hamlet and Lear educated Shakespeare, and I have no doubt that in the process of that education he found out that he was an altogether different man to what he thought himself, and had altogether different beliefs. A dramatist can help his characters to educate him by thinking and studying everything that gives them the language they are groping for through his hands and eyes, but the control must be theirs, and that is why the ancient philosophers thought a poet or dramatist Daimon-possessed.

—W. B. Yeats to Sean O'Casey, *Letters*, ed. Allan Wade (New York, 1955), p. 741, by permission of the publishers, The Macmillan Company.

. . . even Hulme, who, as an anti-romantic, explicitly leads away from the Coleridgean imagination, must, as I shall show, end by returning to a markedly similar theory of poetic creativity.

Hulme feels that the essence of romanticism is located in its idolatry of the individual who, for the romantics, should have unlimited aspirations since he has unlimited powers. . . . For the classicist, according to Hulme, sees man as an extremely limited being who needs all kinds of severely imposed disciplines if he is to function as he should in his proper sphere. Thus Hulme, defending the view of the classicist, rejects a concept of imagination which would substitute a monism for Christian dualism and would make of man a god. For the attribution to man of the power to create absolutely, *ex nihilo*, could mean little less. Thus Hulme explicitly calls for a poetry of fancy rather than the poetry of unbounded imagination which he feels contaminated English verse in the nineteenth and early twentieth centuries. He calls for a poetry that is formally precise and whose pretensions are limited to simple and vivid description. One might say that he calls for a return to a theory of imitation and opposes the reigning theory of expression, the introduction of which was so largely Coleridge's responsibility.

But there is also a quite different side of Hulme. In his essay on Bergson, in which he expounds sympathetically the aesthetic of his master in philosophy, there is a description of the poet's activity that seems nearly as transcendental as Coleridge's. Here Hulme distinguishes between intuition and stock perception and characterizes artistic creativity as the former. It is only the artist, he claims, who can break through the mere static recognition of the world about us which practical life demands; he alone can see through to the dynamic flux which characterizes essential reality. And as artist he makes this vision available to others who, without the artist, could never see beyond the stereotyped world of practicality.

This conception gives the poet a far higher and more romantic function than Hulme has assigned him in his severe "Romanticism and Classicism.". . . For while Hulme, as influenced by Bergson, still wants the poet to be descriptive, he adds a metaphysical dimension to this objective. He would have the poet describe the world about him not merely as it seems to be but rather as it really is behind the veil which hides it from most of us. The poet must not give us as the world "the film of familiarity and selfish solicitude" (note how apt this Coleridgean phrase is here) which our senses normally allow to us; rather he must give us the rare world beyond, which he somehow intuits. Now this is a handsome objective; and the intuitive faculty which is to fulfill it for Hulme seems not far removed from the imagination invoked by Coleridge. Surely we may doubt the power of fancy to operate at these profound levels.

—Murray Krieger, *The New Apologists for Poetry* (Minneapolis, 1956), pp. 33–4, by permission of the University of Minnesota Press.

At this point I shall venture to generalize, and suggest that with this disappearance of the idea of *Original Sin*, with the disappearance of the idea of intense moral struggle, the human beings presented to us both in poetry and in prose fiction to-day, and more patently among the serious writers than in the underworld of letters, tend to become less and less real. It is in fact in moments of moral and spiritual struggle depending upon spiritual sanctions, rather than in those 'bewildering minutes' in which we are all very much alike, that men and women come nearest to being real. If you do away with this struggle, and maintain that by tolerance, benevolence, inoffensiveness and a redistribution or increase of purchasing power, combined with a devotion, on the part of an elite, to Art, the world will be as good as anyone could require, then you must expect human beings to become more and more vaporous.

—T. S. Eliot, *After Strange Gods* (London, 1934), p. 42

[Melville's] letter to Mrs. Hawthorne acknowledging her symbolic interpretation of *Moby-Dick* is remarkable both for what it says and for what it assumes:

But, then, since you, with your spiritualizing nature, see more things than other people, and by the same process, refine all you see, so that they are not the same things that other people see, but things which while you think you but humbly discover them, you do in fact create them for yourself—therefore, upon the whole, I do not so much marvel at your expressions concern'g Moby Dick. At any rate, your allusion for example to the "Spirit Spout" first showed to me that there was a subtle significance in that thing—but I did not, in that case, *mean* it. I had some vague idea while writing it, that the whole book was susceptible of an allegoric construction, & also that *parts* of it were—but the speciality of many of the particular subordinate allegories, were [*sic*] first revealed to me, after reading Mr. Hawthorne's letter, which, without citing any particular examples, yet intimated the part-&-parcel allegoricalness of the whole.

This is the full-blown doctrine of aesthetic impersonality.

—Charles Feidelson, Jr., *Symbolism and American Literature* (Chicago, 1953), p. 176. Published by the University of Chicago Press, and copyright 1953 by the University of Chicago.

Augustine puts this [argument concerning evil] as succinctly as Pope does: As bad men use to ill purpose the goods of the world, God, who is good, uses bad men to good purpose. The painter knows where to place black in the scheme of his picture, and God knows where to place wicked men in the scheme of his world. (*Sermon* CCCI, 5)

All these abstract pieces of his argument Pope [in the *Essay on Man*] catches up like his predecessors in the metaphor of harmony-from-discord that has influenced Western thinking for more than twenty centuries. It may be that the ultimate appeal of this metaphor has lain in giving imaginative configuration to the average human being's sense that he is, and yet is not, at home in a world he never made. At any rate, it has had the special virtue for theodicy of recognizing the fact of evil while restricting its significance. It enabled one to take account of the observed heterogeneity and conflict of things, but reconcile them; as, for example, in the thought of Heraclitus, its probable inventor, who asserted that the universal discord—"everything happens by strife"—was the ground of the universal union—"as with the bow and the lyre, so with the world: it is the tension of opposing forces that makes the structure one." Thus the image brought together in one perspective man's present suffering and his faith, the partial and the whole views; and in such a way that even its commonest linguistic formulations (*concors discordia rerum*) dramatized the triumph of cosmos over chaos, and its commonest analogies (the world as picture, play, poem, building, etc.) all suggested, like the parent image, that in some higher dialectic than men could grasp the thesis and antithesis of experienced evil would be resolved: "All discord, harmony not understood."

—Maynard Mack, ed. Alexander Pope, *An Essay on Man* (Twickenham Edition, London, 1950), Introduction, pp. xxxiv–xxxv, by permission of Methuen and Co., Ltd.

CHAPTER 30

FICTION AND DRAMA: THE GROSS STRUCTURE

§ *Henry James's concern for the novel as an art form in its own right: his debt to Turgenev and Flaubert—II. the novel conceived as an organic and dramatic structure: the action "rendered" rather than "told"—the problem of the narrator and the point of view—the problem of sequence in time, and of the "time-shift" as theorized by Conrad and Ford Madox Ford—III. the connection between this conception of fiction and the Eliot-Pound conception of poetry: an organic and "impersonal" quality shared by both, with differences only in scope and strategy —IV. the reassertion of the claims of plot as made by some recent critics—Francis Fergusson's denial that drama is "primarily" a composition "in the verbal medium": his definition of "action"—V. his indictment of a "lyric" conception of drama, and his appeal for a return to an Aristotelian theory of "imitation"—Elder Olson's "Aristotelian" poetics of the lyric—Henry James's views on objective values and the organic structure of fiction—VI. Eliot on the relation of poetry and drama—the general problem of the genres—VII. "cold-blooded" critics of poetry and "warm-blooded" critics of fiction* §

THE CONCEPTION OF THE NOVEL AS A SPECIAL ART FORM COMES relatively late. Henry James could complain in 1888 that the English novel "had no air of having a theory, a conviction, a consciousness of itself behind it—of being the expression of an artistic faith, the result of choice and comparison." [1] The French novelist, to be sure,

[1] "The Art of Fiction," in *Partial Portraits* (London and New York, 1888), reprinted in *The Art of Fiction and Other Essays by Henry James*, ed. Morris Roberts (New York, 1948), p. 3.

did regard writing as a craft and applied himself to the novel as an art form. But even in France the consciousness of fiction as a craft was relatively new, and James was separated by only one generation from the men whom he regarded as the first serious theorists of the art of fiction to be found anywhere—Ivan Turgenev and Gustave Flaubert. Guy de Maupassant, another of James's conscious artists, was seven years younger than James himself. As a young man James had talked with all of them, and in 1912 he could regard himself as the "last survivor of those then surrounding Gustave Flaubert." [2]

James was willing to concede that the English novel was not "necessarily the worse for" the fact that it proceeded from no special theorizing. But the English novel was "*naif*"; and James was himself too much the artist to rejoice in the "comfortable, good-humoured feeling" so widely held that "a novel is a novel, as a pudding is a pudding, and that our only business with it could be to swallow it." [3] The novel was or ought to be a work of art, and its special potentialities as a form needed to be explored. Flaubert was, for James, "the novelist's novelist," [4] and Flaubert became, especially for novelists like Joseph Conrad and Ford Madox Ford, who derived their theories from James as well as from the 19th-century French novelists, a fountainhead. James disliked, to be sure, the vision of the world that he found in Flaubert and Balzac and Zola. All three saw life as more dreary, more sordid, more mean and limited than James believed the facts to warrant. But whereas Zola conceived himself to be a kind of scientist and Balzac thought of himself as a historian, Flaubert, for all the solidity of his report of human circumstance, had shown himself to be an artist. At any rate, James believed that he could learn from Flaubert's work the principles of fictional construction.

"A novel," James declared in his essay on "The Art of Fiction," "is in its broadest definition a personal, a direct impression of life." [5] It is not clinical and "scientific," since it depends upon the individual artist's imaginative perception; and it is *direct*—not mediated through formulae or general ideas about life. A novel is also to be conceived as an organic thing—"all one and continuous, like any other organism." [6] How fully

---

[2] *The Letters of Henry James*, ed. Percy Lubbock (New York, 1920), II, 258.

[3] In a letter to Hugh Walpole, dated May 19, 1912, James wrote: "Tolstoi and D[ostoevsky] are fluid pudding, though not tasteless, because the amount of their own minds and souls in solution in the broth gives it savour and flavour, thanks to the strong, rank quality of their genius and their experience. But there are all sorts of things to be said of them, and in particular that we see how great a vice is their lack of composition. . . ." See *The Selected Letters of Henry James*, ed. Leon Edel (New York, 1955), p. 171.

[4] "Gustave Flaubert," *The Art of Fiction*, p. 153. He applied the same epithet to Turgenev.

[5] *The Art of Fiction*, p. 8.

[6] *The Art of Fiction*, p. 13.

organic James found Flaubert's best novels to be is well illustrated from a passage in which he discusses Flaubert's attention to the exact phrase:

> It was truly a wonderful success to be so the devotee of the phrase and yet never its victim. Fine as he inveterately desired it should be he still never lost sight of the question Fine for what? It is always so related and associated, so properly part of something else that is in turn part of something other, part of a reference, a tone, a passage, a page, that the simple may enjoy it for its least bearing and the initiated for its greatest.[7]

James praises Turgenev by saying that his work does away with "the perpetual clumsy assumption that subject and style are—aesthetically speaking or in the living work—different and separable things."[8]

II

A VIEW of art so thoroughly organic as this implies as a corollary an impersonal art; that is, that the work grows in accordance with some inner principle of its own being, and is not merely the creature of the writer's ego, either as an expression of his feelings as a man or as an assertion of his opinions. Ford Madox Ford records a conversation in which James said: "There are things that one wants to write all one's life, but one's artist's conscience prevents one. . . . And then . . . perhaps one allows oneself. . . ."[9] James was speaking of one of his failures, "The Altar of the Dead"; and Ford goes on to comment that the bitter lesson that the artist has to learn is "that he is not a man to be swayed by the hopes, fears, consummations or despairs of a man. He is a sensitized instrument, recording to the measure of the light vouchsafed him what is—what *may* be—the Truth."[1]

For the novelist, the problem of securing impersonality for his art has a special connection with management of the point of view. How does the narrator avoid intruding himself into the work? How, when there is information to be conveyed, can he avoid seeming to lecture his reader? How can he avoid spoiling a powerful scene by seeming to bob up before the reader like a prompt-clerk? These were questions that concerned James. But these also were the questions which Ford, and according to Ford, Joseph Conrad, with whom he collaborated on two or three novels, were to give particular attention.

They wished to make the reader forget the writer altogether so

---

[7] "Gustave Flaubert," *The Art of Fiction*, pp. 143–4.
[8] *The Art of Fiction*, p. 120.
[9] *Thus to Revisit* (London, 1921), p. 49.
[1] *Thus to Revisit*, p. 49.

that the story would seem to tell itself and develop with its own life. The novelist was not to "tell the reader" about what happened but to *render* it as action. Moreover, the action was not to be rendered with photographic fidelity but as it would make its impression upon a human observer. Hence Ford's name for the new art, Impressionism. As Ford put it, "Conrad found salvation not in any machined Form, but in the sheer attempt to produce in words life as it presents itself to the intelligent observer." [2] Or as Conrad himself put it (in his Preface to *The Nigger of the Narcissus*): "before all, to make you see."

The general tendency was back toward drama with the emphasis upon direct presentation rather than the mediation of a special expositor, and with a concomitant reliance upon the reader's power to infer, in Henry James's words, "the unseen from the seen, to trace the implication of things, to judge the whole piece by the pattern." [3]

Percy Lubbock, whose scholarly handbook *The Craft of Fiction* (1929) gives what may be regarded as the standard exposition of the tenets of the Flaubert-James school, distinguishes between panorama (the long-range view of the action) and scene (the close-up view), and describes the design of a novel in terms of the presentation of the action through scenes and panoramas, and the proper disposition of these in relation to each other.

It follows that two matters of special concern for critics of this school were those of the narrator and the point of view from which he "sees" the action. The narrator of the story is frequently a character, whose knowledge is limited to what he himself could have seen and heard, and this narrator may be either a major or a minor character. And even when the narrator is omniscient, possessed of all that the author himself knows about the story, he is scarcely to be thought of as merely the author speaking in his own right. Thus Lubbock interprets the celebrated impersonality of Flaubert's art to mean only "that Flaubert does not announce his opinion in so many words. . . . [The impersonality] of Flaubert and his kind lies only in the greater tact with which they express their feelings—dramatizing them, embodying them in living form, instead of stating them directly." [4]

The question about point of view is, of course, not a new one. In some sense it is as old as literature. Ezra Pound remarks: "I have . . . found also in Homer the imaginary spectator, which in 1918 I still thought was Henry James' particular property." [5] But since Flaubert's time the

<hr />

[2] *Thus to Revisit*, p. 46.

[3] *The Art of Fiction*, p. 11. James is actually referring in this passage to a power of the novelist, but it is a power which in some measure any writer using a dramatic method must also demand of his reader.

[4] *The Craft of Fiction* (London, 1921), pp. 67–8.

[5] *The ABC of Reading* (1934), reprinted by New Directions (Norfolk, Conn., 1951), p. 43.

problem has come in for more conscious examination than perhaps it had ever received before.

The handling of time sequence is another such problem that comes in for special treatment by these theorists of fiction. Again, it is an old problem, and one that has received very sophisticated practical solutions in the past, including devices so different as the folk-balladist's abrupt juxtaposition of little discrete scenes without intermediate narration and the classic epic-writer's beginning *in medias res*. But such theorizing as it has received in the past has had to do principally with the drama, and under the rubric of the unities of time and place. In the modern novel, the problem, for obvious reasons, arises with special force.

The modern fiction writer's concern with time goes further than the making of a series of scenes and deciding the relative emphasis to be placed upon each of them. The novelist has frequently found it desirable to alter the chronological arrangement of events, sometimes describing an earlier event *after* portraying a later event, and he has sometimes attempted to achieve an effect of simultaneity of events. Flaubert, in discussing the famous incident of the *comices agricoles* in his *Madame Bovary*, wrote:

> Everything should sound simultaneously; one should hear the bellowing of the cattle, the whisperings of the lovers and the rhetoric of the officials all at the same time.[6]

But, as Joseph Frank points out in his "Spatial Form in Modern Literature," [7]

> since language proceeds in time, it is impossible to approach this simultaneity of perception except by breaking up temporal sequence. And this is exactly what Flaubert does: he dissolves sequence by cutting back and forth between the various levels of action in a slowly-rising crescendo until—at the climax of the scene—Rodolphe's Chateaubriandesque phrases are read at almost the same moment as the names of prize winners for raising the best pigs.

This device of incongruous juxtaposition became the "Time-shift" developed by Conrad and Ford. Ford likened the effect of simultaneity gained by the time-shift to the effect experienced by a person looking out of a window "through glass so bright that whilst you perceive through it a landscape or a backyard, you are aware that, on its surface it reflects a face of a person behind you." [8] Joyce, of course, exploited the device to the limit in his *Ulysses*. But it is by no means confined to

[6] Cited by Joseph Frank; see footnote 7.
[7] *The Sewanee Review*, LI (Spring, 1943); reprinted in *Critiques*, p. 322.
[8] "On Impressionism," *Poetry and Drama*, I (June, 1914), 174.

modern fiction. Frank finds it throughout modern poetry—in Pound's *Cantos* and in Eliot's *Waste Land,* where the poet makes use of a "deliberate disconnectedness" and "superimposes one time scheme upon another." [9]

III

THAT modern poetry and fiction should make use of similar devices and should exhibit what is essentially the same kind of organization is not surprising. For the theorists of fiction we have been discussing were the associates of Hulme, Pound, and Eliot—and in the instance of Flaubert and James, moreover, they were sources from whom Hulme, Pound, and Eliot derived much of their theory. Like the theorists of poetry discussed in the preceding chapter they too display, in reaction against romantic inspirationalism, a concern for craftsmanship, and a stress upon form as opposed to the exploitation of privileged "poetic" materials. Indeed theirs too might be called an "impersonal" art. Even those aspects of it which might be thought of as exclusively "fictional"—*e.g.,* concern with point of view and with time sequence—are aspects of dramatic presentation—of the process of *rendering* as distinguished from *telling.* The time-shift also, with its potentiality for incongruous juxtapositions, finds its corresponding devices in the ironic confrontations characteristic of the poetry of Pound and Eliot.

There is no need to claim too much here. Fiction is set off sharply enough from lyric poetry to preclude any serious danger of our ever confusing the two. Fiction, for example, has an appetite for richness of circumstance, for sheer concretion, that sets it well apart from any lyric. Even short stories so far tilted over toward the lyric sensibility as James Joyce's "Clay," "Araby" and "The Sisters" do not seriously challenge this statement. Yet the lyric shares with the novel a common fictionality. If "character" and "sequence of action" seem to be especially the problems for the novelist, a little reflection will reveal that they confront the poet too. Eliot's Prufrock is a character, and Pound's "Mauberley" involves the problem of handling a sequence of time. Both Eliot's poem and Pound's differ in scope and scale, of course, from any novel. But like any novel, they too are organic structures, and they are forced to exploit to the limit such resources as a smaller compass affords—and because it is smaller, demands. Yet the general principle governing the relation of individual word to the total work is not changed simply because these are poems and not novels. As one writer on James remarks:

> James's concern for form in the novel "implies an elaborate art, often close to poetry, the aim of which is the maximum of expression." [1]

[9] Stallman, *Critiques,* p. 321.
[1] Morris Roberts, Introduction to *The Art of Fiction,* p. xix.

I V

A CONCERN for "character" and "action" as they occur in poem or novel has not always, of course, been complemented by an adequate concern for craftsmanship. (In *Thus to Revisit,* Ford Madox Ford comments with amusement and sometimes bitterness on the slovenliness of the English novel of the 19th century.) Matthew Arnold [2] was confident that if one chose a "fitting action" and allowed oneself to become "penetrated" with "the feeling of its situations," then "everything else [would] follow." This prescription for composing a work might even be described as an implicitly "organic" theory inasmuch as Arnold's basic assumption seems to be that details of style and structure must be consonant with, being dictated by, the larger governing principle: these details, that is, have no merit in themselves but only in virtue of giving substantial form to the entelechy of the whole. About the soundness of this principle, neither Ford nor James could possibly have quarreled, though they might have wondered that Arnold should so scant the intricate problem of working out the details of style and structure, and though they might have been puzzled as to how one could be sure that one had chosen a "fitting action" until one had "fitted" it to words.

Arnold, as we have seen, was asserting the primacy of subject matter and plot against what he felt to be an overemphasis upon lyric sensibility and a preoccupation with the verbal medium as such. In our own times, the criticism stemming from Hulme and Eliot has provoked similar reactions and counterclaims for the primacy of plot. One of a group of critics writing recently at the University of Chicago notes that "the criticism of the last two centuries . . . has . . . been marked by a subsidiary interest in plot and its needful agents." [3] Plot and character delineation, so the argument of this group runs, have been slighted and neglected; the tendency has been to reduce literature to the verbal element. [4] Such counterclaims typically derive from the Aristotelian *Poetics* with its focus upon drama and its stress upon plot as "the soul of

[2] Cf. *ante* Chapter 20.

[3] Norman Maclean, in *Critics and Criticism, Ancient and Modern,* p. 414.

[4] A similar conflict occurred in the 17th century, with Thomas Rymer as the worthy champion of plot, "the foundation," as he termed it, in dealing with which the English dramatists had been defective. Dryden conceded the point but argued that they had been able to attain the end of tragedy through complementary means, namely, through their excellent treatment of the "superstructure" (characters, thoughts, and words). See Frank L. Huntley, *The Unity of John Dryden's Dramatic Criticism* (Chicago, 1944).

Charles Gildon also disparaged the critic who reaches "no farther than Words and Sentences; dealing in the very Scraps of Poetry; a Couplet, an Expression is the utmost he pretends to. But for a Design, or a complete Poem, to meddle with it, he accounts Pedantry, or Imposition" (*The Complete Art of Poetry,* 1718).

tragedy." Such also is the general derivation of a book from another quarter, Francis Fergusson's *The Idea of a Theater* (1949), which is one of the most engaging of these reassertions of the primacy of plot.

Fergusson does not regard drama as "primarily a composition in the verbal medium." Drama is a mixed art to which the actor and even the stage designer make their contributions. Yet the presence of such elements as these does not constitute the real basis for Fergusson's separation of drama from fiction and poetry. Remembering Aristotle, who, though naming "song" and "spectacle" as parts of tragedy, yet spends very little time in discussing them,[5] Fergusson gives scant attention to acting and stage effects as such. He is in search of something more ultimate; he is looking for "that dramatic art which, in all real plays, underlies these as well as the more highly developed arts of language."[6]

His basic direction is indicated in his assertion that whereas the lyric is a composition in the verbal medium, in drama "the words result . . . from the underlying structure of incident and character."[7] But it is not clear upon what kind of substructure the words of a lyric are supposed to rest. What supports *them* or do they simply float on the air? If the question should turn out to be a bogus question—like the ancient question as to what the earth rested upon, upon the back of an immense tortoise, or upon that of a fabulous elephant—its unintelligibility might call in question the distinction that Fergusson makes between lyric poetry and the drama. To this possibility we shall have to recur.

At any rate, Fergusson's search for a "dramatic art" that underlies all the "arts of language" takes him down to a stratum deeper even than plot, for he insists that plot itself rests upon "action." But action is something that Fergusson acknowledges it is difficult to define, and which cannot be "abstractly defined"[8] at all. It seems to be both inside and outside the drama, and thus Fergusson sometimes seems to be talking about an element within the play; at other times, about something outside the play which is to be located in the historical culture—a myth, for example. In considering a concrete instance, the action in *Oedipus Rex*, he is willing to describe the action as a theme: he calls it a quest—the search for the culprit in order to purify human life. He goes on to say:

> Sophocles must have seen this seeking action as the real life of
> the Oedipus myth. . . . Moreover, he must have seen this par-
> ticular action as a type, or crucial instance, of human life in

[5] "The 'visual aspect of the staging' [*opsis*], despite its emotional appeal, is the least artistic of all the elements and has least to do with the art of poetry. . . . moreover the production of scenic effects lies more in the province of the 'costumer and stage-manager' [*skeuopoios*] than of the poet." *Poetics* VI: *Aristotle*, trans. Philip Wheelwright (New York, 1951), p. 299.

[6] *The Idea of a Theater* (Princeton, 1949), p. 9, by permission of the publishers, Princeton University Press.

[7] *Idea of a Theater*, p. 8.   [8] *Idea of a Theater*, p. 230.

general; and hence he was able to present it in the form of the ancient ritual which also presents and celebrates the perennial mystery of human life and action. Thus by "action" I do not mean the events of the story but the focus or aim of psychic life from which the events, in that situation, result.[9]

The *Oedipus Rex* is regarded as the expression of a total culture. "The perspectives of the myth, the rituals, and of the traditional *hodos*, the way of life of the City—'habits of thought and feeling' which constitute the traditional wisdom of the race—were all required to make this play possible."[1] The myths and rituals which were Sophocles' heritage and the heritage of the audience for which he wrote were "actions" upon which the dramatist could draw. Such resources are not available to the dispossessed and alienated modern artist. He must rely merely on his *art*—an observation which helps explain Fergusson's curious remark that Racine and Wagner were "purer artists than Sophocles, as the best modern critics have taught us to understand that idea."[2] The implication would seem to be that great art is not *merely* art but something else (art plus religion?).

V

FERGUSSON has made it clear that the "best modern critics" have been concerned with subtle verbal analysis, to the *neglect* of "action." Certain passages in his book, however, suggest that those qualities of drama that the lyric does *not* possess are outside the bounds of art altogether or at least are outside those of "pure art." They would seem to be cultural elements shared by the artist with his fellow citizens and thus would be mythic, ritualistic, religious, and even philosophical patterns.

In discussing the "action" upon which great drama has been based, Fergusson shows a great concern for what was *available* to a Sophocles and to the audience that saw his plays. T. S. Eliot, in his *Dialogue on Dramatic Poetry* (1928) had a speaker remark that

> Aristotle did not have to worry about the relation of drama to religion, about the traditional morality of the Hellenes, about the relation of art to politics . . . he did not have to read the (extremely interesting) works of Miss Harrison or Mr. Cornford, or the translations of Professor Murray, or wrinkle his brow over the antics of the Todas and the Veddahs. Nor did he have to reckon with the theatre as a paying proposition.[8]

[9] *Idea of a Theater*, p. 36.
[1] *Idea of a Theater*, p. 22.
[2] *Idea of a Theater*, p. 3.
[8] *Selected Essays*, p. 32.

But these are just the topics about which Fergusson feels that he must worry. The remark of Eliot's speaker, he says, is wistful because "we cannot escape the unanswerable questions which Aristotle did not have to ask. The analysis of the art of drama leads to the idea of a theater which gives it its sanction, and its actual time and place. And when the idea of a theater is inadequate or lacking, we are reduced to speculating about the plight of the whole culture." [4] Precisely. And Fergusson realizes that much of his book is just such a speculation. He is too intelligent to chide the modern author for what he cannot help. The problem is communal, and the artist can fairly be asked nothing more than that he should recognize that he is alienated and rootless and try to set his own lands in order.

Fergusson also would persuade the modern artist to abandon idealistic expressionism in favor of some theory of art based on "imitation." But the modern artist, "after three hundred years of rationalism and idealism, with the traditional modes of behavior lost or discredited," [5] finds it difficult to imitate or even to "see" any action other than that of his own subjectivity. Eliot, for example, approaches the drama from the standpoint of lyric poetry, and thus begins "with the Idealistic conception of art as formally prior to the theater itself." [6] Fergusson, on the other hand, would "extend Aristotle's definition to subsequent forms [of the drama]," for it presupposes an objective world, knowable but outside the mind that knows it. The "lyric" conception is hopelessly idealistic and subjective. Fergusson admits that

> The phrase "objective equivalent" [for the poet's feeling] seems to support Eliot's announced classicism. Yet it refers, not to the vision of the poet, but to the poem he is making; and it implies that it is only a *feeling* that the poet has to convey. . . . The emphasis on the poem and its form, to the exclusion of what it represents, recognizes only one of the instincts which Aristotle thought were the roots of poetry in general, the "instinct for harmony and rhythm." [7]

In brief, Fergusson, sensing the tendency of theories of symbolic form to become monistic, urges the counterview that the poet's vision must be objective. Sophocles, he says, "must have believed in the objective reality of the human situation which the tragic theater enabled him to mirror and celebrate." [8] Sophocles was not merely expressing himself but imitating something outside himself.

The question as to whether Eliot's objective correlative is merely

---

[4] *Idea of a Theater*, p. 226.
[5] *Idea of a Theater*, p. 239.
[6] *Idea of a Theater*, p. 8.

[7] *Idea of a Theater*, p. 240.
[8] *Idea of a Theater*, p. 236.

expressionistic has come in for some attention in Chapter 29 (*ante*, p. 668). But in any case, one may wonder whether the only way to avoid the extreme of subjective expressionism is to adopt a theory of "imitation." Fergusson is properly cautious in his speculations as to Sophocles' actual beliefs, and he has to admit that Euripides, though inheriting the "theater of Sophocles," did not believe in the Greek myths at all.[9]

One may come at the matter from the other direction. Fergusson's account of the "action" suggests that it is not an element peculiar to drama but is to be found in all literature, including lyric poetry. For he says action is "the focus or aim of psychic life from which the events . . . result." But every piece of literature is about psychic life in some sense, and the briefest lyric, if it is really a poem and not an aimless farrago, has a focus or an aim. Moreover, though one does not mean to collapse the useful distinction between the song and the drama, the analogies are there. The most fragile lyric has at least one character, that of the implied speaker himself, and it has a "plot"—an arrangement of psychic incidents, with a development, at least of mood.

What Fergusson and Eliot hold in common is the belief that the work of art is an organic whole, and this view of the art work is in some sense more important than the decision to fix our criticism upon the diction or upon the action—upon the "actualization" of the work or upon the "soul" of the work. In an organic work, one implies the other, and we can work from "inner" soul to "outer" manifestation, or *vice versa*. For if the work be truly organic, then each element of structure is a necessary or probable consequence of the larger principle of the whole. But if we do work backwards from the words to the characters who speak them and from the characters on back to the plot in which the characters are involved, small wonder that the final and fundamental governing principle, Fergusson's "action," should prove so difficult to define. Indeed, our only clues to it are its "actualizations," that is, the text of the play itself. If "action" is held to be the most important thing in the work, it yet remains an inference, a hypothesis constructed by the reader. The "action" resembles the Aristotelian *substance*, which is known only through the *accidents* that inhere in it. The *raison d'être* of Fergusson's action would seem to be to provide a ground in which

---

[9] Fergusson thinks that "Sophocles might well have taken myth and ritual as literally 'fictions,' yet still have accepted their deeper meanings—trope, allegory, and anagoge—as valid" (p. 35). This guess may well be correct, but if so, one wonders what to make of the difference between the ancient poet, buoyed up by myth and ritual, and the alienated modern who, "with the traditional modes of behavior lost or discredited," is unable to "see" any action but his own, and is thus unable to "imitate" it. Even William Butler Yeats, it can be claimed, accepted "the deeper meanings" of his *Vision*—"trope, allegory, and anagoge" as "valid." One could claim at least as much, presumably much more, for the symbols of T. S. Eliot's later poetry.

the "accidents" of the play (speeches, characters, gestures) may subsist.

Elder Olson has shown how arbitrary the use of terms taken from an imitative theory of art can be. The occasion is his adjustment of the Aristotelian terms to a poetics of the lyric. Olson arrives at his poetics by remodeling, or perhaps it would be more accurate to say, truncating, the Aristotelian poetics of tragedy. Whereas Aristotle found six parts in a tragedy, Olson requires four in order to deal with the lyric—or rather, to observe his own precision, "that species [of lyric] to which Yeats's *Sailing to Byzantium* belongs." [1] The four necessary parts are choice, character, thought, and diction. "For choice is the activity, and thought and character are the causes of the activity, and diction is the means. The choice, or deliberative activity of choosing, is the principal part for reasons analogous to those which make plot the principal part of tragedy. Next in importance comes character; next thought; and last, diction."

Yet one might argue for "plot" as a fifth necessary part—or at least as a substitute for "choice." Yeats's poem actually has a plot. The speaker in this poem pictures himself as having made the voyage to Byzantium and in excited reverie imagines his visit to St. Sophia and his vision of the holy sages and the prayer that he will utter to them. Conversely, one could argue that the four parts might be reduced to three: *e.g.*, that the term *thought* might be omitted altogether, since there can be neither character nor choice without thought. To conclude, the "four parts" would seem to be more or less convenient terms under which to discuss the poem—not the inevitable and necessary elements of the poem.

The doctrine of imitation has great virtues of its own, and it avoids a difficulty into which expressionist doctrines so easily slip: that of turning the whole work into the subjective fantasies issuing out of the poet's private consciousness. But the doctrine of imitation has its own difficulties. Aristotle himself did not make the artist's "imitation" a literal mirroring. It is in some sense a transformation as well. Fergusson's "action" seems to be at once inside and outside the work of art: sometimes it seems to be the primal structural principle of the drama but, at other times, it is an "aim of psychic life" with mythic antecedents.

Henry James, who was a good enough "Aristotelian" to believe that in his novels he was giving a picture of a real and objective and external world and to declare that "the soul of a novel is its action," faced this problem in his "Art of Fiction." His common sense is refreshing. He writes:

> I cannot see what is meant by talking as if there were a part of a novel which is the story and part of it which for mystical reasons is not. . . . "The story," if it represents anything, repre-

[1] *Critics and Criticism*, p. 563.

sents the subject, the idea, the *donnée* of the novel; and there is surely no "school" . . . which urges that a novel should be all treatment and no subject. There must assuredly be something to treat; every school is intimately conscious of that. The sense of the story being the idea, the starting-point, of the novel, is the only one that I see in which it can be spoken of as something different from its organic whole; and since in proportion as the work is successful the idea permeates and penetrates it, informs and animates it, so that every word and every punctuation-point contribute directly to the expression, in that proportion do we lose our sense of the story being a blade which may be drawn more or less out of its sheath.[2]

We have cited James and Eliot as champions of an organic theory of literature, and we have drawn the inference that for them and their schools the differences between poetry and fiction and drama tend to become less sharp and less radically deep. Whatever the author may owe to an idea as a "starting-point" or to a story as a "subject," informing idea and actualized story become something else in the work itself: they are no longer separable from the work.

V I

BUT it may be only fair to notice that on occasion Eliot himself can write as if poetry and drama were radically different forms. In *Poetry and Drama* he writes:

> I laid down for myself the ascetic rule to avoid poetry which could not stand the test of strict dramatic utility: with such success, indeed, that it is perhaps an open question whether there is any poetry in the play at all.
>
> . . . the self-education of a poet trying to write for the theatre seems to require a long period of disciplining his poetry, and putting it, so to speak, on a very thin diet. . . .[3]

But the stylistic problem described in these passages is precisely that described by Ford Madox Ford in his account of the wrestle with style that went on in his collaborations with Conrad.

[2] *The Art of Fiction*, pp. 17–18.

[3] *Poetry and Drama* (Cambridge, Mass., 1951), pp. 39–40, by permission of the publishers, Harvard University Press. In a recently reported interview, Eliot seems to make a distinction between "pure, unapplied" poetry and dramatic poetry as "applied" poetry. Perhaps we may wonder how much we are allowed to press distinctions made in apparently informal conversation. See *The New York Times Book Review*, November 29, 1953.

The trouble . . . with us was this: we could not get our own prose keyed down enough. . . .

Our most constant preoccupation, then, was to avoid words that stuck out of sentences either by their brilliant unusualness or their "amazing aptness." For either sort of word arrests the attention of a reader, and thus "hangs up" both the meaning and the cadence of a phrase.[4]

Even in *Poetry and Drama* Eliot makes it plain that drama in verse is the ideal. Prose dramatists, even the great prose dramatists, have been "hampered in expression by writing in prose." There is a "peculiar range of sensibility" that lies beyond prose but which "can be expressed by dramatic poetry, at its moments of greatest intensity."[5] If we put this late essay beside the earlier "Dialogue on Dramatic Poetry" (1928) we get some such conception as this: poetry is essentially dramatic and the greatest poetry always moves toward drama; drama is essentially poetic and the greatest drama always moves toward poetry.[6]

The moral would seem to be that anyone, including Mr. Eliot, speaking in a special and limited context, is likely to talk as if poetry and drama were two very different things. For here we come up against the ancient and vexing problem of genres. A recent discussion of genre theory[7] indicates how confused and confusing some of these problems are. The notion of genres, as Austin Warren points out, furnishes a principle of order. If, to borrow his phrase, we reduce lyric, epic, and drama to "a common literariness," how shall we distinguish a play from a story? Such reductions are in the interest of nobody. Yet it is proper to glance at the other extreme: if we multiply the genres indefinitely, we shall ultimately have to recognize a special genre for each art work,[8] and if we make the larger genres watertight compartments, we shall end up with at least three separate "literatures," not one.

[4] *Thus to Revisit*, pp. 52–3.
[5] *Poetry and Drama*, p. 43.
[6] "C: Do you mean that Shakespeare is a greater dramatist than Ibsen, not by being a greater dramatist, but by being a greater poet? B: That is precisely what I mean. For, on the other hand, what great poetry is not dramatic? Even the minor writers of the Greek Anthology, even Martial, are dramatic. . . . E: [Archer] was wrong, as you said, in thinking that drama and poetry are two different things." *Selected Essays*, pp. 38–9.
[7] By Austin Warren, in Wellek and Warren's *Theory of Literature* (New York, 1949). See pp. 235–47.
[8] A possibility less remote than one might think. Elder Olson writes that "the beauty of a tragedy is not the same as the beauty of a lyric, any more than the distinctive beauty of a horse is the same as that of a man," but then the beauty of a lyric of "the species to which Yeats's 'Sailing to Byzantium' belongs" is evidently not that of a poem belonging to another subspecies of the lyric. Would Yeats's "Among School Children" require the postulation of another subspecies? And his Crazy Jane poems, still another? See *Critics and Criticism, Ancient and Modern*, p. 563.

VII

CERTAIN academic critics, however, are not alone in their objection to a criticism that seems to deal "only with words" rather than with "character" and "plot." The more frequent objections come from those who care little for the niceties of genre theory and want only to distinguish "mere words" from "life." They often write as if words were a necessary evil—pale limp things, interposing themselves between the reader and the compelling stuff of experience offered him by the author.

Such objectors are by no means always literary journalists. At their best, one may say that these critics take the necessary mediation of words for granted and want to get on to the qualities in the author—his breadth of view, his compassion, his knowledge of the human heart—, or to an exposition of his views—his political sagacity, the relevance of what he says to the cultural situation, and the like.

At their most careless or most trivial, they express the typical Anglo-Saxon distrust of words. *Art* for them means the "artful" and probably also the "artificial." They frequently write as if the author could lay upon the page warm, quivering chunks of life, if he were only gifted enough, and if he only chose to. They are suspicious of any attempt to talk about words and their interaction.

The editor of *The Kenyon Review* has taken cognizance of the contemporary situation in the following terms:

> So in an age of unusual critical achievement we have managed to arrive rather quickly at an excruciating impasse: with cold-blooded critics of poetry working away at what sometimes appear to be the merest exercises with words; and warm-blooded critics of the critics of poetry [he has already said that these are likely to be "critics of fiction"] reproaching their exercises, and perhaps about to reproach their poetry too.
>
> How confidently, twenty years or so past, were some of us offering a new "understanding of poetry"! I will not say, How brashly; for the innovation was real, it was momentous; but it was not complete, and now it has bogged down at a most embarrassing point.[9]

The protest of the warm-bloods is scarcely new; something like it, we have noted, was to be heard in early Victorian England. John Henry Newman and his friend John Keble, author of *The Christian Year*, expressed this same sort of distrust of "art," technique, and execution. Like the modern warm-blooded "critics of fiction," Newman and Keble as-

---

[9] John Crowe Ransom, *The Kenyon Review*, XIV (Winter, 1952), p. 159.

sociated the difference between cold calculation and warm spontaneity with the difference between "plotted" narrative and the plotless lyric.[1] But Newman and Keble just reversed the modern correlation: with them "plot" is associated with cold-blood; the lyric utterance is warm and effusive. This reversed alignment of the contrasted elements reinforces the deeper commitment that both Victorian and modern warm-blooded critic share: a distrust of art and technique—whether the concern in question is that of poet or critic. As for the impasse apparently reached by modern criticism, we are disposed to offer a different metaphor, not that the caravan "has [now] bogged down at a most embarrassing point" in new and unexplored country, but rather that the hunt has circled and that some of the hounds are once again baying on the trail of the Longinian fox.

SUPPLEMENT

She was largish and of a French figure, that is with a noticeable waist and a more noticeable rear, and she had heels too high for her balance in a spurting bus. . . . She had much trouble getting the two fares in the box, and considerably more trouble getting herself from the box down the aisle, hauling from seat to seat by their shining handles against the momentum of the bus, lurching, as she had to, in all directions save the right one. During the whole business—and this is what I am getting at—she managed by sniffs and snorts, by smiles, by sticking her tongue out very sharp, by batting her very blue eyes about, and generally by cocking her head this way and that, she managed to express fully, and without a single word either uttered or wanted, the whole mixed, flourishing sense of her disconcertment, her discomfiture, her uncertainty, together with a sense of adventure and of gaiety, all of which she wanted to share with her companion behind me, who took it I was sure, as I did myself, all smiles. . . .

That is an example of the gesture that comes before language; but reflecting upon it, it seems also an example of the gesture which when it goes with language crowns it, and so animates it as to make it independent of speaker or writer; reflecting upon it, it seems that the highest use of language cannot be made without incorporating some such quality of gesture within it. How without it could the novelist make his dialogue ring? how could the poet make his cry lyric, his incongruity comic, or his perspective tragic? The great part of our knowledge of life and of nature—perhaps all our knowledge of their play and interplay—comes to us as gesture, and we are masters of the skill of that knowledge before we can ever make a rhyme or a pun, or even a simple sentence. Nor can we master language purposefully without re-mastering ges-

[1] Cf. *ante* Chapter 20.

ture within it. Gesture, in language, is the outward and dramatic play of inward and imagined meaning. It is that play of meaningfulness among words
which cannot be defined in the formulas in the dictionary, but which is defined in their use together; gesture is that meaningfulness which is moving, in
every sense of that word: what moves the words and what moves us.

—R. P. Blackmur, *Language as Gesture* (New York, 1952) pp. 5–6, by
permission of the publisher, Harcourt, Brace and Company.

But who am I to offer such a diagnosis of fiction's ailment? Four years
of instruction under the greatest faculty in English, philosophy and history
that Harvard, or any other American university ever assembled, must have
taught me nothing, because the constitutionally academic critics dismiss my
kind as mere journalists, just as they dismiss any writing with the juice of life
in it as mere journalism. The best I can wish for some of these gentlemen is
that they might be exposed for a brief period of their careers to the bracing
winds of human sympathy and understanding which blow through every
newspaper office.

One trouble with literary criticism in this country today is that too much
of it has been taken over by a group of impenetrably insulated bookworms.
What they have to say about literature interests neither the intelligent public
nor those writers who are worth their salt. Yet they exercise a corrupting influence because many of them are in a position to foist their ideas upon un-
formed, immature minds.

—J. Donald Adams, *The New York Times Book Review* (September 5,
1954). Reprinted by permission of the author and the publishers.

Also, I would hold that a "dramatistic" placement of the lyric is to be
arrived at "deductively" in this sense: one approaches the lyric from the category of *action*, which Aristotle considers the primary element of the drama.
And then by dialectic coaching one looks for a form that will have as its
primary element the moment of *stasis*, or *rest*. We are admonished, however,
to note that there are two concepts of "rest," often confused because we may
apply the same word to both. There is rest as the sheer cessation of motion
(in the sense that a rolling ball comes to rest); and there is rest as the end of action (end as finish or end as aim), the kind of rest that Aristotle conceived
as the *primum mobile* of the world, the ground of motion and action both.
It is proper for the physical sciences, we would grant, to treat experience non-
dramatically, in terms of motion, but things in the realm of the social or human require treatment in terms of action or drama. Or rather, though things
in the realm of the human *may* be treated in terms of motion, the result will
be statements not about the intrinsic, but about the extrinsic (as per our
remarks on an "incongruous" science of the personality).

A treatment of the lyric in terms of action would not by any means require us merely to look for analogies from the drama. On the contrary, the
state of arrest in which we would situate the essence of the lyric is not analogous to dramatic action at all, but is the dialectical counterpart of action. Con-

sider as an illustration the fourteen Stations of the Cross: The concern with them in the totality of their progression would be dramatic. But the pause at any one of them, and the contemplation and deepening appreciation of its poignancy, in itself, would be lyric.

A typical Wordsworthian sonnet brings out this methodological aspect of the lyric (its special aptitude for conveying a *state* of mind, for erecting a moment into a universe) by selecting such themes as in themselves explicitly refer to the arrest, the pause, the hush. However, this lyric state is to be understood in terms of action, inasmuch as it is to be understood as a state that sums up an action in the form of an attitude.

Thus approached, an attitude is ambiguous in this sense: It may be either an incipient act or the substitute for an act. An attitude of sympathy is incipiently an act, for instance, in that it is the proper emotional preparation for a sympathetic act; or it may be the substitute for an act in that the sympathetic person can let the intent do service for the deed (precisely through doing nothing, one may feel more sympathetic than the person whose mood may be partially distracted by the conditions of action). In either case, an attitude is a state of emotion, or a moment of stasis, in which an act is arrested, summed up, made permanent and total, as with the Grecian Urn which in its summational quality Keats calls a "fair Attitude."

—Kenneth Burke, *A Grammar of Motives* (New York, 1945), pp. 475–6. Reprinted with permission of the publishers, from *A Grammar of Motives* by Kenneth Burke. Copyright, 1945, by Prentice-Hall, Inc.

CHAPTER 31

MYTH AND ARCHETYPE

§ *The increasing modern interest in the symbolization
of primitive man: Vico as a pioneer in this field, and modern contributions from anthropology and psychology—*
Ernst Cassirer's Philosophy of Symbolic Forms: *the origin
of language and the origin of myth, the identification of
subject and object in the symbol—II. Cassirer's view of
what poetry expresses and of its relation to the language of
science—W. M. Urban's* Language and Reality: *metaphysics as a symbolic language mediating among such
other symbolic languages as those of science and art—III.
Mrs. Langer's* Philosophy in a New Key *and her* Feeling
and Form: *the "import" of art as a "pattern of sentience,"
her account of lyrics and of more complicated poems—
the strengths and limitations of the doctrine of symbolic form—IV. the distinction between poetry and myth
as maintained by Cassirer and Langer: the assimilation of
poetry to myth made today by the new "myth" critics—
Northrop Frye and the elevation of literary criticism to a
social science—Richard Chase and the equation of poetry
and myth—Leslie Fiedler and the return to the poet's
biography—V. other applications of myth study to literature: Maud Bodkin and W. H. Auden—VI. Carl Jung's influence upon modern literary criticism: his conception of
"purposive" myths and dreams, his application of a "cognitive" criticism to myths and dreams—VII. Jung's distinction between the dream and the work of art—his
specification of what the psychologist can contribute to
the study of literature—Yeats and the uses of myth* §

ONE CONSEQUENCE OF THE SYMBOLIST DEVELOPMENT IN LITERATURE [1]
has been an increasing respect for the symbolism of primitive
man, and specifically for the myths and legends through which
he characteristically expresses himself. If, as Kant argued, the mind is
no passive mirror, merely giving back the world reflected in it, but is

[1] Cf. *ante* Chapter 26.

rather an active force that affects the very shape of reality as perceived by us, then the symbolizations of primitive man are not necessarily childish and absurd, but have their own interest and perhaps make their own contribution to "truth." As we have seen in an earlier chapter,[2] J. G. Herder, who was a younger contemporary of Kant's, boldly derived language from the mythic process and made the special character of poetry reside in the fact that poetry preserves the dynamic quality of myth. Even earlier in his *Scienza Nuova*, the Neapolitan scholar Giambattista Vico had elaborated the theory that myth was a kind of poetic language, the only language that man was capable of in his primitive stage of development, and yet, for all that, a genuine language with its own principle of structure and its own logic.

Vico conjectured that language first began with gesture, then developed through the stages of myth and figurative language to the clarified and ordered language of modern polite societies. Yet if Vico dignified poetry by regarding it as a form of knowledge—and, for the historian of primitive times, an indispensable mode of knowledge—he regarded it as an inferior knowledge which had been superseded as civilization developed.

Vico had very little influence upon the thinkers of his own day. René Wellek writes that "the attempts to prove his influence in France, England, and Germany during the 18th century, especially in aesthetics, have all failed."[3] In our own time, however, Vico has come to exert a very powerful influence. Our modern studies of primitive man have confirmed some of Vico's insights and have, in any case, compelled recognition of his position as a brilliant pioneer. Even some of his more questionable observations find their parallels in those of present-day critics. If, for example, Vico was unable to distinguish poetry from myth, we find modern critics like Richard Chase insisting that myth is only poetry. It is interesting, however, to note that a modern philosopher like Croce, whom Vico influenced directly, displays very little interest in the sort of anthropological speculation in which Herder indulged in the 18th century and of which today Vico is to be regarded as the great pioneer. In spite of his acknowledged debt to the historical empiricism of Vico, Croce developed a rigorous philosophical idealism.

The philosopher of our day who has pushed furthest the concern for the origin of language and the laws that govern the development of primitive ritual and myth is Ernst Cassirer. His *Philosophy of Symbolic Forms* (1923–29) is Kantian in its general orientation, but Cassirer pays high tribute to Herder, calling him "the Copernicus of history."[4] He quarrels, however, with Herder's attempt to derive language from myth,

---

[2] Cf. *ante* Chapter 17.
[3] *A History of Modern Criticism*, I, 135.
[4] *The Philosophy of Symbolic Forms* (New Haven, 1953), I, 41.

insisting that neither is derivable from the other. We are rather to think of language and myth as "two diverse shoots from the same parent stem,"[5] springing from the same impulse of symbolic formulation. This impulse Cassirer calls "a concentration and heightening of simple sensory experience." Cassirer's association of primordial language with intense emotional experience is a matter of some importance for his conception of poetry. We shall return to it. But first it is important to sum up what Cassirer seems to say about the relation of language to reality.

Some of Cassirer's comments promise a great deal. Symbols, he holds, are shaped by man's needs and purposes. The symbol is not an aspect of reality: it *is* reality. In the symbol there is a thoroughgoing identification between subject and object:

> . . . in place of a more or less adequate "expression," we find a relation of identity, of complete congruence between "image" and "object," between the name and the thing.[6]

Indeed, Cassirer insists that we falsify the issues when we describe the symbol as a "meeting-place" of subject and object, for the very concept of the ego and non-ego belong to what is a relatively "late development" of language. Primitive man, Cassirer conjectures, knew no such duality. The distinction between the apprehending self and the apprehended thing required for its recognition the development of the power of reflection and of logic.

In an earlier chapter[7] we remarked upon Coleridge's yearning for the discovery of a realm in which the distinction between words and things should be abolished. But that realm actually exists, Cassirer declares—it exists in the world of the savage mentality. In the mind of primitive man, the flickering mythic perceptions—the "momentary gods" that are generated out of the savage's more vivid experiences—are, through the medium of words, stabilized and given a relative fixity. The word is no mere surrogate. "Often it is the *name* of the deity," Cassirer has observed, "rather than the god himself, that seems to be the real source of efficacy."[8]

Indeed, for Cassirer a local habitation and a name remains even today of the utmost importance; lacking a name, human experience cannot be "stored and stabilized." Only through the habitation afforded by a name can the psychic energy pass over into something like substance—a deposit of meaning that can be contemplated on later occasions, and linked with and related to other such deposits of meaning. The ability

[5] *Language and Myth*, trans. Susanne Langer (New York, 1946), p. 88, by permission of the publishers, Harper and Brothers.
[6] *Language and Myth*, p. 58.
[7] Cf. *ante* Chapter 26.
[8] *Language and Myth*, p. 48.

to make and use such symbols is what renders man a human being: man is the symbol-making animal—the only such animal.[9]

II

BUT as logic and discursive thought develop, language loses its emotional charge; its quality of concreteness is attenuated; and it approaches the state of the language of science. The process is, on the whole, one of deprivation: language is reduced to "a bare skeleton." There remains one area, however, in which, even for sophisticated modern man, language "recovers the fullness of life." [1] That is the realm of "artistic expression," where the original creative power of language is not only "preserved" but "renewed." Poetry expresses, Cassirer writes,

> neither the mythic word-picture of gods and daemons, nor the logical truth of abstract determinations and relations. . . . The world of poetry stands apart from both, as a world of illusion and fantasy—but it is just in this mode of illusion that the realm of pure feeling can find utterance, and can therewith attain its full and concrete actualization.[2]

Cassirer makes it plain that the "pure" feeling that art expresses is not merely the personal emotions of the poet. The lyric poet, he tells us, is not "just a man who indulges in displays of feeling." This realm of pure feeling has its own claim to objectivity. Since we can know reality only through symbolic forms, art constitutes one of the perspectives by which to view reality. Art is no mere entertainment, no mere diversion, no mere act of play. It is a revelation of a genuine aspect of our life.

> What would we know of the innumerable nuances in the aspect of things were it not for the works of the great painters and sculptors? Poetry is, similarly, the revelation of our personal life. The infinite potentialities of which we had but a dim and obscure presentiment are brought to light by the lyric poet, by the novelist, and by the dramatist. Such art is in no sense mere counterfeit or facsimile, but a genuine manifestation of our inner life.[3]

Cassirer seems to conceive of art as in some sense a counterpoise to science. Art gives us a special knowledge of our "inner" life, as science presumably does of our "outer" life. It restores the dimension of emotion

[9] "Hence, instead of defining man as an *animal rationale*, we should define him as an *animal symbolicum.*" *An Essay on Man* (New Haven, 1944), p. 26.

[1] *Language and Myth*, p. 98.

[2] *Language and Myth*, p. 99.

[3] *Essay on Man*, p. 169.

and emotional response and thus offsets the attenuation and abstraction necessary to science. One wishes that Cassirer were somewhat clearer on this matter of the relation of one kind of language to another, and specifically with reference to the relation of art to science. He has, to be sure, some interesting and suggestive passages in which he says that language "moves in the middle kingdom between the 'indefinite' and the 'infinite,' " [4] and that the effort to realize a truly *pure* treatment of either being or of self would necessarily take us outside the realm of language altogether into "a world of silence." He tells us too that since we can know reality only through symbolic forms, the question of what reality is apart from such forms becomes irrelevant. The basic philosophical question, he says in his *Language and Myth*, has to do with the "mutual limitation and supplementation" [5] of myth, art, religion, and science—that is, with a mediation among the various accounts of reality given by the various kinds of language.

But by making science the "last step in man's mental development," by frankly calling it the "highest and most characteristic attainment of human culture," [6] Cassirer seems to give it a priority over the other kinds of language. Though he defends the objectivity of the other kinds of language, he leaves the suggestion that science, by paring away the personal and emotional elements that are so much a constitutive part of the languages of myth, religion, and art, does actually give us a wider and deeper aspect of reality—that in some sense, in spite of his general argument, science does have some very superior access to reality. On the whole, therefore, one must agree with a recent critic who writes that:

> Although Cassirer represents poetry as the regeneration of the creative power of the word. . . , he is ultimately loyal to reason. Truth is the province of the "conceptual sign," and poetry, however valuable, is "a world of illusion and fantasy." [7]

Wilbur Urban, who shares many of Cassirer's fundamental views, has been careful to repudiate any implication that art and religion use more "primitive" languages than do science and philosophy. In his *Language and Reality* he points out that all three are relevant to man, and to modern man.[8] He is also concerned to present them as not merely meaningful but true. That is, Urban is concerned to relate to one underlying reality what is "said" by all the kinds of languages. Urban's way

---

[4] *Language and Myth*, p. 81.
[5] *Language and Myth*, p. 9.
[6] *Essay on Man*, p. 261.
[7] *Symbolism and American Literature*, p. 55. Cf. René Wellek on this aspect of Cassirer, *Rocky Mountain Review*, IX (Summer, 1945), 195.
[8] *Language and Reality* (New York, 1939), *passim*. On pp. 469–70, he writes that it is a fallacy to view the aesthetic symbol "as a mere stage of, or imperfect substitute for, scientific and philosophical knowledge." Reprinted by permission of the publishers, The Macmillan Co.

of solving Cassirer's problem of "mutual limitation and supplementation" is to set up metaphysics as the special discipline whose function it is to interpret what art, religion, and science have "to say" about reality and to mediate their varying "statements."

In a loyal adherence to the doctrine of symbolic form, Urban has to dismiss any hope that we can discover "hypothetical 'pure experience' . . . by stripping [it of] language." [9] But he thinks that there is an approach to some final truth and reality through understanding the "symbolic forms of language" and through becoming "more conscious of the formative principles embodied in these constructions." Urban's deepest difficulty is to penetrate a "symbolic" language fully while respecting the fact that it *is* symbolic. This difficulty comes out especially in his remarks on the problem of art. Like Croce, he holds that a poem is strictly untranslatable.[1] The artistic symbol is not "merely a surrogate for a concept" but is rather the way in which the ideal content is apprehended and expressed. Yet if one wishes to connect what art has to tell us about reality with what science or with what religion has to tell us about reality, one is apparently compelled to make some kind of translation:

> We are apparently faced with a dilemma. If we are to interpret the "sense" of the symbol we must expand it, and this must be in terms of literal sentences. If, on the other hand, we thus expand it we lose the "sense" or value of the symbol *as symbol.* The solution of this paradox seems to me to lie in an adequate theory of interpretation of the symbol. It does not consist in substituting *literal* for symbol sentences, in other words substituting "blunt" truth for symbolic truth, but rather in deepening and enriching the meaning of the symbol.[2]

The fact that Urban ventures such a solution throws some light on our general problem. The autonomy that is conferred upon poetry by a doctrine of symbolic forms is bought at a high price if it leaves that autonomous realm quite isolated from other autonomous realms such as that of science. Yet Urban's solution poses real difficulties; and Mrs. Susanne K. Langer, another philosopher of symbolic form, has had to reject Urban's attempt to "interpret" artistic symbols as not only unsatisfactory but as quite inconsistent with Urban's general position.

III

Mrs. Langer's view appears first in *Philosophy in a New Key,* 1942. The title suggests something of the excitement with which her book is written. She considers that the concept of symbolic transformation, for which

---

[9] *Language and Reality,* p. 374. [2] *Language and Reality,* pp. 434–5.
[1] *Language and Reality,* p. 490.

she gives special credit to Cassirer, strikes a new key in philosophy, a key into which all the great questions of our age must now be transposed.

The end of a philosophical epoch, she argues, comes "with the exhaustion of its motive concepts." [3] Now once more the springs of "philosophical thought have run dry." [4] In our own otherwise arid landscape, the principle of symbolic transformation represents a fresh fountainhead, a generative force providing us with new motives and problems. Activities of our day apparently so diverse as symbolic logic and Freudian psychology reveal themselves to be in fact related when one reflects that each has discovered in its own way the importance of this power of symbolization.

Like Cassirer, Mrs. Langer regards myth as the "primitive phase of metaphysical thought, the first embodiment of *general ideas*." [5] In due course mythic conception gives way when discursive language has been developed. The civilization then moves into a rationalistic period, though Mrs. Langer concedes that a day may come in which, ideas having been "exploited and exhausted, there will be another vision, a new mythology." [6] But Mrs. Langer, though she seems to connect poetry and the arts generally with mythic thinking, is not willing to concede that art is a mere passing phase in man's mental history. On the contrary, art is a "new symbolic form" which is able to live on "side by side with philosophy and science and all the higher forms of thought." [7] Here, of course, Mrs. Langer follows closely Cassirer's statement that poetry presents us with a "world of illusion" in which "the realm of pure feeling can find utterance." In *Philosophy in a New Key* music was her primary example. Music, she says, is "our myth of the inner life—a young, vital, and meaningful myth, of recent inspiration and still in its 'vegetative' growth." [8] In *Feeling and Form*, 1953, she applies her theory of symbolic transformation in detail to the other arts.

All art has meaning, or more precisely, something called "import." Music, for example, has articulated form; it represents an intuition simple or complex, on the part of the composer. It has

> *import*, and this import is the pattern of sentience—the pattern of life itself, as it is felt and directly known. Let us therefore call the significance of music its "vital import" instead of "meaning," using "vital" not as a vague laudatory term, but as a qualifying adjective restricting the relevance of "import" to the dynamism of subject experience. [9]

[3] *Philosophy in a New Key* (Cambridge, Mass., 1942), p. 9.
[4] *Philosophy in a New Key*, p. 13.   [6] *Philosophy in a New Key*, p. 202.
[5] *Philosophy in a New Key*, p. 201.   [7] *Philosophy in a New Key*, p. 202-3.
[8] *Philosophy in a New Key*, p. 245.
[9] *Feeling and Form* (New York, 1953), pp. 31-2, by permission of the publishers, Charles Scribner's Sons.

A vase, a painting, even an abstract design has its import. We are presented not with actual feeling but with "ideas of feeling" and through art we come to recognize and know the "life of sentience."

Since the life of feeling is a stream of tensions and resolutions, and since all vital tension patterns are organic patterns, any work of art must be essentially organic. But Mrs. Langer warns us not to confuse this illusion of the life of feeling with anything so crude as a direct copying of feelings. Indeed, since the artist does not give us a direct copy, he need not have experienced in actual life the feelings that his work expresses. He may, in articulating the work, even discover new possibilities of feeling. "For, although a work of art reveals the character of subjectivity, it is itself objective; its purpose is to objectify the life of feeling." [1]

Mrs. Langer's position is in general a sensitive and highly sophisticated exposition of the symbolist view of art. Her highest praise of a poem is that it should be "entirely expressive"; and in fact her critical position scarcely allows her to offer more in the way of praise. This fact is clearly revealed in the detailed analyses of poems which she gives us in *Feeling and Form*. She is much more convincing when writing on the short lyrics than on more complicated poems. She is, for example, quite excellent in discussing a relatively simple and lyrical poem like William Blake's "The Echoing Green," which she takes to be a symbol "of life completely lived." "Here," she writes, the artistic form is "completely organic, and therefore able to articulate the great vital rhythms and emotional overtones and undertones." [2]

But her observations on Wordsworth's "Intimations Ode" suggest some of the embarrassments to which she is exposed by a poem of greater complexity. This "philosophical" poem, she points out properly enough, is not really a very formidable piece of philosophizing. The poet could not have "elaborated and defended his position." He evidently did not really believe in the doctrine of Platonic anamnesis to which the poem seems to commit him. The logical structure "of the thought is really very loose." [3] What the poem expresses is

> essentially the experience of having so great an idea [as that of transcendental remembrance], the excitement of it, the awe, the tinge of holiness it bestows on childhood, the explanation of the growing commonplaceness of later life, the resigned acceptance of an insight. [4]

The poem expresses what it feels like to have so great an idea. But what of greatness? If the idea seemed trivial to the reader, would

[1] *Feeling and Form*, p. 374.
[2] *Feeling and Form*, p. 227.
[3] *Feeling and Form*, p. 220.
[4] *Feeling and Form*, p. 219.

that fact not make a real difference? It would have been possible for Mrs. Langer to argue that only two things are required: first, as she has actually argued, that the idea should have appeared great to the poet, and second, as her general theory of art implies, that the poet should have been sufficiently competent as a poet to make the idea seem great to us; that is, Mrs. Langer might have argued that the poet's failure could only be the failure of inexpressiveness.[5] But the circular nature of such an argument scarcely needs pointing out: for the reader to whom the idea has been rendered great, it *is* great—that is, within the relevant frame of reference, the experience of the poem.

Mrs. Langer expresses some dissatisfaction with T. S. Eliot's "purer" poems, and she is rather impatient of some of his literary methods, particularly his use of literary allusions. Her reference to Eliot's "desperate nostalgia for a vanished culture," [6] makes one wonder, however, whether her dissatisfaction has to do merely with literary techniques and not also with Eliot's ideas—which may not seem "true and important" [7] to her even though one assumes they must have seemed so to the poet. Yet one may question whether, in terms of her general theory, she is entitled to say more than that Eliot's poems are sometimes inexpressive. For elsewhere in *Feeling and Form* she makes such remarks as these: "Materials [for a poem] are neither good nor bad, strong nor weak"; [8] "Where a theme comes from makes no difference; what matters is the excitement it begets, the importance it has for the poet"; [9] and "There is nothing the matter with an ardent moral idea in poetry, provided the moral idea is used for poetic purposes." [1]

On the negative side, Mrs. Langer's presentation of the doctrine of symbolic form is admirable. She puts cogently the warning that we must not impose our preconceptions on the poem; nor wrench out of context any "statements" that may be imbedded in the poem; nor demand that it be a political or philosophical document answering to our own political or philosophical notions. But as another "answer to science" the doctrine of symbolic form, even as developed by Mrs. Langer, risks claiming at once too little and too much.

It risks claiming too little in stressing as the essential pattern of poetry the "life of sentience." Mrs. Langer is much more sophisticated than, say, Max Eastman. She carefully distinguishes between the pattern of feelings as articulated in the poem and the poet's own outpouring of emotions; she avoids the notion that the poet is simply projecting a subjective experience. But on close scrutiny there actually may be little to differentiate her account of what poetry expresses from Eastman's. He opines that

[5] *Feeling and Form*, p. 234.
[6] *Feeling and Form*, p. 248.
[7] *Feeling and Form*, p. 219.

[8] *Feeling and Form*, p. 406.
[9] *Feeling and Form*, p. 254.
[1] *Feeling and Form*, p. 5.

George Meredith made poetry of happy passion in "Love in the Valley," and of unhappy pain in "Modern Love," and though he was very intellectual, he had nothing to say to us about either one of them [i.e., those feelings] that we have been able to remember, except that there they were.[2]

At the same time, the doctrine of symbolic form risks claiming too much. Even in Mrs. Langer's treatment, and not merely in the obviously extravagant treatments of an Emerson or a Whitman, there is this risk. If all the cards in the deck are "wild" and can be counted as belonging to whatever suit and constituting whatever value we care to assign them, then the game ends. The possibility of conflict disappears. Perhaps Wordsworth's "great idea," Mrs. Langer has argued, was required only to generate the emotion for Wordsworth's poem, as a grain of sand within the oyster is required to generate a pearl. But the power of the idea to excite the poet's awe is not so easily separated from its ability to elicit the reader's awe: for to assume that the poet could have done quite as well with *any* idea that appealed to him is to conclude that ideas do not matter at all or—what amounts to the same thing—to assume that the poet is a kind of god, capable of making up his meanings out of whole cloth. In either case we are back to Emerson's symbolistic monism. If Mrs. Langer avoids this kind of monism, as on the whole she does, it is because in practise she uses more referential criteria than she is perhaps aware that she is using and more than her theory strictly entitles her to use.

IV

THOUGH both Cassirer and Mrs. Langer are, as we have seen, much interested in the relation of poetry to myth, and though they both levy upon myth to illustrate the theory of symbolic form, they are scrupulously careful to distinguish myth from poetry. Mrs. Langer writes, for instance, "Legend and myth and fairy tale are not in themselves literature, they are not art at all, but fantasies; as such, however, they are the natural materials of art." [3] But many of the critics of our time have, more boldly (or shall one say less scrupulously) seized upon the connection between myth and literature as providing a new key to criticism.

These new "myth" critics, now to be discussed, tend to be more conversant with psychology than with philosophy. They have also been heavily influenced by the anthropological studies of the last fifty years. They have been tremendously impressed by the discovery—or the rediscovery—that myth, ritual, and poetry are to be found at the begin-

---

[2] *The Literary Mind*, p. 148.   [3] *Feeling and Form*, p. 274.

nings of every culture. The specifically human estate begins, it has been persuasively argued, with these forms of human expression, and it develops under their influence. The modern myth critic has probably been even more powerfully impressed by the evidence that primitive man still lurks within each of us, and that the 20th-century citizen who dutifully drives to work each morning in an automobile, transacts business by telephone with a firm three thousand miles away, and gets himself ready for sleep by watching entertainment relayed to his living-room by the electronics industry, recreates nightly in his dreams the primordial symbols of ancient myth. Seen in these terms, myth seems to offer to poetry an inviolable refuge against the incursions of a hostile science.

Myth suggests a fresh means by which to study the "laws of the imagination." Mrs. Langer herself is willing to agree that, since these laws are "really just canons of symbolization," the "systematic study of them" may be justly said to have been "first undertaken by Freud." [4] The critics who hope to find in myth the key to artistic creation make much of the number of characteristics that poetry shares with dream. The process that Freud calls the "dream-work" shows startling similarities with "poetic work." In both there is "condensation" (the combining several images in one image), "displacement" (the vesting in some apparently unimportant element the underlying significance of the whole), and "overdetermination" (several quite different significances focused upon the same element so that it bears more than one meaning). In both poetry and dream, logical relationships are frequently evaded or transcended by the mere juxtaposition of images.[5] Not only Freud, but notably among other psychologists Carl Jung, and the cultural anthropologists in general are regarded as having furnished positive and specific directives for the study of poetry. Some of our recent critics, under the stimulus of such studies, write with the excitement of men who have suddenly envisaged a whole new hemisphere.

For Northrop Frye the discovery points to the possibility of turning literary criticism for the first time into a true science. No true science, he argues, can be content to rest in the structural analysis of the object with which it deals. The poet is only the *efficient* cause of the poem, but the poem, having form, has a formal cause that is to be sought. On examination, Frye finds this formal cause to be the archetype.[6]

What Frye calls "total" literary history moves from the primitive to the sophisticated, and so Frye glimpses the possibility of envisaging lit-

---

[4] *Feeling and Form*, p. 241.

[5] Cf. *ante* Chapter 28 for parallels in the modern "semantic" study of poetic language.

[6] "My [Critical] Credo," *The Kenyon Review*, XII (Winter, 1951), pp. 92–110. "Archetype," borrowed from Jung, means a primordial image, a part of the collective unconscious, the psychic residue of numberless experiences of the same kind, and thus part of the inherited response-pattern of the race.

erature as the "complication of a relatively . . . simple group of formulas that can be studied in a primitive culture." [7] In the light of this
possibility, the search for archetypes becomes a kind of "literary anthropology, concerned with the way that literature is informed by preliterary categories such as ritual, myth and folk tale." [8] Since the quest-
myth is central to ritual and myth—and thus to literature—all the literary
genres may be derived from it. Groupings under the rubrics of the four
seasons emerge. That of spring will illustrate what Frye has in mind:

> The dawn, spring, and birth phase. Myths of the birth of the
> hero, of revival and resurrection, of creation and . . . of the de-
> feat of the powers of darkness, winter and death. Subordinate
> characters: the father and mother. The archetype of romance
> and of most dithyrambic and rhapsodic poetry.[9]

Frye not only envisages criticism's taking its place "among the other
social sciences." He has suggestions for bringing this about through
what amounts to a production-line technique. The literary specialists
who will deal with the text in question are disposed as follows: first the
editor ("to clean up the text for us"), then the rhetorician and philol-
ogist, the literary psychologist, the literary social historian, the philosopher and the historian of ideas, and finally at the end of the line, the
literary anthropologist. Frye consistently refers to the work of art as a
"product," an organic commodity that is capable of being sorted, classi-
fied, and graded—a notion that receives some support from the way in
which Frye chooses to suggest how a poem comes into being:

> The fact that revision is possible, that the poet makes changes
> not because he likes them better but because they are better,
> means that poems, like poets, are born and not made. The poet's
> task is to deliver the poem in as uninjured a state as possible, and

---

[7] *Kenyon Review*, XII, 99.

[8] *Kenyon Review*, XII, 99–100.

[9] *Kenyon Review*, XII, p. 104. Joseph Campbell's *The Hero with a Thousand
Faces* (Bollingen Series, XVII, 1949), is one of a number of recent books that
treat the quest-myth. Campbell too feels that his mission is to proclaim the new
dispensation. He tells us that the "great coordinating mythologies . . . now are
known as lies" (p. 388), yet the problems with which they purported to deal
remain. We shall solve these problems, he predicts, by learning "to recognize the
lineaments of God in all the wonderful modulations of the face of man" (p. 390).
Still more extravagant claims for the benefits to spring from our knowledge of the
universal myth are made by James K. Feibleman in his *Aesthetics* (New York,
1949). He argues that the future of modern literature is immense: Though we
moderns have no legends like that of Troy nor myths like that of the House of
Atreus, we do have an extensive knowledge of the master myth, "the myth of the
year god" (p. 426). The possession of this myth gives our artists an even greater
opportunity than that afforded the Greek artist of the fifth century B.C., for the
modern artist not only knows a *greater number* of myths he knows much more
about the very nature of myth!

if the poem is alive, it is equally anxious to be rid of him, and
screams to be cut loose from his private memories and associations, his desire for self-expression, and all the other navel-strings
and feeding tubes of his ego. The critic takes over where the
poet leaves off. . . .[1]

In this lively analogy the poem is evidently the babe, the poet the
mother, and the critic the midwife and nurse, who ties off the cord,
tells the mother the infant is a boy or girl, washes it up for presentation
to the outside world, and presumably gives it an anthropological classification and takes its Bertillion measurements. Yet Frye's analogy fails to
cover what must finally be the crucial question of whether the poem is
still-born and inert, or alive. He merely alludes to this question with the
cautionary "if the poem is alive." In some sense this has always been
the primary question with which criticism has had to concern itself: is
the poem "alive," or is it merely a document, wooden, dead, lifeless, a
mere "exhibit," without literary merit? Frye's midwife-critic, in none of
the special roles portioned out to him as textual editor, historian of ideas,
or even literary anthropologist, can answer that question, and in none of
the many roles that Frye assigns him does he need to answer that question. The inert and valueless "document" will submit to the kind of
classification that Frye specifies just as well as a valuable poem. The
promise that by such means criticism may take its place among the other
social sciences justifies pressing the question suggested by Frye's analogy. For it is a matter of some consequence whether criticism, once it
has become a social science, will become as chary of making evaluations
and rendering normative judgments. In short, is the aim to make criticism a purely descriptive, value-free social science? That eventuality
would prove to be simply a new variant on the old historicism.

In the position developed by Richard Chase in *The Quest for Myth*,
the term "myth" is clearly a value term. A poem that is vibrantly alive
is mythic and vice versa; for Chase absolutely identifies poetry and myth.
"Myth," he writes, "is only art."[2] The adverb *only* in this context is
rather curious. One wants to ask whether Chase is attempting to debunk
myth, on the assumption that myth has close affiliations with religion;
or whether he is striving to enhance art by suggesting that the important
function claimed for myth in past cultures is actually still available
through art for our scientific civilization. A reading of Chase's book
indicates that he means to do something of both.

Poetry and myth, he argues, arise out of the same human needs,
represent the same kind of symbolic structure, succeed in investing experience with the same kind of awe and magical wonder, and perform

[1] *Kenyon Review*, XII, 97–8.
[2] *The Quest for Myth* (Baton Rouge, 1949), p. 110.

the same cathartic function. The last phrase, however, is strictly a misnomer. Here Chase substitutes for Aristotle's metaphor of purgation a figure of his own that has to do with animal taming. We have been made, he says, whether we like it or not, the trustees "of inhumanly powerful forces which were once caged and domesticated by the apparatus of the Christian religion." That cage has been broken and the beasts have escaped and now lurk in the depths of man's unconscious. Ghosts such as haunt the hero in Henry James's "The Beast in the Jungle"

> are terrible and destructive just because they are inadequately projected by their victims. . . . We must do with "the beast" what James himself did: flush it from the jungle so that it may be captured in the texture of aesthetic experience and bent to our will.[3]

The artist is evidently the hound that flushes the beast from the jungle; his art is the cage that holds him when captured, and also, one supposes, the kitchen-chair and whip which the artist lion-tamer uses to force him to take his stand on the pedestal and sit quietly, obedient to the trainer's will. But the complications of Chase's image need not obscure at all the function which he assigns to poetry. It is substantially the role that Matthew Arnold assigned to poetry. The strength of art is that it does not rest upon dogma, and therefore can survive the breakup of dogma. If myth once upon a time tamed the destructive forces within man, and if myth is only art, then art ought to be able to tame them for us now.

The parallel with Arnold will suggest why Chase is so hostile to the proposition that myth originally implied belief. And here, of course, Chase comes into sharp collision with philosophers of symbolic form like Cassirer and Langer, who, as we have seen, firmly insist that in the true "mythical imagination there is always implied an act of *belief*."[4] I. A. Richards once wrote of *The Waste Land* that Eliot had effected a complete severance of poetry and belief, though Eliot himself was to demur. Chase seems to be saying that there never was any effective relation between belief and myth (poetry). The claim is almost heroically desperate. Yet it is easy to see why Chase has to insist upon it. If it could be made good, it would constitute an answer to a question that nowadays is certain to be raised by many voices: namely, how modern man is to profit from the power inherent in myth if in fact no intellectually respectable modern can any longer believe in myth? If, however, myth is "only art," the day is saved.

For Leslie Fiedler, the new perspective now offered by myth leads

[3] *Quest for Myth*, p. 102.   [4] *An Essay on Man*, p. 75.

straight back into the study of message and consequently into the study of biography.[5] Fiedler reacts sharply against recent "formalist" trends in criticism: the emphasis upon an "impersonal art," upon the poem itself rather than the study of its background. He wishes to reaffirm the importance of the poet's personality and the relevance of the poet's "intention." It is easy to see why: the theories that he is attacking tend to minimize the ancient distinction between literary form and content. Fiedler is engaged in reasserting a full dualism. For the archetypal materials are really a privileged poetic subject matter in disguise. He argues that any great poem must be an acceptable rendition of this special poetic content.

At the same time, a study of the poet's response—of the way in which he expresses, and by expressing, stamps, his personal "signature" upon the archetype—forces the critic to take full account of the biography of the poet. For in Fiedler's conception, a poem is not an object to be known; it is rather a clue to an event in the poet's psyche. The poet's psyche is the arena in which *Dichtung* and *Wahrheit* become one: the poetic work itself is incidental to this important process:

> In deed as in word, the poet composes himself as maker and mask, in accordance with some contemporaneous *mythos* of the artist. And as we all know, in our day, it is even possible to be a writer without having written anything! [6]

Literature has come a long way since the day of Thomas Gray and his "mute inglorious Miltons." That our poets may be tongue-tied, or too busy with their psychic struggles to stop and put anything down on paper, may or may not endanger their status as real poets. But, of course, Fiedler expects them normally to put themselves on paper, for then the therapeutic benefits of the process of poetic objectification (compare Chase *ante*) become socially available:

> In the Mask of [the poet's] life and the manifold masks of his work, the poet expresses for a whole society the ritual meaning of its inarticulate selves; the artist goes forth not to "recreate the conscience of his race," but to redeem its unconscious. We cannot get back into the primal Garden of the unfallen Archetypes, but we can yield ourselves to the dreams and images that mean paradise regained.[7]

In the same essay Fiedler writes that the poet is able to take us back "to his unconscious core, where he becomes one with us all in the presence of our ancient Gods, the protagonists of fables we think we no

---

[5] "Archetype and Signature," *The Sewanee Review*, LX (Spring, 1952), 253–73. Reprinted by permission of *The Sewanee Review*.
[6] *The Sewanee Review*, LX, 261.   [7] *Sewanee Review*, LX, 273.

longer believe." [8] But never mind what we *think* on these occasions; do we or do we not believe? That will be the question that some readers will want to put. Can we, by taking a firm hold on our bootstraps, actually lift ourselves to a belief in what we do not "really believe"? Or is "believe" being used in a Pickwickian sense? One is aware that the question may not be easy to answer, but eventually it must at least be faced.

V

THE more literary question that is raised by Fiedler and by the myth critics in general may be put as follows: Have they found in their study of myth and the psychology of dreams an authoritative clue to the interpretation of poems? They certainly write with the excitement of men who have found such a key. Yet their claims are a little incoherent and at points contradictory.

The attempt to apply Freudian theory to poetry runs into a similar problem: Mrs. Langer points out that the peculiar weakness of Freud's theory as applied to poetics is that it tends to "put good and bad art on a par, making all art a natural self-expressive function like dream and 'make-believe.' " [9]

It is possible, of course, to argue that one poet uses a myth more "artistically" or more "powerfully" than another; or one may argue that some myths are more powerful or more significant than other myths and therefore yield greater poems. But to take either alternative would seem to reinstate the traditional critical problems in full force. For our attempt to show that Poem A uses Myth X artistically whereas Poem B does not, brings up what Frye has called the "problem of rhetoric." And so does our argument that Myth X is more significant (and therefore makes for a greater poem) than Myth Y. Considerations of this sort suggest that "mythic" and "archetypal" criticism, whatever other contribution it may make, provides no way of circumventing the basic problems of traditional criticism. [1]

In considering some of the recent "myth" criticism, we have seen how various it is in its emphases: with Frye we are asked to assign an almost monstrous "life of its own" to the poem; with Fiedler, on the other hand, the poem is important as an event in the life of the poet; and there is Chase's concern for the audience in his therapeutic emphasis. But the literary use of the study of myths *can* be centered firmly upon the poetic structure itself. Maude Bodkin's *Archetypal Patterns of*

[8] *Sewanee Review*, LX, 273.
[9] *Feeling and Form*, p. 240.
[1] Cf. Fergusson, *Idea of a Theater*, pp. 17, 77.

Poetry is an excellent demonstration of this possibility. Her archetypal patterns are the primordial images that occur in the poetry of both the past and the present. They are such images as that of the mysterious cavern, of the guilt-haunted wanderer, of the fountain, of the buried corn, and so on. She keeps specific passages of the poems that she discusses steadily in view. In her sensitive commentaries on particular poems, Miss Bodkin is for the most part filling out implications, suggesting comparisons between the symbols in the poem and symbols as they occur in tribal and religious life, and in general employing the special findings of psychology and comparative religion in the same way that she employs other fields of knowledge. Such work is always important, but it scarcely invokes a revolutionary technique—nor does Miss Bodkin regard it as doing so. Her very conception of archetypes implies that images endowed with such universal significance—images rooted so deep in the human psyche—must have yielded much of their significance to both poet and reader in the past. The work left to the modern psychologist can be no more than to make explicit in a particular way what was already in some sense intuited by the earlier reader.

> It is with the complete resources of our minds that we must appreciate, if appreciation is to be genuine. If, for instance, we have found certain elements in experience made newly explicit through the teaching of Freud, that new awareness will enter into our apprehension of *Othello*, or of *Hamlet*, though it was not present in Shakespeare's own thought, nor in the audience for whom he wrote.
>
> One can no more bind within the limits of the author's intention the interactions with new minds of a play or poem that lives on centuries after his death, than one can restrict within its parents' understanding the interrelations of the child that goes forth from their bodies to live its own life in the world.[2]

Thus, Miss Bodkin, refusing to allow the "author's intention" to tyrannize over the meaning of the work, recognizes the possibility of a growth of meaning in the constituent elements of a work and therefore a possible development in the meaning of the work itself. But she is as far as she can be from suggesting that a new "archetypal" criticism will now replace criticism as we have known it. Knowledge of archetypes may be regarded as an acquisition of new artistic materials or else as an enrichment of older artistic materials: it constitutes an enlargement of the poet's (and of the reader's) potential resources; but it is not a "new" method of organization or interpretation.

[2] *Archetypal Patterns of Poetry* (Oxford, 1934), p. 334, by permission of the publishers, Oxford University Press, Inc. Another excellent treatment of this sort of imagery is to be found in W. H. Auden's *The Enchafèd Flood* (1950).

VI

RECENT "myth" criticism, as previous allusions in this chapter indicate, owes more to Carl Jung than to any other man. It may be interesting, therefore, to examine his notions of the relation of the study of myth to literary criticism. There can be no doubt as to the serious role that Jung assigns to myth. One aspect of the seriousness with which he takes the function of myth in our psychic life is his insistence that one must discriminate very carefully among myths and even among dreams. He does not speak of dreaming "skilfully" or "eloquently," but he does assert that one can on occasion dream "significantly." He writes that he is compelled to admit "that the unconscious mind is capable at times of assuming an intelligence and purposiveness which are superior to actual conscious insight." [3] The implications of this statement are large. If the activity of the unconscious in dream and myth is not merely a symptom of psychic disorder but "at times" at least is an intelligent and purposive ordering, then all myths and dreams are not alike; some are evidently more purposive and significant than others. And this judgment, that some are more purposive and significant than others, implies a cognitive criticism and interpretation of myth and dream. Jung means too that the function of "purposive" myths and dreams is not merely or even primarily cathartic; it is knowledge-giving: dreams give us knowledge of ourselves.

This emphasis in Jung perhaps accounts for the fact that he has been more directly influential on recent literary criticism than Freud has been. Miss Bodkin has put the matter very well:

> The difference between the two schools [of Freud and Jung] lies in Jung's belief that a synthetic or creative function does pertain to the unconscious—that within the fantasies arising in sleep or waking life there are present indications of new directions or modes of adaptation, which the reflective self, when it discerns them, may adopt, and follow with some assurance that along these lines it has the backing of unconscious energies. [4]

It may not be too much to say that Jung (in contrast to Freud with his "psychiatric" analysis even of the poem) brings a cognitive criticism to bear even upon the dream.

> The "manifest" dream-picture is the dream itself, and contains the "latent" meaning. If I find sugar in the urine, it is sugar, and not a façade that conceals albumen. When Freud speaks of

[3] *Psychology and Religion* (New Haven, 1938), p. 45.
[4] *Archetypal Patterns*, p. 73.

the "dream-façade," he is really speaking, not of the dream itself, but of its obscurity. . . . We say that a dream has a false front only because we fail to see into it. We would do better to say that we are dealing with something like a text that is unintelligible, not because it is a façade, but simply because we cannot read it.[5]

Some of the dreams that he describes are very elaborate symbolic structures. Their parts are ordered in accordance with a "logic of the imagination" and are therefore, to the proper interpreter, coherent and intelligible. They are in some sense analogous to poems, and the role of the interpreter—if we are to judge from Jung's own procedure in his published analyses—is analogous to that of the literary critic. For example, Jung will write of a particularly elaborate dream that it "speaks of religion and that it means to do so. Since the dream is elaborate and consistent it suggests a certain logic and a certain intention." [6] Moreover the interpretation does not require a secret key: the symbols that it makes use of are remarkably "public" and traditional—not nearly so clandestine as one might have thought. The condensations, juxtapositions and symbolic ambiguities, as Jung interprets this dream, show a remarkable resemblance to those met with in much modern literary criticism.

"A great work of art," Jung writes, "is like a dream." And he specifies two ways in which it is: "for all its apparent obviousness it does not explain itself and is never unequivocal." That is, the poem is not prescriptive; neither the poem nor even the dream says "You ought" or "This is the truth." Moreover, like the dream, the poem requires us to make our own interpretation, for the poem presents an image "in much the same way as nature allows a plant to grow, and we must draw our own conclusions." [7]

VII

IN VERY important ways, Jung's conception of the poem parallels that of the symbolist theorist. A poem is organic; it is filled with implicit meaning; the relation of its parts may transcend that of rational arrangement —may indeed involve the reconciliation of apparent contradictions. This last parallel with certain modern theories of poetry becomes especially apparent if, following up Jung's claim for parallelism between poem and dream, we attribute to poetry on his view the kind of tension which he is emphatic in claiming for dream. Psychic energy in general, he

---

[5] *Modern Man in Search of a Soul* (New York, 1933), p. 15, by permission of the publishers, Harcourt, Brace and Company, Inc.
[6] *Psychology and Religion*, p. 31.   [7] *Modern Man*, p. 198.

tells us, involves "the play of opposites." The healthy growth of the mind involves a shattering of narrow states of consciousness through "the tension inherent in the play of opposites" and a building up thereby of a state of "wider and higher consciousness." [8]

We have thus far stressed the likeness between poem and dream. Jung in fact draws a very sharp distinction between them. The dream is shaped by the unconscious, but the poem, though it may draw upon the depths of man's being, is "apparently intentional and consciously shaped." [9] Moreover Jung is careful to distinguish the psychologist's study of the poet from his study of the poem:

> The truth is that [Freud's view of art] takes us away from the psychological study of the work of art, and confronts us with the psychic disposition of the poet himself. That the latter presents an important problem is not to be denied, but the work of art is something in its own right, and may not be conjured away.[1]

The psychologist, then, is able (if he wishes) to study the poem and not merely the mind of the man who made it.

If we ask what specific contribution the psychologist can make to the study of literature, Jung first offers us a distinction between two broad classes of literary work. There is what he calls "psychological" literature, which

> always takes its materials from the vast realm of conscious human experience—from the vivid foreground of life, we might say. I have called this mode of artistic creation psychological because in its activity it nowhere transcends the bounds of psychological intelligibility. . . .
>
> In dealing with the psychological mode of artistic creation, we never need ask ourselves what the material consists of or what it means.[2]

But this question does force itself upon us as soon as we come to the visionary mode of creation.

> We are astonished, taken aback, confused, put on our guard or even disgusted—and we demand commentaries and explanations. We are reminded in nothing of everyday, human life,

[8] *Modern Man*, p. 117.

[9] *Modern Man*, p. 175. The full context of Jung's discussion makes it quite plain that the intentionality is to be inferred from the work itself and not merely from some statement by the poet. In this matter Jung is emphatic, writing that "the truth is that poets are human beings, and that what a poet has to say about his work is often far from being the most illuminating word on the subject" (p. 186).

[1] *Modern Man*, p. 185.   [2] *Modern Man*, pp. 180–2.

but rather of dreams, night-time fears and the dark recesses of the mind that we sometimes sense with misgiving.[3]

Apparently, the literature of the visionary mode may require the services of the psychologist. What those specific services are, it remains to consider.

In the first place, according to Jung, the psychologist can show us that the kind of experience with which, say, a Dante or a Melville deals is, in spite of its "visionary" nature, important and to be taken seriously. The psychologist can point out that "we must take [the vision] at least as seriously as we do the experiences that underlie the psychological mode of artistic creation," experiences that "no one doubts . . . are both real and serious." [4]

In the second place, the psychologist can point out that however "dark this nocturnal world" with which the visionary artist deals may be, "it is not wholly unfamiliar." [5] The last clause is worth stressing. If what the visionary artist treated were *wholly* unfamiliar, that is, really private and eccentric, its expression might have value for the artist himself and might provide an interesting case-study for the psychologist, but it would cease to be a work of art. The fact is that the nocturnal world is in some sense the world of all of us, and this the psychologist can help us to see.

The work of the psychologist, *qua* psychologist, therefore, turns out to be not so much a work of interpretation as one of vindication. The artist is to be freed from the charge that his vision is merely a symptom of some personal psychic maladjustment and from the charge that his symbols are merely subjective distortions of that world fashioned by those whom Jung calls the "reason-mongers." Actually, as to specific "methods" of interpretation, Jung has in his later writings very little to say. But the clear implication is against the possibility of any special "method" by which the psychologist takes over from, and substitutes himself for, the literary critic. Jung has made it plain that "visionary" literature includes some of the most important literature that we have—*Moby Dick* and even the *Divine Comedy*. But he is careful also to include among instances of "visionary" literature such a work as Rider Haggard's *She*.[6] Jung does not indicate how we know that *She* is not so great a novel as *Moby Dick;* he simply takes it for granted that we do know it. But this judgment of relative literary value is clearly made by the critic, judging by whatever criteria a critic does judge, and not by the psychologist judging as psychologist.

To the question raised earlier as to whether the new "myth" criticism possesses a special key for literary interpretation, the answer of

[3] *Modern Man,* p. 182.   [4] *Modern Man,* p. 185.   [5]*Modern Man,* p. 188.
[6] Jung also says specifically that "Literary products of highly dubious merit are often of the greatest interest to the psychologist" (*Modern Man,* p. 177).

Jung would seem to be an emphatic no. The literary critic will obviously profit by all that he can learn about what human beings are, about how they behave, and especially about the way their minds work.[7] He will also find valuable whatever knowledge he can obtain about the languages in which men express themselves—not only Latin or French or Old Norse, but all those recurrent patterns of symbolism to which the modern anthropologist or the depth psychologist or the student of comparative literature direct our attention. By studying these symbolic languages he will learn again how various is man and yet how much the same man remains. In this area of knowledge Jung furnishes stimulating—even exciting—observations, but by his own confession, his contribution would seem to consist in having added to our knowledge about man's processes of symbolization and the great immemorial symbols—the archetypes—in which man tends to express himself.

So it is also with W. B. Yeats, surely the greatest of the recent poets who have tried to use myth as the basis of their own work. As we have indicated in an earlier chapter,[8] Yeats proposed in writing *A Vision* to create a living myth. But no one knew better than Yeats that this would be literally impossible. We find him saying, therefore, that no mere intellectual revolution can bring back the "old simple celebration of life tuned to its highest pitch." What might be possible for such a revolution to bring about would necessarily have to be "something more deliberate . . . , more systematized, more external, more self-conscious, as must be at a second coming." [9]

Just so. Yeats's own "myth" as embodied in *A Vision* is more fully systematized, more deliberate, more external than any genuine myth can be. *A Vision* is in part a theory of history; in part a psychology of creation, in part—and perhaps most importantly—a dictionary of public and semi-personal symbols—a kind of logbook of the symbols that Yeats had used and was in the future to use in his own poetry. *A Vision* contains some prose wrought almost fully up to the pitch of poetry; and it throws light upon Yeats's own development as a thinker and an artist. But the finest of Yeats's poems do not depend upon it. They transcend it, making use of the "natural" and traditional symbols that he discusses in *A Vision*, or at times ignoring that body of symbols altogether and creating their own symbols. They are poems and their symbols are poetically effective, not because Yeats was a maker of myths but because he was a poet. And we for our part recognize his poems to be poems by whatever means we have for recognizing poetry.

[7] "Psychology and the study of art will always have to turn to one another for help, and the one will not invalidate the other" (*Modern Man*, p. 177).
[8] Cf. *ante* Chapter 26.
[9] *Wheels and Butterflies*, 1934 (New York, 1935), pp. 65–6.

PART FIVE

CHAPTER 32

EPILOGUE

§ *retrospect: from Plato through the Middle Ages—II. the
Renaissance and neo-classic eras—III. the romantic and
post-romantic, to about 1940—IV. the historical method as
a study of the audience, criticism of gross structure, myth
and ritual origins, the century of the common man—V.
the correct view of Plato's rhapsode? the critical problem
of values and emotions, subject and object, relative and
universal, the role of words, accent on experience, light
refracted through a crystal, reality of external values, the
"naive"—VI. aesthetic emotion and real life, tension and
reconciliation, tragic and comic, Plato's* Philebus, *pure and
impure pleasures, aesthetics of "significant form," 18th-
century dismal feelings, opposed to analysis of wit and
irony, problem of pain and destruction, material concreteness, division, conflict, evil in literature, problem of moral
commitment, Manichaean dualism, human substance vs.
philosophic melodrama—VII. irony as metaphoric structure, "form," the metaphysical metaphor, metaphor as universality and concreteness, metaphor and historical information, multiple perspectives, Aristotelian mimetic,
Ricardian affective, Crocean expressionistic and linguistic,
metaphor in criticism, status of the literary "kinds," various focuses—VIII. values sensory, spiritual, and aesthetic
(representative and non-representative), reduction up or
down, opposing and reconciling terms, "speculative,"
"practical," "doing," "making," "useful," "fine," various
simplifications, the difficult alternative: "A theory of poetic or fine art must keep asserting in various idioms, by
various stratagems, in accord with the demands of the dialectic of the time, the special character of poetry as a tensional union of making with seeing and saying"* §

THE HISTORY WHICH WE HAVE JUST BROUGHT TO ONE OF ITS MOMENtary conclusions in the modern theory of mythic archetypes had one of its remote formal beginnings, we remember, in a Platonic dialogue where an ironic dialectician compelled a naive professor and reciter of poetry, a rhapsode, to make some damaging admissions about the kind of science or wisdom which either the rhapsode or his authority the poet might lay claim to. The upshot of the inquisition appeared to be that neither poet nor rhapsode, so far as they were simply poet or rhapsode, "knew" anything at all. They were prompted to their marvelous utterance by a divinely irrational afflatus; they were out of their minds with a power which came directly to the poet and was passed on by him to the rhapsode and to *his* auditors by a kind of magnetism.

The *Ion* was an early and simple preliminary to Plato's more elaborate attacks on the illusionistic and emotive power of poetry (and of rhetoric) in the *Republic, Phaedrus* and other mature dialogues. Aristotle in his *Poetics* answered that a workout of painful emotions is a good thing, effecting a homeopathic purgation, and as for the allegedly deceptive remove at which poetry stood from the universals, the tragic or epic poem was actually a kind of ethical invention which came much closer than the uncontrived chronicle of history to saying something serious and philosophic and universal about the human protagonist. There were hints about a certain blend of goodness and fault in that protagonist and his experience of disastrous results. A comic poem was more abstract, less mythic, and the mistakes made were less painful and less destructive. In his *Rhetoric* Aristotle made some remarks about verbal tricks and heightened metaphoric ways of speaking, and about the character of a speaker and the emotions of his audience. These were inescapable dimensions of discourse, and as they might be used in one way by the sophist, the honest orator had better look well to their opposite use.

A few hundred years later in Augustan Rome we found the urbane lyric and epistolary poet Horace still talking—in a tradition of Peripatetic codifications—about dramatic and epic poetry and speaking casually about Socratic wisdom as a sufficient source of poetic content. It seemed important to him—or he spoke as if it seemed important—to recognize certain well defined types of poetry, their metres, contents, and rules of decorum. He said that correct usage in words was important and along with that a great deal of care and craft in putting them together. Despite his formal textbook talk about tragedy and comedy (the genres a young aspirant would be expected to try his hand at), Horace himself was a conversational, satiric, and epistolary poet—and through this focus on poetry as a kind of skilled and gentlemanly ex ercise in talking he makes his shrewdest observations. But then at Rome less than a century later, we have, in the all but anonymous Greek man of letters who wrote the *Peri Hupsous,* almost the direct opposite of Horace. The *Peri Hupsous* is a celebration of ecstasy and inspiration; it now asserts in full earnestness and enthusiasm the view that was framed half playfully in Plato's *Ion.* The educational prestige of declamation and rhetoric was such in first-century Rome that the treatise of Longinus could not but be much preoccupied with certain technical entanglements, figures and kinds of diction and formulas for amplification. But the special and pulsing accent of Longinus is on the great and impassioned soul of the poet, his flashes and spurts of inspiration, the careless and plunging grandeur of his utterance, the bigness of the objects which inspire him, and the corresponding transport of his audience.

And that accent was something far from alien to the full Roman neo-Platonism which appears two centuries later with the metaphysician and visionary Plotinus. The difference is that whereas Longinus rests his case on the flash of inspiration, the quasi-divine illumination, Plotinus, systematic, meditative, profoundly metaphysical and brooding, would integrate the flash into a comprehensive philosophy of divine intelligence and life radiant through and immanent in all the universe and all human souls and minds. A special instance of that intelligence is the artist, who by some superior access to divinity gives us the better and brighter image of Zeus. The ambitious synthetic reasoning of Plotinus produces some interesting emphases, such as those on the beauty and simplicity of light, on the superiority of the ocular sense which meets and appreciates light, and on the likeness and union of knowing organ and subject with object. The same reasoning produces two such difficult problems as that of the double form (form upon form) in the carved stone, and the conflict between the divine principle of unity and the Stoic principle of beauty in the complexity implied by "symmetry." St. Augustine with a geometric and numerical emphasis on unity and harmony, and Aquinas (despite a nearly Platonic assignment of poetry to the area of sophistry) continue the Plotinian accent on order and radiance and on "connaturality" of subject and object.

The long course of the Christian Middle Ages acknowledges and develops without deviation the philosophy of intelligible unity, being, and beauty, with an accent now on numerical harmony, astronomy and music, now on a cosmological principle of visible radiance, and always on the vast and minutely detailed symbolism of God's illuminated book, the universe. Thus one kind of Platonic strain joins with and, from Patristic times on, helps to develop the ancient allegorical reading of poetry, which is freshly and with unprecedented vigor applied to the exegesis of the Hebrew and Christian Scriptures. The Middle Ages and later the Renaissance make a long period of all-out symbolic reading—though scarcely in the more fluid and "creative" sense in which "symbolism" has been understood in times closer to our own. Finally, the Middle Ages is a period of a certain kind of rhetorical poetics— *Poetria Nova* in the 13th century—which means Hellenistic prescriptions for how to use all the figures, and on what occasions.

II

DURING all that period Aristotle was not known as a literary authority, and there was no other authority. But with the 16th century in Italy Aristotle's *Poetics* had to be dealt with (perhaps for the first time directly as a dead system of partly cryptic notes), and Horace too, who became "fused" with Aristotle in a newly completed code. But meanwhile there was the luxuriance of vernacular literature from Dante to Ariosto to be coped with by the theoretical arbiters, vernacular problems of diction and of metrics, and of burlesque and "errant" romance forms of epic. There was the heroic love theme of Tasso, the pastoral mixture innovated by Guarini. Hence a series of denunciations and spirited defences. Romantic freedoms were won, but the classic professors were stout champions too—and from Scaliger and Castelvetro, though for different reasons, emerged the hyper-Aristotelian dramatic unities of action, time and place, destined to become for French dramatists of the next century and for Dryden a theoretical precedent and challenge of great meaning. During the later 16th century in Italy the question about levels of symbolism appears in somewhat simpler forms than in the Middle Ages, and there appears too the grand question, implied in the whole classical debate from Plato and Aristotle on, as to whether poetry is an "icastic" (or literal, or realistic) image, or whether it has some kind of warrant to be imaginative or "fantastic." *Aut prodesse aut delectare* too is much debated—and all possible combinations of the aims of pleasing and teaching are contrived, including in the French mid-17th century at least as early as the Abbé D'Aubignac's *Pratique du Théâtre*, 1657, the notion that poetry is to please *through* instructing —a notable, if somewhat cramped, anticipation of the later famous idea that aesthetic values are one kind of end in themselves. Sir Philip Sidney is the Elizabethan English man of letters who gives us the best epitome of all these continental themes, especially the didactic and moral. His phrase about the poet "ranging within the zodiac of his own wit" and his dictum that the poet "nothing affirmeth and therefore never lieth" are brilliant, if perhaps only incidental, announcements of poetic freedom and might. And beside these may be set Bacon's passage about science buckling and bowing the mind to reality, poetry "submitting the shews of things to the desires of the mind."

In the generation of the Jacobeans, Ben Jonson's more ruggedly assertive didactic and satiric classicism includes a surprisingly severe, almost agelastic, version of Aristotle's meager dictum that the comic is a form of the ugly. Jonson furnishes also a lively demonstration, through free and virile Englishing, how little the classic mind thought that previous realization of an idea could tarnish it.

The most long-lived, productive and important English critic of the 17th century is Dryden, who in his several phases—as the "new" English dramatic theorist against the French norms, as heroic dramatist, court wit and conversationalist, as Shakespearian critic, as satirist or refined executioner of dullness, as translator of the classics, as translator and appreciator of Chaucer—shows us the meaning of such gradually shifting neo-classic debates as those concerning the stage unities and rhyme in drama (matters of intensity and realization disguised as matters of verisimilitude), those concerning verbal decorum, the real, the marvelous and the heroic, and those concerning such various topics as "poetic justice," the serious aims of laughter, the rivalry between ancients and moderns, the possibility and the meaning of translation and imitation. The "heroic" focus (so far as it really was a theoretical focus) was a momentary juncture of Aristotelian ideas about the hero with inflational notions of grandeur and inspiration. Concurrently (in a confused alliance with the heroic) came the quieter and tougher revival of Horatian courtly urbanity the kind of wit that was destined to succeed "metaphysical" wit (a thing uncelebrated in contemporary theory), the kind of poetry that would persist longest into the severe era of reason that was being ushered in.

The 17th century saw the end of Ciceronian and medieval and early Renaissance rhetorical culture; it was a century of decline in the prestige of words and the mysteries of auditory doctrine, of a soaring new prestige for seeing and diagramming, for the simplifying and classifying spirit of science. We have observed the variations in meaning of the index word "wit"—the gradual discountenancing of the metaphysical and imaginative meaning (one which might be used to describe the poetry of Donne, Herbert, Milton, or Shakespeare) and the evolution of the new concept of "true" wit as only judgment after all, propriety of thought and speech, "nature to advantage dressed"—until literary criticism centered in a highly ambiguous *new* key term. The term "wit" might now be either viewed suspiciously in its older poetic meaning, as by Locke or Addison, or applied in its safer new meaning (by reason of an ingeniously evasive submission to good sense on the part of the best English poets) in a deceptive way to current poetry.

In that crisis of the accomplished dissociation of sensibility, with Cartesian and Newtonian rationality running ahead to apparently limitless conquests of clarity, and with the verbal arts lavishing themselves

on patterns of oratorical trim, on repeated metaphorical recommenda-
tions of a lost sense—was heard the new accent on ocular and auditory
pleasure ("pleasures of the imagination"), on sensation, on the aesthetic,
on landscape, on supposed weddings of the arts in forms like oratorio,
song, and opera. And there was heard also, more and more plainly, the
new accent on feeling, on tender and sympathetic feeling, on the pleasures of painful feeling. The Platonic universal of Samuel Johnson and
Sir Joshua Reynolds was merged in the neo-Longinian sublime. Despite
much stalwart talk about norms and species, Johnson's classic garment
flies in tatters in the strong affective breezes. Yet classical precedents
were always invoked: for the sensational, the Horatian *ut pictura poesis;*
for the emotive, both Longinian ecstasy and sentimentalized versions of
Aristotelian catharsis. In the sublimity of awful and threatening natural
phenomena, in the physiognomy of emotive expressions, the aesthetic
of sensation and the aesthetic of emotion conclusively joined. The new
movement, for all its sources in antiquity, was headlong toward the
future and would be "modern" for at least two centuries to come. Add
the subtly pervasive principle of "association." This was first only a way
of breaking up traditional patterns of expectancy and of value. But in
a second phase (in conjunction with a new fondness for particularity
and especially for picturesque details of nature) it became a principle
of positive, creative, emotionally warm and plastic power—a principle
of imaginative "coalescence."

III

A CERTAIN kind of classicism persisted long in England under the name
and in the actuality of "poetic diction"—that curious species of glossy
ornament which was demolished by Wordsworth in the first phases of
his primitivism and simplism. After that the scene was clear for both
Wordsworth and Coleridge to proceed from "association" in its simpler
Hartleyan and mechanical phase to the more emotive and plastic notion
which, by pushing ahead only a slight distance and by showing in their
mature poems what the fullness of the doctrine could mean, they
established in the glorious (though momentary) status of "imagination." Coleridge added the deepening and fortification of German metaphysics—the epistemology of "object" and "subject," or the imaginative
reconciliation of these two opposites and along with them of art and
nature, emotion and thought, the universal and the particular, and other
satellites. Coleridge and Wordsworth show in a manageable landscape
vignette what the larger and more varied movement of German romanticism, the poetry and theory of Goethe and Schiller and Novalis,
the lectures of the Schlegels, the philosophy of Kant, Schelling and

Fichte, was in process of doing for the whole history of modern poetry and aesthetics in the West.

The romantic theory was in effect a highly ambiguous and double claim—a claim both for poetic freedom and for poetic responsibility. It was thus the cloud-capped starting point for certain quite opposite lines of poetic theory that came down through the 19th century toward our own day. One of these, moving from Kantian disinterest, formality and beauty, through French academic aesthetics and then early symbolist and Parnassian poetics, resulted in what we look back on as Art for Art's Sake—the end-of-the-century gilded celebration of autonomous poetic power. At the level of general aesthetics and linguistic, the philosophy of Benedetto Croce is the voraciously systematic expression of this view. Not so far removed from art-for-art's sake as we might wish to think, and in some phases part of it, was the thing, technically so much more subtle and more interesting to us, which came out of romantic "imagination" and "symbol" and became "symbolism." This seems to have come not so much directly from the German philosophers as through Coleridge and Poe, and Heine and Baudelaire, to the era of Mallarmé and the Wagnerians. Here was a more subtle "music" of "ideas" than the neo-classic theory of painting the passions had conceived—and a new quasi-spiritual reaction against the philosophy of science.

But those kinds of theory, both pure art and symbolism, were directly at odds with three other main kinds which developed the opposite accent of the romantic heritage—not that on autonomous privilege but that on moral and social power and evolutionary responsibility. Here were three versions of didacticism: one, the earliest and most fully romantic—what we may call the rhapsodic, the bardic, the prophetic, as it is brandished for instance in the *Defense of Poetry* by Shelley or the *Heroes and Hero Worship* of Carlyle; a second, the most nearly allied to a proper literary interest, the classical humanism, severity, and loftiness, both German and French in origin, which is fully expressed in English by Matthew Arnold; a third, owing much to Hegelian dialectic, getting under way more slowly, but more modern and more resolute, the Franco-Russian complex of ideas under the heads of the real, the natural, the social or sociological. This last was the most urgently didactic and the most confidently evolutionary of all. Tolstoy is the greatest literary artist who gave himself to this kind of theory. Tolstoy on what is true and telling in literature, on what is effete, jaded, hedonistic, and merely aristocratic, hits hard, and we may have to take him into account in a way that we do not have to take into account Zola on the novel as an experiment in a social science laboratory.

If we look around the critical scene and especially the American critical scene during the first decades of our own century, we see distinct aftermaths of all the 19th-century events which we have just been tracing: For one thing the exotic and flashy tail-ends of the art-for-art's sake tradition, the cosmopolitanism of the *Smart Set* and *Mercury* writers. For another, the continuation of Arnoldian humanism in the long influence of P. E. More and Irving Babbitt and the approximate end of that humanism in the twin detonations of the anthologies for and against it in 1930. There was also a strong socio-real tradition, under the names of naturalism, Responsibilities of the Novelist, and the uglier name of Muck-Raking, and also the coming of age of honest America, a matter of smoke and steel, the Prairie Schooner, and slabs of the sunburnt west. And then the most acutely didactic accent of all, in the Marxist criticism of the 1930's—rampaging until it becomes obvious to the literary intelligences connected with it that this kind of thing will never do.

One of the most novel strains of literary criticism produced by the 20th century has been that which we may roughly sum up under the name of psychologism. On the one hand, and perhaps most conspicuously: the Freudian kind, in the shape of new motivations drawn out of the unconscious for novels and poems, and literary biographies rewritten into case histories and ordeals. (Groping for tragic and comic motives in depth psychology and anthropology goes back through Freud to Nietzschean rhapsody and repose and Hegelian conflict of ethical substance.) And on the other hand: the quieter kind of affectivism, the equipoise, the beautiful harmony of impulses, promoted by Richards and his colleagues in the 'twenties. And this slips back through the exquisitely refined hedonism of Santayana to the affectivism connected with utilitarian ethics during the 19th century. J. S. Mill's two essays on poetry show how this 18th-century heritage could get into criticism. Mill echoes the way it had already done so in Wordsworth and Coleridge.

But by and large the literary discussion of the 19th century, unlike that of the 18th, had not been notable for any systematic affectivism. And when this romantic and aesthetic plea reappeared with Richards in the 1920's, it had so much to say about mere incipience of impulses and their equipoise that it was a new witness for something like a classical disinterest or detachment. With its up-to-date paraphernalia of verbal analysis, Ricardian aesthetic was readily available, or at least convertible, for purposes of cognitive literary discussion.

Richards connected readily enough with the "neo-classicism" which was represented in the same era by the conspicuous figures of Pound and Eliot. Twentieth-century "neo-classicism" derived attitudes from the intuitionist but classical philosopher T. E. Hulme, from the precise grammatical statements of Gourmont, and from the whole tide of the French symbolist and musically ironic poetics. (With Pound there was too the thing called "imagism," and at least a flourish of something supposed or pretended to be due to the fact of Chinese ideographic writing. But that can hardly be important.) Impersonality, craftsmanship, objectivity, hardness and clarity of a kind, a union of emotion with verbal object, a norm of inclusiveness and reconciliation and hence a close inter-dependence of drama, irony, ambiguity, and metaphor, or the near equivalence of these four—such ideas made up the neo-classic system as it worked its way into practical criticism about 1935 or 1940. And, however far short the system fell of being able to convince old-line historians or to demonstrate beyond appeal or cavil that this or that poem meant this much or that much or was excellent or not, the arrival of this kind of criticism did mean a new technical and objective interest in poetry.

IV

THE past fifteen years on the critical front have seen several new, or newish, large claims making headway. Let us move somewhat more slowly now for a few pages and let us restate and bring together certain themes which have appeared more or less separately in earlier chapters (21, 24, 31). The most academic of the new claims, the most profes-sional, the most scholarly, is that relatively new kind of graduate school study that seeks to substitute for the poem, not the author, as in former more romantic phases of historicism, but precisely and deliberately the audience for which the author may in any sense be proved to have written the poem. If we look back to the mid-18th century and the first clear start of the modern historical method in such documents as Thomas Warton's *Observations on the Faerie Queene*, Bishop Hurd's *Letters on Chivalry and Romance*, or even Samuel Johnson's *Preface to Shakespeare*, we note that their sympathy for the Gothic or the Eliza-bethan hesitates somewhat between a plea for tolerance of antique authors, despite the barbarous ages in which they wrote, and a plea for appreciation of the inspirational opportunities afforded by those very ages. But the decisive concept for the time was personal "genius." That is, criticism was on the side of Shakespeare in spite of his handicaps. In the 19th century, there were nationalism, folklorism, and cultural de-terminism, the race, milieu, and moment of Taine's *History*. But literary studies still tended to marshal such interests rather squarely behind the author. That is, they were important because they showed the mind of the author, what made him write the way he did. Sainte-Beuve's pro-fession of intense interest in the author's boyhood, his brothers and sisters, his parents and his grandparents, is an extreme yet typical in-stance of such Shandean depth in criticism. Despite the somewhat con-trary cultural massiveness of Courthope's *History of English Poetry*, it is mainly right to say that English and American literary research (following good continental models) continued until fairly recent years to be a pursuit of the author, his whole history, both internal and external, and his habitat. It requires perhaps only a tilt of the mirror to turn the habitat into the author's audience. And the audience had of course all along received attention. It was clearly one name for the socio-real focus. But to shift the accent of value in academic research (the accent on both the value of poetry itself and the value of research into poetic history) was yet another step, and it has been a fairly recent one. Until recently it was the normal aim of academic research to be able to announce: "And thus we prove what the author was trying to say," "thus we prove his learning and accuracy," "thus we prove his sincerity," or "thus we prove his deep feeling." But the new mode, one which is more comprehensive and difficult, and has yet advanced so little as to have perhaps a large and dangerous future, seems to entertain the aim of announcing: "And thus we prove that the author's poem was addressed to the audience of his day, or to the real audience, or to the audience that mattered." "Thus he knew what he was doing, and thus he was a good author." More and more articles in journals and books from university presses nowadays have titles referring to *Shakespeare's Audience*, to *The Social Mode of Restoration Comedy*, to *Paradise Lost and the Seventeenth Century Reader*, to *Box, Pit, and Gallery, The Theatrical Public in the Time of Garrick*, to the rise of a reading public, to the number of Victorian persons who bought Macaulay's *History of England* or Tennyson's *Maud*.

It is not difficult to suggest sympathies between the new kind of historicism turned toward the audience and a second recent critical trend, the bad conscience which has been developing in some critics with regard to nice verbal analysis. This is being expressed not only in direct misgivings about analysis, or pleas for a more "open" contextual reading, but also partly in the form of proclamations about the need for doing justice to the overall structures of stories and dramas, their motives, plots, actions, tragic rhythms, their deeper, wider, and more bulky symbolism, their bigger meaning—in short, all that part and aspect of them which may be supposed to be too massive and too important to be penetrated by the technique known as verbal criticism. This kind of conscience had a summary and rather impressive exposition about 100 years ago in Matthew Arnold's Preface to his *Poems* of 1853, where he repented of the inaction, or the suicidally limited action, of his *Empedocles*, appealed to the great serious action of the Greek tragedies, and thought that Shakespeare enjoyed such rhetorical virtuosity that he had been a bad influence on romantic poets, notably on Keats. (Keats, like a modern critic summoned before the bar in Chicago, was too much interested in words and images.) Arnold was giving Germanic and post-romantic moral resonance to an older classical plea—heard, for instance, in Rymer, with echoes by Dryden, and in Gildon—that Shakespeare was defective and not to be imitated in the fundamental matter of plot, and that a critic ought indeed to concern himself with the plot, with the whole poem, the grand design, and not be a "criticaster" of words, a "piece-broker." It was a theme heard in the classically severe Lessing too, whose ideas on drama were parallel to his Lockean and Cartesian notion that the colors of painting were unreal and hence inferior to the reality of sculptural mass and shape. The ideas of Arnold were part of his ambitious humanistic and moralistic program for literature. That, as we have been saying, was one branch of post-romantic didacticism. Later on there was a new criticism concerning prose fiction, not the criticism of Zola, but that of Flaubert, James and Ford, and this was not so far from the spirit of symbolist poetics. It does not appear that Henry James was much afraid of being caught in the mesh of words or of piddling away his effort on the texture or surface of things. If a woman put her hand on a table and looked at him in a certain way, that was for James, or for one of his characters, an event. And the event interlocked with every other event in the world. (The artist tried to conjure or pretend some kind of circle around it.) It is not in these great theorists of prose fiction that we find the scruple against dallying with the details of the medium.

But we do find it again more recently, and not only in the fortifications of a certain kind of academic neo-Aristotelianism but in more momentous campaigns under the standard of myth and the ritual origins. Here metaphor is action, and big action. For the first time since Dryden and Le Bossu the literary gist is supposed to be big enough and solid enough so that you would think it could be rendered essentially from one language to another. The rhythm of the tragic idea—the going out in quest, the confrontation and passion, the discovery or education—is the big thing. We have observed that the book which gives this theory the most persuasive articulation is Francis Fergusson's *Idea of a Theatre*. Here we have the most imposing of the several recent critical trends. Surely the hugest cloudy symbol, the most threatening, of our last ten or fifteen years in criticism is the principle of criticism by myth and ritual origins.

It is true that this new mythologism is not always associated with any strong mistrust of rhetorical inspection. Expression and symbolism can make a ready enough alliance with myth and ritual. For all four are theories of the creative imagination, the fiat of the human spirit as deity or as participating in deity. Herder and Schelling and Cassirer join Lévy-Bruhl and Frazer and the Cambridge classical anthropologists in the secularization of the spirit according to the philosophy of symbolic form. Philip Wheelwright's *Burning Fountain*, the most recent important book in the mythic mode, is a magnificent synopsis of relations between a special semantics on the one hand and on the other ritual anthropology interpreted by the darkness visible of depth psychology. The semantics states the difference between a scientifically bare "steno-language" and

the "plurisignations," the trans-logical "depth-language" common to poetry, myth, religion, and metaphysics. The anthropology dwells on he-
reditary and "preconsciously rooted" symbols, symbols of the "threshold,"
the world view of primitive man, the death and rebirth of the vegetation
god. (The *Fire Sermon* of Buddha, the *Oresteia* of Aeschylus, the *Four
Quartets* of Eliot may be cited to define the infra-red range of illustration.) To a writer who participated strongly in the new yearning for a
gross structural poetics Wheelwright's book might well look like a deplorable re-celebration of imagery and thematic "paraplots."

But myth and ritual are, as we have already said, patterns of action
and of large action. In that way they can have their easy enough connection with an anti-verbal poetics. And both these interests involve a stress
on what is important about poetry in a large and public way, what can
give it religious and social dignity and didactic claims. The validation for
the new myth philosophy is thought to lie in the primitive racial unconsciousness. Thus it eschews the risky appeal to objectivity, but plunges in
the vast reservoir of racial and prelogical unconsciousness for an intersub-
jective base of universality. It arrives at the phase of apocalyptic and prophetic vision. Along with the Greeks and the Hindus (from whom Friedrich Schlegel also once drew inspiration), there is Milton, there is Blake,
there is Melville, there is Yeats, there is Eliot, there is Joyce, and maybe
there is Faulkner. The three main trends of recent criticism which we
have just sketched—that toward the audience, that toward gross structure, and that toward myth—have in common a horizontal or folkways
alignment (in contrast, for instance, to the vertical and aristocratic alignment of the neoclassic formalism). All three show to some degree the
didactic and evangelizing interest which was prepared in the 19th-century
socio-real tradition. Despite the fact that sociology does come out of the
19th century, the humanism and literary theory in English and French
during that century were mainly inspirational, individualistic, and heroic.
It is the present century, as we all know, which is the century of the common man. The literary trends we have named conceive man, whether
common or elite, in large multiples, thinking and responding in classes.
Plato's rhapsode makes a strong bid for the recovery of his weeping
thousands.

V

WHAT is the real status, the correct status, of Plato's rhapsode and of the
poet whose inspired representative the rhapsode is? After Aristotle and
throughout antiquity—in the Peripatetic and Horatian tradition, in the
Isocratean and Ciceronian tradition of wisdom in oratorical eloquence, in
the emotive and mysterious phases of neo-Platonism, the poetic power
enjoyed a certain fairly high prestige, perhaps we may say an approxi-

mately sufficient degree and kind of prestige. During the Middle Ages both for theological reasons and because of the growing, strongly implicit scientific aims of the whole scholastic effort, poetry went through an era of theoretically low esteem. The Renaissance was a rebirth exactly of the humanistic classical literary claim, though this was vastly complicated now by codifications drawn out of the authority of the ancient writings and by the dialectic engendered from literary practice in the emergent spirit of "romance." The waning of the Renaissance into the era of literary neo-classicism and the first centuries of modern science brought a decline in the prestige of verbal power comparable to what Plato, at least in moments of the *Republic* and in the *Ion,* would seem to have thought desirable. The reawakening or German romantic renascence of poetic power drew plentifully enough on the classical heritage, but was also in a new way emotive, subjective, associational, "imaginative," creative, the claimant of a markedly new kind of authority. Since the day of the high romanticizing, literary theory has included perhaps the whole range of possible claims for poetry: the autonomy of various expressionisms, and of art for art's sake, the biographical and environmental substitutions made possible by improved historical methodology, the deterministic and evolutionary aspects of sociological theory, and the varied didacticisms of the 19th century, reappearing in the claims of the 20th-century archetypal myth.

We can study the history of changes in opinion, writes T. S. Eliot in his short history of English criticism, "without coming to the stultifying conclusion that there is nothing to be said but that opinion changes." The present writers have not written this short history of literary opinion without seeing in it a pattern of effort pointed toward at least a certain kind of goal.

The most difficult moment, the most insistently recurring moment under the most varying forms, in the history and dialectic of literary theory is that which touches values and emotions—or what human beings like and dislike and the experience of their liking and disliking. And one of the most sustained trends of modern critical history—paralleling and shadowing the course of modern metaphysics and psychology—has been toward the reduction of values to subjectivity, that is, toward the doctrine that what human beings like and dislike is a question that refers precisely and only to the experience itself of their liking and disliking. It would be difficult, perhaps impossible, for a literary critic or a historian of literary criticism to contrive within the limit of his own idiom and decorum a sufficient account of the difficult metaphysics that make the problem of value. Yet a literary theorist ought to be at least moderately aware of the relation his thoughts may show to that problem.

The great variety of human tastes for pleasure and of emotive responses to experience, the variety even for a single person from moment to moment and under this or that condition, may at times cast a chilly light over our speculations about value. These facts are scarcely matters which the theorist of poetry can dispute as facts. He can scarcely re-verify or re-count them, or balance or redress them by fresh statistics. He may, however, have a deeper or a shallower perspective in the under-standing of such facts. A sense of order, of hierarchy, of unity in the uni-verse of our experience—a sense of purpose, if one may whisper the word—can do something to dispel the cold illusion of the neutral substrate, the opaque ground below good and evil.

Let us say first that the situation of the person confronting his world of values is a vastly complicated one. He confronts not any single type and grade of thing constituting an objectively insulated and external "value," but various objects in various kinds of relations to himself. In each value situation there is both an objective and a subjective aspect—but the accent falls now upon one and now upon the other of these, and with various degrees of weight. A man is hurt by a knife or a club, and he feels the hurt and the damage as something that happens to a part of himself—not as a quality of the knife or club, the inflicting external entity. He tastes salt or sugar, and the taste with the liking or disliking of it is a subtle union of that specific new entity from outside both with his own mouth and with whatever may just previously have been tasted. And then, at a third level, he views red or blue, and whatever any theory may tell him about the relation of light to his eye (whatever sophistica-tion in theory of vision he is equal to) he experiences the pleasant or un-pleasant quality as a quality outside himself. (Such at least is the "phe-nomenology" of the event.) He looks at a landscape, and the complexity of the visual pattern and of the meanings inevitably attached to it place the locus of value even more emphatically—and stereoptically—outside. (To tickle one's foot, to "tickle" one's palate, to "tickle" one's fancy—these three grades in the semantics of the word "tickle" will summarize the series of values which we have just sketched.) Finally, suppose that a given man sees or hears of a murder (a knife stuck in another man); here the value implicated exhibits a very distinct and superior kind of external firmness and objectivity—that of the ethical realm. And yet this value is rooted in the pain and destruction inflicted upon a certain subject. To say that a value is relative to a subject is not to say that the value is relative in the sense that anybody's opinion about it may be as correct as anybody else's. Or, to say that a value is not objective, or not purely and simply objective, is not to say that it is not *universal*, or valid in relation to all subjects. Some such term as *inter-subjective* may perhaps be invoked to describe the accent that falls on some universals. It is surely true, for in-stance, that any human subject whatever will suffer pain and damage from knife wounds—even though this truth is not sufficient to establish a property of evil intrinsic to the knife itself.

But here let us revert, with some insistence, to the fact that the present discussion is concerned not directly with knives and persons, with sensory pleasures or moral values, but with poetry and hence with words. The problem of value which we are sketching is made even more complicated for the poetic theorist—and perhaps a certain distance from the basic value problem is created for him—by the fact that poetry is composed of words. For words introduce a special kind of valuing "subject," the subject who not only responds to values with emotions or feelings but formulates and utters (if only to himself) his awareness of both value and response. Not that such persons are unusual, but by the very fact of utterance a person values in a special way.

And most likely he values in a very subtly mingled way:—by exclamations and by the rhythmic aspects of utterance achieving something like a direct expression at least of vaguer feeling; by the names of pleasures and pains and of emotions and of their correlative values (hate, anger, love, and joy, the good and the bad, the beautiful and the ugly) achieving a firmer if more abstract delineation; by the neutral-sounding names of all sorts of objects, qualities, actions, and relations (of man, animal, and stone, of color, shape, and movement) achieving a deeper substantiation. The words of the last category do not name either responses or values directly, yet in real contexts they may have intense emotive import. For the purpose of poetic criticism it would appear to be significant to divide this large group into two great parts: the names of objects and actions which are causes, or motives, of an emotive response (the characters and the plot of the poem), and the names of the large world of symbols and associations which, though not direct objects of emotion, often fortify emotive interpretation (the black, the white, the crow, and the dove). No one of these classes of words carries very far in creating the expression (or in promoting the contagion) of emotive experience. They operate always by a complex meshing and nowhere more than in the verbal constructions which are poems. The complexity of their operation forbids all the more extreme simplifications of poetic theory—both the simply mimetic (theories of either real or metaphysically ideal imitation of the objective world) and the simply emotive or sentimental (pure theories of emotive expression or pure theories of emotive result).

One of the main lessons of critical history would seem, indeed, to be that the stress of literary theory must fall on the *experience* (subjective and emotive) rather than on the *what*, the object of value so far as that is outside *any* experiencing subject. Yet, for reasons which we have been sketching, this lesson need not be interpreted as relegating the values of poetry to the realm of the whimsical and undebatable. A refraction of light through a crystal tells something about the light, something about the crystal; the refraction itself is a kind of reality, interesting to observe. Let us say that poetry is a kind of reality refracted through subjective responses. This refraction itself is an area of reality. Does the refraction tell us something unique and profound about the reality beyond itself? We need not actually say much about this for the purposes of a workable poetics. (Much will depend on what we conceive the ultimate character of that reality to be.)

The norm of wit and cunning word-play entertained by Horace and centuries later, with a stress on the imitation of gentlemanly polite conversation, by Boileau, Dryden, and Pope, was one version of this important truth:—that if poetry is to "imitate," it will imitate what is alive with the human spirit. And no less relevant to the same truth was the fully self-conscious, creative and expressionist romantic theory. The following resonant statement by Shelley has been partly quoted in an earlier chapter:

> . . . as the lyre trembles and sounds after the wind has died away, so the child seeks, by prolonging in its voice and motions the duration of the effect, to prolong also a consciousness of the cause. In relation to the objects which delight a child, these expressions are, what poetry is to higher objects. The savage . . . expresses the emotions produced in him by surrounding objects in a similar manner; and language and gesture, together with plastic or pictorial imitation, become the image of the combined effect of those objects, and of his apprehension of them. Man in society, with all his passions and his pleasures, next becomes the object of the passions and pleasures of man; an additional class of emotions produces an augmented treasure of expressions; and language, gesture, and the imitative arts, become at once the representation and the medium, the pencil and the picture, the chisel and the statue, the chord and the harmony.

In a more soberly grammatical passage of the *Biographia* (Chapter XXII) Coleridge wrote:

> Be it observed . . . that I include in the *meaning* of a word not only its correspondent object, but likewise all the associations which it recalls. For language is framed to convey not the object alone, but likewise the character, mood and intentions of the person who is representing it.

A capsule symbol of the situation for the theorist might be made out of the *Poetics* of Aristotle, which talks about *mimēsis* or the imitation (through words and music and scenes and an outward story) of certain objects, but the objects are characters, passions, and *praxeis*, that is, actions or farings, adventures, experience—objects of the inner realm of spirit.

Yet we have been implying, and let us now say more plainly, that to entertain such a theory of poetic value is not to *deny* the reality and the value of the outer realm, the *what* which is at various levels external to each valuing subject. The theory cannot make such a denial, even at what may appear the most superficial levels, without dissolving the grounds on which it hopes to talk about poetic experience. As we move into the inner moral and spiritual experience of man in search of our most clearly absolute, our most securely universal, concepts of value, it may seem that we leave behind, abandon to an uncertain and merely academic fate, the values, pleasant or unpleasant, which in a more superficial scheme we might assign to such external phenomena as the colors red and blue. Neither the poet nor the theorist, however, is in a good position to leave these behind. If there were nobody else at all—no metaphysician, moralist, or theologian—who cared to speak in defence of sensory values—yet the poet, in his indirect and obscure way, would have to go on confessing them, and his theorist would have to think about them. For they contribute the symbolic, the external, the phenomenological language by which the poet speaks about the inner and deeper realities of value. And if they did not constitute at least an inter-subjectively universal and reliable set of values, they could not be used as signs in the poet's communication. Most likely it is not necessary for the theorist of poetry to decide the nice metaphysical question as to the *locus* of each sensory value—*in* object or *in* subject. Perhaps the very question is illusory. But both poet and theorist can be sure of one minimum thing: that at least inter-subjective viability is required for poetic communication. It will not be enough for a reader to be instructed (by a theorist or by a historian) that once upon a time, here and there, this meant that, purple was royal, black meant death, Dorian was martial, Lydian erotic, flutes were sweet, thunder frightening. If a poem is actually experienced and valued, these things, no less than (and as a condition for) the deeper poetic meanings of spirit, must lie somehow within the range of experience.

"We see how . . . [Schiller] plagued himself," says Goethe, "with the design of perfectly separating sentimental from *naive* poetry. For the former he could find no proper soil, and this brought him into unspeakable perplexity. As if . . . sentimental poetry could exist at all without the *naive* ground in which, as it were, it has its root." [1] A theorist of poetry may be driven to be some kind of idealist about the nature of poetry itself or the area of its operation. But if he remains close to the objects of his scrutiny—that is, to actual poems—he will be equally driven to remain a realist in his conception of the universe in which the poetic area is contained and in which poetry finds its reasons. Theories of sheer affectivity and subjective valuing have suffered the paradox of promoting not enthusiasm for value but distance, detachment, cooling, neutrality. The sterner metaphysical, cognitive theories, talking about

[1] *Conversations*, November 14, 1823.

real right and wrong, real beauty and ugliness, are the theories which actually sustain value and make responses to value possible. For response cannot feed indefinitely on itself.[2]

VI

WHAT is the relation of the poetic or aesthetic emotion to the emotions of real or ordinary life? This difficult question has been implicit in the critical debate from ancient days, with the catharsis of Aristotle or the transport of Longinus, to the recent past, with the incipience and equipoise of Ricardian psychology or the Freudian varieties of worked-off inhibitions. If one has to make a stark choice between the simply realistic theory—that poetry deals with straight emotions of pity, fear, or erotic passion, and that is why we like it—and some theory of artistic modification—that poetry works some distinctive change in real-life emotions, and that is why we like it—one must clearly choose the latter. But then this alternative, the theory of modification, is itself perhaps susceptible of a puzzling refinement into alternatives. Is the emotion which is characteristic of poetry only a modification of real-life emotion (anger toned down, for instance, or anger caught or embodied in an expression), or is the modified and expressed real-life emotion the ground or object of some further distinct emotion, not anger at all, but precisely the aesthetic emotion? Something like the latter would seem to be required if we are to range poetry under the time-honored heading of the "beautiful"—or the aesthetic. The correct response to the beautiful or the aesthetic is presumably not anger, even in an ameliorated form. Yet that correct response is something that can hardly be the proper business of the critic or theorist of poetry, simply because it *is* an ultimate emotive response to the poetic object and not a part of that object. This correct response will have to take care of itself. If it *is* the aim of poetry, it is an aim beyond the direct aim, which is to make an utterance.

---

[2] The situation of the poet in general is well described in the following recent account of symbolism. "The conscious symbolist will find himself in a curious position. . . . Poetic form presupposes the rational world. . . . And the more thoroughly the symbolist conceives of language as symbol, the more likely it is that he will lose touch with language as sign; to the extent that he attains his aim, it would seem that his sense of direction must waver, since he cannot locate his work with reference to himself or an external world. Deliberate symbolism is hazardous in its quest for a pure poetry, for poetry can be pure only by virtue of the impurities it assimilates. In the degree that the poem shakes loose from the poet himself and from the world of objects, in the degree that the poetic world is free from logical bonds, poetry will be deprived of material; in performing its function, it will destroy its subject matter."—Charles Feidelson, Jr., *Symbolism and American Literature* (Chicago, 1953), pp. 70–1. Published by The University of Chicago Press and copyrighted (1953) by the University of Chicago.

We move thus from the epistemological problem—whether the value expressed by poetry is something objective or something subjective—to a kind of ontological problem arising perhaps precisely out of the specific mixed or half-way epistemology of the poetic act. For if we say poetry is to talk of beauty and love (and yet not aim at exciting erotic emotion or even an emotion of Platonic esteem) and if it is to talk of anger and murder (and yet not aim at arousing anger and indignation)—then it may be that the poetic way of dealing with these emotions will not be any kind of intensification, compounding, or magnification, or any direct assault upon the affections at all. Something indirect, mixed, reconciling, tensional might well be the strategem, the devious technique by which a poet indulged in all kinds of talk about love and anger and even in something like "expressions" of these emotions, without aiming at their incitement or even uttering anything that essentially involves their incitement. This problem has been touched on obliquely all through critical history—in all discussions of the tragic and painful and all hints about the comically defective and about the tragicomic—in all theories of irony, paradox, and reconciled opposites.

One part of the difficulty about the modern myth and ritual claims has all along been their solemnity:—the deep cathartic function and the vast canonical subject matters, the cycles of death and rebirth which they impute to or prescribe for the poetry of serious worth. These ideas may be called unhistorical. Like 18th-century Gothicists and Druidists, the myth critics want to push us back into some prelogical and hence preliterary supposed state of very somberly serious mentality. And hence they are forgetting where they are in history and are overlooking at least two great types of lesson—the lesson of religion, especially that of the Hebrew and Christian religion—which is the lesson of genuine solemnity —and the lesson of accomplished poetry, in Homer, let us say, in Horace, Dante, Shakespeare, Pope—which is surely a different kind of lesson. Let us run the risk of seeming frivolous by saying that it is much less like a lesson of solemnity than a lesson of strife and fun. And to round out our pattern of competing principles, let us add a third modern lesson, that of abstract philosophy.

The ancient division of poetry into tragic and comic, while it is a division, is also an inclusion, and it involves a suggestion that the tragic and the comic may be complementary. On the other hand, there was Plato, in his *Republic*, complaining about the promotion of strife and division by poetry, the feeding and watering of the passions, and in his *Philebus* (or as the recent Cambridge version calls it, *Plato's Examination of Pleasure*) saying that both tragedy and comedy are impure pleasures arising from pain and certain kinds of triumph over pain (like life itself, which is at once tragic and comic), but that a better kind of pleasure is the pure kind arising, for instance, from the knowledge of geometric forms. We can see this kind of Platonism, the numerical and geometric, reappearing here and there down through the centuries, in Augustine and Boethius, for instance (where the orientation is musical), in 18th-century reasoners on order and harmony like Hutcheson (where the orientation again may be visual and geometric). During the early part of our own century the same thing, with frequent appeals to Plato's *Philebus*, has appeared in the aesthetic of "significant" form. The ideas of Bell, Fry, and Wilenski, or of Jay Hambidge, on painting and sculpture, have a clear enough resemblance to art for art's sake in the phase of Whistler and Wilde, and this whole school of formalism (intent on the "significance" of the cube, the "significance" of the cylinder, as well as on the porcelain nicety of certain French verse forms) has contributed a shade of meaning to the term "formalist" when it has been used in an unfriendly way during the more or less recent course of literary debate. Nevertheless, the school of significant form provides us with a sufficiently sharp contrast to the kind of "formalist" criticism which in recent years has been so much concerned with principles of tension, drama, metaphor, paradox, irony, and wit. Another early modern solution to the problem of evil in art was the opposite of the Platonic, and just as extreme. This was the 18th-century resolution by surrender to dismal or to tender feelings. The analysis of wit has been equally an opponent of that. Thus the authors of this history find little difficulty in explaining to themselves a strong sympathy for the contemporary neo-classic school of ironic criticism and for what it has in common with the theory that prevailed in the time of Coleridge and the Germans.

We have observed that the reconciliation of opposites as it was meditated by Schelling and Coleridge had a largely metaphysical bearing. How to get subject and object together and yet explain their distinctness; how to unify inner and outer, general and particular, thought and emotion, art and nature, or a longer series of almost any such opposites one might name—this was the speculation that preoccupied these deeply introspective, transcendentally minded men. An irony of a more darkly moral coloring, a sardonic self-transcendence, was known to Friedrich Schlegel and others. The 20th-century neo-classic irony of poetic inclusiveness, looking back to conversational ironic symbolism, and finding a theoretical hint in quotations from Coleridge by Eliot and Richards, has had a strongly emotive and at times moral accent. There is a direct concern with human affairs and human values here (human "interests"), good and evil, pleasure and pain, rather than with the mysteries of knowledge and creation, the activity of that "synthetic and magical power" the imagination. And so it seems to us that the recent ironists have put a hard problem very compellingly.

Pain and destruction are the two great components of the problem. You can show that pleasure is only an elusive and phantasmal by-product of things and qualities; it cannot be pursued in itself with any success; and you can subsume pleasure under the head of interest, which is the general affective counterpart of knowledge and objects. But pain is not like that; it can sometimes be avoided (that is, it does not always increase through flight, as pleasure diminishes through pursuit); and when it cannot be avoided, we wish it could be. It is one of the most positive experiences we have. (Pain has the two dominant aspects of being a thing we don't like and of being a kind of intensity. The artist, we may speculate, in achieving a certain distance from the aspect of what we don't like is able to take advantage of the intensity.) On the other hand, destruction is clearly enough negative, the termination of experience, being, and interest. The question here is: Why? There is a religious answer that speaks of patience and atonement. This answer is not at odds with poetry, but neither is it available to poetry as a formal solution to the poetic problem.

Of course the reflective and responsible theorist will say that he doesn't call evil itself, or division, or conflict, desirable things. He is sure, however, that facing up to them, facing up to the human predicament, is a desirable and mature state of soul and the right model and source of a mature poetic art. But again, with a certain accent, that may sound somewhat like telling a boy at a baseball game that the *contest* is not really important but only his *noticing* that there *is* a contest.

Let us say that we recognize the fact of material concreteness in human experience, and though matter itself be not evil (as in the Persian scheme), yet it does seem the plausible enough ground for some kind of dualism, division, tension, and conflict, the clash of desires, and evil and pain. Spirit and matter, supernatural and natural, good and evil, these tend to line up as parallel oppositions. Even so refined and geometric a material concept as that of symmetry has its danger for the concept of beauty through unity. How *could* symmetry be part of the definition of beauty? Think, says Plotinus, what that doctrine leads to. "Only a compound can be beautiful, never anything devoid of parts" (I, vi, 1). But parts and composition (and decomposition) seem to be inescapable in the human situation, and on the modern view, art, especially verbal art, confronts this fact. The theorist says that art ought to have the concreteness which comes from recognizing reality and including it. Art ought to have tension, balance, wholeness. Anybody will have to admit that there could never be any drama or story, either comic or tragic, without tension, without conflict, without evil. It may not be at first glance so obvious, but it is nevertheless true, that without some shade of these same elements there could never be any pastoral or idyllic retreat, any didactic or satiric warning, any lyric complaint—or, for that matter, any lyric rejoicing,[3] so far are the springs of human rejoicing buried in the possibility, the threat, the memory of sorrow, so far is human life an experience of mutation, of struggle, of stasis only momentarily and dynamically attained.[4] The great works and the fine works of literature seem to need evil—just as much as the cheap ones, the adventure or detective stories. Evil or the tension of strife with evil is welcomed and absorbed into the structure of the story, the rhythm of the song. The literary spirit flourishes in evil and couldn't get along without it.

The problem can be put succinctly in the following way: Is the unity and order of beauty (and poetry) something that comes about *in spite of* diversity of parts or only *in virtue of* such diversity? The obvious facts in tragedy and comedy and the less obvious facts in other poetic genres would seem to say that the kind of unity required can come about only in virtue of diversity—only in virtue of a certain strife. In certain arts of abstract visual design and perhaps even in some kinds of music, we can see the diversity necessary for the art appearing without much, or without any, idea of strife or painful emotion attached to it. There may well be certain Platonic forms of truly fine art—notably certain forms of drawing and carving, arts which Plato himself was apparently concerned to

[3]

> Yet if we could scorn
>   Hate and pride and fear;
> If we were things born
>   Not to shed a tear,
> I know not how thy joy we ever should come near.
> —P. B. Shelley, *To a Skylark*

Shelley's brief statement concerning pain and poetry in his *Defense* (ed. Cook, p. 35) is much to the point. The following is one of many fine glimpses in Wordsworth's *Prelude:*

> To fear and love,
> To love as prime and chief, for there fear ends,
> Be this [imaginative wisdom] ascribed; to early intercourse,
> In presence of sublime or beautiful forms,
> With the adverse principles of pain or joy—
> Evil as one is rashly named by men
> Who know not what they speak.
> —(1850), XIV, 163

[4] Somewhat more extremely: ". . . it is not possible for imagination to acquaint us with any other world. . . . without the horror we should never focus the beauty; without death there would be no relish for life; without danger, no courage; without savagery, no gentleness; and without the background of our frequent ignominy, no human dignity and pride. (These are excellent and rather Hegelian commonplaces.) . . . there is provided traditionally, betwixt the residence of the soul in one world and its residence in another world, a Lethean bath to bring forgetfulness of that nature which the soul has just lived with; in order that it may adapt to whatever nature may be next in order" (John Crowe Ransom, "The Concrete Universal: Observations on the Understanding of Poetry, II," *The Kenyon Review*, XVII, Summer, 1955, 405–6; also in Ransom's *Poems and Essays*, New York 1955, Vintage Books, Inc.). The Nietzschean version of these commonplaces has been sampled *ante* Chapter 25, pp. 562–4.

purify in the geometric direction, and perhaps certain kinds of music. But as soon as we get into the realm of verbal art, we see the accent of strife in diversity very prominent, and in the major poetic forms, either narrative or dramatic, that element is unmistakable and unavoidable.

One might look on the concept of "poetry" as a kind of central locus where a pull for duality and conflict coming in from the direction of tragedy and comedy encounters and has its own kind of conflict with a pull for harmony coming in from the direction of general aesthetics, "beauty," and beyond that the philosophy of order, being, and the unity of God. "Human interest" confronts Kantian "disinterest" and Thomist "ipsa apprehensio."

Perhaps we face here some kind of problem concerning *The Marriage of Heaven and Hell*. If we take the relatively cautious course of saying that in poetry there has to be an ironic balance of impulses, rather than clear Fourth-of-July choices and celebrations, it will sound to a moralist as if we entertained only wavering beliefs and purposes, no moral commitments.[5] And if we talk more boldly about evil being "reconciled" in poetry, we may sound as if we were actually propitiating evil, giving some dark earth spirit its rightful place in the scheme of things. We may look like a set of Manichaean dualists, some kind of split personalities, or pagans trying to stand on tiptoe.[6]

The lineaments of a response to such difficulties may be discerned in the well-enough-known fact that poetic art is neither the comic-strip melodrama of good and evil as separate agents, hero and villain, nor any kind of philosophic melodrama, truth and falsity disguised as personages and fighting out their duel to one only canonical conclusion, the triumph of truth. For the theater of poetic conflict is human substance itself, ethical substance, as Hegel put it; the conflict is of man with himself or of good and evil in man. Even if the conflict is externally so simple as man against a flood or a forest fire, the poetic conflict is what happens inside the man fighting or the man observing the man fighting. The desire expressed by a few recent theorists for some kind of literary substance as opposed to either Platonic idea or Platonic semblance may be invoked here as a witness. We have alluded in an earlier chapter to what we may call the "no-angelism" of Allen Tate in his volume of "Didactic and Critical Essays" entitled *The Forlorn Demon*. And thus Miss Elizabeth Sewell:

> I have repeated one essential thing about what I conceive to be the true life of the imagination, that in it the life of the mind depends for its liberation upon a kind of submission to the life of the body (and the human), and that the two must live together, according to the way of man, and not of angels or demons.

[5] Cf. *ante*, Chapter 29, pp. 672–4, the view of Yvor Winters.
[6] Cf. H. M. McLuhan, review of D. E. S. Maxwell on T. S. Eliot in *Renascence*, Spring, 1955.

> This submission is, superficially, a scandal, but, more profoundly viewed, it is a way of freedom.[7]

Other writers in this vein have touched more emphatically on the intimacy which obtains between human substance and the fact of evil both as suffering and as division and destruction. Thus Father William Lynch:

> True tragedy has always been a sober calculation of the relation of human energy to existence. Such calculating has always required profound honesty and the rejecting of the cheaper forms of mysticism. St. Paul himself had weighed the matter well and found it impossible to work out the equation. And he therefore cried out: "Who shall deliver me from the body of this death?"[8]

The patristic idea of the "Fortunate Fall," variously expressed by Ambrose, by Augustine, by Gregory the Great, and in the liturgy ("*O felix culpa, quae talem ac tantum meruit habere Redemptorem*")[9] is probably a closer analogue to an adequate literary theory than such neo-Platonic ideas as Augustine entertained about the beauty of the triangle or the circle. The writers of the present history have not been concerned to implicate literary theory with any kind of religious doctrine. It appears to us, however, relevant, as we near our conclusion, at least to confess an opinion that the kind of literary theory which seems to us to emerge the most plausibly from the long history of the debates is far more difficult to orient within any of the Platonic or Gnostic ideal world views, or within the Manichaean full dualism and strife of principles, than precisely within the vision of suffering, the optimism, the mystery which are embraced in the religious dogma of the Incarnation.

And let us say furthermore: that if verbal art has to take up the mixed business of good and evil, its most likely way of success and its peculiar way is a mixed way. And this means not simply a complicated correspondence, a method of alternation, now sad, now happy (as in some neo-classic theories of tragicomedy), but the oblique glance, the vertical unification of the metaphoric smile. To pursue the ironic and tensional theories in the way most likely to avoid the Manichaean heresy will require a certain caution in the use of the solemn and tragic emphasis. Dark feelings, painful feelings, dismal feelings, even tender feelings move readily toward the worship of evil. And they have the further disadvantage that they run readily into pure feeling itself, its indulgence and the theory of that, as in the 18th century. There was a girl in Mrs. Thrale's set at

[7] "The Death of the Imagination," *Thought*, XXVIII (Autumn, 1953), 443.
[8] "Confusion in Our Theater," *Thought*, XXVI (Autumn, 1951), 359–60.
[9] Cf. A. O. Lovejoy, *Essays in the History of Ideas* (Baltimore, 1948), pp. 285–94, "Milton and the Paradox of the Fortunate Fall."

Streatham who could weep so prettily that she was sometimes called upon
for a parlor demonstration.

It is true that pure laughter too has its limitations. It may be idiotic.
There is a certain kind of optimistic writing that sounds like the result
of laughing gas. But bright feelings and the smile go with metaphor and
wit, and when playing on serious topics, wit generates a certain mimicry
of substance which is poetry. There was another member of the
Streatham set who in a *Preface to Shakespeare* noticed that "Shakespeare
has united the powers of exciting laughter and sorrow not only in one
mind, but in one composition." By this line of suggestion and by quoting
further authorities of this tenor we might arrive at a theory that sounded
too much like the homely formula "Grin and bear it," or perhaps like a
prescription for *The Most Lamentable Comedy and Most Cruel Death of
Pyramus and Thisbe.* But the theory also could be made to sound like a
phrase in Aristotle's *Poetics*—the four words *anōdunon kai ou phthartikon*
—not painful and not destructive, a description which Aristotle meant for
the comic object as distinguished from the hideously suffering tragic object. But the phrase, even in Aristotle's system, can easily be lifted so as
to operate not only at the level of poetic object but at that of poetic utterance, poetry itself, and then it will refer not only to comedy but to tragedy too.

VII

ONE apparently needs to insist nowadays that the term "irony" need not
always be taken with a strongly emotive and moral accent. "Irony" may
be usefully taken rather as a cognitive principle which shades off through
paradox into the general principle of metaphor and metaphoric structure
—the tension which is always present when words are used in vitally new
ways. The ultimate advantage of the theory of irony and metaphor is that
it is a theory that involves both poetic content and poetic "form" and demands the interdependence of these two. There are certain kinds of
contentual meaning which can scarcely be discussed except under the
aspect of technique, style, "form." These meanings are pre-eminently the
ironic-metaphoric.

The term "form," perhaps it will be well to assert briefly at this
point, is one which we have been content to use throughout this history
in a provisional but convenient Renaissance and modern manner [1] to refer

[1] See, for instance, Gilbert, pp. 202, 470, 492, 500, Dante (*Letter to Can
Grande*) and Tasso (*Discorsi*); Gregory Smith, I, 266, William Webbe; René le
Bossu, *Traité du poème épique*, 1675, "Livre Second, De la matière du poème
épique"; "Livre Troisième, De la Forme du poème épique"; and *ante*, Chapter 22,
p. 484, Arnold on Wordsworth; p. 488-9, Gautier on *Emaux et Camées* and Wilde
("Form is everything"). And see Chapter 2, p. 33.

to all those elements of a verbal composition—rhythm, metrics, structure, coherence, emphasis, diction, images—which can more or less readily be discussed as if they were not a part of the poem's "content," message, or doctrine. "Form," as we have suggested by apposition just above, is technique and style. "Form" includes all those elements which an aesthete might conceive as justifying a view of art as pure, non-conceptual, non-didactic. It is all that the old rhetorical theory might call either "disposition" or "elocution." It is what Aristotle in the *Poetics* calls "medium" (diction and music) and "manner" (spectacle). Thus "form" is not identical, at first glance anyway, with *all* the character that a work may have, as in the radical view of monistic expressionism. "Form" in the sense implied by the last three or four hundred years of literary criticism is only a dim analogy of the Aristotelian idea or essence by which "matter" is *formed* into some kind of thing (stone into a statue, or something less identifiable than stone into stone itself). Only a dim or inferior analogy, we say. Yet it is at least as clear and good as the opposed more Platonic analogy (found in Scaliger and more recently in the Chicago critics) by which "matter" is the sheer meaningless phonetics, the physical sound, of words (if such a thing can be conceived) and "form" is the idea of the story or other meaning imposed upon the words. Our exposition has preferred to make use of the readily definable and widely understood convention that "matter" is the content or message of literary works, so far as that may be extricated from their dense formality, and "form" is all that complication and stylization which in past ages has in one way or another been looked on as extraneous to matter—a kind of ornament, recommendation, fortification, dress, or the like. Nevertheless our final view, implicit in our whole narrative and in whatever moments of argument we may have allowed ourselves, has been that "form" in fact embraces and penetrates "message" in a way that constitutes a deeper and more substantial meaning than either abstract message or separable ornament. In both the scientific or abstract dimension and in the practical or rhetorical dimension there *is* both message and the means of conveying message, but the poetic dimension is just that dramatically unified meaning which is coterminous with form. This is true both in the sense that all verbal discourse, no matter how unpoetic, has this poetic aspect, and in the more special sense that certain instances of verbal discourse are almost insusceptible of abstractive message reading, and these are poems (in verse and prose) in the most special and excellent sense.

Poetry is truth of "coherence," rather than truth of "correspondence," as the matter is sometimes phrased nowadays. We have heard Sir Philip Sidney say that the poet "nothing affirmeth and therefore never lieth." And Wilde, in the vein of wit peculiar to him: "After all, what is a fine lie? Simply that which is its own evidence."

A close internal relation exists of course between this kind of "form" and the tension of values and emotions on which we were insisting a few pages back. Such tension can occur at structural levels or in local detail of symbols and metaphors. It can be read as metaphoric meaning here and there in poems or as metaphoric character or dimension extending all through poems and constituting their very "imitative" relation to the world of reality which with their aid and in them we come to know. For excellent reasons the *discordia concors* of the metaphysical metaphor or simile has seemed to some critics of our generation the very type and acme of the poetic structure. Such a figure is at least a small-scale model, a manageable miniature, in which a critic may more or less readily scrutinize certain features: the non-literal confrontation of vehicle and tenor, the pull of opposite values and feelings—the lovers, their sighs and anguish, and the willed control, the restraint, the geometry and the compasses.

Let us speak briefly here in praise of metaphor. Let us observe that metaphor combines the element of necessity or universality (the prime poetic quality which Aristotle noticed) with that other element of concreteness or specificity which was implicit in Aristotle's requirement of the mimetic object. Metaphor is the union of history and philosophy which was the main premise of Sidney's *Defence*. And metaphor would seem to be the only verbal structure which will accomplish this feat. We can have our universals in the full conceptualized discourse of science and philosophy. We can have specific detail lavishly in the newspapers and in records of trials and revelations of psychiatric cases. But it is only in metaphor, and hence it is *par excellence* in poetry, that we encounter the most radically and relevantly fused union of the detail and the universal idea. Detail in itself is contingent on information and it is the characteristic object of the historian's research. Still it gets into poems, and poems start with it and from it, and the historian is in the happy position of not necessarily renouncing criticism. Metaphor is the universal amber for the preservation and enhancement of the scraps and trifles of historic fact. "Pretty! in amber to observe the forms, Of hairs, or straws, or dirt, or grubs, or worms! The things, we know, are neither rich nor rare, But wonder how the devil they got there." For it is not a universal fact and not universally admired that men should wear cork-heeled "shoon." But joined with certain ideas of vanity and frivolity and with salt water (in the ballad of *Sir Patrick Spens*), the shoes make a permanent and important, a universally conceivable, human meaning. A "superannuated" British warship of the year 1838 becomes by modern naval norms a highly vulnerable smallish wooden tub. But in the high slant perspective, the orange and bloody sunset, of Turner's illumination we still have *The Fighting Téméraire*. Metaphors are poetry's permanent and necessary conclusions drawn from variable and contingent premises. Other universals are abstract and to that extent *a priori*, even tautological. (A rose is a rose. . . .) Metaphor is a substantive—or a mock-substantive—universal.

It is true that metaphor in poetry is not the same thing as metaphor in poetic theory. Yet a metaphoric theory of poetry is almost necessarily a theory of multiple focuses and hence a historic theory and a perspective theory. It entertains not historically separate and opaque conceptions but a translucent continuous view of history as vista and development. The theory implicit in our narrative sees three main focuses or three most radical ideas in the history of literary criticism, believes them interrelated and reconcilable, and aspires to discard no one of the three. Thus, we recognize: (1) the mimetic or Aristotelian, which does justice to the world of things and real values and keeps our criticism from being merely idealistic; (2) the emotive (as developed with most subtlety perhaps by Richards), which does justice to human responses to values and keeps criticism from talking too much about either ethics or physics; (3) the expressionistic and linguistic (*par excellence* the Crocean), which does justice to man's knowledge as reflexive and creative and keeps criticism from talking about poetry as a literal recording of either things or responses. Our account of critical history says that the second and the third of these radical ideas are present in Aristotle along with the first, though the third, the expressionistic, is surely the weakest of the three and least explicitly developed. It appears to us that these ideas can be made the main points of reference for an indefinitely variable criticism of *all* poems. That is, there are no poems which, as one academic school of our day would have it, are in some exclusively proper way "mimetic" and which hence should not be permitted an expressionistic or symbolic reading; and conversely, all "symbolic" poems, if they are real poems, are in some important sense "mimetic" and dramatic. It seems to us, finally, that metaphor is not only in a broad sense the principle of all poetry but is also inevitable in practical criticism and will be active there in proportion as criticism moves beyond the historical report or the academic exercise.

These observations imply the principle too by which we evaluate the history of the celebrated, perhaps notorious, "genres," literary "species," "types," or "kinds"—not wishing to adopt either these genres or any modification of them as authoritative points of reference or fixations in our scheme of literary valuing, nor on the other hand to follow the Crocean sweep in refusing to allow any worth at all to or make any use of such technically defined entities. The evolution of criticism has produced four, perhaps five, genre conceptions dominant enough in their eras to serve as focusses for the poetic whole. Each of these (with perhaps one exception) seems to have had its advantages; each has enabled a certain understanding not only of one literary genre but of the whole poetic structure and problem. Aristotle's view was dramatic, or more precisely tragic (with intimations of a twin comic view), and this had the great advantage of opening up the more broadly "dramatic," the ethically

problematic and tensional, aspect of poetry as a whole. *Peri Poiētikēs*—
On the Art of Fiction. Aristotle, if read rightly, has something to say
about all the poetic genres. The next basic view is that of Horace, conversational, epistolary, idiomatic, ironic, satiric—despite all the defunct
doctrines about drama which Horace manages to embalm in his gentlemanly wit. This view has the advantage of opening up the linguistic, the
idiomatic, the metaphoric and in that sense again the "dramatic" aspect
of all poetry. Next is the high, the grand, the ecstatic view of Longinus—
which on the whole opens up more dangers and confusions perhaps than
affective advantage, and is not a view according to literary species (but
just the opposite) unless we look on it as making a large contribution
(via Boileau) to the new genre of the "heroic" in the third quarter of the
17th century. Here was a perspective that was almost altogether inflationary and bad, looking not into the realm of spirit and word, where poetry really is, but into a gigantorama of grossly direct stimulations, of
pageantry, drums, duels, warfare, spectres, loud protestations of lust,
honor, and valor. Meanwhile, in the same essays of Dryden which defend the heroic, a theory of courtly wit and ridicule is asserted, and by
the time of Pope and Swift, this can be considered a second focussing of
the Horatian conversational and satiric ideal. And in close liaison, appears the mocking genre of the anti-heroic or burlesque. (Both these, it
is true, are, as with the original Horatian satire, genre norms more by
the implication of prevalent and successful practice than by any clearly
enunciated theory.) Lastly, the cycle of genres is completed in the era
of the romantics with the now affectionately remembered lyric ideal and
its attendant opinion that a long poem is a contradiction in terms. This
had the advantage of exploiting a new view of "expression," a view of
subjectivity both as cognition and as feeling, and of metaphor as the
small-scale model and touchstone of the whole poetic business. After that
Copernican revolution, from dramatic, epic and satiric forms to the lyric,
there were no new genre theories.[2] Theories after that were returns ei-

---

[2] "Those forms which he [Friedrich Schlegel] finds appropriate to his own
taste and time and which are congenial, above all, to the reflective, ironic temper
of the modern mind are the fragment, the dialogue (*das Gespräch*), the rhapsody,
the arabesque, the ironic comedy, and the speculative, satirical, or polemical
aphorism. All these are 'mixed' forms ('All pure, classical forms,' he says in *Lyceum*
fragment 60, 'are now absurd'). . . . The lyrical soliloquy, so indicative of a later
and different sort of nineteenth-century romanticism, is for Schlegel an enviable
but certainly a primitive and inferior manner. Unlike these forms, which have at
least a sporadic historical character in common, the form of the novel is radically
new and certainly without a continuous history. The novel (*der Roman*) represents
for Schlegel the most significant invention of the modern analytical sensibility. It is
related by its philosophical and discursive purpose not to the classical epic but to
the didactic poem, whose greatest single specimen is the *Divine Comedy*. . . . the
novel is not a consistent art form; it is not, in a strict sense, a genre . . ." (Victor
Lange, "Friedrich Schlegel's Literary Criticism," *Comparative Literature*, VII, Fall,
1955, 299).

ther to the classic idea of bigness, as with Arnold, or to the romantic idea of the lyrically intense moment, as with the imagists of the early 20th century. Or they were more and more subtly and dialectically blended obliterations of the old genre idea, as with the 19th-century dramatic monologues and idylls, and then the varieties of symbolism, post-symbolism, and latterly surrealism. The interlude of the porcelain verse genres with the Parnassians scarcely counts.

VIII

ONE perhaps will look about for some comprehensive issue, some paradoxical junction, that will catch, if only in a precarious and momentary stasis, the whole of the problem. This seems to appear nowadays in the question so often asked or implied: whether a poetic theory should be Platonic (concerned with meanings, even though only with analogical meanings) or Aristotelian, concerned, some critics appear to suppose, only with structures—structures of meaning which are somehow, in themselves, as structures, devoid of any meaning and not a modification or enablement of the meanings which are thought to be structured. Which view should poetic theory lean toward? Or, perhaps better, why should such a question be asked? The reason appears to lie in a kind of three-story pattern of human values which may be expounded roughly as follows: There is (1) easiest and lowest, the level of sensory pleasure and pain, terminal in its own way, unexplainable, more or less opaque. There is—to jump to the other extreme—(3) spiritual value, ethical and religious, terminal too, in a different way, in the sense that there is no higher appeal or sanction. And then in between there is (2) something like what Kant saw (which made him close a gap in his system with the *Critique of Judgment*). That is, there is aesthetic pleasure, pleasure of art, and this divides into two kinds: (A) the non-referential and Platonic, a form of sensory-intellectual pleasure (like wall paper and arabesques), terminal again in its own way—and (B) the referential or symbolic, the anti-Platonic art pleasure, especially the pleasure of poetry. But this kind of aesthetic value is an unstable conception. It almost inevitably invites being reduced—either up or down—to (1) sensory values, pleasure and pain (the portrayal of flowers and perfumes in Eden, says Addison, is more delightful than the portrayal of brimstone and smoke in Hell)—or to (3) conceptualized ethical and religious values (poetry, says the old didactic theory, is to teach correct lessons).

The grand problem for the theorist would appear to be how to evade these temptations, or, perhaps better, how to embrace them both and thus have a double or paradoxical theory. His best chance to do this, we have suggested, is found in the curious fact of metaphor, which is a combination of concreteness and significance, a reconciliation or simultaneous embodiment of diverse emotive pulls, a way of facing and even asserting something serious while at the same time declining the didactic gambit which nature is always pushing forward—both to artist and to theorist.

A theory of art will not be able to get along without at least two key terms—to stand in partial opposition to each other and keep the theory from collapsing into tautology or into literalism. At the same time it will hardly be a theory at all unless it tries to bring these two terms into a reconciled and necessary relation, or to see each in and through the other. The two best critical terms, the most simple, inclusive, and unavoidable, are perhaps *making* and *saying* (if the latter be understood to include its expressionist complement the term *seeing*—"Always the seer is a sayer"). Or *Creation and Discovery*, as the title of an aesthetic philosopher's recent book has it. *Making*, the Aristotelian emphasis, and *saying-seeing*, the Platonic and romantic. The justification of this polar arrangement is the impossibility that the two can ever come completely together without the collapse and loss of poetry, and the equal impossibility of their being taken in strict dichotomy or separation without the same loss. Under these two complementary but opposed heads we can marshal an indefinite list of the antitheses that emerge in various phases of critical argument: drama vs. statement, metaphor vs. literal fact, concrete vs. abstract, whole vs. part, whole structure vs. Longinian or Crocean flash, inclusion vs. exclusion, pleasure *and* pain vs. pleasure *or* pain, Aristotelian *harmonia* vs. Aristotelian *mimēsis*, art in full vs. either romantic or classical art; finally, and again basically, the work vs. either the author or the audience. Art or poetry is the peculiar situation where we see each member of each pair only in or through its opposite: making through saying and saying through making.

Something can be learned, something perhaps ultimate, from the most abstract schemes of the philosophers. Let us take a concluding look at an Aristotelian and scholastic classification of human mental activities recently readvertised in the aesthetic writings of the neo-scholastic philosopher Jacques Maritain. Systematic mental activities (arts and sciences), says the tradition, are either speculative (like metaphysics and mathematics) or practical, and the practical are either concerned with doing (ethics and politics) or with making (arts), and then these activities of making are further divisible into useful arts and fine arts—the last being the category where we find poetry. Perhaps, though we will not urge this in a quarrelsome way against aestheticians of painting or music, poetry is *the* fine art. Mr. Maritain thinks that something he calls "poetry," a principle of subjective communion with objective reality, is the essence of all the fine arts. And indeed the verbal principle as it works in poetry more pronouncedly than in other arts does at least put a special emphasis on the relation of tension which holds between fine art (especially poetry) and the other arts and between art in general and the sciences. There is a doubling of art and fine art, in two stages, from their generic non-speculative direction back through the status of *making* (as distinct from doing) to the status of *fine* (as distinct from useful). This last, the status of *fine*, is one where acting takes on in a peculiar way the aspect of speculation (seeing-saying). Let us imagine a tabular arrangement as follows:

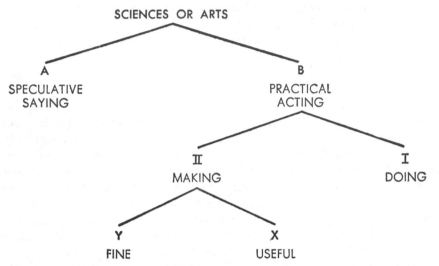

SCIENCES OR ARTS

A
SPECULATIVE
SAYING

B
PRACTICAL
ACTING

II
MAKING

I
DOING

Y
FINE

X
USEFUL

And let us recite thus the broadest lessons of critical history: (1) A pragmatic general philosophy collapses A and B, and hence there is no possibility that a problem about art can really arise. "When we look at a picture, or read a poem, or listen to music," says Richards, "we are not doing something quite unlike what we were doing on our way to the Gallery or when we dressed in the morning." [3] (2) Functionalism in art theory (even in a scholastic frame of general reference) collapses X and Y, echoing and complementing the general pragmatic reduction of A to B. "To make a drainpipe," says Eric Gill, "is as much the work of an artist as it is to make paintings or poems." [4] (3) Platonic versions of art and beauty (including perhaps the neo-scholastic theory of Mr. Maritain) and fully idealist versions of expressionism, like that of Croce, put a transcendental "beauty" somehow specially under Y, though by definition as a transcendental this beauty is also everywhere else and is hence the proper object of the most generalized speculative activity. "If an epigram be art," says Croce, "why not a simple word?" [5] (4) Didactic art theory, from Plato to the present day, completes too in its own way the motion of return (from right to left in our spatial representation) and rules art

[3] *Principles of Literary Criticism* (New York, 1934), p. 16.
[4] Eric Gill, *Art* (London, 1935), p. 4.
[5] *Aesthetic,* trans. Douglas Ainslie (London, 1922), p. 13.

by the straight norms of A, conceptual truth. Poetry, that is, becomes the art of *saying* something *correct* either about God or nature or about some human activity. Would a pilot or a poet know better, asks Socrates, how to steer a boat in a storm?

It remains that a theory of poetic or fine art must do something yet different. It must keep asserting in various idioms, by various stratagems, in accord with the demands of the dialectic of the time, the special character of Y (poetry) as a tensional union of making with seeing and saying.

INDEX

i